Hong Kong

"All you've got to do is decide to go
and the hardest part is over.

So go!"

TONY WHEELER, COFOUNDER – LONELY PLANET

**Lorna Parkes,
Piera Chen, Thomas O'Malley**

Contents

Plan Your Trip — 4

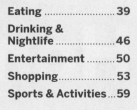

Explore Hong Kong — 64

Understand Hong Kong — 231

Survival Guide — 259

Hong Kong Maps — 296

(left) Nan Lian Garden (p137), located at Chi Lin Nunnery.

(above) View of Victoria Harbour from Victoria Peak (p88).

(right) Cantonese barbecue restaurant in Wan Chai (p108).

WITHDRAWN

Kowloon
p132

Central
District
p68

The Peak &
Northwest
Hong Kong Island
p86

Wan Chai &
Northeast
Hong Kong Island
p101

Aberdeen
& South
Hong Kong Island
p122

Welcome to Hong Kong

Hong Kong welcomes with an iconic skyline, a legendary cuisine, and lush, protected nature where rare birds and colourful traditions thrive.

Neighbourhoods & Islands

Hong Kong's neighbourhoods and islands offer a sensory feast. You may find yourself swaying along on a historic double-decker tram, cheering with the hordes at the city-centre horse races, or simply gazing out at the glorious harbour. What most visitors don't immediately realise is that over 70% of Hong Kong is mountains and sprawling country parks, some also home to geological and historical gems. Escape the city limits on one of the world's smoothest transport systems and spend your day wandering in a Song dynasty village, hiking on a deserted island or kayaking among volcanic sea arches.

Cuisine

One of the world's top culinary capitals, the city that worships the God of Cookery has many a demon in the kitchen, whether the deliciousness in the pot is Cantonese, Sichuanese, Japanese or French. So deep is the city's love of food and so broad its culinary repertoire that whatever your gastronomic desires, Hong Kong will find a way to sate them. The answer could be a bowl of wonton noodles, freshly steamed dim sum, a warm pineapple bun wedged with butter, a pair of the sweetest prawns, your first-ever stinky tofu, or the creations of the latest celebrity chef.

Shopping

From off-the-rack Chinese gowns to bespoke speciality knives (and vice versa), the sheer variety of products in Hong Kong's shops is dizzying. Every budget, need and whim is catered for in 'can do' spirit by a similarly impressive assortment of venues: glitzy malls where the moneyed shop, chic side-street boutiques and vintage dens where fashionistas find their gems, nerdy gadget bazaars, and a mix of markets where you can haggle to your heart's content. The city has no sales tax so prices are generally attractive to visitors.

Culture

Underneath the glass and steel of Hong Kong's commercial persona is a dynamic cultural landscape where its Chinese roots, colonial connections and the contributions of its home-grown talent become intertwined. Here you're just as likely to find yourself dissecting art in the dizzying number of contemporary galleries as joining in dawn taichi or reading the couplets of a local poet to the drumbeat of a dragon boat. Culture could also mean indie music by the harbour or Chinese opera in a bamboo theatre, not to mention the thousands of shows staged year-round at the city's many museums and concert halls.

PISAPHOTOGRAPHY / SHUTTERSTOCK ©

Why I Love Hong Kong

By Lorna Parkes, Writer

Hong Kong has to be the most beguiling city on earth. One minute I can be straining to get an eyeful of the city's neck-breaking verticality, and the next I'm seeking shade under trailing Chinese banyan trees that convince me I'm in a subtropical place far away from Central's hustle. It's exotic yet familiar. Hong Kong's complexity and diversity is astounding and its confident cultural melee never fails to woo me – particularly in the kitchen, where Hong Kong chefs create love letters to their food-adoring fans. If I had one last meal? It would be dim sum in Hong Kong.

For more about our writers, see p320

Above: Aqua Luna's (p85) traditional Chinese junk on Victoria Harbour

Hong Kong's
Top 16

Star Ferry *(p264)*

1 A floating piece of Hong Kong heritage and a sightseeing bargain, the legendary Star Ferry was founded in 1880 and plies the waters of Victoria Harbour in the service of regular commuters and tourists. At only HK$2.70, the 15-minute ride with views of Hong Kong's iconic skyline must be one of the world's best-value cruises. While the vista is more dramatic when you're Island-bound, the art deco Kowloon pier, resembling a finger pointing at the Island, is arguably more charming.

⊙ *Central District*

The Peak *(p88)*

2 Rising above the financial heart of Hong Kong, Victoria Peak offers superlative views (pictured) of the city and the mountainous countryside beyond. Ride the hair-raising Peak Tram – Asia's first cable funicular, in operation since 1888 – to the cooler climes at the top, as skyscrapers and apartment blocks recede into the distance. Escape the crowds by striking out on little-worn paths that encircle the mountain. At dusk Victoria Harbour glitters like the Milky Way on a sci-fi movie poster, mysterious and full of promise, as the lights come on.

⊙ *The Peak & Northwest Hong Kong Island*

DANIEL FUNG / SHUTTERSTOCK ©

DANIEL FUNG / SHUTTERSTOCK ©

Food-Lover's Paradise (p39)

3 Hong Kong is a city that lives and breathes seemingly just to eat and drink. It's also one of the only cities in the world where Michelin-starred meals can be had for a song. You could be ripping gourmet roast goose (pictured) with your bare hands in a humble street cafe one night and dining on fusion delicacies with harbour views the next. Ease into the day with a 'pantyhose' milk tea at a *cha chaan tang* (teahouse) then roll your sleeves up for a dim sum bun fight at lunch.

✗ *Eating*

Man Mo Temple (p89)

4 Experience Chinese folk religiosity in Soho. Permanently wreathed in sandalwood smoke from the hanging incense coils, this famous temple is dedicated to Man (god of literature) and Mo (god of war) and the gods who govern them. Formerly a cultural and political focal point for the local Chinese, the temple now commands a following beyond conscientious students and the martially inclined, as locals and tourists come to perform age-old rites and have their fortunes told.

⊙ *The Peak & Northwest Hong Kong Island*

Temple Street Night Market (p135)

5 Beneath the glare of naked bulbs, hundreds of stalls sell a vast array of booty, from sex toys to Nepalese daggers. You can browse for handy gadgets or quirky souvenirs, and test your bargaining skills. Nearby, fortune-tellers beckon in English from dimly lit tents, and Cantonese opera singers strike a pose. If you're hungry, the many open-air stalls offer snacks or a seafood feast. Sure it's touristy, but its mesmerising and impenetrable aura makes everyone – including locals – feel like a welcome visitor.

🔒 *Kowloon*

Hong Kong Wetland Park (p175)

6 Surreally nestled under an imposing arc of apartment towers, this 61-hectare ecological park in crowded Tin Shui Wai is a swampy haven of biodiversity. This is urban/nature juxtaposition at its best and, curiously, most harmonious. Precious ecosystems in this far-flung yet easily accessible part of the New Territories provide tranquil habitats for a range of waterfowl and other wildlife. Try to forget the human-made world for a moment and delve into a landscape of mangroves, rivers and fish-filled ponds.

⊙ Day Trips from Hong Kong

Happy Valley Races (p118)

7 Every Wednesday night the city horse-racing track in Happy Valley comes alive, with eight electrifying races and a carnival of food and beer. You can try your luck at betting or simply enjoy the collective exhilaration and the thunder of shod hooves. Races were first held here in the 19th century by European merchants who imported stocky stallions from Mongolia, which they rode themselves. Now there are races every week except in the sweltering months of July and August.

☆ Wan Chai & Northeast Hong Kong Island

Tai Kwun (p71)

8 Almost a village within a city, the reimagining of the former Central Police Station at Tai Kwun on Hollywood Rd is the biggest heritage project to open in Hong Kong in more than a decade. Vocal silhouettes of former inmates (including Vietnamese revolutionary Ho Chi Minh) leap about in unlocked cells, and confronting art consumes visitors in the startling Herzog & de Meuron–designed JC Contemporary block. Dedicate several hours to exploring the maze of heritage blocks crammed with exhibitions and artsy musings; then process what you've seen in the complex's bars and restaurants.

⊙ *Central District*

Big Buddha (p160)

9 A favourite with local day trippers and foreign visitors alike, the world's biggest outdoor seated Buddha lords over the western hills of Lantau Island. Visit this serene giant via the Ngong Ping 360 cable car. Negotiate the 268 steps to the three-platform altar on which it is seated and check out the three halls along the way. Reward yourself with some monastic food at the popular vegetarian restaurant in Po Lin Monastery below. Buddha's Birthday in May is a colourful time to visit this important pilgrimage site.

⦿ **Day Trips from Hong Kong**

PMQ (p90)

10 Soho's old married police quarters is one of Hong Kong's greatest heritage reinvention successes. This buzzy lifestyle arena is where small Hong Kong designers hawk their wares in modernist units punctuated by artisan coffee bars, restaurants, a world-class sake education centre and sweet treats galore: it's Hong Kong's most diverting shrine to commercialism, and with bagloads more local character than you'll find in the luxury megamalls of Central. Pop-up creative events and flashes of street art fill the central courtyard; a cathedral-like gallery in the rafters crowns the complex.

⌂ **The Peak & Northwest Hong Kong Island**

Riding the Trams (p268)

11 Nicknamed 'ding dings' by locals, trams have been sedately chugging back and forth between the Eastern and Western districts of the Island since 1904. A century later the world's largest fleet of still-operating double-decker trams continues to negotiate pathways through the city's heavy traffic. This is low-carbon transport at its finest, and there's something fun and just a little bit Harry Potter–esque about these ultra-skinny, creaking gliders. Board in Central and watch the city unfold like a carousel of images as you relax and ponder tomorrow's itinerary.

🏃 **Transport**

Exploring
Lamma (p179)

12 If there were a soundtrack for the island of Lamma, it would be reggae. The island's laid-back vibe attracts herb-growers, musicians and New Age therapists from a rainbow of cultures. Village shops stock *prosecco*, and island mongrels respond to commands in French. If you hike to the nearest beach, your unlikely compass will be three coal-fired plants against the skyline, looking more trippy than grim. Then, in the glow of the day's final rays, head back for fried calamari and beer by the pier at Sok Kwu Wan (pictured), for example.

🏃 **Day Trips from Hong Kong**

Walled Villages
of Yuen Long *(p175)*

13 Yuen Long's walled villages take you back over half a millennium to a wild time when piracy was rife along the South China coast. Isolated from China's administrative heart, Hong Kong, with its treacherous shores and mountainous terrain, was a hideout for pirates. Its earliest inhabitants built villages with high walls, some guarded by cannons. Inside these walls today you'll see carefully restored ancestral halls, courtyards, pagodas and ancient farming implements. The villages are linked by the Ping Shan Heritage Trail.

 *Day Trips from Hong Kong*

Hiking the Hong
Kong Trail *(p60)*

14 Once you've made it past the windy Dragon's Back ridge (pictured), the Hong Kong Trail sweeps you into rolling hills, secluded woodland and lofty paths that afford sumptuous views of the rugged south and its wavy shore. Starting from the Peak, the 50km route snakes across the entire length of Hong Kong Island, past beautiful reservoirs, cobalt bays and WWII battlefields. Spread over five country parks, this wonderful trail invites both easy perambulations and harder hikes.

🏃 *Sports & Activities*

Ruins of the Church of St Paul (p198)

15 Macau's most famous landmark is a dramatic gate perched on a hill 26m above sea level, smack in the middle of the city. A sweep of stairs with landings and balustrades takes you to it, and then to nowhere. Once part of a 17th-century Jesuit church destroyed in a fire, the facade, with fine carvings and detailed engravings displaying Christian, Chinese and Japanese influences, is a captivating historical fragment and a document in granite of Macau's unique 'Mediterrasian' culture.

👁 *Macau*

Mong Kok Markets (p153)

16 With its eclectic speciality markets Mong Kok makes for a rewarding shopping crawl. Ladies' Market has a 1.6-km-long wardrobe covering everything from 'I Love HK' rugby shirts to granny swimwear. Exotic seeds and gardening tools sit next to buckets of fragrant florals in the flower market (pictured). Stalls displaying colourful aquatic life in softly humming, UV-lit tanks line the streets of the goldfish market. There are vertical markets too – a buzzing computer mall, and a multistorey gadget-lovers' heaven.

🏠 *Kowloon*

What's New

Tai Kwun

After years of wrangling, the former Central Police Station on Hollywood Rd has finally reopened as Tai Kwun. The restoration job is a thing of beauty, as are the high-tech history exhibitions and Herzog & de Meuron–designed art gallery. (p71)

Craft Beer Tours

Local craft beer has finally been welcomed into the fold in Hong Kong's bars, and now it's possible to get behind the scenes of some of the city's most exciting, innovative breweries with tours led by Humid with a Chance of Fishballs. (p100)

West Kowloon Train Station

A HK$9-billion infrastructure investment, the new high-speed Kowloon West rail terminus opened in autumn 2018, promising to whisk passengers to mainland China in half the time; just 48 minutes to Guǎngzhōu. (p262)

Blue House Cluster

A community-run cluster of 1920s wooden tenement buildings in Wan Chai, sensitively restored and partially opened to the public with shops and eateries. (p105)

Kennedy Town

Once a sleepy waterside suburb in the far west of Hong Kong Island, K-Town is looking ripe for gentrification. In the past couple of years, brunch spots have proliferated and the Aussie-import Little Creatures microbrewery has opened on the Praya. (p99)

The Murray

Touted as one of Asia's hottest new hotel openings in 2018, the 1960s Murray has been hailed as a best-in-class example of how to reinvent heritage buildings for the 21st century. (p224)

Gin Craze

The West's 'ginaissance' has caught on and Hong Kong Island now has several quirky dens with world-class lists of craft batches; check out Ping Pong Gintoneria (p98) and Dr Fern's Gin Parlour (p78).

Mojo Nomad

Flashpacking has landed in Hong Kong thanks to Mojo Nomad, a design-led hostel concept that quickly took off in Aberdeen and then spread its wings to Sheung Wan – one of Hong Kong Island's most desirable locations, within touching distance of Soho and Central. (p227)

Cinematheque Passion

In the wake of Macau's fledgling International Film Festival & Awards, the territory's first arthouse cinema and film archive has opened inside a magnificent old Portuguese house adjacent to the Ruins of St Paul. (p207)

Disneyland's Marvel section

Disneyland is upping its game with a raft of new areas to appeal to older children, including an entire Marvel-themed zone that's being launched in phases from 2018 to 2023. (p182)

Hong Kong–Zhūhǎi–Macau Bridge

In 2018 the long-anticipated Hong Kong–Zhūhǎi–Macau Bridge opened to traffic, reducing transit times and costs for getting around the Pearl River Delta. (p261)

For more recommendations and reviews, see **lonelyplanet. com/hong-kong**

Need to Know

For more information, see Survival Guide (p259)

Currency
Hong Kong dollar (HK$)

Language
Cantonese, English

Visas
Visas are not required for Brits (up to 180 days); or Australians, Canadians, EU citizens, Israelis, Japanese, New Zealanders and US citizens (up to 90 days).

Money
ATMs are widely available; international debit/credit cards are accepted in most places except budget Cantonese restaurants.

Mobile Phones
Any GSM-compatible phone can be used here. If you have an unlocked handset, buying a local SIM card with 4G mobile data and free local calls is convenient and easy.

Time
Hong Kong Time (GMT/UTC plus eight hours)

Tourist Information
Hong Kong Tourism Board (www. discoverhongkong.com) visitor centres have helpful and welcoming staff, and reams of information – most of it free. There are two branches in town, as well as visitor centres in the airport.

Daily Costs

Budget:
Less than HK$800
➡ Guesthouse or dorm bed: HK$180–450

➡ Meals at a *cha chaan tang* (teahouse) or *dai pai dong* (food stall): HK$60–150

➡ Museums (free); night markets (free); horse races (HK$10)

➡ Bus, tram, ferry ticket: HK$2.60–15

Midrange:
HK$800–2500
➡ Double room in a hostel or budget hotel: HK$450–1100

➡ Chinese dinner with three dishes: HK$300

➡ Drinks and live music: HK$500

Top End:
More than HK$2500
➡ Double room in a boutique or four-star hotel: HK$2200

➡ Dinner at a top Chinese restaurant: from HK$800

➡ Cantonese opera ticket: HK$200

Advance Planning

Two months before Check dates of Chinese festivals; book accommodation, tickets for major shows, and a table at a top restaurant.

One month before Check listings and book tickets for fringe festivals; book nature tours and a table at a popular restaurant.

Two weeks before Book harbour cruises and your Tai Kwun pass; sign up for email alerts from events organisers.

One week before Check the weather forecast.

Useful Websites

Lonely Planet (lonelyplanet. com/china/hong-kong) Destination information, hotel bookings, traveller forum and more.

Discover Hong Kong (www. discoverhongkong.com) The Hong Kong government's user-friendly website for travel information.

Urbtix (www.urbtix.hk) Tickets to movies, shows and exhibitions.

Time Out Hong Kong (www. timeout.com.hk) What to eat, drink and do in Hong Kong and Macau.

Hong Kong Observatory (www. hko.gov.hk) Weather information including forecasts.

WHEN TO GO

October to early December is the best time to visit. June to August is hot and rainy. Beware of typhoons in September.

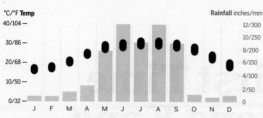

Arriving in Hong Kong

Hong Kong International Airport Airport Express MTR train to city centre from 5.54am to 12.48am, HK$110 (with Octopus) or HK$115; 'A' buses to various parts of Hong Kong from 6am to 12.30am, HK$19 to HK$45; taxi to Central/Kowloon around HK$370/270.

Lo Wu and Lok Ma Chau MTR train to city centre from 5.55am to midnight (Lo Wu), from 6.38am to 10.55pm (Lok Ma Chau), HK$44 to HK$53.

Hong Kong–Macau Ferry Terminal MTR train (Sheung Wan) to Central/Kowloon from 6.05am to 12.56am, HK$5 to HK$10; taxi HK$24 to HK$100.

China Ferry Terminal Star Ferry to Central from 6.30am to 11.30pm, HK$2.20 to HK$3.70; taxi HK$34 to HK$44.

For much more on **arrival** see p260

Getting Around

MTR The ultramodern Mass Transit Railway is the quickest way to get to most urban destinations. Most lines run from 6am to just after midnight.

Bus Extensive and as efficient as the traffic allows, but can be bewildering for short-term travellers.

Ferry Fast and economical, and throw in spectacular harbour views at no extra cost.

Tram Runs east to west along Hong Kong Island; convenient and great fun if you're not in a hurry.

Taxi Cheap compared with Europe and North America. Most taxis are red; green ones operate in certain parts of the New Territories; blue ones on Lantau Island. All run on meter.

Minibus Vans with a green or red roof that cover areas not reachable by bus; green are the easiest for travellers to use.

For much more on **getting around** see p264

Sleeping

Hong Kong hotels have small rooms. That said, service is usually very good and there's plenty on offer, from dorm beds to presidential suites. Most hotels on Hong Kong Island are between Sheung Wan and Causeway Bay; in Kowloon, they are located around Nathan Rd, where you'll also find budget places.

Useful Websites

Lonely Planet (lonelyplanet. com/china/hong-kong/hotels) Hostels, B&B and hotel listings, and an online booking service.

Hong Kong Hotels Association (香港酒店業協會; HKHA; Map p184, D2; ☑852 2769 8822, 852 2383 8380; www.hkha. org; Hong Kong International Airport; ⊙7am-midnight) For booking midrange and high-end hotels that are members of the association.

Discover Hong Kong (www. discoverhongkong.com) The tourist board has a large database of hotels, including those accredited by the Quality Tourism Services scheme, searchable by location and facilities.

For much more on **sleeping** see p221

First Time Hong Kong

For more information, see Survival Guide (p259)

Checklist

→ Make sure your passport is valid for at least one month past your intended stay

→ Inform your debit-/credit-card company you're going away

→ Arrange for appropriate travel insurance

→ Check if your mobile-phone service provider has a roaming agreement with a Hong Kong operator

What to Pack

→ Good walking shoes for the city and the countryside

→ Light rain gear – Hong Kong has a subtropical climate with monsoons in summer

→ Smart-casual staples to move from day to night

→ Mosquito repellent, sunscreen and sunglasses in summer

→ Travel electric adaptor for Hong Kong

→ A small day pack

Top Tips for Your Trip

→ Hong Kong's efficient Mass Transit Railway (MTR) system and buses can take you to most sights; rural areas are mostly easily accessible from the city centre by public transport.

→ If you have more than two days, visit the countryside or outlying islands for a completely different impression of Hong Kong.

→ Hong Kong has some of the world's best Chinese food; indulge in at least one excellent Chinese meal.

→ To get a feel for local culture, explore the main areas of the city by foot.

→ Take the Star Ferry and the trams at least once. They are living heritage and are well connected to some of the main sights.

What to Wear

Hong Kong has its share of fashion-obsessed people, but in general, Hong Kongers are casual. That said, many up-market restaurants and bars (especially in Central) enforce dress codes so check ahead; no shorts for men and no flip-flops is common.

Summer is hot and humid. Dress lightly but bring a jacket for air-conditioned facilities.

When hiking in summer, pack your swimsuit and goggles for an impromptu dip.

Be Forewarned

Hong Kong is generally a safe city to travel around, even alone at night, but always use common sense.

After dark Stick to well-lit streets if walking; note the MTR is perfectly safe to use at night.

Shopping scams Retailers of genuine antiques should be able to provide certification proving authenticity; as a general rule, assume trinkets in markets are reproductions.

Theft Hong Kong has its share of pickpockets. Carry as little cash and as few valuables as possible, and if you put a bag down, keep an eye on it. If robbed, obtain a loss report for insurance purposes at the nearest police station. See 'e-Report Room' at www.police.gov.hk.

Key Transport

Central–Mid-Levels Escalator
A long, covered escalator that links up areas built on slopes in Central, Soho and the Mid-Levels.

Cross-harbour taxi A taxi going from Hong Kong Island to Kowloon Peninsula or vice versa; passengers must pay a cross-harbour toll.

MTR Nine lines serving Hong Kong Island, Kowloon and the New Territories; the Airport Express; a light-rail network in northwestern New Territories; and intercity trains to Guǎngdōng, Běijīng, and Shànghǎi.

Octopus card A rechargeable 'smart card' that can be used on most forms of public transport.

City street

Taxes

There is no value-added tax (VAT) or sales tax in Hong Kong, except on alcohol and tobacco. Shops levy a HK$0.50 charge for plastic-bag usage.

Tipping

Bars and cafes Not expected unless table service is provided, in which case 10% will often be automatically added to your bill.

Hotels A HK$10 or HK$20 note for the porter at luxury hotels; gratuity for cleaning staff at your discretion.

Restaurants Most eateries, except very cheap places, impose a 10% to 15% service charge. At budget joints, just rounding off to the nearest HK$10 is fine.

Taxis Tips are never expected, but many people leave the small change.

Etiquette

Though informal in their day-to-day dealings, Hong Kong people do observe certain rules of etiquette.

Bargaining Haggling over the price of goods is not expected in shops. Do bargain when buying from street vendors (but not in food markets).

Dining At budget places, people think nothing of sticking their chopsticks into a communal dish. More high-end restaurants provide separate serving spoons with each dish; if they're provided, use them. Don't be afraid to ask for a fork if you can't manage chopsticks.

Greetings Just wave and say 'Hi' and 'Bye' when meeting for the first time and when saying goodbye.

Queues Hong Kongers line up for everything. Attempts to 'jump the queue' are frowned upon.

Language

Many people in Hong Kong speak some level of English, especially those working in the service industries (shops, restaurants, bars). Don't be afraid to ask for directions in English. Most restaurants have English menus. Fewer taxi drivers speak English than you might expect.

If you know Mandarin, you can try using it in Hong Kong. Most people understand the dialect; some speak it reasonably well.

For more on language and a useful glossary, see p277.

Top Itineraries

Day One

Central District (p68)

 Armed with your prebooked pass, start early at **Tai Kwun** heritage and arts complex. Then head west down Hollywood Rd checking out antiques shops and **PMQ**'s local designers. Stop at **Man Mo Temple** for a taste of history and explore the hip community on **Tai Ping Shan Street**.

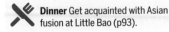 **Lunch** Queue for heavenly beef brisket noodles at Kau Kee (p92).

The Peak & Northwest Hong Kong Island (p86)

Work your way back to Central via Sheung Wan's **Dried Seafood Street**, to catch the legendary **Peak Tram** up to **Victoria Peak**. Stunning views of the city will greet you; perhaps tackle one of the trails. Descend and take a scenic ride on the vintage tram to **Kennedy Town** for beers at **Little Creatures** and a peek at this old-school neighbourhood.

Dinner Get acquainted with Asian fusion at Little Bao (p93).

Central District (p68)

Dedicate the evening to bar-hopping around **Soho**. Don't miss Asian-accented cocktails in **Dr Fern's Gin Parlour** and **Quinary**, perhaps also catching live jazz at **Peel Fresco**. In the wee hours of the morning, head back west to Kennedy Town for 4am dim sum at **Sun Hing**.

Day Two

Wan Chai & Northeast Hong Kong Island (p101)

 Embrace (manufactured) nature at lovely **Hong Kong Park**, not forgetting to check out the **Flagstaff House Museum of Tea Ware**, then head over to the **Blue House** cluster; if it's Saturday, join a free guided tour of these restored wooden tenement buildings.

Lunch Kam's Roast Goose (p109) for arguably the best roasted meat in town.

Kowloon (p132)

Take the **Star Ferry** to Kowloon. Enjoy the views along **Tsim Sha Tsui East Promenade** and savour your stroll to the **Hong Kong Museum of History**. Take afternoon tea in style at the **Peninsula** hotel. After that, if you have the stamina, bus it north to **Yau Ma Tei**, where you can check out **Tin Hau Temple**, the **Jade Market** and traditional shops along **Shanghai Street**.

Dinner Temple Street Night Market (p135) for cheap food under the stars.

Kowloon (p132)

Have your fortune told and catch some Cantonese opera at **Temple Street Night Market**. Then it's not too far a hoof to **Horizonte Lounge** at the Madera Hotel, where awesome urban skyline views await. If there's an indie gig on at **This Town Needs**, head over there to hang with the hipsters.

Day Three

Aberdeen & South Hong Kong Island (p122)

Take the bus to Aberdeen for a walk along **Aberdeen Promenade**, from where you can hop on a sampan to go shopping (for bargain designer furniture and clothing) at Horizon Plaza on the island of **Ap Lei Chau**. Coffee and cakes are available at several of the furniture shops here. If it's a Saturday, book onto a boozy tour of Hong Kong's own brewery, **Young Master**.

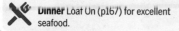

Lunch Jumbo Kingdom Floating Restaurant (p129) – so kitsch it's fun.

New Territories (p161)

Make your way from Aberdeen to **Sai Kung Peninsula** after lunch. Check out Sai Kung Town or hop on a ferry at the waterfront to a nearby beach for a late afternoon dip.

Dinner Loaf On (p167) for excellent seafood.

Kowloon (p132)

After a busy day, head to **Kowloon Taproom** for local craft beers and good people-watching. If after a few beers you're in need of late-night munchies, crispy fried Korean chicken at **Chicken HOF & Soju** will be music to your ears.

Day Four

Macau (p197)

Hop on an early boat to Macau. When you arrive, take a bus or a cab to the legendary **Lung Wah Tea House**. Have dim sum for breakfast. Buy some tea leaves from them before you go and explore the bustling **Red Market** next door. Have a leisurely stroll to the cultural parts of **Northern Macau Peninsula** to work off your breakfast. Check out the designer shops and the cobbled streets of the atmospheric **St Lazarus Church District**, and buy a few souvenirs.

Lunch Clube Militar de Macau (p206) for old-school Portuguese dining.

Macau (p197)

Explore the sights around the **Largo do Senado**. Walk along Rua Central through much of the Unesco-listed **Historic Centre of Macau**, including the **ruins of the Church of St Paul**. Nibble on Portuguese egg tarts and almond cookies as you do so. Then head to lovely **Taipa Village** for a look.

Dinner António (p211) dishes up sumptuous Portuguese classics.

Macau (p197)

Check out the **Studio City** casino complex. Try your hand at the tables or just have a drink at the bar. Then head back to Macau Peninsula to catch the ferry back to Hong Kong.

If You Like...

Views

Victoria Peak Pilgrims the world over come here for unbeatable views of the city. (p88)

Sevva A million-dollar view in every sense. (p78)

InterContinental Lobby Lounge Afternoon tea and late-night drinks come with some of the best harbour views in Kowloon. (p147)

High Island Reservoir Climb the dramatic East Dam to survey this engineering feat and the polygonal rock formations below. (p169)

Tai Long Wan Hiking Trail Gasp and whip out your camera every time a bay comes into view. (p168)

Tai Po Waterfront Park Telescopes at the viewing tower rein in views of the hills and retro factory premises. (p170)

Tung Ping Chau Mother Nature's flight of fancy brought stunning sedimentary rocks resembling layered sponge cakes. (p169)

Pak Nai Drink in the sunset at this westernmost edge of Hong Kong. (p175)

Sai Wan Swimming Shed Rickety local swimming pier on the western edge of Hong Kong Island. (p92)

Modern Architecture

HSBC Building The Norman Foster masterpiece commands a special place in the city's hearts and minds. (p72)

GUOZHONGHUA / SHUTTERSTOCK ©

Nan Lian Garden (p137), Kowloon

Bank of China Tower Some scoff at IM Pei's ingenious design as a futuristic meat cleaver. (p72)

Old Bank of China Building Six decades on, this art deco gem still exudes terrific modernity. (p72)

Asia Society Hong Kong Centre A beautiful roof garden grows out of an overgrown former military site. (p104)

Lippo Centre 'Hugging Koalas' was designed by American architect Paul Rudolph. (p104)

Hong Kong Convention & Exhibition Centre A stingray washed up on an artificial island. (p105)

Parks & Gardens

Victoria Peak Garden The peak above the Peak. This landscaped haven of calm commands untrammelled views. (p88)

Tai Po Waterfront Park A charming park by the Tolo Harbour with picnic lawns and a viewing tower. (p170)

Kowloon Walled City Park The former sin city par excellence reincarnated as a traditional Jiāngnán (southern Yangtze) garden. (p142)

Nan Lian Garden A splendid Tang-style garden at Chi Lin Nunnery, adorned with a pagoda, tea pavilion, koi pond and Buddhist pines. (p137)

Hong Kong Zoological & Botanical Gardens Enveloped by skyscrapers, this stronghold of nature has graced the city since 1871. (p72)

Hong Kong Park A rainforest-like aviary and the city's oldest colonial building lie in this human-made leisure space. (p103)

Ocean Park A huge aquarium and thrilling rides draw families

to this highly popular amusement park. (p124)

Cheung Kong Park A petite oasis favoured by lunching office workers in the middle of Central. (p74)

Astropark This park appeals to the stargazer within, with Chinese and western astronomical instruments. (p169)

Kowloon Park An oasis of green off Nathan Rd. (p138)

Unusual Eats

French toast, Hong Kong–style Popular comfort food, liberally served at *cha chaan tang* (teahouses). Try it at Chau Kee. (p95)

Snake soup A winter favourite trusted for its warming properties. Served at Ser Wong Fun. (p77)

Chiu Chow pig's blood with chives A timeless delicacy of jiggly russet cubes. Served at Chan Chun Kee. (p93)

Cow innards Cheap and nutritious, simmering away in vats of stock behind steamy noodle-shop windows. Try City Hall Maxim's Palace. (p75)

Turtle jelly A mildly bitter concoction of turtle shell and Chinese herbs. Good for skin. Available at Kung Lee. (p82)

Yin yeung Born of colonialism, the quintessential Hong Kong drink of tea mixed with coffee. Served at Mido Café. (p145)

Stinky tofu Fermented, bacterium-rich goodness. Smells more pungent than it tastes. Available at Chuen Cheong Foods. (p110)

'Russian' borscht Hardly Russian but still delectable, it epitomises 'soy sauce western' cuisine. Served at Tai Ping Koon. (p113)

24 herbs This common bitter drink the colour of wrath will

For more top Hong Kong spots, see the following:
➡ Eating (p39)
➡ Drinking & Nightlife (p46)
➡ Entertainment (p50)
➡ Shopping (p53)
➡ Sports & Activities (p59)

PLAN YOUR TRIP IF YOU LIKE...

cool your system. Enjoy at Lui Seng Chun. (p141)

Hiking

Tai Long Wan Hiking Trail Emerge from the luxuriant mountains to find the idyllic Tai Long Wan beach. (p168)

Dragon's Back A popular see-the-sea ramble that undulates to the somnolent village of Shek O. (p60)

Lamma Take a gentle 4km hike across the leafy island to the embrace of waterside seafood restaurants. (p179)

High Island Reservoir East Dam The only volcanic site of Hong Kong Geopark that humans (and stray cattle) can access on foot. (p169)

Lai Chi Wo Any walk from Wu Kau Tang or Luk Keng passes this ancient Hakka village surrounded by woodlands and mangroves. (p173)

Hong Kong Cemetery Wander through this hilly, overgrown, deeply atmospheric resting place of Hong Kong's good and naughty. (p107)

Morning Trail Dappled path encircling the Peak, with stellar city-skyline views. (p88)

Tai Mo Shan Several hiking trails thread up and around Hong Kong's tallest mountain. (p161)

Colonial & Fusion Architecture

Old Supreme Court Building The most imposing colonial edifice left in town, though perhaps not the most beautiful. (p79)

Former Marine Police Headquarters Even blatant commercialism cannot detract from the poise and beauty of this neoclassical monument. (p138)

Tao Fong Shan Christian Centre Christian buildings with Buddhist characteristics designed by a Dane sit on a hill in Shatin. (p165)

Tai Kwun Stern edifices that trace the history of law enforcement in Hong Kong. (p71)

Lui Seng Chun A surprisingly harmonious marriage between a Chinese 'shophouse' and an Italian villa. (p141)

St John's Cathedral Criticised for blighting the colony's landscape when it was first built, today it's a reminder of dear old Blighty. (p72)

Béthanie Two octagonal cowsheds plus a neo-Gothic chapel equal a performing-art space. (p125)

Traditional Culture

Tai O Visit the stilt houses in Hong Kong's southwestern corner for a glimpse of the city's fishing culture. (p182)

Aberdeen (p124) and **Ap Lei Chau** (p125) The Water People's culture is palpable at the markets and food stalls, and on dragon boats.

Walled villages Dotted around the New Territories, villages like Lai Chi Wo preserve traces of an agricultural way of life. (p173)

Folk voodoo In full swing every March after the first (mythological) thunder of the year rouses the animal world. (p107)

Cantonese opera The endangered Unesco-listed art is conserved at the Sunbeam and Yau Ma Tei theatres. (p119)

Pok Fu Lam Village This 'urban' village features an old way of life among relics of a dairy and a fire dragon. (p125)

Dried Seafood Street Hold your nose browsing the stalls around Des Voeux Rd West, where Cantonese cooks shop. (p97)

Tsim Sha Tsui TST's little-known side comprises colonial-era recreation clubs and the homes of early Shanghainese migrants. (p139)

North Point Hong Kong's Little Fújiàn since the turn of the last century, particularly evocative at Chun Yeung Street Market. (p107)

Yau Ma Tei Kowloon's grassroots street culture is still very much alive at places like Tin Hau Temple. (p140)

Chinese Architecture

Kang Yung Study Hall A beautiful study hall that used to function as a private school in a far-flung Hakka village. (p174)

Tang Clan Ancestral Hall Hong Kong's most magnificent ancestral hall sits in Ping Shan alongside other worthy village structures. (p175)

Tin Hau Temple A fine Tin Hau Temple that has kept many of its original elements, including the elaborate roof ornaments. (p106)

Tsz Shan Monastery An impressive ancient-inspired modern Buddhist complex in Tai Po. (p173)

Chi Lin Nunnery A meticulous modern replica of Tang dynasty Buddhist architecture. (p137)

Man Mo Temple Creaking, headily-scented behemoth on Hollywood Rd. (p89)

Markets

Temple Street Night Market Hong Kong's liveliest night market, with occasional free Cantonese opera performances. (p135)

Cat Street Daytime street market selling Chinese repro antiques, vintage Bruce Lee posters and old Hong Kong photos. (p91)

Graham Street Market A vestige of old Hong Kong, this Central street market still sells fermented beans, Asian fruits and vegies. (p73)

Chun Yeung Street Market Atmospheric Fújiànese spot amid old tenement buildings. (p107)

Bowrington Road Market Outdoor and indoor wet market with lively late-night *dai pai dong* (food stalls; p113)

Tai Po Market Outdoor wet market in the New Territories selling dried seafood and sugarcane juices. (p171)

Vintage Market Find recycled fashions from all over the world and handmade jewellery at this Macau market. (p210)

Month by Month

TOP EVENTS

Chinese New Year, January/February

Birthday of Tin Hau, April/May

Cheung Chau Bun Festival, April/May

Dragon Boat Festival, May/June

Hungry Ghost Festival, August

February

The marquee of clammy clouds may seal up the city in perfect hibernation mode, but nothing can dampen the spirits around Chinese New Year, the most important festival on the cultural calendar.

✯✯ Chinese New Year

Vast flower markets herald the beginning of this best-loved Chinese festival. Wear red and be blessed at Sik Sik Yuen Wong Tai Sin Temple (p136). Then find a spot by Victoria Harbour (or failing that, a TV) and be awed by fireworks.

✯✯ Spring Lantern Festival

Lovers are the focus as colourful lanterns glowing under the first full moon of the lunar year mark the end of New Year celebrations, and a day known as Chinese Valentine's Day.

☆ Hong Kong Arts Festival

Lasting five to eight weeks, Hong Kong's premier cultural event (p50) scintillates with a feast of music and performing arts, ranging from classical to contemporary, by hundreds of local and international talents.

🏃 Hong Kong Marathon

Around 70,000 athletes compete in this top Asian marathon. The annual event also includes a half-marathon, a 10km race and a wheelchair race.

March

Rain and warm weather return, triggering the whirr of dehumidifiers in every home and office – as flowers and umbrellas bloom across the city.

☆ Hong Kong International Film Festival

One of Asia's top film festivals, the four-decade-old HKIFF (p50) screens the latest art-house and award-winning movies from Asia and around the world. Timing straddles Easter each year.

◉ Hong Kong Flower Show

For approximately 10 days, Victoria Park turns into a colourful sea of fragrant floral displays as horticulturalists from over 20 countries experiment with their green fingers.

🔒 Art Basel

Hong Kong becomes the epicentre of the international art world for three days as the world's top art fair (p53) takes the Hong Kong Convention and Exhibition Centre by storm.

April

☆ Hong Kong Sevens

Hong Kong's most famous sporting event – and probably its most original. The Rugby Sevens (p61) was invented here in 1975 and the eternally popular tournament promises fierce competition, as well as a reliable glut of carnivalesque partying from the fans.

✯ Birthday of Tin Hau

A festival dedicated to the patroness of fisherfolk and one of the harbour city's most popular deities. Key celebrations include a colourful float parade in Yuen Long and traditional rites at the 'Big Temple' in Joss House Bay. It falls on the 23rd day of the third lunar month.

May

The city steams up, especially in the urban areas, as the long summer months begin. The first heavy showers of the year cleanse the air as religious celebrations heat up the mood.

✯ Cheung Chau Bun Festival

This unique, weeklong festival (p187) on Cheung Chau climaxes on Buddha's birthday when children 'float' through the island's narrow lanes dressed up as mythological characters and modern-day politicians, while the more daring townsfolk scramble up bun-studded towers at midnight.

✯ Buddha's Birthday

Devotees stream to Buddhist monasteries and temples all over the territory on the eighth day of the fourth lunar month to pray to the founder of Buddhism and bathe his likenesses with scented water.

🎨 Affordable Art Fair

This three-day event in May attracts more than 115 local and international galleries, selling pieces from HK$1000 to HK$100,000: a bargain compared with prices in many of Hong Kong's galleries the rest of the year.

☆ Le French May

Misleadingly named, this celebration of all things Gallic (p53) often starts in April and ends in June – so much the better, as it returns with a rich arts program of consistently high quality, plus the obligatory fine food and wine.

June

The heavens are truly open, the mercury spikes and strong air-conditioning switches on citywide to soothe the nerves of locals and visitors alike.

☆ Dragon Boat Festival

Thousands of the world's strongest dragon-boaters meet in Hong Kong over three days of intense racing and partying (p36) at Victoria Harbour, while smaller but equally heart-stopping races happen in waterways all over the city.

August

Seven million souls palpitate and perspire in the sweltering heat. Torrential downpours are common but there is always a sun-toasted beach near you in this sprawling archipelago of 260-plus islands.

✯ Hungry Ghost Festival

Restless spirits take leave from hell to roam the earth during the seventh moon. Hell money, food and earthly luxuries made of papier mâché are burned to propitiate the visitors. Fascinating folk traditions come alive across the city. It falls on the 15th day of the seventh lunar month.

September

Good old summer lingers but the humidity factor starts to recede. Stay close to the ocean coastlines for free respite as school kids swap their buckets and spades for mighty dunes of homework.

✯ Mid-Autumn Festival

Pick up a lantern and participate in a moonlit picnic on the 15th night of the eighth lunar month (13 September 2019). This family occasion commemorates a 14th-century anti-Mongol uprising with much cheerful munching of the once-subversive moon cakes.

November

At long last Hong Kong mellows. Temperatures sensibly cool down to around 22°C (72°F) and rainfall ceases significantly, much to the delight of ramblers and other countryside merrymakers.

☆ Clockenflap

Hong Kong's largest outdoor music festival (p51) incorporates international, regional and local live music of a mostly indie variety, as well as art installations and pop-ups. Acts that have played the festival include New Order, the Libertines, A$AP and Massive Attack.

(Top) Dragon Boat Festival, Stanley (p127), Hong Kong Island
(Bottom) Durian moon cake, Mid-Autumn Festival

OSTILL IS FRANCK CAMHI / SHUTTERSTOCK ©

NEWROADBOY / SHUTTERSTOCK ©

🏃 Oxfam Trailwalker

What began as a fundraising exercise drill by local Ghurkha soldiers in 1981 is today a celebrated endurance test that challenges hikers in teams of four to complete the 100km MacLehose Trail in 48 hours.

🎎 Hong Kong International Literary Festival

Held over 10 days in autumn, the festival features established and emerging writers from around the world. Past authors have included luminaries Margaret Atwood and Louis de Bernières.

December

Arguably the best time of the year to visit the city. Sunny days and clear-blue skies reign. The delightful weather is perfect for all outdoor activities, though brace for the Christmas shopping crowds.

⊙ Hong Kong Winterfest

Rejoice as neon Yuletide murals appear on the Tsim Sha Tsui harbourfront (p138). Ferry across to Statue Sq to see illuminated Christmas trees and fake snow. Join teenage revellers around Times Sq to ring in Christmas day.

☆ Hong Kong International Races

Billed as the Turf World Championships, master horsemen and equine stars from across the planet descend on the beautifully set Sha Tin Racecourse (p166) to do battle. Expect fanatical betting from the 60,000-plus who pack the stands.

Travel with Kids

In a city where skyscrapers tower over city streets, subtropical trees swoop low, and excellent museums are connected by characterful trams and ferries, there's a lot for kids to get excited about. Food and sanitation are of a high standard, but crowds, traffic and pollution might spook more timid mini travellers.

Hong Kong Museum of History (p134)

Child-Friendly Museums

Hong Kong Science Museum

The three storeys of action-packed displays at Hong Kong's liveliest museum (p139) are a huge attraction for toddlers to teens. There's a theatre where staff in lab coats perform wacky experiments.

Hong Kong Museum of History

This excellent museum (p134) brings the city's history to life in visually and aurally colourful ways. Kids will enjoy the 'Hong Kong Story' exhibition with its splendid replicas of local traditions, and a life-sized fishing junk.

Hong Kong Space Museum & Theatre

Kids eager to test their motor skills will go berserk – there are buttons to push, telescopes to peer through, simulation rides and computer quizzes. Older kids will enjoy the Omnimax films shown on the convex ceiling of the theatre (p140).

Hong Kong Maritime Museum

Even if the exquisite ship models at this museum (p73) don't do the trick, there's plenty to fire junior's imagination – gun-toting pirate mannequins, real treasures salvaged from shipwrecks, a metal diving suit... Plus there's an environmental angle with 'Water Jai' and his tears for plastic waste in the ocean.

Hong Kong Railway Museum

Thomas and his friends jolt to life at this open-air museum (p171) converted from a historic railway station; it comes complete with old coaches and a train compartment.

Hong Kong Heritage Museum

Though some youngsters may appreciate the displays, the real gem is the hands-on children's discovery gallery where they can dress up, play puzzle games and enjoy an exhibition of vintage toys (p165).

Transport Geekery

Peak Tram

Children will be fascinated by the ride on the gravity-defying Peak Tram (p268).

EWILDING / SHUTTERSTOCK ©

Star Ferry

Cruise liner, barge, hydrofoil, fishing junk... Your mini-mariners will have a blast naming passing vessels, as their own tugboat (p264) chugs serenely across Victoria Harbour.

Trams

Looking out of the window of a Harry Potter-esque, skinny double-decker tram (p12) that rattles, clanks and sways amid heavy traffic can be exhilarating.

MTR

The metro is interestingly colour-coded, full of myths and futuristic enough to enthral younger travellers.

Symphony of Lights

Children will be awestruck by the dance of laser beams (p151) projected from skyscrapers on both sides of the harbour, to accompanying music. Bring the Darth Vader costume.

Shopping with Kids

All the essential toiletries you need for younger kids and babies can be found in Hong Kong's chain-store pharmacies, such as Mannings.

Hong Kong Book Centre (Map p302, H3; ☑852 2522 7064; www.hkbookcentre.com; Lower Level, On Lok Yuen Bldg, 25 Des Voeux Rd, Central; ◷9am-6.30pm Mon-Fri, to 5.30pm Sat; ⓜHong Kong, exit B) has a good range of English-language children's books. Horizon Plaza (p131) has megastores selling kids' books and clothing. Tai Yuen St is known for traditional toy shops catering to youngsters of all ages.

For dozens of outlets dedicated to children, head to **Ocean Terminal** (Map p314, B5; www.oceanterminal.com.hk; Salisbury Rd, Tsim Sha Tsui; ◷10am-9pm; 🚢Star Ferry, ⓜEast Tsim Sha Tsui, exit J) at Harbour City, Elements mall (p154) or Festival Walk (p154) in Kowloon, or Times Square (p121) in Causeway Bay.

Dolphin-Watching

See the second-smartest animal on earth in the wild – and here it's in bubble-gum pink! Hong Kong Dolphinwatch (p155) runs three four-hour tours a week to waters where Chinese white dolphins may be sighted.

Theme Parks & Green Spaces

Ocean Park

Hong Kong's premier amusement park (p124) offers white-knuckle rides, a top-notch aquarium, real giant pandas and a cable-car ride overlooking the sea.

Hong Kong Park

Ducks, swans and turtles inhabit the ponds here (p103), and the massive forest-like aviary has an elevated walkway that lets visitors move through the tree canopy to spy on the birds.

Hong Kong Zoological & Botanical Gardens

After a visit to this park (p72), your offspring will have seen the American flamingo, the Burmese python, the two-toed sloth and may even be able to tell a buff-cheeked gibbon from a cheeky child.

Hong Kong Wetland Park

Patience may be required for appreciation of the wetland habitats, but not for the themed exhibition galleries, the theatre and 'Swamp Adventure' play facility (p175).

Kowloon Park

This large verdant space (p138) has lakes with waterfowl, two playgrounds, swimming pools, an aviary and dragon dances on Sundays.

Hong Kong Disneyland

This famous theme park (p182) is continually upping its game; a fancy new Marvel-themed area is being launched in phases from 2018 to 2023.

Ocean Park (p124), Aberdeen

Tips for Visiting Ocean Park or Disneyland

Practicalities

➡ Both Ocean Park (p124) and Disneyland (p182) are extremely popular with mainland Chinese tourists. For a quieter visit, avoid Chinese public holidays, in particular Labour Day (1 May) and the ensuing two days, National Day holidays (1 to 7 October), Ching Ming Festival in April, and Chinese New Year in January or February. The summer months of July and August are also very busy. At the weekend, Sunday is slightly less busy than Saturday.

➡ Some of the rides have height restrictions.

➡ There's plenty of decent Chinese and western food at both parks.

Ocean Park

➡ Most teens and grown-ups will prefer Ocean Park to Disneyland; it's much bigger, has a lot more to offer, and the rides are more intense.

➡ Ocean Park consists of two parts – Waterfront near the entrance, and Summit on the headland. You can't walk between the two, but you can take the scenic Cable Car or the subterranean Ocean Express train. The former is busiest in the morning and just before closing. To avoid long lines, take the Ocean Express up and the Cable Car down.

➡ Younger children may like Whisker's Harbour, the age-appropriate play area, and Pacific Pier where they can look at and feed seals and sea lions. Note that it may seem like a lovely idea but animal-welfare groups suggest interaction with sea mammals held in captivity creates stress for these creatures.

Disneyland

➡ Although Disneyland has historically catered for younger audiences, it is in the process of adding new attractions that will appeal to older kids. A hotly anticipated Marvel-themed area will open between 2018 and 2023; an Iron Man Experience flight simulation was already in operation at our last visit.

➡ Though Hong Kong Disneyland is comparatively small, do bring a stroller if you have one. It's stroller-friendly with parking near the rides. The park also has a limited number of strollers for rent.

➡ There are lockers on Main Street, USA, where many of the shops are located.

➡ Fantasyland is by far the best for the very young set. Here's where you'll find Dumbo, Mad Hatter's Teacups, It's a Small World and the Many Adventures of Winnie the Pooh. The highly popular Toy Story Land and Grizzly Gulch usually have the longest lines.

➡ Taking the train on Disneyland Railroad is nice if you're tired, but note it does not take you all the way around the park. There are two stops – at the entrance and in Fantasyland.

➡ There's no need to stake out a position to watch the fireworks that come on at 8pm, unless you're looking to take awesome photos. On the other hand, watching near the entrance will allow a quick exit.

➡ Going to Disneyland in the afternoon may let you make flexible use of your time and avoid long lines. The park also takes on a special magic in the twilight hours (6pm to 9pm), when some rides are lit up.

Like a Local

Certain values and habits permeate everyday life in Hong Kong, but while they're prevalent, your experience of the city's cultural mores depends on the locals who cross your path – not everyone is the same. Here are some tips to help you navigate the social seas of this metropolis.

DESIGN / GETTY IMAGES ©

Dim sum

Cultural Etiquette

Greetings

Some locals find hugging and cheek kissing too intimate; others secretly wish for more. Generally speaking, a simple 'Hello, how are you?' and a light handshake will do. Remove your shoes before entering someone's home.

Face

The cornerstone of human relations in this part of the world. Think status and respect: be courteous and never lose your temper in public.

Gifts

If you present someone with a gift, they may appear reluctant for fear of seeming greedy, but insist and they'll give in. Don't be surprised if they don't unwrap a gift in front of you, though; to do so is traditionally considered impolite.

Dining Out

Most Hong Kongers like to 'go Dutch' when dining out with friends. The usual practice is to split the bill evenly, rather than for each person to pay for what they ordered or asking for separate cheques.

Colours

Red symbolises good luck, happiness and wealth (though writing in red can convey anger and unfriendliness). White is the colour of death in Chinese culture, so think twice before giving white flowers or attending an elderly person's birthday celebration in white.

Table Manners

Sanitary Consumption

Dishes are meant to be shared at Chinese meals. Expensive restaurants provide serving chopsticks or spoons with each dish; most budget places don't, but you can ask for them.

Mind Your Chopsticks

Don't stand your chopsticks upright in the middle of a bowl – that resembles two incense sticks at a graveside offering. Nearly all restaurants have forks; don't be afraid to ask for one.

Spirit of Sharing

Take a few pieces of food from a communal dish at a time, preferably those nearest to you. It is not necessary to shove half the dish into your bowl in one go. For shared staples, it is fine to fill up your whole bowl.

Tea Language

When someone refills your dainty teacup, you can tap two fingers (index and middle) gently on the table twice instead of saying thank you with your mouth stuffed. Mastering this (allegedly) centuries-old gesture will endear you to your hosts.

Bones & Tissues

Your plate is the preferred spot for bones, but at budget places diners put them on the table beside their plates or bowls. If you find that disconcerting, place a tissue under or over your rejects.

Food Obsessions

Open Rice

Legions of food critics, amateur or otherwise, post reports and photos on the user-driven, bilingual restaurant-review website www.openrice.com every day.

Dim Sum

Morning dim sum is a daily ritual for many retirees and a tasty excuse for a family reunion at the weekend. Now family and food vie for attention with smartphones.

Tea Break

When mid-afternoon comes, *cha chaan tang* (teahouses) are full of elderly folks debating the morning's meat prices and stock-market fluctuations. These humble cafes function as community focal points for the aged and housewives to swap gossip and commentary. They're also bolt-holes for many a stressed office worker.

Late-Night Sweets

After dinner, locals like to head to a dessert shop for sweet soups and other Chinese-style or fusion desserts, such as black sesame soup and durian crepes.

Steamy Winter

In winter, a hotpot at a *dai pai dong* (food stall) or even a restaurant is a soul-warming, convivial experience. Dip slivers of meat, seafood and vegetables in a vat of steaming broth. Consume and repeat.

Local Hoods

Full-scale gentrification has yet to arrive in these areas, but urban development is already changing their character.

Aberdeen & Ap Lei Chau

Go on a boat ride in the city's famous typhoon shelter, watch the dragon boat races, and explore the markets (p129) and temples of Hong Kong's 'People of the Water'.

Yau Ma Tei

Stroll Shanghai Street (p140) for traditional barbers, Chinese wedding costume–makers and artisans of other time-honoured crafts.

Sham Shui Po

Find flea markets, 1930s shophouses, post-war housing estates and even an ancient tomb in this resilient working-class district.

Sai Ying Pun

West of Sheung Wan, the pungent smells of dried seafood and Chinese herbal medicine lead up to hilly residential streets (p97) and neighbourhood restaurants.

Money Matters

Jockey Club

Step into any Jockey Club off-course betting centre (often found in public housing estates, near markets or in transport terminals) on any race day or night, and you'll be assailed by a maelstrom of emotions as punters struggle to defy the odds. Occasionally, you'll hear a squeal of joy, but more often than not invective peppers deep sighs of desperation as numerals streak across the TV screens every 30 minutes. Outside, high rollers squat on the pavement en masse, heads buried in race cards, in search of the forever elusive winning formula.

Stocks & Shares

Similarly, look out for the hole-in-the-wall brokerage firms on weekdays and you'll find crowds of (not all small-time) investors deeply engrossed in the live stock-market updates on the wall-mounted panels.

For Free

Hong Kong is not a cheap place to visit and prices creep up at every opportunity, as any local can testify. But don't despair: many of the city's best attractions – skyscrapers, nature trails, vintage transport – are free or cheap. With a bit of planning, you can save your pennies for indulgences.

Flagstaff House Museum of Tea Ware (p104)

Museums

Many of Hong Kong's major museums are now free; those that are not still sometimes offer free entry on Wednesdays.

Museum of History

Get context on all of Hong Kong's history all in one place (p134).

Heritage Museum

Features (p165) exhibits on folk traditions, the life of Bruce Lee and Cantonese opera.

Flagstaff House Museum of Tea Ware

An elegant showcase (p104) of vintage teaware inside Hong Kong Park.

University Museum & Art Gallery

Rotating art and sculpture (p92) alongside permanent Chinese antiques.

Railway Museum

Featuring Hong Kong's railway history with disused train carriages (p171) for the kids.

Museum of Coastal Defence

A museum (p108) detailing Hong Kong's coastal defence over six centuries.

Tours

Tai Kwun

The former Central Police Station (p71) on Hollywood Rd is a complex of a dozen or so heritage buildings.

Blue House Cluster

Hong Kong's last remaining wooden tenement building (p105) is a heritage success story.

Asia Society Hong Kong Centre

A former explosives magazine (p104) that stages top-notch exhibitions.

Heritage of Mei Ho House Museum

This museum (p142) shows the development of public housing in Hong Kong with photos and replicas.

Tai O Heritage Hotel

This former police station (p186) guarded the coast against pirates (book online).

Festivals & Events

Dragon Boat Races

Dragon boat racing (香港國際龍舟邀請賽; www.hkdba.com.hk; ⊘May or Jun) against a backdrop of decorated fishing junks.

Hungry Ghost Festival

Elaborate rites to appease roaming spirits in the seventh lunar month at this festival (p28) when the gates of hell are believed to be open.

Fire Dragon Dance

A smoky dance by a straw dragon stuck with glowing incense sticks during the Mid-Autumn Festival (p28).

Cheung Chau Bun Festival

Modern re-enactment of a Qing ritual where climbers scramble up bun towers and try to pocket as many buns as possible at this festival (p28).

Freespace Happening

Annual kaleidoscope of live music, film, dance, parkour and handicrafts, in West Kowloon (www.westkowloon.hk/en/freespacehappening).

Nature Escapes

Hills

Hike, cycle or take long walks in Hong Kong's beautiful countryside.

Beaches

Hong Kong's beaches come with lifeguards; just bring sunblock and beer.

Cheap & Cheerful

Not quite free, but near enough to warrant inclusion.

Tram

For a couple of dollars you can rattle your way through the urban canyon of highrises on a tram (p12).

Star Ferry

Give up pocket change for the voyage of a lifetime on the Star Ferry (p264).

Off-Peak-Hour Dining

Many Chinese restaurants offer discounted prices on either side of the noon to 2pm lunch hours. *Cha chaan tang* (teahouses) and fast-food chains have good-value afternoon tea.

Happy Hours

Around sundown, generous happy hours are a feature of many bars.

Movie Tuesday

On Tuesdays, a movie ticket costs from HK$10 to HK$25 less than usual.

Horse Racing

For only HK$10, you can experience a night at the races at Happy Valley Racecourse (p119).

Guided Tours

Hong Kong's world-class public transport and English-language heritage make it a relatively easy place to tour independently; however, there's something to be said for having a helping hand if you're short on time or want to scratch beneath the surface of Hong Kong culture.

There are tours available to just about anywhere in the territory. There are also speciality tours covering topics such as WWII relics, feng shui, antique buying and architecture, although many of these run infrequently and require a minimum number of participants. The Hong Kong Tourism Board (www.discoverhongkong.com) has some recommendations listed on its website.

Hong Kong's food tours are especially prolific, fascinating and easy to access, allowing tourists to get truly stuck in to what can feel like a bewildering facet of local life, fraught with mysterious customs, etiquette and other-worldly scrumptiousness.

Harbour Tours

The easiest way to see the full extent of Victoria Harbour from sea level is to join an hour-long circular Star Ferry Harbour Tour (www.starferry.com.hk) , of which there are a number of different options. Most of the tours depart from the Star Ferry Pier in Tsim Sha Tsui, but there are also departures from the piers at Central and Wan Chai; buy tickets at the pier.

Single daytime round trip Departs from Tsim Sha Tsui hourly between 11.55pm and 5.55pm daily and less regularly from Central Pier and Wan Chai; costs HK$105 for adults and HK$95 for concessions (children aged three to 12 years, seniors over 65).

Night round trip Departs at 6.55pm and 8.55pm from Tsim Sha Tsui and 8.15pm from Central Pier, though times can sometimes differ slightly for winter/summer (check online). Costs HK$190 for adults, HK$171 concessions.

Symphony of Lights Harbour Cruise Departs at 7.55pm from Tsim Sha Tsui and 7.15pm from Central Pier, timed for the nightly sound-and-light show over Victoria Harbour; it costs HK$215 for adults, HK$194 concessions.

Some operators offer tours with drinks, food and even buffet.

Aqua Luna (p85) Highly recommended cruises on a traditional Chinese wooden junk boat, with professional staff and comfy deck seating.

Watertours (p155) Six different tours of the harbour, as well as dinner and cocktail cruises, aboard a junk-style boat. Its one-hour Symphony of Lights Tour (HK$290) includes unlimited free alcoholic and soft drinks.

ADRIENNE PITTS / LONELY PLANET ©

Aqua Luna (p85) junk crossing Victoria Harbour

Hong Kong Ferry Group (☎852 2802 2886; www.cruise.com.hk; adult/child from HK$350/ 250) Offers two harbour cruises, including a Symphony of Lights tour, in a (pink!) ferry-style vintage boat with buffet dinner and a live band.

Nature Tours

Eco Travel (綠恆生態旅遊; ☎852 3105 0767; www.ecotravel.hk) This eco-travel company offers tours exploring Hong Kong's fishing and ocean culture, wetlands tours, a nature bike tour, and a trip to the Geopark of the northern New Territories. Some are only in Cantonese – phone or email ahead to check the availability of tours in English as its website is in Chinese.

Hong Kong Dolphinwatch (p155) Offers three- to four-hour cruises to see dolphins in their natural habitat.

Kayak and Hike (p168) The seven-hour Sai Kung Geopark kayak tour provides an exciting option for exploring the beauty of Sai Kung.

Walk Hong Kong (☎852 9187 8641; www. walkhongkong.com) Offers a range of hiking tours to some of the most beautiful places in Hong Kong, including deserted beaches in Sai Kung (HK$800 per person, 8½ hours), Dragon's Back in Shek O (HK$500, four hours) and WWII battlefields (HK$500, four hours). Urban cultural and heritage tours are also available. The meeting point is usually 2 Connaught Pl in Central.

Sea Kayak Hong Kong (p181) Based on Lamma Island, this environmentally conscious operator runs self-guided paddling trips as well as a raft of expeditions.

Recommended Geopark Guide System (www. hkr2g.net/en_index.htm) The government's R2G website has trained guides and agency recommendations for tours of Hong Kong Global Geopark.

Food Tours

Little Adventures in Hong Kong (☎852 9853 6746; www.littleadventuresinhongkong.com; per person from US$115) Tours are a little more pricey than some of its competitors, but its guided walks are led by food writers, journalists and chefs who provide insights few other tour guides can. Weekly group walks to Wan Chai or Kennedy Town (per person US$115) cover food, local history and culture; other options include a four-hour Wonton-a-thon walk, a cook's tour, and a smorgasbord of customisable options, depending on your interest.

Hong Kong Foodie Tour (☎852 2850 5006; www.hongkongfoodietours.com; adult/child from HK$750/540; ◷Mon-Sat) Regular group tours sampling Hong Kong's local food joints with native guides, and one of the only operators covering further-flung food haunts in the New Territories. There are four options: Central and Sheung Wan, Sham Shui Po, the Tai Po Market and Temple Street Night Market. Walks run every day of the week except Sunday. The Central and Sheung Wan trip departs Monday to Saturday at 1.45pm or 2.15pm and visits up to six locations: come hungry!

Humid with a Chance of Fishballs (p100) Personable Canadian–Hong Konger Virginia gets rave reviews and offers one of the cheapest food tours in the city: a guided dim-sum lunch in a chaotic 1950s parlour for HK$220. Or try eating typhoon-shelter crab on a sampan boat. She's also the only guide in the city offering a craft-beer breweries tour, which calls at three brewers most Saturdays (per person HK$608).

Aqua Luna (p85) Not guided per se, but Aqua Luna has a reasonably priced (HK$400) harbour cruise on its beautifully nostalgic Chinese wooden boat with an excellent dim-sum lunch of truffled har gow, char siu bao (barbecue pork bun) and creamy egg-custard tarts: a great way to combine two of Hong Kong's favourite pastimes – scoffing and sailing. The weekly cruise departs Mondays.

City & Culture Tours

Big Foot Tours (☎852 8192 9928; www.bigfoot tour.com; group tour HK$750, 1-2-person private tour HK$2200) Professional small group and private tours that really get behind the scenes of daily Hong Kong life. Group tours focus on New Territories neighbourhoods, their monasteries and so on. Private itineraries can focus on food (wanna try snake soup?), architecture, nature or whatever strikes your fancy, and guides are full of interesting facts.

Big Bus Company (Map p314, C6; ☎852 3102 9021; www.bigbustours.com; Unit KP-38, 1st fl, Star Ferry Pier, Tsim Sha Tsui; adult/child from HK$480/430; ◷9am-6pm; ⊕) A good way to get your bearings in the city is on the hop-on, hop-off, open-topped double-deckers. Three tours are available: the Kowloon Route takes in much of the Tsim Sha Tsui and Hung Hom waterfront; the Hong Kong Island Route explores Central, Admiralty, Wan Chai and Causeway Bay; and the Green Tour goes to Stanley Market and Aberdeen.

Eating

One of the world's most delicious cities, Hong Kong offers culinary excitement whether you're spending HK$50 on a bowl of noodles or HK$2000 on a seafood feast. The best of China is well represented, be it Cantonese, Shanghainese, Northern or Sichuanese. Similarly, the smorgasbord of non-Chinese – French, Italian, Japanese, Thai, Vietnamese, Indian – is the most diverse in all of Asia.

Cantonese Cuisine

The dominant cuisine in Hong Kong is Cantonese and it's easily the best in the world. Many of China's top chefs fled to the territory around 1949; it was therefore here and not in its original home, Guǎngzhōu, that Cantonese cuisine flourished.

This style of cooking is characterised by an insistence on freshness. Seafood restaurants display tanks full of finned and shelled creatures in their final moments. Flavours are delicate and balanced, obtained through restrained use of seasoning and light-handed cooking techniques such as steaming and quick stir-frying.

Cantonese cuisine refers to the culinary styles of Guǎngdōng province, as well as Chiu Chow (Cháozhōu) and Hakka cuisines. Chiu Chow dishes reflect a penchant for seafood and condiments. Deep-fried soft-boned fish comes with tangerine oil; braised goose with a vinegar and garlic dip. Hakka cuisine is known for its saltiness and use of preserved meat. Salt-baked chicken and pork stewed with preserved vegetables fed many hungry families and famished workers back in leaner times.

Hong Kong's chefs are also an innovative bunch who'll seize upon new ingredients and find wondrous ways of using them. For example, dim sum has expanded to include mango pudding, and shortbread tarts stuffed with abalone and chicken. Black truffles – the kind you see on French or Italian menus – are sometimes sprinkled on rolled rice sheets and steamed. And it works.

Dining Local

DIM SUM

Dim sum are Cantonese tidbits consumed with tea for breakfast or lunch. The term literally means 'to touch the heart' and the act of eating dim sum is referred to as yum cha, meaning 'to drink tea'.

In the postwar period, yum cha was largely an activity of single males, who met over

---

WALLED VILLAGE CUISINE

The modern history of Hong Kong begins with the First Opium War, but the roots of its cuisine go much further back. The local inhabitants who dwelt here ate what they could herd, grow or catch from the sea. Certain ancient food traditions from these peoples remain, most notably walled village cuisine, best known for the 'basin feast' (盆菜; *poon choi*). The story has it that the last emperor of the southern Song dynasty (AD 1127–1279), fleeing from the Mongols, retreated to a walled village in Hong Kong with his entourage. The villagers, lacking decent crockery, piled all kinds of food into a large basin to serve the royal guests. *Poon choy* has become a dish for festive occasions in the New Territories ever since.

NEED TO KNOW

Opening Hours

➡ Lunch 11am–3pm

➡ Dinner 6pm–11pm

Some restaurants are open through the afternoon, while others are also open for breakfast. Most restaurants open on Sunday (some close Mondays) and close for at least two days during the Lunar New Year.

Price Ranges

The prices below are based on a two-course meal.

$ less than HK$200

$$ HK$200 to HK$500

$$$ more than HK$500

Reservations

Most restaurants (midrange or above) take reservations. At popular addresses booking is crucial, especially for weekend dinners, and some may serve two or even three sittings a night.

Tipping

Tipping is not a must as every bill (except at the cheapest Cantonese joints) includes a 10% service charge, but this almost always goes into the owner's coffers, so if you're happy with the service, tip as you see fit. Most people leave behind the small change.

Resources

Good Eating (www.scmp.com) The restaurant guide and directory of a local English-language newspaper.

Hungry Hong Kong (http://hungryhk. blogspot.hk) Food and travel, with hunger-inducing photography.

Open Rice (www.openrice.com) Popular local site with restaurant reviews penned by the city's armchair gourmands.

Sassy Hong Kong (www.sassyhongkong. com) Definitive city blog that's particularly strong on food and drink.

Time Out (www.timeout.com.hk) An authoritative fortnightly guide and listings of what's on.

WOM Guide (www.womguide.com) A guide to the city's dining scene, new trends and sustainable food features.

their breakfast tea to socialise or exchange tips about job-seeking. Soon yum cha became a family activity.

Each dish, often containing two to four morsels steamed in a bamboo basket, is meant to be shared. In old-style dim sum places, just stop the waiter and choose something from the cart. Modern venues give you an order slip, but it's often in Chinese only. However, as dim sum dishes are often ready-made, the waiters should be able to show you samples to choose from.

The holy trinity of Hong Kong dim sum consists of *har gow,* translucent steamed parcels of chunky chopped shrimp; *siu mai,* a thicker skin encasing minced pork, topped with fish roe; and *char siu bao,* the classic barbecue pork bun. Other staples include molten custard buns and chicken feet in black bean sauce. To truly be initiated into Hong Kong dining, you must try all of these.

SOY SAUCE WESTERN

'Soy sauce western' *(si yau sai chaan)* features western-style dishes prepared with a large dollop of wisdom from the Chinese kitchen. It's said to have emerged in the 1940s when the ingenious chef of Tai Ping Koon decided to 'improve' on western cooking by tweaking recipes, such as replacing dairy products with local seasoning – lactose intolerance is common among East Asians – and putting rice on the menu.

His invention met its soulmate in White Russians, who had fled to Shànghǎi after the Bolshevik Revolution and sought refuge in Hong Kong in 1949; they soon cooked up what's known as Shanghainese–Russian food.

The two schools of western-inspired cuisine offered affordable and exotic dining to locals at a time when authentic western eateries catered almost exclusively to expatriates. Eventually the two styles mingled, spawning soy sauce western as we know it today. Popular dishes include Russian borscht, baked pork chop over fried rice and beef stroganoff with rice.

DAI PAI DONG

A *dai pai dong* (大牌檔) is a food stall, hawker-style or built into a rickety hut crammed with tables and stools that sometimes spill out onto the pavement. After WWII the colonial government issued food-stall licences to the families of injured or deceased civil servants. The licences were

Above: *Dai pai dong* (food stall), Central District

Right: Dim sum dishes

big so the stalls came to be known as *dai pai dong* (meaning 'big licence stalls').

Dai pai dong can spring up anywhere: by the side of a slope, in an alley or under a tree. That said, these vintage places for trillion-star dining are fast vanishing; most have now been relocated to government-run, cooked-food centres.

The culinary repertoire of *dai pai dong* varies from stall to stall. One may specialise in congee while its neighbour whips up seafood dishes that give restaurants a run for their money. In places where there's a cluster of *dai pai dong,* you can order dishes from different operators.

CHA CHAAN TANG

Teahouses (茶餐廳; *cha chaan tang*) are cheap and cheery neighbourhood eateries that appeared in the 1940s serving western-style snacks and drinks to those who couldn't afford Earl Grey and cucumber sandwiches. Their menus have since grown to include more substantial Chinese and soy sauce western (p40) dishes.

Some teahouses have bakeries creating European pastries with Chinese characteristics, such as pineapple buns (菠蘿包; *bo law bao*), which don't contain a trace of the said fruit, and cocktail buns, which have coconut stuffing (雞尾包; *gai may bao*).

How Hong Kongers Eat

Many busy Hong Kongers take their breakfast and lunch at tea cafes. A full breakfast at these places consists of buttered toast, fried eggs and spam, instant noodles and a drink. The more health-conscious might opt for congee, with dim sum of rolled rice sheets *(cheung fan)* and steamed dumplings with pork and shrimp *(siu mai).*

Lunch for office workers can mean a bowl of wonton noodles, a plate of rice with Chinese barbecue or something more elaborate.

Afternoon tea is popular at the weekends. On weekdays it is the privilege of labourers and ladies of leisure *(tai-tais).* Workers are said to vanish, Cinderella fashion, at 3.15pm sharp for their daily fix of egg tarts and milk tea. For *tai-tais,* tea could mean scones and rose-petal jam with friends or a bowl of noodles at the hairdresser.

Dinner is the biggest meal of the day. If prepared at home, what's on the table depends on the traditions of the family,

SHARK FIN – UNDERSTANDING THE ISSUES

Shark fin has been considered a delicacy in China for centuries. Though eaten since the Song dynasty (960–1279), shark fin became a luxury food item during the Ming dynasty (1368–1644), at a time when sea trade between China and Southeast Asian countries became more prominent. Shark-fin soup was served during emperors' banquets and has been passed down within Chinese culture as a food status symbol. Though the fin itself is relatively tasteless, its exoticism and difficulty to procure led to shark fin becoming a symbol of wealth and honour.

China's rapid economic expansion following its opening in the 1980s led to an increase in wealthier classes who could afford luxury food items, which in turn has led to overfishing, including several species of shark that are now considered endangered. Most estimates say between 75 and 100 million sharks are killed each year to meet the demands for meat and fin, with Hong Kong being the centre of the shark-fin trade. According to the International Union for Conservation of Nature (IUCN) Red List, upwards of 30% of shark populations are now listed as threatened or near-threatened.

In addition to this are the cruel methods by which shark fin is fished. Preparing the dish involves cutting the fin off and then often throwing the shark back into the water where it cannot swim, or leaving it to suffocate – either way enduring a painful and lingering death.

You will still find shark fin on many menus and for sale in markets across China, and especially in Hong Kong and Guǎngdōng, where it first became a delicacy. However, as awareness has grown globally and in the region about the animal-welfare issues, endangerment of species and knock-on environmental effects of shark-fin consumption, public outcry has increased.

but usually there's soup, rice, veggies and a meat or fish dish. Everyone has their own bowl of rice and/or soup, with the rest of the dishes placed in the middle of the table for sharing. Dining out is also extremely common, with many families eating out three to five times a week. Eating is a communal affair in Hong Kong and few people eat alone; menus are designed around sharing.

International Cuisine

From monkfish-liver sushi to French molecular cuisine, Hong Kong has no shortage of great restaurants specialising in the food of other cultures. The variety and quality of Asian cuisines is outstanding, surpassing even that of Tokyo. Then there's the exceptional array of western options. Hong Kong's affluent and cosmopolitan population loves western food, especially European. This is evidenced by the number of international celebrity chefs with restaurants here, such as Joël Robuchon, Pierre Gagnaire and Gordon Ramsey. Prices at these and other top addresses can be steep, but there's also a burgeoning number of excellent eateries specialising in rustic French or Italian that cater to food lovers with medium-sized pockets.

Self-Catering

The two major supermarket chains, PARKnSHOP (www.parknshop.com) and Wellcome (www.wellcome.com.hk), have megastores that offer groceries as well as takeaway cooked food. But do seek out the many food markets that still exist around the city, too.

Wet markets for fresh produce (open 6am to 7pm) can be found all over town.

Vegetarians Beware

There are 101 ways to accidentally eat meat in Hong Kong. A plate of greens is probably cooked in meat stock and served with oyster sauce. Broth made with chicken is a prevalent ingredient, even in dishes where no meat is visible. In budget restaurants, chicken powder is used liberally. The safe bet for veggies wanting to go Chinese is to patronise vegetarian eateries or upscale establishments. Restaurants specialising in other cuisines are often more sympathetic to vegetarians when planning menus; life can be even harder for vegans.

Cooking Classes

Dim-sum classes are nigh-on impossible to come by at a reasonable price (too fiddly/time-consuming), but Hong Kong is a good place to hone your skills in the other arts of Chinese cookery. Try these:

Home's Cooking (www.homescookingstudio. com; per person HK$750; ◷Mon–Fri) This highly rated cooking class offers three-hour morning sessions from the owner's home in the east of Hong Kong Island. Students cook a three-course Chinese meal: think spring rolls, lotus-leaf chicken and ginger pudding. Classes include a trip to a local wet market and lunch. There's a class minimum of two people.

Martha Sherpa (☏852 2381 0132; https:// marthasherpa.com; Flat F, 14th fl, Wah Lai Mansion, 62-76 Marble Rd, North Point; courses HK$1680; ♿; ⓂNorth Point, exit A2) Expert Cantonese home-cook Martha Sherpa (her last name comes from her Nepali husband) has taught the likes of former Australian PM Julia Gillard how to cook Hong Kong favourites. Small-group classes cover topics like restaurant-style Hong Kong Cantonese cuisine, Cantonese barbecue, Chinese regional cuisines, dim sum and vegetarian Chinese cookery. Half-day, full-day and evening classes are available.

Eating by Neighbourhood

➜ **Central District** (p74) Michelin-starred restaurants in five-star hotels, but also some of Hong Kong's most storied old cheap eats and cafes.

➜ **The Peak & Northwest Hong Kong Island** (p92) Sai Ying Pun and Sheung Wan have some of the city's most inventive fusion options.

➜ **Wan Chai & Northeast Hong Kong Island** (p108) Everything from the world's best *char siu* (roast pork) to bustling late-night cooked-food centres.

➜ **Aberdeen & South Hong Kong Island** (p128) Laid-back beach cafes and British-style pubs dot the island's sunny south side.

➜ **Kowloon** (p143) Cheap Indian dives sit next to glittering Cantonese banquet halls along Kowloon's screaming neon boulevards.

Lonely Planet's Top Choices

Kam's Roast Goose (p109) The crispiest, juiciest roast goose in the territory.

Aberdeen Fish Market Yee Hope Seafood Restaurant (p128) Seafood feast inside a wholesale fish market.

Little Bao (p93) Hong Kong's most raved-about fusion invention is this fist-sized Asian burger *bao* (bun).

Sun Hing Restaurant (p95) Point at dim-sum baskets and sit down to eat; don't miss the salty-sweet custard buns.

Kau Kee Restaurant (p92) Humble setting for the best beef brisket noodles in town; bring tissues to mop your face.

Old Bailey (p77) Classy menu, classy Tai Kwun setting and oh-so-tasty Chinese dishes you might not have seen before.

Best by Budget

$

Sun Kwai Heung (p114) Excellent low-key Cantonese barbecue.

Tai Cheong Bakery (p74) Serving Hong Kong's favourite egg tarts for half a century.

Kau Kee Restaurant (p92) Pull up a plastic pew at this holy grail for beef brisket noodle soup fans.

ABC Kitchen (p94) The cheapest western food you'll find in Hong Kong, in the incongruous environs of a local cooked-food centre.

Yat Lok (p74) Michelin-starred greasy roast goose heaven; Anthony Bourdain approved this joint.

Chi Lin Vegetarian (p146) Refined Chinese veggie dishes in an ornamental garden.

$$

Old Bailey (p77) Exquisite Shanghainese dishes in an architect-designed space that could come from the pages of a magazine.

Black Salt (p96) Creative takes on South Asian food, presented as scrumptious sharing dishes.

Ho Lee Fook (p77) Playful underground diner dishing out its own unique take on retro Chinatown cuisine.

Din Tai Fung (p144) Beloved Taiwanese chain serving perfectly formed *xiao long bao* (Shànghǎi-style dumplings).

Spring Deer (p144) This old old-timer of Northern Chinese cooking always delivers.

$$$

Seventh Son (p110) Top-notch dim sum and Cantonese fare.

Rōnin (p94) It's counter seating only at this trendy Japanese bar with inventive dishes and slick, knowledgeable servers.

Duddell's (p76) Refined Cantonese cuisine paired with excellent sommelier service in a cool, gallery-worthy space.

Lung King Heen (p76) The Chinese restaurant that upped the game for Cantonese chefs.

Bo Innovation (p112) Michelin-starred molecular Chinese cuisine with stratospheric prices fit for dedicated foodies.

Best Dai Pai Dongs

Stanley Street (p75) One of the few surviving *dai pai dong* (food stall) clusters in Central.

Gi Kee Seafood Restaurant (p114) Gourmet seafood above a wet market.

Sei Yik (p130) Queues form for breakfast toast at this half-hidden Stanley mainstay.

Ap Lei Chau Market Cooked Food Centre (p129) Where the fisherfolk hang out.

Best Dim Sum

Sun Hing Restaurant (p95) Working-class Kennedy Town staple with the best custard buns in town.

Yum Cha – Central (p75) Instagrammable buns take the limelight at this contemporary dim sum hall.

Lin Heung Tea House (p74) Old-school cart dim sum; prepare to fight for your meal.

Tim Ho Wan (p75) The first-ever budget dim sum place to earn a Michelin star.

Fook Lam Moon (p145) Celeb haunt in Macau with swanky menu but reasonably priced dim sum.

Lung King Heen (p76) Three-Michelin-starred dim sum for weekend brunch? Yes please.

Best Dining Away from the Crowds

Chung Kee Store (p174) Seafood and Hakka dishes deep in the hills.

Pirate Bay (p187) Family-friendly, pirate-themed French crepes opposite the water.

Amalfitana (p129) Pizza parlour within toe's dipping distance of the sea at Repulse Bay.

Yue Kee Roasted Goose Restaurant (p164) Primo roast goose in a far-flung village.

Foo's Cafe (p174) Farm-to-table village cafe serving Chinese goodies.

Best Western

8½ Otto e Mezzo Bombana (p76) Considered by many the finest Italian in Hong Kong.

Little Creatures (p99) Aussie-run microbrewery with excellent mod European carb-loaders, tacos etc.

Catch (p95) The best place in town for a fancy brunch.

Aberdeen St Social (p94) Chef Jason Atherton cooks up fancy takes on Brit food inside PMQ.

Best Japanese

Okra (p96) Friendly neighbourhood joint in Sai Ying Pun with playful creations and sake pairing.

Rōnin (p94) Buzzing Soho restaurant with masterful raw and cooked creations.

Yardbird (p93) Itty-bitty yakitori skewers; a hipster favourite in Sheung Wan.

Butao Ramen (p75) Queues tell you this Central lunch favourite has the winning ramen formula.

Best Asian Fusion

Bo Innovation (p112) Michelin-starred fusion gastronomy from Hong Kong's Alvin Leung.

Little Bao (p93) If China did burgers they would be made with... bao.

Kasa (p111) Chinese meat patty Scotch eggs anyone?

Man Mo Café (p93) Truffled brie and foie gras are some of the French ingredients in these delicious dim sum.

Tung Po Seafood Restaurant (p115) Lively Cantonese fusion in a wet market; opt for the late sitting.

Chifa Dumpling House (p76) Peruvian Chinese cuisine is the deal at this laid-back reggae-playing dumpling house.

Best Noodles

Ho To Tai Noodle Shop (p176) Shrimp-filled wonton noodles earn a devoted following.

Mak's Noodle (p74) Beloved shrimp-wonton shop with multiple locations.

Ho Hung Kee (p112) Making noodles, wontons and congee for 70 years.

Kau Kee Restaurant (p92) The best beef brisket noodles in town, served with or without a curry infusion.

Best Seafood

Aberdeen Fish Market Yee Hope Seafood Restaurant (p128) Seafood in a wholesale fish market; preordering required.

Ap Lei Chau Market Cooked Food Centre (p129) Seafood you buy from the market below is prepared here.

Loaf On (p167) Low-key but high-end seafood in seaside village of Sai Kung.

Chuen Kee Seafood Restaurant (p167) Classic seafood palace on Sai Kung waterfront.

Sam Shing Hui Seafood Market (p177) Bustling working seafood market in the New Territories.

Best Sweets

Atum Desserant (p112) Confectionary presented as art.

Mammy Pancake (p93) Arguably the city's best egg puffs/waffles.

Yuen Kee Dessert (p95) Dessert-only restaurant selling just one thing: hot, sweet Cantonese soups.

Tai Cheong Bakery (p74) The ultimate in Hong Kong egg tarts.

Honeymoon Dessert (p167) HK-based chain serving up sweet soups and icy treats.

Best Cha Chaan Tang (Teahouses)

Lan Fong Yuen (p74) *The* place to sample Hong Kong's famous milk tea.

Cheong Kee (p114) Above a wet market, some say it has the best thick toast in town.

Cafe Match Box (p112) Retro decor and fluffy egg sandwiches at this throwback joint.

Mido Café (p145) A charmingly retro spot overlooking the Tin Hau temple.

Cross Cafe (p95) Modern take on a *cha chaan tang*, with red-bean iced teas and truffled scrambled eggs.

Chau Kee (p95) Locals have been known to queue for the decadent 'lava' French toast with molten custard.

Best Vegetarian

Pure Veggie House (p109) Standout veggie dim sum and Cantonese classics.

Chi Lin Vegetarian (p146) Delightful Buddhist cuisine beside a gorgeous nunnery.

Sum Yuen (p212) Modern vegetarian cuisine at a Macau temple.

Mana! Fast Slow Food (p75) Vegan and raw food heaven with veggie flatbreads, smoothies and coffees.

Lock Cha Tea Shop (p108) Traditional-style Chinese tea shop inside leafy Hong Kong Park serving vegetarian dim sum.

Bookworm Cafe (p180) Beloved hippie haunt on laid-back Lamma.

Drinking & Nightlife

Energetic Hong Kong knows how to party and does so visibly and noisily. That said, don't be surprised that many of the city's bars are hidden inside skyscrapers; would it be Hong Kong if it were otherwise? You can find any type of bar or pub you want, but boozing will cost you dearly as alcohol is one of the few things that are taxed in this city: follow the happy hours.

What's Your Tipple?

A growing number of bars are dedicated to connoisseurship of one particular drink, such as whisky, gin or sake. Expect hand-carved ice, obscure bottles and nerdily expert bartenders.

Ever the faddy drinkers, Hong Kong has recently waded into the global gin craze with an increasing number of bars competing over who can mix the fanciest G&T. Sake is another area where Hong Kongers really know their stuff, with a growing number of bars dedicated to education and impressive import lists. Before this there was the whisky trend, and the city is still an excellent place to savour the amber liquid, with stylish Japanese whisky bars and European-style dens.

Cafes

Starbucks and Pacific Coffee are out – artisan coffee is in. Hong Kong has lately sprouted a very decent independent coffeehouse scene, complete with organic beans, micro-roasteries and cupping events.

LGBTQ+ Nightlife

For a world city of its size and status, Hong Kong has a surprisingly small LGBTQ+ scene. That said, it's made big strides in recent years and is slowly growing in confidence. The nightlife is relatively low-key and does not focus heavily on one particular area of the city. The biggest concentration of venues can be found around Kowloon and Central/Sheung Wan.

In 2018 a cluster of bars in Sheung Wan launched a 'Gaybarhood' (www.gaybarhood. net) collaboration in an effort to encourage more of a local scene.

Useful resources include:

Dim Sum (http://dimsum-hk.com) A free, monthly gay magazine with listings.

Travel Gay Asia (www.travelgayasia.com) An excellent resource for listings of LGBT+ bars across Hong Kong, including details of happy hours, 'free-flow' vodka hours and drag shows.

Utopia Asia (www.utopia-asia.com/hkbars.htm) A website with listings of gay-friendly venues and events in town.

HONG KONG'S PANTYHOSE TEA

Teahouses (茶餐廳; *cha chaan tang*) are perhaps best known for their Hong Kong–style 'pantyhose' milk tea (奶茶; *nai cha*) – a strong brew made from a blend of several types of black tea with crushed egg shells thrown in for silkiness. It's filtered through a fabric that hangs like a stocking, hence the name, and drunk with evaporated milk. 'Pantyhose' milk tea is sometimes mixed with three parts coffee to create the quintessential Hong Kong drink, tea-coffee or *yin yeung* (鴛鴦), meaning 'mandarin duck', a symbol of matrimonial harmony.

Karaoke

Karaoke clubs are as popular as ever with the city's young citizens, with a sprinkling of clubs in Causeway Bay and Wan Chai, and local dives in Mong Kok, Kowloon. The aural wallpaper at these clubs is most often Canto-pop covers, compositions that blend western rock or pop with Chinese melodies and lyrics, but there is usually a limited selection of 'golden oldies' and pop in English.

Cocktails

Hong Kong's Central district is home to some of the world's best cocktail bars, combining Asian flavours with western mixology. The city receives attention from the World's Top 50 Bars and Asia's Top 50 Bars awards each year, and while a night on the town crawling these venues ain't cheap, it really is an experience not to be missed. Ready your wallet for some world-class mixology action.

Craft Beer

The days when imported lagers ruled Hong Kong's draught taps are over: every bar worth its salt is now stocking something home-grown and microbreweries can be found shoehorned into high-rises and suburban warehouses. Breweries to look out for include Gweilo, Young Master, Lion Rock and Moonzen. Young Master Brewery (p124) runs guided tours of its Wong Chuk Hang facility every Saturday, and Australian-import microbrewery Little Creatures (p99) has a popular bar and restaurant in Kennedy Town. Humid with a Chance of Fishballs (p100) runs informative tours that get behind the scenes at a handful of craft breweries, allowing beer lovers to chew the ears of the brewers.

Drinking & Nightlife by Neighbourhood

→ **Central District** (p78) The epicentre of Hong Kong's partying scene is here in Lan Kwai Fong (LKF) and Soho; ready your wallet for some of the world's best cocktail bars.

→ **The Peak & Northwest Hong Kong Island** (p96) More laid-back than Central, expect speakeasies and craft beer; the LGBTQ+ crowd favours Sheung Wan.

→ **Wan Chai & Northeast Hong Kong Island** (p115) A delicious cocktail of the classy, the hidden and the hip alongside hostess bars and cheap raucous thrills.

NEED TO KNOW

Opening Hours

→ Bars open noon or 6pm and stay open until 2am to 6am; Wan Chai bars stay open the latest.

→ Cafes usually open between 8am and 11am and close between 5pm and 11pm.

Dress Code

Smart casual is usually good enough for most clubs, but patrons wearing shorts and flip-flops will not be admitted. Jeans are popular in Hong Kong and these are sometimes worn with heels or a blazer for a more put-together look. Hong Kong's clubbers can be style-conscious, so dress to impress! The dressiest area is Central, where locals move straight from the office to the bars wearing suits – expect to feel out of place in travel comfies.

Happy Hour

During certain hours of the day, most pubs, bars and even certain clubs give discounts on selected drinks or offer two-for-one deals. Happy hour is usually in the late afternoon or early evening – 3pm or 5pm until 8pm, say – but times can vary widely; some even start up again after midnight.

How Much?

It's downright expensive to drink in Hong Kong. An all-night boozy tour can set you back at least HK$800. Thrifty drinkers often buy from convenience stores as there is no law against drinking alcohol in public in Hong Kong. Alternatively, plan your nights around happy-hour hopping, which can halve the cost of drinks.

Price Ranges

→ Beer: HK$45 to HK$100 per pint

→ Wine: HK$50 to HK$150 per glass

→ Whisky: HK$50 to HK$250 per shot

→ Cocktails: HK$65 to o HK$200

→ Cover charge for clubs (including one drink): HK$200 to HK$700

→ **Aberdeen & South Hong Kong Island** (p130) Options are slim heading south, but bring a bottle to the waterfront and you have your own party.

→ **Kowloon** (p147) Waterholes with a local flavour abound in TST; as do belting karaoke bars.

Lonely Planet's Top Choices

Quinary (p80) Justifiably lauded as one of the world's top bars, with Instagram-ready cocktails and Asian accents.

Old Man (p96) Intimate, hidden and serving some of the most unusual cocktail concoctions you'll ever taste.

Ping Pong Gintoneria (p98) Gin swigging in a former ping-pong hall.

Cheng's Store (p164) Eccentric and nuanced tea offerings by a quirky master in Tsuen Wan.

Executive Bar (p118) Exclusive whisky and cocktail bar where you can catch serious Japanese mixology in action.

Pontiac (p80) A dive bar at its best, with an alternative soundtrack that kicks the rest of LKF's ass.

Best for Clubbing

Volar (p82) Young crowd partying underground (literally) against a futuristic backdrop.

Dusk Till Dawn (p117) The place to be rocking out to live music when the other bars close.

Behind (p78) Roving club night hosted by classy venues on Hong Kong Island.

Petticoat Lane (p81) Central's friendliest LGBTQ+ club has it all: topless bartenders, free-flow vodka hours and, of course, a dance floor.

Best for Tea Time

Peninsula Hong Kong (p230) The most elegant afternoon tea in the territory.

Lock Cha Tea Shop (p108) Antiquey environs and tradi-tional music accompany tea here in Hong Kong Park.

Cheng's Store (p164) Mr Cheng's rather costly concoc-tions are uniquely Hong Kong.

Teakha (p98) Wake up and smell the jasmine at this elegant tea lounge.

Lan Fong Yuen (p74) The classic spot to try Hong Kong's famous milk tea.

Best for Cocktails

Quinary (p80) Creative Asian-inspired cocktails in an elegant setting.

Butler (p149) Japanese cocktail bar in a quiet part of TST.

Executive Bar (p118) It's appointment-only at this swanky whisky lounge.

Old Man (p96) A homage to Hemingway with unique con-coctions that would make even Papa fall off his bar stool.

Iron Fairies (p80) Magical drinking den channelling an old industrial vibe.

Honi Honi (p78) Tropical tiki vibes, classy terrace in the sky and freshly juiced cocktail mixers.

Best for People-Watching

Peak Cafe Bar (p81) Watch the Central–Mid-Levels Elevator roll by from this Soho spot.

Club 71 (p80) A mainstay of artists and writers.

Cheng's Store (p164) Mr Cheng making tea is interesting enough.

Beer Bay (p78) Locals promenading and suits com-muting home at Central Pier.

Best for Quirky Vibes

Ned Kelly's Last Stand (p151) Dixieland jazz, Aussie decor and expat crowds.

Wanch (p119) Rock out with tourists, locals, sailors, junkies and other assorted weirdos at this live-music spot.

Missy Ho (p96) Turn up late to this Kennedy Town restaurant–bar and post-dinner drinkers will get the dress-up box out.

Iron Fairies (p80) 'It is very bad luck to steal a fairy' read the table signs at this fantastical basement cocktail bar.

Best for Unpretentious Drinking

Café 8 (p78) Social spot with a harbourside roof terrace atop the Hong Kong Maritime Museum.

Club 71 (p80) As unpretentious as you can get in the Soho area.

Beer Bay (p78) Drinking on the steps of Central Pier with beer, BYO snacks and friendly faces.

Pontiac (p80) Friendly vibes, an all-female bar team and great soundtrack make this dive bar a winner.

Agave (p117) Enough tequila will help anyone lose their pretensions.

Buddy Bar (p118) A low-key neighbourhood pub in hip but friendly Tai Hang.

Best Views

Sevva (p78) Beautiful people and beautiful harbour views, within air-kissing distance of the HSBC Building.

Skye Bar (p117) Magnificent harbour views, hidden on the roof of a Causeway Bay hotel.

Ben's Back Beach Bar (p130) Overlooking a deserted Shek O beach.

Cé La Vi (p81) Get right amid the business towers at this rooftop party bar in LKF.

Sugar (p118) Dizzying views from atop an Island East hotel.

Intercontinental Lobby Lounge (p147) Floor-to-ceiling glass overlooks Victoria Harbour.

Best for Watching Sports

Dickens Bar (p118) This British-style pub plays any rugby and football to be found.

Slide on 79 (p81) More sophisticated than your average LKF sports pub – hello cocktails!

Globe (p81) British pub with Narnia-style space and comfy booths.

Delaney's (p130) An Irish pub with TVs and friendly crowds.

Canny Man (p117) Hong Kong's only Scottish pub, with sports screens, haggis and stovies.

Best for Craft Beer

65 Peel (p80) Neon-tinged beer bar with flights of local beers and Hong Kong–themed bites.

Craftissimo (p98) Trendy bottle shop with a back-alley patio for drinking takeaways or a rotating draught offering.

Little Creatures (p99) Roomy Aussie-import microbrewery in local hood Kennedy Town.

Second Draft (p117) Local beers are the star at this comfy neighbourhood gastropub affiliated with Young Master brewery.

Kowloon Taproom (p149) Open-fronted, grungy bar pouring local Lion Rock beers.

Beer Temple (p206) Huge selection in Macau, backed by a pumping soundtrack.

Best for Whisky

Butler (p149) It's either whisky or cocktails here, or whisky-based cocktails.

Angel's Share Whisky Bar (p81) It's all about the whisky, including its own special barrel.

Executive Bar (p118) The Japanese mixologist knows his whisky.

Best Coffee Champions

Elephant Grounds (p118) Great brews including 'bulletproof coffee' and much-loved ice-cream sandwiches.

NOC (p99) Cafe, brunch spot and roastery in one, in a light and bright contemporary space.

Cupping Room (p98) Popular Hong Kong mini-chain with rotating single-origin brews and a roastery in Tai Ping Shan.

Valor (p187) Ice-drip coffee served in baby coconut shells, island style.

Bound (p150) Excellent coffee is the lynchpin of this art-touting cafe-bar.

Accro Coffee (p177) The best brews in the New Territories.

Best for Gin O'Clock

Ping Pong Gintoneria (p98) Gin-based concoctions in an old ping-pong hall.

Dr Fern's Gin Parlour (p78) Enter through the waiting room in the basement of Landmark mall to be treated by the doctors.

Botanicals (p115) Come after dark for negronis with house-infused gin.

Best LGBTQ+ spots

Petticoat Lane (p81) Central club with topless bartender hours, drag shows and a friendly crowd.

Zoo (p98) Local vibe for late-night dancing and drinking in Sheung Wan.

Behind (p78) Sophisticated roaming club night.

Boo (p150) Don't expect a quiet drink, but do expect to be entertained at this karaoke and DJ bar in Kowloon.

Boom (p213) Macau's only gay bar has live music, themed nights and occasional go-go dancers.

T:ME (p82) Low-key cocktail lounge in a Central back alley.

Best Happy Hours

Honi Honi (p78) Very few of Hong Kong's classiest cocktail bars throw happy hours like Honi Honi.

Colette's Art Bar (p81) Enjoy the marathon-long happy hour on the balcony at this bar in an old dairy farm.

Stone Nullah Tavern (p115) Unlimited house spirits, wines, Pabst Blue Ribbon beer, fried chicken and maple bacon for HK$100. Rejoice!

Pontiac (p80) Do HK$15 happy hour beers make this the cheapest deal in town?

Cé La Vi (p81) Rooftop bars don't usually partake in happy hours; grab this two-for-one deal with both hands.

⭐ Entertainment

Hong Kong's arts and entertainment scene is healthier than ever. The increasingly busy cultural calendar includes music, drama and dance hailing from a plethora of traditions. The schedule of imported performances is nothing short of stellar. And every week, local arts companies and artists perform anything from Bach or stand-up to Cantonese opera and English versions of Chekhov plays.

The Arts

Local western music ensembles and theatre troupes stage weekly shows, while famous foreign groups are invited to perform often, particularly at the **Hong Kong Arts Festival** (香港藝術節; www.hk.artsfestival.org; from HK$150; ⊘Feb-Mar). The annual event attracts world-class names in all genres of music, theatre and dance, including the likes of the Bolshoi Ballet, Anne-Sophie Mutter and playwright Robert Wilson.

Cantonese Opera

Unsurprisingly, Hong Kong is one of the best places on earth to watch Cantonese opera. The best time to catch a performance is during the Hong Kong Arts Festival (p50) and the Mid-Autumn Festival, when outdoor gigs are staged in Victoria Park. You can also catch a performance at the Temple Street Night Market (p135) or during Chinese festivals.

There are irregular performances at the historic Sunbeam Theatre (p119) and regular shows at the Yau Ma Tei Theatre (p141) and Ko Shan Theatre (www.lcsd.gov.hk/kst), both in Kowloon. If you don't speak Cantonese, the best way to book tickets for any performance is through Hong Kong Ticketing (p51), Urbtix (p51) or **Cityline** (☎852 2314 4228; www.cityline.com.hk).

Cinema

Hong Kong is well served with cinema, screening both mainstream and art-house films. Cinemas usually show local productions and Hollywood blockbusters. The vast majority of films have both English and Chinese subtitles. Book tickets and seats online or in person well before the show.

Cinema buffs from all over Asia make the pilgrimage to the annual **Hong Kong International Film Festival** (香港國際電影節; www.hkiff.org.hk; from HK$45; ⊘Mar-Apr). Cine Fan (www.cinefan.com.hk), run by the same folks, has offerings all year round.

Live Music

Hong Kong's live-music scene has seen a growing number of venues hosting independent musicians (imported and local) several nights a week. The options range

---

AVENUE OF STARS

Much of Kowloon's prime waterfront is dedicated to stars of the Hong Kong cinema, honoured through statues and hand prints. Though foreigners may not recognise many of the names, everyone loves to pose in front of the Bruce Lee statue. The giant bronze pig, in case you're wondering, is McDull, a beloved Hong Kong children's cartoon. In early 2019 it is due to re-emerge more starry eyed than ever after a sprucing up.

from a smooth evening of jazz to a raucous night of goth metal, not to mention dub step, post-rock, drum 'n' bass and electronica.

Peel Fresco (p82) and Grappa's Cellar (p82) are popular venues. And don't miss the clandestine dive This Town Needs (p151).

The **Hong Kong International Jazz Festival** (www.hkijf.com; from HK$200; ⊙Sep, Oct or Nov) caters to jazz lovers.

CONCERTS

Hong Kong is a stop on the big-name concert circuit, and a growing number of internationally celebrated bands and solo artists perform here. These include mainstream acts and those on the edge of the mainstream – from U2, Guns N' Roses and Madonna, to Kings of Convenience, Deerhoof and Mogwai.

CLOCKENFLAP

The highlight in Hong Kong's live-music calendar is the excellent multi-act outdoor music festival known as **Clockenflap** (香港 音樂及藝術節; www.clockenflap.com; Central harbourfront; tickets 1-day HK$820-890, 3-day HK$1410; ⊙Nov or Dec). The three-day event has featured dozens of local, regional and international acts performing at the West Kowloon promenade.

Entertainment by Neighbourhood

→ **Central District** (p82) Jazz is being played every night of the week somewhere in Central, along with alternative theatre and high-roll shows.

→ **The Peak & Northwest Hong Kong Island** (p99) Drag shows draw LGBTQ+ drinkers to Sheung Wan.

NEED TO KNOW

Show Tickets

Expect to pay around HK$80 for a seat up the back for a local ensemble and from about HK$600 for a performance by big-name international acts or an international musical such as *Chicago*.

Movie Tickets

Movie tickets cost between HK$65 and HK$100, but can be cheaper at matinees, at the last screening of the day (usually 11.30pm), on weekends and on holidays, or on certain days of the week. Almost all non-English-language films have both Chinese and English subtitles.

Booking

Urbtix (☑ticketing enquiries 10am-8pm 852 3761 6661; www.urbtix.hk) and **Hong Kong Ticketing** (☑ticket hotline 10am-8pm 852 3128 8288; www.hkticketing.com) have tickets to every major event in Hong Kong. You can book through them or purchase tickets at the performance venues; Urbtix tickets can be collected from a handful of kiosks around town.

→ **Wan Chai & Northeast Hong Kong Island** (p119) Comedy, Cantonese opera, theatre, live music – you name it, it's here.

→ **Aberdeen & South Hong Kong Island** Beaches and fishing outposts flank this area; what more entertainment do you need?

→ **Kowloon** (p150) Home to Hong Kong's big-shot, multimillion-dollar theatre complexes.

Lonely Planet's Top Choices

Hong Kong International Film Festival (p50) Asia's top film festival features both esoteric titles and crowd pleasers.

Clockenflap (p51) Everyone in town attends this massive rock festival.

Hong Kong Arts Festival (p50) Hong Kong's most exciting outdoor music festival.

This Town Needs (p151) The city's most visible clandestine live-music venue.

Peel Fresco (p82) Intimate live-jazz venue that regularly features recording artists.

Best Live Music

Peel Fresco (p82) Groovy jazz and arty crowds in a tiny club.

This Town Needs (p151) HK's most famous music dive has a line-up of solid indie acts.

Wanch (p119) Wan Chai's venerable live-music spot is tops for rock, jazz and lots of beer.

Grappa's Cellar (p82) This Italian restaurant turns to rock, jazz and comedy.

Fringe Club (p82) Jazz, world music and more play inside this Victorian building.

Best Movie Theatres

Broadway Cinematheque (p152) Hong Kong's best art-house theatre shows indie films that don't play elsewhere.

AMC Pacific Place (p120) In the plush Pacific Place mall, watch Hollywood and Hong Kong releases in comfort.

HKAC Cinema (p120) In the Hong Kong Arts Centre, this small space plays festival releases on a limited basis.

Cinematheque Passion (p207) Macau's first art-house cinema and film archive.

Palace IFC (p82) Eight screens of blockbusters in plush surrounds.

Best Theatre

Hong Kong Arts Centre (p120) Theatre, dance and more.

Hong Kong Academy for the Performing Arts (p120) All manner of performances grace this school's stage.

Hong Kong Cultural Centre (p152) If it's culture, it's here.

Fringe Club (p82) Think of it as Hong Kong's off-Broadway.

Cattle Depot Artist Village (p143) Esoteric performance art in a former slaughterhouse.

Best Kooky or Underground

This Town Needs (p151) The underground music spot in Hong Kong, so cool the government wants to shut it down.

Canton Singing House (p150) Temple St's best singalong parlour – think old-school Cantonese karaoke.

Petticoat Lane (p81) Drag queens appear at the stroke of midnight at this popular LGBTQ+ nightclub.

Cattle Depot Artist Village (p143) A Kowloon slaughterhouse turned artists' village and music venue.

🛍 Shopping

Hong Kong is renowned as a place of neon-lit retail pilgrimage. This city is positively stuffed with swanky shopping malls and brand-name boutiques. All international brands worth their logos have stores here. These are supplemented by the city's own retail trailblazers and an increasing number of creative local designers. Together they are Hong Kong's shrines and temples to style and consumption.

Antiques

Hong Kong has a rich and colourful array of Asian antiques on offer, and is one of the best markets in the world to shop for genuine Chinese antiques (tombware, Qing dynasty furniture, Ming dynasty pottery etc). That said, forgeries and expert reproductions abound, and serious buyers should restrict themselves to reputable antique shops and auction houses. Ask for certification that proves authenticity; remember that there is no such thing as a bargain in a hunting ground this high profile. Most of the highest-quality pieces are sold through auction houses such as Christie's, especially at its spring and autumn sales.

The epicentre of Hong Kong's street-level antiques retail scene has traditionally been Hollywood Rd, but spiralling rents in Central are pushing shops to the western end of this historic thoroughfare; most are now bunched around the area between Tai Ping Shan St and Upper Lascar Row (Cat St). The market is also moving increasingly upmarket as the value of Chinese antiques has skyrocketed beyond all imagination in the past six to eight years. A piece that would have been HK$10,000 is now HK$40,000 to HK$50,000; the midrange market is disappearing, as are many of the old stalwart shops along Hollywood Rd.

Cat Street Market (p91) hawks cheaper paraphernalia, including magazines, Chinese propaganda posters and badges from the Cultural Revolution. For old-style Chinese handicrafts, the main places to go are the large emporiums.

Art

Whether it is true or not, Hong Kong is now being touted as one of the best places in the world to shop for contemporary art. An increasing number of art galleries in Hong Kong sell paintings, sculptures, ceramic works and installations – some very good – by local artists, as well as international names-in-the-making. The city's swankiest commercial galleries are firmly entrenched in the area once occupied by antiques shops on and around Wyndham St and Hollywood Rd in Central.

Art Basel (香港巴塞爾藝術展; www.artbasel.com/hong-kong; ☺Mar), **Le French May** (www.frenchmay.com; ☺Apr-Jun) and **Fotanian** (www.fotanstudios.org; ☺Oct) offer great opportunities to acquire art or simply acquaint yourself with the city's interesting visual-arts scene.

Cameras

Increasingly, Tsim Sha Tsui in Kowloon has become the go-to place for electronics, including cameras. Service in the big electronics chain stores here is reassuring, the products legitimate and the prices competitive. Some low-level bargaining may be possible but don't expect giant discounts on the ticket prices. These days many shops that don't carry price tags are still legitimate, but do shop around to ensure the figures you're being quoted are fair. In Mong Kok, check out Showa Film & Camera (p153) for retro film cameras, lenses and first-class film-developing services.

NEED TO KNOW

Opening Hours

→ Central: generally 10am to 8pm

→ Causeway Bay: 11am to 9.30pm or 10pm

→ Tsim Sha Tsui: 11am to 8pm

→ Most shops open on Sunday

→ Winter sales in January; summer sales in late June and early July

Duty-Free

There's no sales tax in Hong Kong so ignore the 'Tax Free' signs in some stores. However, you will pay duty on tobacco and alcohol. In general, almost everything is cheaper when you buy it outside duty-free shops.

Refunds & Exchanges

Most shops won't give refunds, but they can be persuaded to exchange purchases if they haven't been tampered with and you have a detailed receipt.

Service

Service is attentive and credit cards are widely accepted.

Shipping Goods

Many shops – especially furniture and antiques stores – will package and post large items for you, but check whether you'll have to clear the goods at the destination country. Smaller items can be shipped from the post office or try DHL (www.dhl.com.hk/en).

Warranties & Guarantees

Some imported goods have a Hong Kong–only guarantee. If it's a well-known brand, you can sometimes return the warranty card to the Hong Kong importer to get one for your country. Grey-market items imported by somebody other than the official agent may have a guarantee that's valid only in the country of manufacture, or none at all.

Clothing

DESIGNER BRANDS & BOUTIQUES

The best places to find global designer brands and luxury stores are in malls such as IFC (p84) and the **Landmark** (置地廣場; Map p302; ☑852 2500 0555; www.centralhk.com; 1 Pedder St, Central; ☎; ⓜCentral, exit G) in Central, Pacific Place (p120) in Admiralty and Festival Walk (p154) in Kowloon Tong. Some of these shops, such as Prada, have outlets at Horizon Plaza (p131) in Ap Lei Chau selling off-season items at discounted prices.

For something unique, there are cool independents run by, or featuring, local designers in Central, Sheung Wan, Wan Chai and Tsim Sha Tsui. The pricing, while not as high as luxury retail, is certainly not cheap. Sometimes the quality doesn't live up to the price tag, but there are some lovely original pieces to be had. Central has some fabulous local designer boutiques; the area in Sheung Wan around Tai Ping Shan St is a little more affordable.

STREET MARKETS & MINI-MALLS

The best hunting grounds for low-cost garments are in Tsim Sha Tsui at the eastern end of Granville Rd, and Cheung Sha Wan Rd in Sham Shui Po. The street markets on Temple St in Yau Ma Tei and Tung Choi St in Mong Kok have the cheapest clothes. You may also try Li Yuen St East and Li Yuen St West, two narrow alleyways linking Des Voeux Rd Central with Queen's Rd Central. They are a jumble of inexpensive clothing, handbags, backpacks and costume jewellery.

For a truly local shopping experience, the mini-malls in Tsim Sha Tsui are teeming with all things young and trendy, both locally designed and imported from the mainland or Korea. Usually you can negotiate a lower price when you purchase more than one item. And if you have a good eye, you can end up looking chic for very little.

Gems & Jewellery

The Chinese attribute various magical qualities to jade, including the power to prevent ageing and accidents. The Jade Market (p154) in Yau Ma Tei is diverting, but unless you're knowledgeable about jade, limit yourself to modest purchases. Some guided tours of Kowloon include a visit here, which can give a better insight than what you'll learn on your own.

Hong Kong also offers a great range of pearls – cultured and freshwater. Retail prices for other precious stones are only marginally lower than elsewhere. The more reputable jewellery-shop chains – and there are many in Tsim Sha Tsui and Mong Kok catering to tourists from the mainland – will issue a certificate that states exactly what you are buying and guarantees that the shop will buy it back at a fair market price.

Handicrafts & Souvenirs

For old-school Chinese handicrafts and other goods such as hand-carved wooden pieces, ceramics, cloisonné, silk garments and place mats, head to the large Chinese emporiums, such as Chinese Arts & Crafts. Mountain Folkcraft (p83) in Central is also good for both Chinese and Southeast Asian handicrafts. You'll find a small range of similar items (but of a lesser quality) in the alleyways of Tsim Sha Tsui and stalls lining Cat Street (p91) in Sheung Wan, but remember to check prices at different vendors and bargain.

If you prefer something in a modern Chinese style, Shanghai Tang (p83), the fashion boutique with branches all over town, has a range of cushions, tableware, photo frames and other home accessories – at luxury prices.

The homewares, fashion and accessories store G.O.D. (p82) is an excellent home-grown brand with a cheeky Hong Kong twist and several stores across the city.

Leather Goods & Luggage

All the brand names – such as Louis Vuitton, Samsonite and Rimowa – are sold at Hong Kong department stores, and you'll also find some local vendors in the luggage business. The popularity of hiking and travel has triggered a proliferation of outdoor-products shops that carry high-quality backpacks. If you're looking for a cheap casual bag or daypack, check out Li Yuen St East and Li Yuen St West in Central or Stanley Market (p127).

Local Brands & Designers

Hong Kong doesn't have a profusion of quirky, creative one-offs or unique vintage items as in London, New York or Copenhagen. (Have you seen the rent landlords charge here?) But the city has a small, passionate band of local designer boutiques offering value, character and style across a range of goods, especially in fashion, design and homewares. A small army of them have conveniently taken up residence inside the excellent PMQ complex (p90) on the borders of Sheung Wan and Central; don't miss it.

Soho, Wan Chai, Causeway Bay and Tsim Sha Tsui are other hot spots for these stores. Some, such as **Homeless Workplace** (Map p312; ☑852 9309 7120; www.homeless. hk; 12th fl, unit 1203, The Factory, 1 Yip Fat St, Wong Chuk Hang; ⊘noon-7pm Mon-Fri; MWong Chuk Hang, exit A2), carry a smattering of chic, design-oriented goods (local and imported) while others, such as homewares and fashion store G.O.D. (p83) and fashion boutiques Shanghai Tang (p83) and **Initial** (Map p302; ☑852 2259 5112; www.initialfashion. com; G01, Man Yee Bldg, 60-68 Des Voeux Rd, Central; ⊘11am-9.30pm; MCentral, exit C), have in-house design teams.

Watches

Shops selling watches are ubiquitous in Hong Kong and you can find everything from a Rolex to Russian army timepieces and diving watches. Avoid the shops without price tags. **City Chain** (時間廊; Map p302; ☑852 2537 6518; www.citychain.com; ground fl, Yat Fat Bldg, 44-46 Des Voeux Rd Central, Central; ⊘10.30am-9pm; MCentral, exit C1) is a reputable high-street store and the big department stores are other places worth trying, but do compare prices.

Bargaining

Sales assistants in department or chain stores rarely have any leeway to give discounts, but you can try bargaining in owner-operated stores and certainly in markets.

Some visitors believe that you can always get the goods for half of the price originally quoted. But if you can bargain something down that low, perhaps you shouldn't be buying it from that shop anyway. Remember, you may be getting that DSLR cheap but paying high mark-ups for the memory card, or worse, it may have missing components or no international warranty.

Don't be too intent on getting the best deals. Really, what's HK$5 off a souvenir that's being sold for HK$50? Probably not much to you, but it may mean a lot to the old lady selling it.

The Low-Down on High-Tech Shopping

Once upon a time Hong Kong's very favourable tax laws meant the city was a fertile ground for bargain-hunters looking to buy

PMQ (p90), Soho

the latest electronics gear. But with the advent of the internet in recent years, there are fewer and fewer bargains to be had on high-end goods (and if you think you've found one, beware). Prices are certainly extremely competitive, though, and Hong Kong has a plethora of specialist shops and big chains in which you can confidently shop. In smaller stores, shopkeepers are generally honest but some have been known to sell display or secondhand items as new ones. For reputable electronics centres, head to Wan Chai or Kowloon; Sham Shui Po is the place to go for cut-price computer centres.

Shopping by Neighbourhood

➡ **Central District** (p82) Posh malls and designer brands abound in Hong Kong's business district.

➡ **The Peak & Northwest Hong Kong Island** (p99) Trendy Sheung Wan is fast becoming the go-to spot for quirky boutiques and local designers.

➡ **Wan Chai & Northeast Hong Kong Island** (p120) From street markets to fancy malls to funky hipster enclaves, Wan Chai has it all.

➡ **Aberdeen & South Hong Kong Island** (p130) Ap Lei Chau is the place for outlet hauls; Stanley has a fun outdoor souvenir market.

➡ **Kowloon** (p152) Shop for designer goodies and knock-offs galore along with half of China.

Lonely Planet's Top Choices

G.O.D. (p130) Awesome lifestyle accessories, fashionable cheongsam, homewares and gifts – Hong Kong to the bone with a whiff of mischief.

Wattis Fine Art (p83) Antique maps, nostalgic photographs and rare lithographs of Hong Kong, Macau and elsewhere in Asia.

PMQ (p90) A one-stop-shop for affordable local design, fashion and jewellery, all jostling for your dollars inside a dynamic heritage arts complex.

Chan Shing Kee (p99) Classical Chinese furniture and decorative antiques.

Shanghai Tang (p83) A peek into the world of contemporary luxury fashion and homewares – Chinese style.

Yue Hwa Chinese Products Emporium (p153) Old Chinese department store *grande dame* with embroidered slippers, chopsticks and calligraphy equipment.

Best Antiques & Vintage

Andy Hei (p83) Rare Chinese antiques in *huanghuali* wood.

Capital Gallery (p99) Tiny shop selling curios from several thousand years ago.

Chan Shing Kee (p99) *The* place for classical Chinese furniture.

Arch Angel Antiques (p83) Authentic Chinese tombware in all shapes and sizes.

Cat Street Market (p91) Not genuine antiques, but interesting repro goodies, vintage posters and old photos.

Best Art

PMQ (p90) Affordable, Hong Kong–focused art in a collection of small independent stores.

C&G Artpartment (p141) Edgy local art.

Pearl Lam Galleries (p84) Contemporary Hong Kong and international art.

H Queen's (p73) Contemporary-art haven in the sky, with galleries from top international dealers.

Blindspot Gallery (p126) One of the best places to acquaint yourself with Hong Kong and Asian photography.

Chiu Kee Porcelain Studio (p183) Painted Chinese porcelain in traditional Hong Kong style.

Best Beauty & Fragrance

Two Girls (p121) Hong Kong's cheap-and-cheerful local beauty brand, with fun vintage packaging.

Joyce (p84) High-end beauty products and scents from across the world.

Hysan Place (p121) The 6th-floor Garden of Eden is a paradise for hard-to-find, youth-oriented Asian cosmetics.

Candle Company (p84) Diffusers, candles and incense from Hong Kong designer Carroll & Chan.

Best Books

Eslite (p121) Massive Taiwanese bookstore/cafe/gallery/toy store.

Hong Kong Reader (p154) Bilingual bookstore with an intellectual edge.

Kubrick Bookshop Café (p150) Excellent selection of highbrow fiction, art books and literary journals.

Swindon Books (p153) Independent, and crammed with Hong Kong–related reads.

Bookworm Cafe (p180) A secondhand island bookshop island inside a vegetarian cafe.

Best Fashion

Kapok (p120) Hipster fashions from local and international designers.

Horizon Plaza (p131) Cut-rates on luxury goods and clothing in a 27-floor warehouse.

Pacific Place (p120) High-end couture in a pleasant mall environment.

Fashion Walk (p121) High-street names and local brands.

Only Alice (p99) Chic, affordable Hong Kong fashion and accessories boutique on trendy Tung St.

Best Food & Beverages

Kowloon Soy Company (p83) A Central institution since 1917, selling artisanal soy, yellow bean and oyster sauces.

Shanghai Street (p140) Woks, mooncake moulds and other cooking implements galore.

Lam Kie Yuen Tea Co (p100) Friendly tea specialist with gorgeous teaware.

Yiu Fung Store (p121) Hong Kong's most famous emporium for Chinese pickles and other cooks' ingredients.

Papabubble (p121) Hard candies in a variety of quirky local flavours.

Best Gadgets

Wan Chai Computer Centre (p120) A warren of all things electronic.

Golden Computer Arcade (p154) Computers and components for extra low prices.

Apliu Street Flea Market (p154) A huge digital-products flea market.

Mong Kok Computer Centre (p154) Cheap computer mall.

Showa Film & Camera (p153) Retro film cameras and accessories.

Best Gifts

Temple Street Night Market (p135) Everything from chopsticks to jewellery – bargain hard.

G.O.D. (p83) Playful accessories and homewares paying homage to Hong Kong pop culture.

Stanley Market (p127) Carved name chops, satin baby shoes and more in a touristy but fun street market.

Mountain Folkcraft (p83) Folk crafts from Chinese minorities and Southeast Asian countries.

Lam Kie Yuen Tea Co (p100) Venerable tea shop with huge selection.

Best Malls

IFC Mall (p84) Swanky and always-crowded Central mall.

Pacific Place (p120) Ultra-luxe international clothing and accessories.

Elements (p154) One of Kowloon's fanciest shopping centres.

Festival Walk (p154) More than 200 shops plus an ice rink.

Rise Shopping Arcade (p152) Cheap, fun shopping mall.

Hysan Place (p121) The finest in Japanese and Korean fashions.

Best Markets

Stanley Market (p127) Touristy street market, good for souvenirs.

Apliu Street Flea Market (p154) Massive electronics flea market.

Temple Street Night Market (p135) Iconic night market of kitsch and souvenirs.

Ladies' Market (p153) Clothing, mobile-phone covers, knock-off purses and more.

Ap Lei Chau Market (p129) A seafood extravaganza just a floor below the Ap Lei Chau Cooked Food Centre.

Yau Ma Tei Wholesale Fruit Market (p141) The oldest market buildings in Hong Kong.

Best Quirky Items

Sino Centre (p154) Geek out at this anime mall.

Chan Wah Kee Cutlery Store (p153) One of Asia's few remaining master knife sharpeners.

Cat Street (p91) Junk stalls hawk communist kitsch and Bruce Lee posters at this touristy street market.

Island Beverly Mall (p121) Eye-popping Japanese youth fashions.

Niin (p99) Eco-conscious jewellery and accessories fashioned out of reclaimed wood and abalone shells.

Soul Art (p83) Polymer clay dim sum and Chinese cult figurines, straight from Běijīng.

Sports & Activities

Despite the metropolis of glass and steel at its heart, Hong Kong is an outdoorsy city offering countless ways to enjoy the water and the outlandish natural environment that pushes against the city's urban spaces. Hiking trails abound, there's a thriving keep-fit culture and dozens of spas and massage centres cater for relaxation-seekers.

Climbing

Hong Kong is peppered with excellent granite faces and volcanic rocks in some striking wilderness areas. The best place to climb is on Tung Lung Chau, which has a technical wall, a big wall and a sea gully. Shek O beach has some excellent bouldering as well.

The Hong Kong Climbing website (www. hongkongclimbing.com) is a handy resource for climbers.

Cycling

Hong Kong's natural terrain makes for some fabulous cycling.

The longest bicycle track runs from Sha Tin through Tai Po to Tai Mei Tuk, taking you through parks, and past temples and the waterfront. The Hong Kong Cycling Alliance (http://hkcyclingalliance.org) has information on road rules and safety for cyclists.

You need a (free) permit for mountain biking. Check with the Mountain Biking Association (www.hkmba.org) for permit details.

SNAKES ALIVE

Take care when bushwalking in the New Territories, particularly on Lamma and Lantau islands. Poisonous snakes are a hazard, although they will not attack unless surprised or provoked. Go to a public hospital if bitten; private doctors do not stock antivenene.

Dragon Boat Racing

Hong Kong is possibly the best place in the world to watch dragon boat racing because the traditions underlying the practice are still very much alive. The city has more than 20 races a year with most taking place from May to July. The Hong Kong Tourism Board (www. discoverhongkong.com) has information on the main events.

Football (Soccer)

Hong Kong has a fairly lively amateur football league. Games are played at the Happy Valley Sports Ground (p119), a group of pitches inside the Happy Valley Racecourse, and at **Mong Kok Stadium** (旺角大球場; Map p319; ☎852 2380 0188; 37 Flower Market Rd, Mong Kok; Ⓜ Prince Edward, exit B1). For schedules and venues, check the sports sections of the English-language newspapers or check the Hong Kong Football Association website (www. hkfa.com). For information on casual football matches, visit http://casualfootball.net.

Golf

Hong Kong has only one public golf course, but some private clubs open their doors on weekdays for a green fee.

The Hong Kong Golf Association (www. hkga.com) has a list of driving ranges and tournaments held in the territory, including the Hong Kong Open Championships, one of Asia's leading professional golf tournaments (usually played in November or December).

NEED TO KNOW

Maps

The Map Publications Centre sells excellent maps detailing hiking and cycling trails; buy online (www.landsd.gov.hk/mapping/en/pro&ser/products.htm) or at one of its many retail outlets.

Information & Facilities

Enjoy Hiking (www.hiking.gov.hk) A government site with comprehensive information; select trails by area, level of difficulty, duration etc.

Environmental Protection Department (www.epd.gov.hk) Lists of country and marine parks.

Hong Kong Birdwatching Society (www.hkbws.org.hk) In the process of building an English-language website.

Hong Kong Tourism Board (www.discoverhongkong.com) Has a full list of sporting events.

Leisure and Cultural Services Department (www.lcsd.gov.hk) Lists of fields, stadiums, beaches, swimming pools, water-sports centres etc, including equipment for hire.

South China Athletic Association (南華體育會; Map p310; ☑enquiries 852 2577 6932, membership 852 2577 4427; www.scaa.org.hk; 5th fl, South China Sports Complex, 88 Caroline Hill Rd, Causeway Bay; non Hong Kong resident membership per month HK$60; ⊗8am-9.30pm; ⊒31) Has sports facilities for hire.

Gyms, Yoga & Meditation

Yoga and fitness are big business here, with the largest slices of the pie shared out among a few big names. Pure Fitness (p85) has comprehensive gym facilities (including yoga classes) and several branches, with day rates for drop-ins. If sightseeing is leaving you frazzled, you can also meditate (with or without sound therapy) at the Samadhi Training Centre for the Soul (p100) in trendy Sheung Wan.

Hiking

Many visitors are surprised to learn that Hong Kong is an excellent place for hiking. Lengthy wilderness trails criss-cross the territory and its islands through striking mountain, coast and jungle terrain. The four main ones are the MacLehose Trail, at 100km the longest in the territory; the 78km-long Wilson Trail, which runs on both sides of Victoria Harbour; the 70km-long Lantau Trail; and the Hong Kong Trail, which is 50km long. Hong Kong's excellent public-transport network makes it feasible to tackle these trails a section at a time.

Local hiking guidebooks with suggested itineraries are widely available in Hong Kong bookshops. Or consult Enjoy Hiking (www.hiking.gov.hk), a government-affiliated website and mobile app with maps of many of Hong Kong's walking trails, plus information on route closures and facilities in country parks. It is always a good idea to check for updates on weather and the condition of the trails (landslides can sometimes mean route closures or diversions) before setting out.

Horse Racing

Horse racing is Hong Kong's biggest spectator sport. There are two racecourses: one in Happy Valley (p119) and one at Sha Tin (p166). Attending one of the Wednesday race meetings (7pm, HK$10) at Happy Valley during the racing season (September to June) is a great way to experience horse racing in Hong Kong.

THE HONG KONG TRAIL

If you want to hike without exerting yourself too much, the Hong Kong Trail (港島徑) on Hong Kong Island is a great choice. The 50km route comprises eight sections of varying difficulty, beginning on the Peak (take the tram up to the Peak and follow the signs) and ending near Shek O, in the south of Hong Kong Island.

One of the easiest and most scenic sections runs for about two hours along a mountain ridge called **Dragon's Back**. It takes you past woods, then up to the windy spine of the dragon where there are views of sun-drenched beaches and billowing hills streaked with cloud shadow. Then it's all the way down to Shek O Rd, where you can hoof it or bus it to Shek O's beach (p128) for a rewarding meal, a swim or a game of frisbee.

If you're a solo budget traveller eager to see what all the fuss is about, Hong Kong Pub Crawl (p85) offers a Wednesday evening crawl (per person HK$10) on race days that includes a couple of hours at Happy Valley, a beer voucher and a quick how-to on betting.

For a blowout experience, join the Come Horseracing Tour (per person from HK$1390) offered by **Gray Line Tours** (☑852 2368 7111; www.grayline.com.hk). The package includes transport, meals, all-you-can-drink wine or beer, and admission to the members' area; packages are available on race days for both courses.

Martial Arts

Hong Kong has a glut of martial-arts programs, but only a few have special arrangements for English-speaking visitors.

Hong Kong Shaolin Wushu Culture Centre (p185) on Lantau offers overnight stays, while Wan Kei Ho International Martial Arts Association (p100) has a local and foreign following, and open classes twice a week in Sheung Wan.

Rugby

The **World Rugby Sevens** (www.hksevens.com.hk; Hong Kong Stadium; ⊙late Mar or early Apr) sees teams from all over the world come to Hong Kong for three days of lightning-fast 15-minute matches at the 40,000-seat Hong Kong Stadium (p119) in So Kon Po. Even non-rugby fans scramble to get tickets, because the Sevens is a giant, international, three-day party, complete with costumes and Mardi Gras levels of drunkenness.

Running

The best places to run on Hong Kong Island include Harlech and Lugard Rds on the Peak; Bowen Rd above Wan Chai; the waterfront promenade running west from the Hong Kong–Macau Ferry Terminal in Sheung Wan; the track in Victoria Park; and the Happy Valley racecourse – as long as there aren't any horse races! In Kowloon, a popular place to run is the Tsim Sha Tsui East Promenade. Lamma makes an ideal place for trail runners, with plenty of paths and dirt trails, great views and, best of all, no cars.

Scuba Diving

Hong Kong has some surprisingly worthwhile diving spots, particularly in the far northeast, and there is certainly no shortage of courses. Sai Kung–based Splash Hong Kong (p168) in the New Territories is a five-star PADI operator offering courses (from HK$1200) and fun dives (from HK$500).

Spa Treatments & Therapies

Whether you want to be spoilt rotten with thousand-dollar caviar facials or have a simple foot rub, Hong Kong's extensive pampering sector can assist. Most of the luxury hotels operate their own spas. For less elaborate routines, you'll find plenty of places in Central and Kowloon offering spa treatments, massages and reflexology. Be aware that some massage venues, especially in Wan Chai, may be 'happy ending' establishments.

Wakeboarding

Most operators of this popular sport are based in Sai Kung (New Territories) and Tai Tam (Hong Kong Island). Rates are about HK$850 per hour. Try **Hong Kong Wakeboard** (☑852 9454 5772; www.wakeboard.com.hk; Tai Tam Tuk, Tai Tam; per hr HK$850-1500; ⊙6am-7pm).

Windsurfing, Kayaking & Canoeing

The best time for windsurfing is October to December. Check the Leisure and Cultural Services Department website (www.lcsd.gov.hk) for government-run water-sports centres providing canoes, windsurfing boards, kayaks and other equipment for hire, some only to holders of the relevant certificates. Kayak and Hike (p168) and Sea Kayak Hong Kong (p181) both offer excursions to the Hong Kong Global Geopark (p159).

Activities by Neighbourhood

➡ **Central District** (p84) Hong Kong's business district is the place for five-star spas and quick massage appointments.

➡ **The Peak & Northwest Hong Kong Island** (p100) Climbing (or riding) up the Peak is an essential experience; and there are good hiking trails up top.

➡ **Wan Chai & Northeast Hong Kong Island** (p121) Hiking trails abound, there's a thriving keep-fit culture and dozens of spas and massage centres.

➡ **Aberdeen & South Hong Kong Island** (p131) Southside is all about beaches and family fun, with the city's biggest amusement park.

➡ **Kowloon** (p155) City parks are perfect for people-watching on this crowded peninsula.

Above: Hiking, Lantau Trail (p183)

Left: Kayaking, Sai Kung Peninsula (p167)

WILLIAM GRAY / GETTY IMAGES ©

Lonely Planet's Top Choices

Dragon boat racing (p36) Feel the heart-pounding excitement of these atmospheric races; Stanley Beach, Tai-O and Aberdeen offer some of the best events.

Hiking Hong Kong's trails (p131) A palette of hills, history, grottoes and rural culture.

Horse racing in Happy Valley (p119) The thunderous action at this urban racecourse makes for an unforgettable experience.

World Rugby Sevens (p61) Join rugby fans for three days of lightning matches and wild partying.

Kayaking in Sai Kung (p168) Paddle in clear waters surrounded by hills and geological wonders.

Best Martial Arts

Hong Kong Shaolin Wushu Culture Centre (p185) Teaches the ancient Shaolin style of martial arts.

Wan Kei Ho International Martial Arts Association (p100) Kung fu for locals and foreigners.

Yip Man Martial Arts Athletic Association (p155) Runs six-week intensive courses.

Best Scenic Hikes

Tai Long Wan Hiking Trail (p168) A glorious hike to an even more glorious beach.

Tai Tam Waterworks Heritage Trail (p131) Nature and history come together.

Dragon's Back (p131) Hong Kong Island's best scenery, running through Shek O.

Morning Trail (p88) A shady paved path around the Peak, with stunning city views.

Sunset Peak (p183) On Lantau, Hong Kong's third-highest peak.

Lamma Island Family Trail (p179) A two-hour stroll between this outer island's two main villages.

Best Swimming

Lamma Island (p179) Small and laid-back.

Lantau Island (p181) Large, remote and good for water sports.

Cheung Chau Island (p188) Tops for windsurfing.

Sai Kung (p167) Scuba diving, kayaking and blue water galore.

Island South (p128) Sometimes crowded but gorgeous waters around Stanley and Shek O.

Kennedy Town Swimming Pool (p100) Excellent spot for an outdoor urban dip, with peeking views of the harbour.

Best Pampering

Spa at the Four Seasons (p85) Luxury, luxury and more luxury.

Iyara (p85) Urban bolt-hole with free wine and mesmerising Central–Mid-Levels Escalator views.

Ten Feet Tall (p85) Foot massages, pressure points and aromatherapy with cold-pressed fruit juices.

Happy Foot Luxe (p85) Central's go-to foot-rub spot.

Best Watery Escapades

Hong Kong Dolphinwatch (p155) Seek out Hong Kong's bubble-gum-pink dolphins in the Pearl River estuary.

Kayak and Hike (p168) Explore the geopark and its clear waters on a guided kayak tour.

Aqua Luna (p85) Set sail on a timbered junk boat to experience Victoria Harbour with local fanfare.

Splash Hong Kong (p168) Find the coral beds of far northeastern Hong Kong on a fun dive in the New Territories.

Explore Hong Kong

HONG KONG'S TOP SIGHTS

Big Buddha (p160), Lantau

Neighbourhoods at a Glance

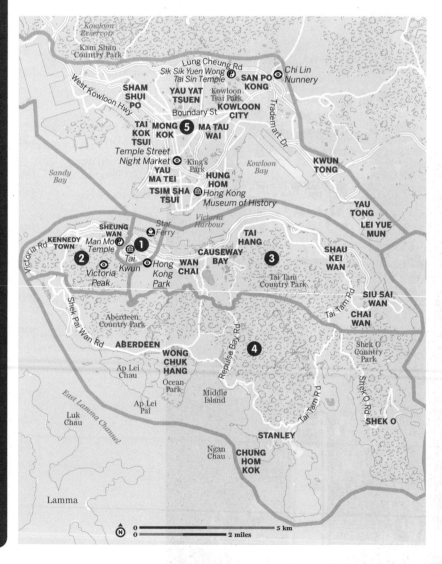

❶ Central District p68

The minted heart of Asia's financial hub is crammed with corporate citadels, colonial relics and massive monuments to consumerism. It's where you'll find the stock exchange, the Mandarin Oriental, Prada and world-class restaurants and bars, all housed in a compelling mix of modern architecture and heritage digs. Dynamic day and night, Central and its raucous bedfellows, Lan Kwai Fong and Soho, are where well-heeled Hong Kongers come to work and play.

❷ The Peak & Northwest Hong Kong Island p86

Soaring Victoria Peak is Hong Kong's most alluring attraction and offers a great vantage point from which to gaze back on the city. Down below, one by one, the charming old neighbourhoods of Sheung Wan, Sai Ying Pun and Kennedy Town are slowly gentrifying. Between them they offer something for everyone, whether it's history, antiques and fine art, stylish hedonism or a generous slice of local life as it has been lived in these hoods for decades.

❸ Wan Chai & Northeast Hong Kong Island p101

Wan Chai is Hong Kong distilled: a towering, tireless showcase of the old and new, arts and folk traditions, people upon people, and a god of cookery. To its west, Admiralty is home to government headquarters and mind-blowing hill and sea views, and offers quality over quantity for your shopping, dining and lodging needs. In the shopping mecca of Causeway Bay, traffic, malls and restaurants jockey for space with a racecourse and a cemetery, while at its periphery, East greets West in pockets of tranquillity.

❹ Aberdeen & South Hong Kong Island p122

The southern district is not only a showcase of history – Pok Fu Lam has the island's last surviving village alongside vestiges of a Victorian dairy – but Aberdeen and Ap Lei Chau are also the homes of Hong Kong's boat-dwelling fisherfolk and as such, offer wonderful seafood and boat rides. In addition, Ap Lei Chau has great shopping, and Wong Chuk Hang, contemporary art. The south is also Hong Kong Island's backyard playground – from beaches and seaside dining, to a waterfront bazaar and an amusement park.

❺ Kowloon p132

Tsim Sha Tsui is endowed with marvellous museums, an unbeatable harbour setting and all the superlatives Central has to offer on a more human scale. Other assets include leafy parks, colonial gems and the most diverse ethnic mix in all of Hong Kong. Indigenous Yau Ma Tei is old Hong Kong at its most captivating – a mosaic of neon, night markets, guesthouses and martial-arts dens, while Mong Kok is all sardine-packed commercialism. In New Kowloon, a Buddhist nunnery and a Taoist temple beckon the spiritually inclined.

For coverage of the New Territories, see p161; for information on the outlying islands, see p177; for Shēnzhèn, p189; and for Macau, p197.

NEIGHBOURHOODS AT A GLANCE

Central District

CENTRAL | LAN KWAI FONG | SOHO | MID-LEVELS

Neighbourhood Top Five

1 Star Ferry (p70) Cruising on the iconic green-and-white ferries, the midcentury vessels that cross Victoria Harbour all day and into the night.

2 Tai Kwun (p71) Admiring how art and heritage are cleverly celebrated in this long-awaited reinvention of the old Central Police Station.

3 Skyscrapers (p72) Getting up close and personal with skyscrapers made famous by the big screen, checking out stacks like the Bank of China Tower and HSBC Building.

4 Cantonese cuisine (p74) Chowing down on Michelin-starred street food at Yat Lok one night, then

high-end Cantonese fare at Duddell's (p76) the next.

5 Bar-hopping (p80) Sauntering between some of the world's best cocktail bars in Lan Kwai Fong and Soho, witnessing Asian-infused mixology magic, sipping wine on rooftops and drinking craft beer.

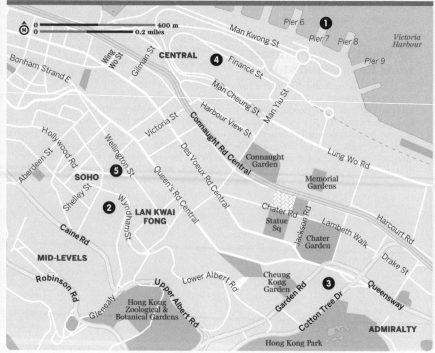

For more detail of this area see Maps p298, p302 and p306 ➡

Explore Central District

The dust never seems to settle in Hong Kong's central business district. Shops don't close until 8pm or 9pm, office workers never seem to leave and once the sun sets, the bars of Lan Kwai Fong and Soho compete with hundreds of restaurants for after-work action.

Central has few top museums, but don't miss Tai Kwun, the former Central Police Station, now reimagined as a major arts and heritage complex. Afterwards, check out other memorials to Hong Kong's past – Central is where much of Hong Kong's colonial architecture is clustered.

Take in some retail therapy at the luxury malls if you have cash to burn, or hop around dozens of intimate high-end art galleries, but don't forget to eat and drink because this is what Central does best. Try to have lunch outside the noon-to-2pm insanity when hordes of hungry suits descend on every table in sight. Hong Kongers may be busy, but they'll always stop for lunch.

In between pounding the pavements, look up: Central's glass-and-steel modernity is another world in the sky and skyscrapers like the HSBC Building and Bank of China Tower deserve your attention. The perfect way to end the day? With a fresh breeze on the historic Star Ferry to Kowloon.

Local Life

→ **Lil' Manila** Every Sunday, Filipino domestic helpers take over Statue Square (p72) and the surrounding area to eat, sing, chat and play cards.

→ **Contemplation** Amid the bars of Lan Kwai Fong, look out for tiny temples where office workers light incense sticks; there's one at the end of Wo On Lane and another on the Peel St steps at the intersection with Staunton St.

→ **Shopping** Graham Street Market (p73) is where locals have been shopping for fruit, tofu, duck eggs and fermented beans for almost 200 years.

Getting There & Away

→ **MTR** Central station on the Island and Tsuen Wan lines.

→ **Tram** Runs east and west along Des Voeux Rd Central; very handy for trying to get to places in between MTR stations and only costs HK$2.60 per ride (Octopus or exact change only).

→ **Peak Tram** Runs from the lower terminus (33 Garden Rd) to the Peak.

Lonely Planet's Top Tip

To enjoy Central's top-notch restaurants without breaking the bank, go for the midday specials. Most restaurants offer these for the convenience of office workers but they're a lifeline for frugal foodies. Unless you're dining alone, it's best to make both lunch and dinner reservations in advance, or risk being disappointed.

Best Places to Eat

→ Old Bailey (p77)
→ Yat Lok (p74)
→ Tai Cheong Bakery (p74)
→ Duddell's (p76)
→ Ho Lee Fook (p77)
→ Chifa Dumpling House (p76)

For reviews, see p74. ➡

Best Places to Drink

→ Quinary (p80)
→ Pontiac (p80)
→ Iron Fairies (p80)
→ Sevva (p78)
→ Beer Bay (p78)
→ Behind Bars (p80)

For reviews, see p78. ➡

Best Places to Shop

→ G.O.D (p82)
→ Wattis Fine Art (p83)
→ Kowloon Soy Company (p83)
→ Shanghai Tang (p83)
→ Soul Art (p83)
→ Mountain Folkcraft (p83)

For reviews, see p82. ➡

CENTRAL DISTRICT

KAPI NG / SHUTTERSTOCK ©

TOP SIGHT
STAR FERRY

You can't say you've 'done' Hong Kong until you've taken a ride on a Star Ferry, that legendary fleet of electric-diesel vessels with names such as Morning Star and Twinkling Star. At any time of day the ride, with its riveting views of skyscrapers and soaring mountains, is one of the world's best-value cruises.

The Star Ferry was founded in 1888 by Dorabjee Nowrojee, a Parsee from Bombay. At the time, most locals were crossing the harbour on sampans. Nowrojee bought a steamboat for his private use, and this eventually became the first Star Ferry.

The Star Ferry features prominently in Hong Kong's history. On Christmas Day 1941, the colonial governor Sir Mark Aitchison Young took the ferry to Tsim Sha Tsui, where he surrendered to the Japanese at the Peninsula. In 1966 thousands gathered at the pier to protest against a proposed 5¢ fare increase. It evolved into a riot that is seen as the trailblazer of local social protests leading to colonial reforms.

The pier on Hong Kong Island is an Edwardian replica that replaced the old art deco pier at Edinburgh Pl that was demolished despite vehement opposition from Hong Kong people. The Kowloon pier remains untouched. Take your first trip on a clear night from Tsim Sha Tsui to Central. It's less dramatic in the opposite direction. The lower deck (only open on the Tsim Sha Tsui–Central route) costs a few cents less but gets the full thrust of the ferry's engine noise and diesel fumes. At the end of the 10-minute journey, watch as a crew member at the back of the boat casts a hemp rope to his colleague who catches it with a billhook, the way it was done in 1880 when the first boat docked.

The Star Ferry operates on two routes: Tsim Sha Tsui–Central and Tsim Sha Tsui–Wan Chai. The first is more popular. Get tickets at the piers.

DON'T MISS

→ The views
→ Kowloon pier
→ The hemp rope and billhook routine

PRACTICALITIES

→ 天星小輪
→ Map p298, F2
→ ☑852 2367 7065
→ www.starferry.com.hk
→ Pier 7, Central
→ adult HK$2.20-3.70, child HK$1.50-2.20
→ ⊘every 6-12min, 6.30am-11.30pm
→ Ⓜ Hong Kong, exit A2

TOP SIGHT
TAI KWUN

Contemporary Swiss design fuses with colonial relics at Tai Kwun, a reimagining of the old Central Police Station and one of Hong Kong Island's most significant preservation projects. Renovations took eight years, during which time one of the original blocks collapsed, but this long-awaited behemoth heritage and arts complex finally opened in May 2018.

The site was founded in 1841 for the British army when it occupied Hong Kong during the First Opium War. When the Chinese ceded the territory in 1842 it became the flag-bearer for colonial law and order, and a rare example of a police station, magistracy and prison in one complex. Buildings were added over time until the early 20th century, and the complex became a declared monument in 1995. Visits should start in the Barrack Block, where the Main Heritage Gallery explores the site's full history.

The complex is vast, comprising 18 blocks that mix history exhibitions, art galleries, shopping and dining. Info boards tell little-known stories collected from locals and officers who once worked here. Leave time for the prison cells of B Hall (Block 12), where animated silhouettes of prisoners bring to life the conditions for inmates – including Vietnam revolutionary Ho Chi Minh, who was interred here in the 1930s, and for the old entranceway to Victoria Prison (off Arbuthnot Rd), which was once a makeshift chapel.

JC Contemporary (a contemporary art gallery) and JC Cube (a performance venue) are masterpieces of modern design, conceived by Swiss architects Herzog and de Meuron using aluminium bricks to echo the Victorian red brick around them. Architecturally, the rest of the complex is symptomatic of its colonial roots – a fusion of European neoclassical and local Chinese style.

DON'T MISS

➡ Police Headquarters Block exhibition

➡ Barrack Block Main Heritage Gallery

➡ B Hall 'Life in Victoria Prison' exhibition

➡ JC Contemporary art gallery

➡ Victoria Prison chapel frescos

PRACTICALITIES

➡ Map p302, D4

➡ ☎852 3559 2600

➡ www.taikwun.hk

➡ 10 Hollywood Rd, Lan Kwai Fong

➡ admission free

➡ ⏱10am-11pm, visitor centre to 8pm

⊙ SIGHTS

Central Hong Kong has the bulk of the territory's colonial-era buildings, as well as some of the world's tallest and most gawk-worthy modern skyscrapers; expect a sore neck.

⊙ Central

★ PEAK TRAM
FUNICULAR

Map p298 (☏852 2522 0922; www.thepeak.com. hk; Lower Terminus, 33 Garden Rd; 1-way/return adult HK$37/52, child 3-11yr & seniors over 65yr HK$14/23; ⊙7am-midnight; MCentral, exit J2) This cable-hauled funicular railway has been scaling the 396m ascent to the highest point on Hong Kong Island since 1888. A ride on this clanking tram is a classic Hong Kong experience, with vertiginous views over the city as you ascend up the steep mountainside. It's become so popular in recent years that plans are afoot to move the terminal further up the hill, to better accommodate ever-growing queues that have become a public nuisance at peak times.

The Peak Tram runs every 10 to 15 minutes from 7am to midnight; using an Octopus card to pay for the ticket will help reduce your queuing time. Note that the ticket office will push the fare that includes entry to the Sky Terrace 428 viewing deck (one way/return HK$84/99).

BANK OF CHINA TOWER
NOTABLE BUILDING

Map p298 (中銀大廈, BOC Tower; 1 Garden Rd; MCentral, exit K) The awesome 70-storey Bank of China Tower, designed by IM Pei and completed in 1990, rises from the ground like a cube, and is then successively reduced, quarter by quarter, until the south-facing side is left to rise on its own. Some geomancers believe the four prisms are negative symbols; being the opposite of circles, these triangles contradict what circles suggest – money, union and perfection.

ST JOHN'S CATHEDRAL
CHURCH

Map p298 (聖約翰座堂; ☏852 2523 4157; www. stjohnscathedral.org.hk; 4-8 Garden Rd; ⊙7am-6pm Mon-Tue & Thu-Fri, to 6.30pm Wed, to 7.30pm Sat & Sun; MCentral, exit K) FREE Services have been held at this Anglican cathedral since it opened in 1849, with the exception of 1944, when the Japanese army used it as a social club. It suffered heavy damage during WWII, and the front doors were sub-

sequently remade using timber salvaged from HMS *Tamar,* a British warship that guarded Victoria Harbour. You walk on sacred ground in more ways than one here: it is the only piece of freehold land in Hong Kong. Enter from Battery Path.

HONG KONG ZOOLOGICAL & BOTANICAL GARDENS
PARK

Map p298 (香港動植物公園; www.lcsd.gov. hk; Albany Rd; ⊙terrace gardens 5am-10pm, greenhouse 9am-4.30pm; ♿; ⍟3B, 12) FREE This Victorian-era garden has a welcoming collection of fountains, sculptures and greenhouses, plus a zoo and some fabulous aviaries. Some 160 species of bird reside here. The small zoo has a collection of monkeys, sloths, lemurs and orangutans, all in a leafy setting. Albany Rd divides the gardens, with the plants and aviaries to the east, close to Garden Rd, and most of the animals to the west.

★ HSBC BUILDING
NOTABLE BUILDING

Map p298 (滙豐銀行總行大廈; www.hsbc.com. hk/1/2/about/home/unique-headquarters; 1 Queen's Rd; ⊙escalator 9am-4.30pm Mon-Fri, to 12.30pm Sat; MCentral, exit K) FREE This unique building, designed by British architect Sir Norman Foster in 1985, has stood the test of time – more than 30 years on, its magnetism can still be felt in Central. On completion it was the world's most expensive building and considered an engineering marvel, reflecting Foster's wish to break the mould of previous bank architecture. The ground floor is an inviting two-storey walk-through public space, housing an exhibition of HSBC's Hong Kong history and architecture.

OLD BANK OF CHINA BUILDING
NOTABLE BUILDING

Map p298 (1 Bank St; MCentral, exit K) Constructed in 1950, the old Bank of China building now houses the bank's Central branch and, on its top floors, the exclusive members-only China Club, which evokes the atmosphere of old Shànghăi. The BOC is now headquartered in the awesome Bank of China Tower to the southeast, and was designed by Chinese-born American architect IM Pei and completed in 1990.

STATUE SQUARE
SQUARE

Map p298 (皇后像廣場; Edinburgh Pl; MCentral, exit K) This leisurely square used to house effigies of British royalty. Now it pays tribute to a single sovereign – the founder of HSBC. In the northern area (reached via an underpass) is the **Cenotaph** (和平紀念碑; Map p298; Chater Rd; Ⓜ Central, exit J1), built in 1923 as a memorial to Hong Kong residents killed during the two world wars. On the south side of Chater Rd, Statue Sq has a pleasant collection of fountains and seating areas – a perennially popular spot thanks to the free wi-fi available here.

★ **HONG KONG MARITIME MUSEUM**   MUSEUM

Map p298 (香港海事博物館; ☑852 3713 2500; www.hkmaritimemuseum.org; Central Ferry Pier 8; adult/child & senior HK$30/15; ⊙9.30am-5.30pm Mon-Fri, 10am-7pm Sat & Sun; ⛴; Ⓜ Hong Kong, exit A2) This multilayered museum records 2000 years of Chinese maritime history and the development of the Port of Hong Kong. Exhibits include ceramics from China's ancient sea trade, shipwreck treasures and old nautical instruments. Modern displays on topics such as diving and conservation are on the upper levels; some of the most eye-opening artefacts are in the basement galleries dedicated to the Canton Trade, including a replica of the first junk to make it to New York in 1847.

H QUEEN'S   ARTS CENTRE

Map p302 (☑852 2343 1738; www.hqueens.com.hk; 80 Queens Rd; Ⓜ Central, exit D2) Most things in Hong Kong exist in the sky, and the contemporary art scene is no different. H Queen's is a vertical arts centre right in the heart of Central Hong Kong, housing some big-ticket international names that include David Zwirner, Pace and Hauser & Wirth. There are 24 galleries in total, with a selection of restaurants for nibbles afterwards too. Business hours differ, but the galleries are mostly open around 11am to 7pm Tuesday to Saturday.

GRAHAM STREET MARKET   MARKET

Map p302 (嘉咸街; Graham St; ⊙8am-6pm; ☐5B) This busy street market has been providing Central Hong Kong with fruit, vegies, tofu, duck eggs and all variety of fermented beans and sauces for nearly 200 years. Graham St has been in peril for some years, but urban authorities' plans to replace it with hotels and apartments are moving extremely slowly and, for now, this remains one of the most convenient places to see Hong Kong street life in action.

◉ Lan Kwai Fong & Soho

TAI KWUN   MUSEUM, ARTS CENTRE

See p71.

CENTRAL–MID-LEVELS ESCALATOR   LANDMARK

Map p302 (Soho; ⊙down 6-10am, up 10.30am-midnight) The world's longest covered outdoor people-mover zigzags from Central's offices to homes near Conduit Rd in the Mid-Levels using an 800m system of escalators and walkways. Embark and watch the streets unveil – do so early evening, heading uphill from where it starts on Queen's Rd Central, and you'll see one of the world's most serene daily commutes. It's also very handy for reaching the bars of Soho without having to sweat and puff your way up the steep ladder streets.

◉ Mid-Levels

DR SUN YAT-SEN MUSEUM   MUSEUM

Map p302 (孫中山紀念館; ☑852 2367 6373; http://hk.drsunyatsen.museum; 7 Castle Rd; ⊙10am-6pm Mon-Wed & Fri, to 7pm Sat & Sun; ☐40M) FREE Dr Sun Yat-Sen was a key figure in the fight to establish a Chinese republic and served as its first president in the days after the revolution in 1911, later founding the Kuomintang – Chinese Nationalist Party. Housed in a grand Edwardian building, this museum of archival material dedicated to his life is fascinating but confusingly laid out – start on the 2nd floor, which is the best place to learn why Yat-Sen is considered the father of modern China.

JAMIA MOSQUE   MOSQUE

Map p302 (些利街清真寺; Lascar Mosque; ☑852 2523 7743, 852 2838 9417; 30 Shelley St; ⊙tours 11.30am-8pm Tue-Thu, Sat & Sun, 3-8pm Fri) Also called Lascar Mosque after the Indian sea people it was originally built for, Hong Kong's oldest mosque is a mint-green beauty now dwarfed by the Mid-Level highrises. The first mosque on this site was erected in 1849 and called Mohammedan; the one here today was built in 1915. Non-Muslims can enter on casual guided tours during opening hours, or just drop by to admire its facade from the terrace. Jamia Mosque is accessible from the Central–Mid-Levels Escalator.

OASES IN THE CITY

Starting to lose your mind amid the skyscrapers and frenetic streets of Central? Escape to these urban oases, hidden in unlikely locations.

Cheung Kong Park Sandwiched between St John's Cathedral and the Former French Mission Building, this tiny, hillside park has water features and photo-worthy pocket-sized views of the Bank of China and HSBC tower tips.

Exchange Square Skyscrapers guard world-class sculptures on this elevated terrace between walkways and the IFC Mall, with fountains that soothe harried office workers at lunchtime.

IFC Mall Roof Garden Get takeaway dim sum from Tim Ho Wan, or pick up booze at the 7-Eleven in Hong Kong Station, and take the lift to the 4th floor of IFC Mall (p84). You'll emerge on this manicured roof garden with greenery, bar-like public seating and unexpectedly wow-factor harbour views.

✖ EATING

Many of the city's poshest, multi-Michelin-starred restaurants are in Central, though there's also no shortage of down-to-earth Cantonese cheapies. Where possible, book ahead. Expect to queue at many of the best no-reservations restaurants and cafes.

✖ Central

★YAT LOK
CHINESE $

Map p302 (一樂燒鵝; ☑852 2524 3882; 34-38 Stanley St; meals HK$56-180; ☺10am-9pm Thu-Tue, to 5.30pm Sun; ⓂCentral, exit D2) Be prepared to bump elbows with locals at this tiny, basic joint known for its roast goose. Anthony Bourdain gushed over the bird. The leg is the most prized cut and the general rule is the more you pay, the better your meat will be – meals, including rice or slippery noodles, start at HK$56 and rise to HK$170. Little English is spoken, but there's a menu. Takeaway is also available.

★TAI CHEONG BAKERY
BAKERY $

Map p302 (泰昌餅家; ☑852 3960 6262; 35 Lyndhurst Tce; pastries from HK$6; ☺8am-8.30pm; Ⓠ40M) Tai Cheong was best known for its lighter-than-air beignets (deep-fried dough rolled in sugar; *sa yung* in Cantonese) until former governor Chris Patten was photographed wolfing down its egg-custard tarts. Since then 'Fat Patten' egg tarts have hogged the limelight – the buttery BBQ-pork pastries are just as wonderful; frankly it's all delicious.

★LAN FONG YUEN
CAFE $

Map p302 (蘭芳園; ☑852 2854 0731, 852 2544 3895; 2 & 4A Gage St; meals from HK$60, minimum spend HK$28; ☺7am-6pm Mon-Sat; Ⓠ5B) This rickety facade hides an entire *cha chaan tang* (tea cafe). Lan Fong Yuen (1952) is believed to be the inventor of the 'panty-hose' milk tea and droves of Instagrammers come to worship here, drink in hand. Over a thousand cups of the strong and silky brew are sold daily alongside pork-chop buns, instant noodles and other delicious tasties.

MAK'S NOODLE
NOODLES, CANTONESE $

Map p302 (麥奀雲吞麵世家; ☑852 2854 3810; www.maksnoodle.sg; 77 Wellington St; noodles from HK$42; ☺11am-9pm; ⓂCentral, exit D2) Mak's founder emigrated to Hong Kong from China in WWII and established this now-legendary noodle stop, first as a *dai pai dong* (food stall) and then a shop – although now a chain, this Central branch with small street-facing kitchen is the original. Green 1920s chinoiserie decor makes it feel more restaurant-like than its competitors. Try the shrimp wonton soup with beef brisket.

LIN HEUNG TEA HOUSE
CANTONESE, DIM SUM $

Map p302 (☑852 2544 4556; Ground fl, 160-164 Wellington St; meals from HK$60; ☺6am-10pm, dim sum to 3.30pm; ⓂSheung Wan, exit E2) In the morning, this famous 1950s teahouse is packed with older men reading newspapers. Eating here can be overwhelming for the uninitiated: dim sum (from HK$15) is served from trolleys and servers are swamped with locals frantically waving order sheets as soon as they emerge from the kitchen. Little English is spoken; hover near the kitchen if you want to eat.

The *har gow* (shrimp) dumplings are coveted morsels, as are the chicken feet in black-bean sauce, but you may just have to take what you can get. This is the type of place where regulars have their own special teapots and get preferential service. For the rest of us, it's an eye-opening bun fight.

YUM CHA – CENTRAL
DIM SUM $

Map p298 (☑3708 8081; www.yumchahk.com; 2nd fl, Nan Fung Place, 173 Des Voeux Rd Central; dishes from HK$50; ⊗11.30am-3pm & 6-11pm, happy hour 6-8pm; ☎; Ⓜ Sheung Wan, exit E3) With four branches across Hong Kong, Yum Cha is one of Hong Kong's most loved modern dim sum chains. Why? Mainly thanks to the super Instagrammable (and admittedly gimmicky) pork buns that look like pigs, and gooey custard buns with eyes. Themed dishes accompany a mix of traditional and twist-on-the-classic dim sum offerings, served with a generous selection of tea.

BUTAO RAMEN
JAPANESE $

Map p302 (豚王; ☑852 3189 1200; www.butao-ramen.com; 69 Wellington St; ramen from HK$89; ⊗11am-11pm; Ⓜ Central, exit D2) From the line of customers waiting out front, you can believe that this joint serves the best ramen in town. Choose from the signature Butao with rich pork broth, the spicy Red King, the fusion-y parmesan-enhanced Green King, or the squid-inky Black King. You can also customise how long the noodles should be cooked and the intensity of the broth.

TIM HO WAN
DIM SUM $

Map p298 (添好運點心專門店; ☑852 2332 3078; www.timhowan.com; Shop 12A, Level 1, Hong Kong Station; meals HK$100-150; ⊗9am-8.30pm; Ⓜ Hong Kong, exit E1) Opened by a former Four Seasons chef, Tim Ho Wan was the first-ever budget dim sum place to receive a Michelin star. Many relocations and branches later, this iteration beneath IFC Mall (p84) may be bland-looking but the star is still tucked snugly inside its tasty titbits (the shrimp dumplings are excellent). Expect to wait 15 to 40 minutes for a seat.

MANA! FAST SLOW FOOD
VEGAN $

Map p302 (☑852 2851 1611; www.mana.hk; 92 Wellington St; meals HK$100-200; ⊗10am-10pm; ☎✐; Ⓜ Central, exit D2) ✐ Craving fresh fruit and veggies? Drop by this vegan and raw-food haven that whips up smoothies, salads and flatbreads (available gluten-free). The latter are baked in-shop by the cheerful staff then smothered with organic greens and Mediterranean dips. Besides tasty, guilt-free food, Mana offers a chilled-out vibe that makes you forget its physical smallness and not-so-bohemian prices.

There's now a second branch close to Tai Ping Shan St in Sheung Wan, with made-for-lingering canopied outdoor seating in a ladder street and more of a coffee-shop feel.

DUMPLING YUAN
DUMPLINGS $

Map p302 (餃子園; ☑852 2525 9018; 98 Wellington St; meals from HK$55; ⊗10am-11pm; ☑40M) Without exception, everybody in this simple restaurant with booths and plastic chairs is noshing on one thing: bowls piled with heavenly bundles of steamed dumplings. Varieties include mutton and green onion, beef and celery, and pork and chive.

WANG FU
DUMPLINGS $

Map p302 (王府; ☑852 2121 8006; Ground fl, 65 Wellington St; meals HK$40; ⊗11am-3pm & 6-10pm Mon-Sat; ☑40M) Wellington St is jam-packed with quality dim sum cafes and this one is known for its handmade Běijīng-style steamed bundles, which you'll see visitors from the mainland demolishing plate after plate of. Look for the daily special dumpling advertised in the window, alongside hearty noodle and rice dishes.

CITY HALL MAXIM'S PALACE
DIM SUM $

Map p298 (美心皇宮; ☑852 2521 1303; 2nd fl, Lower Block, Hong Kong City Hall, 1 Edinburgh Pl; meals from HK$150; ⊗11am-3pm & 5.30-11.30pm Mon-Sat, 9am-3pm & 5.30-11.30pm Sun; ☎♿; Ⓜ Central, exit K) This 'palace' offers the quintessential Hong Kong dim sum experience. It's cheerful, it's noisy and it takes place in a huge kitschy hall with dragon decorations and hundreds of locals. A dizzying assortment of dim sum is paraded on trolleys the old-fashioned way. There's breakfast on Sunday from 9am, but people start queuing for a table at 8.30am.

DAI PAI DONG
STREET FOOD $

Map p302 (盛記; Stanley St; meals HK$100; ⊗11am-3pm & 6-11pm; ♿; Ⓜ Central, exit D2) In the fine-dining enclave of Soho, finding a good, cheap meal can be tricky. Stanley St is home to a small strip of *dai pai dong* (food stalls) that have withstood gentrification, retaining a working-class, laugh-out-loud character. There's no signage at any of them and very little, if any, English spoken, though the menus usually have translations.

Go-tos here include Hong Kong classics such as garlic prawns, fried noodles and sweet-and-sour pork.

CHIFA DUMPLING HOUSE
FUSION $$

Map p302 (☑852 2311 1815; www.chifa.hk; Ground fl, 26 Peel St; dinner from HK$300; ⏰noon-11pm Sun-Thu, to 11.30pm Fri & Sat; 🖥🍴) Since the mid-19th century there has been a Chinese diaspora in Peru, cooking home cuisine using Peruvian ingredients. This interpretation of Chinese food is what you'll find at retro-styled Chifa. Dumplings like the violet *xiao long bao* (soup dumplings) with beetroot sauce are supposed to be the main event, but there's a lot more to the menu – all tasty and beautifully presented.

There's a good lunch deal for two to three courses (HK$128 or HK$168), but many of the most interesting dishes are only available in the evening. Book ahead.

LUK YU TEA HOUSE
CANTONESE $$

Map p302 (陸羽茶室; ☑852 2523 5464; 24-26 Stanley St; meals from HK$200; ⏰7am-9.30pm, dim sum to 6pm; 🚇; Ⓜ Central, exit D2) This gorgeous formal teahouse (c 1933) with original art deco decor was the haunt of opera artists, writers and painters who came to give recitals and discuss the national fate. The food is old-school Cantonese plus a variety of dim sum dumplings. Prices reflect the grand setting: come for the aesthetics, not a good deal on your dinner.

★DUDDELL'S
CANTONESE $$$

Map p302 (都爹利會館; ☑852 2525 9191; www.duddells.co; Level 3 & 4 Shanghai Tang Mansion, 1 Duddell St; dim sum from HK$65, lunch from HK$380, dinner HK$500-1000; ⏰noon-2.30pm & 6-10.30pm Mon-Sat; 🖥; Ⓜ Central, exit G) Light Cantonese fare is served in riveting spaces enhanced by artwork at this one-Michelin-starred restaurant-gallery. There's a graceful dining room, marble-tiled '50s salon and leafy terrace; it's a lovely spot to splash out on exquisite dishes such as barbecued Ibérico pork with honey. Style-wise the contemporary setting blows far outweighs the competition; the sommelier is also excellent.

AMBER
EUROPEAN $$$

Map p302 (☑852 2132 0066; www.mandarinoriental.com/landmark; Landmark Oriental, 15 Queen's Rd Central; set lunch HK$628-1518, set dinner HK$2098-2628; ⏰noon-2.30pm & 6.30-10.30pm; Ⓜ Central, exit G) 🍃 Two-Michelin-starred Amber was set to receive a complete physical reinvention at the time of writing, but one thing that won't be changing is Chef Ekkebus or his masterful fusion of traditional French food with modern Asian flavours and ingredients – think Hokkaido sea urchin with lobster jelly and seaweed waffles or duck foie gras with daikon radish fondant.

LUNG KING HEEN
CANTONESE, DIM SUM $$$

Map p298 (龍景軒; ☑852 3196 8880; www.fourseasons.com/hongkong; Four Seasons Hotel, 8 Finance St; meal HK$350-700, weekday set lunch HK$640, yum cha degustation HK$1650; ⏰noon-2.30pm Mon-Fri, 11.30am-3pm Sat & Sun, & 6-10pm daily; 🖥; Ⓜ Hong Kong, exit E1) The world's first Chinese restaurant to receive three Michelin stars still retains them. The Cantonese food, though by no means peerless in Hong Kong, is excellent. The dining experience is a dichotomy: harbour views and impeccable service, combined with a simple setting devoid of the bells and whistles of Four Seasons' other restaurants, and reasonable prices for the quality.

8½ OTTO E MEZZO BOMBANA
ITALIAN $$$

Map p298 (☑852 2537 8859; www.ottoemezzobombana.com; Shop 202, 18 Chater Rd, Landmark Alexandra; lunch/dinner from HK$700/1380; ⏰noon-2.30pm & 6.30-10.30pm Mon-Sat; 🖥; Ⓜ Central, exit H) Asia's only Italian restaurant with three Michelin stars lives up to its name, and Chef Bombana is here to see that it does. 'Eight and a Half' is the place for white truffles, being the host of the local bidding for these pungent diamonds. Book two months ahead for weekends; weekday lunch tables are easier to bag.

🍴 Lan Kwai Fong & Soho

MOTORINO
PIZZA $

Map p302 (☑852 2801 6881; www.motorinopizza.com; 14 Shelley St, Soho; meals HK$170-380; ⏰noon-midnight; 🖥🚇; Ⓜ Central, exit D2) This skinny, buzzing outpost of the famed NYC pizzeria puts out charcoal-kissed Neapolitan pizza with a bubbly and flavourful crust that will give your jaws a delectable workout. The brussels-sprout and smoked-pancetta version is especially glorious. Reservations accepted for lunch; the fixed-price weekday lunch menu is a good deal at HK$138 for pizza and a soft drink.

FLYING PAN
AMERICAN $

Map p302 (☑852 2140 6333; www.the-flying-pan.com; Ground fl, 9 Old Bailey St, Soho; breakfast combos HK$50-140; ⏰24hr; 🛜🅿; 🚌26) It's kitsch, *almost* untouched by Instagrammers, and huge breakfasts roll all day and night at this 24-hour faux-1950s American diner, blaring Guns N' Roses at 10am. Local and expat families flock here for brunch on weekends; the deliciously oozy, doorstop grilled-cheese toasted sandwich with scrambled egg and streaky bacon (HK$50) is probably the best-value western-style breakfast you'll find in Central.

SER WONG FUN
CANTONESE $

Map p302 (蛇王芬; ☑852 2543 1032; 30 Cochrane St, Soho; meals HK$100-480; ⏰11am-10.30pm; Ⓜ Central, exit D1) This snake-soup specialist with starched service whips up old Cantonese dishes that are as tantalising as its celebrated broth, and the packed tables attest to it. Many regulars come for the homemade pork-liver sausage infused with rose wine – perfect over a bowl of immaculate white rice. Booking advised for dinner.

★OLD BAILEY
CHINESE $$

Map p302 (☑852 2877 8711; www.oldbailey.hk; 2nd fl, JC Contemporary, Tai Kwun, Old Bailey St, Soho; meals from HK$300; ⏰noon-3pm & 6-11pm Mon-Sat, lounge bar noon-11pm; 🛜🅿; 🚌26) The joy of Old Bailey begins with its snazzy Herzog & de Meuron–designed interior that mixes mid-century-modern Scandi with Chinese design principles, and the sweeping outdoor terrace overlooking Tai Kwun and Soho's skyscrapers. The food lives up to its surroundings, with dishes like Longjing-tea-smoked pigeon and juicy *xiao long bao* (soup dumplings) with Sichuan peppercorns.

HO LEE FOOK
HONG KONG $$

Map p302 (☑852 2810 0860; http://holeefook hk.tumblr.com; Ground fl, 1-5 Elgin St, Soho; meals HK$250-500; ⏰6-11pm Sun-Thu, to midnight Fri & Sat; 🛜; Ⓜ Central, exit D2) As irreverent as its name suggests, this buzzy underground spot does a winkingly modern take on retro Chinatown cuisine. Fat prawn toasts are served with Kewpie mayo, the *char siu* uses upmarket Kurobuta pork, and prawn *lo mein* is spangled with crunchy fried garlic and slicked with shellfish oil. It's justifiably popular and the atmosphere is see-and-be-seen, despite nightclub-level darkness.

SOUL FOOD
THAI $$

Map p302 (☑852 2177 3544; www.soulfoodthai.com.hk; 26-28 Elgin St, Soho; meals HK$200-400; ⏰6-10.45pm Mon-Wed, to 11.45pm Thu-Sat, noon-10pm Sun, happy hour 6-9pm; 🛜; 🚌26) This Bangkok import has nailed its own spin on classic Thai cuisine with satisfying dishes like soft-shell-crab pad Thai, southern Thai samosas and creamy coconut ice cream with salted caramel and crunchy peanuts. The dimly lit interior is pared back and grown up, with a single row of seating; book ahead for dinner. To get here, take the Central–Mid-Levels Escalator (p73).

CHOM CHOM
VIETNAMESE $$

Map p302 (☑852 2810 0850; www.chomchom.hk; 58-60 Peel St, Soho; meals HK$350-500; ⏰5pm-late Sat-Wed, from 6pm Thu-Fri; 🛜; Ⓜ Central, exit D1) Wildly popular and always lively, Chom Chom re-creates Vietnamese street food with bold flavours and charcoal grills, which are best washed down with its craft beers on tap. The corner location makes for great people-watching and is often crowded with queuers. Pho fans take note: Chom Chom's version is a refreshing noodle roll with beef, baby garlic and Thai basil.

YUNG KEE RESTAURANT
CANTONESE $$

Map p302 (鏞記; ☑852 2522 1624; www.yung kee.com.hk; 32-40 Wellington St, Lan Kwai Fong; lunch from HK$150, dinner HK$250-500; ⏰11am-11.30pm; 🅿; Ⓜ Central, exit D2) The roast goose here, made from fowl raised in the restaurant's farm and roasted in coal-fired ovens, has been the talk of the town since 1942. It's thanks to the special sauce; a light and aromatic, meaty gravy served with yellow beans marinated in Chinese five spice. Cheaper rice and meat dishes, including the signature goose, are available 2pm to 5.30pm.

CARBONE
ITALIAN $$$

Map p302 (☑852 2593 2593; www.carbone.com.hk; 9th fl, LKF Tower, 33 Wyndham St, Lan Kwai Fong; mains HK$220-600, set lunch for 2 HK$388pp; ⏰noon-2.30pm Mon-Sat, 6-11.30pm Sun-Thu, to midnight Fri & Sat) The only foreign outpost of the over-the-top New York Italian-American joint, Carbone makes you feel like Frank Sinatra having dinner in 1963. Walls are panelled in dark wood, chairs are red leather, waiters rock maroon tuxedos and desserts come on a rolling cart. Retro classics include a a bigger-than-your-head veal parmesan and a huge, satisfying tangle of spaghetti and meatballs.

🍷⚓ DRINKING & NIGHTLIFE

Expect all-night street parties in Lan Kwai Fong, and occasionally in Soho. The dress code is smart-casual as a minimum; if you want to get in anywhere glam in Central, don't wear flip-flops or trainers.

⚓ Central

DR FERN'S GIN PARLOUR COCKTAIL BAR
Map p302 (📞852 2111 9449; Shop B31A, Landmark Atrium, 15 Queen's Rd; ⊙noon-1am Sun-Thu, to 2am Fri & Sat; 🐾; Ⓜ Central, exit G) Just what the doctor ordered: lying somewhere between a Victorian hothouse and a scientific lab, Dr Fern's draws on gin's botanical biology for its trippy look. It's hidden behind a 'Waiting Room' door in the basement of the Landmark mall (enter from Pedder St) and it's table service; wait to be greeted by a doctor. Book ahead for the evening.

There are more than 300 gins on the menu. Can't decide? Use the gin flavour wheel at the front of the menu to guide you through the different categories. G&Ts start at HK$95 and climb to about HK$220.

SEVVA COCKTAIL BAR
Map p298 (📞852 2537 1388; www.sevva.hk; 25th fl, Prince's Bldg, 10 Chater Rd; ⊙noon-midnight Mon-Thu, to 2am Fri & Sat; 🐾; Ⓜ Central, exit H) If there was a million-dollar view in Hong Kong, it's the one from the balcony of flashy Sevva: with skyscrapers so close you can see their steel arteries, with harbour and Kowloon views. At night it takes your breath away, but the prices will too – expect to pay a minimum HK$160 for a glass of wine. Book ahead if you want a couch on the balcony in the evening, though you can also perch at a standing table or simply go out for photos.

BEER BAY BAR
Map p298 (Hong Kong Central Ferry Pier 3; ⊙3-11pm Mon-Thu, 2-11.30pm Fri & Sat, noon-9.30pm Sun; Ⓜ Hong Kong, exit A1, A2) Still wearing your sightseeing grubbies and don't feel up to the glam nightspots of Central? Head to this ultralocal open-air beer kiosk at the ferry pier, a favourite of outer-island dwellers looking for a quick tipple before heading home. Grab a pint of local Gweilo craft beer

and sit on the concrete steps watching the water; bring your own snacks.

HONI HONI COCKTAIL BAR
Map p302 (📞852 2353 0885; www.honihonibar.com; 3rd fl, Somptueux Central Bldg, 52 Wellington St; ⊙4pm-2am Mon-Sat, to midnight Sun, happy hour 4-7pm Mon-Fri; 🐾; Ⓜ Central, exit D2) The terrace at Honi Honi is a tropical-island oasis that literally rises above the mayhem of Lan Kwai Fung. It was Hong Kong's first tiki bar and although no longer the only one, it's still the best, with a decent happy hour (cocktails from HK$40, unusual for Hong Kong's top bars), classy '70s furniture and excellent cocktails with fresh fruit. Also look out for the Uncensored Cabaret – an anything-goes gathering of local acts one Sunday a month.

CAFÉ 8 CAFE
Map p298 (📞852 3791 2158; http://cafe8.org; Roof Level, Hong Kong Maritime Museum, Central Pier 8; ⊙10am-8pm; 🐾; Ⓜ Hong Kong) This social-enterprise cafe on the top deck of Pier 8 provides employment and training for students of the Nesbitt Centre, a local NGO helping adults with learning disabilities. It's a casual place that attracts locals with occasional live music and inexpensive drinks (HK$55 Prosecco), cakes and lunches. What makes it remarkable is the astounding harbour view from its outdoor terrace.

BEHIND CLUB
(www.facebook.com/clubbehind; ⊙last Sat of month) Behind started at one of the first gay clubs in Hong Kong, Club 97 in Lan Kwai Fong (now closed), and has gone on to become a roving club night. It's an inclusive night, popular within the LGBT+ community but not exclusively so, regularly attracting about 600 people. Venues change every couple of months; check online.

GOOD SPRING CO TEAHOUSE
(春回堂; 📞852 2544 3518; 8 Cochrane St, Central; tea HK$10-35; ⊙9am-7.30pm; Ⓜ Central, exit D2) This Chinese medicine shop has a counter selling herbal teas – for detoxing, getting rid of water, cooling the body or treating colds. The most popular is the bitter 24-herb tea. There's also the fragrant chrysanthemum infusion. Watch the staff at the back wrapping precious roots and powder prescriptions as you stand and sip your tea alongside local office workers.

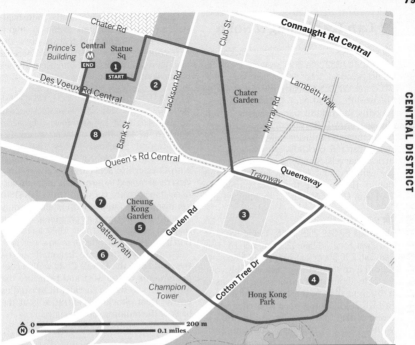

Neighbourhood Walk
Exploring Hong Kong's Heart

START STATUE SQ, CENTRAL
END CENTRAL MTR STATION
LENGTH 1.5KM; ONE HOUR

Begin the walk at **❶ Statue Square** (p72), which is a good place to see Hong Kong life congregate – particularly on Sundays when Filipino domestic workers on their day off take over the space, playing cards, chatting over lunch, dancing and singing karaoke. Take in the handsome outline of the neoclassical **❷ Old Supreme Court Building** (前立法會大樓; Former Legislative Council Building; 8 Jackson Rd), one of the few colonial-era survivors in the area and the former seat of Hong Kong's modern legislature.

Walk southwest through Chater Garden park and cross over Queensway to the angular, modern lines of the **❸ Bank of China Tower** (p72), guarded by water features and sculptures.

Head east, crossing Cotton Tree Dr, into Hong Kong Park for the free **❹ Flagstaff House Museum of Tea Ware** (p104), displaying valuable pots, cups and other elegant tea ware. Sample some of China's finest teas in the serene teahouse next door.

From here, head west through the park past the ornamental lake to take elevated walkways west over Cotton Tree Dr. Head through Champion Tower, over Garden Rd and through **❺ Cheung Kong Park** (p74) – perhaps pausing here to take photos of the HSBC Building and Bank of China Tower – to modest **❻ St John's Cathedral** (p72), dating from 1849. Towering corporate cathedrals now surround it, and it is an important historic Hong Kong monument.

Follow Battery Path past the red-brick **❼ Former French Mission Building** (前法國外方傳道會大樓; 1 Battery Path) and take the steps down to Queen's Rd Central. Cross over to the **❽ HSBC Building** (p72) and up the escalator (if it's open) to the large, airy atrium. Walk through the ground-floor plaza to pat Stephen and Stitt, the two lions guarding the exit to Des Voeux Rd Central. The closest Central MTR station entrance is a short distance to the north, between Statue Sq and Prince's Building.

📍 Lan Kwai Fong & Soho

★QUINARY
COCKTAIL BAR

Map p302 (☑852 2851 3223; www.quinary.hk; 56-58 Hollywood Rd, Soho; ⏰5pm-1am Mon-Sat; 📶; Ⓜ Central, exit D2) Consistently voted one of the world's top 50 bars, Quinary is a sleek, moodily lit cocktail bar attracting a well-dressed crowd. Its gifted mixologists create homemade infusions of spirits and the Asian-inspired cocktails are delicious, theatrical marvels. Signature creations include the Quinary Sour (whisky, liquorice syrup, bonito flakes) and the Instagram-killing Earl Grey Caviar Martini with whipped air.

★PONTIAC
BAR

Map p302 (☑852 2521 3855; 13 Old Bailey St, Lan Kwai Fong; ⏰5pm-12.30am Mon-Fri, from 3pm Sat, 3-10.30pm Sun, happy hour 5-8pm; 📶; 🚇26) There's something indescribably comfortable about the Pontiac, which rocks to a different tune to most of the cheesy bars in LKF. It's a skinny, open-fronted, graffiti-covered dive that's wholly run by women, with a string of bras hanging behind the bar to let you know who's in charge. Alternative music, friendly vibe, HK$15 happy-hour beers: what's not to love?

★IRON FAIRIES
COCKTAIL BAR

Map p302 (☑852 2603 6992; www.facebook.com/theironfairieshongkong; Lower ground fl, 1-13 Hollywood Rd, Lan Kwai Fong; ⏰6pm-2am Mon-Thu, 5pm-3am Fri & Sat, 5pm-2am Sun; 📶; 🚇26) Australian Ashley Sutton is a master of theatre and this bar is unlike anything else in Hong Kong. Ten thousand butterflies flutter from copper threads attached to the ceiling, in an underground cave designed to mimic a blacksmith's foundry where tables are piled with fairies forged from iron. It's beautifully surreal, and the mixology ain't bad either. Enter from Pottinger St.

65 PEEL
CRAFT BEER

Map p302 (☑852 2342 2224; www.facebook.com/65peel; Ground fl, 65 Peel St, Soho; ⏰4pm-midnight Mon-Sat, from 2pm Sun; 📶) Everything you need to know about Hong Kong's craft-beer scene is on page one of 65 Peel's beer menu, dedicated to local taps from breweries like Young Master, Lion Rock and Moonzen. Beers are listed from 1 to 12 by strength, and bitterness is indicated by the IBU ranking; try a beer flight of four 200ml serves for HK$140.

Quiet during the day, this industrial-style craft-beer bar gets going at night, when its pink-neon wall feature gives the bare-concrete space an eerie glow. There's a food menu of reinvented Hong Kong dishes to line your stomach.

STOCKTON
COCKTAIL BAR

Map p302 (☑852 2565 5268; www.stockton.com.hk; 32 Wyndham St, Lan Kwai Fong; ⏰6pm-2am Mon-Wed, to 4am Thu-Sat; Ⓜ Central, exit D2) Hard-to-find Stockton evokes the ambience of a private club in Victorian London with Chesterfield sofas and wood panelling cleverly arranged to form dark, intimate corners. Its signature cocktails (from HK$130) are inspired by famous writers and quirkily served in vessels such as ceramic pots with rosemary fronds to garnish. Make a reservation if you're coming after 9pm on a weekend.

From the big iron gate diagonally across the road from the Fringe Club, walk a couple of doors to the west and turn into the open doorway with a corridor lit by candles on the floor. Stockton's entrance is at the back of the building, up the stairs.

CLUB 71
BAR

Map p302 (☑852 2858 7071; Basement, 67 Hollywood Rd, Soho; ⏰5pm-1am Mon-Sat, happy hour 5-9pm; 📶; 🚇26, Ⓜ Central, exit D1) This friendly, unassuming bar with a bohemian vibe is named after a protest march on 1 July 2003. It's a favourite haunt of local artists and activists who come for cheap beer and jamming sessions. In the public garden out front, revolutionaries plotted to overthrow the Qing dynasty a hundred years ago. Enter from the alley next to 69 Hollywood.

BEHIND BARS
BAR

Map p302 (www.facebook.com/behindbars.hk; E-Hall, Tai Kwun, Arbuthnot Rd, Soho; ⏰4pm-midnight Tue-Sun; 🚇26) A series of interlinking jail cells in the former Central Police Station, now Tai Kwun (p71) heritage complex, have been given a clever makeover to create this quirky bar. Inside red-brick 'Block 15', the whitewashed cells now have mirrored walls and nooks to sit in, while a communal table fills the central aisle where wardens would have once paced.

COLETTE'S ART BAR
BAR

Map p302 (☑852 2521 7251; www.hkfringe.com.hk; 2nd fl, 2 Lower Albert Rd, Lan Kwai Fong; ⏰noon-2.30pm Mon-Fri, 4.30-10pm Tue-Thu, to midnight Fri & Sat; Ⓜ Central, exit D1) Bargain-hunters and thirsty shoestringers rejoice:

happy hour runs 4.30pm to 10pm at artsy Colette's, which makes it one of the cheapest bars in Central. It's in a lovely corner heritage building that was once a dairy farm, and has a hidden balcony with alfresco seating. It packs out for its weekday vegetarian lunch buffet (HK$118 with drink). Colette's is part of the Fringe Club (p82), which also houses a rotating gallery, basement Vault coffee shop, performance spaces and old-fashioned Foreign Correspondents' Club where expat hacks hang out.

CÉ LA VI
ROOFTOP BAR

Map p302 (☑852 3700 2300; http://hk.celavi. com; 25th fl, California Tower, 32 D'Aguilar St, Lan Kwai Fong; ☺3pm-late, happy hour 5-8pm Mon-Fri; ☎; ⓂCentral, exit D2) Take the elevator to the 25th floor and then keep going up until you reach the Skydeck; this glam bar has three floors but there's only one place you want to be and that's on the roof amid the sky-scraping turrets. Reserve a table if you want a seat, but the best sunset views are to be had standing. The soundtrack is Latin and the dress code is smart after 6pm; no shorts or open shoes for men, no flip-flops for ladies. Happy hour is two-for-one.

PETTICOAT LANE
GAY & LESBIAN

Map p302 (☑852 2808 2738; www.petticoat lane.club; Basement, 57-59 Wyndham St, Lan Kwai Fong; ☺6pm-2am Tue & Thu, to 3am Wed, to 4am Fri, 8pm-4am Sat; ⓂCentral, exit D2) Central's best LGBT night out is Petticoat Lane, a basement club with sparkling foliage hanging above the bar, a dance floor, small outdoor terrace and gender-neutral toilets. The vibe is inclusive and its weekly 'Wednesgay' evenings with topless bartenders include free-flow Absolut vodka (10pm to 11pm) for all and sundry. There's a drag show every night at midnight.

SLIDE ON 79
SPORTS BAR

Map p302 (☑852 2779 9279; www.slideon79. com; Harilela House, 79 Wyndham St, Lan Kwai Fong; ☺11.45am-midnight Mon & Tue, to 1am Wed & Thu, to 3am Fri & Sat, 3pm-12.30am Sun, happy hour 3-8pm; ☎) If you're looking for sports screens but reluctant to set foot in a mock English or Irish pub, Slide on 79 has you covered. But with its cocktail menu, live gigs, mural wall and pleasant open frontage in the middle of LKF, it's a good spot any time – this is far from your average sports bar. Enter from Pottinger St. Happy hour is buy-one-get-one-free.

ANGEL'S SHARE WHISKY BAR
BAR

Map p302 (☑852 2805 8388; www.angelsshare. hk; 2nd fl, Amber Lodge, 23 Hollywood Rd, Lan Kwai Fong; ☺3pm-2am Mon-Thu, to 3am Fri & Sat, happy hour 5-9pm; ⓂCentral, exit D1) One of Hong Kong's best whisky bars, Angel's Share emulates the look of a European gentleman's club and has more than 100 whiskies from the world over – try a whisky flight with four 25ml drams for HK$450, or its special barrel selection, which comes straight out of a large 180L oak barrel at the bar's entrance. Gets busy from 10pm.

GLOBE
PUB

Map p302 (☑852 2543 1941; www.theglobe.com. hk; 45-53 Graham St, Soho; ☺10am-midnight Sun-Thu, to 2am Fri & Sat, happy hour 10am-8pm; ☎; ⓂCentral, exit D2) It may look like your average, petite LKF bar, but inside the Globe is a vast, pubby beer hall with an impressive list of 150 beers, including 13 on tap; look for local craft brews such as Gweilo and Young Masters. Long wooden tables and comfortable banquettes are popular with diners scoffing decent British pub grub. Good for sports events.

PEAK CAFE BAR
BAR

Map p302 (☑852 2140 6877; www.cafedeco group.com; 9-13 Shelley St, Soho; ☺11am-2am Mon-Fri, 9am-2am Sat & Sun, happy hour 3-8pm; ☎; ☐13, 26, 40M) This welcoming bar with cheap, classic cocktails is decorated with the charming fixtures and fittings of the old Peak Cafe from 1947, which was replaced by the Peak Lookout (p94). It's in two parts, with the lower area reserved for diners, both next to the Central–Mid-Levels Escalator (p73). Plant yourself by the window during happy hour and watch commuters glide by.

KUNG LEE
JUICE BAR

Map p302 (公利真料竹蔗水; ☑852 2544 3571; 60 Hollywood Rd, Soho; juice from HK$14; ☺11am-10pm; ☐26) This institution in the heart of Soho has been quietly selling herbal teas and fresh sugar-cane juice since 1948 – its quality is unchanged, as are the charming vintage tiles, posters and signs. There's 'turtle jelly' too, made with the powdered shell of a certain type of turtle and a variety of Chinese herbs. It's good for cooling and detoxing.

T:ME   GAY

Map p302 (☑852 2332 6565; www.time-bar.com; 65 Hollywood Rd, Soho; ☺6pm-2am Mon-Sat, happy hour 6-9.30pm; Ⓜ Central, exit D1) This small, chic gay bar is located in a back alley facing a small park, and serves cocktails with Asian ingredients such as ginger liqueur, lychee and plum wine. Daily drinks deals keep prices down, especially the second happy hour after midnight on Fridays and Saturdays. Enter through the alley off Peel St just north of Hollywood Rd.

VOLAR   CLUB

Map p302 (☑852 2810 1510; Basement, 38-44 D'Aguilar St, Lan Kwai Fong; entry Tue-Thu HK$200, Fri & Sat HK$300; ☺6pm-1am Tue, to 6am Wed-Fri, 10pm-6am Sat; Ⓜ Central, exit D2) A staple of the Lan Kwai Fong nightlife scene, this futuristically lit underground (literally) club grinds out the jams until the sun comes up. Expect a sweaty, international crowd of 20-somethings partying *hard*. Entry fees kick in when the club starts to fill up, usually around 1am to 2am.

☆ ENTERTAINMENT

★PEEL FRESCO   JAZZ

Map p302 (☑852 2540 2046; www.peelfresco. com; 49 Peel St, Soho; ☺5.30pm-late Tue-Sun; 🚌13, 26, 40M) Charming Peel Fresco has live jazz six nights a week, with local and overseas acts on an intimate stage close enough for listeners to chink glasses with musicians. It's small, relaxed and friendly, and there's no better place in Soho than here curled up with a drink when the action starts around 9.30pm; come at 9pm to secure a seat.

A cover charge of up to HK$200 can apply if the act is an international recording artist, but often the gigs are free.

FRINGE CLUB   LIVE MUSIC

Map p302 (藝穗會; ☑852 2521 7251, theatre bookings 852 2521 9126; www.hkfringe.com.hk; 2 Lower Albert Rd, Lan Kwai Fong; 🚇; Ⓜ Central, exits D1, D2, G) The Fringe offers original music most Friday and Saturday nights, with jazz, rock and world music getting the most airplay. The intimate theatre hosts eclectic local and international performances other nights. It's in a Victorian listed building (c 1892) that was part of a dairy farm, and the distinctive red-and-white brickwork on its facade is known as 'blood and bandages'.

TAKEOUT COMEDY CLUB   COMEDY

Map p302 (☑852 6220 4436; www.takeout comedy.com; Basement, 34 Elgin St, Soho; 🚌26) In need of some LOL? Hong Kong's first full-time comedy club, founded by Chinese-American Jameson Gong, has stand-up and improv acts in English, Cantonese and Mandarin. It also hosts visiting comedians from overseas. See website for program.

PALACE IFC   CINEMA

Map p298 (☑852 2388 6268; Podium Level 1, 8 Finance St, IFC Mall, Central; ☺10am-10pm Mon-Fri, 8.30am-midnight Sat, 8.30am-10pm Sun; Ⓜ Hong Kong, exit F) This eight-screen cinema complex in the IFC Mall (p84) is arguably the most advanced and comfortable in the territory.

GRAPPA'S CELLAR   LIVE MUSIC

Map p298 (☑852 2521 2322; http://elgrande. com.hk/restaurant/grappas-cellar; 1 Connaught Pl, Central; ☺11am-midnight; Ⓜ Hong Kong, exit B2) For at least two weekends a month, this subterranean Italian restaurant morphs into an entertainment venue hosting jazz and other live music – chequered tablecloths and all. Call or visit the website for event and ticketing details.

🛍 SHOPPING

Central's enormous, interconnected network of malls and office buildings have all the luxury goods one might desire. Head south, up the hill, for interesting upmarket independent shops. The eastern end of Hollywood Rd is packed with antiques and art galleries.

★G.O.D.   GIFTS, HOUSEWARES

Map p302 (Goods of Desire; ☑852 2805 1876; www.god.com.hk; 48 Hollywood Rd, Soho; ☺11am-9pm) Goods of Desire – or G.O.D. – is a cheeky local lifestyle brand, selling homewares, clothes, books and gifts with retro Hong Kong themes. Fun buys include aprons printed with images of Hong Kong's famous neon signs, bed linen with themes like koi fish, and reasonably priced cheongsam tops in modern fabrics and colours; great for souvenirs. There's another branch in PMQ (p90).

★**WATTIS FINE ART** ANTIQUES
Map p302 (www.wattis.com.hk; 2nd fl, 20 Hollywood Rd, Lan Kwai Fong; ⊙10.30am-6pm Mon-Sat; ▣26) This upstairs gallery has an outstanding collection of antique maps, lithographs, photos and posters for sale. Rarely will you find such an extensive homage to Asian history, covering not just Hong Kong and Macau, but also Chinese cities like Shànghǎi and Southeast Asian destinations such as Borneo, Myanmar (Burma), Malaka and Mumbai. Enter from Old Bailey St.

★**KOWLOON SOY COMPANY** FOOD & DRINKS
Map p302 (九龍醬園; ☑852 2544 3695; www.kowloonsoy.com; 9 Graham St, Central; ⊙8.30am-6.15pm Mon-Fri, to 6pm Sat; Ⓜ Central, exit D1) *The* shop (c 1917) for artisanal, naturally fermented soy sauce, premier cru yellow-bean sauce (Chinese miso) and other high-quality condiments; it also sells preserved eggs (*pei darn,* 皮蛋) and pickled ginger (*suen geung,* 酸姜), which are often served together at restaurants. Did you know that preserved eggs, being alkaline, can make young red wines taste fuller-bodied? Just try it.

The owner speaks excellent English and can help guide you through the range.

★**SHANGHAI TANG** CLOTHING, HOMEWARES
Map p302 (上海灘; ☑852 2525 7333; www.shanghaitang.com; 1 Duddell St, Shanghai Tang Mansion, Central; ⊙10.30am-8pm; Ⓜ Central, exit D1) This elegant four-level store is a local institution, and one of the few places in Central that specialises in luxury Chinese style. It's the place to go if you fancy a body-hugging *qípáo* (cheongsam) with a modern twist, a Chinese-style clutch or a lime-green mandarin jacket. Shanghai Tang also stocks beautiful chinoiserie-style homewares; don't expect to find much below HK$1000.

SOUL ART ARTS & CRAFTS
Map p302 (☑852 2857 7786; www.soulartshop.com; Ground fl, 24-26 Aberdeen St, Soho; ⊙11am-8pm; ▣26) This Běijīng import brings traditional Chinese culture to life in the form of handmade polymer clay and cloth figurines – and it's actually a lot cooler and more beautiful than it sounds. The dainty baskets of rainbow-coloured dumplings and cloth tigers hand-stitched and then hand-

painted with peonies are both adorable – as is the shop's fluffy ginger cat, Tiger.

LIANCA FASHION & ACCESSORIES
Map p302 (☑852 2139 2989; www.liancacentral.com; Basement, 27 Staunton St, Soho; ⊙11.30am-8pm; ▣26) An understated boutique offering Hong Kong–made leather goods – handbags and wallets, mostly – in classic designs. All items except a few imported accessories are lovingly crafted in Lianca's own workshop. Enter from Graham St.

MOUNTAIN FOLKCRAFT GIFTS & SOUVENIRS
Map p302 (高山民藝; ☑852 2523 2817; www.mountainfolkcraft.com; 12 Wo On Lane, Lan Kwai Fong; ⊙10am-6.30pm Mon-Sat; Ⓜ Central, exit C) This is one of the nicest shops in the city for folk craft, and one of the most reasonably priced for vintage Asian artefacts. It's piled with bolts of batik and sarongs, clothing, wood carvings, lacquerware and paper cuts made by ethnic minorities in China and other Asian countries.

ARCH ANGEL ANTIQUES ANTIQUES
Map p302 (☑852 2851 6848; 70 Hollywood Rd, Lan Kwai Fong; ⊙9.30am-6.30pm Mon-Sat, to 6pm Sun; ▣26) Though the specialities are ancient porcelain and tombware, Arch Angel packs a lot more into its two floors: it has everything from old ink drawings and terracotta horses to palatial furniture, with friendly staff to help you navigate the well-displayed stock. Prices range from about HK$3000 to HK$1 million.

ANDY HEI ANTIQUES
Map p302 (研木得益; ☑852 3105 2002; www.andyhei.com; 72 Hollywood Rd, Lan Kwai Fong; ⊙10am-12.30pm & 1.30-6pm Mon-Sat; ▣26, Ⓜ Central, exit D2) This world-class furniture dealer specialises in classical Chinese furniture from the Ming and Qing dynasties, and scholar's objects. It also restores rare *huanghuali* wood and *zitan* pieces, mainly from the 18th century. Hei is the founding chairman of Fine Art Asia (www.fineartasia.com), which showcases art and antiquities of Asian heritage.

CANDLE COMPANY HOMEWARES
Map p302 (☑852 2545 0099; www.carrolland chan.com; 11 Lyndhurst Tce, Central; ⊙10am-8pm Mon-Sat, from noon Sun) The flagship store for Hong Kong's Carroll & Chan brand of candles and diffusers sells gift-worthy products

like ecofriendly beeswax candles, paper lotus-flower diffusers, incense sticks and fragranced wooden mushrooms in linen bags. The mosquito-ridding citronella candles are particularly handy for Hong Kong summer nights. Look out for the fragrance based on white Michelia – a popular local flower.

CUFFS
CLOTHING

Map p302 (⏳852 2413 8098; www.cuffs.hk; 2/F, Yuen Yick Bldg, 27-29 Wellington St, Central; ⏳11.30am-8pm Mon-Sat) The funkiest of Hong Kong's new generation of tailoring stores, Cuffs offers fashion-forward fabrics and custom-makes not only suits, shirts and tuxes, but 'cool-dry' chinos and womenswear as well. There's even a Shirt Bar and a Suit Bar to guide dithering dandies to their desired look. A two-piece suit starts from HK$4200. The shop stocks off-the-rack garments and accessories too.

POTTERY WORKSHOP GALLERY
ART, HOMEWARES

Map p302 (樂天陶社; ⏳852 2525 7949; www.potteryworkshop.com.cn; Room 305, 3rd fl, Lyndhurst Bldg, Lyndhurst Tce, Central; ⏳1-6pm Tue-Sun; ⏳26) This 3rd-floor gallery showcases playful ceramic objects made by local ceramic artists and artisans from the mainland and overseas. The lovely pieces range from crockery to sculptures. Pottery classes are also offered. The entrance is next to the HSBC (p72).

GIORDANO LADIES
CLOTHING

Map p302 (⏳852 2921 2955; www.giordanoladies.com; ground & 1st fl, Lansing House, 43-45 Queen's Rd Central, Central; ⏳11am-9pm Mon-Sat, to 8pm Sun; ⏳Central, exit D1) Giordano Ladies is a midrange Hong Kong brand that channels a Scandi-chic aesthetic with graceful clothing in a neutral palette. Its offering is a lot less staid than the brand name suggests; expect well-tailored office attire, utility-wear and leisurewear that will fit seamlessly into most wardrobes. Prices start at about HK$800.

PEARL LAM GALLERIES
ART

Map p302 (藝術門; ⏳852 2522 1428; www.pearllam.com; 601-605 Peddar Bldg, 12 Peddar St, Central; ⏳10am-7pm Mon-Sat; ⏳Central, exit D1) This elegant space showcases mainland Chinese, Hong Kong and Asian, as well as European, contemporary art – mostly paintings and sculptures. The owner, Pearl Lam, has been a fervent promoter of Chinese contemporary art and design since the 1990s. She also has galleries in Shànghǎi and Singapore, and recently opened a new flagship gallery in nearby H Queen's (p73).

LINVA TAILOR
FASHION & ACCESSORIES

Map p302 (年華時裝公司; ⏳852 2544 2456; Ground fl, 38 Cochrane St, Central; ⏳9.30am-6pm Mon-Sat; ⏳26) Fancy a cheongsam aka qípáo (body-hugging Chinese dress)? Bring your own silk or choose from the selection at this old-fashioned tailor shop (est 1965). If you're pushed for time, the bespoke tailors, Mr and Mrs Leung, are happy to mail the completed items to you.

JOYCE
FASHION & ACCESSORIES

Map p302 (⏳852 2810 1120; www.joyce.com; Ground fl, 16 Queen's Rd Central, New World Tower, Central; ⏳10.30am-7.30pm; ⏳Central, exit D1) This boutique fashion and beauty department store is a good choice if you're short of time rather than money. Comme des Garçons, Chloé and Alexander McQueen are just some of the international luxury brands stocked here: it's so upmarket, you get sofa service with tea, if you like. For the same threads at half the price, visit **Joyce Warehouse** (Map p312; ⏳852 2814 8313; www.joyce.com; 21st fl, Horizon Plaza Arcade, 2 Lee Wing St, Ap Lei Chau; ⏳10am-7pm; ⏳South Horizons, exit C).

IFC MALL
MALL

Map p298 (⏳852 2295 3308; www.ifc.com.hk; 8 Finance St, Central; ⏳Hong Kong, exit F) This luxurious shopping mall boasts 200 high-fashion boutiques linking the One and Two IFC towers and the Four Seasons Hotel. Outlets include Gucci, Céline, Bottega Veneta, Chloé...we could go on. The Hong Kong Airport Express Station and bag drop is on the ground floor. Its most alluring feature, though, is the awesome roof terrace on the 4th floor.

🏃 SPORTS & ACTIVITIES

★IYARA
SPA

Map p302 (⏳852 2545 8638; www.iyaradayspa.com; 1st fl, 26 Cochrane St, Lan Kwai Fong; manicure/pedicure from HK$160/250, massage from HK$380; ⏳10am-9pm Mon-Thu, to 8pm Fri & Sat, 11am-8pm Sun) Many of Hong Kong's city spas are positively cave-like, in low-lit high-rises with no windows. Iyara, however, is more like a secret garden. It's run by friendly Thais who use organic, natural products. Floor-to-ceiling windows at eye level with the Central–Mid-Levels Escalator provide entertainment while getting a manicure or foot massage with a (free) glass of wine.

AQUA LUNA   BOATING
Map p298 (☑852 2116 8821; www.aqualuna. com.hk; Central Pier 9, Central; from HK$160) Professional harbour tours on traditional Chinese wooden junk boats, with a covered upper level and comfy deck seating. Lots of options run on different days, including a hop-on, hop-off harbour tour, trip to Stanley, Symphony of Lights (p151) evening cruise, and a recommended dim sum lunch cruise (HK$400) on Mondays. Tours depart from Central and then pick up from Tsim Sha Tsui Pier 2. Most tours include one free wine or beer.

HONG KONG PUB CRAWL   FOOD & DRINK
(www.hongkongpubcrawl.com; HK$100; ⊘Wed, Thu) These friendly weekly drinking events pull in a young crowd, including many solo travellers from Hong Kong's hostels. The HK$100 ticket gets you one free beer and several watered-down shots, plus cheap drinks deals at every venue (great value in Hong Kong terms). Thursday nights are the main event, but the Wednesday race night takes in Happy Valley Racecourse (p119) too.

SPA AT THE FOUR SEASONS   SPA
Map p298 (☑852 3196 8900; www.fourseasons. com/hongkong/spa.html; Four Seasons Hotel, 8 Finance St, Central; ⊘8am-11pm, last appointment 10pm; ⋈Hong Kong, exit F) A 1860-sq-metre, ultra-high-end spa with ice fountain and 'herbal cocoon room', and prices to match its Four Seasons location. Its signature treatment is jade-stone massage, but no matter what you book you'll get use of the spa's jacuzzi, steam room and sauna – come in the morning or after 6pm if you want the jacuzzi, because it's off limits 2pm to 6pm.

WORLD WIDE FUND
FOR NATURE HONG KONG   ECOTOUR
(WWFHK; ☑852 2526 1011; www.wwf.org.hk) The World Wide Fund for Nature Hong Kong can arrange guided visits to the Mai Po Nature Reserve (p176) and Hoi Ha Wan Marine Park (p168). Book online.

IMPAKT   MARTIAL ARTS
Map p302 (☑852 2167 7218; www.impakt.hk; 110-116 Queen's Rd Central, 2nd fl, Wings Bldg, Central; ⊘7am-10pm Mon-Fri, 8am-7pm Sat, 10am-5pm Sun; ⋈Central, exit D2) Impakt is one of the few martial-arts centres with female trainers. They teach Muay Thai, kickboxing, jujitsu, karate etc to *GI Jane* wannabes and experienced fighters alike. You can walk in for a one-off class or to use the gym facilities for HK$250. Private sessions cost from HK$325 per person per hour. Excellent English spoken.

TEN FEET TALL   MASSAGE
Map p302 (☑852 2971 1010; www.tenfeettall.com. hk; 20th & 21st fl, L Place, 139 Queen's Rd Central; ⊘11am-1am Mon-Fri & Sun, 10.30am-2am Sat; ⋈Central, exit D2) This sprawling, dimly lit comfort den (745 sq metres) offers a range of treatments, from foot reflexology and shoulder massage to hard-core pressure-point massage and aromatic oil treatments. There's a menu of cold-pressed fruit juices to sip on while you're being pampered.

HAPPY FOOT LUXE   SPA
Map p302 (知足樂; ☑852 2522 1151; www.happy foot.hk; 19th & 20th fl, Century Sq, 1 D'Aguilar St, Lan Kwai Fong; ⊘10am-1am; ⋈Central, exit D2) Getting intense, Chinese-style foot massages is a regular treat for many hard-driving Hong Kong business people. Foot/body massage starts at HK$218/270 for 50 minutes at Happy Foot, or retreat into one of its dark spaces for Thai massage or nail treatments.

PURE FITNESS   GYM
Map p298 (☑852 8129 8000; www.pure-fitness. com; Level 3, 8 Finance St, IFC Mall, Central; day rate HK$350; ⊘6am-midnight Mon-Sat, 8am-10pm Sun; ⋈Hong Kong, exit F) A sleek urban gym offering comprehensive facilities and classes, plus short-term contracts (from one month – ideal for longer-stay travellers) and a drop-in day rate (HK$350). The IFC branch focuses on fitness and beginners' yoga, but other branches across Hong Kong have different offerings, including kickboxing, Pilates and dance fitness. It's a favourite among the professionals working in Central.

The Peak & Northwest Hong Kong Island

SHEUNG WAN | THE PEAK | SAI YING PUN | KENNEDY TOWN

Neighbourhood Top Five

① **Victoria Peak** (p88) Taking the white-knuckle ascent to Victoria Peak on the Peak Tram (p268) for views and strolls around the summit.

② **Sheung Wan** Strolling the streets of Sheung Wan to uncover the fascinating history of 19th-century Hong Kong.

③ **PMQ** (p90) Foraging for Hong Kong–designed jewellery, clothes and homewares at this huge heritage site with coffee, cocktails and art.

④ **Man Mo Temple** (p89) Breathing in the heady scent of Hong Kong Island's biggest temple, creaking

under the gaze of a dozen skyscrapers.

⑤ **Kennedy Town** (p99) Supping craft beers and eating old-school dim sum in this up-and-coming hood, where the skyscrapers finally give way to waterside living.

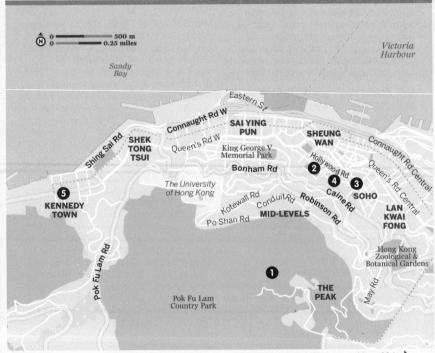

For more detail of this area see Map p304 ➡

Explore The Peak & Northwest Hong Kong Island

Of all the neighbourhoods strung west along Hong Kong Island, Sheung Wan captures the imagination best with its balance of modernity and tradition. Begin by exploring this fascinating enclave in the morning when the temples and shops of dried seafood get into full swing.

Browse the antiques shops and art galleries around Hollywood Rd, and stop for artisan coffee and brunch at a roastery, or a traditional Hong Kong milk tea and French toast at a *cha chaan tang* (teahouse). Even if you're not into shopping, PMQ is worth visiting as an artsy heritage site.

After Sheung Wan you might need a breath of fresh air; consider hiking up Mt Davis, browsing art at the University Museum & Gallery, or heading to Little Creatures in Kennedy Town for craft beers and a waterside meander. Before dusk, head to Central to take the Peak Tram up Victoria Peak; wait to see the lights come on in the city. Descend and return to Sheung Wan for Asian fusion food and cocktails.

Local Life

➝ **Exercising** Join local runners making tracks along the waterside promenade that courses through Sun Yat Sen Memorial Park.

➝ **Shopping** Des Voeux Rd West is known as 'Dried Seafood Street'; a pungent area where Cantonese cooks come to stock up on ingredients like dried shrimp, fish maw and sea cucumbers.

➝ **Hanging out** Belcher Bay Park in Kennedy Town is a leafy community hub where local teenagers socialise and retirees come to exercise and play mahjong.

Getting There & Away

➝ **Ferry** Sheung Wan is home to the **Hong Kong–Macau Ferry Terminal** (Shun Tak Centre; Map p304; Shun Tak Centre, 200 Connaught Rd Central, Sheung Wan), with regular ferry departures to Macau and some departures to Guangdong in mainland China.

➝ **Bus** City buses heading to all parts of Hong Kong Island and Kowloon depart from the **Macau Ferry Pier Bus Terminus** (Map p304; Connaught Rd Central, Sheung Wan), outside the Shun Tak Centre.

➝ **Tram** The double-decker heritage tram runs along Des Voeux Rd Central and Des Voeux Rd West, linking Central with Sheung Wan, Sai Ying Pun and Kennedy Town.

Lonely Planet's Top Tip

Don't miss the neighbourhood around Tai Ping Shan St in Sheung Wan. Once a tenement area where the bubonic plague broke out in the 19th century, it is now a burgeoning boho haven, with cafes, galleries and boutiques – all quite low-key and tasteful – mushrooming alongside weather-beaten shrines.

THE PEAK & NORTHWEST HONG KONG ISLAND

✗ Best Places to Eat

➝ Kau Kee Restaurant (p92)

➝ Little Bao (p93)

➝ Rōnin (p94)

➝ Sun Hing Restaurant (p95)

➝ Man Mo Café (p93)

➝ Black Salt (p96)

For reviews, see p92.➡

🍷 Best Places to Drink

➝ Old Man (p96)

➝ Ping Pong Gintoneria (p98)

➝ Little Creatures (p99)

➝ Craftissimo (p98)

For reviews, see p96.➡

🔒 Best Places to Shop

➝ PMQ (p90)

➝ Cat Street (p91)

➝ Capital Gallery (p99)

➝ Niin (p99)

➝ Only Alice (p99)

➝ Lam Kie Yuen Tea Co (p100)

For reviews, see p99.➡

HELLORF ZCOOL / SHUTTERSTOCK ©

 TOP SIGHT
VICTORIA PEAK

Standing at 552m, Victoria Peak is the highest point on Hong Kong Island. It is also one of the most visited spots by tourists, and it's not hard to see why. Sweeping views of the metropolis, verdant woods, easy but spectacular walks – all reachable in just eight minutes from Central by Hong Kong's earliest form of transport – the 125-year-old, gravity-defying Peak Tram (p268).

Predictably, the Peak has become a moneymaking circus with restaurants, two shopping malls and various entertainment businesses, but there's still magic up here if you can get past that. Make the pilgrimage up to the Sky Terrace 428 – so named because it stands at 428m above sea level – for the 360-degree views and perfect photo op, but leave time for further exploration.

Some 500m to the northwest of the upper terminus, up steep Mt Austin Rd, is the site of the old governor's summer lodge, which was burned to the ground by Japanese soldiers during WWII. The stately gatehouse and beautiful gardens remain, however, and have been refurbished with faux-Victorian gazebos and stone pillars. It takes about 30 minutes to get up here and your reward is that it's blissfully peaceful. Head past the gardens and you'll find a second lookout point with island and sea views.

The dappled Morning Trail, a recommended 3.5km circuit of the Peak that takes at least an hour, starts from Peak Galleria heading north up Lugard Rd. It's also possible to hike to Pok Fu Lam Reservoir or descend to Central via two different paths, one which passes through the Zoological & Botanical Gardens and another that follows the Tramway Path. The 50km Hong Kong Trail also starts on the Peak. The Hong Kong Tourist Board Centre (p275) beside the Peak Tower has maps, or download the Easy Hiking Hong Kong app.

DON'T MISS
➡ Peak Tram
➡ Peak trails
➡ Victoria Peak Garden

PRACTICALITIES
➡ 維多利亞山頂
➡ ☎852 2522 0922
➡ www.thepeak.com.hk
➡ combined Peak Tram Sky Pass adult/child return HK$99/47, adult/child single HK$84/38
➡ ⏱24hr
➡ 🚌15 from Central, below Exchange Sq, 🚊Peak Tram Lower Terminus

TOP SIGHT
MAN MO TEMPLE

One of Hong Kong's oldest temples, atmospheric Man Mo Temple is dedicated to the god of literature (Man), who's always holding a writing brush, and the god of war (Mo), who wields a sword.

History

Built in 1847 during the Qing dynasty by wealthy Chinese merchants, it was, besides a place of worship, a court of arbitration for local disputes when trust was thin between the Chinese and the colonialists. Oaths taken at this Taoist temple (often accompanied by the ritual beheading of a rooster) were accepted by the colonial government.

The Temple Today

Outside the main entrance are four gilt plaques on poles that used to be carried around at processions. Two describe the gods being worshipped inside, one requests silence and a show of respect within the temple's grounds, and the last warns menstruating women to keep out of the main hall.

Inside the temple (on the left as you go in) are two 19th-century sedan chairs with elaborate carvings, which used to carry statues of the two gods during festivals.

Lending the temple its beguiling and smoky air are rows of large earth-coloured spirals suspended from the roof, like strange fungi in an upside-down garden. These are incense coils burned as offerings by worshippers.

On the western side of the temple is Lit Shing Kung (the Saints' Palace), a place of worship for other Buddhist and Taoist deities. Another hall, Kung Sor (Public Meeting Place), used to serve as a court of justice to settle disputes among the Chinese community before the modern judicial system was introduced. A couplet at the entrance urges those entering to leave their selfish interests and prejudices outside. Fortune-tellers beckon from inside.

DON'T MISS

➡ The main temple
➡ Lit Shing Kung
➡ Fortune-tellers

PRACTICALITIES

➡ 文武廟
➡ Map p304, G4
➡ ☏852 2540 0350
➡ 124-126 Hollywood Rd, Sheung Wan
➡ admission free
➡ ⊙8am-6pm
➡ 🚌26

◉ SIGHTS

You'll find many of Hong Kong's most intriguing sights around the Peak and in the neighbourhoods below it, from quirky museums and historic buildings to fragrant temples.

◉ Sheung Wan

MAN MO TEMPLE TAOIST TEMPLE
See p89.

★PMQ ARTS CENTRE
Map p304 (元創方; ☑852 2870 2335; www.pmq.org.hk; S614, Block A, PMQ, 35 Aberdeen St, Soho; ⊙building 7am-11pm, shops noon-8pm; ▣26, ⓂCentral, exit D2) This arts and lifestyle hub occupies the multistorey modernist building complex of the old married police quarters (c 1951). Dozens of small galleries and shops, including a branch of G.O.D (p82), hawk local design in the form of hip handmade jewellery, clothing, housewares and more, making the PMQ a terrific place to hunt for nontacky souvenirs. There are also several restaurants and cafes, a breezy central courtyard hosting pop-ups and street art, and a large space on the top floor with rotating free exhibitions.

The site's earliest incarnation was a temple built in 1843, which was subsequently replaced by Central School, where Nationalist leader Dr Sun Yatsen once studied. Remnants of the school remain. PMQ is bounded by Hollywood Rd (north), Staunton St (south), Aberdeen St (east) and Shing Wong St (west).

★PAK SING ANCESTRAL HALL TEMPLE
Map p304 (廣福祠; Kwong Fuk Ancestral Hall; 42 Tai Ping Shan St; ⊙8am-5pm; ▣26) In the 19th century many Chinese who left home in search of better horizons died overseas. As it was the wish of traditional Chinese to be buried in their home towns, this temple was built in 1856 to store corpses awaiting burial in China, and to serve as a public ancestral hall for those who could not afford the expense of bone repatriation. Families of the latter have erected 3000 memorial tablets for their ancestors in a room behind the altar.

PALACE OF MOON & WATER KWUN YUM TEMPLE BUDDHIST TEMPLE
Map p304 (水月觀音堂; 7 Tai Ping Shan St; ⊙9am-6pm; ▣26) Not to be confused with Kwun Yum Temple nearby, this dimly lit temple honours Kwun Yum of a Thousand Arms. Kwun Yum (aka Guanyin) is the Goddess of Compassion. According to legend, Buddha gave her a thousand arms so she could help everyone who needed it. For a small donation, you can give the small wooden windmill at the entrance a spin; it will presumably change your luck.

KWUN YAM TEMPLE BUDDHIST TEMPLE
Map p304 (觀音廟; Kwun Yum; 34 Tai Ping Shan St; ⊙7.30am-5.30pm; ▣26) Built in 1840, Sheung Wan's oldest temple honours Kwun Yam, the Goddess of Mercy. It's a quaint-

---

HONG KONG ISLAND'S WILD WEST

Ride the MTR's Island line to its most westerly point (or take the double-decker tram) and you'll emerge in Kennedy Town, a quiet neighbourhood at the foot of Mt Davis that feels a lot further away from Central's skyscrapers than it actually is. This is where Hong Kong life meets the edge of Victoria Harbour and fishers still plunge their rods into the sea straight off the Praya.

A good place to start the day is at Kennedy Town Swimming Pool (p100), where you can join locals who come for laps in the fabulous 50m outdoor pool fronting the harbour. Just across the road, Belcher Bay Park is a favourite among retirees and where mahjong marathons take over public tables.

Kennedy Town's low-rise streets are mostly unremarkable and untainted by gentrification, and that's part of its charm. It's a good jumping off point for a hike up Mt Davis (p92), or gazing out to sea at the Sai Wan Swimming Shed (p92) – a wobbly pierlike structure frequented by locals (and Instagrammers), and the last of its kind. Hong Kong's foodies know Kennedy Town for one thing alone: dim sum at Sun Hing (p95). Arrive early (as in, 5am) or extremely late to see taxi drivers and city workers get their fix at this working-class joint. Finish your explorations with craft beers at Aussie microbrewery Little Creatures (p99); the surest sign that gentrification is coming this way.

looking structure, with a magnificent and intricate brass carving just above the doorway. The temple has been renovated with funky structural additions – orange iron railings and a yellow awning printed with Buddhist swastika symbols.

LIANG YI MUSEUM
MUSEUM

Map p304 (兩依博物館; ☑852 2806 8280; www. liangyimuseum.com; 181-199 Hollywood Rd, Soho; HK$200; ☺by appointment 10am-6pm Tue-Sat; MCentral, exit D2) This private three-floor museum houses two exquisite collections: antique Chinese furniture from the Ming and Qing dynasties, and Chinese-inspired European vanities from the 19th and 20th century. The former is one of the world's best. The precious collection is displayed through rotating themed exhibitions that change every six months, paired with museum pieces called in from world-class galleries all over the globe. The museum itself is a stunning space; visits are by appointment only (book at least a day ahead) and by guided tour. Visitors can touch or sit on the pieces, which are not separated by rope or glass.

CAT STREET
AREA

Map p304 (摩囉街; Upper Lascar Row; ☺10am-6pm; ☑26) Just north of (and parallel to) Hollywood Rd is Upper Lascar Row, aka 'Cat Street', a pedestrian-only lane lined with antique and curio shops and stalls selling Bruce Lee movie posters and old Hong Kong photos, cheap jewellery and newly minted ancient coins. It's a fun place to trawl through for souvenirs, but expect most artefacts to be mass-produced fakes.

HONG KONG MUSEUM OF MEDICAL SCIENCES
MUSEUM

Map p304 (香港醫學博物館; ☑852 2549 5123; www.hkmms.org.hk; 2 Caine Lane, Mid-Levels; adult/concession HK$20/10; ☺10am-5pm Tue-Sat, 1-5pm Sun; ☑3B) Although this museum's focus is medical sciences, there are several interesting exhibits for tourists – in particular the section dedicated to the history of the Tai Ping Shan District in which the museum stands, now a hipster hood of little indie shops, bars and cafes, but once a vast slum area of tenement housing. It was here in 1894 that an outbreak of bubonic plague originated, turning Hong Kong into a quarantine port and making the British rethink health and medicine in the colony.

The museum building itself is a lovely Edwardian-style, brick-and-tile structure (1905) fronted by bauhinia trees. If you take the bus, alight at the Ladder St bus stop on Caine Rd.

MAN WA LANE
AREA

Map p304 (文華里; Man Wa Lane; ☺10am-6pm; MSheung Wan, exit A1) Kiosks in this alley just east of the Sheung Wan MTR station specialise in name chops: a stone (or wood or jade) seal with the owner's name carved in Chinese on its base. It's combined with Chinese red ink or cinnabar paste to make a seal imprint that can be used in lieu of a handwritten signature. Tell the shop owner your name and they will create an auspicious Chinese version for you.

WESTERN MARKET
HISTORIC BUILDING

Map p304 (西港城; ☑852 6029 2675; 323 Des Voeux Rd Central & New Market St; ☺9am-7pm; ☑Sheung Wan, exit B) Textile vendors driven off nearby streets in the 1990s moved into this renovated market building (1906) with its bold red-and-white facade, four-corner towers and other Edwardian features. Now bolts of cloth flank the corridors of the 1st floor. Souvenir shops and the **Grand Stage** (大舞臺飯店; Map p304; ☑852 2815 2311; meals from HK$100; ☺11.30am-3pm; ☑; MSheung Wan, exit E2) restaurant occupy the ground and top floors, and there are a couple of cafes inside the entrance.

⊙ The Peak

VICTORIA PEAK
VIEWPOINT

See p88.

⊙ Sai Ying Pun & Kennedy Town

UNIVERSITY OF HONG KONG
UNIVERSITY

Map p304 (香港大學; ☑852 2859 2111; www.hku.hk; Pok Fu Lam Rd, Pok Fu Lam; ☑23, 40 from Admiralty) Established in 1911, HKU is the oldest university in Hong Kong. The Edwardian-style Main Building, with its pastel-pink edifice, colonnaded verandahs and red-brick core, dates to 1912 and is a declared monument. Several other early 20th-century buildings on the campus, including the domed Hung Hing Ying (1919), opposite the main entrance, and Tang Chi Ngong Buildings (1929), are also protected.

UNIVERSITY MUSEUM & ART GALLERY
MUSEUM

Map p304 (☑852 2241 5500; www.hku.hk/hkumag; Fung Ping Shan Bldg, 94 Bonham Rd, Pok Fu Lam; ⊙9.30am-6pm Mon-Sat, 1-6pm Sun; ▣23, 40M) FREE The University of Hong Kong Museum & Art Gallery houses collections of ceramics and bronzes spanning 5000 years, including exquisite blue-and-white Ming porcelain; early Qing dynasty furniture; and almost 1000 fascinating small Nestorian (Church of the East) crosses from the Yuan dynasty, the largest such collection in the world. It also hosts temporary exhibitions from around the world, covering everything from Italian Medici sculpture to photojournalism in Mongolia.

The museum is to the east of the university's main building and opposite the start of Hing Hon Rd.

SAI WAN SWIMMING SHED
WATERFRONT

(Victoria Rd, Western District; ▣1) Local Instagrammers and wedding photographers know all about Sai Wan Swimming Shed, a dreamy spot below Mt Davis where old-school Hong Kongers come for bracing sea dips with hazy views of Hong Kong's toothsome skyline in the distance. There used to be a series of swimming sheds along the waterfront but this is the only surviving one. It's charming and rickety, with a couple of wooden platforms, mini shrines, makeshift showers and a walkway disappearing into the sea.

To get here take bus 1, which runs through Sheung Wan, Sai Ying Pun and Kennedy Town, and alight at the Caritas Jockey Club stop on Victoria Rd. The steps leading down to the swimming shed are a couple of minutes' walk east along Victoria Rd.

Note that although there are showers here and locals do use the swimming shed, the signs in Chinese warn visitors of the dangers of swimming here. Enter the water at your own risk.

MT DAVIS
RUINS

(Mt Davis Path, Victoria Rd; ▣1) Leafy and deserted in a slightly dystopian way, Mt Davis is one of the last remaining adventures on Hong Kong Island's busy northern belt. In the early 20th century it was home to the Mount Davis Battery, tasked with defending the western end of Hong Kong Island, and the eery abandoned military ruins of barracks and gun battalions are here for all to see, along with unmanicured harbour views, butterflies and unmarked trails. Take bus 1 to the Mt Davis Path stop and walk up.

The battery received heavy damage during the WWII Japanese occupation in 1941 and was abandoned to the wild shortly after. With the whistling breeze and deafening silence, it's not hard to buy into the urban myths that this peak is haunted. Locals sometimes visit on weekends, but you'll likely have it to yourself midweek.

The Mt Davis path is a 10-minute bus journey on the number 1 from Kennedy Town MTR, or a HK$40 taxi if you'd prefer to drive up and walk back down (the path is a road, albeit a very quiet one). There are also helter-skelter steps leading through the Jurassic foliage, but they are not maintained and you may find them obstructed. Expect the walk to take about 45 minutes up and 30 minutes back down.

✖ EATING

The quality of restaurants on the Peak is increasing, but you'll still find better food and prices down below. Sheung Wan has some excellent fusion choices; Sai Ying Pun has a more low-key neighbourhood vibe but the quality is equally high. Book ahead for dinner if restaurants take reservations. Western-style brunch is becoming increasingly popular and far-flung waterside Kennedy Town has an appealing cluster of options.

✖ Sheung Wan

★KAU KEE RESTAURANT
NOODLES $

Map p304 (九記牛腩; ☑852 2850 5967; 21 Gough St, Central; meals from HK$50; ⊙12.30-10.30pm Mon-Sat; Ⓜ Sheung Wan, exit E2) You can argue till the noodles go soggy about whether Kau Kee has the best beef brisket in town. Whatever the verdict, the meat – served with toothsome noodles in a fragrant beefy broth – is hard to beat. During the 90 years of the shop's existence, film stars and politicians have joined the queue for a table. Besides regular brisket, you can order – and many of the locals do – the beef tendon (牛筋; ngau gun) served in a curry sauce. But know that the best cuts of meat are reserved for the classic dish.

MAMMY PANCAKE
STREET FOOD $

Map p304 (媽咪雞蛋仔; 32 Bonham Strand E; waffles from HK$16; ⏱noon-9pm) Hong Kong is a city of foodie fad-followers and one of its original inventions is the bulbous egg puff/waffle, sometimes filled with treats like red bean or peanut butter. Many locals will argue that Michelin-recommended Mammy Pancake whips up the fluffiest and best. Place your order at the counter and wait for your paper bag. Add an iced tea for extra street cred.

CHAN KAN KEE
GUANGDONG $

Map p304 (陳勤記鹵鵝飯店; ☎852 2858 0033; 11 Queen's Rd W; meals HK$100-300; ⏱11am-10.30pm; ☎; ⊠5) For an authentic Chiu Chow treat, this family-run restaurant serves hearty marinated goose, baby oyster omelette and duck soup. It's jam-packed during lunch hours. Chiu Chow is a city in the northeastern part of Guǎngdōng province, but its cooking is so refined and distinctive that it's often mentioned separately from Cantonese cuisine.

CHAN CHUN KEE
GUANGDONG $

Map p304 (陳春記; ☎852 3542 5793; Shop 5, Queen St Cooked Food Market, 1 Queen St; meals from HK$30; ⏱noon-7pm; ☎) Warning to vegetarians: different parts of a pig will confront you in every repast at this Chiu Chow eatery. The locals flock to this unpretentious kitchen for its pig's blood and innards soup (豬紅豬雜湯). For a less exotic adventure, try the fish-skin dumplings or fish balls with noodles.

★LITTLE BAO
FUSION $$

Map p304 (☎852 2194 0202; www.little-bao.com; 66 Staunton St; meals HK$200-400; ⏱6-11pm Mon-Fri, noon-4pm & 6-11pm Sat, noon-4pm & 6-10pm Sun; ☎☑; ⓜCentral, exit D2) A trendy diner that wows with its *bao* (Chinese buns) – snow-white orbs crammed with juicy meat and slathered with Asian condiments – and fusion sharing dishes. Its signature porkbelly *bao* with hoisin ketchup, and truffle fries with shiitake tempeh might just be the greatest, most unique meal you have in Hong Kong. Go early to put your name on the waiting list – no reservations.

★MAN MO CAFÉ
DIM SUM $$

Map p304 (☎852 2644 5644; www.manmo dimsum.com; 40 Upper Lascar Row; meals HK$300-500; ⏱noon-10.30pm Mon-Sat, to 5pm Sun; ☎☑; ⓜCentral, exit D2) At this welcoming place, chefs from culinary giants in Taiwan (Din Tai Fung) and France (Robuchon) team up to create high-end fusion dim sum. Portions are dainty but unique and utterly delicious. Rich foie gras explodes out of *xiao long bao* (soup dumplings), Nutella oozes from sesame-speckled balls, and truffle brie dumplings bewitch vegetarians. The chic interior reflects both its French influences and antique-y Cat St location.

CHACHAWAN
THAI $$

Map p304 (☎852 2549 0020; www.chachawan. hk; Ground fl, 206 Hollywood Rd; meals HK$200-450; ⏱noon-3pm & 6.30-11pm, happy hour 5-7pm; ☎☑; ⓜSheung Wan, exit A2) Specialising in the spicy cuisine of northeastern Thailand's Isaan region, this hip little spot is always jam-packed and plenty noisy. No curries or pad thai here, just bright, herb-infused, chilli-packed salads and grilled fish and meat (vegetarian options too). Wash it all down with cocktails incorporating Thai flavours such as sweet tea and lychee. No reservations – expect a wait in the evening.

YARDBIRD
JAPANESE $$

Map p304 (☎852 2547 9273; www.yardbird restaurant.com; 154-158 Wing Lok St; meals from HK$250; ⏱6pm-midnight Mon-Sat; ⓜSheung Wan, exit 2, ⓕMacau Ferry Terminal) Yardbird is a hipster's ode to the chicken. Every part of the cluck-cluck, from thigh to gizzard, is seasoned, impaled with a stick then grilled, yakitori-style. The resulting skewers are flavourful with just the right consistency. It's highly popular and doesn't take reservations, so sample the sakes in the convivial bar area while you wait for a table.

TIM'S KITCHEN
CANTONESE $$

Map p304 (桃花源; ☎852 2543 5919; www.tims kitchen.com.hk; 84-90 Bonham Strand; lunch HK$130-500, dinner HK$300-1000; ⏱11am-3pm & 6-11pm; ⓐ; ⓜSheung Wan, exit A2) This two-floor formal restaurant is considered one of Hong Kong's best – as evidenced by the Michelin honour and the praises lavished by local gourmets. It serves extraordinarily delicate and subtle Cantonese fare, and at lunchtimes a reasonably priced dim sum menu too. Signature items such as the crab claw poached with wintermelon and crystal king prawn require preordering a day ahead. Reservations essential.

ABC KITCHEN
EUROPEAN $$

Map p304 (☑852 9278 8227; www.abckitchen. com.hk; Shop 7, Queen St Cooked Food Centre, 1 Queen St; lunch HK$45-65, dinner HK$150-350; ☺12-2.30pm Mon-Sat, 7-10pm Mon-Sun; Ⓜ Sheung Wan, exit B) Serving elegant European cuisine in the unexpected environs of a wet market's food court, ABC Kitchen is an experience you won't find elsewhere. And the food's terrific too – the menu changes, but the suckling pig is a reliable favourite. If you're craving western food, you won't find better for the price. Dinner reservations essential; save money by bringing your own wine. Cash only.

MRS POUND
ASIAN $$

Map p304 (☑852 3426 3949; www.mrspound. com; 6 Pound Lane; meals HK$200-400; ☺noon-3pm & 5pm-midnight; ☎; ☐26) When Mrs Pound first opened, it was a stamp shop. Now it's masquerading as a traditional locksmiths; tap a lock near the door and it swings open to reveal a playful dive-y diner serving up Asian fusion street food such as sriracha-drizzled corn and beef-rendang poutine. Happy hour (5pm to 8pm) includes 50% off many cocktails and nibbles. No reservations. Later on in the evening it becomes a fun bar.

GOUGH'S ON GOUGH
BRITISH $$

Map p304 (☑852 2473 9066; www.goughs ongough.com; 15 Gough St, Soho; meals HK$400-800; ☺noon-2.30pm Sun-Fri, 6.30pm-midnight daily; ✷; Ⓜ Sheung Wan, exit E1) This funky British restaurant, designed by interiors expert Timothy Oulton, is a stunning space. A spiral staircase, an aquarium, a monochrome geometric floor and mismatched ornaments are just begging to be Instagrammed. The menu is modern British (think classic seafood and meat dishes), and even if you can't get a reservation, the intimate bar upstairs does a neat range of inventive cocktails.

CHAIRMAN
CANTONESE $$

Map p304 (大班樓; ☑852 2555 2202; www.the-chairmangroup.com; 18 Kau U Fong; meals from HK$300; ☺noon-3pm & 6-11pm; ☎; Ⓜ Sheung Wan, exit E2) Understated faux-retro decor and warm service impart a homely feel at this upmarket place serving Cantonese classics with a healthy twist. Ingredients are sourced locally; cured meat and pickles are made at its own farm. No surprise – almost all the dishes hit all the right notes, from flavour to presentation. Reservations essential.

ABERDEEN ST SOCIAL
BRITISH $$

Map p304 (☑852 2866 0300; www.aberdeen streetsocial.hk; Ground fl, PMQ, 25 Aberdeen St, Central; downstairs meals HK$150-300, upstairs meals HK$400-800; ☺noon-11pm; ☎; Ⓜ Sheung Wan) Run by British celebrity chef Jason Atherton, trendy Aberdeen St Social is really two restaurants in one. Downstairs is an all-day cafe where hip Sheung Wan dwellers eat avocado toast and fancy fish and chips on the patio. Upstairs is pricey, avant-garde dining (think smoked eel with foie gras). Its lunch deal is a snip compared with usual prices: HK$298 for three courses. Happy hour runs 5pm to 8pm Sunday to Friday.

★RŌNIN
JAPANESE $$$

Map p304 (☑852 2547 5263; www.roninhk. com; Ground fl, 8 On Wo Lane, Central; meals from HK$500; ☺6pm-midnight Mon-Sat; ☎; Ⓜ Sheung Wan, exit E2) With just 24 counter seats locked down behind an unmarked door, Rōnin has all the hallmarks of a coveted Soho dining spot before you've even seen the daily changing menu. Plates – all delicious and inventive – are organised by raw, smaller and bigger, and include revelations like succulent black-pilsner-battered smoked tilefish and crunchy palm-sized crabs with *yuzu* and sesame.

Ask the staff to recommend sake or shochu from the extensive menu to pair with your meal; they really know their stuff.

UPPER MODERN BISTRO
FRENCH $$$

Map p304 (☑852 2517 0977; www.upper-bistro. com; 6-14 Upper Station St; 2-course set lunch HK$168-248, dinner from HK$500; ☺noon-10.30pm Mon-Thu, to 11pm Fri & Sat, 11.30am-10pm Sun; Ⓜ Central, exit D2) Just around the corner from trendy Tai Ping Shan St, the 'bistro' label undersells the chic, contemporary interiors of this large restaurant, where petal-like 'eggs' are whimsically overlaid on the ceiling. The food is haute French cuisine by Michelin-starred Philippe Orrico, with clever Asian touches.

✗ The Peak

PEAK LOOKOUT
INTERNATIONAL, ASIAN $$

(太平山餐廳; ☑852 2849 1000; www.peaklook out.com.hk; 121 Peak Rd; meals from HK$200;

⊙10.30am–midnight Mon-Thu, to 1am Fri, 8.30am–1am Sat, 8.30am–midnight Sun; 🚌15, 🚋Peak Tram) This 60-year-old colonial establishment has more character than all the other Peak restaurants combined, and it's the only place to eat up here that's not inside a mall. It's looking a little shabby around the edges these days, but the food is still good – especially the western selections – and the views from the outdoor terrace are worth lingering over.

🍴 Sai Ying Pun & Kennedy Town

⭐ **SUN HING RESTAURANT**   DIM SUM $

(新興食家; 🕿852 2816 0616; Ground fl, 8C Smithfield Rd, Kennedy Town; meals HK$50; ⊙3am–4pm; 🚌101) Many a drunken Soho reveller has trudged westward after a long night seeking cheap dim sum, but to no avail. Then just before they pass out, there appears, vision-like, Sun Hing in all its scrumptious glory! They weep. True story, though some say tears are shed over the runny 'Golden Sauce' custard bun (流沙包) – don't leave without ordering some.

Little English is spoken, but there's an English menu and staff will also wave you over to point at what you want in baskets on a table at the side of the cafe.

CROSS CAFE   CAFE $

Map p304 (十字冰室; 🕿852 2887 1315; www.facebook.com/crosscafehk; Shop 12, Ground fl, Hang Sing Mansion, 48-78 High St, Sai Ying Pun; breakfast/meals from HK$30/40; ⊙7.30am–8.30pm Mon-Sun; Ⓜ Sai Ying Pun, exit B2, minibus 12) Taking its cue from the traditional Hong Kong *cha chaan tang* (tea restaurants), this cafe with minimalist white seating and red neon signs offers a contemporary twist on the much-loved original. Dishes such as oatmeal in Trappist mango papaya milk, or fluffy pineapple bun with truffled scrambled egg, make for a satisfying breakfast. There's no English sign; look for the neon Chinese characters.

KWUN KEE RESTAURANT   CANTONESE $

Map p304 (坤記煲仔小菜; 🕿852 2803 7209; Wo Yick Mansion, 263 Queen's Rd W, Sai Ying Pun; meals from HK$80; ⊙11am–2.30pm & 6-11pm Mon-Sat, 6-11pm Sun; 🚌101) Hong Kong's top brass make pilgrimages to this local place for its claypot rice (HK$80 to HK$105,

available only at dinner) – a meal-in-one in which rice and toppings such as chicken are cooked in claypots over charcoal stoves until the grains are infused with the juices of the meat and a layer of crackle is formed at the bottom. Enter from Kwai Heung St.

There's a second branch on Des Voeux Rd West, but this is the original and has the best atmosphere, with diners spilling out into the street.

CHAU KEE   CANTONESE $

Map p304 (周記; 🕿852 2559 2389; Ground fl, Tung Lee Mansion, 1H Water St, Sai Ying Pun; meals from HK$50; ⊙8am–6pm Tue-Sun; 🚌) What do you get if you cross a traditional Chinese custard bun with Hong Kong's traditional crispy French toast? You get Chau Kee's 'lava' French toast. This modern *cha chaan tang*, with retro sepia photos of Hong Kong on the walls, found local fame with this deliciously indulgent dish, but it's a good cheap eat for any meal of the day.

BA YI RESTAURANT   CHINESE $

Map p304 (巴依餐廳; 🕿852 2484 9981; 43 Water St, Sai Ying Pun; meals from HK$150; ⊙noon–3pm & 6-10pm Tue-Sun; Ⓜ Sai Ying Pun, exit B2) This rustic halal restaurant serving the cuisine of northwestern China's Xinjiang province is a lamb lover's paradise. Here you can savour mutton in all its glory – grilled, braised, fried or boiled with lashings of spices. Bookings essential; specials such as roasted lamb leg require advance order. It's a five- to 10-minute walk uphill from Sai Ying Pun MTR station.

CATCH   EUROPEAN $

(🕿852 2855 1289; www.catch.hk; 95 Catchick St, Kennedy Town; brunch HK$68-148, set lunch HK$128-148, dinner HK$160-400; ⊙5pm–midnight Mon-Wed, noon-3pm & 5pm-midnight Thu & Fri, 9am-4.15pm & 6pm-midnight Sat & Sun; 🛜; Ⓜ Kennedy Town, exit B) Want to track down Hong Kong's casualistas? Chances are they're eating (or queueing for a table) at Kennedy Town's Catch, an Australian-style streetside cafe popular for its weekend brunch classics such as avocado on sourdough and seriously good coffee. Tuesday is two-for-one steak night, and happy hour runs 5pm to 8pm Monday to Thursday.

YUEN KEE DESSERT   DESSERTS $

Map p304 (源記甜品專家; 🕿852 2548 8687; 32 Centre St, Sai Ying Pun; desserts from HK$25; ⊙1-11pm; 🚌101, 104) This old-timers' favourite has been whipping up its famous sweet mulberry mistletoe tea soup with lotus seeds and egg (桑寄蓮子雞蛋茶) since 1855. The restaurant specialises in *tong shui* (traditional sweet, warm soups), and that's literally all it sells. Alternatives to the oriental tea include almond, walnut or red bean; if you're unsure, try the egg-custard version.

BLACK SALT   ASIAN $$

Map p304 (☑852 3702 1237, reservations by Whatsapp 852 5173 3058; www.blacksalt.com.hk; Ground fl, 14 Fuk Sau Lane, Sai Ying Pun; meals from HK$300; ⏰5.30-11pm Tue-Sat, to 10pm Sun, noon-3pm Sat & Sun; 🈂🍴; ⓜSai Ying Pun, exit B2) Black Salt is the friendly neighbourhood restaurant we'd all like to have around the corner. It's tiny inside (so book ahead), and tables spill out onto a small laneway terrace. Dishes are a delicious, accomplished mash-up of South Asian cuisines, including fancy Kathmandu *momo* dumplings, Sri Lankan *kothu roti* and Indian *mattar paneer* with melt-in-the-mouth homemade curds. Service is split into two sittings.

Note that dishes are designed to share, but if you're eating alone the excellent staff are happy to tailor a meal with smaller portions (and prices) so you can still try a variety of items on the menu. Brunch is served on weekends.

OKRA   JAPANESE $$

Map p304 (☑852 2806 1038; www.okra.kitchen; Ground fl, 110 Queen's Rd W, Sai Ying Pun; meals from HK$400; ⏰6-11.30pm Mon-Sat; 🈂; ⓜSai Ying Pun, exit A1) This relaxed *izakaya* (informal Japanese pub) in Sai Ying Pun is as much about sake sampling as it is the food, but the enthusiastic staff nail both. The team work closely with trusted producers to bring the best natural and unpasteurised sakes to Hong Kong, then match them with creative dishes such as crispy brussels sprouts with homemade XO sauce and smoked *yuzu* jam ribs.

POTATO HEAD   INDONESIAN $$

Map p304 (☑852 2858 6066; www.ptthead.com; Ground fl, 100 Third St, Sai Ying Pun; meals HK$150-400; ⏰restaurant noon-11pm Mon-Fri, from 11am Sat & Sun; ✳🈂; ⓜSai Ying Pun, exit B2) The Hong Kong outpost of Potato Head, which started as a hipster beach club in Bali with killer cocktails, isn't so much a restaurant as a multiconcept events space with food and decks. It consists of an excellent Indonesian restaurant, Kaum, where you eat small plates off a long wooden table; a fun cocktail lounge; and a hidden Music Room at the back.

MISSY HO'S   ASIAN $$

(☑852 2817 3808; www.facebook.com/Missy HosHK; Ground fl, 48 Forbes St, Kennedy Town; ⏰dinner 6-10pm Mon-Sat, bar to 11pm; 🈂; ⓜKennedy Town, exit A) Missy Ho's was once famed for its indoor swing that was unfurled from the ceiling after dinner service, but health-and-safety complaints eventually forced them to ditch it. Still, you get the picture: fun is high on the agenda at this K-Town restaurant-bar, stuffed with Hong Kong-inspired paraphernalia including bird cages. It's popular for lively weekend dinners; the menu is Asian fusion. Happy hour 4pm to 7pm.

🍷 DRINKING & NIGHTLIFE

Neighbourhoods west of Soho offer a more relaxed nightlife scene and the further west you travel, the quieter it generally gets. Sheung Wan has a blossoming LGBT scene around Jervois St and Bonham Strand. Sai Ying Pun has a couple of excellent cocktail bars.

🍷 Sheung Wan

★OLD MAN   COCKTAIL BAR

Map p304 (☑852 2703 1899; www.theoldmanhk.com; Lower ground fl, 37-39 Aberdeen St, Soho; cocktails HK$100; ⏰5pm-2am Mon-Sat, to midnight Sun; ⓜCentral, exit D2) If Ernest Hemingway was still alive today, chances are he'd love this tiny no-sign speakeasy named after his novel *The Old Man And The Sea*, with a neo-cubist portrait of Papa himself looking down approvingly from behind the bar. The atmosphere is friendly rather than pretentious and the mixology is exceptionally creative, with elements like gruyere, sous-vide pandan leaves and nori dust.

Try to get a seat at the communal table in front of the intimate bar to see the bartenders work their magic: the strip down the middle is iced, to keep your drinks cool. The entrance isn't advertised – look for the steps heading down into a dead-end alleyway off Aberdeen St.

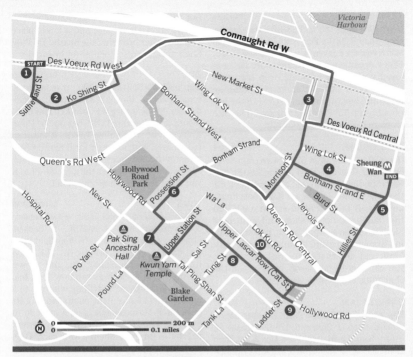

🏃 Neighbourhood Walk
Hong Kong's Wholesale District

START SUTHERLAND ST STOP, KENNEDY TOWN TRAM
END SHEUNG WAN MTR STATION, EXIT B
LENGTH 1.5KM; ONE HOUR

Set off from the Sutherland St stop of the Kennedy Town tram. Have a look at (and a sniff of) Des Voeux Rd West's many ❶ **dried seafood shops** piled with all manner of desiccated sea life. Walk south on Sutherland St to Ko Shing St to browse the medieval-looking goods on offer from the ❷ **herbal-medicine traders**.

At the end of Ko Shing St, re-enter Des Voeux Rd West and head northeast. Continue along Connaught Rd West, where you'll find the attractive colonial building that houses the ❸ **Western Market** (p91). At the corner of Morrison St, walk south past Wing Lok St and onto Bonham Strand East where you'll find ❹ **Lam Kie Yuen Tea Co** (p100). This friendly tea shop might let you sample some of its astounding selection of Chinese brews.

If you're hungry, take a quick detour down Bonham Strand to ❺ **Mammy Pancake** (p93) for a takeaway egg waffle and iced tea. Backtrack to climb up ❻ **Possession Street**, where British marines planted the Union Jack flag in 1841 (look out for the plaque), then take a left into Hollywood Rd, before ascending Pound Lane to Tai Ping Shan St. Here you'll see three charming temples (p90), including the ❼ **Palace Of Moon & Water Kwun Yum Temple**.

Head southeast down trendy Tai Ping Shan St, keeping an eye out for street art, then left to descend Upper Station St to the start of Hollywood Rd's ❽ **antique shops** with curios and rare, mostly Chinese, treasures. Continuing east on Hollywood Rd brings you to ❾ **Man Mo Temple** (p89), one of the oldest and most significant temples in the territory.

Take a short hop to the left down Ladder St to Upper Lascar Row, home of the ❿ **Cat Street Market** (p91), which is well stocked with inexpensive Chinese memorabilia. Ladder St brings you back to Queen's Rd Central; head north until you hit Wing Lok St and you'll find yourself at exit A1 of Sheung Wan MTR station.

TEAKHA
TEAHOUSE

Map p304 (茶家; ☑852 2858 9185; www.teakha. com; Shop B, 18 Tai Ping Shan St; ⊙9am-6pm Mon & Wed-Fri, 8.30am-7pm Sat & Sun; 🛜; ☲26) Fancy organic tea concoctions are best enjoyed with the homemade drop scones in this modern interpretation of a Chinese teahouse, just off the main street in the impossibly hip Tai Ping Shan St area. The cute teaware makes a good souvenir.

CRAFTISSIMO
CRAFT BEER

Map p304 (☑852 6274 3130; www.craftissimo. hk; Shop D, Ground fl, 22-24 Tai Ping Shan St; ⊙1-10pm Sun-Thu, to 11pm Fri & Sat; ☲26) Look for the kegs turned into squat bar stools down an alley off Tai Ping Shan St and you'll find this laid-back bottle shop and craft-beer bar. There's no seating inside, just six rotating draught taps and a wall crammed with local and international craft beers that you can buy to take away or drink on the charming, rough-and-ready patio.

BARISTA JAM
COFFEE

Map p304 (☑852 2854 2211; www.baristajam. com.hk; Shop D, Ground fl, 126-128 Jervois St; ⊙8am-6pm Tue-Fri, from 10am Mon & Sat, from 11am Sun; 🛜; Ⓜ Sheung Wan, exit A2) Connoisseurs should make the pilgrimage to this small, concrete-walled institution that also sells coffee beans and professional coffee-making equipment. Toasted sandwiches, scrambled eggs and salads can be ordered alongside a mean flat white if you want to linger.

CUPPING ROOM
COFFEE

Map p304 (☑852 3705 0208; www.cupping room.hk; Shop 8, Silver Jubilee Mansion, Po Hing Fong; ⊙9am-5pm Mon-Fri, to 6pm Sat & Sun; 🛜; ☲26) The moreish, heady scent of freshly roasting coffee is amplified in this speciality coffee shop, thanks to the roasting room directly behind the counter. Cupping Room has several branches in Hong Kong

but this is where the magic happens. The cafe is atypically roomy, and a lovely place to pause after browsing the nearby Tai Ping Shan area. It's also popular for brunch.

ZOO
GAY & LESBIAN

Map p304 (☑852 3583 1200; www.facebook. com/ZooBarHK; Ground fl, 33 Jervois St; ⊙7pm-4.30am; 🛜; Ⓜ Sheung Wan, exit A2) The open frontage makes this LGBT bar one of Hong Kong's most welcoming. Inside, it's glitterball heaven with a mostly local crowd propping up the bar. Doesn't get busy until late. Almost opposite, there's the gay club FLM if you want to take things up a notch.

WINK
GAY & LESBIAN

Map p304 (☑852 3568 1402; www.facebook. com/winkhongkong; Ground fl, 79 Bonham Strand; ⊙5.30pm-3am Mon-Fri, from 8pm Sat & Sun, happy hour 5-9pm Mon-Fri; 🛜) This playfully named bar is clubby, chic and known for its cocktails, such as rainbow fruit tea. Black walls provide a striking contrast to a backlit row of succulent plants ringing its perimeter. Management is on a mission to team up with other LGBT-friendly venues nearby to promote Sheung Wan as a 'Gaybarhood'. Happy hour (5pm to 9pm Monday to Friday) is buy-one-get-one-free.

🍷 Sai Ying Pun & Kennedy Town

PING PONG GINTONERIA
BAR

Map p304 (☑852 9835 5061; www.pingpong129. com; 135 Second St, Sai Ying Pun; ⊙4.30pm-midnight Sun-Thu, to 1am Fri & Sat; 🛜; Ⓜ Sai Ying Pun, exit B2) Behind a closed red door, stairs lead down into a cavernous former ping-pong hall, now one of Hong Kong's coolest bars. The drink here is gin – the neon-illuminated bar stocks more than 50 types from across the globe, served in a variety of cocktails both classic and creative (G&Ts

---

SHEUNG WAN'S LGBT SCENE

Hong Kong's LGBT scene is surprisingly small for the city's size and worldliness, but a community does exist and it is friendly, inclusive and growing in confidence. In recent years a pocket of bars and clubs has put down roots in Sheung Wan and in 2018 three of them joined together to promote the area as a 'Gaybarhood'. Its epicentre is around Jervois St and Bonham Strand and so far the hood includes Zoo, Wink and FLM, which are all within easy crawling distance. Keep an eye on the website (www.gaybarhood.net) and Facebook page for deals, events and local LGBT news.

from HK$110). The crowd is artsy, and the decor is even artsier.

LITTLE CREATURES   MICROBREWERY
(☑852 2833 5611; www.littlecreatures.hk; Ground fl, 5A New Praya, Kennedy Town; ⏱9am-11.30pm Mon-Fri, 8am-11pm Sat & Sun; 🛜) This Australian import has the most visitor-friendly microbrewery set-up in Hong Kong. It occupies a vast space (for Hong Kong) just back from the waterfront; a cathedral of reclaimed wood and hoppy aromas. You'll find all the classic brews here, plus an increasing selection of local experiments like mangosteen ale. The western-style pub grub and brunch is top-notch.

JUNELS RESTO BAR   BAR
Map p304 (☑852 5182 8725; Ground fl, 11 Lai On Lane, Water St, Sai Ying Pun; ⏱noon-late; Ⓜ️Sai Ying Pun, exit B3) A local favourite among Western District residents, Junels Resto Bar is a Philippine restaurant with a difference (basically, you won't come here for the food). After dark, it turns into a free-for-all karaoke joint, with groups of friends screeching through a generous selection of hits. The San Miguels are cheap and it's decorated like a Christmas tree all year round.

NOC   COFFEE
Map p304 (☑852 3611 5300; www.noccoffeeco.com; Ground fl, Bohemian House, 321 Des Voeux Rd W, Sai Ying Pun; ⏱8am-6pm; 🛜; 🍴) Light, bright and echoey with barista clatter, NOC's cathedral-like roastery and coffee shop is a pleasant spot to worship the beans, and a relaxing place to work, chat or brunch at long communal tables in a cool minimalist setting.

☆ ENTERTAINMENT

SHEUNG WAN CIVIC CENTRE   THEATRE
Map p304 (上環文娛中心; ☑bookings 852 2853 2678, enquiries 852 2853 2689; www.lcsd.gov.hk/en/swcc/; 5th fl, Sheung Wan Municipal Services Bldg, 345 Queen's Rd Central, Sheung Wan; ⏱9am-11pm, box office 10am-6.30pm; Ⓜ️Sheung Wan, exit A2) This government-run performance venue shares a building with a wet market and cooked food centre. Its year-round program leans towards drama by local theatre troupes – some engagingly experimental – and occasional concerts by independent musicians and bands.

🛍 SHOPPING

Gentrifying Hollywood Rd, which stretches from Central to Sheung Wan, is home to some of Hong Kong's best art galleries and antique shops. The area around Tai Ping Shan St is one of the best for independent fashion.

CAPITAL GALLERY   ANTIQUES
Map p304 (長安美術; ☑852 2542 2271; 27E Tung St, Sheung Wan; ⏱10am-6pm Mon-Sat, by appointment Sun; 🚌26, Ⓜ️Central, exit D2) Located on a slope between Upper Lascar Row and Hollywood Rd, this tiny, friendly shop specialises in ceramics and is crammed with sculptures and other curios dating from 4000 to 5000 years ago. Silk Road pieces, such as minority textiles from northwest China, are also a highlight.

CHAN SHING KEE   ANTIQUES
Map p304 (陳勝記; ☑852 2543 1245; www.chanshingkee.com; 228-230 Queen's Rd Central, Sheung Wan; ⏱9am-6pm Mon-Sat; 🚌101, 104) This shop with a three-storey, museum-like showroom is run by Daniel Chan, the third generation of a family that's been in the business for 70 years. Chan Shing Kee is known to collectors and museums worldwide for its fine classical Chinese furniture (16th to 18th century). Scholars' objects, such as ancient screens and wooden boxes, are also available.

NIIN   JEWELLERY
Map p304 (☑852 2878 8811; www.niinstyle.com; 200 Hollywood Rd, Sheung Wan; ⏱10am-7pm Mon-Wed & Fri, 11am-8pm Thu, 11am-6pm Sat) 🐚 Ever wondered what happens to all the abalone shells thrown out by Hong Kong's restaurants? Some of them end up here, reimagined as beautiful pendants, rings, bracelets and handbags. Australian–Hong Kong designer Jeanine Hsu uses shells, reclaimed wood, brass and natural gemstones in her unusual but very wearable creations. Prices start at about HK$1200.

ONLY ALICE   FASHION & ACCESSORIES
Map p304 (☑852 3464 0772; www.theonlyalice.com; Ground fl, 55 Tung St, Sheung Wan; ⏱9.30am-6.30pm Tue-Fri, 10am-7pm Sat & Sun; 🚌26) In an area spoilt for choice with independent fashion, this contemporary Hong Kong brand stands out with its wearable clothing and reasonable prices. Playful tees, flattering utility wear and feminine florals

are all present in this small Tai Ping Shan store, along with accessories like headbands and off-the-wall stockings. Expect to pay well under HK$1000 for most pieces.

SELECT 18   VINTAGE

Map p304 (☑852 2858 8803; Ground fl, Grandview Garden, 18 Bridges St, Soho; ⊙noon-9pm Mon-Wed, to 11pm Thu-Sat, noon-8.30pm Sun) An eclectic hoarder's den of European and Asian collectibles including plenty of local Hong Kong ephemera. Old photos, ad posters, Happy Valley race cards and Chinese comics are just some of the gems waiting to be discovered. The store also carries a convincing range of retro-style modern jewellery.

LAM KIE YUEN TEA CO   FOOD & DRINKS

Map p304 (林奇苑茶行; ☑852 2851 0018; www. lkytea.com; Ground fl, 105-107 Bonham Strand E, Sheung Wan; ⊙9am-6pm Mon-Sat; Ⓜ Sheung Wan, exit A2) This shop, which has been around since 1955, is testament to just how much tea there is in China. From unfermented to fully fermented, and everything in between, there's simply too much to choose from. But don't panic – the owner will offer you a tasting. Lovely (pricey!) teaware is also sold here.

QUEEN'S ROAD WEST INCENSE SHOPS   ARTS & CRAFTS

Map p304 (Queen's Rd W, Sheung Wan; ⊙8am-7pm; ⊞26) At 136-150 Queen's Rd West, there are shops selling incense and paper offerings for the dead. The latter are burned to propitiate departed souls and the choice of combustibles is mind-blowing – dim sum, iPads, Rolexes, Viagra tablets and even solar-powered water heaters. You may buy them as souvenirs, but keeping rather than burning them is supposed to bring bad luck.

🏃 SPORTS & ACTIVITIES

KENNEDY TOWN
SWIMMING POOL   SWIMMING

(☑852 2817 7973; 2 Sai Cheung St North, Kennedy Town; adult/child Mon-Fri HK$17/8, Sat & Sun HK$19/9; ⊙6.30am-noon, 1-5pm & 6-10pm,

closed Wed 10am-5pm; Ⓜ HKU, exit C2) To build the Kennedy Town MTR an old public swimming pool had to be demolished and this architecturally arresting beast on the harbourfront was built to replace it. Al ways full of locals, it includes heated indoor pools, a jacuzzi and a kids' play pool, but the best bit is the 50m by 25m outdoor pool with peeping harbour views.

Conveniently, you can pay with Octopus at the turnstiles.

HUMID WITH A CHANCE OF FISHBALLS   FOOD & DRINK

(☑852 9139 5761; www.humidwithachanceof fishballs.com; dim sum tour HK$220-270; ⊙dim sum tour Wed & Sat) Dim sum novices who want a deeper insight into yum cha culture and etiquette can book this excellent guided dim sum lunch at one of Sheung Wan's craziest local parlours. The tour guide, Virginia, is a Canadian–Hong Konger and consummate foodie who knows all the tricks to get the best morsels. She also runs Hong Kong's only craft-breweries tour (selected Saturdays; HK$610).

SAMADHI TRAINING CENTRE FOR THE SOUL   MEDITATION

Map p304 (☑852 9311 2915; www.facebook. com/samadhicentre; 2-4 Tai Ping Shan St, Sheung Wan; ⊙11am-7pm Wed-Mon; ⊞26) Finding Hong Kong a bit full-on? Samadhi is here to help. At ground level there's a soothing meditation drop-in space that welcomes frazzled peace-seekers (tourists included), and above that there's a second space for weekly guided sessions, which often involve sound healing. The program is on its Facebook page; most events are free, but book ahead.

WAN KEI HO INTERNATIONAL MARTIAL ARTS ASSOCIATION   MARTIAL ARTS

Map p304 (尹圻瀰國際武術總會; ☑852 9506 0075, 852 2544 1368; www.kungfuwan.com; 3rd fl, Yue's House, 304 Des Voeux Rd Central, Sheung Wan; Ⓜ Sheung Wan, exit A) English-speaking Master Wan teaches northern Shàolín kung fu to a wide following of locals and foreigners. Group classes are offered between 7pm and 8pm on Mondays and Thursdays, or you can sign up for private tuition.

Wan Chai & Northeast Hong Kong Island

ADMIRALTY | WAN CHAI | CAUSEWAY BAY | HAPPY VALLEY | ISLAND EAST

Neighbourhood Top Five

1 Blue House Cluster (p105) Uncovering heritage architecture around Queen's Rd East, alongside hipster bars, temples, wet markets and open-air bazaars.

2 Happy Valley Racecourse (p119) Feeling your adrenalin soar at an urban racecourse on a Wednesday night, beer in hand.

3 Fashion Walk (p121) Trawling through the streets and malls for designer fashion among the hordes of teeny-boppers in Causeway Bay.

4 Flagstaff House Museum of Tea Ware (p104) Experiencing culture, history and gastronomy at this heritage museum and its

resident restaurant in Hong Kong Park.

5 Chun Yeung Street Market (p107) Riding the North Point tram through the heart of this hyperlocal Fújiànese market, then disembarking to join the throngs.

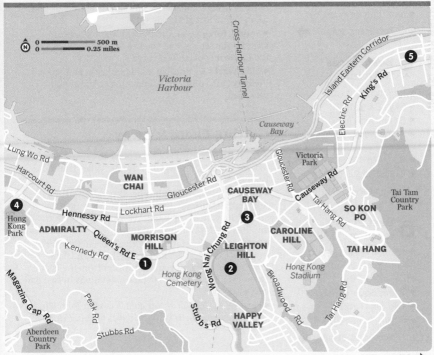

For more detail of this area see Maps p306, p308 and p310 ➡

Lonely Planet's Top Tip

Viewing the Island's east districts from a moving tram imparts a charming cinematic quality to your impressions, as these primarily residential areas can underwhelm on foot. Add speed to the uniformity of housing blocks and you get rhythm and pattern. The bonus is that you can hop off when something tickles your fancy. The district is served by some 30 stops on the eastbound tramline.

✕ Best Places to Eat

➡ Bo Innovation (p112)

➡ Kam's Kitchen (p113)

➡ Seventh Son (p110)

➡ Samsen (p110)

➡ Kam's Roast Goose (p109)

➡ Yee Tung Heen (p113)

For reviews, see p108.➡

🍺 Best Places to Drink

➡ Second Draft (p117)

➡ Skye Bar (p117)

➡ Botanicals (p115)

➡ Stone Nullah Tavern (p115)

➡ Sugar (p118)

➡ Executive Bar (p118)

For reviews, see p115.➡

🛍 Best Places to Shop

➡ Fashion Walk (p121) Pacific Place (p120)

➡ Kapok (p120)

➡ Times Square (p121)

➡ Two Girls (p121)

➡ Kevin Cheung (p120)

For reviews, see p119.➡

Explore Wan Chai & Northeast Hong Kong Island

From Admiralty MTR, plot a course through the marble sea of Pacific Place mall to Hong Kong Park, where skyscrapers peer over carp-filled pools and turtles bask on sunbaked rocks. Then make your way east, detouring at the modern heritage marvel that is Asia Society Hong Kong Centre before a stroll along Queen's Rd East, the former coastline of 'old' Wan Chai. Stop for a drink or snack in the hip Star St hood, then make your way towards Stone Nullah Lane, passing a temple and colonial-era post office until you reach Blue House, Wan Chai's heritage gem. Dine on nouveau Hong Kong food in Wan Chai or Causeway Bay, a tram ride away (arrive after the lunch crowds). Shop for books and fashion, sit under a tree in Victoria Park, then enjoy happy-hour drinks in Causeway Bay's civilised Tai Hang neighbourhood. Or just hop on an eastbound 'ding ding' and play it by ear.

Local Life

➡ **Neighbourly charm** The leafy streets of Tai Hang are full of intimate corner cafes, civilised bars and hole-in-the-wall galleries.

➡ **Fújiàn town** North Point is the colourful stronghold of Hong Kong's Fújiànese community, centred around Chun Yeung Street Market (p107).

➡ **Foodie forays** Wan Chai's local wet markets are a feast for the senses, and you can dine on fresh fare at the 1st-floor cooked-food centres.

➡ **Lil' Jakarta** Indonesian maids gather in and around Victoria Park (p106) on Sundays to eat, pray and socialise.

Getting There & Away

➡ **Tram** Hennessy Rd is a good place to catch trams to Central and Causeway Bay. Happy Valley trams use Percival St.

➡ **Bus** Useful bus routes linking Central with Admiralty, Causeway Bay and Happy Valley are 5, 5B and 26, which stop along Yee Wo St. Take green minibus 40 if travelling to Stanley.

➡ **MTR** Admiralty station is where you can transfer from the east–west Island Line to the South Island Line. At North Point, you can transfer from the Island Line to the Tseung Kwan O Line for stations in east and north Kowloon.

➡ **Ferry** Wan Chai ferry pier connects with Tsim Sha Tsui, Kowloon. North Point pier goes to Hung Hom.

TOP SIGHT
HONG KONG PARK

Designed to look anything but natural, the hillside oasis of Hong Kong Park emphasises artificial creations such as its fountain plaza, cascading waterfall, playground and aviary, connected by terraced landscaping and tree-lined pathways. With a wall of skyscrapers on one side and mountains on the other, this 8-hectare park makes for dramatic photographs.

The standout feature of Hong Kong Park is the **Edward Youde Aviary** (尤德觀鳥園; Map p306; ☉9am-5pm) FREE. Home to some 80 bird species, it's something akin to a rainforest planted in the middle of the city. Visitors walk along a wooden gantry several metres above the ground. The aviary is named after a former Hong Kong governor (1982–86).

At the park's northernmost tip is the elegant colonial Flagstaff House (p104). Built in 1846 for a British major general, it now houses a museum of antique Chinese tea ware. The adjacent Lock Cha Tea Shop (p108) is a great place to recharge over fine tea and vegetarian dim sum.

The exquisite **KS Lo Gallery** (羅桂祥茶藝館; Map p306; ☎852 2869 0690; 10 Cotton Tree Dr; ☉10am-6pm Wed-Mon) FREE above Lock Cha Tea Shop (p108) contains rare Chinese ceramics from renowned kilns in ancient China, as well as stone seals owned by the eponymous collector.

On the eastern edge of the park, the **Hong Kong Visual Arts Centre** (香港視覺藝術中心; Map p306; ☎852 2521 3008; 7A Kennedy Rd; ☉10am-6pm Wed-Mon; ☐3B, 12, 12A) FREE, housed in part of the former Victoria Barracks, stages occasional exhibitions of multimedia works by local and Asian artists.

DON'T MISS

➡ Edward Youde Aviary
➡ Flagstaff House Museum of Tea Ware
➡ KS Lo Gallery
➡ Hong Kong Visual Arts Centre

PRACTICALITIES

➡ 香港公園
➡ Map p306, C4
➡ ☎852 2521 5041
➡ www.lcsd.gov.hk/en/parks/hkp/index.html
➡ 19 Cotton Tree Dr, Admiralty
➡ admission free
➡ ☉park 6am-11pm
➡ ♿
➡ Ⓜ Admiralty, exit C1

◉ SIGHTS

Wan Chai and its environs might have fewer traditional sights than Kowloon and Central, but this claustrophobic, east–west jumble of high-rise prosperity *is* the sight. The section of Wan Chai between Queen's Rd East and Johnston Rd, where the original coastline was, is rich with ancient and modern heritage, while the new harbourfront has monuments to culture, commerce and sovereignty. You'll find scenic stretches of manicured green amid the urban jungle, along with temples whirled in incense, and one or two good museums and galleries.

◉ Admiralty

HONG KONG PARK   PARK
See p103.

★ASIA SOCIETY HONG KONG CENTRE   CULTURAL CENTRE
Map p306 (亞洲協會香港中心; Hong Kong Jockey Club Former Explosives Magazine; ☑852 2103 9511; www.asiasociety.org/hong-kong; 9 Justice Dr; ⊙gallery 11am-5pm Tue-Sun, to 7pm last Thu of month; Ⓜ Admiralty, exit F) FREE Hong Kong's Asia Society moved to these fabulous new digs in 2012, enclosing an art gallery, theatre, restaurant (p109) and gift shop all open to the public. The hillside complex is a lovely place to wander, incorporating heritage buildings and former ammunition stores artfully linked by raised walkways and rooftop gardens. Architects Tod Williams and Billie Tsien opted for a low-rise design that deferred to history and the natural lie of the land, in contrast to the skyscrapers nearby.

Monthly English-language tours delve more deeply into the military history of the site. Check the website for scheduling.

FLAGSTAFF HOUSE MUSEUM OF TEA WARE   MUSEUM
Map p306 (旗桿屋茶具文物館; ☑852 2869 0690; 10 Cotton Tree Dr; ⊙10am-6pm Wed-Mon; Ⓜ Admiralty, exit C1) FREE Built in 1846 as the home of the commander of the British forces, Flagstaff House is the oldest colonial building in Hong Kong still standing in its original spot. Its colonnaded verandahs exude a Greek Revival elegance, complemented by the grace of the tea ware from the 11th

to the 20th centuries: bowls, brewing trays, sniffing cups (used particularly for enjoying the fragrance of the finest oolong from Taiwan) and teapots made of porcelain or purple clay from Yíxìng.

The adjacent Lock Cha Tea Shop (p108) is a great place to recharge over a pot of fine tea. Flagstaff House sits on Hong Kong Park's northernmost tip.

TAMAR PARK   PARK
Map p306 (添馬公園; Harcourt Rd; Ⓜ Admiralty, exit A) This harbourfront park on the site of the New Central Government Offices (新政府總部) is an inviting sprawl of verdant lawns where you can sunbathe while watching the ships go by. It's part of a 4km promenade along the northern shoreline of Hong Kong Island, from Central Piers, outside the IFC mall, past Wan Chai, all the way to North Point. Concerts and art events take place here occasionally, as did the major protest known as the Umbrella Movement in 2014.

LIPPO CENTRE   ARCHITECTURE
Map p306 (力寶中心; 89 Queensway; Ⓜ Admiralty, exit B) Though the HSBC (Hongkong & Shanghai Bank) Building (p72) and the Hong Kong International Airport (p260), both by English architect Norman Foster, may be Hong Kong's best-known examples of modern architecture, the city also features quite a number of fine modern buildings designed by old masters. The Lippo Centre, which evokes koalas hugging a tree, is a pair of office towers designed in the 1980s by American architect Paul Rudolph, who also built Rudolph Hall at the Yale School of Architecture.

◉ Wan Chai

★PAK TAI TEMPLE   TAOIST TEMPLE
Map p308 (北帝廟; 2 Lung On St; ⊙8am-5pm; Ⓜ Wan Chai, exit A3) A short stroll up Stone Nullah Lane takes you to a majestic Taoist temple built in 1863 to honour a god of the sea, Pak Tai. The temple, the largest on Hong Kong Island, is adorned with ceramic roof-ridge ornaments made in the Guǎngdōng pottery centre of Shíwān that depict scenes from Cantonese opera. The main hall of the temple has a shadowy, 3m-tall copper likeness of Pak Tai cast during the Ming dynasty.

BLUE HOUSE CLUSTER
....

A rare heritage protection success story, the 1920s Blue House is one of Hong Kong's last surviving wooden tenement buildings. The graceful, four-storey structure, featuring cast-iron balconies reminiscent of New Orleans, and its adjoining neighbours the Yellow House and Orange House, were taken over by a local community trust, painstakingly restored and are now partially open to the public. Several apartments still house descendants of the original residents.

Two eateries, a thrift store, community library and an organic veg shop in the **cluster** (藍屋; Map p308; ☑852 2835 4376; www.vivabluehouse.hk; 72-74A Stone Nullah Lane, Wan Chai; Ⓜ Wan Chai, exit D) **FREE** are being run as social enterprises, with all profits returning to the Blue House. Free guided tours in English (◷11am Sat) take you into a residential unit preserved as it was in the mid-20th century – you'll be astonished at how many families shared the same room. The **House of Stories** (◷10am-6pm; Thu-Tue) – a museum and exhibition space on the ground floor – is a rich source of info on yesteryear Hong Kong.

The Blue House was built atop a temple to the god of Chinese medicine, which was preserved within the new tenement. You can see the temple facade at the corner of King Sing St and Stone Nullah Lane.

KING YIN LEI   HISTORIC BUILDING

(景賢里; ☑852 2848 6230; www.heritage.gov.hk; 45 Stubbs Rd; ☐15, 15B on Sun & public holidays) **FREE** This stunning 17,000-sq-ft mansion (c 1937) owes its unique appearance to the Chinese Renaissance style associated with the 1920s when the Chinese government called for a revival of traditional culture, and architects in Shànghǎi set about merging eastern and western styles.

Designed by a British architect for a wealthy Chinese merchant's wife, the opulent King Yin Lei complex is not only a wonder to look at – its halls and rooms are gorgeous – it's also testimony to the rising social and financial status of the Chinese on Hong Kong Island before WWII.

Parts of *Soldier of Fortune* (1955) starring Clark Gable were set here, but in 2007 King Yin Lei literally saw the bulldozers at its gates until outraged conservationists managed to pressure the government into declaring it a monument.

King Yin Lei opens to the public for just a couple of weekends a year, in June and July, and you must reserve in advance. Check the website for opening days. Green minibus 26 departing from Lee Garden Rd in Causeway Bay stops there.

HUNG SHING TEMPLE   BUDDHIST TEMPLE

Map p308 (洪聖古廟; 129-131 Queen's Rd E; ◷8.30am-5.30pm; ☐6, 6A, Ⓜ Wan Chai, exit A3) Nestled in a nook on the southern side of Queen's Rd East, this dark and rather forbidding temple is built atop huge boulders that used to overlook the harbour. It was erected around 1850 in honour of a deified Tang dynasty official known for his virtue (important) and ability to make predictions of value to traders (ultra-important).

A narrow staircase leads to the upper floor, where a fortune-teller (Chinese only) can divine your future for a hefty fee.

SOUTHORN PLAYGROUND   PARK

Map p308 (修頓球場; Hennessy Rd; ◷6am-11.30pm; Ⓜ Wan Chai, exit B2) This unspectacular-looking sports ground is in fact the social hub of old Wan Chai, offering a cross-section of life in the hood at any time of the day. Seniors come to play chess, students and amateur athletes to shoot hoops and kick ball. There are hip-hop dance-offs, homemakers shaking a leg, outreach social workers, cruisers looking for a booty call, and a daily trickle of lunchers from the banks and construction sites.

HONG KONG CONVENTION
& EXHIBITION CENTRE   NOTABLE BUILDING

Map p308 (香港會議展覽中心; www.hkcec.com.hk; 1 Expo Dr; ☐18) This enormous waterfront expo centre, a leading venue for large trade fairs and conventions including Art Basel Hong Kong (p53), was built in 1988. Architecturally, it has been compared with a bird's wing, a banana leaf and a lotus petal. Walk through it on your way to Golden Bauhinia Square (p151), and soak up the terrific harbour views through a soaring wall of glass.

POLICE MUSEUM
MUSEUM

(警隊博物館; ☑852 2849 7019; www.police.gov. hk/ppp_en/01_about_us/pm.html; 27 Coombe Rd, The Peak; ☉2-5pm Tue, 9am-5pm Wed-Sun; ♿; ☐15) FREE Crime-thriller fans should make a trip to this small museum in lush Wan Chai Gap. The protagonist in this former police station is the Hong Kong police force, formed in 1844, but the real stars are the Triads (ie Hong Kong mafia). The eye-opening Triad Societies & Narcotics Gallery uncovers their secret rituals and a historical account of Kowloon Walled City. Kids will enjoy the weaponry display.

Photography is forbidden inside. If taking the bus, alight at the stop between Stubbs Rd and Peak Rd.

LOVERS' ROCK
LANDMARK

(姻緣石; off Bowen Rd; ☐green minibus 24A) Lovers' Rock or Destiny's Rock (Yan Yuen Sek) is a phallus-shaped boulder on a bluff at the end of a track above Bowen Rd. Adorned with incense and offerings, it's a favourite pilgrimage site for women with relationship or fertility problems. It's busy during the Maidens' Festival, held on the seventh day of the seventh moon (mid-August).

The easiest way to reach here is to take green minibus 24A from the Admiralty bus station. Get off at the terminus (Shiu Fai Tce; 肇輝台) and walk up the path behind the housing complex.

CENTRAL PLAZA
NOTABLE BUILDING

Map p308 (中環廣場; 18 Harbour Rd; ☐18, ⓂWan Chai, exit A5) Central Plaza, one of Hong Kong's tallest buildings, looks garish with its glass skin of three colours – gold, silver and terracotta. It's possible to access the 46th floor for panoramic harbour views. Central Plaza provides direct connection to Hong Kong Convention & Exhibition Centre (p105) and Wan Chai MTR station through an elevated pedestrian footbridge.

COMIX HOME BASE
CULTURAL CENTRE

Map p308 (動漫基地; ☑852 2824 5303; www. comixhomebase.com.hk; 7 Mallory St; ☉10am-8pm; ♿; ⓂWan Chai, exit A3) FREE Housed in repurposed heritage buildings, this cultural cluster is entirely themed on the medium of comics and anime. A brief ground-floor display introduces Hong Kong's own comic-book history, from wartime classics (Renjian Pictorial) and colonial-era satires (Old Master Q), through Ma Wing-shing's martial-arts comics, to the pensive creations of younger artists such as Chi Hoi.

⊙ Causeway Bay

★ TIN HAU TEMPLE
TEMPLE

Map p310 (天后廟; 10 Tin Hau Temple Rd; ☉7am-5pm; ⓂTin Hau, exit B) Hong Kong Island's most famous Tin Hau (Goddess of the Sea) temple has lent its name to an entire neighbourhood, a metro station and a street. It has been a place of worship for 370 years and, despite renovations, imparts an air of antiquity, particularly in the intricate stone carvings near the entrance and the ceramic figurines from Shíwān decorating the roof. The main altar contains an effigy of the goddess with a blackened face.

VICTORIA PARK
PARK

Map p310 (維多利亞公園; www.lcsd.gov.hk/en/ ls_park.php; Causeway Rd; ☉park 24hr; ♿; ⓂTin Hau, exit B) FREE Built on land reclaimed from the **Causeway Bay Typhoon Shelter** (銅鑼灣避風塘; Map p310; off Hung Hing Rd; ⓂCauseway Bay, exit D1), Victoria Park is the biggest patch of public greenery on Hong Kong Island. The best time to go is on a weekday morning, when it becomes a forest of people practising the slow-motion choreography of taichi. The park becomes a flower market just before the Lunar New Year and a lantern museum during the Mid-Autumn Festival. The swimming pool (previously outdoor), built in 1957, is Hong Kong's oldest.

The park has 13 standard tennis courts, two lawn-bowls greens and swimming pools, as well as football pitches, basketball courts and jogging trails.

NOONDAY GUN
HISTORIC SITE

Map p310 (香港怡和午炮; 221 Gloucester Rd; ☉7am-midnight; ⓂCauseway Bay, exit D1) The sun may have long since set on the British Empire, but this Hotchkiss 3lb naval gun still fires forlornly into history each day at noon, a colonial tradition dating to the mid-1800s. The gun stands in a small waterfront compound across the busy road from the Excelsior Hotel, where its noon-on-the-dot firing by a white-gloved attendant always draws a small crowd.

Operated by British conglomerate Jardine Matheson, the noonday gun was made famous by its mention in the Noël Coward song 'Mad Dogs and Englishmen'. It's

RENT-A-CURSE GRANNIES

Under the Canal Rd Flyover between Wan Chai and Causeway Bay, you can hire little old ladies to beat up your enemy. From their perch on plastic stools, these rent-a-curse grannies will pound paper cut-outs of your romantic rival, office bully or whiny celeb with a shoe (their orthopaedic flat or your stilettos – your call) while rapping rhythmic curses. All for only HK$50. Hung Shing Temple (p105) has a 'master' who performs the same with a symbolic 'precious' sword for the exorbitant sum of HK$100.

Villain hitting or villain exorcism (打小人; da siu yan) is a practice related to folk sorcery. It's performed throughout the year, but the most popular date is the Day of the Awakening of Insects when the sun is at an exact celestial longitude of 345° (usually between 5 and 20 March on the Gregorian calendar). It's believed to bring reconciliation or resolution, though that too could be symbolic.

tricky to find, accessible via an underpass through a basement car park. Look for a silver door in the alley just west of the World Trade Centre.

☉ Happy Valley

F11 PHOTOGRAPHIC MUSEUM MUSEUM
(F11攝影博物館; ☎852 6516 1122; http://f11.com; 11 Yuk Sau St; ☉2-6pm Tue-Sat; ☒Happy Valley) FREE Photography exhibitions are held three or four times a year inside this 1930s art-deco residence restored and opened as a museum by a former Hong Kong lawyer and vintage Leica collector. Past shows have featured Elliott Erwitt, Bruno Barbey and Robert Capa. Visits are by appointment only (by phone or email). There might be more going on at its sister venue, **F22** (Map p308; ☎852 9698 1122; www.f22.com; 5th fl, Amber Commercial Bldg, 70-74 Morrison Hill Rd, Wan Chai; ☉2-6pm, Tue-Sat; ☒Happy Valley) FREE.

HONG KONG CEMETERY CEMETERY
Map p308 (香港墳場; Wong Nai Chung Rd; ☉7am-6pm or 7pm; ☒Happy Valley) FREE Crowded and cosmopolitan, dead Hong Kong is no different from the breathing city. Tombstones jostle for space at this Christian cemetery (c 1845) located alongside the Jewish, Hindu, Parsee and Muslim cemeteries, and St Michael's Catholic Cemetery. Burial plots date from the mid-1800s and include colonialists, tycoons and silverscreen divas.

HONG KONG RACING MUSEUM MUSEUM
Map p308 (☎852 2966 8065; 2nd fl, Happy Valley Stand, Wong Nai Chung Rd; ☉noon-7pm, to 9pm

race days; ☒Happy Valley) FREE Hong Kong Racing Museum showcases the celebrated trainers, jockeys and horses that have thrilled the crowds at Happy Valley over the years. The British wasted no time in setting up the racetrack – the earliest photo on display, depicting a turf oval on a bare plain hemmed in by hills, was taken in 1865.

The most important event in the history of the Happy Valley Racecourse – individual winnings notwithstanding – was the terrible fire in 1918 that killed almost 600 people. The **Race Course Fire Memorial** (馬場先難友紀念碑; So Kon Po, Wan Chai; ☒5B, 8H, Ⓜ Causeway Bay, exit F1) pays tribute to the victims.

☉ Island East

★**CHUN YEUNG STREET MARKET** MARKET
(春秧街街市; Chun Yeung St, North Point; ☉8am-6pm; Ⓜ North Point, exit A4) Hop on a tram bound for North Point, and past Fortress Hill you'll turn into a narrow street teeming with market stalls and old tenement buildings. This is the famous Chun Yeung Street Market, and at 5pm it's so busy the tram has to squeeze between traders and cart-pullers. Many stores here sell foodstuffs from Fújiàn that you can't find elsewhere in Hong Kong. North Point has a huge Fújiànese community and you'll hear their dialect spoken on Chun Yeung St.

As the tram turns the corner into King's Rd, you'll pass the nondescript **Wah Fung Chinese Goods Centre** (華豐國貨公司; ☎852 2856 0333; Kiu Kwan Mansion, 395-421 King's Rd, North Point; ☉10.30am-9.30pm; Ⓜ North Point, exit A4). Once Hong Kong's

LOCAL KNOWLEDGE

YIK CHEONG BUILDING: HONG KONG IN FILM

Like a sci-fi set from *Blade Runner*, this gritty, impossibly dense and vertiginous cluster of colourful **apartments** (益昌大廈; Monster Building; King's Rd, Quarry Bay; Ⓜ Tai Koo, exit B) is one of the most Instagrammed sights in the city (especially since it appeared in a *Transformers* film). As a result, photography has been banned for the sake of the residents, but you can sneak a (quiet) peek by entering at 1026–28 King's Rd.

largest Chinese department store, the building it's in, Kiu Kwan Mansion (僑冠大廈), served as a hideout for underground communists during the 1967 riots.

★ **HONG KONG MUSEUM OF COASTAL DEFENCE**   MUSEUM
(香港海防博物館; ☑ 852 2569 1500; http://hk.coastaldefence.museum; 175 Tung Hei Rd, Shau Kei Wan; ⊙ 10am-6pm Fri-Wed Mar-Sep, to 5pm Oct-Feb; 🚹; Ⓜ Shau Kei Wan, exit B2) **FREE** Housed in a coastal fort (c 1887) that guarded the eastern sea entrance into Hong Kong harbour (via the narrow Lei Yue Mun Channel), this excellent museum whisks visitors through six centuries of coastal warfare, from marauding Ming dynasty pirates to the Battle of Hong Kong against the Japanese in 1941. Exhibitions are housed inside the old redoubt; outside, views are magnificent, and a historical walking trail winds through gun emplacements, tunnels and observation posts almost down to the coast.

As you leave the MTR, follow the museum signs on Tung Hei Rd for about 15 minutes. Bus 85, which is accessible via exit A3 and runs along Shau Kei Wan Rd between North Point and Siu Sai Wan, stops on Tung Hei Rd outside the museum.

HONG KONG FILM ARCHIVE   MUSEUM
(香港電影資料館; ☑ bookings 852 3761 6661, enquiries 852 2739 2139, resource centre 852 2119 7360; www.filmarchive.gov.hk; 50 Lei King Rd, Sai Wan Ho; ⊙ 10am-8pm, box office noon-8pm, resource centre 10am-7pm Mon & Wed-Fri, to 5pm Sat, 1-5pm Sun; Ⓜ Sai Wan Ho, exit A) **FREE** The archive is a cinephile's heaven. Its resource centre has over 6300 reels and tapes, as well as magazines and scripts related to

Hong Kong cinema through the ages. You can browse through its comprehensive bilingual online catalogue before visiting. The archive also holds thematic exhibitions and has regular screenings in its **cinema**. Check online for programs.

From the MTR station, walk north on Tai On St and west on Lei King Rd.

PARA SITE   GALLERY
(藝術空間; ☑ 852 2517 4620; www.para-site.org.hk; 22/F, Wing Wah Industrial Bldg, 677 King's Rd, Quarry Bay; ⊙ noon-7pm Wed-Sun; Ⓜ Quarry Bay, exit C) **FREE** Art fans will be genuinely thrilled to discover this hidden gem of a gallery and exhibition space on the top floor of an office tower. Created and curated by long-established independent art group Para Site, the exhibitions usually have a Hong Kong or Asian focus but universal relevance.

✖ EATING

Wan Chai, with its wealth of cuisines at all price points, is Hong Kong's undisputed food capital, whether you crave Michelin-starred molecular Cantonese, traditional roast goose or the hyperlocal buzz of a 'cooked food market'. Causeway Bay is an eclectic amalgam of fast casual eateries, while North Point is an emerging destination for in-the-know foodies. Further afield, Shau Kei Wan and Sai Wan Ho offer good-value Canto staples and street eats.

✖ Admiralty

★ **LOCK CHA TEA SHOP**   VEGETARIAN, CHINESE **$**
Map p306 (樂茶軒; ☑ 852 2801 7177; www.lockcha.com; Ground fl, KS Lo Gallery, 10 Cotton Tree Dr, Hong Kong Park; dim sum HK$28-35, tea from HK$38; ⊙ 10am-8pm, to 9pm weekends, closed 2nd Tue of month; 🖉; Ⓜ Admiralty, exit C1) Set in the lush environs of Hong Kong Park, Lock Cha serves fragrant Chinese teas and vegetarian dim sum in an antique-styled environment designed to resemble a scholar's quarters. There are traditional music performances on Saturday (7pm to 8.30pm) and Sunday (4.30pm to 6.30pm). Do call to reserve a seat.

Talks on tea, as well as tea-appreciation classes on weekdays, can be arranged one day in advance (HK$1000 for three tea tastings for up to five people). Call for details.

GREAT FOOD HALL
SUPERMARKET, INTERNATIONAL $

Map p306 (☑852 2918 9986; www.greatfoodhall. com; Basement, Pacific Pl; meals from HK$100; ☉10am-10pm; ⌖; ⓜAdmiralty, exit F) In the basement of the swish Pacific Place (p120) mall, Great Food Hall is part upscale deli, part posh supermarket. Load up on stacked sandwiches, filled rolls, imported cheeses and boxed salads for a picnic in neighbouring Hong Kong Park (p103), or avail yourself of a Triple O fast-food-style hamburger.

AMMO
MEDITERRANEAN $$

Map p306 (☑852 2537 9888; www.ammo.com. hk; Asia Society Hong Kong Centre, 9 Justice Dr; mains around HK$250; ☉noon-11pm Sun-Thu, to midnight Fri & Sat; ⓜAdmiralty, exit F) 'Military-chic' is the design theme at this modern European restaurant with decorative copper flourishes intended to evoke the site's past as a former British explosives magazine. Whether it succeeds or not, AMMO is an undeniably special setting for a lunch, brunch or dinner of creative, small-plate Mediterranean fare.

AMMO is at the Asia Society Hong Kong Centre (p104). Afternoon tea is served daily between 3pm and 5pm.

PURE VEGGIE HOUSE
VEGETARIAN, CHINESE $$

Map p306 (心齋; ☑852 2525 0556; 3rd fl, Coda Plaza, 51 Garden Rd, Mid-Levels; meals HK$250-500; ☉10.30am-10.30pm; ⌖; ☐12A from Admiralty MTR) This Mid-Levels Buddhist restaurant goes beyond the usual tofu and broccoli to serve innovative and delicious vegetarian dishes employing ingredients sourced from organic farms around the Guǎngdōng city of Héyuán. Dishes are cooked with natural salt and cold-pressed peanut oil; no MSG or other hidden nasties. Excellent all-vegie dim sum, served at lunch, will please even dedicated carnivores.

SAN XI LOU
SICHUAN $$

Map p306 (三希樓; ☑852 2838 8811; 7th fl Coda Plaza, 51 Garden Rd, Mid-Levels; meals HK$200-400; ☉11am-10.30pm; ☐12A from Admiralty MTR) Fresh ingredients and masterful use of spices make this isolated eatery one of Hong Kong's best Sichuan restaurants. Indecisive chilli heads can go for the hotpot, but

hard-core fans of the cuisine should try the 'water-cooked fish' (水煮魚), which consists of fish slices and shredded vegetables swimming in a vermilion broth infused with dried chillies and Sichuan peppercorns.

Many restaurants are known to use frozen fish for this fiery dish, but here you can actually taste the delicate sweetness of the fresh fish and feel its silken texture through the heat. Book a window table for views of the Botanic Gardens.

✖ Wan Chai

KAM'S ROAST GOOSE
CANTONESE $

Map p308 (甘牌燒鵝; ☑852 2520 1110; www. krg.com.hk; 226 Hennessy Rd; meals HK$80-200; ☉11.30am-9pm; ⓜWan Chai, exit A2) Expect to queue for half an hour or more to worship at the oily alter of perfectly roast goose. One of two spin-offs from Central's famed Yung Kee Restaurant (p77), Michelin-starred Kam's still upholds the same strict standards in sourcing and roasting. The best cut is the upper thigh (succulent but less fatty), which can be had with steamed rice or seasoned noodles.

Besides the crisp-skinned fowl, other barbecued meats such as roast suckling pig are well worth sinking your teeth into. If you don't mind ordering your goose to go, you can get it almost straight away.

PICI
ITALIAN $

Map p306 (☑852 2755 5523; https://pici.hk; 16 St Francis Yard; pasta around HK$130; ☉11.30am-10.30pm; ⓜAdmiralty, exit F) Typical of Hong Kong's 'fast-casual 2.0' trend, along with the likes of Thai joint Samsen (p110), neighbourhood pasta bar Pici is hip, chef-focused and as geared towards a solo lunch as it is a wine-soaked evening with friends. Pasta dishes range from the namesake *pici* (fat Tuscan spaghetti) with pecorino and pepper to pappardelle with slow-cooked beef-cheek *ragu*. Expect a wait at busy periods.

LE PETIT SAIGON
SANDWICHES $

Map p306 (☑852 2455 2499; http://legarcon saigon.com; 12-18 Wing Fung St; banh mi HK$88; ☉noon-9pm; ⌖; ⓜAmiralty, exit F) For when Hong Kong's humdrum egg sandwich just won't cut it, upgrade to a *banh mi* (Vietnamese sandwich). The test of authenticity is the bread; thankfully, the baguettes at this counter eatery are fluffy and crisp, crammed generously with pork, chicken or tofu, and all those herby aromatics and zingy salad accoutrements you'd expect from a Saigon street stall.

HONBO
BURGERS $

Map p306 (☑852 2567 8970; https://honbo.hk; 6-7 Sun St; burgers from HK$88; ⊘noon 4pm & 5-10pm; ⓂAdmiralty, exit F) The juicy *honbo* here (Cantonese for hamburger) are dainty, delicious and local, employing New Territories beef and vegies, and buns baked down the road. Like the mini dining room, the Cantonese chef-owner keeps the menu trim (beef and cheese, battered soft-shell crab or seared scallops), accompanied by excellent fries and a couple of Hong Kong craft beers on tap.

DIMDIMSUM
DIM SUM $

Map p308 (點點心點心灣仔店; ☑852 3568 2770; www.dimdimsum.hk; 7 Tin Lok Lane; dim sum HK$18-40; ⊘10am-11.30pm; ⓂCauseway Bay, exit A) There are few reliably good restaurants around town that continue to serve dim sum late into the evening (it's typically eaten for brunch). Then there's DimDimSum. The Cantonese chain, which has several branches across Hong Kong, has all the classics: turnip cake, fluffy char siu bao (barbecue pork buns), pork and shrimp dumplings and crispy rice rolls, which are served to steaming-hot perfection.

LA CREPERIE
FRENCH $

Map p306 (☑852 2529 9280; 1st fl, 100 Queen's Rd E; savoury galettes from HK$98, crêpes from HK$68; ⊘noon-midnght Mon-Fri, 11.30am-11pm Sat, 11am-10pm Sun; ⓂWan Chai, exit A3) Decked out like a seaside town in Brittany, this quaint little crêperie whips up sumptuous savoury galettes with hearty fillings such as Reblochon cheese and diced bacon, along with airy crêpes daubed in ice cream, fruit and chocolate. Wash it down with imported cider served in bowls.

CHUEN CHEONG FOODS
CHINESE $

Map p308 (泉昌美食; ☑852 2575 8278; 150 Wan Chai Rd; 2 pieces of stinky tofu HK$15; ⊘12.30-9pm Mon-Sat; ⓂWan Chai, exit A4) So you're walking through Wan Chai and you smell something...wait, is there a *horse stable* nearby? Nope, that's just the manure-like stench of stinky tofu, a paradigmatic case of 'tastes better than it smells'. This popular street stall (no English sign) serves the beloved snack Hong Kong–style, which means

deep-fried and slathered with chilli sauce and sweet hoisin sauce.

CHRISLY CAFE
HONG KONG $

Map p308 (華星冰室; ☑852 2666 7766; www.chrislycafe.com.hk; Shop B1, Ground fl, Kwong Sang Hong Bldg, 6 Heard St; meals from HK$38; ⊘7am-11pm; ⓂWan Chai, exit A4) Dine on buttery pineapple buns, fluffy scrambled eggs, and toast with condensed milk and peanut butter at this retro-styled faux *cha chaan tang* (teahouse) opened by the founder of a Mandopop record label.

★SEVENTH SON
CANTONESE $$

Map p308 (家全七福; ☑852 2892 2888; www.seventhson.hk; 3rd fl, Wharney Guangdong Hotel, 57-73 Lockhart Rd; meals from HK$350; ⊘11.30am-3pm & 6-10.30pm; ⓂWan Chai, exit C) Worthy spin-off from the illustrious and famously wallet-unfriendly Fook Lam Moon (p145; aka Tycoon's Canteen), for its clientele of movie stars and politicians, Seventh Son reproduces to a T FLM's homestyle dishes and a few extravagant seafood numbers as well. The food here is excellent, prices are fair, plus you get the treatment FLM reserves for regulars.

★SAMSEN
THAI $$

Map p308 (泰麵; ☑852 2234 0001; 68 Stone Nullah Lane; dishes from HK$118; ⊘12-2.30pm & 6.30-11pm; ⓂWan Chai, exit D) One bite of Samsen's delectable pad thai and Queen's Rd East becomes Khao San Rd; but at this hip little gem presided over by an Aussie chef, the good ol' backpacker staple is pimped up with plump tiger prawns, paired with zingy Thai salads and washed down with Moonzen craft beer. Expect to queue.

LIU YUAN PAVILION
SHANGHAI $$

Map p308 (留園雅敍; ☑852 2804 2000; 3rd fl, The Broadway, 54-62 Lockhart Rd; meals HK$200-600; ⊘noon-2.30pm & 6-10.30pm; ⓂWan Chai, exit C) This bright, pleasant restaurant in airy yellows makes superb Shanghainese classics, from *xiao long bao* (soup dumplings) with crabmeat to a jiggly, melt-in-your-mouth braised ham hock. It has a loyal following among the local Shanghainese community, so do book ahead. Sharing dishes and large tables suit groups.

KIN'S KITCHEN
CANTONESE $$

Map p308 (留家廚房; ☑852 2571 0913; 5th fl, W Sq, 314-324 Hennessy Rd; meals HK$180-450; ⊘noon-3pm & 6-11pm; ⓂWan Chai, exit A2)

Art-critic-turned-restaurateur Lau Kin-wai infuses his artistic sense and passion for local ingredients into this understated restaurant specialising in Cantonese classics with a twist. Lau, looking quite the bon vivant with silver hair and rosy cheeks, is sometimes seen discussing the merits of the four kinds of white rice on the menu with customers.

Exquisite dim sum, which you can order by the piece at a minimum of two pieces, is only served at lunch.

KASA
CANTONESE, SWEETS **$$**

Map p308 (家香; ☑852 2659 9189; Suite 103, 1/F Shui On Centre, 6-8 Harbour Rd; mains from HK$120; ⊗8am-9.30pm Mon-Fri, noon-9pm Sat; Ⓜ Wan Chai, exit C) Resourceful, affordable Kasa tinkers with Chinese and Western classics inside its simple open kitchen. Grey mullet is served with fermented bean sauce, claypot rice features pork cooked *sous vide*, braised short ribs use a Shànghǎi-inspired '*dongpo*' seasoning, while 'Scotch eggs' switches ground pork for Cantonese *lap cheung* sausage.

22 SHIPS
TAPAS **$$**

Map p308 (☑852 2555 0722; www.22ships.hk; 22 Ship St; tapas HK$88-198; ⊗noon-3pm & 6-11pm; Ⓜ Wan Chai, exit B2) This tiny, trendy tapas spot doesn't take reservations, so expect to line up to gorge on the playful small plates of young Brit chef Aaron Gillespie – dishes such as scallop ceviche with *yuzu*, a sour Asian citrus (HK$138), or beautifully bronzed suckling pig with pineapple and *piquillo* peppers (HK$198).

PAWN KITCHEN
BRITISH **$$**

Map p308 (☑852 2866 3444; www.thepawn.com.hk; 62 Johnston Rd; mains from HK$200; ⊗11am-2am Mon-Sat, to midnight Sun; Ⓜ Wan Chai, exit A3) Occupying the 2nd floor of a historic balconied building, the Pawn impresses with modern British cooking: mussels steamed in malt beer with 'big chips', rustic fish pie and founding chef Tom Aiken's signature macaroni cheese with braised beef, lobster or truffle. Try to book an alfresco balcony table.

HONG ZHOU RESTAURANT
ZHEJIANG **$$**

Map p308 (杭州酒家; ☑852 2591 1898; 1st fl, Chinachem Johnston Plaza, 178-186 Johnston Rd; HK$200-800; ⊗11.30am-2.30pm & 5.30-10.30pm; Ⓜ Wan Chai, exit A5) A food critics' favourite, this establishment excels at Hángzhōu cooking, the delicate sister of Shanghainese cuisine. Dishes such as shrimp stir-fried with tea leaves show how the best culinary creations should engage all your senses. Its version of Dongpo pork (東坡肉), a succulent braised pork-belly dish named after a gluttonous poet, is cholesterol heaven.

MEGAN'S KITCHEN
CANTONESE, HOTPOT **$$**

Map p308 (美味廚; ☑852 2866 8305; 5th fl, Lucky Centre, 165-171 Wan Chai Rd; hotpot per person HK$200-300; ⊗noon-3pm & 6-11.30pm; Ⓜ Wan Chai, exit A3) Broth choices like tom yum and lobster borscht make for a modern twist on the classic hotpot experience at Megan's, though standbys such as spicy Sichuan soup are just as good. The vast menu of items runs the gamut from the standard (mushrooms, fish slices, tofu) to the avant garde (don't miss the fabulous rainbow cuttlefish balls).

Like all hotpot restaurants, Megan's is best visited with a crowd of at least four. Subdivided hotpots mean you can sample up to three broths, so the more the merrier. Call ahead for reservations, especially on weekends. If you're out to party, add two hours of free-flow wine for HK$168 per person.

WAN CHAI'S MARKETS

The area sandwiched by Queen's Rd East and Johnston Rd in Wan Chai is a lively outdoor bazaar thronged with vendors, shoppers and parked cars. Cross St and Wan Chai Rd feature **wet markets** (灣仔街市; Map p308; Zenith, 258 Queen's Rd E; ⊗6am-8pm; Ⓜ Wan Chai, exit A3) in all their screaming splendour. **Tai Yuen St** (Map p308; ⊗10am-7.30pm; Ⓜ Wan Chai, exit A3), aka 'toy street' (玩具街; *woon gui kaai*) to locals, has hawkers selling goldfish, plastic flowers and granny underwear, but it's best known for a dwindling number of traditional toy shops, where you'll find not only kiddies' playthings, but clockwork tin and other kidult collectibles. Spring Garden Lane and Wan Chai Rd are a treasure trove of quirky shops selling everything from spices to funerary offerings and electronic gadgets.

BO INNOVATION CHINESE $$$

Map p308 (廚魔; ☎852 2850 8371; www.bo innovation.com; 1st fl, 60 Johnston Rd; lunch set HK$750, tasting menu HK$900, dinner tasting menu HK$2280-2680; ☺noon-2pm Mon-Fri, 7-10pm Mon-Sat; ⓂWan Chai, exit B2) Committed foodies with dollars to burn will be determined to try this three-starred gastro-lab presided over by the 'Demon Chef', aka Hong Kong's own Alvin Leung. Celebrated for his self-styled 'X-Treme Cuisine', Leung rips up the rule book and reimagines Chinese classics in bold and often outrageous ways.

✖ Causeway Bay

CAFE MATCH BOX HONG KONG $

Map p310 (喜喜冰室; ☎852 2868 0363; www. cafematchbox.com.hk; 57 Paterson St; breakfast sets from HK$36; ☺8am-11pm; ⓂCauseway Bay, exit D1) Whimsical Match Box is a hip shrine to the *bing sutt* of the 1950s (literally 'ice room'), the Western-style cafe predecessor of the *cha chaan tang*. Mandopop paraphernalia, an antique coke fridge and retro public bus booths set the scene for red-bean drinks, fluffy egg sandwiches, macaroni, oatmeal and toast. Lots of toast. The alleyway location adds to the atmosphere.

NAGI RAMEN JAPANESE $

Map p310 (凪豚骨拉麵; 3 King St, Tai Hang; ramen from HK$82; ☺noon-3pm & 6-8.45pm Tue-Sun; ⓂTin Hau, exit B) Straight outta Shibuya, this micro ramen joint has just four tables from which to slurp the Japanese-trained chef's near-perfect noodle and pork-bone broth creations. Customise your bowl down to the fine details using the bilingual tick sheet, from spice, salt and garlic levels to extras such as soft-boiled eggs.

SISTER WAH NOODLES $

Map p310 (華姐清湯腩; ☎852 2807 0181; 13 Electric Rd, Tin Hau; noodles HK$48; ☺11am-10.45pm; ⓂTin Hau, exit A2) Locals and tourists pack out this steamy corner eatery to slurp flat rice noodles topped with wobbly beef brisket or tendon in a clear soup broth. Old timers like to chase theirs with a bowl of cooked white radish.

ATUM DESSERANT DESSERTS $

Map p310 (☎852 2377 2400, 852 2956 1411; www. atumhk.com; 16th fl, The L Square, 459-461 Lockhart Rd; desserts from HK$138; ☺1-11.30pm; ☝; ⓂCauseway Bay, exit C) Hop on to a stool at this Scandi-styled dessert bar and watch gallery-worthy creations materialise with some help from liquid nitrogen and the owner's years as a pastry chef at the Mandarin Oriental. Improvisation (HK$348 for two) is confectionery, fruits and ice cream 'painted' on a slab in front of you like a Jackson Pollock crossbred with a Monet.

HO HUNG KEE NOODLES $

Map p310 (何洪記; ☎852 2577 6028; 12th fl, Hysan Pl, 500 Hennessy Rd; noodles from HK$40; ☺11.30am-11.30pm; ⓂCauseway Bay, exit F2) The tasty noodles, wontons and congee here are cooked according to the Ho's heirloom recipes (the brand has a 70-year history), and clearly they still work, as do the dim sum and Cantonese classics more recently offered. Though the windowless mall location lacks atmosphere, Ho Hung Kee is always packed during lunch, even before it was awarded one Michelin star.

There's also a branch in the airport.

LAB MADE ICE CREAM DESSERTS $

Map p310 (分子雪糕專門店; ☎852 9355 4476; www.labmade.com.hk; 6 Brown St, Tai Hang; ice creams from HK$47; ☺2pm-midnight, to 11pm Sun; ☝; ⓂTin Hau, exit B) A delicious science experiment, the ice cream at Lab Made is created with liquid nitrogen and a mixer, each scoop made to order and emerging with a puff of vapour. A rotating menu offers four flavours daily, a blend of the prosaic (chocolate or mango for example) and the only-in-Hong-Kong magical (condensed milk and peanut butter, purple rice, even mooncake!).

YU SICHUANESE, NOODLES $

Map p310 (渝酸辣粉; ☎852 2838 8198; 4 Yiu Wa St; meals from HK$100; ☺noon-5pm & 6-11pm; ⓂCauseway Bay, exit A) Addicts of the Sichuanese peppercorn flock to this guileless little shop for that tingling and numbing *'ma la'* taste, which only happens when the Sichuanese fare is done right. You can choose the level of spiciness for your noodles, from tame to full-blown; there are some nonspicy offerings too.

BOWRINGTON ROAD MARKET MARKET $

Map p308 (鵝頸街市; 21 Bowrington Rd; meals from HK$35; ☺6am-8pm; ⓂCauseway Bay, exit A) One of the area's most buzzy indoor (and outdoor) wet markets, with a cooked-food centre of *dai pai dong* (大牌檔, food stall) on the floor above that sell cheap meals until 2am.

DELICIOUS KITCHEN
SHANGHAI $

Map p310 (☑852 2577 8350, 852 2577 7720; 9-11B Cleveland St; meals HK$55-120; ⊙11am-11pm; Ⓜ Causeway Bay, exit E) Shanghainese rice cooked with shredded Chinese cabbage and topped with meat or seafood is the big draw at this buzzy little eatery (listed on the menu as 'steamed rice with vegetables'). It's best with the legendary honey-glazed pork chop. Fat, vegie-stuffed wontons and perfectly crispy fried tofu are also winners.

★ KAM'S KITCHEN
CANTONESE $$

Map p310 (甘飯館; ☑852 3568 2832; 5 Mercury St, Tin Hau; lunch HK$60-300, dinner from HK$200; ⊙11.30am-3pm & 6-10.30pm; Ⓜ Tin Hau, exit A1) A family feud at the venerable Yung Kee in Central created this excellent-value spin-off. Kam's Kitchen serves classic, labour-intensive Cantonese dishes like prawn stuffed with crab roe and oysters sizzling with ginger and onion. And, of course, the famous goose is still here, as a roasted bird or with its fat drizzled into fried rice.

For lunch only, you can order roast goose on rice for HK$60 – dingy dining room aside, the bird is every bite the equal to Michelin-lauded Kam's Roast Goose (p109), and without the lines.

CHOI'S KITCHEN
CANTONESE $$

Map p310 (私房蔡; ☑852 3485 0501; Shop C, Ground fl, Hoi Kok Mansion, 9 Whitfield Rd, Tin Hau; claypot rice HK$138; ⊙11am-10pm Mon-Sat; Ⓜ Tin Hau, exit A2) Originally a *dai pai dong* (大牌檔; food stall), this friendly neighbourhood Canto joint is known for claypot rice topped with preserved sausage, steamed chicken or smoked duck. The rice is cooked to order (30 minutes) and only available at dinner. Use the metal spoon provided to chip away at the precious crispy bits stuck to the claypot.

PAK LOH CHIU CHOW
CANTONESE $$

Map p310 (百樂潮州; ☑852 2576 8886; www.pakloh.com; 23-25 Hysan Ave; lunch/dinner from HK$200/300; ⊙11am-11pm; Ⓜ Causeway Bay, exit A) The clean renovated setting belies Pak Loh's status as a veteran of Chiu Chow (Teochew) cooking, a Cantonese cuisine famed for its masterful seafood dishes. Whether you keep to classics such as salt-and-pepper Bombay duck fish (ask for tangerine oil to dip), marinated goose, a hearty oyster omelette, or splurge on a giant steamed crab, eaten cold, Pak Loh delivers.

TAI PING KOON
CHINESE $$

Map p310 (太平館餐廳; ☑852 2576 9161; www.taipingkoon.com; 6 Pak Sha Rd; meal sets from HK$170; ⊙11am-11.30pm; Ⓜ Causeway Bay, exit F) Just like Chinese dishes have been adapted to western palates overseas, here the tables are turned. Throwback fare such as baked escargots, 'Swiss' chicken wings and Russian borscht are served in neat, if slightly worn, surrounds by waiters who've been here for decades.

'Soy sauce western' cuisine, as it is known, is believed to have been invented by the original Tai Ping Koon in Guǎngzhōu. There are several branches around town.

YEE TUNG HEEN
DIM SUM, CANTONESE $$$

Map p310 (怡東軒; ☑852 2837 6790; 2nd fl, Excelsior Hotel, 281 Gloucester Rd; lunch/dinner from HK$200/500; ⊙noon-3pm & 6-10pm; Ⓜ Causeway Bay, exit D1) This elegant and underhyped restaurant is an expert at haute Cantonese cuisine. Managed by the Mandarin Oriental, it delivers MO-quality food and service at two-thirds of the price; it's easier to book too. The best ingredients are painstakingly prepared and presented to impress, as exemplified by lunchtime dim sum offerings such as eggplant pastry and the award-winning mushroom assortment.

FORUM
CANTONESE, DIM SUM $$$

Map p310 (富臨飯店阿一鮑魚; Ah Yat Abalone; ☑852 2869 8282; www.forumrestaurant1977.com; 1st fl, Sino Plaza, 255-257 Jaffe Rd; meals HK$500-1600; ⊙11am-2.30pm & 5.30-10.30pm; Ⓜ Causeway Bay, exit D4) The flagship of a fine-dining brand with over a dozen branches worldwide, this two-Michelin-star eatery serves exquisite Guǎngdōng classics (including lunchtime dim sum). But Forum is most renowned for its braised abalone prepared from a recipe by the award-winning chef-owner Yeung Koon-yat. The bad news: it starts at HK$2100 (cheaper with the set menu, but you'll need six diners).

FARM HOUSE
CANTONESE $$$

Map p310 (農圃飯店; ☑852 2881 1331; www.farmhouse.com.hk; 1st fl, Taiping Tower, 8 Sunning Rd; meals HK$500-1500; ⊙11am-2.30pm & 6-10.30pm; Ⓜ Causeway Bay, exit F1) It's easy to see why well-to-do families living nearby dine at this long-established restaurant when their maids are on leave. The masterful takes on home cooking, such as steamed pork patty with duck egg, and fancier Cantonese fare, like the deep-fried deboned chicken wings stuffed with glutinous rice, are hard to beat. Ambience is relaxing and upscale.

Book a few days in advance for Friday or the weekend.

WEST VILLA CANTONESE, DIM SUM **$$$**
Map p310 (西苑酒家; ☑852 2882 2110; 5th fl, Lee Gardens One, 33 Hysan Ave; meals from HK$500; ◷11am-11.30pm; Ⓜ Causeway Bay, exit A) Above a ritzy shopping mall, prepare to be intimidated by tanks of king crab, rows of Chateau Margaux wines and a menu heavy on wallet-busting abalone. This posh spot does *char siu* (barbecued pork, HK$198) well too – slightly charred at the edges, with a golden lean-to-fat ratio and a stellar soy-sauce chicken. Dim sum, served at lunch, is also exquisite.

✖ Happy Valley

CHEONG KEE HONG KONG **$**
(昌記; ☑852 2573 5910; 2nd fl, Wong Nai Chung Market & Cooked Food Centre, 2 Yuk Sau St; meals from HK$30; ◷7am-4.30pm; 🚌1 from Des Voeux Rd Central, 🚋Happy Valley) This scrappy little *dai pai dong* above a wet market is one of Hong Kong's most venerable *cha chaan tangs,* beloved for its ultrathick toast drenched in condensed milk and peanut butter. Milk tea is silky-sweet, while local comfort foods such as porkchop noodles and *char siu* with egg are well above average.

It's the first stall you come to as you enter the cooked food centre. No English menu but some of the staff speak a little.

GI KEE SEAFOOD RESTAURANT DAI PAI DONG, CANTONESE **$**
(鉌記海鮮飯店; ☑852 2574 9937; Shop 4, 2nd fl, Wong Nai Chung Wet Market & Cooked Food Centre, 2 Yuk Sau St; meals from HK$150; ◷11am-1.30pm & 5-11pm; 🚌1 from Des Voeux Rd Central, 🚋Happy Valley) You might have to queue for a plastic stool at this *dai pai dong* perched above a wet market for delicious Cantonese fare like chicken with fried garlic. Chan Chung-fai, the man in the kitchen, had a huge following some years back, including the likes of Zhang Ziyi and Jackie Chan.

It's the third stall on the left as you enter the cooked-food centre, two along from Cheong Kee.

✖ Island East

★ON LEE NOODLE NOODLES **$**
(☑852 2513 8398; 22 Main St E, Shau Kei Wan; noodles from HK$40; ◷9am-7pm Fri-Wed; Ⓜ Shau Kei Wan, exit B2) Quiveringly tender beef brisket is the big draw here, eaten with noodles either in a soup or 'stirred' with soy sauce (you still get a little bowl of beefy soup to drink). Add extras such as fish balls, wontons, or more brisket if hungry. It's the perfect pit stop when visiting the nearby Hong Kong Museum of Coastal Defence (p108).

★TIM HO WAN – NORTH POINT DIM SUM **$**
(添好運; ☑852 2979 5608; www.timhowan.com.hk; 2-8 Wharf Rd, Seaview Bldg, North Point; dim sum from HK$18; ◷10am-9.30pm; Ⓜ North Point, exit A3) This less hectic outpost of Hong Kong's famously cheap (for the quality) dim-sum chain, is now a global brand with branches in Asia, Australia and the US. The quality is consistent – that is to say, great but not gourmet – while the wall of windows and bigger tables makes it a far nicer experience than the original Mong Kok shop.

★SUN KWAI HEUNG CHINESE **$**
(新桂香燒臘; ☑852 2556 1183; 17, Kam Tam Yun House, 345 Chai Wan Rd, Chai Wan; meals from HK$47; ◷8am-9pm; Ⓜ Chai Wan, exit C) This off-the-beaten-track shop has unbeatable Cantonese barbecue and none of the lines of better-known places. *Char siu* (barbecued pork) emerges from the roaster, edges beautifully bronzed and caramelised, several times a day.

SIU WAH KITCHEN CANTONESE **$**
(紹華小廚; ☑852 8199 8188; Shop CF3, Aldrich Bay Market Cooked Food Centre, Aldrich Bay, Shau Kei Wan; claypot rice from HK$72; ◷10am-10pm Tue-Sun; Ⓜ Shau Kei Wan, exit B3) This humble stall prepares claypot rice the old way using charcoal, which cooks more evenly than gas and gives a beautiful layer of crust. More unusual ingredients include taro with pork (芋頭肉碎飯) and mutton and cumin (疆土羊肉). After drizzling the sweet soy sauce, wait a few minutes for it to caramelise with the rice crackling. Your taste buds will thank you.

MASTER LOW KEY
FOOD SHOP $\qquad$ SWEETS $

(低調高手大街小食; ☑852 6986 8500; 76A Shau Kei Wan Main St E, Shau Kei Wan; eggettes from HK$16; ⊗noon-10pm Mon-Fri, 11am-10pm Sat & Sun; ☑; Ⓜ Shau Kei Wan, exit B1) Master Low Key's eggettes, aka egg waffles (雞蛋仔), are among the town's best. These fluffy balls of goodness with a golden exterior and a melty, eggy centre are Hong Kong's favourite snack. The Master also does 'Belgian' waffles, which come drizzled with peanut butter and condensed milk, Hong Kong–style, or with jam.

The shop is just outside exit B1 of Shau Kei Wan MTR station.

★ TUNG PO SEAFOOD
RESTAURANT $\qquad$ MARKET, CANTONESE $$

(東寶小館; ☑852 2880 5224, 852 2880 9399; 2nd fl, Java Rd Wet Market, Municipal Services Bldg, 99 Java Rd, North Point; meals HK$200-600; ⊗5.30pm-midnight; Ⓜ North Point, exit A1) You're guaranteed a hearty repast at any *dai pai dong* dai atop Java Rd Wet Market, but at Tung Po (and its sister spot, 店小二), you'll discover fusion Cantonese with a higher price tag and a dash of eccentricity. Thursday to Saturday, it's Hong Kong's most riotous dinner, as bowls of beer are downed to blaring '90s R & B.

Dishes to try include the roasted crispy chicken, Thai-style stir-fried clams and chargrilled sea prawns. Book ahead (reservations 2.30pm to 5.30pm) or turn up before 7pm. The 9pm sitting is the livelier one. Big tables here are best suited to groups.

🍷 DRINKING & NIGHTLIFE

Salubrious, after-hours fun on Lockhart Rd used to be the main reason drinkers ventured east of Central, but a proliferation of unique watering holes off Queen's Rd East has improved Wan Chai's nightlife considerably. Hip-casual bars serving local craft beers and cocktails have mushroomed around Sun, Moon and Star Sts, and near the Blue House. Likewise, the drinking scene in Causeway Bay has evolved beyond upstairs Japanese whiskey dens to include speciality bars and street-corner cafes in Tai Hang and 'Caroline Haven'. A gourmet-coffee culture has also taken root.

🍷 Admiralty

CAFE GREY $\qquad$ BAR
Map p306 (☑852 2918 1838; www.upperhouse. com; 88 Queensway, Pacific Pl; ⊗6-10.30pm, to midnight Fri & Sat; Ⓜ Admiralty, exit F) On the 49th floor of the Upper House (p227), Cafe Grey pulls in a suited after-office crowd for drinks, dinner and corporate back-slapping in an atmosphere of clubby exclusivity. Even if you're not on the company expense account, it's worth stretching to one drink at the 14m-long stone bar simply to experience the sensational harbour views.

Cafe Grey is also a popular spot for daily afternoon tea, from 3.30pm to 5.30pm.

🍷 Wan Chai

★ BOTANICALS $\qquad$ BAR
Map p308 (Botanical Bar; ☑852 2866 3444; www.thepawn.com.hk; 1st fl, 62 Johnston Rd; ⊗11.30am-1am Sun-Thu, to 2am Fri & Sat; Ⓜ Wan Chai, exit A3) On the 1st floor of gorgeous heritage pile the Pawn (p111), Botanicals draws after-work imbibers to its stylish twin bars and colonial-chic verandah for wines by the glass, craft beers and playful cocktails (after 5pm) including 10-cask negronis (HK$100 to HK$140) concocted from a variety of gin infusions, boutique vermouths and herbal additions.

DJs spin after 8pm on Friday and Saturday evenings. Once a month, the bar holds cocktail classes on the roof; see the website to book.

★ STONE NULLAH TAVERN $\qquad$ BAR
Map p308 (☑852 3182 0128; www.stone nullahtavern.com; 69 Stone Nullah Lane; ⊗noon-1am; Ⓜ Wan Chai, exit A3) The Americana theme is downplayed at this corner tavern that packs in punters for Wan Chai's best happy hour, boasting unlimited house spirits, wines, Pabst Blue Ribbon beer, fried chicken and maple bacon (5pm to 7pm, $HK100). The rest of the time, it's a convivial hang-out for well-mixed cocktails ($HK99), bourbon or Young Master craft beer in a hip, historic neighbourhood.

WAN CHAI & NORTHEAST HONG KONG ISLAND DRINKING & NIGHTLIFE

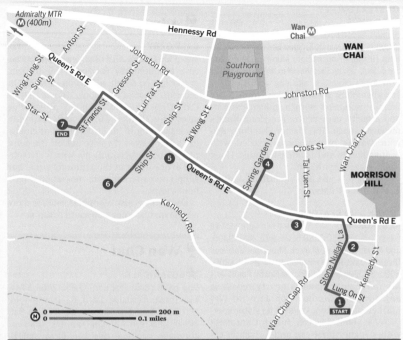

🏃 Neighbourhood Walk
Old Wan Chai's Forgotten Streets

START PAK TAI TEMPLE
END STAR ST
LENGTH 1.2KM; TWO HOURS

A short stroll from the main bus routes and Wan Chai metro (exit A3), you'll start to get a feel for the neighbourhood as it was in the 19th century at **1 Pak Tai Temple** (p104), a stunning temple built 150 years ago by local residents. Further down the slope, the **2 Blue House** (p105), one of Hong Kong's last surviving wooden tenement buildings, will show you what life was like in Wan Chai in the last century via its fascinating House of Stories.

The Streamline Moderne exterior of the original Wan Chai Market (corner Queen's Rd East and Wan Chai Rd) is all that remains of the place, which now fronts a shopping centre. Once the hub of the neighbourhood, the market was used as a mortuary by Japanese forces in WWII (the new, air-conditioned market is at number 258). To the west, the pocket-sized **3 Old Wan Chai Post Office** (舊灣仔郵政局; 221 Queen's Rd E; ⏰10am-5pm Mon-Wed) is Hong Kong's oldest post office.

Take a quick look at **4 Spring Garden Lane**, one of the first areas developed by the British, and imagine what it was like in the 1900s. Then head along Queen's Rd East to peep inside the mysterious **5 Hung Shing Temple** (p105), once a seaside shrine in the days when the sea came right up to the temple doors.

Just west of the temple, turn up the hill along Ship St and stand before the now-derelict **6 Ghost House** at 55 Nam Koo Tce. Its history is a wretched one: it was used by Japanese soldiers as a brothel housing 'comfort women' in WWII.

The **7 Star St neighbourhood** is a quietly hip corner of town with street names (Star, Sun, Moon) that indicate this was the site of Hong Kong's first power plant. On 31 Wing Fung St is a six-storey balconied building in art deco style.

Admiralty MTR can be reached by an escalator and underground travelator entered at the bottom of Wing Fung St.

DJIBOUTII BAR

Map p306 (☏852 9449 0777; 2 Landale St; ☺noon-1am Mon-Thu, to 3am Fri, 5pm-3am Sat; Ⓜ️Wan Chai) Awash in purple neon, funky furnishings and African-inspired curios, Djiboutii is a back-alley bar with bags of personality. Choose your perch – at bar stools under a crystal chandelier or outside in the mural-adorned passageway – and set yourself up with a citrus- and fruit-laced signature cocktail (from HK$120). Bar snacks include assorted skewers, rotisserie chicken, homemade dips and minipizzas.

TAI LUNG FUNG BAR

Map p308 (大龍鳳; ☏852 2572 0055; 5-9 Hing Wan St; ☺noon-1am Mon-Thu, to 1.30am Fri & Sat, happy hour noon-9pm; Ⓜ️Wan Chai, exit A3) This retro-styled backstreet bar takes its name from a 1960s Cantonese opera troupe. In common parlance, Tai Lung Fung (Big Dragon Phoenix) means 'much ado'. Appropriately, the decor is ostentatious and the vibe relaxed and convivial, tarnished only slightly by a dull drinks menu.

MANSON'S LOT CAFE

Map p308 (☏852 2362 1899; www.mansonslot. com; 15 Swatow St; ☺8am-6.30pm, to 8pm Thu-Sat; Ⓜ️Wan Chai, exit D) Impeccable Australian-roasted coffee is the draw at this pretty little boho cafe popular for its lunch sets. Some relevant trivia as you enjoy your flat white – in the 19th century, the ground under you belonged to the founder of Hong Kong's first dairy farm, a Scottish surgeon called Patrick Manson.

CANNY MAN PUB

Map p308 (精伶吧; ☏852 2861 1935; www.the-cannyman.com; Basement, Wharney Guangdong Hotel, 57-73 Lockhart Rd; ☺noon-2am, to 3am Fri & Sat; Ⓜ️Wan Chai, exit C) Pair your pint of ale with haggis, lamb stovies (a kind of stew) or 'mince and tatties' at Hong Kong's only Scottish pub, a wood-panelled, sport-watching sort of place under a hotel. Set lunches are especially good value, and as you'd expect, it has a super selection of scotch. Happy hour is noon to 9pm daily.

AGAVE BAR

Map p308 (☏852 2866 3228; www.epicurean. com.hk; Shop C & D, 93 Lockhart Rd; ☺noon-1am Sun-Thu, to 2am Fri & Sat, happy hour 3-8pm; Ⓜ️Wan Chai, exit C) Fans of tequila will be ecstatic – there are dozens of varieties on offer and the bartenders are heavy-handed

with it. Most come for the margaritas (from HK$82), with chips and salsa if hungry. Themed interiors are bright and colourful; snag a perch facing Lockhart Rd to watch the weird and wonderful residents of Wan Chai wander (or stagger) by.

There's another, newer branch on Hollywood Rd, Central.

DUSK TILL DAWN BAR

Map p308 (☏852 2528 4689; Ground fl, 76-84 Jaffe Rd; ☺noon-5am Mon-Fri, 3pm-6am Sat & Sun; Ⓜ️Wan Chai, exit C) It's either your nightlife nightmare or everything you hoped Honkers would be, but true to its name, when the other bars peter out, Dusk Till Dawn is just getting started. A Filipino band bashes out the hits to a beery crowd of locals and expats dancing until the sun comes up. Beers from HK$80.

🍷 Causeway Bay

★**SECOND DRAFT** CRAFT BEER

Map p310 (☏852 2656 0232; 98 Tung Lo Wan Rd, Tin Hau; ☺noon-1am; Ⓜ️Tin Hau, exit B) Tall windows wrap around a magisterial sweep of wooden bar at this Tai Hang neighbourhood gastropub, the sort of civilised joint where everybody knows everybody. A curated line-up of local beers favours the faultless Young Master brewery (450ml pours around HK$80), or go for an organic wine, paired with creative nibbles such as edamame with crispy chicken skin.

During the day, it's a breezy spot to stop by for lunch or single-origin coffee.

★**SKYE BAR** BAR

Map p310 (☏852 2839 3327; 22nd fl, Park Lane Hotel, 10 Gloucester Rd; ☺noon-1am; Ⓜ️Causeway Bay, exit E) The views are to die for at this open-air rooftop gem jutting out from the corner of the Park Lane Hotel. Treat yourself to a glass of Perrier-Jouët champers (HK$170) at the curvaceously sociable bar as you drink in one of the most magnificent harbour panoramas in the city. Ah, Hong Kong.

★**EXECUTIVE BAR** LOUNGE

Map p310 (☏852 2893 2080; http://executivebar-com-hk-1.blogspot.hk; 27th fl, Bartlock Centre, 3 Yiu Wa St; ☺5.30pm-1am Mon-Fri, to 2am Sat; Ⓜ️Causeway Bay, exit A) There are just 20 seats at this discrete gem of a bar overlooking the racecourse, which means Japanese owner

LOCAL KNOWLEDGE

FIRE DRAGONS IN TAI HANG

Tai Hang, a quietly hip residential neighbourhood of old temples, intimate cafes and a few high-rises, is famed for its fire-dragon dance. For three nights during the Mid-Autumn Festival, some 300 residents parade a handmade dragon measuring 67m and stuck with 70,000 incense sticks through the streets to the throb of drum and gong. The tradition has been happening annually since 1880, when Tai Hang was a tiny Hakka village in the throes of a plague. The fierce two-hour affair lasts from 8.15pm to 10.30pm, with spectators thronging close to the dragon to get a closer look, amid shouts of 'Watch it! Watch it!' More at www.taihangfiredragon.hk.

and bartender Ichiro (it's a one-man operation) can give you his undivided attention. Perfectionist spins on classic cocktails employ fresh fruits imported from Japan, hand-chipped ice and house-infused bitters that change with the seasons. Ichiro has a terrific whiskey selection too.

HONG KONG ISLAND

TAPHOUSE   CRAFT BEER

Map p310 (✆852 3705 9901; 1A-1B Tsing Fung St, Tin Hau; ☺1pm-2am; Ⓜ Tin Hau, exit A2) A dazzling chrome cliff face of around 50 taps showcases Hong Kong beers from Young Master, Moonzen, Kowloon Bay, Lion Rock, Gweilo, Mak's and more at this sporty neighbourhood bar. You'll pay around HK$80 for a 400ml pour. The kitchen turns out respectably lip-smacking wings, too, slathered in a choice of 10 sauces.

ELEPHANT GROUNDS   CAFE

Map p310 (✆852 2253 1313; www.elephantgrounds.com; Shop C, 42-48 Paterson St, Fashion Walk; ☺10am-9.30pm, to 10pm Sat & Sun; Ⓜ Causeway Bay, exit E) Founded in 2013, Elephant Grounds has quickly become Hong Kong's go-to chain for third-wave coffee and hipster brunch fare such as avo toast or eggs Benny. This branch stands out for having an ice-cream counter, offering wacky homemade flavours like Thai iced tea and Earl Grey cookie.

DICKENS BAR   BAR

Map p310 (✆852 2837 6782; www.mandarinoriental.com/excelsior/dining/dickens_bar; Basement, Excelsior Hong Kong, 281 Gloucester Rd; ☺noon-1am Mon-Thu, to 2am Fri & Sat, happy hour 4-8pm; Ⓜ Causeway Bay, exit D1) A long-lived bastion of expat boozing, this British pub lookalike pours its own Master Dickens lager along with craft beers from Gweilo, Young Master and Hong Kong Beer Co.

You can also get English beer Boddingtons on tap, and old-fashioned bottled ales like Black Sheep. Expect the best of Britpop on loop and live sport on the big screens.

BUDDY BAR   BAR

Map p310 (✆852 2882 9780; 22 School St, Tai Hang; ☺5.30pm-2am Thu-Tue; Ⓜ Tin Hau, exit B) This low-key corner bar is the kind of place where everybody knows your name (or they would, if you lived in Tai Hang). The drink selection is limited, but at least your dog is welcome to snooze at your feet while you down a pint of Belgian ale.

🍸 Island East

★**SUGAR**   LOUNGE

(✆852 3968 3738; www.east-hongkong.com; 32nd fl; ☺5.30pm-1am Mon-Thu & Sun, to 1.30am Fri & Sat) Enviable East Island views are the drawcard at this stylish terrace bar atop designer business hotel **East** (香港東隅; ✆852 3968 3808; 29 Taikoo Shing Rd, Taikoo Shing, Quarry Bay; Ⓜ Tai Koo, exit D1). With signature peach mojito in hand, take in the prosperity: the glass towers of Taikoo Pl to the west, the Kai Tak cruise terminal (formerly the old airport runway) in the bay in front. Reserve a table for Thursday to Saturday evenings.

☆ ENTERTAINMENT

★**HAPPY VALLEY**
RACECOURSE   HORSE RACING

Map p310 (跑馬地馬場; ✆852 2895 1523; www.hkjc.com/home/english/index.asp; 2 Sports Rd, Happy Valley; HK$10; ☺7-10.30pm Wed Sep-Jun; 🚋 Happy Valley) An outing at the races is one of the quintessential Hong Kong things to do, especially if you're around during the weekly Wednesday-evening races. Punters pack into the stands and trackside, with branded beer stalls, silly wigs and live music setting up an electric party atmosphere.

To bet, you must first exchange cash for betting vouchers inside the stands, then use the machine terminals (which have English settings and instructions). Stewards will help.

The first horse races were held here way back in 1846. Now meetings are held both here and at the newer and larger (but less atmospheric) Sha Tin Racecourse (p166) in the New Territories. Check the website for details on betting and tourist packages. Take the eastbound Happy Valley tram to the final stop and cross the road to the racecourse. You can use an Octopus card to enter the turnstiles.

WANCH
LIVE MUSIC

Map p306 (☑852 2861 1621; www.thewanch. hk; 54 Jaffe Rd, Wan Chai; MWan Chai, exit C) Decked out in old Hong Kong paraphernalia, the Wanch, so called for Wan Chai district's nickname, has live music (mostly classic rock, blues and folk) nightly from 9.30pm. Jam night is Monday from 8pm. There's no cover charge. Happy hour is 5pm to 9pm.

HONG KONG STADIUM
STADIUM

Map p310 (香港大球場; ☑852 2895 7926; 55 Eastern Hospital Rd, So Kon Po; ☐Happy Valley) The 40,000-seat Hong Kong Stadium in So Kon Po, a division of Causeway Bay, is Hong Kong's largest sports venue. The Hong Kong World Rugby Sevens (p61) takes place here.

Plans were in place at time of research to build a newer, larger stadium at Kai Tak.

SUNBEAM THEATRE
THEATRE

(新光戲院; ☑852 2563 2959, 852 2856 0161; www.sunbeamtheatre.com/hk; 423 King's Rd, Kiu Fai Mansion, North Point; opera HK$160-380; MNorth Point, exit A4) Cantonese opera is performed at this vintage theatre throughout the year. Shows generally run five days a week from 7.30pm for about a week, with occasional matinees at 1pm or 1.30pm.

There's also a cinema that stages classic and new-release films from Hong Kong, China and Japan.

HONG KONG ACADEMY FOR THE PERFORMING ARTS
DANCE, THEATRE

Map p306 (香港演藝學院; ☑852 2584 8500; www.hkapa.edu; 1 Gloucester Rd, Wan Chai; MAdmiralty, exit E2) With its striking triangular atrium and an exterior Meccano-like frame (a work of art in itself), the APA (1985) is a Wan Chai landmark and a major performance venue for music, dance, theatre and scholarship. Check out its online event calendar for exhibits and performances.

AMC PACIFIC PLACE
CINEMA

Map p306 (☑852 2265 8933; www.amccinemas. com.hk; 1st fl, 1 Pacific Pl, Admiralty; MAdmiralty, exit F) With six screens (or 'houses' as they are called in Hong Kong), including a VIP screen with waitress service called the Oval Office, this cinema inside the Pacific Place (p120) mall in Admiralty is one of the fanciest in town.

HONG KONG ARTS CENTRE
ARTS CENTRE

Map p308 (香港藝術中心; www.hkac.org.hk; 2 Harbour Rd, Wan Chai; MWan Chai, exit A1) A popular venue for dance, theatre and music, the Hong Kong Arts Centre also contains the two-floor **Pao Galleries** (包玉剛及包兆龍畫廊; Map p308; ☑852 2582 0200; ◯10am-8pm during exhibitions) FREE which hosts retrospectives and group shows in all visual media. There are also a few boutiques, an art bookshop, the HKAC Cinema and a cafe.

HKAC CINEMA
CINEMA

Map p308 (☑852 2582 0200; Upper basement, Hong Kong Arts Centre, 2 Harbour Rd, Wan Chai; ☐18) This basement cinema in the Hong Kong Arts Centre shows mostly art films and occasional Chinese classics with English subtitles. The ticket office is on the 2nd floor.

🛍 SHOPPING

Admiralty boasts one of the city's best luxury malls in Pacific Place, but the retail heart of this part of Hong Kong is Causeway Bay. Wan Chai, with markets both indoors and out, is better for bargain hunters, while North Point offers a more traditional Chinese shopping experience.

🏠 Admiralty

★ PACIFIC PLACE   MALL

Map p306 (太古廣場; ☑852 2844 8988; www.
pacificplace.com.hk; 88 Queensway; ⊙10am-
10pm; ⓂAdmiralty, exit F) A polished marble
sea of high-end couture and accessories,
posh Pacific Place manages to avoid the
malady of mall fatigue via its expansive design, relatively light footfall and skylights
which let the natural light pour in.

🏠 Wan Chai

★ KAPOK   FASHION & ACCESSORIES

Map p306 (☑852 2549 9254; www.ka-pok.com;
3 Sun St; ⊙11am-8pm, to 6pm Sun; ⓂAdmiralty,
exit F, ⓂWan Chai, exit B1) In the hip Star St
area, this Hong Kong–born boutique stocks
a fastidiously curated selection of luxe-cool
menswear labels (plus their own, Future
Classics), along with bags and quirky design gifts. A cafe counter means you can
sip single-origin espresso as you browse.
A more fashion-oriented sister boutique is
around the corner at 5 St Francis Yard.

KEVIN CHEUNG   GIFTS & SOUVENIRS

Map p308 (張瑋晉; ☑852 6033 2102; http://
kevin-cheung.com; 2nd fl, 4 Hing Wan St;
ⓂWan Chai, exit D) Product designer Kevin
Cheung's workshop is also his home, occupying a lovely heritage unit in Wan Chai's
Blue House (p105) cluster. Cheung collects
Hong Kong waste (old carpets, bicycles etc)
and upcycles it into useful and beautiful
products. Curios such as bicycle bells made
from old rice cookers and his 'wallpaper
wallets' make uniquely local gifts. You'll
need to contact Cheung to arrange a visit.

WAN CHAI
COMPUTER CENTRE   ELECTRONICS

Map p308 (灣仔電腦城; 1st fl, Southorn Centre, 130-138 Hennessy Rd; ⊙10am-9pm Mon-
Sat, noon-8pm Sun; ⓂWan Chai, exit B1) Buy a
drone, build a custom gaming PC, or repair
the iPhone screen you cracked on that Lan
Kwai Fong bar crawl. You can do it all and
more at this gleaming, beeping warren of
tiny electrical shops.

KUNG FU SUPPLIES   SPORTS & OUTDOORS

Map p308 (功夫用品公司; ☑852 2891 1912;
www.kungfu.com.hk; Room 6A, 6th fl, Chuen Fung
House, 192 Johnston Rd; ⊙10am-7pm Mon-Sat;

🚌6, 6A, 6X, ⓂWan Chai, exit A5) If you're looking to stock up on martial-arts accessories,
including uniforms, nunchaku and safety
weapons for practice, or just want to thumb
through a decent collection of books and
DVDs, this is the place to go.

🏠 Causeway Bay

★ FASHION WALK   CLOTHING

Map p310 (www.fashionwalk.com.hk; ⊙office
10am-11pm; ⓂCauseway Bay, exit D4) A mostly
street-level fashion-shopping mecca spanning four streets in Causeway Bay – Paterson, Cleveland, Great George and Kingston.
It's where you'll find big names such as
Comme des Garçons, Sandro and Kiehl's,
but also high-street favourites, up-and-
coming local brands and shops with off-
the-rack high-street labels.

★ TIMES SQUARE   MALL

Map p310 (時代廣場; www.timessquare.com.
hk; 1 Matheson St; ⓂCauseway Bay, exit A) The
hyperkinetic buzz at the heart of Causeway Bay, Times Square is retail nirvana for
Hong Kong's shoppers, with mainstream
brands over 13 floors (it was the first 'vertical mall' in the city), restaurants, cafes, a
cinema and the famous clock on the forecourt outside – like with its namesake in
NYC, revellers congregate here on 31 December for the countdown.

Before the mall existed, this formerly
residential neighbourhood was home to the
Sharp St tram depot. This history is captured, delightfully, in a large scale model
on display inside the Lego Store (9th floor),
complete with working trams, teahouses
and crowded tenements.

★ ESLITE   BOOKS

Map p310 (誠品; ☑852 3419 6789; 8th-10th
fl, Hysan Pl, 500 Hennessy Rd; ⊙10am-10pm
Sun-Thu, to 11pm Fri & Sat; 🚻; ⓂCauseway Bay,
exit F2) You could waste hours inside this
swanky three-floor Taiwanese bookshop,
which features a massive collection of English and Chinese books and magazines,
a shop selling gorgeous stationery and
leather-bound journals, a cafe, a bubble-
tea counter and a huge kids' toy and book
section.

TWO GIRLS   COSMETICS

Map p310 (雙妹嘜; ☑862 2504 1811; www.two-
girls.hk; Shop 283, 2-10 Great George St, Cause-

way Pl; ⊙noon-9pm; Ⓜ Causeway Bay, exit E) Hong Kong's first cosmetics brand has been selling fragrant, highly affordable creams, potions, perfumes and talcs since 1898. The pretty, retro packaging featuring two cheongsam-clad beauties makes these excellent gifts.

On the 2nd floor of Causeway Place, a mazelike warren of ministores, Two Girls takes a bit of finding.

G.O.D.   HOMEWARES, CLOTHING

Map p310 (Goods of Desire; 🗹852 2890 5555; www.god.com.hk; 9 Sharp St E; ⊙noon-10pm; Ⓜ Causeway Bay, exit A) The Causeway Bay branch of this playful born in Hong Kong store is great for getting those vintage mailbox fridge magnets, iconic T-shirts and its infamously disrespectful lucky cats (you'll understand when you see them). There are bigger branches in Central.

PAPABUBBLE   FOOD

Map p310 (🗹852 2367 4807; www.papabubble. com.hk; 34 Tung Lo Wan Rd, Tai Hang; ⊙11am-10pm; 🚾; Ⓜ Tin Hau, exit B) This Spanish artisan candy company's Hong Kong outpost sells unique-to-here flavours such as lemon tea and durian, featuring local designs like Chinese zodiac animals and the character for 'double happiness'. Great gifts. Kids will love watching the hot sugar being pulled behind the counter.

YIU FUNG STORE   FOOD

Map p310 (么鳳; 🗹852 2576 2528; http://yiufungstore.hk; Foo Ming St; ⊙11am-10.30pm; Ⓜ Causeway Bay, exit A) Now with several branches around town, Hong Kong's most famous store (c 1960s) for Chinese pickles and preserved fruit features sour plum, liquorice-flavoured lemon, tangerine peel, pickled papaya and dried longan. Just before the Lunar New Year, it's crammed with shoppers.

SOGO   DEPARTMENT STORE

Map p310 (崇光; 🗹852 2833 8338; www. sogo.com.hk; 555 Hennessy Rd; ⊙10am-10pm; Ⓜ Causeway Bay, exit B) The range is mind-boggling at this Japanese-owned department store, with 17 floors of high-end fashion and accessories, cosmetics, homewares and much more. Prices drop dramatically during the sales (check the website) and the store becomes a madhouse.

A highlight is the basement supermarket and food hall hawking all manner of Japanese treats such as *onigiri* (fish-stuffed rice balls), fried-octopus pancakes, almost-too-pretty-to-eat *mochi* (sweet glutinous rice cakes) and oceans of sake.

HYSAN PLACE   MALL

Map p310 (🗹852 2886 7222; www.hp.leegardens. com.hk; 500 Hennessy Rd; ⊙10am-10pm Sun-Thu, to 11pm Fri & Sat; Ⓜ Causeway Bay, exit F2) This shiny 17-storey mall is filled with hundreds of ever-trendy Japanese, Korean and local clothing and beauty brands in a more upmarket environment than other local teeny-bopper havens, but more affordable than most malls in Causeway Bay. The supermarket, Jason's Food & Living, in the lower basement, has an awesome bakery.

ISLAND BEVERLY MALL   MALL

Map p310 (金百利商場; 1 Great George St; Ⓜ Causeway Bay, exit E) Crammed into cubicles, up escalators and in the back lanes of this unassuming mall next to Sogo are microshops selling local designer threads, garments, toys, and cosmetics from Japan and Korea, not to mention a kaleidoscope of kooky accessories. Great place to get those Jimmy Choo lookalikes to go with your jeans. Shops are open from afternoon till late.

🏃 SPORTS & ACTIVITIES

EASTERN NATURE TRAIL   HIKING

(東區自然步道) Stage 5 of the Hong Kong Trail, this 9km, three-hour nature trail, known for the indigenous trees and migratory birds it passes, starts on Mount Parker Rd in Quarry Bay and ends on Wong Nai Chung Gap Rd in Tai Tam. The trail also features WWII military relics and a former sugar refinery. You'll pass beautiful Tai Tam Country Park on your descent to Tai Tam Reservoir. Following Tai Tam Reservoir Rd, you'll reach Wong Nai Chung Gap Rd.

To get to the starting point, take exit B from Tai Koo MTR station, head 600m west and turn into Quarry St. The start of the trail is near the Quarry Bay Municipal Services Building at 38 Quarry St.

Aberdeen & South Hong Kong Island

ABERDEEN | AP LEI CHAU | POK FU LAM | DEEP WATER BAY | REPULSE BAY | STANLEY | SHEK O

Neighbourhood Top Five

❶ Aberdeen Promenade (p124) Watching the goings-on on moored boats then hopping on a sampan to cross the typhoon shelter the way it was done decades ago.

❷ Wong Chuk Hang (p126) Gallery-hopping, touring a brewery and

chilling at the latest industrial-chic cafe.

❸ Béthanie (p125) Revisiting a time in Hong Kong history when French missionaries crossed paths with dairy cowboys and a fire dragon in Pok Fu Lam.

❹ Stanley Downing a pint or two at the British-style

pubs in this seaside town and taking a dip at one of its beaches.

❺ Shek O Beach (p128) Lounging on the shaded sand at this laid-back, cliff-framed beach village.

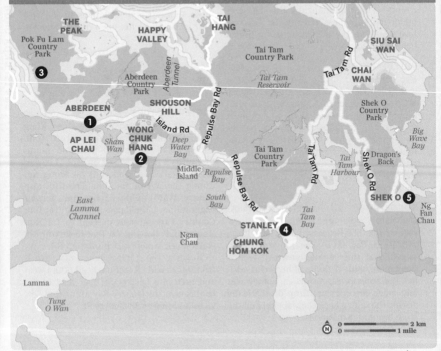

For more detail of this area see Map p312 ➡

Explore Aberdeen & South Hong Kong Island

The southern district is not only a showcase of history – Pok Fu Lam has the island's last surviving village alongside vestiges of a Victorian dairy – but Aberdeen and Ap Lei Chau are also the homes of Hong Kong's boat-dwelling fisherfolk, and as such, offer wonderful seafood and boat rides. In addition, Ap Lei Chau has great shopping, and Wong Chuk Hang, contemporary art. The south is also Hong Kong Island's backyard playground, from beaches and seaside dining, to a waterfront bazaar and an amusement park.

Local Life

➡ **Drinking** After dinner in Ap Lei Chau or Aberdeen, grab drinks from a convenience store and head to the seafront promenade.

➡ **Shopping** When shopping in the mammoth Horizon Plaza (p131), wear sensible shoes like the locals.

➡ **Seafood** It's common for foodies to buy their own seafood in a wet market and have it cooked in a *dai pai dong* (food stall) of their choice for a by-weight cooking fee. Ap Lei Chau Market and its associated Cooked Food Centre (p129) offer this.

➡ **Swimming** Glowing algae (completely harmless) are common in the waters of Stanley, Middle Bay and Repulse Bay during the summer months.

Getting There & Away

➡ **MTR** There is no station in downtown Aberdeen, but the South Island Line runs from Admiralty to Ap Lei Chau (South Horizons and Lei Tung stations), Wong Chuk Hang and Ocean Park.

➡ **Bus for Shek O** Bus 9 from Shau Kei Wan MTR station (exit A3).

➡ **Bus for Stanley** Buses 6A, 6X and 260 go to **Stanley Market Bus Terminus** (赤柱市集巴士總站; Map p313; cnr Stanley Village Rd & Stanley Beach Rd) from Central (below Exchange Sq). They also stop at Deep Water Bay. **Minibus 40** (Map p313; Stanley Village; ⊘24hr) also runs from Jardine's Bazaar (Causeway Bay).

➡ **Bus for Aberdeen** Buses 73 and 973 from Stanley call at Aberdeen Main St. Bus 107 from Kowloon Bay stops at **Aberdeen Bus Terminus** (香港仔巴士總站; Map p312; btwn Aberdeen Praya Rd & Wu Nam St). **Shum Wan Bus Terminus** (深灣道巴士站, 雅濤閣裡; Map p312; inside Broadview Court) is where buses depart for Causeway Bay and Central.

➡ **Bus for Pok Fu Lam** Bus 40 from Wan Chai Pier. Buses 7, 90B and 91 link Pok Fu Lam with Aberdeen Praya Rd.

Lonely Planet's Top Tip

The beaches on the south side of Hong Kong are best enjoyed on weekdays when you can have them to yourself. The discreet St Stephen's Beach (p128) boasts fine water quality and near-perfect sunset views.

◉ Best Spots for Fresh Air

➡ Dragon's Back (p131)
➡ Tai Tam Waterworks Heritage Trail (p131)
➡ Shek O Beach (p128)
➡ Waterfall Bay Park (p126)
➡ Aberdeen Promenade (p124)
➡ Deep Water Bay (p127)

For reviews, see p124.➡

✖ Best Places to Eat

➡ Ap Lei Chau Market Cooked Food Centre (p129)
➡ Aberdeen Fish Market Yee Hope Seafood (p128)
➡ Amalfitana (p129)
➡ Lighthouse (p129)
➡ Nam Long Shan Road Cooked Food Market (p128)

For reviews, see p128.➡

🍷 Best Places to Drink

➡ Komune (p130)
➡ Ben's Back Beach Bar (p130)

For reviews, see p130.➡

ABERDEEN & SOUTH HONG KONG ISLAND

◉ SIGHTS

The southern part of Hong Kong Island lays claim to Hong Kong's richest fishing culture. You'll see the homes, markets and temples, both traditional and modern, of Hong Kong's 'people of the water'. Aberdeen Harbour is widely believed to be what gave Hong Kong its name. Its Cantonese name, 'Heung Gong Zai', translates as 'Little Hong Kong' or 'Little Fragrant Harbour'. It was here that incense trees from the New Territories were brought via Tsim Sha Tsui for export to China, lending the harbour a lingering perfume.

◉ Aberdeen

ABERDEEN DOWNTOWN   AREA

Map p312 (香港仔市中心; M Wong Chuk Hang, exit B) Downtown Aberdeen's minibus-thronged streets may seem little different from other small suburban towns in Hong Kong. But dried seafood shops are in abundance here and snippets of Tanka dialect can be overheard. Locals are known to throw rowdy banquets at the old-fashioned restaurants here after dragon boat races. For most outsiders though, it's where you pass to reach Aberdeen Promenade, and board the sampan to Ap Lei Chau. Buses to/from Central, Causeway Bay and other parts of Hong Kong Island stop here as well.

★ ABERDEEN PROMENADE   WATERFRONT

Map p312 (香港仔海濱公園; Aberdeen Praya Rd; ☐70, 72, 72; M Wong Chuk Hang, exit B) **FREE** Tree-lined Aberdeen Promenade runs from west to east on Aberdeen Praya Rd across the water from Ap Lei Chau. On its western end is sprawling **Aberdeen Wholesale Fish Market** (香港仔魚市場; Map p312) with its industrial-strength water tanks teeming with marine life. It's pungent and grimy, but 100% Hong Kong. Before reaching the market, you'll pass berthed house boats and seafood-processing vessels. (We detected a karaoke parlour or two as well.)

★ YOUNG MASTER BREWERY   BREWERY

Map p312 (少爺麥啤; www.youngmasterales.com; Ground fl, Sungib Industrial Centre, 53 Wong Chuk Hang Rd, Wong Chuk Hang; tour HK$100; ☺9am-6pm Mon-Sat, closed Sun; M Wong Chuk Hang, exit A2) Young Master Ales has moved to a new street-level location in Wong Chuk Hang. Merchandise is sold in the front, while at the back, the brewing system, ageing barrels, and bottling line whir, hiss and grind away. The small-batch, nonfiltered, chemical-free beers range from crisp to robust, and have funky names inspired by Hong Kong pop culture like fake blood, a tribute to kung fu movies. Book online for the Saturday hour-long guided tours (English 1pm, Cantonese 4pm). You cannot imbibe on the premises, but you can buy beer to take away.

The brand name is a playfully nostalgic tribute to a bygone era in Hong Kong, then still under British rule, when industries such as textile, plastics and electronics were taking off.

OCEAN PARK   AMUSEMENT PARK

(海洋公園; ☑852 3923 2323; www.oceanpark.com.hk; Ocean Park Rd; adult/child 3-11yr HK$385/193; ☺10am-7.30pm; ♿; M Ocean Park) Despite the crowd-pulling powers of Disneyland on Lantau, Ocean Park remains the most popular theme park in Hong Kong. Constant expansion, new rides and thrills, and the presence of four giant pandas and two rare red pandas ensure the park remains a huge draw for families. Be aware that in part of the park, Marine World, cetaceans are kept in captivity and performances involving dolphins and orcas are a feature, which scientific studies suggest is harmful to these animals. Ocean Park is undergoing a mega expansion that will see the launch of the 3716-sq-metre Tai Shue Wan Water World in 2019/20.

The park is divided into two main sections. The main entrance is on the Waterfront (lowland) side and is linked to the main section on the Summit (headland) via a scenic cable car ride and a marine-themed funicular train called the Ocean Express.

The major attractions at the Waterfront are Amazing Asian Animals and Aqua City. The Grand Aquarium, which boasts the world's largest aquarium dome, is home to 5000 fish representing over 400 species. Old Hong Kong is a replica of the old buildings that once graced Wan Chai and older parts of Kowloon. To the north is Whiskers Harbour, which thrives on an assortment of kid-oriented rides.

On the Summit, Thrill Mountain has plenty of white-knuckle rides, such as the celebrated roller coaster, Hair Raiser. Meanwhile, the Chinese Sturgeon Aquarium showcases a living gift from the mainland.

TIN HAU TEMPLE — TEMPLE

Map p312 (天后廟; 182 Aberdeen Main Rd; ☺8am-5pm; 🚌70) Caught between a church and the thoroughfare, this temple has an eclectic deity collection, two moon gates and hovering incense coils. The stone columns, ridge ornaments featuring a legendary female warrior, and copper bell (rumoured to have been salvaged from the seabed by a fisher) are Qing dynasty, but the dragon-and-phoenix murals look decidedly 20th century. The temple worships the Goddess of the Sea, with nods to Wong Tai Sin, wish-granter extraordinaire.

OLD HOUSE NO. 10 — VILLAGE

(黃竹坑新圍10號; ☺9am-1pm & 2-5pm Sat & Sun; 🚌260, 6A, 6X, 73, 973, 65) History buffs may be interested to know that there's an ancient village close to Ocean Park. Wong Chuk Hang 'San Wai' ('New Village'), founded in the 1860s, is the branch of a 200-year-old 'old village'. The old village still stands, close to Aberdeen Tunnel, but has been reduced to a tiny shanty town of sorts. The highlight of New Village is a graded century-old vernacular residence with attractive clay sculptures of carp, flowers, bats and dragons. The house is open on Saturday, Sunday and public holidays. Get off the bus at Wong Chuk Hang San Wai (黃竹坑新圍村), the same stop you would for Ocean Park, or take exit C from Ocean Park metro station.

⦿ Ap Lei Chau

AP LEI CHAU — AREA

Map p312 (鴨脷洲) Ap Lei Chau retains some of its sleepy charm despite developments spurred by the opening of the South Island MTR line. There are shipyards along its shore, warehouses in the south around Horizon Plaza (p131), low-rise homes, gritty public housing built in the '70s and '80s to rehouse the boat-dwelling community, and dozens of newly built gleaming high-rises to exploit the 'sea view' premium. Around Ap Lei Chau Main St you'll find machinery workshops, seafood galore and the highly recommended Cooked Food Centre (p129). Ap Lei Chau is served by the South Horizons and Lei Tung stations.

HUNG SHING TEMPLE — TAOIST TEMPLE

Map p312 (洪聖古廟; Hung Shing St; ☺8am-5pm; Ⓜ Lei Tung, exit A1) Renovated many times since it was built in 1773 by local fishermen, Ap Lei Chau's major temple is dedicated to Hung Shing, the protector of seafarers. Its major features are a sea-facing orientation (which is believed to bring good feng shui), the fine Shiwan figurines on the roof ridges (which denote its significance), and the two timber 'dragon poles' in its forecourt, which are said to counter the 'death-like aura' of the Aberdeen Police Station across the water.

AP LEI CHAU WATERFRONT PROMENADE — WATERFRONT

Map p312 (鴨脷洲海濱長廊; Ⓜ Lei Tung, exit A1) Directly facing Aberdeen Promenade across the typhoon shelter, Ap Lei Chau Waterfront Promenade is where commuter ferries from Aberdeen stop. People in the neighbourhood come here to fish in the evening. It has a pleasant walking trail and a plaza where you'll find the old Hung Shing Temple.

⦿ Pok Fu Lam

POK FU LAM VILLAGE — VILLAGE

(薄扶林村; ☎ Ms So 852 6199 9473; www.pflv archives.org.hk; 🚌7, 40, 40M, 90B, 91) Built on a sloping hillside, peaceful Pok Fu Lam Village looks like a shanty town compared to the high-density middle-class residences around it. Though no stunner, it's valued by historians not only for the famous fire dragon dance at the Mid-Autumn Festival, but equally for its ties to Hong Kong's dairy industry. Other highlights include Béthanie and Li Ling Pagoda.

As the sites are scattered, the best way to see them all is to join a walking tour. Four-hour English tours are available upon request for about HK$700 per person. Email or call two weeks ahead to book.

BÉTHANIE — HISTORIC BUILDING

(伯大尼; ☎852 2584 8918; www.hkapa.edu/ about/getting-here/; 139 Pok Fu Lam Rd; HK$25; ☺11am-6pm Mon-Sat, from noon Sun; 🚌7, 40, 40M, 90B, 91) Perched on hilly Pok Fu Lam, a college and residential area northwest of Aberdeen, this beautiful restoration is a highlight in this part of town. The complex, which now houses a film school, was built by the French Mission in 1875 as a sanatorium for priests from all over Asia to rest and recover from tropical diseases before they returned to their missions.

NEW LIFE IN WONG CHUK HANG

Spurred by the opening of the MTR South Island Line and Wong Chuk Hang station, this area is gentrifying into a hip enclave of galleries, cafes and breweries, which have taken up residence in old factories and warehouses. The Special Administrative Region's homegrown Young Master Brewery (p124) is now based here and there's also **Black Kite Brewery** (Map p312; www.blackkite.hk; 11B Derrick Industrial Building, 49 Wong Chuk Hang Rd; tour HK$100; ☉11am-6pm Tue-Sat; Ⓜ Wong Chuk Hang, exit A2) on the 11th floor of an industrial building, which offers two-hour tours in English (email to book). **Sensory Zero** (感味宮匠; Map p312; ☑853 2511 6011; www.sensoryzero.com; Shop G01, One Island South, 2 Heung Yip Rd; lunch set HK$85-165; ☉8am-8pm; Ⓟ❄🛜; Ⓜ Wong Chuk Hang, exit A2), a warehouse coffee roastery with exposed pipes and bare walls, makes a good pit stop for Japanese-inspired eats at long communal tables.

Art is one of the area's big attractions. Our pick of the burgeoning gallery scene:

Empty Gallery (Map p312; ☑852 2563 3396; www.emptygallery.com; 18th & 19th fl, Grand Marine Centre, 3 Yue Fung St, Tin Wan; ☉11am-7pm Tue-Sat) More than 420 sq metres of black-box space, entered via a car park, favouring experimental works from established and emerging artists.

de Sarthe (Map p312; ☑852 2167 8896; www.desarthe.com/about.html; 20th fl, Global Trade Square, 21 Wong Chuk Hang Rd; ☉11am-7pm Tue-Sat; Ⓜ Wong Chuk Hang, exit A2) This 900-sq-metre French gallery has exhibited an array of western and Asia artists, from French impressionists and post-war artists to contemporary and emerging talent.

Rossi & Rossi (Map p312; ☑852 3575 9417; www.rossirossi.com; 3rd floor, unit C, Yally Industrial Building, 6 Yip Fat St; ☉11am-6pm Tue-Sat; Ⓜ Wong Chuk Hang, exit A2) Specialises in Asian art, particularly from India, the Himalaya and Southeast Asia, both classical and contemporary; Tibetan art is a forte.

Blindspot Gallery (刺點畫廊; Map p312; ☑852 2517 6238; www.blindspotgallery.com; 15th fl, Po Chai Industrial Bldg, 28 Wong Chuk Hang Rd, Aberdeen; ☉10am-6pm Tue-Sat, by appointment only Sun & Mon; Ⓜ Wong Chuk Hang, exit A2) Arguably one of the best places to acquaint yourself with Hong Kong and Asian photography and video, including works by Stanley Wong, Ken Kitano and Maleonn.

Pékin Fine Arts (北京藝門畫廊; Map p312; ☑852 2177 6190; www.pekinfinearts.com; 16F Union Industrial Bldg, 48 Wong Chuk Hang Rd, Aberdeen; ☉10am-6pm Tue-Sun; Ⓜ Wong Chuk Hang, exit A2) At this small Hong Kong outpost of the Běijīng-based gallery, hidden deep within a gritty industrial building, visitors can expect an eclectic selection of pieces by Chinese contemporary artists.

The 30-minute guided tour includes a visit to the neo-Gothic Béthanie Chapel, a theatre in the two octagonal Dairy Farm cow sheds, and a tiny museum housed in a converted wine cellar, which displays the history of the mission. Tours are run hourly and two are in English. It's wise to call ahead, as some venues may not be accessible if they've been hired. The nearest bus stop is at the junction of Pok Fu Lam Reservoir and Pok Fu Lam Rd.

WATERFALL BAY PARK   PARK

(瀑布灣公園; Waterfall Bay Rd; 🚌4, 970, minibus 69) The cascade and the bay here are serene and quite lovely. Barges and fishing junks streak the waters; Lamma is surpris-

ingly near; figurines of gods – both Chinese and Hindu – stand on rocks. Overlooking the sea is a pillbox from WWII when British troops used Aberdeen as a bunker in the battle against the Japanese. The bay is also where the fire dragon of Pok Fu Lam village spectacularly enters the water in the finale of the Mid-Autumn Festival dance.

It was the availability of potable water at Waterfall Bay that first drew the attention of the British and Europeans en route to other ports in Asia, and when they asked the locals the name of the place, they were told 'Heung Gong', ie 'Hong Kong'.

Take Wah Fu Estate–bound buses like routes 4 and 970. Disembark at Wah Fu Commercial Complex (華富商場). Follow

Waterfall Bay Rd for 10 minutes and you'll see Waterfall Bay Park. Once inside, head right in the direction of the towering Residence Bel-Air. You'll see two flights of stairs; the ones descending takes you to the bay.

CYBERPORT WATERFRONT PARK   PARK
(數碼港公園; Telegraph Bay, 100 Cyberport Rd, Cyberport; ⏰7am-11pm) Sandwiched between luxury residences and the sea, this beautiful park has lots of lawns for picnics, a seafront jogging trail, a cycling trail, and trees for shady reading. Local residents come here to walk their dogs and relax; people are friendly and everyone smiles at everyone else.

⊙ Deep Water & Repulse Bays

DEEP WATER BAY   BEACH
(深水灣; 🚌6, 6A, 6X, 260) A quiet little inlet with a beach flanked by shade trees, Deep Water Bay is a few kilometres northwest of Repulse Bay. There is a handful of places to eat and have a drink, and some barbecue pits at the southern end of the beach. If you want a dip in the water, this spot is usually less crowded than Repulse Bay. The beach is a centre for wakeboarding.

REPULSE BAY   BEACH
(淺水灣; 🚌6, 6A, 6X, 260) The long beach with tawny sand at Repulse Bay is visited by Chinese tourist groups year-round and, needless to say, is packed on weekends in summer. It's a good place if you like people-watching. The beach has showers and changing rooms and shade trees at the roadside, but the water is pretty murky.

Middle Bay (中灣) and South Bay (南灣), about 10 and 30 minutes to the south respectively, have beaches that are much less crowded. Middle Bay is popular with gay beachgoers, while French expats are drawn to South Bay.

KWUN YAM SHRINE   TAOIST TEMPLE
(觀音廟; 🚌6, 6A, 6X, 260) Towards the southeast end of Repulse Bay beach is a colourful shrine dedicated to Kwun Yam, the Goddess of Mercy. In the surrounding area, you'll find an assembly of deities and figures – goldfish, rams, the money god, and statues of Tin Hau – expressed in gloriously garish cartoon kitsch. Most of the statues were commissioned by local personalities and businessmen in the 1970s.

⊙ Stanley

STANLEY   VILLAGE
Map p313 (赤柱) This crowd-pleaser is best visited on weekdays. **Stanley Market** (赤柱市集; Map p313; Stanley Village Rd; ⏰9am-6pm; 🚌6, 6A, 6X, 260) is a maze of alleyways that has bargain clothing (haggling is a must!), while **Stanley Main Beach** (赤柱正灘; Map p313; 🚌6A, 14) is for beach-bumming and windsurfing. With graves dating back to 1841, **Stanley Military Cemetery** (赤柱軍人墳場; ☎852 2557 3498; Wong Ma Kok Rd; ⏰8am-5pm; 🚌14, 6A), 500m south of the market, is worth a visit.

ST STEPHEN'S COLLEGE HERITAGE TRAIL   HISTORIC SITE
Map p313 (聖士提反書院文物徑; ☎852 2813 0360; www.ssc.edu.hk/ssctrail/eng; 22 Tung Tau Wan Rd; 🚌6, 6A, 6X, 260) **FREE** WWII history buffs can visit the beautiful campus of St Stephen's College, which sits right next to Stanley Military Cemetery. Founded in 1903, the school was turned into an emergency military hospital on the eve of the Japanese invasion of Hong Kong in 1941 and became an internment camp after the city fell. On Christmas Eve in 1941, Japanese soldiers stormed into the building and killed 56 British and Canadian soldiers who were still wounded in their beds. The austere chapel was built in 1950 on the highest point of the campus in memory of the war victims. The austere chapel was built in 1950 on the highest point of the campus in memory of the war victims. Admission to the trail is by a two-hour guided tour only, run by students who take you to eight sites on the campus. Reserve between one and three months in advance via the website.

PAT KAN UK

At the southern end of Stanley Main St is a row of eight one-storey houses with red bricks and green doors. Quaint and eye-catching, they sit facing the sea in the shade of old trees like the elderly folks who still live in them. These were relocation homes in the 1930s when the government took over farmland to build barracks for better coastal defence in Stanley.

Pat Kan Uk (八間屋) is a transliteration of the Cantonese for 'eight houses'.

ST STEPHEN'S BEACH
BEACH

(聖士提反灣泳灘; 🚌6A, 14) A short walk south of Stanley village is this great little bolt-hole that handily comes with a cafe, showers and changing rooms. In summer you can hire windsurfing boards and kayaks from the water-sports centre.

MURRAY HOUSE
HISTORIC BUILDING

Map p313 (美利樓; Stanley Bay; 🚌6, 6A, 6X, 260) Across the bay from Stanley Main St stands this three-storey colonnaded affair. Built in 1846 as officers' quarters, it took pride of place in Central, on the spot where the Bank of China Tower now stands, for almost 150 years until 1982. It was re-erected here stone by stone and opened in 2001. Today it's home to a number of restaurants, many with lovely sea views.

👁 Shek O

SHEK O BEACH
BEACH

(石澳; 🚌9 from Shau Kei Wan MTR, exit A3) Shek O beach has a large expanse of sand, shady trees to the rear, showers, changing facilities and lockers for rent. It's not quiet by any means, except on typhoon days, but the laid-back beach framed by rocky cliffs is quite pleasant.

BIG WAVE BAY
BEACH

(大浪灣; Ⓜ Shau Kei Wan, exit A3, Shek O-bound minibus) This fine, often deserted beach located 2km to the north of Shek O is little known outside the surfing community. To get there, follow the road north out of town, travel past the 18-hole Shek O Golf & Country Club, then turn east at the roundabout

and keep going until the road ends. One of eight prehistoric rock carvings discovered in Hong Kong is located on the headland above Big Wave Bay.

✕ EATING

✕ Aberdeen

NAM LONG SHAN ROAD COOKED FOOD MARKET
HAWKER $

Map p312 (南朗山道熟食市場; 1 Nam Long Shan Rd, Wong Chuk Hang; meals from HK$60; Ⓜ Wong Chuk Hang, exit B) This two-storey indoor market is what remains of a working-class community after its affiliated housing estate was razed. The fan-cooled, fluorescent-lit market is full of affordable *cha chaan tang* (teahouses) and stir-fry hawkers. Business is thriving as residents from the new swanky high-rises nearby come for meals.

★ ABERDEEN FISH MARKET YEE HOPE SEAFOOD RESTAURANT
CANTONESE, SEAFOOD $$

Map p312 (香港仔魚市場二合海鮮餐廳; ☏852 2177 7872, 852 5167 1819; 102 Shek Pai Wan Rd; meals from $350; ⊗4am-2.30pm; 🚌107, Ⓜ Wong Chuk Hang, exit B) Hidden in Hong Kong's only wholesale fish market, this understated eatery run by fishers is an in-the-know place for ultrafresh seafood. There's no menu, but tell them your budget and they'll source the best sea creatures available, including ones not often seen in restaurants, and apply their Midas touch to them.

BEACH BARBECUE, HONG KONG–STYLE

Show up at any Hong Kong beach or country park on a weekend and you'll see dozens, if not hundreds, of locals enthusiastically brandishing long sharp metal forks. Ancient Hong Kong ritual? Sort of. Here in the Special Administrative Region (SAR), barbecue parties at public beaches and parks replace the kind of indoor or backyard entertaining done in countries where the average home size is larger. Throwing your own barbecue is surprisingly easy and makes for a great day out. Just show up early enough to claim a pit in a public area.

Some of our favourite free public barbecue spots:

Shek O Beach

St Stephen's Beach

Silvermine Bay Beach at Mui Wo in Lantau (Map p184; 🚢Mui Wo)

Lo So Shing Beach in Lamma (蘆鬚城; Map p180; 🚢Yung Shue Wan)

Lion Rock Country Park (望夫石; Lion Rock Country Park; Ⓜ Tai Wai)

The restaurant serves as a canteen for the fishers in the market and you'll see men in gumboots dropping in for beer, Hong Kong–style French toast and other *cha chaan tang* (teahouse) staples throughout the day. Walk-in customers can do the same. There's no English sign; look for the nondescript one-storey yellow building with a green roof at the end of the fish market.

You'll need a Cantonese-speaking friend to help you if you'd like to book a table; organise at least two days in advance (two weeks for weekends).

JUMBO KINGDOM FLOATING RESTAURANT CANTONESE $$

Map p312 (珍寶海鮮舫; ☎852 2553 9111; www.jumbo.com.hk; Shum Wan Pier Dr, Wong Chuk Hang; meals from HK$200; ⊙11am-11.30pm Mon-Sat, from 9am Sun; ❋ ♿; ☎90 from Central, Ⓜ Wong Chuk Hang, exit B) Recently refurbished, Jumbo Kingdom comprises two restaurants: Jumbo Floating Restaurant and Tai Pak Floating Restaurant. The three-storey 'floating' extravaganzas (they're fastened by concrete) look like Běijīng's Imperial Palace crossbred with Macau's Casino Lisboa – so kitsch they're fun. Eschew the overpriced Dragon Court on the 2nd floor and head to the 3rd floor for dim sum.

✗ Ap Lei Chau

★ AP LEI CHAU MARKET COOKED FOOD CENTRE SEAFOOD $

Map p312 (鴨利洲市政大廈; 1st fl, Ap Lei Chau Municipal Services Bldg, 8 Hung Shing St; dishes HK$45-100; ☐ minibus 36X from Lee Garden Rd, Causeway Bay, Ⓜ Lei Tung, exit A1) Above an indoor market, *dai pai dong* (food stall) operators cook up a storm in a sprawling hall littered with folding tables and plastic chairs. **Pak Kee** (柏記; ☎852 2555 2984; seafood meals from HK$160; ⊙6-10.30pm) and **Chu Kee** (珠記; ☎852 2555 2052; seafood meals from HK$180; ⊙6pm-midnight) offer simple but tasty seafood dishes. You can also buy seafood from the wet market downstairs and pay for it to be cooked the way you want. It's packed and noisy on weekends.

Every evening fishers and dragon boaters come here for the cheap beer and food. The market is served by the metro or you can reach it from Aberdeen Promenade by taking a sampan.

TREE CAFE CAFE $

Map p312 (☎852 2870 1582; www.tree.com.hk/cafe; 28th fl Horizon Plaza, 2 Lee Wing St; meals from HK$80; ⊙10.30am-7pm; ♿; ☎90 from Central, Ⓜ South Horizon, exit C) The Horizon Plaza shopping mall has a hundred shops, so if you're feeling peckish after a shopping spree, why not rest your legs in this eco-chic cafe hidden in the eponymous furniture shop on the very top floor of the building? The coffee is good and there is a play area for the little ones.

✗ Repulse Bay

AMALFITANA PIZZA $

(☎852 2388 7787; www.amalfitana.hk; Shop 105, Ground fl, The Pulse, 28 Beach Rd; pizzas HK$140-250; ⊙noon-10.30pm; ❋ ✈ ♿; ☎40, 90, 6X) Open frontage and its location a flip-flop's throw from the beach mean Amalfitana's delicious Italian-style pizzas can be enjoyed between dips in the water. Toppings are classic, with four 'bambino' versions for the little ones. You can order to take away too.

LIGHTHOUSE EUROPEAN $$

(☎852 2889 5939; www.facebook.com/hkthelighthouse; Shop 303, Level 3, The Pulse, 28 Beach Rd; meals/brunch from HK$380/428; ⊙noon-3.30pm Wed-Fri, 11.30am-5.30pm Sat & Sun; ❋ ♿; ☎40, 90, 6X) At this marine-themed bistro, a light-brown-and-blue palette complements sea views through floor-to-ceiling windows. The simply curated menu covers all the popular seafood items – fresh oysters, salt-crusted sea-bass, mussels with French fries, even clam chowder and fish and chips – all executed with finesse by a chef from Britanny.

VERANDAH INTERNATIONAL $$$

(露台餐廳; ☎852 2292 2822; www.therepulsebay.com; 1st fl, 109 Repulse Bay Rd; meals from HK$600; ⊙noon-2.30pm, 3-5.30pm & 7-10.30pm Wed-Sat, 11am-3pm, 3.30-5.30pm & 7-10.30pm Sun; ☎6, 6A, 6X, 260) A meal in the grand Verandah, run by the Peninsula, is a special occasion indeed. The large restaurant is dripping with colonial nostalgia, what with the grand piano at the entrance, the wooden fans dangling from the ceiling, and the marble staircases with wooden banisters.

The Sunday brunch is famous (HK$700) and the afternoon tea (from HK$300 per person) is the best this side of Hong Kong Island. Book ahead.

ABERDEEN & SOUTH HONG KONG ISLAND EATING

LIMEWOOD
INTERNATIONAL

(☎852 2866 8668; www.limewood.hk; Shops 103 & 104, 1F, The Pulse, 28 Beach Rd; ⏱lunch noon 2.30pm Mon-Wed, to 4pm Thu-Sun, dinner 6-10.30pm Mon-Sat, to 9.30pm Sun; ❓40, 90, 6X) Limewood has an island-themed menu that works well, though the fruit-laced fusion food may be a tad predictable. Fish tacos and slow-cooked beef ribs are concisely seasoned; and the guacamole with pork crackling, fish roe and sea urchin is a surprise. You can chill on the wooden stools near the front or rest your sunburnt thighs on a plush banquette with colourful cushions.

✖ Stanley

SEI YIK
CANTONESE $

Map p313 (泗益; ☎852 2813 0507; 2 Stanley Market St; meals from HK$30; ⏱6am-4pm Wed-Mon; ❓6, 6A, 6X, 66) Weekenders flock to this small tin-roofed *dai pai dong* (food stall), opposite the Stanley Municipal Building, for its fluffy Hong Kong–style French toast with *kaya* (coconut jam). There's no English sign; look for the long queue of pilgrims and the piles of fruits that hide the entrance.

TOBY INN
CANTONESE, DIM SUM $

Map p313 (赤柱酒家; ☎852 2813 2880; U1-U2, 126 Stanley Main St; mains HK$80-240, dim sum HK$17-25; ⏱5.30am-10.30pm; ❓6, 6A, 6X, 260) This humble place is Stanley's neighbourhood restaurant, with elderly people dropping in for dim sum at the crack of dawn, dragon boaters feasting on good-value seafood after practice, and families coming in for simple dishes throughout the day.

🍷 DRINKING & NIGHTLIFE

KOMUNE
ROOFTOP BAR

Map p312 (www.komune.com.hk; 64 Wong Chuk Hang Rd; ⏱6.30am-11pm; 🚇Wong Chuk Hang, exit A2) Komune serves beer, bubbles and cocktails, alongside Latin American– and Asian-inspired nibbles on the roof of the Ovolo Southside (p228). Sweeping views are a bonus. Happy hour is 3pm to 7pm.

BEN'S BACK BEACH BAR
BAR

(石澳風帆會; ☎852 2809 2268; Shek O back beach, 273 Shek O Village; ⏱7pm-midnight Thu & Fri, from 11am Sat & Sun; ❓9 from Shau Kei Wan MTR, exit A3) Hidden on Shek O's quiet back beach, Ben's is the neighbourhood watering hole where everyone knows everyone else. You'll find villagers, resident urbanites, and expats sipping cold brews to reggae beats and the sound of the lapping waves. A sea-facing shrine stands next to this rugged ensemble.

From Shek O bus terminal, turn right into the path that leads to an abandoned school and a health centre. The beach is at the end of the path.

DELANEY'S
PUB

(☎852 2677 1126; Shop 314, The Arcade, 100 Cyberport Rd, Pok Fu Lam; ⏱noon-10pm Mon-Thu, 11.30am-late Fri & Sat; 🐾; ❓30X, 42C, 73, 73P, 107P, 970) The clientele at this far-flung branch of the Irish pub are mostly folks from nearby offices and luxury residences. The terrace with giant parasols and ocean views is lively on weekends. While the grown-ups sip champagne or watch live sports on the large screens, young ones can enjoy themselves in the children's play area.

Happy hour is 4pm to 8pm. If you prefer taking the metro, ride to Wong Chuk Hang station and change to minibus 69A.

🛍 SHOPPING

The old warehouses dotting Aberdeen's Wong Chuk Hang offer everything from modern art to made in Hong Kong beer and designer bikes, while those in the southern tip of Ap Lei Chau have designer chairs and off-season fashion. If dried seafood is what you're after, downtown Aberdeen and the area around Ap Lei Chau Main St are the best places to look. Stanley Market is a one-stop shop for casual wear and Chinese-themed paraphernalia.

★G.O.D.
CLOTHING, HOUSEWARES

Map p313 (Goods of Desire; ☎852 2673 0071; www.god.com.hk; Shop 105, Stanley Plaza, 22-23 Carmel Rd, Stanley; ⏱10.30am-8pm Mon-Fri, to 9pm Sat & Sun; ❓6, 6A, 6X, 260) One of the coolest born in Hong Kong shops around, G.O.D. does irreverent takes on classic Hong Kong iconography. Think mobile-phone covers printed with pictures of Hong Kong housing blocks, light fixtures resembling the ones in old-fashioned wet markets, and pillows covered in lucky koi print. There are a handful of G.O.D. shops in town, but this is one of the biggest.

★ HORIZON PLAZA | MALL

Map p312 (新海怡廣場; www.horizonplazahk. com; 2 Lee Wing St, Ap Lei Chau; ◷10am-7pm; Ⓜ South Horizons, exit C) Tucked away on the southern coast of Ap Lei Chau, this enormous outlet housed in a converted factory building contains 100 shops over 25 storeys. Most locals come here to buy furniture, but you'll also find Alexander McQueen on offer and Jimmy Choos at knock-down prices. Heaps of kiddies' stuff as well, from books and toys to clothing and furniture.

★ EDIT X EDITECTURE | CLOTHING

Map p312 (☑852 2548 8682; www.editecture. com; 10F, Unit B, Shui Ki Industrial Bldg, 18 Wong Chuk Hang Rd, Wong Chuk Hang) This large office-shop-showroom belongs to two friends who have won awards designing everything from restaurants to clothes. The highlight here is the edgy streetwear under the house brand, Edit. The shop also has a library and hosts design events. A space to watch.

🏃 SPORTS & ACTIVITIES

Seven beaches, two golf courses, numerous hiking trails, and a plethora of water-sport opportunities all close to the urban centre mean you can always keep the endorphins flowing in this neighbourhood.

★ DRAGON'S BACK | HIKING

(龍脊) The city's most famous trail begins in a forest, soars to a mountain ridge evoking a dragon's spine, before dipping to fine sands and surf. Though Hong Kong has no shortage of visually and culturally superior trails, 8.5km Dragon's Back is relatively easy to access. And it *is* impressive. On days when the golf greens, the sea and the luxury homes are all gleaming in the sun, dotted with cloud shadow, it's downright surreal.

Bus 9 and minibuses with the 'Shek O' sign depart from Shau Kei Wan Bus Terminus, right next to exit A of Shau Kei Wan MTR station. Alight at the trail head – To Tei Wan (土地灣) on Shek O Rd.

★ TAI TAM WATERWORKS HERITAGE TRAIL | HIKING

(大潭水務文物徑) This scenic 5km trail runs past reservoirs and a handsome collection of 20 historic waterworks structures – feats of Victorian utilitarian engineering that include bridges, aqueducts, valve houses, pumping stations and dams, many still working.

The trail, which ends at Tai Tam Tuk Raw Water Pumping Station, takes about two hours. Enter at Wong Nai Chung Gap near the luxury flats of Hong Kong Parkview, or at the junction of Tai Tam Rd and Tai Tam Reservoir Rd. On weekends you'll see residents taking a walk with their dogs, kids, maids, chauffeurs and nannies.

From Admiralty MTR station, bus 6 takes you to Wong Nai Chung Reservoir. Walk east along Tai Tam Reservoir Rd.

HONG KONG AQUABOUND CENTRE | WATER SPORTS

Map p313 (☑852 8211 3876; www.aquabound. com.hk; Stanley Main Beach, Stanley; kayak rental per hour HK$80; ◷9am-6.30pm; ☐6A, 14) You can rent kayaks, stand-up paddle boards, as well equipment for windsurfing and wakeboarding at this place on Stanley Main Beach. You can also hire an instructor to teach you or your child. Prices vary according to class size. Make contact online to see rates, enquire for details or book.

HONG KONG YACHTING | BOATING

Map p312 (☑852 2526 0151; www.hongkong-yachting.com; 18A Gee Chang Hong Centre, 65 Wong Chuk Hang Rd, Aberdeen; junk-boat party per person from HK$680; ◷9am-6pm Mon-Sat; ☐4C, 90) Hong Kong Yachting has vessels you can hire from Aberdeen Harbour to various destinations in Hong Kong and the outlying islands. Through it, you can also buy tickets for a harbour tour or throw a boat party for your friends.

Kowloon

TSIM SHA TSUI | YAU MA TEI | MONG KOK | SHAM SHUI PO | NEW KOWLOON

Neighbourhood Top Five

1 **Symphony of Lights** (p151) Seeing the Hong Kong skyline ablaze at this nightly light show on both sides of Victoria Harbour.

2 **Peninsula Lobby** (p230) Enjoying scones and a cup of Earl Grey in the palatial lobby of the 'Pen', while serenaded by a string quartet.

3 **Temple Street Night Market** (p135) Soaking up the intoxicating mix of commerce, culture and street food at Hong Kong's liveliest night market.

4 **Sik Sik Yuen Wong Tai Sin Temple** (p136) Witnessing a Taoist ceremony or having your fortune told

at this thriving spiritual complex.

5 **Chi Lin Nunnery** (p137) Wandering the serene garden surrounds of this Buddhist enclave and its neighbouring ornamental park.

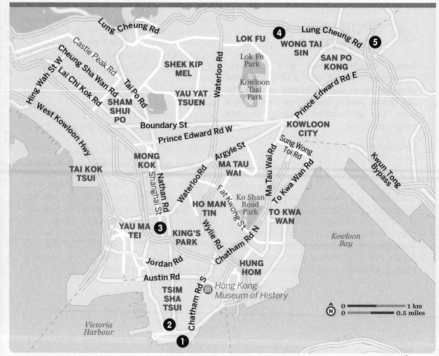

For more detail of this area see Maps p314, p316, p318 and p319 ➡

Explore Kowloon

Start your day by spending a couple of hours at the Museum of History, then take a leisurely half-hour stroll to the Star Ferry Concourse via the scenic Tsim Sha Tsui East Promenade, which in early 2019 completed a three-year refurbishment. Check out the sights along the way, such as the Cultural Centre and the clock tower, and follow up with lunch at an Indian or Shanghainese restaurant.

Walk to Yau Ma Tei, stopping at St Andrew's Church and Kowloon British School. Spend an hour or so exploring Tin Hau Temple, the Jade Market and Shanghai St. Then visit Sham Shui Po and the Apliu Street Flea Market; and if there's time, go to Diamond Hill to immerse yourself in the tranquillity of Chi Lin Nunnery.

Have dinner at one of the roadside stalls in Yau Ma Tei, then it's on to the Temple Street Night Market. Wrap up your day with drinks in Tsim Sha Tsui (TST).

Local Life

➜ **Hang-out** Film buffs and the artsy crowd like to chill on the upper floor of Mido Café (p145).

➜ **Shopping** Fashionistas seek affordable additions to their wardrobes at the Rise Shopping Arcade (p152) and street-level shops at Granville Circuit.

➜ **Singalong parlours** College kids like to celebrate birthdays in Yau Ma Tei's singalong parlours, such as Canton Singing House (p150).

Getting There & Away

➜ **Boat** For Macau Ferries, the China Ferry Terminal is on Canton Rd (Tsim Sha Tsui). Star Ferries leave from the Star Ferry Pier at the western end of Salisbury Rd.

➜ **Bus** Buses leave from the Star Ferry Bus Terminal for points across Kowloon, Hong Kong Island and the New Territories. Useful routes include N21 (airport), 5A (Kowloon City) and 8 (Kowloon Station). Eternal East Cross Border Coach (p261) buses leave from various points in Tsim Sha Tsui.

Lonely Planet's Top Tip

Kowloon has a diverse eating scene. Chungking Mansions has the best Indian grocery stores and kitchens; Kimberley St and Austin Ave are good for Korean food and minimarts; the streets around Temple Street Night Market have Nepalese; and try Kowloon City for Thai.

Best Places to Eat

➜ Chi Lin Vegetarian (p146)
➜ Yè Shanghai (p144)
➜ Tim Ho Wan (p146)
➜ Din Tai Fung (p144)
➜ Kung Wo Tofu Factory (p146)
➜ Mido Café (p145)

For reviews, see p143.➜

Best Places to Drink

➜ Kowloon Taproom (p149)
➜ Bound (p150)
➜ Horizonte Lounge (p150)
➜ InterContinental Lobby Lounge (p147)
➜ Aqua (p149)
➜ Butler (p149)

For reviews, see p147.➜

Best Places to Shop

➜ Ladies' Market (p153)
➜ Yue Hwa Chinese Products Emporium (p153)
➜ K11 Select (p152)
➜ Rise Shopping Arcade (p152)
➜ Showa Film & Camera (p153)

For reviews, see p152.➜

KOWLOON

◉ TOP SIGHT
HONG KONG MUSEUM OF HISTORY

If you have time for only one museum, make it the Hong Kong Museum of History. Its whistle-stop overview of the city's natural history, ethnography and indigenous culture provides some lively context to your impressions of Hong Kong.

The eight galleries of the Hong Kong Story exhibition take you on a fascinating walk through the territory's history, starting with the natural environment and prehistoric Hong Kong (about 6000 years ago), and ending with the territory's return to China in 1997. Don't linger in the earlier galleries, as the best is yet to come.

You'll encounter colourful replicas of a Chinese marriage procession, and the dwellings of the Tanka boat people and the Puntay, who built walled villages. You'll see traditional costumes and re-created shophouses from 1881, and board a tram from 1913. You'll watch WWII footage that features interviews with Chinese and foreigners taken prisoner by the Japanese.

The section devoted to Hong Kong urban culture contains replicas of a retro grocery store, a soda fountain and home interiors. There's even a cinema decorated in '60s-style daily screenings of old Cantonese films.

DON'T MISS

➡ The Hong Kong Story
➡ Special exhibitions

PRACTICALITIES

➡ 香港歷史博物館
➡ Map p316, B2
➡ ☎852 2724 9042
➡ http://hk.history.museum
➡ 100 Chatham Rd S, Tsim Sha Tsui
➡ admission free
➡ ⏰10am-6pm Mon & Wed-Sat, to 7pm Sun
➡ ♿
➡ Ⓜ Tsim Sha Tsui, exit B2

TOP SIGHT
TEMPLE STREET NIGHT MARKET

When night falls and neon buzzes, Hong Kong's liveliest market rattles into life. Temple St extends southwards from Man Ming Lane to Nanking St, cut in two by the historic Tin Hau Temple (p140). It's great for the bustling atmosphere, dai pai dong (food stalls), free Cantonese opera performances and fortune-telling. The market is liveliest between 7pm and 10pm.

Back at the turn of the 20th century, snack and trinket vendors would gather around Tin Hau Temple, the social and spiritual heart of Yau Ma Tei, to hawk their wares to temple-goers. By the 1920s, this commerce had grown into a regular market as vendors would set up further and further from the temple itself. It wasn't until the 1980s, however, that 'Thieves Market', as it was then known, started to appear in the tourist guidebooks.

For alfresco dining, head for Woo Sung St, running parallel to the east, or to the section of Temple St north of the temple. You can get anything from a bowl of wonton noodles to oyster omelettes and Nepalese curries. There are also seafood and hotpot restaurants in the area. For an unusual experience, take a seat at a singalong parlour and order delivery.

Every evening a gaggle of fortune-tellers sets up tents in the middle of the market where they make predictions about your life (from HK$100) by reading your face and palm, or based on your date of birth. Some keep birds that have been trained to pick out 'fortune' cards. Most operators speak some English.

If you're in luck, you'll catch snippets of a Cantonese opera performed under the stars. Some of the most famous stars of the opera stage began their careers in this humble fashion – or so they say.

DON'T MISS

➡ Shopping
➡ Street food
➡ Fortune-tellers
➡ Temple St singalong parlours

PRACTICALITIES

➡ 廟街夜市
➡ Map p318, A1
➡ Temple St, Yau Ma Tei
➡ ⏱6-11pm
➡ Ⓜ Yau Ma Tei, exit C

TOP SIGHT
SIK SIK YUEN WONG TAI SIN TEMPLE

A devout ensemble of halls, shrines, pavilions and altars, this busy Taoist temple is a destination for all walks of life, from pensioners to young professionals. Some come simply to pray, others to divine the future with *chim* (bamboo 'fortune sticks'), which are shaken out of a box on to the ground and interpreted by a fortune-teller.

The complex, built in 1973, is dedicated to a deified healer named Wong Tai Sin who, as a shepherd in Zhèjiāng province, was said to have transformed boulders into sheep. In fact, the whole district is named after him – ironic given he is said to have been a hermit. When he was 15 an immortal taught Wong how to make a herbal potion that could cure all illnesses. He is thus worshipped both by the sick and those trying to avoid illness. The term 'Wong Tai Sin' is sometimes used to describe people who are generous to a fault.

Taoist ceremonies take place at the main altar. The image of the deity was brought to Hong Kong from Guǎngdōng province in 1915. Behind the main altar and to the right are the Good Wish Gardens, replete with pavilions (the hexagonal Unicorn Hall, with carved doors and windows, is the most beautiful), zigzag bridges and carp ponds.

Accessed via stairs beneath the main temple is a glittering, ultramodern chamber of worship added in 2011 at the cost of HK$100 million. Looking like something out of a Las Vegas casino, it couldn't be more of a departure from the traditional environs above. Entry is HK$100.

DON'T MISS

➡ The architecture
➡ *Chim*
➡ The main altar
➡ Ceremonies
➡ Fortune-tellers
➡ Gardens

PRACTICALITIES

➡ 嗇色園黃大仙祠
➡ ☏852 2327 8141, 852 2351 5640
➡ www.siksikyuen.org.hk
➡ 2 Chuk Yuen Village, Wong Tai Sin
➡ donation HK$2
➡ ⏰7am-5pm
➡ Ⓜ Wong Tai Sin, exit B2

TOP SIGHT
CHI LIN NUNNERY

One of the most beautiful and arrestingly built environments in Hong Kong, this large Buddhist complex, originally dating from the 1930s, was rebuilt of wood in the style of a Tang dynasty monastery in 1998. It's serene with lotus ponds, bonsai tea plants, bougainvillea and silent nuns delivering offerings of fruit and rice to Buddha or chanting behind intricately carved screens.

Built to last a thousand years, Chi Lin Nunnery is the world's largest cluster of handcrafted timber buildings, exhibiting a level of artistry rarely found in other faux-ancient architecture. The design, involving interlocking sections of wood joined without a single nail, is intended to demonstrate the harmony of humans with nature.

You enter through the Sam Mun, a series of 'three gates' representing the Buddhist precepts of compassion, wisdom and 'skilful means'. The first courtyard, which contains the delightful Lotus Pond Garden, gives way to the Hall of Celestial Kings, with a large statue of the seated Buddha surrounded by deities. Behind that is the Main Hall, containing a statue of the Sakyamuni Buddha.

Connected to the nunnery is **Nan Lian Garden**, a graceful, Tang-style park with a number of sights including a golden pagoda, koi ponds, flower displays and ornamental rockeries. Nan Lian Garden is also the setting for Chi Lin Vegetarian (p146) and Song Cha Xie (p150).

DON'T MISS

➡ Tang-style architecture
➡ Sam Mun
➡ Lotus Pond Garden
➡ Hall of Celestial Kings
➡ Main Hall
➡ Nan Lian Garden

PRACTICALITIES

➡ 志蓮淨苑
➡ ☑852 2354 1888
➡ www.chilin.org
➡ 5 Chi Lin Dr, Diamond Hill
➡ admission free
➡ ⏱nunnery 9am-4.30pm, garden 6.30am-7pm
➡ Ⓜ Diamond Hill, exit C2

◉ SIGHTS

Kowloon has most of Hong Kong's major museums, its busiest and most beguiling Taoist temple complex (p136), and some of the liveliest street markets. Pockets of fading colonial heritage, including old churches and police stations, reward the casual wanderer, while Yau Ma Tei is the place to go to soak up what vibes linger of yesteryear Hong Kong, especially along Shanghai St. Many of Kowloon's attractions revolve around views of the Hong Kong Island skyline, which can be best appreciated from the Kowloon waterfront and various well-positioned bars and restaurants.

◉ Tsim Sha Tsui

HONG KONG MUSEUM
OF HISTORY   MUSEUM
See p134.

★ TSIM SHA TSUI
EAST PROMENADE   HARBOUR
Map p316 (尖沙嘴東部海濱花園; Salisbury Rd; MEast Tsim Sha Tsui, exit J) One of the finest city skylines in the world has to be that of Hong Kong Island, and the promenade here is one of the best ways to get an uninterrupted view. It's a lovely place to stroll around during the day, but it really comes into its own in the evening, during the nightly Symphony of Lights (p151), a spectacular sound-and-light show involving dozens of buildings on the Hong Kong Island skyline.

The Avenue of Stars, revamped with a new design in 2019, pays homage to the Hong Kong film industry and its stars, with more than 100 handprints and sculptures.

ⓘ BEWARE FAKE MONKS
....

Real monks never solicit money. But during your stay, you may be approached by con artists in monk outfits who try to make you part with your money. Some may even offer Buddhist amulets for sale, or force 'blessings' on you then pester you for a donation. When accosted, just say 'no' firmly and ignore them.

The promenade starts just west of the |under-construction Victoria Dockside parallel to Salisbury Rd, an ambitious 279,00-sq-metre development of offices, retail, art galleries and the forthcoming ultraluxe Rosewood Hotel. It then carries on eastwards almost all the way to the Hong Kong Coliseum and Hung Hom train station.

It gets especially crowded during the Chinese New Year fireworks displays in late January/early February and in June during the Dragon Boat Festival.

★ KOWLOON PARK   PARK
Map p314 (九龍公園; www.lcsd.gov.hk; Nathan & Austin Rds; ⏰6am-midnight; 👪; MTsim Sha Tsui, exit C2) Built on the site of a barracks for an Indian regiment of the British Army, Kowloon Park is an oasis of greenery and a refreshing escape from the Nathan Rd hustle. Pathways wind between banyan trees, gardens, fountains and a flamingo pond; go early to see elderly locals performing taichi.

On Sunday afternoons from 2.30pm, martial-arts and dragon dances are performed at 'Kung Fu Corner' at the park's Sculpture Walk. The Hong Kong Heritage Discovery Centre (free) has exhibitions relating to old Hong Kong, but kids will prefer the Aviary and the extensive swimming facilities (p155).

FORMER MARINE
POLICE HEADQUARTERS   HISTORIC BUILDING
Map p314 (前水警總部; ☎852 2926 8000; www.1881heritage.com; 2A Canton Rd; ⏰10am-10pm; 🚢Star Ferry, MEast Tsim Sha Tsui, exit L6) ⒻⓇⒺⒺ Built in 1884, this gorgeous Victorian complex is one of Hong Kong's four oldest government buildings. It was used continuously by the Hong Kong Marine Police until the 1990s, except during WWII when the Japanese navy took over. The complex is now a nakedly commercial property called 'Heritage 1881'. The original building contains restaurants and Hullet House, a suite-only boutique hotel, all sitting atop high-end shopping, naturally.

Several original features are still here, including cells, carrier-pigeon houses, a bomb shelter and stable block. Why 1881 instead of 1884? Because '4' has a similar pronunciation to 'death' in Chinese, and the developer was superstitious. Free guided tours are available – call to book.

AVENUE OF STARS
WATERFRONT

Map p314 (星光大道; Tsim Sha Tsui East Promenade) The Avenue of Stars, located on the spectacular Tsim Sha Tsui East Promenade, pays homage to the Hong Kong film industry and its stars, with handprints, sculptures and information boards.

Reopened in early 2019 after a three-year renovation, the redesigned waterfront promenade features more greenery and seating. Information about the 107 sets of local celebrity handprints is available through QR codes, while the perennially popular Bruce Lee and Anita Mui statues remain present, but with added augmented reality technology.

NATHAN ROAD
STREET

Map p314 (彌敦道; MTsim Sha Tsui, Jordan) Named after Hong Kong's only Jewish governor, Matthew Nathan, Kowloon's main drag is a bit of a traffic- and pedestrian-choked scrum of malls, jewellery stores and fashion boutiques. It's nonetheless an iconic Hong Kong scene where guesthouses rub shoulders with luxury hotels. And it's completely safe – which is just as well since you won't be able to avoid using it if you spend any time in the area.

Be sure to wander as far as the stretch running parallel with and north of Kowloon Park, shaded by a glorious canopy of banyan trees.

HONG KONG SCIENCE MUSEUM
MUSEUM

Map p316 (香港科學館; 852 2732 3232; http://hk.science.museum; 2 Science Museum Rd; adult/concession HK$25/12.50, Wed free; 10am-7pm Mon-Wed & Fri, to 9pm Sat & Sun; ; MTsim Sha Tsui, exit B2) Younger kids will go wild for the vast array of hands-on exhibits at this modern museum. The boring old laws of physics, chemistry and biology are entertainingly presented via robots, VR, video games and more, along with traditional museum displays like model vehicles and dinosaur skeletons.

KOWLOON MOSQUE
& ISLAMIC CENTRE
MOSQUE

Map p314 (九龍清真寺; 852 2724 0095; 105 Nathan Rd; 5am-10pm; MTsim Sha Tsui, exit C2) With its splendid dome, quartet of 11m-high minarets and lattice window tracery, the Kowloon Mosque is a captivating building and an important place of worship for the territory's 300,000-strong Islamic population. Built in 1984 (the previous mosque suffered damage during MTR construction), it can accommodate up to 3000 worshippers across three halls. The original mosque was established to serve the Indian Muslim troops of the British army who were stationed at what is now Kowloon Park.

Muslims are welcome to attend services, but non-Muslims should ask permission to enter. Remember to remove your footwear.

ROSARY CHURCH
CHURCH

Map p316 (玫瑰堂; 852 2368 0980; http://rosarychurch.catholic.org.hk; 125 Chatham Rd S; 7.30am-7.30pm; MJordan, exit D) Kowloon's oldest Catholic church was built in 1905 with money donated by a Portuguese doctor in Hong Kong, initially for the benefit of the Catholics in an Indian battalion stationed in Kowloon, and later for the burgeoning local Catholic community. Set in a plant-filled courtyard, Rosary Church features a classic Gothic style with a yellowish facade reminiscent of churches in Macau.

English Mass is at 8am and 6.30pm Monday to Saturday, and 8.45am, 12.30pm and 7pm Sunday.

FORMER KOWLOON
BRITISH SCHOOL
HISTORIC BUILDING

Map p314 (前九龍童學校; www.amo.gov.hk; 136 Nathan Rd; MTsim Sha Tsui, exit B1) One of the oldest surviving school buildings in Hong Kong, the Kowloon British School was established in 1902 to teach the children of expat residents. Built in Victorian red-brick style, it was subsequently modified to incorporate verandahs and high ceilings, prompted possibly by the fainting spells suffered by its young occupants.

The school now houses the Antiquities & Monuments Office (古物古蹟辦事處), which has information and exhibits on current efforts towards the preservation of traditional Chinese and colonial architecture.

ST ANDREW'S
ANGLICAN CHURCH
CHURCH

Map p314 (聖安德烈堂; 852 2367 1478; www.standrews.org.hk; 138 Nathan Rd; 7.30am-10.30pm, church 8.30am-5.30pm; MTsim Sha Tsui, exit B1) Sitting atop a knoll adjacent to the Former Kowloon British School is this charming building in English Gothic style that houses Kowloon's oldest Protestant church. St Andrew's was built in 1905 in granite and red brick to serve Kowloon's Protestant population; it was turned into

KOWLOON SIGHTS

a Shinto shrine during the Japanese Occupation. Nearby you'll see the handsome Old Vicarage with its columned balconies (c 1909). Enter from the eastern side of Nathan Rd via steps or a slope.

HONG KONG MUSEUM OF ART   MUSEUM

Map p314 (香港藝術館; ☑852 2721 0116; http://hk.art.museum; 10 Salisbury Rd; adult/concession HK$10/5, Wed free; ⊙10am-6pm Mon-Fri, to 7pm Sat & Sun; ⛴Star Ferry, ⓂEast Tsim Sha Tsui, exit J) This excellent museum was closed at time of research while it undergoes a multimillion-dollar renovation. When open, it has galleries spread over six floors exhibiting Chinese antiquities, fine art, historical pictures and contemporary Hong Kong art. Highlights include the Xubaizhi collection of painting and calligraphy, contemporary works, and ceramics and other antiques from China.

FORMER KCR
CLOCK TOWER   HISTORIC BUILDING

Map p314 (前九廣鐵路鐘樓; Tsim Sha Tsui Star Ferry Concourse; ⛴Star Ferry, ⓂEast Tsim Sha Tsui, exit L6) This 44m-high clock tower (1915) in red brick and granite on the southern tip of Salisbury Rd was once part of the southern terminus of the Kowloon–Canton Railway (KCR). The station was demolished in 1978 after operations moved to the modern train station at Hung Hom, but you can see what it looked like at the Hong Kong Railway Museum in Tai Po.

HONG KONG SPACE
MUSEUM & THEATRE   MUSEUM

Map p314 (香港太空館; ☑852 2721 0226; www.lcsd.gov.hk; 10 Salisbury Rd; adult/concession HK$10/7, shows HK$36/16; ⊙1-9pm Mon & Wed-Fri, 10am-9pm Sat & Sun; ♿; ⓂEast Tsim Sha Tsui, exit J) Updated in 2016, this golf-ball-shaped museum on the waterfront has a new permanent exhibition, 'journey of space exploration', together with high-tech 3D shows several times a day in the Stanley Ho Space Theatre. Be prepared to queue outside to get tickets for a two-hour time slot to enter the museum.

INTERNATIONAL
COMMERCE CENTRE   NOTABLE BUILDING

(環球貿易廣場; ICC; www.shkp-icc.com; 1 Austin Rd W; Sky100 adult/concession HK$188/128; ⊙10am-9pm; ⓂKowloon, exit C1) Hong Kong's tallest building (484m) is a lonely one, standing all by itself in West Kowloon. If you want to ogle the view, you can either head up to the **Ritz-Carlton** (麗思卡爾頓酒店; ☑852 2263 2263; www.ritzcarlton.com; 1 Austin Rd W, ⓂKowloon, exit C1, D1) on the 12th floor, or visit Sky100, an observation deck on the 100th floor. From Element's 2nd-floor 'Metal Zone,' you'll see signage showing you the way. Last entry is at 8pm.

FOOK TAK
ANCIENT TEMPLE   BUDDHIST TEMPLE

Map p314 (福德古廟; 30 Haiphong Rd; ⊙6am-8pm; ⓂTsim Sha Tsui, exit C2) Tsim Sha Tsui's only temple is a smoke-filled hole in the wall with a hot tin roof. Little is known about its ancestry except that it was built as a shrine in the Qing dynasty and renovated in 1900. Before WWII, worshippers of its Earth God were the unskilled labourers from Kowloon Wharf nearby, where the Ocean Terminal (p31) now stands. Today most incense offerers are octogenarians – the temple specialises in longevity.

◉ Yau Ma Tei

TEMPLE STREET
NIGHT MARKET   MARKET

See p135.

★SHANGHAI STREET   STREET

Map p318 (上海街; ⓂYau Ma Tei, exit C) Strolling down Shanghai St will return you to a time long past. Once Kowloon's main drag, it's flanked by stores selling Chinese wedding gowns, sandalwood incense and Buddha statues, plus mahjong parlours and an old pawn shop (at the junction with Saigon St). This is a terrific place for souvenirs – fun picks include wooden moon-cake moulds stamped with images of fish, pigs or lucky sayings, bamboo steamer baskets, long chopsticks meant for stirring pots and pretty ceramic bowls.

The main business here is kitchen goods. Check out dozens of shops hawking woks, cleavers, tree-trunk carving boards and other necessities of Chinese cookery.

TIN HAU TEMPLE   TAOIST TEMPLE

Map p318 (天后廟; ☑852 2385 0759; www.ctc.org.hk; cnr Temple & Public Square Sts; ⊙8am-5pm; ⓂYau Ma Tei, exit C) This incense-filled sanctuary built in the 19th century is one of Hong Kong's most famous Tin Hau (Goddess of the Sea) temples, though restorations have lent it a modern feel. The public

BADASS MAHJONG

Shanghai St in Yau Ma Tei is still home to a few mahjong parlours (麻將舘). In the 1950s, the four-player game of mahjong was so popular that the British, despite their antigambling policy, began issuing licences to mahjong parlours. In their heyday, there were over 150; now only a few dozen are left.

Brightly lit and filled with cigarette smoke, mahjong parlours were often featured in gangster films as they were associated with the triads – the Hong Kong Mafia. Now with the police keeping a close eye on proceedings, they're little more than the noisy playgrounds of hardcore players.

Most of these places have signs reading 麻將娛樂 ('mahjong entertainment'). You can enter for a peek, but picture-taking is forbidden.

square out front is Yau Ma Tei's communal heart where fishers once laid out their hemp ropes in the sun next to Chinese banyans that today shade chess players and elderly locals.

YAU MA TEI
POLICE STATION   HISTORIC BUILDING

Map p318 (油麻地警署; 627 Canton Rd; ⓜYau Ma Tei, exit C) A stone's throw from Tin Hau Temple (p140) is this handsome Edwardian police station (c 1923) with arcades and arches. You may have caught a glimpse of it in the film *Rush Hour 2*. Some of its architectural features have been adapted for feng shui reasons – crime-fighting is a high-risk profession. For instance, the portico at the main entrance is set in an indented corner to better protect the building's inhabitants.

YAU MA TEI WHOLESALE
FRUIT MARKET   MARKET

Map p318 (油麻地果欄; cnr Waterloo Rd & Reclamation St; ⊗24hr; ⓜYau Ma Tei, exit B2) This historic market, founded in 1913, is a cluster of one- and two-storey brick and stone buildings with pre-WWII signboards above the stalls. Although it remains a hive of wholesale activity after dark (especially just before dawn), since 2012 it has been also a retail market, so you can visit by day for freshly cut durian (though not advised if sharing a room!).

In the '80s the market was a hotbed of Triad gang activity.

YAU MA TEI THEATRE   NOTABLE BUILDING

Map p318 (油麻地戲院; ☑852 2264 8108, tickets 852 2374 2598; www.lcsd.gov.hk/ymtt; 6 Waterloo Rd, cnr Reclamation St; ⊗box office 1-8pm; ⓜYau Ma Tei, exit B2) Adjacent to the Wholesale Fruit Market, historic Yau Ma Tei

Theatre (1930) stages regular performances of Cantonese opera. For decades, the art deco–styled theatre had kept market coolies and rickshaw drivers entertained, but losing business to modern cinemas in the '80s, it began showing erotic films and selling porn videos to stay afloat. It closed in 1998 and reopened in 2012.

⊙ Mong Kok & Sham Shui Po

LUI SENG CHUN   HISTORIC BUILDING

Map p319 (雷春生堂; ☑852 3411 0628; http://scm.hkbu.edu.hk/lsctour; 119 Lai Chi Kok Rd, cnr Tong Mi Rd, Mong Kok; ⊗guided tour 2.30pm & 4pm Mon-Fri, 9.30am & 11am Sat, consultation 9am-1pm & 2-8pm Mon-Sat, 9am-1pm Sun; ⓜPrince Edward, exit C2) FREE Hugging a street corner is this beautiful four-storey Chinese 'shophouse' belonging to a school of Chinese medicine. Constructed circa 1931, it features a mix of Chinese and European architectural styles – verandahs, urn-shaped balustrades and other fanciful takes on a neoclassical Italian villa. The well-preserved ground floor, which has a herbal tea shop, is open to the public. Free guided tours (45 minutes) to the upper-floor clinics are available by registration. They're in Cantonese, but exhibits have bilingual labels.

An English tour can be arranged for groups of more than four. Make an appointment if you want to have your pulse taken by a Chinese doctor.

C&G ARTPARTMENT   GALLERY

Map p319 (☑852 2390 9332; www.candg-artpartment.com; 3rd fl, 222 Sai Yeung Choi St S, Mong Kok; ⊗2-7.30pm Thu, Fri, Sun & Mon, from 11am Sat; ⓜPrince Edward, exit B2) Clara and Gum, the founders of this edgy art space up three flights of stairs in a residential building, are passionate about nurturing the local art scene and representing socially minded artists. C&G also runs art courses. See website for details and current exhibitions. The art space is in a building behind the Pioneer Centre (始創中心).

HERITAGE OF MEI HO HOUSE MUSEUM
MUSEUM

(美荷樓生活館; ☑852 3728 3500; Block 41, Shek Kip Mei Estate, 70 Berwick St, Sham Shui Po; ◷9.30am-5pm Tue-Sun; ◨A2, Ⓜ️Sham Shui Po, exit D2) FREE This museum inside the Mei Ho House Youth Hostel (p228) introduces the history of Mei Ho House, which was among the first batch of resettlement blocks built to house the survivors of a devastating blaze that broke out in 1953 and left nearly 58,000 homeless. Mei Ho House marked the beginning of Hong Kong's public housing policies. Using artefacts and replicas of old residences, the museum introduces the way of life and culture in Hong Kong during the 1950s to 1970s.

LEI CHENG UK HAN TOMB MUSEUM
MUSEUM

(李鄭屋漢墓博物館; ☑852 2386 2863; www.lcsd.gov.hk; 41 Tonkin St, Sham Shui Po; ◷10am-6pm Fri-Wed; Ⓜ️Cheung Sha Wan, exit A3) FREE Don't expect a Terracotta Army, but for those interested in the area's ancient history, this is a significant burial vault dating from the Eastern Han dynasty (AD 25–220). The tomb consists of four barrel-vaulted brick chambers set around a domed central tomb. It's encased in a concrete shell for protection and visitors can only peep through a plastic window.

◉ New Kowloon

CHI LIN NUNNERY
BUDDHIST MONASTERY

See p137.

SIK SIK YUEN WONG TAI SIN TEMPLE
TAOIST TEMPLE

See p136.

KOWLOON WALLED CITY PARK
PARK

(九龍寨城公園; ☑852 2716 9962; www.lcsd.gov.hk; Tung Tau Tsuen, Tung Tsing, cnr Carpenter & Junction Rds, Kowloon City; ◷park 6.30am-11pm, exhibition 10am-6pm Thu-Tue; MTR Lok Fu, exit B) Try to imagine that this 1.2-hectare ornamental park, built by the British in the early 1990s, was just a few years earlier one of the most infamous residential estates the world had ever seen. Completely unplanned, it was home to a claustrophobic press of 40,000 Chinese people living in teetering shanty towers 15 storeys high, connected by a network of narrow passageways and staircases that never saw daylight, hence its Cantonese nickname, 'City of Darkness'.

Kowloon Walled City was also infested with gangs, brothels and opium dens, and neither government wanted anything to do with it. The British eventually relocated all the residents, tore it down and put this park in its place, which harkens back to the original Chinese military fort that was built here in 1847. The fort remained a Chinese-run enclave throughout British rule, which partly explains its unregulated rise into Kowloon Walled City.

Surprisingly, traces of the original fort, including cannon and the partly rebuilt almshouse, remain (it now houses a small

---

WORKING ARTISTS IN NEW KOWLOON

Artist villages are interesting to visit, but unless you go during open studios, you may not see many artists. The majority have day jobs, returning to their studios only at the weekends. That said, your visit to places such as Cattle Depot Artist Village (p143), **Jockey Club Creative Arts Centre** (賽馬會創意藝術中心; JCCAC; www.jccac.org.hk; 30 Pak Tin St, Shek Kip Mei; ◷10am-10pm; Ⓜ️Shek Kip Mei, exit C) and **ACO in the Foo Tak Building** (艺鵠; Map p308; ☑852 2893 4808; www.aco.hk; 14th fl, Foo Tak Bldg, 365 Hennessy Rd, Wan Chai; ◷noon-7pm Tue-Sun; Ⓜ️Causeway Bay, exit B) can still be rewarding. There are galleries, bookstores and cafes that keep regular hours; the architecture of these places is interesting – abandoned factories, retro buildings, a former abattoir...

While some artists don't mind visitors, many prefer to work in solitude, even if they leave their doors ajar for the neighbour's cat. Always ask if you're welcome before you enter. Some studios open by appointment only, so check the websites and make contact before you go.

history exhibit on the Walled City). You can also see exhumed sections of the original south gate and sign. A scale model of the Walled City by the park's entrance gives an indication of its staggering density.

Confusingly, Kowloon Walled City Park is effectively inside the larger and more prosaic Carpenter Road Park, delineated, appropriately, by an encircling stone wall.

**CATTLE DEPOT
ARTIST VILLAGE** VILLAGE

(牛棚藝術村; 63 Ma Tau Kok Rd, To Kwa Wan; ⊙10am-10pm; ☐106, 12A, 5C, 101, 111) This century-old slaughterhouse deep in the entrails of Kowloon has been reincarnated into an artists' village, its red-brick buildings housing studios and exhibition halls. Depending on when you come, there might not be much on. One of the most active residents is nonprofit visual-art organisation **1a Space** (☑852 2529 0087; www.oneaspace.org.hk; Unit 14, Cattle Depot Artist Village, 63 Ma Tau Kok Rd, To Kwa Wan; ⊙11am-7pm Tue-Sun; ☐106, 12A, 5C, 101, 111), which holds regular exhibitions of local and international art, concerts and theatrical performances.

Cattle Depot Artist Village is next to a Town Gas storage facility, in the northern part of To Kwa Wan, an area on Kowloon's east coast.

✖️ EATING

Kowloon doesn't have quite as many upmarket restaurants as Hong Kong Island but there's a riveting assortment of Chinese and Asian eateries to fit all budgets in Tsim Sha Tsui. For hearty local fare, head to Yau Ma Tei or Mong Kok. Kowloon City is renowned for its many authentic Thai eateries.

✖️ Tsim Sha Tsui

⭐ **NEW CHETTTINAD** SOUTH INDIAN $

Map p314 (Shop 17, Ground fl, Chungking Mansions, 36-44 Nathan Rd; meals from HK$35; ⊙8am-11pm; Ⓜ Tsim Sha Tsui, exit N5) Rub shoulders with Indian business people, tailors and traders at this tiny halal kitchen, the best of many in the marvellously multicultural maze that is Chungking Mansions. Perfectly crisp dosa the size of skateboards come with masala potato and dhal, or go

for a multidish thali. Finish with a sweet and fiery masala ginger tea.

OWLS CHOUX GELATO ICE CREAM $

Map p316 (32 Mody Rd; gelato from HK$38; ⊙3.30-10.30pm; Ⓜ Tsim Sha Tsui, exit N1) Take a break in this cutesy dessert store where everything, from the gelato to the caramel sauce, is made in-house. Rich flavours such as pistachio, Earl Grey and black sesame can be enjoyed in a cone or sandwiched between creative choux, and smothered in sweet toppings.

YUM CHA DIM SUM $

Map p316 (飲茶; ☑852 2751 1666; http://yumchahk.com; 3/F 20-22 Granville Rd; meals HK$100-250; ⊙11.30am-11pm; ⛾; Ⓜ Tsim Sha Tsui, exit B2) Kids will love the adorable, animal-shaped dumplings and buns at this gimmicky yet delicious dim sum eatery. Barbecue pork buns are adorned with tiny piggy faces, custard buns are anthropomorphic eggs, and bird-shaped pineapple puffs are served in little cages. Don't miss the fun takes on Canto snacks such as 'lollipop' sweet and sour chicken wings.

MAMMY PANCAKE DESSERTS $

Map p314 (媽咪雞蛋仔; 8-12 Carnarvon Rd; egg waffles HK$20-33; ⊙11.30am-9pm Sun-Thu, to 10.30pm Fri & Sat; ⛾; Ⓜ Tsim Sha Tsui, exit D2) This takeaway counter serves up some of Hong Kong's best eggettes, those bubble-wrap waffles beloved of locals of all ages. Go plain or choose inventive flavours such as matcha, chestnut, sweet potato or pork floss. Or just pig out with a waffle sandwich oozing peanut butter and condensed milk. Expect a 15-minute wait.

WOODLANDS INDIAN $

Map p316 (活蘭印度素食; ☑852 2369 3718; www.woodlandshk.com; Upper ground fl, 16 & 17 Wing On Plaza, 62 Mody Rd; meals HK$90-200; ⊙noon-3.30pm & 6.30-10.30pm; ⛾; Ⓜ East Tsim Sha Tsui, exit P1) Located inside a drowsy, old-fashioned mall, Woodlands has been dishing up good-value Indian vegetarian food to compatriots and the odd local since 1981. Dithering gluttons should order the thali meal (HK$90 to HK$135), which is served on a round metal plate with 10 tiny dishes, a dessert and bread. Dosa are recommended.

SWEET DYNASTY CANTONESE, DESSERTS $

Map p314 (糖朝; ☑852 2199 7799; www.sweetdynasty.com; Shop A, Basement, Hong Kong

KOWLOON EATING

Pacific Centre, 28 Hankow Rd; meals HK$70-300; ⊗8am-midnight Sun-Thu, to 1am Fri & Sat; MTsim Sha Tsui, exit A1) Sweet Dynasty's extensive menu encompasses a retinue of casual Cantonese dishes, but the desserts, noodles and congee, for which they became famous years ago, are still the best. Ride the escalator down to the cave-like dining space. Dim sum served until 8pm.

★ YÈ SHANGHAI DIM SUM $$

Map p314 (夜上海; ☑852 2376 3322; www. elite-concepts.com; 6th fl, Marco Polo Hotel, Harbour City, Canton Rd; meals HK$400-800; ⊗11.30am-2.30pm & 6-10.30pm; MTsim Sha Tsui, exit C2) Dark woods and subdued lighting inspired by 1920s Shànghǎi impart an air of romance to this otherwise bustling restaurant serving exquisite Shanghainese and Zhèjiāng classics – tea-smoked duck, sweet and sour 'squirrel' fish, unctuous steamed pork belly. The only exception to this Jiāngnán harmony is the Cantonese dim sum being served at lunch, though that too is excellent.

★ DIN TAI FUNG SHANGHAI $$

Map p314 (鼎泰豐; ☑852 2730 6928; www. dintaifung.com.hk; Shop 130, 3rd fl, Silvercord, 30 Canton Rd; meals HK$150-300; ⊗11.30am-10.30pm; ⛾; MTsim Sha Tsui, exit C1) DTF's steamers of perfectly pleated *xiao long bao* (Shànghǎi-style dumplings) have made this Taiwanese chain an Asia-wide institution. Order them wrapped with pork, crab, veggies or even truffle. Queues are the norm and there are no reservations, but service is excellent. Must-eats also include the fluffy steamed pork buns and the greasy-but-oh-so-good fried pork chop.

★ SPRING DEER PEKING DUCK $$

Map p316 (鹿鳴春飯店; ☑852 2366 4012; 1st fl, 42 Mody Rd; meals HK$150-500; ⊗11.30am-3pm & 6-11pm; MEast Tsim Sha Tsui, exit P3) Hong Kong's most authentic Northern Chinese–style roast lamb is served at this long-standing locals' favourite. Better known is the perfectly bronzed Peking duck, carved thick and served with traditional *shāobǐng* bread as well as the more usual steamed pancakes. Service can sometimes be as welcoming as a Běijīng winter, c 1967. Booking is essential.

GAYLORD INDIAN $$

Map p314 (爵樂印度餐廳; ☑852 2376 1001; 1st fl Ashley Centre, 23-25 Ashley Rd; meals from HK$250; ⊗noon-3pm & 6-11pm; ⛾; MTsim Sha Tsui, exit L5) Dim lighting and nightly live music set the scene for enjoying the excellent rogan josh, dhal and vegetarian dishes at Hong Kong's oldest – and Kowloon's classiest – Indian restaurant, in operation since 1972. You'll pay more than at other Indian joints in town, but the plush alcoves, natural lighting and attentive service justify the outlay.

Or stretch those pennies with the good-value lunchtime buffet (HK$128) or lunch sets (from HK$70).

T'ANG COURT CANTONESE, DIM SUM $$$

Map p314 (唐閣; ☑852 2375 1133; www.hong kong.langhamhotels.com; 1st fl, Langham Hotel, 8 Peking Rd; lunch/dinner from HK$700/1100; ⊗noon-2.30pm & 6-10.30pm; MTsim Sha Tsui, exit L4) Deep carpets, fine silks and burgundy drapes equal a rarefied ambience at this highly praised, high-rolling Cantonese eatery with three Michelin stars inside the Langham Hotel. Tasting menus, from HK$1080 per person, are the most fuss-free way to sample the considerable kitchen skills on show here.

Unlike at most upscale Cantonese restaurants, solo diners are well looked after – there's a special tasting menu for one, with the optional add-on of a half-bottle of champers.

SUN TUNG LOK CANTONESE, DIM SUM $$$

Map p314 (新同樂; ☑852 2152 1417; www.suntun glok.com.hk; 4th fl, Miramar Shopping Centre, 132 Nathan Rd; lunch HK$250-3000, dinner HK$500-5000; ⊗11.30am-3pm & 6-10.30pm; MTsim Sha Tsui, exit B2) Crowned with two Michelin stars, Sun Tung Lok (c 1969) proudly upholds the fine traditions of Cantonese cooking. It's evident in the dim sum (available at lunch) and dishes such as braised abalone, which are a litmus test of culinary skill. Chandeliers and tablecloths can't disguise the windowless mall location, however.

Sun Tung Lok is pricey but sets are available and several dim sum can be ordered in half portions on request.

WOO COW HOTPOT $$$

Map p316 (禾牛薈火焗館; Great Beef Hot Pot; ☑852 3997 3369; 1st & 2nd fl, China Insurance Bldg, 48 Cameron Rd; meals HK$350-600; ⊗5.30pm-2am; ⛾; MTsim Sha Tsui, exit B3) Indecisive gluttons will scream at the mind-blowing hotpot choices here – 200 ingredients (the majority fresh or homemade),

20 kinds of broth (from clam soup to fancy herbal concoctions) and an embarrassment of condiments (all-you-can-dip)! There's no escaping the menu either – the lights are too bright! Now on to the sashimi options... Bookings essential.

Like most hotpot restaurants, dish sizes dictate that you'll need at least four diners to get any bang for your buck (and avoid waste).

DONG LAI SHUN CHINESE $$$
Map p316 (東來順; ☑852 2733 2020; www.rghk.com.hk; B2, Royal Garden Hotel, 69 Mody Rd; meals HK$500-1500; ⏰11.30am-2.30pm & 6-10.30pm; 🛜; ⓜEast Tsim Sha Tsui, exit P2) A rarified setting to dine on rustic Northern Chinese fare such as mutton hotpot, which involves dunking paper-thin slices of mutton into boiling soup and eating it with sesame sauce. But this Běijīng export justifies its Michelin star with fancy Shanghainese, Sichuanese and Cantonese dishes, as well as Peking duck (HK$600), which must be ordered in advance.

TIN LUNG HEEN CANTONESE $$$
(天龍軒; ☑852 2263 2270; www.ritzcarlton.com/hongkong; 102nd fl, Ritz-Carlton Hong Kong, 1 Austin Rd W, International Commerce Centre; dinner from HK$1000; ⏰noon-2.30pm & 6-10.30pm; ❇; ⓜKowloon, exit C1) Though the decor is imposing – Xi Jinping would feel quite at home – the service is personable and the views phenomenal at this two-Michelin star palace. The signature *char siu* (roast pork) made with Spanish Iberico pork is the priciest plate of barbecue in town, but might well be the best.

Lunchtime dim sum sees Tin Lung Heen at its most economical (and the views are better, too).

GADDI'S FRENCH $$$
Map p314 (☑852 2696 6763; www.peninsula.com; 1st fl, The Peninsula, 19-21 Salisbury Rd; set lunch/dinner HK$700/2200; ⏰noon-2.30pm & 7-10.30pm; ⓜTsim Sha Tsui, exit E) Collars are required for gentlemen dining at Gaddi's, a baronial French restaurant with splendid heritage interiors and a history stretching back to just after WWII. The food is traditional French (glazed duck, burgundy snails, dessert souffles), supported by a spectacular wine list. Some might find the live dinner band gratuitous, but the old-world atmosphere is palpable.

FOOK LAM MOON CANTONESE, DIM SUM $$$
Map p316 (福臨門; ☑852 2366 0286; www.fooklammoon-grp.com; Shop 8, 1st fl, 53-59 Kimberley Rd; meals HK$400-2000; ⏰11.30am-2.30pm & 6-10.30pm; ⓜTsim Sha Tsui, exit B1) Locals call FLM 'celebrities' canteen'. And even if you're not rich and famous, FLM will treat you as though you are. The huge menu contains costly items such as abalone, costing at least HK$1000 per head. But it's OK to stick to the dim sum (from HK$60 a basket), which is divine and available only at lunch.

🍴 Yau Ma Tei

⭐ MIDO CAFÉ CAFE $
Map p318 (美都餐室; ☑852 2384 6402; 63 Temple St; meals HK$40-90; ⏰9am-10pm; ⓜYau Ma Tei, exit B2) Kowloon's most famous tea cafe, this highly instagrammable *cha chaan tang* (teahouse; c1950) with mosaic tiles and metal latticework stands astride a street corner that comes to life at sundown. Go upstairs and take a seat next to a wall of iron-framed windows overlooking Tin Hau Temple (p140).

The food is as retro as the surrounds; luncheon-meat sandwiches, macaroni soup, baked rice and other grub that sounds like it came out of a British Army cookbook circa 1939.

AUSTRALIA DAIRY COMPANY CAFE $
Map p318 (澳洲牛奶公司; ☑852 2730 1356; 47-49 Parkes St, Jordan; meals HK$30-50; ⏰7.30am-11pm Wed-Mon; ⓜJordan, exit C2) Long waits and hurried service are the standard at this beloved Hong Kong *cha chaan tang* (teahouse), famed for its steamed milk or egg puddings (HK$30), which are best gobbled up ice-cold. Locals breakfast here on scrambled-egg sandwiches and macaroni in a soup with ham. An experience to be had, for sure, but not a relaxing one!

SUN SIN NOODLES $
Map p318 (新仙清湯腩; ☑852 2332 6872; 37 Portland St; meals HK$40-65; ⏰11am-midnight; ⓜYau Ma Tei, exit B2) A stylish brisket shop in a hood known for brothels, Sun Sin serves succulent cuts of beef in a broth with radish, in a tomato soup or as a curry. If you just fancy a snack, you can get a ladle of chunky brisket dolloped inside a hollowed-out bread roll.

KOWLOON EATING

NATHAN CONGEE & NOODLE NOODLES $

Map p318 (彌敦粥麵家; ☑852 2771 4285; 11 Saigon St; meals HK$60; ⏰7.30am-11.30pm; MJordan, exit B2) This humble shop has been serving up tasty Canto fare for the past half-century. Order a side of fritters to dunk in your congee, tackle a pyramidal rice dumpling, or conquer the blanched fish skin tossed with parsley and peanuts.

Go after dark to grab a snap of the snazzy neon facade of Sik Heung Yuen Cafe, a few doors away at number 17.

HING KEE RESTAURANT CANTONESE $

Map p318 (興記菜館; ☑852 2384 3647; 19 Temple St; meals from HK$65; ⏰6pm-midnight; MYau Ma Tei, exit C) Previously a roadside stall that started out by whipping up hearty claypot rice and oyster omelettes for night revellers and triads, Hing Kee now serves the same under a roof but without the atmosphere. Expect to queue.

✖ Mong Kok & Sham Shui Po

★TIM HO WAN DIM SUM $

(添好運點心專門店; ☑852 2788 1226; www.timhowan.com.hk; 9-11 Fuk Wing St, Sham Shui Po; dim sum from HK$28; ⏰10am-9.30pm, from 9am Sat & Sun; MSham Shui Po, exit B1) Renowned as the first budget dim sum eatery to receive a Michelin star way back in 2010, Tim Ho Wan has spread from its Mong Kok roots (opened by a former Four Seasons dim sum chef) into a miniempire, with five restaurants in Hong Kong (this is the second branch, the original closed) and global franchises everywhere from Sydney to Singapore.

Tim Ho Wan isn't the best dim sum in Hong Kong, but it can still be very good (it retained its star), and the value-for-money is astonishing. Best of all, since the hype has died down it's fairly easy to rock up and get a table most hours of the day.

★KUNG WO TOFU FACTORY TOFU $

(公和荳品廠; ☑852 2386 6871; 118 Pei Ho St, Sham Shui Po; dishes HK$8-30; ⏰9am-9pm; MSham Shui Po, exit B2) Regulars come to this charming 50-year-old shop for fresh soy milk, pan-fried tofu and sweet tofu pudding (HK$12), made the traditional way from beans ground with a hand-operated millstone. The silky tofu has nutty notes, and the hue is off-white – reassuringly imperfect, just like the service.

Established in 1893, Kung Wo wears its name proudly in red clerical script.

ONE DIM SUM DIM SUM $

Map p319 (一點心; ☑852 2789 2280; Shop 1 & 2, Kenwood Mansion, 15 Playing Field Rd, Mong Kok; meals HK$40-100; ⏰10.30am-midnight, from 9.30am Sat & Sun; MPrince Edward, exit A) This cheery little place is known for all-day, bang-for-the-buck dim sum. Tick your selections on the menu card; the quality is more than a match for Tim Ho Wan nearby. One Dim Sum didn't retain the Michelin star it bagged in 2012, but it did keep the crowds. That said, the wait is usually under 30 minutes.

Nonpeak hours are 3pm to 5pm, and 9pm to midnight.

GOOD HOPE NOODLE NOODLES $

Map p318 (好旺角麵家; ☑852 2384 6898; Shop 5-6, 18 Fa Yuen St, Mong Kok; meals HK$30-90; ⏰11am-12.45am; MMong Kok, exit D3) This 40-year-old shop has retained its Michelin commendation and fan following. Now the al dente egg noodles, bite-sized wontons and silky congee that have won hearts for decades continue to be cooked the old way, but are served in neat, modern surrounds.

The braised pork trotters here are the most popular noodle addition, but might be too piggy even for assured carnivores.

✖ New Kowloon

★CHI LIN VEGETARIAN VEGETARIAN, CHINESE $

(志蓮素齋, 龍門樓; Long Men Lou; ☑852 3658 9388; 60 Fung Tak Rd, Nan Lian Garden; meals from HK$200; ⏰noon-9pm Mon-Fri, 11.30am-9pm Sat & Sun; ⏏; MDiamond Hill, exit C2) Savour organic wild mushrooms with rice or noodles, and impeccable veggie dim sum such as steamed asparagus with lily bulbs and truffle, as an artificial waterfall cascades over enormous windows at this refined Chinese restaurant in the ornamental Nan Lian Garden. If you're coming to the Chi Lin Nunnery (p137) next door, it's a must visit.

Do reserve ahead, especially on weekends, and note the minimum charge of HK$120 per person at lunch (and a little more for dinner).

LEI YUE MUN VILLAGE

This ramshackle fishing village on an outcrop of industrial Kowloon gained prominence in the 1960s as the place to go for alfresco seafood dining. Veteran restaurants such as Lung Mun and Lei Yue Mun have been steaming and stir-frying seafood for generations of Hong Kongers and are still at it today.

About two dozen restaurants wrap around market stalls of spiny lobster, abalone, spider crab and more; you select your catch, pay for it, then take it to the restaurant of your choosing to be cooked in a variety of ways (around HK$100 to HK$150 per person). Despite the old fishing boats bobbing in the typhoon shelter, today virtually all the live seafood on sale is flown in from overseas.

Lei Yue Mun is a 10-minute walk south from Yau Tong MTR. Follow Cha Kwo Ling Rd and Shung Shun St south for 15 minutes or catch green minibus 24M from outside the station. If coming from HK Island, you can take a ferry across the channel from Sai Wan Ho to Sam Ka Tsuen.

TÀI UK — THAI $

(泰屋; ☑852 4510 6228; 47 South Wall Rd; dishes from HK$45; ⊗noon-midnight; Ⓜ Lok Fu, exit B) Real Thai cooks, heads twirled in bandannas, sling yellow and red curries and authentic pad Thai at this rough-and-ready budget eatery that even sells cheap Chang beer. All it needs is a laser-disc movie projector playing *Spider-Man 2* and you'll feel like you're back on Koh Pha-Ngan.

To get here, it's a 15-minute walk south from Lok Fu MTR station, or you can hop on bus 75X.

CHEONG FAT — THAI, NOODLES $

(昌發泰國粉麵屋; ☑852 2382 5998, 852 2382 0280; 25-27 South Wall Rd, Kowloon City; noodles from HK$30; ⊗noon-11.30pm; Ⓜ Lok Fu, exit B) Dine on tasty Northern Thai fare like *khao soi* noodles, *larb* (a Thai/Laotian meat salad), and fried fish with lemongrass at this cheap and cheerful eatery in the midst of Kowloon City's 'Little Thailand'. After eating, roam the streets and you'll encounter stores selling imported herbs, chillies, incense and mangoes.

Note that there are two restaurants side-by-side – both are Cheong Fat. To get here, it's a 15-minute walk south from Lok Fu MTR station, or you can hop on bus 75X.

QUEEN'S CAFE — RUSSIAN $

(☑852 2265 8288; www.queenscafe.com; Shop 18, L1/F, Festival Walk, 80 Tat Chee Ave, Kowloon Tong; lunch/dinner from HK$150/300; ⊗11am-11pm; Ⓜ Kowloon Tong, exit C1) Queen's specialises in 'soy sauce western' – the earliest fusion cuisine in Hong Kong bearing the influence of White Russian chefs who fled to Shànghǎi after the Bolshevik victory and

opened cafes there. The highlights here are baked dishes, grilled lamb shashlik, cold cuts and the Hong Kong version of Russian borscht.

🍷 DRINKING & NIGHTLIFE

Kowloon has after-dark action for all walks of life and ethnicities, from ritzy hotel bars to grungy Korean *hof*. The strip of bars along Knutsford Tce, just east of Nathan Rd, is packed with revellers every night. Likewise, East Tsim Sha Tsui, in and around Hart Ave, has enough open-fronted drinking dens for a helluva hangover. Craft beer is making its mark, with personality-rich brewpubs popping up all over.

🍷 Tsim Sha Tsui

★ INTERCONTINENTAL LOBBY LOUNGE — CAFE, BAR

Map p316 (☑852 2721 1211; www.hongkong-ic.intercontinental.com; Hotel InterContinental Hong Kong, 18 Salisbury Rd; ⊗7am-12.30am; 🛜; Ⓜ East Tsim Sha Tsui, exit J) What's that sound? No, not the chink of cup and saucer, that's your jaw hitting the marble floor as you gaze, enraptured, at Hong Kong's most fabulous harbour views through a wall of glass. It's enough to make anybody feel like a somebody, and all you have to do is order a (very expensive) drink. Lobby Lounge is also an ideal venue from which to watch the evening light show (p151) at 8pm.

🏃 Neighbourhood Walk
Kowloon's Teeming Market Streets

START PRINCE EDWARD MTR STATION, EXIT A
END JORDAN MTR STATION, EXIT A
LENGTH 4.5KM; TWO HOURS

A 10-minute walk from Prince Edward station (exit A) will get you to Flower Market Rd, lined with fragrant and exotic blooms. Double back and start heading south on Tung Choi St. Walk two blocks to the **❶ Goldfish Market**, a dozen or so shops trading in these extravagantly hued fish. You'll see an amazing variety, with the real rarities commanding high prices.

Now sharpen your elbows! Tung Choi St Market, also known as the **❷ Ladies' Market** (p153), is crammed with shoppers and stalls selling mostly inexpensive clothing and trinkets.

Head west and south to Waterloo Rd and you'll pass by the art deco–styled **❸ Yau Ma Tei Theatre** (p141) before reaching historic **❹ Yau Ma Tei Wholesale Fruit Market** (p141). It was founded here in 1913 and later became a hotbed of Triad gang activity. Go south on Reclamation St, turning left on to Man Ming Lane until you hit the top of Temple St.

Beneath naked light bulbs, hundreds of stalls at the **❺ Temple Street Night Market** (p135) sell a vast array of booty from sex toys to luggage. The market runs right down to Jordan Rd; look out for impromptu open-air Cantonese opera performances, and consider ducking into one of the **❻ Cantonese Singing Houses** (p150) for a hyperlocal karaoke-type experience.

Fragrant smoke curls from incense spirals at **❼ Tin Hau Temple** (p140); it was here that the market started in the 1920s, as hawkers congregated to sell food and trinkets to worshippers. You might still see fortune-tellers nearby.

A good place to pick up an inexpensive gift (though avoid actual jade unless you know your stuff), the large covered **❽ Jade Market** (p154) contains dozens of stalls. At Jordan Rd turn east, then south into Nathan Rd to find Jordan MTR station.

KOWLOON

★ KOWLOON TAPROOM
CRAFT BEER

Map p314 (☑852 2861 0355; www.kowloon-taproom.com; 26 Ashley Rd; ☺2pm-2am Mon-Fri, from 1pm Sat & Sun; 🚇; MTsim Sha Tsui, exit H) Plugging a crafty gap in the market between TST's hotel bars and same-same sports dives, Kowloon Taproom pours a dozen, local-only craft beers from Lion Rock, Heroes and the like, astride a fry-heavy snack list including battered 'IPA' fish and chips. The grungy, open-fronted space, its bare walls pasted with posters, is a fine people-watching perch. Beers from HK$60.

CHICKEN HOF & SOJU
BEER HALL

Map p316 (李家; Chicken; ☑852 2375 8080; 84 Kam Kok Mansion, Kimberley Rd; beer from HK$32; ☺5pm-4am; MJordan, exit D) In the middle of a Korean neighbourhood, this dark little venue hides an authentically tatty *chimeak* (chicken and beer) bar. Korean lager starts at a wallet-friendly HK$32, and you'll need plenty of it (*soju* chasers optional) to wash down a hearty order of crisp fried chicken.

You can also gorge on Korean sausage and seafood pancakes. If you need to ask directions, people sometimes refer to this place as 'Lee Family Chicken'.

BUTLER
COCKTAIL BAR

Map p316 (☑852 2724 3828; 5th fl, Mody House, 30 Mody Rd; drinks around HK$200; ☺6.30pm-3am Tue-Sat, to 1.30am Sun; 🚇; MEast Tsim Sha Tsui, exit N2) A discreetly upscale drinking den hidden in the residential part of Tsim Sha Tsui, this Japanese bar is split over two floors, with whisky on top and cocktails beneath. Flip through whisky magazines as you watch the unfailingly polite bartenders mix up potent concoctions with precision.

OZONE
ROOFTOP BAR

(☑852 2263 2263; www.ritzcarlton.com; Ritz-Carlton Hotel, 118th fl, ICC, 1 Austin Rd; ☺5pm-1am Mon-Wed, to 2am Thu, to 3am Fri, 3pm-3am Sat, noon-midnight Sun; 🚇; MKowloon, exit U3) Ozone might be the highest bar in Asia, but you're so far up in the stratosphere that the other-worldly views lack oomph. Grab a seat on the windproof outdoor balcony and smoosh right up against the glass. Cocktails and mixed drinks start north of HK$200, or blow your inheritance on a HK$171,000 bottle of vintage Cristal. Or maybe don't.

Oh, that temptingly empty corner table? That's HK$6000 just to park your bum there.

AQUA
ROOFTOP BAR

Map p314 (☑852 3427 2288; www.aqua.com.hk; 29 & 30th fl, 1 Peking Rd; ☺4pm-2am, happy hour 4-6pm; 🚇; MTsim Sha Tsui, exit L5) Drink in harbour views from this mezzanine cocktail bar, although the best window seating is reserved for fine-dining haunt Hutong below. Creative cocktails (from HK$138) are reasonably priced considering you're subsidising all that panoramic glass. Fridays and Saturdays inject life into the otherwise dormant DJ booth. Snacks include excellent tempura shrimp.

VIBES
LOUNGE

Map p314 (☑852 2315 5999; www.themiraho-tel.com; 5th fl, Mira Hong Kong, 118 Nathan Rd; ☺5pm-midnight Sun-Wed, to 1am Thu-Sat; 🚇; MTsim Sha Tsui, exit B1) Open to the elements, this showy 5th-floor lounge bar in the Mira Hotel has greenery, water features, and exotic cabana seating (for a hefty minimum charge). Resident DJs spin downtempo electronic beats every Thursday to Saturday from 8pm. A long list of cocktails and beers is complemented by bar snacks and shisha.

N1 COFFEE & CO
CAFE

Map p316 (☑852 3568 4726; www.n1coffee.hk; 34 Mody Rd, East Tsim Sha Tsui; ☺9am-7pm; 🚇; MEast Tsim Sha Tsui, exit N4) The best place to come when craving a high-quality caffeine fix in East Tsim Sha Tsui. Sandwiches and bagels are good here, too.

FATT'S PLACE
BAR

Map p316 (☑852 3421 1144; 2 Hart Ave; ☺noon-1am, to 3am Fri & Sat; MEast Tsim Sha Tsui, exit N2) You could park up in any of the lively, open-fronted bars along TST's boozy Hart Ave, but Fatt's stands out for its better-than-most beer selection, sociable vibe, warm service and free peanuts, the shells of which carpet the floor like a circus elephant's stable.

FELIX BAR
BAR

Map p314 (☑852 2315 3188; 28th fl, Peninsula Hong Kong, Salisbury Rd; ☺5.30pm-1.30am; 🚇; MTsim Sha Tsui, exit E) Admire the views with a champagne cocktail at this Philippe Starck–designed modern European restaurant that has several distinct bar areas.

AMUSE
BAR

Map p316 (☑852 2317 1988; 4 Austin Ave; ☺5pm-4am Mon-Fri, 6pm-4am Sat, 6pm-3am Sun; 🚇; MJordan, exit D) All flickering candles and exposed brick, this stylish neighbourhood bar pulls in a mix of white-collar locals and university students. Cocktails are just so-so, but you won't mind too much if you can bag a leather sofa facing the row of windows. Note that the regulars and staff here play fairly loose with Hong Kong's smoking ban.

BOO
BAR, KARAOKE

Map p318 (☑852 2736 6168; 5th fl, Pearl Oriental Tower, 225 Nathan Rd, Jordan; ☺7pm-2am Sun-Thu, to 4am Fri, 9pm-4am Sat, happy hour 7-9pm; Ⓜ Jordan, exit C1) This low-key gay bar overlooking Nathan Rd pours good-value cocktails (HK$78). It's a friendly, easygoing place to hang out, though the blare of karaoke isn't conducive to a quiet drink. A DJ spins on Saturdays after 7pm.

🍷 Yau Ma Tei & Mong Kok

★HORIZONTE LOUNGE
ROOFTOP BAR

Map p318 (☑852 2121 9888; www.hotelmadera.com.hk; Madera Hotel, 1-9 Cheong Lok St, Yau Ma Tei; ☺5pm-1am; 🛜; Ⓜ Jordan, exit B1) You'll feel like Rapunzel atop her tower at this lofty perch in the Kowloon skyline. From all four (low) walls, panoramic vistas reveal the great mass of urban jungle-meets-island paradise in all its chaotic glory. Order a drink at the counter below then take your seat outside for sunset. Don't look down.

TAP: THE ALE PROJECT
CRAFT BEER

Map p319 (☑852 2468 2010; 15 Hak Po St, Mong Kok; ☺noon-1am; 🛜; Ⓜ Mong Kok, exit E2) On a lively strip of independent eateries and bars, Tap pours around 20 local craft ales in its exposed brick, blue-painted space. Staff aren't the friendliest, but they will let you taste before you buy. You'll love the excellent sandwiches, from sourdough grilled cheese to grander fusion assemblages, some of which can be bought by half.

KUBRICK BOOKSHOP CAFÉ
CAFE

Map p318 (☑852 2384 8929; www.kubrick.com.hk; Shop H2, Prosperous Garden, 3 Public Sq St, Yau Ma Tei; ☺11.30am-9.30pm; 🛜; Ⓜ Yau Ma Tei, exit C) An eclectic, student-y crowd packs out this bookshop-cafe attached to the Broadway Cinematheque (p152). Pop in for a coffee and browse through a collection of art, film and cultural-studies titles. You can also chow on a burger or pasta bowl.

KNOCKBOX COFFEE COMPANY
COFFEE

Map p319 (☑852 2781 0363; http://knockboxcoffee.hk; 21 Hak Po St, Mong Kok; ☺11am-10pm Mon-Thu, to 11pm Fri-Sun, last orders 9pm; 🛜; Ⓜ Mong Kok, exit E) Pull up a stool at the counter of this hip independent cafe and perk up with a designer coffee poured by specialists who know their beans. If you need to refuel, there are pastries, bagels, salads and more substantial plates like fish and chips.

🍷 New Kowloon

★BOUND
BAR

Map p319 (32 Boundary St, Prince Edward; ☺11am-2am; 🛜; Ⓜ Prince Edward, exit D) You could squish a dozen Hong Kong bars together and they still wouldn't have as much personality as this boho hang-out with its art-adorned walls, flashes of pink neon, indie playlist and craft-beer fridge. Bound could almost be the HQ of a hip marketing agency, but don't be put off – staff are really nice, and the coffee is fabulous.

SONG CHA XIE
TEAHOUSE

(松茶樹; Pavilion of Pine & Tea; ☑852 3658 9390; 60 Fung Tak Rd, Nan Lian Garden; tea from HK$160; ☺noon-6.30pm; Ⓜ Diamond Hill, exit C2) This delightful tea pavilion has graceful wooden corridors and intimate alcoves, which provide the serenity required for savouring good Chinese tea. It's a lovely space with photogenic garden views, but the staff can be rather unobliging if you just want to have a look. If you do stop in for tea, you'll be required to pad about in slippers.

There's a minimum charge of one serving of tea per guest. A selection of dim sum is available. The teahouse is inside Nan Lian Garden, in front of Chi Lin Nunnery (p137).

☆ ENTERTAINMENT

★CANTON SINGING HOUSE
LIVE MUSIC

Map p318 (艷陽天; 49-51 Temple St, Yau Ma Tei; HK$20; ☺3-7pm & 8pm-5am; Ⓜ Yau Ma Tei, exit C) The oldest and most atmospheric of Temple St's singalong parlours, Canton resembles a film set with mirror balls and glowing shrines. Singers take to the stage one after another to belt out the oldies; some customers applaud between glugs of

TEMPLE STREET'S SINGALONG PARLOURS

A highlight of Yau Ma Tei is its old-fashioned singalong parlours (歌廳). These originated 20 years ago to offer shelter to street singers on rainy days.

Most parlours have basic set-ups – tables, a stage and Christmas lights for an upbeat atmosphere. All have their own organist and a troupe of freelance singers – women who'll keep you company and persuade you to make a dedication or sing along with them for a fee. Their repertoire ranges from Chinese operatic extracts to English oldies. You'll see many regulars at these places – kooky types from the neighbourhood or old men who drink from whisky flasks and know all the dames...

It's more fun to go after 9pm. As parlours don't provide food, you're welcome to order delivery. Some sell beer but you can also bring your own from convenience stores.

beer, others are too busy with card games. Every character in here looks like they have a story to tell.

Each session features 20 singers, all with fan following. Patrons tip a minimum of HK$20 if they like a song. Even if you don't, it's nice to tip every now and then for the experience – just slip your money into the box on stage. For HK$100, you can sing a number yourself. They have a few western classics, and you can bet the keyboard player will know them.

★ **THIS TOWN NEEDS**   LIVE MUSIC
(www.facebook.com/thistownneeds; 1st fl, 6 Shung Shun St, Yau Tong; local bands HK$150, overseas HK$200-500; Ⓜ Yau Tong, exit A2) This Town Needs...more underground music venues like this, staging 10 to 15 gigs monthly in a hip warehouse space in the coastal Kowloon burb of Yau Tong. Formerly known as Hidden Agenda, TTN is a much expanded rebranding, now offering an exhibition space, movie screenings and cafe (noon to 7pm, days vary) as well as a bar during live shows.

Shows could be anything from post-rock to reggae, jazz, techno or punk. Hidden Agenda hopped around locations in Hong Kong for years, setting up in abandoned factories when the rent was cheap, then getting turfed out when landlords began to develop the area and neighbours complained about the noise. At prior locations, they've hosted underground bands from mainland China (Chochukmo, Hungry Ghosts, Carsick Cars) and overseas (Tahiti 80, The Chariot, Anti-Flag, Alcest, Pitchtuner). For up-to-date listings, go to their Facebook page.

The entrance is one door to the west of the flashy Ocean One apartment building entrance.

★ **SYMPHONY OF LIGHTS**   LIGHT SHOW
(Kowloon waterfront; ⊗8-8.20pm) Illuminating both sides of Victoria Harbour every night, symphony of lights is a kitsch paean to all that bling real estate (and a middle finger to Earth Hour). Dancing lasers, searchlights and LEDs are timed to music by the Hong Kong Philharmonic Orchestra, piped along the waterfront at Hong Kong Cultural Centre on the Kowloon side and **Golden Bauhinia Square** (金紫荊廣場; Map p308; 1 Expo Dr, Wan Chai; ◻18, Ⓜ Wan Chai, exit A5) across the water.

If you're lucky enough to be watching from a harbour-view hotel room or fancy restaurant, you can download the official mobile app ('A Symphony of Lights'), which plays the music in real time.

NED KELLY'S LAST STAND   JAZZ
Map p314 (☏852 2376 0662; 11A Ashley Rd, Tsim Sha Tsui; ⊗11.30am-2am, happy hour 11.30am-9pm; Ⓜ Tsim Sha Tsui, exit L5) A Kowloon institution, Ned's marked its 45th anniversary in 2017, making it one of Hong Kong's oldest pubs. Named after a gun-toting Australian bushranger, most of the expat regulars here come for the Dixieland jazz band that plays nightly and cracks jokes between songs. The timeworn interior has an old saloon vibe, with lanterns, faded posters and Oz-related paraphernalia.

HONG KONG
CULTURAL CENTRE   THEATRE, MUSIC
Map p314 (香港文化中心; www.lcsd.gov.hk; 10 Salisbury Rd, Tsim Sha Tsui; ⊗9am-11pm; ☏;

Ⓜ East Tsim Sha Tsui, exit L6) Overlooking the most beautiful part of the harbour, the aesthetically challenged and windowless Cultural Centre is a world-class venue containing a 2085-seat concert hall, a Grand Theatre that seats 1750, a studio theatre for up to 535, an impressive Rieger pipe organ, and rehearsal studios.

On the building's south side is the beginning of a viewing platform from where you can gain access to the Tsim Sha Tsui East Promenade (p138).

WEST KOWLOON
CULTURAL DISTRICT   PERFORMING ARTS
(西九文化區; WKCD; ☑852 2200 0000; www. westkowloon.hk; West Kowloon Waterfront Promenade; ⊘6am-11pm; Ⓜ Kowloon, exit D) Taking up a dramatic spot on the West Kowloon harbourfront, WKCD is slowly developing into Hong Kong's cultural quarter. Construction of cultural spaces is ongoing, including the hotly touted M+ Art Museum, and the area is occasionally used for large events and festivals. Parts of the site are open to the public even when there are no events on, but given the construction, it's barely worth it.

DADA BAR + LOUNGE   LIVE MUSIC
Map p316 (www.dadalounge.com.hk; 2nd fl, Luxe Manor, 39 Kimberley Rd, Tsim Sha Tsui; ⊘11am-2am Mon-Sat, to 1am Sun; Ⓜ Tsim Sha Tsui, exit B1) 🆓 Jazz and blues performers take to the stage nightly at this hotel-bar, which looks something like the Moulin Rouge with its scarlet carpets, heart-shaped armchairs and chandeliers. The music plays 7pm to 10pm Monday to Thursday and from 9pm until after midnight on weekends (when there's a minimum bar spend of HK$180 per person).

BROADWAY CINEMATHEQUE   CINEMA
Map p318 (百老匯電影中心; ☑852 2388 3188; Ground fl, Prosperous Gardens, 3 Public Sq St, Yau Ma Tei; Ⓜ Yau Ma Tei, exit C) New art-house releases, rerun screenings and blockbusters are shown across four screens here. Also has a world-cinema DVD and poster store. Pop next door to Kubrick Bookshop Café (p150) for good coffee and simple meals.

🛍 SHOPPING

In Kowloon, shopping equals crowds, whether you're battling through the bargain hunters in Harbour City, Hong Kong's mightiest mall, or running the ever-changing gauntlet of glitzy, grungy commerce that is Nathan Rd. Further north, Yau Ma Tei is a great place to rummage for local Chinese goods and unique gifts, or tackle the Temple Street Night Market, while Mong Kok is a congested press of everything from electronics to clothing to sporting goods. The highlight of shopping in New Kowloon is the cut-price computer centres of Sham Shui Po.

🛍 Tsim Sha Tsui

★ K11 SELECT   ACCESSORIES, CLOTHING
Map p316 (Shop 101, K11 Mall, 18 Hanoi Rd; ⊘10am-10pm; Ⓜ East Tsim Sha Tsui, exit D2) In the K11 (p152) mall, this shop – like a mini department store – is a funky destination for clothing and accessories, much of it by Hong Kong designers. Matter Matters employs bold colours and iconic geometric graphics on its bags and gifts. Hip multi-brand store Kapok has menswear and unisex accessories.

RISE SHOPPING ARCADE   CLOTHING
Map p316 (利時商場; 5-11 Granville Circuit; ⊘3-9pm; Ⓜ Tsim Sha Tsui, exit B2) Bursting the seams of this minimall is cheap streetwear from Hong Kong, Korea and Japan, with a few knock-offs chucked in for good measure. Patience and a good eye could land you purchases fit for a *Vogue* photo shoot. It's best visited between 4pm and 8.30pm when most of the shops are open.

K11 ART MALL   MALL
Map p316 (18 Hanoi Rd; ⊘10am-10pm; Ⓜ East Tsim Sha Tsui, exit D2) With international clothing brands plus some edgier local offerings, K11 is modern, compact and manageable, and also features exhibition spaces for local artists, hence its 'art mall' title. The basement is a sweet-lover's paradise, with a global array of chocolate shops. It's right above the MTR station.

HARBOUR CITY   MALL
Map p314 (www.harbourcity.com.hk; 3-9 Canton Rd; ⊘10am-10pm; Ⓜ Tsim Sha Tsui, exit C1) A magnet for millions of tourists, this never-ending retail and dining mecca has some 700 shops arranged over four zones: kids, sport, fashion and cosmetics. You'll also find food, cafes and a cinema complex.

For posh global groceries and a food court hawking Asian cuisine, seek out Cty'super.

BROWN'S TAILOR
CLOTHING

Map p314 (☑852 3996 8654; www.brownstailor. com; Unit E, 2nd fl, Comfort Bldg, 88 Nathan Rd; ◷11am-7pm Mon-Fri, to 6.30pm Sat; Ⓜ Tsim Sha Tsui, exit B1) Brown's belongs to a new generation of bespoke tailoring shops for men. They're adept at both making traditional gentlemen's attire and instilling modern elements into a classic look. Depending on the fabric used, a suit will cost you between HK$7500 and HK$12,000. You'll need to allow 10 days for various fittings and a further two weeks for the finished article.

HEAVEN PLEASE
CLOTHING

Map p314 (☑852 3107 0839; www.heaven please.com; Shop 230, 2nd fl, Mira Pl 1, 132 Nathan Rd; ◷noon-9pm; Ⓜ Tsim Sha Tsui, exit B1) Lady Gaga meets punk Lolita at this store opened by two Hong Kong designers, one of whom was previously fashion editor at *Marie Claire*. Both are liberal with the lace and the '80s glam.

SWINDON BOOKS
BOOKS

Map p314 (☑852 2366 8001; www.swindon books.com; 13-15 Lock Rd; ◷9am-6pm Mon-Fri, to 1pm Sat; Ⓜ Tsim Sha Tsui, exit H) A locally run bookshop strong on Hong Kong–related titles. Go upstairs for a bargain selection of used or shop-worn books.

PREMIER JEWELLERY
JEWELLERY

Map p314 (愛寶珠寶有限公司; ☑852 2368 0003; Shop G14-15, Ground fl, Holiday Inn Golden Mile Shopping Mall, 50 Nathan Rd; ◷10am-7.30pm Mon-Sat, to 4pm Sun; Ⓜ Tsim Sha Tsui, exit G) This third-generation family firm is run by a suited and silk-tongued gemologist selling diamonds, white gold and jade on Nathan Rd for over 40 years. A loyal following of shoppers, especially airline cabin crew, come here for bespoke jade pieces and diamond engagement rings. Allow about two to four days to have a piece made.

CURIO ALLEY
GIFTS & SOUVENIRS

Map p314 (btwn Lock & Hankow Rds; ◷10am-8pm; Ⓜ Tsim Sha Tsui, exit C1) This is a fun place to rummage for name chops, soapstone carvings, fans and other Chinese bric-a-brac. It's in an alleyway between Lock and Hankow Rds, just south of Haiphong Rd.

🏠 Yau Ma Tei & Mong Kok

★LADIES' MARKET
MARKET

Map p319 (通菜街, 女人街; Tung Choi Street Market; www.ladies-market.hk; Tung Choi St, Mong Kok; ◷noon-11.30pm; Ⓜ Mong Kok, exit D3) The Tung Choi Street Market is a cheek-by-jowl affair offering cheap clothes and trinkets. Vendors start setting up their stalls as early as noon, but it's best to get here between 1pm and 6pm when there's much more on offer. Beware, the sizes stocked here tend to suit the lissom Asian frame. A terrific place to soak up local atmosphere.

★YUE HWA CHINESE PRODUCTS EMPORIUM
DEPARTMENT STORE

Map p318 (裕華國貨; ☑852 3511 2222; www. yuehwa.com; 301-309 Nathan Rd, Jordan; ◷10am-10pm; Ⓜ Jordan, exit A) This five-storey behemoth is one of few old-school Chinese department stores left in the city. Products include silk scarves, traditional Chinese baby clothes and embroidered slippers, cheap and expensive jewellery, pretty patterned chopsticks and ceramics, plastic acupuncture models and calligraphy equipment. The top floor is all about tea, with vendors offering free sips. Food is in the basement.

SHOWA FILM & CAMERA
VINTAGE

Map p319 (☑852 6541 5621; www.showa-store. com; 3rd fl, 66 Sai Yeung Choi St, Mong Kok; ◷2-9pm; Ⓜ Mong Kok, exit D3) Shutterbugs and vintage shoppers will love this boho store hawking retro film cameras, lenses, accessories and gifts. Staff are passionate and chatty, and they also have a first-rate film-developing service.

Showa has another branch in Causeway Bay, at 1-5 Foo Ming St.

CHAN WAH KEE CUTLERY STORE
HOMEWARES

Map p318 (陳華記刀莊; ☑852 2730 4091; 278 Bowring St, Yau Ma Tei; ◷11am-6pm Thu-Tue; Ⓜ Jordan, exit C2) At this humble shop, octogenarian Mr Chan, one of Asia's few remaining master knife-sharpeners, uses nine different stones to grind each blade, and alternates between water and oil. If you buy from him (he has a great selection), he'll sharpen it there and then. Prices range from HK$200 for a small paring knife to around HK$2000 for a Shun knife.

His customers include chefs, butchers, tailors and homemakers from all over the world. He's had clients send him Japanese willow knives for his magic touch. Choppers, cleavers, slicers, paring knives, even scissors – he's done them all.

JADE MARKET
MARKET

Map p318 (玉器市場; Battery St & Kansu St, Yau Ma Tei; ◎10am-6pm; MYau Ma Tei, exit C) Enclosed by looping Battery St, this covered market has hundreds of stalls selling all varieties and grades of jade. But unless you know your nephrite from your jadeite, it's not wise to buy expensive pieces here. Some of the best buys are not jade at all, but pretty, vintage-y ceramic-bead necklaces and bracelets, or coloured wooden beads with double happiness signs.

SINO CENTRE
MALL

Map p318 (信和中心; 582-592 Nathan Rd, Mong Kok; ◎10am-10pm; MYau Ma Tei, exit A2) The go-to place for all things related to Asian comics and anime, the tiny stores in this mall sell everything from kidult figurines to vintage Casio watches and video games.

LANGHAM PLACE MALL
MALL

Map p319 (朗豪坊; ☑852 3520 2800; www.langhamplace.com.hk/en; 8 Argyle St, Mong Kok; ◎11am-11pm; MMong Kok, exit C3) This 15-storey supermall has some 300 shops that stay open as late as 11pm. The hordes of people here, including what seems like millions of mainland shoppers, can feel intolerable, especially on weekends.

MONG KOK
COMPUTER CENTRE
ELECTRONICS

Map p319 (旺角電腦中心; www.mongkokcc.com; 8-8A Nelson St, Mong Kok; ◎1-10pm; MMong Kok, exit D3) Prices at this computer mall are cheap but language can be a barrier, and you'll see more finished products than computer components.

HONG KONG READER
BOOKS

Map p319 (序言書室; ☑852 2395 0031; www.hkreaders.com; 7th fl, 68 Sai Yeung Choi St S, Mong Kok; ◎1-11pm; MMong Kok, exit D3) Run by a handful of young Hong Kongers, this is a bilingual bookstore-cafe with an intellectual bent. If you're looking for the likes of Derrida or Miłosz, this is the place to go. Check the website for the latest literary readings, though most are conducted in Cantonese.

When you find number 68, you'll have to walk up some steps to the clunky old elevator.

🔒 New Kowloon

★GOLDEN COMPUTER ARCADE & GOLDEN SHOPPING CENTER
ELECTRONICS

(黃金電腦商場、高登電腦中心; www.golden-narcade.org; 146-152 Fuk Wa St, Sham Shui Po; ◎11am-9pm; MSham Shui Po, exit D2) Occupying three floors of a building just across from Sham Shui Po MTR station, Golden Computer Arcade is where the techies go for their low-cost computers and peripherals. The 3Cs are generally considered the best shops – Centralfield, Capital and Comdex.

APLIU STREET FLEA MARKET
MARKET

(鴨寮街; Apliu St, btwn Nam Cheong & Yen Chow Sts, Sham Shui Po; ◎noon-midnight; MSham Shui Po, exit A1) A geek's heaven, this grungy flea market specialises in all things digital and electronic. The market spills over into Pei Ho St.

CHEUNG SHA WAN ROAD
MARKET

(長沙灣道; Cheung Sha Wan Rd, Sham Shui Po; ◎10am-6.30pm Mon-Fri, to 4pm Sat; MSham Shui Po, exit C1) This long road is a riot of shops selling fabrics, trimmings, buttons, ribbons and other raw materials, as well as prêt-à-porter clothing. You'll bump into fashion designers here.

ELEMENTS
MALL

(圓方; www.elementshk.com; 1 Austin Rd W, West Kowloon; ◎11am-9pm; MKowloon, exit C1) Located inside the ICC (p140), Kowloon's most upmarket shopping mall is a confusing maze divided into five zones each themed to one of the five natural elements. As well as ample shopping and dining, it's also home to Hong Kong's largest cinema complex.

FESTIVAL WALK
MALL

(又一城; www.festivalwalk.com.hk; 80-88 Tat Chee Ave, Kowloon Tong; ◎11am-10pm; MKowloon Tong, exit C1) All polished floors and gleaming silver escalators, Festival Walk's design lends it an airiness that makes it more pleasant than most other malls in town. As well as some 200 shops, it has a cinema and an ice-skating rink.

🏃 SPORTS & ACTIVITIES

HONG KONG

DOLPHINWATCH
WILDLIFE WATCHING

Map p314 (香港海豚觀察; ☎852 2984 1414; www.hkdolphinwatch.com; 15th fl, Middle Block, 1528A Star House, 3 Salisbury Rd, Tsim Sha Tsui; adult/child HK$460/230; ⏲cruises Wed, Fri & Sun) 🌿 Hong Kong Dolphinwatch was founded in 1995 to raise awareness of Hong Kong's endangered pink dolphins. The organisation conducts dolphin-spotting cruises (three to four hours) three times weekly as long as enough people sign up. Advance booking is required. It claims that 97% of cruises sight at least one dolphin; if none are spotted, passengers are offered a free trip.

Guides assemble in the lobby of the **Kowloon Hotel** (九龍酒店; Map p314; ☎852 2929 2888; www.thekowloonhotel.com; 19-21 Nathan Rd; Ⓜ Tsim Sha Tsui, exit E) in Tsim Sha Tsui at 8.50am for the bus to Tung Chung via the Tsing Ma Bridge, from where the boat departs; the tours return in the afternoon.

It is estimated that 100 to 200 misnamed Chinese white dolphins *(Sousa chinensis)* – they are actually bubblegum pink – inhabit the coastal waters around Hong Kong, finding the brackish waters of the Pearl River estuary to be the perfect habitat. Unfortunately, these glorious mammals, which are also called Indo-Pacific humpback dolphins, are being threatened by environmental pollution and their numbers are dwindling.

WATERTOURS
BOATING

Map p314 (☎852 2926 3868; www.watertours. com.hk; 6th fl, Carnarvon Plaza, 20 Carnarvon Rd, Tsim Sha Tsui) Hong Kong is perhaps best admired by boat, and this company offers a range of 'cruises' on junk-style crafts. Most worthwhile are the one-hour excursions such as the 'Symphony of Lights Tour' (HK$290), which includes unlimited free alcoholic and soft drinks.

CHIN WOO ATHLETIC ASSOCIATION
MARTIAL ARTS

Map p318 (精武體育館; ☎852 2384 3238; www. chinwoo.com.hk; Flat B & C, 13th fl, Wah Fung Bldg, 300 Nathan Rd, Yau Ma Tei; ⏲2.30-9pm; Ⓜ Jordan, exit B1) This is the 88-year-old branch of the Chin Woo Athletic Association, founded 100 years ago in Shànghǎi by the famed kung-fu master Huo Yuanjia (霍元甲). The Shànghǎi school was featured in Bruce Lee's *Fist of Fury* and Jet Li's *Fearless*. You can visit the school during opening hours. Classes, however, are taught mainly in Cantonese.

YIP MAN MARTIAL ARTS ATHLETIC ASSOCIATION
MARTIAL ARTS

Map p314 (葉問國術總會; ☎852 2723 2306; www.yipmanwingchunasso.com; 54 3/F Mirador Mansion, 58 Nathan Rd, Tsim Sha Tsui; Ⓜ Tsim Sha Tsui, exit D) This *wing chun* kung-fu school looks the part with its rack of dummy training weapons and outdoor terrace for sunrise roundhouse kicks. Experienced teachers speak a bit of English, and there's a basic guesthouse for extended training programs.

The cost for three lessons a week (two or three hours each) for a month is HK$500. A six-month intensive course (six hours a day, six days a week) is around HK$5000, depending on the student.

KOWLOON PARK SWIMMING COMPLEX
SWIMMING

Map p314 (九龍公園游泳池; ☎852 2724 3577; Nathan & Austin Rds, Tsim Sha Tsui; adult/concession HK$19/9; ⏲6.30am-noon, 1-5pm & 6-10pm; ♿; Ⓜ Tsim Sha Tsui, exit C2) Kids will love this huge, ageing swimming complex with four indoor pools and several lagoon-like outdoor swimming areas. It's a cheap, fun way to cool off when the Hong Kong blast furnace is blazing. Avoid summer weekends when you'll struggle to find the water.

KOWLOON SPORTS & ACTIVITIES

Day Trips from Hong Kong

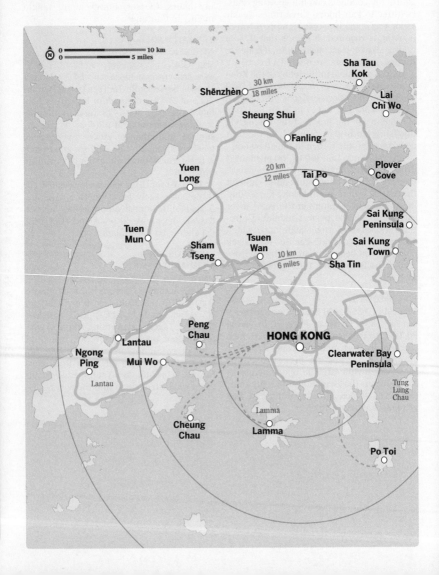

NEW TERRITORIES P161

Clearwater Bay Peninsula p162
The name says it all – beaches with crystal-clear water.

Tsuen Wan p162
Home to some of Hong Kong's most important monasteries.

Sha Tin p165
A New Town with a historical feel, temples and a heritage museum.

Sai Kung Peninsula p167
Beautiful beaches and deserted coves, and half of Hong Kong Global Geopark.

Tung Ping Chau p169
Isolated in Mirs Bay, this island is surrounded by abundant sea life.

Tai Po p170
Lively markets and temples, plus an encyclopaedia of flora and fauna.

Fanling & Sheung Shui p172
A heaven for history buffs, with fortified villages and historic ruins.

Plover Cove p173
Plover Cove is where you go to hike, hike, hike or bike, bike, bike!

Sha Tau Kok p173
Hong Kong's frontier town and home to an ancient walled Hakka village.

Yuen Long p175
Hong Kong Wetland Park, laid-back Pak Nai and old walled villages.

Tuen Mun p177
Visit at leisure the temples and monasteries that dot the landscape.

OUTLYING ISLANDS P177

Lamma p179
The quickest island escape from downtown Hong Kong, laid-back Lamma exudes a bohemian charm and is home to many a commuter who prefers more space and greenery.

Lantau p181
The largest of the islands boasts bountiful sights and recreational possibilities: country parks, hiking trails, fishing villages, beaches, monasteries and the unmissable Big Buddha.

Cheung Chau p186
Think seafood and seafaring culture on this bustling isle with great windsurfing beaches and temples dedicated to water deities. The annual Bun Festival is a highlight.

SHĒNZHÈN P189

Just across the border in mainland China, this skyscraping metropolis of 12 million people has thriving shopping, arts and nightlife scenes.

TOP SIGHT
PING SHAN HERITAGE TRAIL

This meandering 1km trail through three old but lively villages in northwestern New Territories features 12 thoughtfully restored historic buildings and a museum at Ping Shan dedicated to the powerful Tang clan, the founders of the spectacular 500-year-old Ping Shan Village. The Tangs are believed to be some of Hong Kong's earliest immigrants.

Start with the **Ping Shan Tang Clan Gallery** (屏山鄧族 文物館; ☑852 2617 1959; Hang Tau Tsuen, Ping Shan, Yuen Long; ⊙10am-5pm Tue-Sun; ⊠Ping Shan) **FREE** at the eastern end of the trail. Housed in a former police station, the gallery showcases the history of the Tangs. The colourful collections include a traditional sedan chair, ritual wares and a giant wooden bed. The building itself was constructed in 1899 and was a colonial outpost to monitor 'untoward' villagers.

Leaving the Tang Clan Gallery, retrace your steps to Ping Ha Rd and turn right. The small Hung Shing Temple is on your right-hand side, followed by Ching Shu Hin Chamber and Kun Ting Study Hall when you turn right again.

North of Hung Shing Temple, Shu Hin Chamber and Kun Ting Study Hall (pictured) are the Tang Clan Ancestral Hall (p175) and Yu Kiu Ancestral Hall, two of Hong Kong's largest ancestral halls. The Tangs justifiably brag about them, especially the one that bears their name, as it follows a three-halls-two-courtyards structure indicative of the clan's prestigious status in the imperial court.

There are some more temples and an old well ahead. At the end of the heritage trail is small, three-storey **Tsui Sing Lau Pagoda** (聚星樓; Ping Ha Rd, Ping Shan Heritage Trail; ⊙9am-1pm & 2-5pm, closed Tue; ⊠Tin Shui Wai) **FREE**, the only surviving ancient pagoda in Hong Kong.

DON'T MISS

➤ Ping Shan Tang Clan Gallery

➤ Tang Clan Ancestral Hall

➤ Yu Kiu Ancestral Hall

PRACTICALITIES

➤ 屏山文物徑

➤ ☑852 2617 1959

➤ Hang Tau Tsuen, Ping Shan, Yuen Long, New Territories

➤ ⊙ancestral halls & Tsui Sing Lau Pagoda 9am-1pm & 2-5pm, closed Tue

➤ Ⓜ Tin Shui Wai, exit E

TOP SIGHT
HONG KONG GLOBAL GEOPARK

The breathtaking, Unesco-listed Hong Kong Global Geopark spans 50 sq km across the eastern and northeastern New Territories and comprises two regions of spectacular rock formations – volcanic (140 million years ago) and sedimentary (400 million years ago). The best way to experience either region is by joining a guided boat tour. The Volcano Discovery Centre website (www.volcanodiscoverycentre.hk) has details.

DON'T MISS

➡ Sea stacks and sea arches
➡ Red siltstone and secluded islands

PRACTICALITIES

➡ 香港地質公園
➡ New Territories
➡ www.geopark.gov.hk

Sai Kung Volcanic Rock Region

The beautiful Sai Kung Volcanic Rock Region features interlocking hexagonal volcanic rock columns with a honeycomb-shaped cross-section lined up in tilting clusters like fingers pointing at the sky. They may cover an entire rock face like the pipes of a giant organ or stick out above a secluded bay like a metaphor for the city.

The formations are similar to the grey basaltic lava formations in Giant's Causeway in Northern Ireland, but Hong Kong's acidic, silica-rich rocks are a luminous yellow, which is rare and looks stunning against the blue of the sea and, on a sunny day, the sky.

The columns were made by lava and volcanic ash that cooled and contracted after violent volcanic eruptions in the Cretaceous Period. In some places, including this region's only walkable section at High Island Reservoir East Dam (p169), you can see rocks buckled by gravity before they managed to cool completely.

Boat tours for this region cover some of the following: Ung Kong group of islands, Ninepin group of islands, High Island Reservoir East Dam and Sharp Island, and allow you to see at reasonably close range, depending on the weather, massive sea stacks, precipitous rock cliffs, sea arches and sea caves.

Tours cost about HK$300 per person. They leave from the **Volcano Discovery Centre** (火山探知館; Map p168; ☑852 2394 1538; www.volcanodiscoverycentre.hk; Sai Kung Waterfront Park; ☺9am-5pm, exhibition 9.30am-4.30pm; 🛒; 🚌92, 299X) near the Sai Kung waterfront and last for about three hours.

NE New Territories Sedimentary Rock Region

This region features old villages and Hong Kong's oldest rocks formed during the Devonian Period. You'll see eccentrically shaped, red-coloured oxidised conglomerate, sandstone and siltstone from 400 million years ago, including a famous one called Devil's Fist. You'll also get to visit old villages, including Lai Chi Wo (p173) and some of Hong Kong's most secluded islands, peer at rocks to examine the sedimentary layers, and pass a shuttered pearl farm – the only remaining testimony to the pearl industry that thrived in Hong Kong from 900 years ago through WWII to the 1960s.

Boat tours pass through Tolo Channel, a channel south of Plover Cove, which lies over a deep fracture zone running all the way to Shēnzhèn, Fújiàn, Taiwan and Zhèjiāng, which, millions of years ago, was all land.

Most boat tours for this region cover some combination of the following: Double Haven, Ma Shi Chau, Lai Chi Wo (p173), Joss House Bay Tin Hau Temple (p162), Bluff Head, Kat O Island (吉澳), Crooked Island (鴨洲, aka Duck Island) and Tung Ping Chau (p170). They usually leave from the Ma Liu Shui Pier near the Chinese University and last half a day. There is a new weekend ferry service between Ma Liu Shui pier, Kat O and Crooked Island. The boat departs from Ma Liu Shui for Kat O at 8.30am, from Kat O for Crooked Island at 10.15am, from Crooked Island for Kat O at noon, and from Kat O back to Ma Liu Shui at 3.30pm. The service operates Saturday, Sunday and public holidays.

TOP SIGHT
PO LIN MONASTERY & BIG BUDDHA

No trip to Hong Kong is complete without visiting Ngong Ping Plateau for the seated Tian Tan Buddha statue. It can be seen aerially as you fly into Hong Kong, or on a clear day from Macau, but nothing beats coming up close and personal with this much-loved spiritual icon over 500m up in the western hills of Lantau.

Commonly known as the 'Big Buddha', the Tian Tan Buddha is a representation of Lord Gautama some 23m high (or 26.4m with the lotus). It was unveiled in 1993, and still holds the honour as the tallest seated bronze Buddha statue in the world. It's well worth climbing the 268 steps for a closer look at the statue and the surrounding views. The Buddha's birthday, a public holiday in April or May, is a lively time to visit when thousands make the pilgrimage. Visitors are requested to observe some decorum in dress and behaviour. It is forbidden to bring meat or alcohol into the grounds.

On the second level of the podium is a small museum containing oil paintings and ceramic plaques of the Buddha's life and teachings.

Po Lin Monastery, a huge Buddhist complex built in 1924, is more of a tourist honeypot than a religious retreat, attracting hundreds of thousands of visitors a year, and it's still being expanded. Most of the buildings you'll see on arrival are new, with the older, simpler ones tucked away behind them. **Po Lin Vegetarian Restaurant** (寶蓮禪寺齋堂; Map p184; ☑852 2985 5248; Ngong Ping; set meals regular/deluxe HK$110/150; ☹11.30am-4.30pm; ☑) in the monastery is famed for its inexpensive food.

The most spectacular way to get to the plateau is by the 5.7km **Ngong Ping 360** (昂平360纜車; Map p184; www.np360.com.hk; adult/child/concession one-way from HK$145/70/95, return from HK$210/100/140; ☹10am-6pm Mon-Fri, 9am-6.30pm Sat, Sun & public holidays; ☒), a cable car linking Ngong Ping with the centre of Tung Chung (downhill and to the north). The journey over the bay and the mountains takes 25 minutes, with each glassed-in gondola carrying 17 passengers. The upper station is at the skippable theme park–like Ngong Ping Village just west of the monastery.

DON'T MISS

➡ Tian Tan Buddha
➡ Po Lin Monastery
➡ Ngong Ping 360

PRACTICALITIES

➡ 寶蓮禪寺
➡ Lantau
➡ Map p184, C3
➡ ☑852 2985 5248
➡ ☹9am-6pm

New Territories

Explore

The New Territories offer world-class hiking. Exploring one or more sections of the MacLehose Trail or the Pat Sin Leng Nature Trail is likely to be very rewarding. Alternatively, you can do a round-the-island walk of stunning Tung Ping Chau, encircle Plover Cove Reservoir, or combine stargazing and hiking on Tap Mun Island.

If you don't plan on heading to the hills, Sha Tin and Tai Po can more or less be visited on the same day, as can Tsuen Wan and Tuen Mun. Yuen Long, with its heritage trails and nature reserves, requires a full day. And of course, Hong Kong Global Geopark deserves a trip. Depending on whether you're joining a boat or walking tour, kayaking or hiking there, it will take up (at least) a good part of a day.

The Best...

➡ **Sight** Hong Kong Global Geopark (p159)

➡ **Place to Eat** Yue Kee Roasted Goose Restaurant (p164)

➡ **Place to Drink** Accro Coffee (p177)

Top Tip

Kaitos, ferries plying Hong Kong's lesser known waterways, are useful when visiting the New Territories and Outlying Islands. The Transport Department has reliable information on sailings (www.td.gov.hk).

Getting There & Away

➡ **Metro** The MTR East Rail Line stops at Sheung Shui, Fanling, Tai Po and Sha Tin. The Ma On Shan Line serves Sha Tin while the Tseung Kwan O Line is good for Sai Kung. The West Rail Line takes you to Tsuen Wan, Yuen Long and Tuen Mun. The MTR Light Rail network in Western New Territories serves areas in Yuen Long and Tuen Mun. The MTR also operates feeder bus routes within Tuen Mun, Yuen Long and Tai Po, connecting villages with bus terminals near railway stations.

➡ **Bus** Many Tuen Mun–bound buses call at Tsuen Wan and Yuen Long, while most Tai Po–bound buses call at Tai Wai, Sha Tin, Sheung Shui and Fanling.

Need to Know

➡ **Area Code** ☑852

➡ **Location** North and east of Kowloon; Clearwater Bay Peninsula is 15km east of Tsim Sha Tsui, while the Ping Shan Heritage Trail in Yuen Long is 30km northwest of Kowloon.

WORTH A DETOUR

TAI MO SHAN

Hong Kong's tallest mountain is not Victoria Peak but Tai Mo Shan, the 'big, misty mountain' that, at 957m, is nearly twice as high as that relative molehill (552m) on Hong Kong Island. Several hiking trails thread up and around it. You can always start your hike with breakfast at Choi Lung (p164) or Duen Kee (p164), but you will need to bring your own food and water for longer trails.

Tai Mo Shan Country Park Visitor Centre (大帽山郊野公園遊客中心; ☑852 2498 9326; cnr Route Twisk & Tai Mo Shan Rd; ⊗9.30am-4.30pm, closed Tue; ☐51 from Ⓜ️Tsuen Wan West Bus Terminus) is at the junction of Route Twisk (the name is derived from 'Tsuen Wan into Shek Kong') and Tai Mo Shan Rd, which is crossed by the 100km MacLehose Trail, the territory's longest hiking path.

The nearest MTR station is Tsuen Wan. From there, catch bus 51 on Tai Ho Rd North, alighting at the junction of Route Twisk and Tai Mo Shan Rd in Tsuen Kam Au. Follow Tai Mo Rd, which forms part of Stage 9 of the MacLehose Trail, east to the summit. On the right-hand side, about 45 minutes from the bus stop, a fork in the road leads south along a concrete path to the **Sze Lok Yuen Hostel** (施樂園; ☑852 2488 8188; Tai Mo Shan, Tsuen Wan; dm HK$85-115, campsites HK$20-30). Bus 64 also links Tai Mo Shan with Yuen Long and Tai Po Market, and bus 25K runs between Tai Po Market and Tai Mo Shan.

Clearwater Bay Peninsula

Tseung Kwan O, accessible via the MTR station of the same name, is the springboard to the Clearwater Bay Peninsula. There are several wonderful beaches for whiling away an afternoon. The most beautiful and popular are Clearwater Bay First Beach and Clearwater Bay Second Beach. In summer try to go during the week, as both beaches get very crowded on the weekend.

Seafood lovers will not want to miss Po Toi O Village: this is where you can enjoy sumptuous seafood and home-style cooking at its best.

◎ SIGHTS & EATING

★JOSS HOUSE BAY

TIN HAU TEMPLE　　　　　　　TEMPLE

(糧船灣天后古廟, Big Temple; ☑852 2519 9155; ◐8am-5pm; minibus 16) This far-flung structure along Tai Au Mun Rd is the largest, oldest and one of the territory's most important Tin Hau temples, hence the title 'Big Temple' ('Tai Miu'). It has lovely protruding eaves, a display of miniature boats, and a courtyard where fishermen are often seen drying silver bait. 'Big Temple' was built in 1266 by Fújiànese salt traders. Behind it is a large rock with an inscription made in 1274 (Song dynasty) documenting a visit by a salt administrator and his friend, and the history of two temples. It's the oldest dated inscription found in Hong Kong.

'Big Temple' has three statues of Tin Hau, including one used for parading during the Tin Hau Festival, of which it is a prime celebration venue. The deity is accompanied by her usual attendants – red-faced General See-all and green-faced General Hear-all. Their names 觀 ('*guan*' to watch) and 音 ('*yin*' sound) make up the deity's name 觀音 (Guanyin).

From Tai Miu, hikers can follow the 6.6km-long High Junk Peak Country Trail up to Tin Ha Shan (273m) and then continue on to High Junk Peak (Tiu Yu Yung; 344m) before heading eastward back to Tai Au Mun.

SEAFOOD ISLAND　　　CANTONESE, SEAFOOD $$

(海鮮島海鮮酒家; ☑852 2719 5730; Shop B, 7 Po Toi O Chuen Rd; meals from HK$280; ◐11am-11pm) Crustaceans of every kind are on full display at this energetic restaurant hidden in discreet Po Toi O Village. A totally non-luxe setting with no-nonsense fare, Seafood Island is famed for its squid sashimi and razor clams. It's more a group activity to dine here. Grab some friends and enjoy all the treats on offer. Set meals for groups of 12 from HK$3380 to HK$4680.

✦ SPORTS & ACTIVITIES

CLEARWATER BAY

COUNTRY PARK　　　　　　　OUTDOORS

(清水灣郊野公園; ☐103) The heart of the country park is Tai Au Mun, from where trails go in various directions, through the **Clearwater Bay Country Park Visitor Centre** (清水灣郊野公園遊客中心; ☑852 2719 0032; ◐9.30am-4.30pm, closed Tue; ☐91 from Choi Hung to Tai Au Mun) to the southeast in Tai Hang Tun. Take Lung Ha Wan Rd north from Tai Au Mun to the beach at Lung Ha Wan (Lobster Bay) and return via the 2.3km Lung Ha Wan Country Trail.

Tsuen Wan

Exploring the outskirts of residential town Tsuen Wan can be very rewarding, especially if you are an early bird. Having yum cha in the morning at one of the teahouses in Chuen Lung Village is an experience. After breakfast, hikers usually continue up to Tai Mo Shan Country Park. If you want to see vibrant temples, head back to the town centre and take a minibus bound for the palatial Western Monastery and colourful Yuen Yuen Institute.

◎ SIGHTS

YUEN YUEN INSTITUTE　　　TAOIST TEMPLE

Map p163 (圓玄學院; ☑852 2492 2220; Lo Wai Rd, Sam Dip Tam; ◐8.30am-5pm; ☐green minibus 81) FREE Stuffed with vivid statuary of Taoist and Buddhist deities plus Confucian saints, the Yuen Yuen Institute, in the hills northeast of Tsuen Wan, gives a fascinating look into Hong Kong's tripartite religious system. The main building is a replica of the Temple of Heaven in Běijīng.

On the upper ground floor are three Taoist immortals seated in a quiet hall; walk down to the lower level to watch as crowds of faithful pray and burn offerings to the 60 incarnations of Taoist saints lining the walls.

Tsuen Wan

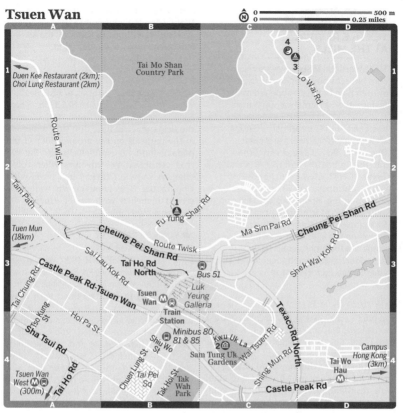

CHUK LAM SIM MONASTERY
BUDDHIST MONASTERY

Map p163 (竹林禪苑; ☎852 2416 6557; Fu Yung Shan Rd; ◎9am-5pm; 🚌green minibus 85) A monastery in a bucolic setting outside the tourist circuit, the large Bamboo Forest Monastery was first built in 1932 by an elderly monk who carved it out of a hillside with six disciples. The lovely Buddhist frescoes, miniature landscapes and fish ponds were added later. The second hall holds three of the largest golden Buddhas in Hong Kong. Locals come to worship the four-faced Brahma (Phra Phrom) statue from Thailand, going round in circles in prayer – clockwise or anticlockwise depending on the request.

WESTERN MONASTERY
BUDDHIST MONASTERY

Map p163 (西方寺; ☎852 2411 5111; Lo Wai Rd, Sam Dip Tam; ◎8.30am-5.30pm; 🚌green minibus 81) FREE Built in Lo Wai Village, one of

Tsuen Wan

◉ Sights

Tsuen Wan's oldest villages, in the 1970s, this tranquil complex is styled as a Chinese palace and calls to mind a period movie set. The various halls are large and spacious, connected to each other by stairs running up a hillside. Near the entrance is an interesting little garden with miniature landscapes, Bodhisattva grottoes and reclining Buddhas. Depending on the time of day, you may witness monks chanting mantras in the main hall. To reach the monastery, take minibus 81 from Shiu Wo St. A taxi from the MTR station will cost around HK$50.

LOCAL KNOWLEDGE

TEXTILE REVIVAL AT THE MILLS

The cavernous **Mills** (www.themills. com.hk) is a converted textile factory in Tuen Wan that has reopened as a fashion-themed creative hub that includes workshops for budding fashion designers and entrepreneurs, shops showing local craftwork and cafes. One of the old mills has been turned into the Centre for Heritage, Arts and Textile (CHAT; www.mill6chat.org), with a rooftop garden where you can walk your dog. Hong Kong's textile industry was started in the 1950s by Shanghainese emigres like the family behind the Mills, and went on to dominate the city's economy for four decades until lower labour costs elsewhere lured factories away.

SAM TUNG UK MUSEUM   MUSEUM

Map p163 (三棟屋博物館; ☑852 2411 2001; 2 Kwu Uk Lane; ⊙10am-6pm, closed Tue; Ⓜ Tsuen Wan) FREE This well-tended museum aims to portray rural life as it was lived in this late-18th-century Hakka walled village, the former residents of which (the Chan clan) were resettled in 1980. Within the complex, a dozen three-beamed houses contain traditional Hakka furnishings, kitchenware, wedding items and agricultural implements, most of which came from two 17th-century Hakka villages in Guǎngdōng province. Behind the restored halls is the old village school, with interactive displays and videos on Hakka women, traditional crafts and food.

At the Tsuen Wan MTR station, take exit E and walk five minutes southeast along Sai Lau Kok Rd to Kwu Uk Lane and the museum.

✖ EATING & DRINKING

★CHOI LUNG RESTAURANT   CANTONESE $
(彩龍茶樓; ☑852 2490 4711; 27 Chuen Lung Village, Route Twisk; dim sum HK$18-30; ⊙5.30am-3pm; ⌂ minibus 80 from Tsuen Wan) This 40-year-old establishment near the village entrance uses spring water to make tofu dessert. It's self-service – pick up your dim sum from the kitchen, make your tea, and plonk yourself down on a plastic stool.

The best time to go is between 8am and 10am when the widest choices are available and the bustling atmosphere makes you feel you're starting the day right.

DUEN KEE
RESTAURANT   CANTONESE, DIM SUM $
(端記茶樓; ☑852 2490 5246; 57-58 Chuen Lung Village, Route Twisk; dim sum HK$16-55; ⊙6am-2pm; ⌂ minibus 80 from Tsuen Wan) Close to the fields, you can have dim sum under one of the parasols on the ground floor of this popular no-frills yum-cha joint. But the true attraction lies upstairs where older villagers show off their caged birds while sipping tea. The home-grown watercress served blanched with oyster sauce is the signature vegetable.

★YUE KEE ROASTED
GOOSE RESTAURANT   CANTONESE $$
(裕記大飯店; ☑852 2491 0105; www.yuekee. com.hk/en; 9 Sham Hong Rd, Sham Tseng; meals HK$180-500; ⊙11am-11pm; ⌂ minibus 302 from Ⓜ Tai Wo Hau) In an alley lined with roast-goose restaurants, 60-year-old Yue Kee is the king. Order gorgeous plates of coppery-skinned charcoal-roasted goose (half is plenty for four people) and sample house specialities including soy-braised goose web (feet), wine-infused goose liver and stir-fried goose intestines. If that's not your speed, there are plenty of standard Cantonese dishes on offer. Book ahead. Yue Kee is a Michelin-star restaurant.

CHENG'S STORE   TEAHOUSE
(鄭記士多; ☑852 2491 6628; 10 Sham Hong Rd, Sham Tseng; tea/coffee HK$70-150; ⊙1-10pm; ⌂ minibus 302 from Ⓜ Tai Wo Hau) Tea connoisseurs may like this eccentric store that whips up lattes with Iron Buddha leaves and 'yin yeung' with Blue Mountain. The boss Mr Cheng charges hotel prices, but his concoctions are nuanced and unusual. He also makes an Instagram-worthy performance of his labour, talks about tannin and tea-making in the Song dynasty, and serves his drinks in bowls.

⊨ SLEEPING

★CAMPUS HONG KONG   HOSTEL $
(香港校園旅舍; ☑852 2945 1111; www.campushk.com; 123 Castle Peak Rd, Yau Kom Tau; dm from HK$220, r from HK$880; ▣; Ⓜ Tsuen Wan) Fabulous hostel for university students that also entertains backpackers when rooms

are available, but especially during the summer months. The 48 rooms with four beds each have nifty communal and study spaces, kitchenette and shower. It's part of a serviced apartment complex (Bay Bridge Hong Kong) and hostel guests also get to enjoy the sea views, the fitness room and the swimming pool.

Sha Tin

You're likely to arrive in New Town Plaza, a bustling mall connected to Sha Tin MTR station, if you visit this part of the New Territories. There are three noteworthy religious establishments in the area – 10,000 Buddhas Monastery, Po Fook Hill columbarium and Che Kung Temple. The town's other key drawcard is the Heritage Museum.

Try to time your visit with one of the rip-roaring weekend race days at the beautifully set Sha Tin Racecourse.

◎ SIGHTS

★HONG KONG HERITAGE MUSEUM
MUSEUM

Map p166 (香港文化博物館; ☎852 2180 8188; www.heritagemuseum.gov.hk; 1 Man Lam Rd; ⊙10am-6pm Mon & Wed-Fri, to 7pm Sat & Sun; ⑭; MChe Kung Temple, exit A) Southwest of Sha Tin town centre, this spacious, high-quality museum inside an ugly building gives a peek into local history and culture. Highlights include a children's area with interactive play zones, the New Territories Heritage Hall with mock-ups of traditional villages, the Cantonese Opera Heritage Hall, where you can watch old operas with English subtitles, and an elegant gallery of Chinese art. There's also a Jin Yong exhibit, with some 300 items illustrating the life and works of martial arts novelist Louis Cha, aka Jin Yong. To reach the Hong Kong Heritage Museum from Che Kung Temple MTR station, walk east along Che Kung Miu Rd, go through the subway and cross the footbridge over the channel. The museum is 200m to the east.

10,000 BUDDHAS MONASTERY
TEMPLE

Map p166 (萬佛寺; ☎852 2691 1067; ⊙10am-5pm; MSha Tin, exit B) FREE Built in the 1950s, this quirky temple actually contains more than 10,000 Buddhas. Some 12,800 miniature statues line the walls of the main temple and dozens of life-sized golden stat-

ues of Buddha's followers flank the steep steps leading to the complex. There are several halls and pavilions, as well as a nine-storey pagoda. It's kitsch but so unlike any other temple in Hong Kong that it's worth the uphill hike to visit.

TAO FONG SHAN CHRISTIAN CENTRE
ARCHITECTURE

Map p166 (道風山基督教叢林; ☎852 2694 4038; www.tfscc.org/en; 33 Tao Fong Shan Rd) FREE A representative of the 'Chinese Revival' architectural style, Tao Fung Shan is a Protestant retreat centre, seminary and hostel. In 1929 a Norwegian Lutheran missionary passionate about Buddhism bought land in Sha Tin and commissioned a Danish architect to design a place where Christians and Buddhists could interact – Tao Fong Shan's symbol is a cross interwoven with a lotus. The resulting buildings have black-thatched roofs, light-blue ridges and red pillars – temple-like, sort of, but with clean silhouettes and a restrained Northern European palette.

✕ EATING

FOODY
TAIWANESE, INTERNATIONAL $

(伙食工業; ☎852 3586 0863; Shop 3, Ground fl, Leader Industrial Centre, 57-59 Au Pui Wan St, Fo Tan; meals HK$80-200; ⊙noon-6pm Mon-Thu, to 10.30pm Fri-Sun) Taiwanese-style noodles and fried chicken as well as pastas and burgers served in a spacious, shabby chic cafe full of retro furniture and vintage objects. The food is decent though not exceptional, but slouchy chairs and friendly service make it great for chilling. Taiwanese R&B is played during the day, with occasional gigs by singer-songwriters or talks on cultural themes at night.

★SHA TIN 18
CANTONESE, CHINESE $$

(沙田18; ☎852 3723 7932; www.hongkong.shatin.hyatt.com; Hyatt Regency Hong Kong, 18 Chak Cheung St; meals HK$350-800; ⊙11.30am-3pm & 5.30-10.30pm; MUniversity) Sha Tin 18's Peking duck (whole HK$788, half HK$500) has put this hotel restaurant, adjacent to the Chinese University, in the gastronomic spotlight. Book your prized fowl 24 hours in advance, and tantalise your taste buds in three ways – pancakes with the crispy skin, meat and leeks; duck soup; and wok-fried minced duck. The Asian fusion desserts here are also famous.

Sha Tin

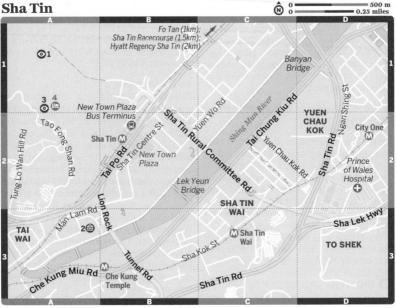

Sha Tin

⊙ Sights

⊜ Sleeping

☆ ENTERTAINMENT

SHA TIN RACECOURSE HORSE RACING

(沙田賽馬場; www.hkjc.com; Penfold Park, Sha Tin; race-day public stands HK$10, members' enclosures HK$100-150; Ⓜ Racecourse) Northeast of Sha Tin town centre is Hong Kong's second racecourse, which can accommodate up to 80,000 punters. Races are usually held on Sunday afternoon (and sometimes on Saturday and public holidays) from September to early July; a list of race meetings is available on the website.

The Racecourse East Rail station, just west of the track, opens on race days only.

⊨ SLEEPING

**TAO FONG SHAN
ASCENSION HOUSE** HOSTEL $

Map p166 (道風山昇天屋; www.ascension-househk.com; 33 Tao Fong Shan Rd; dm HK$180, d HK$350, q HK$650; ⊜ ❋; Ⓜ Sha Tin, exit B) Located at the edge of the Tao Fong Shan compound is Ascension House with four basic air-conditioned dorms accommodating two or three people. Bathrooms are shared and guests have use of a kitchen. It's managed by volunteers from Scandinavia, who also lead daily prayers, host cookouts and arrange weekend outings. Participation is optional.

**TAO FONG SHAN
PILGRIM'S HALL** HOSTEL $

Map p166 (道風山雲水堂; ☑ 852 2691 2739; www.tfssu.org/pilgrim.html; 33 Tao Fong Shan Rd, Sha Tin; r without bathroom HK$310-480; ⊜ ❋; Ⓡ Sha Tin, exit B) This Lutheran Church-affiliated hostel, part of the Tao Fong Shan complex, is set on a peaceful hillside above Sha Tin. The rooms are clean and quiet. The canteen provides simple and healthy meals (for a fee), but you need to reserve in advance.

HYATT REGENCY SHA TIN   HOTEL $$$

(沙田凱悅酒店; ☑852 3723 1234; www.hong-kong.shatin.hyatt.com; 18 Chak Cheung St, Sha Tin; r HK$2500-3000, ste HK$3500-12,500; ▣ 🕊 ❄ @ 🛜 ≋; ▣University) An excellent option if you don't mind being a few MTR stations removed from the action. To make up for that, you get views of Tolo Harbour or the rolling hills of Sha Tin and an exceptional Chinese restaurant. Prices for a standard room could go down to the hundreds during low season, and there are long-stay packages.

Sai Kung Peninsula

Sai Kung Peninsula is one of the last havens left in Hong Kong for hikers, swimmers and boaters, and most of it is one beautiful 7500-hectare country park. Small ferries depart from the waterfront for nearby island beaches, a journey to any of which is rewarding. Moored boats sell seafood to customers on the pier. The atmosphere is unbeatable.

The MacLehose Trail, a 100km route across the New Territories, begins at Pak Tam Chung on the Sai Kung Peninsula. On top of this, Sai Kung Town boasts excellent Chinese seafood restaurants, especially along the attractive waterfront.

◉ SIGHTS

HONG KONG
GLOBAL GEOPARK   PARK
See p159.

SAI KUNG TOWN   AREA

Map p168 (西貢市中心; ▣92, Ⓜ Choi Hung minibus 1A, 1M, ▣299X, ⓂSha Tin East Rail) Sai Kung Town is a wonderful base for exploring the rugged and massive countryside that defines the Sai Kung Peninsula. This eclectic waterfront town has a cluster of seafood restaurants and is also a stopping point and transport hub out from the surrounding countryside. Ferries depart regularly for offshore islands with secluded beaches and villages. From terminals by the waterfront, buses, minibuses and taxis take you to various locations in the country park, including points on the MacLehose Trail.

✖ EATING & DRINKING

HONEYMOON DESSERT   DESSERTS $

Map p168 (滿記甜品; ☑852 2792 4991; Units B&C, 10A Po Tung Rd, Sai Kung; desserts from HK$25; ⏱1pm-1am Sun-Fri, to 2am Sat; ▣1) This shop specialises in Chinese dessert soups made with nuts, pulses, and yam, or fruit, coconut milk and sago. It also whips up crepes and puddings with tropical fruits like mango and banana, and – famously – durian.

★LOAF ON   CANTONESE, SEAFOOD $$

Map p168 (六福菜館; ☑852 2792 9966; 49 See Cheung St, Sai Kung; dishes from HK$150; ⏱11am-10pm; ▣1) The motto here is: eat what they hunt. This three-storey Michelin-star restaurant is where fish freshly caught from Sai Kung waters in the morning lands on customers' plates by midday. The signature fish soup and steamed fish sell out fast. There is no English signage, but it's identifiable by a lone dining table set outside and the shiny brass sign. Reservations recommended.

CHUEN KEE SEAFOOD
RESTAURANT   SEAFOOD $$$

Map p168 (全記海鮮菜館; ☑852 2792 6938; 87-89 Man Nin St, Sai Kung; seafood meals from HK$350; ⏱11am-11pm; ▣1) Chuen Kee impresses with its range of fish, crustaceans and molluscs on offer – all displayed alive in tanks at the entrance, of course. The preparation is similar, but you'll get palm-length mantis shrimp, king crab and 30cm-long razor clams, among other prized creatures.

CLASSIFIED   WINE BAR

Map p168 (☑852 2529 3454; 5 Sha Tsui Path, Sai Kung; ⏱8am-midnight) Classy Classified is the place to go in Sai Kung for good wine and cheese. Wooden communal tables and open frontage make it ideal for people-watching too.

MOMENTAI   BAR

Map p168 (無問題; ☑852 2792 8991; Kiosk 1 Waterfront, Wai Man Rd, Sai Kung; ⏱noon-11pm Tue-Sat, to 10pm Sun) Situated right next to the Sai Kung waterfront promenade, Momentai is convenient for a beer or a glass of wine when you hop off the boat from the beach islands nearby. The views are hard to beat, but you might want to eat somewhere else.

Sai Kung Town

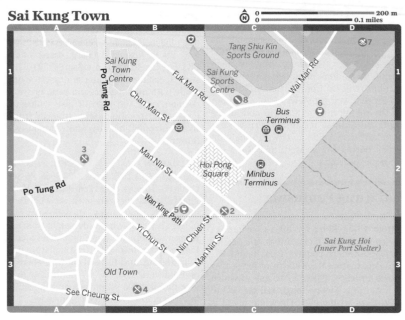

Sai Kung Town

◎ Sights
1 Volcano Discovery Centre.................C2

✦ Eating
2 Chuen Kee Seafood Restaurant.........C2
3 Honeymoon Dessert..........................A2
4 Loaf On...B3

◒ Drinking & Nightlife
5 Classified...B2
6 Momentai..D1

◔ Sports & Activities
7 Sai Kung Swimming Pool...................D1
8 Splash Hong Kong.............................C1

🏃 SPORTS & ACTIVITIES

★ TAI LONG WAN HIKING TRAIL   HIKING
(大浪灣遠足郊遊徑; 🚌village bus 29R) The
northern end of Sai Kung Peninsula has
several wonderful hikes that will take you
through some of Hong Kong's most pris-
tine scenery. The breathtaking 12km Tai
Long Wan Hiking Trail, which starts from
the end of Sai Wan Rd and passes through
beautiful coves including Sai Wan, Tai
Long Wan and Chek Keng, is a perennially

popular option. On weekdays you're likely
to have the trail to yourself. The walk takes
five to six hours.

KAYAK AND HIKE   HIKING, WATERSPORTS
(📞852 9300 5197; www.kayak-and-hike.com)
The seven-hour Sai Kung Geopark kayak
tour provides an exciting option for exploring the beauty of Sai Kung. It takes you to
a kayak base at nearby Bluff Island in a
speed boat or junk, from where you paddle
to a beach to enjoy swimming and snorkelling. Departs 8.30am at Sai Kung old pier
(HK$800 per person).

HOI HA WAN MARINE PARK   OUTDOORS
(海下灣海岸公園; 📞1823; Hoi Ha; 🚌green
minibus 7) A rewarding 6km walk here starts
from the village of Hoi Ha, part of the Hoi
Ha Wan Marine Park, a 260-hectare protected area blocked off by concrete booms
from the Tolo Channel and closed to fishing vessels. There are mangroves along the
coast, coral growing in abundance under-
water, starfish and Nemo's friends.

SPLASH HONG KONG   DIVING
Map p168 (📞852 2792 4495; www.splashhk.
com; Unit 5, 1st fl, Ko Fu House, 58-72 Fuk Man Rd,
Sai Kung; courses from HK$1200, fun dives from
HK$500) Hong Kong has some surprisingly

HIGH ISLAND RESERVOIR EAST DAM

Handsome architecture, the South China Sea and 14-million-year-old volcanic rocks make **High Island Reservoir East Dam** (萬宜水庫東霸; www.ecotoursaikung.com) one of Hong Kong's most breathtaking places. It is the most easily accessible part of Hong Kong Global Geopark (p159) and the only place where you can touch the hexagonal rock columns. The scenery is surreal and made even more so by the presence of thousands of dolosse blocks (huge cement barriers shaped like jacks) placed along the coast to break sea waves.

High Island was Hong Kong's second reservoir built by sealing off the coast with dams (Plover Cove was the first). This was done to provide fresh water to the territory after mainland China shut down supply during the 1967 riots. High Island was designed by Binnie & Partners of London and constructed by an Italian company, Vianini Lavori. At the southern end of East Dam, you'll see a giant, light blue dolos block, a memorial to those who died on the project. Nearby is a concrete slab that commemorates, in Chinese and English, the inauguration of the reservoir in 1978. The construction of the reservoir had one unintentional effect – it made a part of what 30 years later became Hong Kong Global Geopark accessible on foot. Off the coast of the southern end of the dam is Po Pin Chau (literally, Broken-Sided Island), a massive sea stack with rock columns all over its face like a giant pipe organ.

East Dam of High Island Reservoir is in Stage 1 of the MacLehose Trail, which means you can hike here. Alternatively, you can join a Geopark tour that makes a stop at East Dam. See the website for the list and to enrol.

At the time of research, a dedicated green minibus (route 9A) had just been launched to take passengers between Sai Kung's Pak Tam Chung and East Dam. During the trial period the route (HK$11.30) operated on Sundays and public holidays, between 3pm and 6pm. You could also take bus 94 from Sai Kung Bus Terminus to Pak Tam Chung, then walk 9km along Tai Mong Tsai Rd and Sai Kung Man Kee Rd, following MacLehose Trail Stage 1, to East Dam.

A taxi to East Dam from Sai Kung Town takes about 30 minutes and costs HK$160. But you may need to call a taxi service for the return trip. Try 852 8103 1189. Be prepared to offer an extra HK$50 or more when placing your request in order to land a ride.

worthwhile diving spots, particularly in the far northeast, and Sai Kung–based Splash is a five-star PADI dive centre offering courses at all levels, shore dives, boat dives and equipment rental.

SAI KUNG SWIMMING POOL   SWIMMING
Map p168 (852 2791 3100; Wai Man Rd, Sai Kung; ⊙6.30am-noon, 1-6.30pm & 7.30-10pm Apr-Oct; 92, 94, 99, 299, 1, 1A) Consists of a 50m main pool, a teaching pool for learners and a leisure pool. The water is heated in the cooler months. Closed every Wednesday (or Thursday if Wednesday is a public holiday) for cleaning.

**CHONG HING WATER
SPORTS CENTRE**   WATER SPORTS
(創興水上活動中心; 852 2792 6810; www.lcsd.gov.hk/en/watersport/hiring/hiring_craft/hiri_book1.html; West Sea Cofferdam, High Island

Reservoir, Sai Kung; canoe, dinghy & board hire per hr HK$20-30) Government-run watersports centre with a vast artificial lake, a campsite and **Astropark** (天文公園; 852 2721 0226; www.astropark.hk.space.museum; ⊙24hr). You can hire crafts for sailing, canoeing and windsurfing. It also offers camping facilities and operates canoe tours to sea caves.

Tung Ping Chau

The easternmost point of Hong Kong, kidney-shaped Tung Ping Chau (東平洲) sits in splendid isolation in Mirs Bay in the far northeast of the New Territories. At one time the island, which is called Tung Ping Chau (East Peace Island) to distinguish it from Peng Chau (same pronunciation in Cantonese) near Lantau, supported a population of 3000, but now it is virtually deserted. The distance from Ma Liu Shui to the southwest, from where the ferry serving the island departs, is around 25km.

The island is part of Hong Kong Global Geopark (p159), which encompasses eight sites of special geologic significance that are protected from development. Together with the waters around it – which teem with sea life (especially corals) – it forms Hong Kong's fourth marine park.

🏃 SPORTS & ACTIVITIES

TUNG PING CHAU TRAIL   HIKING

(東平洲環島遊) This 6km trail starts from Tung Ping Chau ferry pier and encircles the island. As you weave in and out of old hamlets, you'll see spectacular geological features like sedimentary rocks, wave-cut platforms and sea stacks. Near the water, incoming waves leave puddles with a thriving ecology of starfish, sea anemones and krill-like mini aquariums.

🛏 SLEEPING

TUNG PING
CHAU CAMPSITE   CAMPGROUND

(東平洲營地) **FREE** This campground is next to Kang Lau Shek (更樓石), a spectacular stack overlooking the sea. There is also a huge wave-cut platform near the site. Fa-

cilities include barbecue pits, benches and tables, drains and clotheslines.

Tai Po

Formed from two former market towns on either side of the Lam Tsuen River, Tai Po has a lively waterfront downtown ringed by housing estates and, beyond, rolling rural hills. On offer are quirky temples, a cute railway museum and several nature areas. But the best thing about this ever-changing region is the street life. Barter for lychees in the crowded street markets, queue for tofu or noodles at hole-in-the-wall stalls, or watch proud parents photograph their babies toddling along the pedestrian bridge crossing the river. This is old-school Hong Kong living at its finest.

◎ SIGHTS

TAI PO WATERFRONT PARK   PARK

(大埔海濱公園; ⊙Insect House 8am-7pm, tower from 7am, park 24hr; 🚌72A, 73, 73X, 75X, 271, 275R, 275S, 275, 74K) Hong Kong's largest public park and one of the most beautiful has tree-framed lawns for picnics and kite-flying, an amphitheatre with white sail canopies, a cycling track along Tolo Harbour from which you can watch dragon

Tai Po

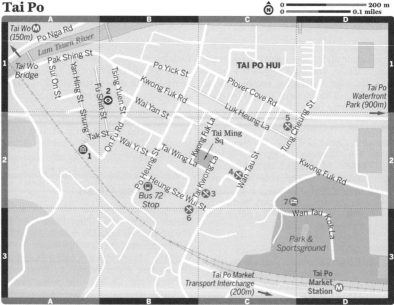

boat races during the Dragon Boat Festival, and an Insect House. The highlight is a quirky lookout tower resembling a rocket in a hoop skirt. It has telescopes to view the harbour and high-rises in the distance, and the dystopian '70s industrial landscape of Tai Po Industrial Estate.

TAI PO MARKET   MARKET

Map p170 (大埔街市; Fu Shin St; ⊘6am-8pm; MTai Wo) Not to be confused with the MTR station of the same name, this street-long outdoor wet market is one of the most winning in the New Territories. Feast your eyes on a rainbow of fruit and vegetables, tables lined with dried seafood, old ladies hawking glutinous Hakka rice cakes, and stalls selling fresh aloe and sugar cane juices.

KADOORIE FARM
& BOTANIC GARDEN   FARM

(嘉道理農場暨植物園; ☑852 2483 7200; www.kfbg.org.hk; Lam Kam Rd; adult/child HK$30/15, under 5yr & seniors free; ⊘9.30am-5pm; ⊛; ☐64K) Set in a valley, the 148-hectare Kadoorie Farm & Botanic Garden is primarily a conservation and teaching centre, but it has a few animals, and the woods and the gardens are especially lovely, with lots of indigenous flora and fauna. You can buy organic produce here as well. Bus 64K goes to the farm.

HONG KONG
RAILWAY MUSEUM   MUSEUM

Map p170 (香港鐵路博物館; ☑852 2653 3455; www.heritagemuseum.gov.hk/en_US/web/hm/museums/railway.html; 13 Shung Tak St; ⊘10am-6pm, closed Tue; ⊛; MTai Wo) FREE Housed in the former Tai Po Market train station (built in 1913 in traditional Chinese style),

this small museum is a fun stop for trainspotters and families with train-crazy kids. There are a few exhibits about the history of the Hong Kong railways, but the real draws are the historical train carriages open to visitors.

✖ EATING

TAI PO HUI MARKET   STREET FOOD $

Map p170 (大埔墟街市大樓; 8 Heung Sze Wui St; meals HK$30-50; ⊘market 6am-8pm, cooked food centre to 2am; MTai Po Market, exit A2) This modern silver building houses a large, clean and always-busy wet market, with a spacious cooked-food centre on top. Favourites include stall 27 (東記) for Shanghainese pork-chop noodles, stall 20 (有記) for sticky Hakka dumplings, stall 14 (錦華) for congee and stalls 8 and 9 (林記) for dim sum. Tables are shared. You can buy from different shops.

CHAN HON KEE   CANTONESE $

Map p170 (陳漢記; ☑852 2658 2277; 91B Wan Tau St; claypot rice HK$50-80, rice rolls HK$17-27; ⊘11am-4am; MTai Po Market, exit A2) People flock to this neighbourhood restaurant for its silken rice-flour rolls, which are steamed to translucence with meat or seafood, or simply drizzled with soy sauce, and its hearty claypot rice (all 26 varieties available only at dinner). There's always a line outside, so go early.

AH PO TOFU   DESSERTS $

Map p170 (亞婆豆腐花; Shop 2A, Tai Kwong Lane; tofu pudding HK$8; ⊘10am-8pm; MTai Po Market, exit A2) You'll recognise this beloved *dau fu fa* (sweet silky tofu pudding) shop by the line snaking down the busy pedestrian street. Sprinkle on palm sugar to taste, then eat while standing before returning the bowl to the counter.

CHOI YUN KEI   NOODLES, CANTONESE $

Map p170 (蔡潤記; ☑852 2657 6460; 7 Tung Cheung St; ⊘7.30am-4pm; MTai Po Market, exit A1) This famous old shop sells only four things – beef brisket (牛腩), fish balls (魚蛋), fish slices (魚片) and tripe (牛肚) – and they're delicious. You can have them with soup noodles – flat rice noodles (河粉) are a good idea – with a side of fried fish skin (炸魚皮) and poached greens (郊外油菜).

Service is slow; be patient.

☘ SPORTS & ACTIVITIES

TAI PO KAU NATURE RESERVE   HIKING

(大埔滘自然護理區; Tai Po Rd; 🚌70, 72) The thickly forested 460-hectare Tai Po Kau Nature Reserve is Hong Kong's most extensive woodlands. It is home to many species of trees and insects, and is a superb place for a quiet walk or a small workout. The reserve is criss-crossed with four main tracks ranging in length from 3km to 10km, plus a short nature trail of under 1km. If possible, avoid the reserve on Sunday and public holidays, when the crowds descend upon the place.

The reserve is well served by buses. Bus 70 passes through Jordan and Mong Kok on its way here. Bus 72 can be used to get here from the nearby Sha Tin and Tai Po Market East Rail stations. A taxi from Tai Po Market East station will cost around HK$40, and from the University East station about HK$55.

🛏 SLEEPING

⭐GREEN HUB   HOSTEL $

Map p170 (綠匯學苑; ☎852 2996 2800; www.greenhub.hk; 11 Wan Tau Kok Lane; s/tw/tr from HK$400/650/900; ❄🛜; Ⓜ Tai Po Market, exit A2) 🏅 This fabulous hostel is part of the repurposed Old Tai Po Police Station complex now run by Kadoorie Farm. Guestrooms have high ceilings and double-tiled roofs. Four come with air-conditioners; the rest rely on fans and natural ventilation. The canteen, open from 10am to 3.30pm, prepares vegetarian meals with local, Fair Trade ingredients. There are monthly barter parties. Booking essential.

Fanling & Sheung Shui

Fanling's highlights are the impressive Fung Ying Sin Temple, located just a stone's throw from the Fanling East Rail station, and the immersive Lung Yeuk Tau Heritage Trail that strings together five ancient walled villages. Sheung Shui is home to a stately 19th-century mansion with Chinese and western features.

For the more adventurous, off-the-beaten-path options include the seldom-visited walled village of Ping Kong or the village of Sha Tau Kok, where Japanese pillboxes from WWII lie intact in the (still) unspoilt countryside.

⊙ SIGHTS

TAI FU TAI MANSION   HISTORIC BUILDING

(大夫第; San Tin, Yuen Long; ⊙9am-1pm & 2-5pm, closed Tue; 🚌76K) Located between Yuen Long and Sheung Shui, this splendid Mandarin-style building complex dating from 1865 is eclectically fused with western design. Members of the Man clan, another powerful family in the New Territories, lived here for well over a century until they moved out in 1980. The courtyard is encircled by stone walls with a guarded checkpoint. Inside, auspicious Chinese symbols are found in the woodcarvings along with art nouveau glass panels, and there is a European fountain.

FUNG YING SIN TEMPLE   TAOIST TEMPLE

(蓬瀛仙館; ☎852 2669 9186; www.fysk.org; 66 Pak Wo Rd, Fanling; ⊙8am-6pm; Ⓜ Fanling) This brightly coloured Taoist temple perched on a hillside opposite Fanling MTR station is one of Hong Kong's most important Taoist temples. It was founded in 1926 and has been meticulously renovated over the years. There are wonderful exterior murals of Taoist immortals, an orchard terrace, a wall inscribed with Laotzu's Tao Te Ching (Classic of the Tao and of Virtue), and a **vegetarian restaurant** (Ground & 1st fl, Building A7; ⊙11am to 5pm). There's a columbarium (a storage place for cinerary urns) behind the temple.

🍴 EATING

⭐KWAN KEE BEEF BALLS & PORK KNUCKLES   NOODLES $

(群記牛肉丸豬手; ☎852 2675 6382; 5 Luen Cheong St, Luen Wo Hui, Fanling; meals HK$50; ⊙11am-5.45pm) There's always a wait at this unpretentious shop for the bouncy beef balls and the chewy, collagen-laden pork knuckles served in blue plastic bowls and (optional) drizzled with aromatic home-made chilli sauce. It sells out fast and customers may be asked to return an hour later for the next batch.

⭐SUN HON KEE   HAKKA, CANTONESE $$

(新漢記; ☎852 2683 0000; 5 Luen Wo Rd, Fanling; mains HK$88-288; Ⓜ Fanling, exit C) Well-executed Hakka cuisine, known for its use of preserved ingredients as well as stews and braises, is on offer at this busy two-floor restaurant. Dishes tend to be boldly flavoured, as they're meant to go with rice. Try the chicken cooked in yellow wine (黃酒煮雞), braised pork belly (客家炆豬肉) and pan-seared squid with shallots (紅蔥爆吊桶). Best with beer or rice with lard and sweetened soy sauce (豬油撈飯). Booking advised for weekend dinners.

🏃 SPORTS & ACTIVITIES

**LUNG YEUK TAU
HERITAGE TRAIL**   WALKING

(龍躍頭文物徑; ◻54K) This 4.5km-long trail northeast of Fanling meanders through five relatively well-preserved walled villages, home to the Tang clan. The oldest (800 years), most attractive and most intact village is Lo Wai, identifiable by its 1m-thick fortified wall. Unfortunately, it's not open to the public. Admire the exterior, before continuing to the more welcoming villages of Tung Kok Wai to the northeast and Sun Wai towards the trail's northern end.

Plover Cove

Apart from a visit to Tsz Shan Monastery, Plover Cove has only two real draws: hiking and cycling. Large parts of it are designated geopark areas, so you'll see rugged rocks and mineral marvels, especially around Plover Cove Reservoir. Plan a full day here. For an easy walk, the 4.4km Pat Sin Leng Nature Trail is a good alternative.

◉ SIGHTS

TSZ SHAN MONASTERY   MONASTERY

(慈山寺; ☑852 2123 8666; www.tszshan.org; 88 Universal Gate Rd, Tai Po; ⊙9.30am-5pm; Ⓜ Tai Po Market, Tai Wo) Spanning 46,000 sq metres, Tsz Shan is state-of-the-art antiquity that cost HK$1.5 billion and took 12 years to build. At a glance, it's a graceful Tang dynasty complex. But inside the shell of precious *zitan* wood is a steel structure that does away with the need for the pillars and interlocking eave brackets found in ancient architecture. This gives the monastery a more modern look. Tsz Shan does not entertain walk-ins. Book online up to a month ahead. Tsz Shan also runs meditation retreats, as well as tea and zen calligraphy workshops. See the website for details.

🏃 SPORTS & ACTIVITIES

★ PLOVER COVE RESERVOIR   OUTDOORS

(船灣淡水湖; ◻75K) Part of Hong Kong Global Geopark, this reservoir was completed in 1968, in a very unusual way. Rather than build a dam across a river, of which Hong Kong has very few, a barrier was erected across the mouth of a great bay. The sea water was siphoned out and fresh water was pumped in. The area around the reservoir is glorious hiking and cycling country, and well worth a full day's exploring.

PAT SIN LENG NATURE TRAIL   HIKING

(八仙嶺自然教育徑; ◻75K) This excellent 4.4km-long trail, which should take from two to 2½ hours, leads from the Plover Cove Country Park Management Centre at Tai Mei Tuk and heads northeast for 4km to Bride's Pool where it ends. There are signboards numbered 1 to 22, so there is little danger of getting lost. The scenery is excellent and the two waterfalls at Bride's Pool are delightful, but the place gets packed on the weekend.

Sha Tau Kok

An off-limits frontier area for more than 60 years, Sha Tau Kok Village (沙頭角), which lies 11km northeast of Fanling, was sealed off from the rest of Hong Kong in 1951 following the communist takeover of China. While access to the border town itself is still restricted to local residents, the 400 hectares of land – and the patchwork of time-warped villages that it contains – to the west and southwest have been partially open since 2012.

◉ SIGHTS

★ LAI CHI WO   VILLAGE

(荔枝窩; hakkahomelcw@gmail.com; Plover Cove Country Park) Part of Hong Kong Global Geopark, 400-year-old Lai Chi Wo is Hong Kong's best-preserved Hakka walled village and has an intact woodland. With 200 houses, ancestral halls, temples, and a breezy square fringed by old banyans, it is a sight to behold. There are 90-minute guided tours every Sunday and public holiday (11am and 1.30pm). Register at the village square or email before you go to ensure a place. Bespoke tours can be arranged on weekdays; make contact two weeks in advance.

Lai Chi Wo is one of Hong Kong's most biologically diverse freshwater wetlands. If you follow the stream leading out of the village, you'll see looking-glass mangroves with buttress roots in a lace-like pattern. Also here is the white-flower Derris, a climbing vine with long, supple branches like elongated arms that form a natural swing. It is a poisonous plant and its root when crushed can be used as a fish stunner and insecticide. There are butterflies and dragonflies aplenty here, hovering over scuttling mangrove crabs.

Lai Chi Wo was once the most affluent Hakka walled village in the northeastern New Territories. A 5- to 7-hectare crescent-shaped wood embraces the village from behind – ideal for feng shui as the backing of a forest is believed to bring luck. Thickly grown trees are also a natural protective barrier.

The village has become a model for rural resurrection in Hong Kong. Though almost completely abandoned in the 1960s, it is quite lively now, thanks to the efforts of villagers and conservationists.

The growing of rice and vegetables has resumed, pig and cow sheds have been restored, and shuttered village houses now function as education and research facilities, and eventually, holiday homes.

A ferry departs for Lai Chi Wo on Sunday and public holidays at 9am from the Ma Liu Shui Pier near the Chinese University and returns at 3.30pm. It's HK$80 return and takes 90 minutes.

Most Hong Kong Global Geopark Sedimentary Rock tours make a stop at Lai Chi Wo, or just hike there from Wu Kau Tang or Luk Keng, and lunch at Foo's Cafe.

You can also hike to Lai Chi Wo. Green minibus 20C, operating between Tai Po Market MTR station and Tai Mei Tuk, goes beyond Tai Mei Tuk to Wu Kau Tang once every one to two hours between 5.45am to 7.45pm daily, with the last minibus returning from Wu Kau Tang at around 8.15pm.

From Wu Kau Tang, it's 4.6km to Lai Chi Wo.

On Sundays and public holidays, bus route 275R goes from Tai Po Market MTR station to Bride's Pool, which is only 750m from Wu Kau Tang.

Green minibus 56K leaves Fanling MTR station for Luk Keng at 30-minute intervals on weekdays, and 10-minute intervals on Saturdays, Sundays and public holidays. From Luk Keng, it's 9.6km to Lai Chi Wo.

KANG YUNG STUDY HALL
HISTORIC BUILDING

(鏡容書屋; ⊘9am-1pm & 2-5pm, closed Tue) **FREE** This graceful study hall in the Hakka village of Sheung Wo Hang (上禾坑村) was a private school in the 18th century and once had students from as far away as Sha Tin. The building's hibiscus-framed doorway leads to two grey-bricked halls with cocklofts. Every Mid-Autumn Festival (15th day of the eighth lunar month), the Li brothers of the village, one of whom is a sculptor, make enormous sky lanterns from about 7pm and send them off from an open lawn.

✕ EATING

CHUNG KEE STORE
HAKKA $

(松記士多; ☑852 2679 9148; Kuk Po Village, Luk Keng, Sha Tau Kok; meals from HK$120; ⊘11am-6pm Sat, Sun & public holidays, closed Jul & Aug) Deep in the hills, a Hakka villager with a passion for cooking has turned his seafront store into a restaurant. Patrons feast under trees on seafood and Hakka classics like steamed mullet, braised pork belly and broiled clams. But if you just want the hikers' staple – Spam and egg instant noodles – Mr Yeung is fine with that too.

FOO'S CAFE
CAFE $

(富記茶室; Lai Chi Wo Village; ⊘9.30am-4pm Sun & public holidays) This farm-to-table cafe in the village of Lai Chi Wo sources produce locally and turns it into soul-warming delicacies. Organic pork wontons, flaxseed noodles tossed with scallions, winter melon and dried shrimp soup with rice are some of the items you may encounter depending on the season. Don't miss the Hakka sweet tea made from the village's last remaining wild sweet tea tree. Infusions of butterfly pea flower, marigold and lemongrass are other thirst-quenching options.

FOOK LEE TEA HOUSE
HAKKA $

(福利茶室; ☑852 2679 9421; 1 Sam A Tsuen, Sha Tau Kok; dishes HK$50-160; ⊘morning-sundown Sat, Sun & public holidays) Delicious village kitchen with tables on the patio serving Hakka braised pork, salt and pepper squid, and other hearty Hakka and Cantonese dishes. It curdles its own tofu and grows its own veggies. Open every weekend for brunch, lunch and very late lunch in the cool hiking-friendly seasons; call for hours at the height of summer.

Take minibus 20R near Tai Po Market MTR station and get off at the last stop – Wu Kau Tang (烏蛟騰村) – and turn into the path near the lamp post to enter Wu Kau Tang Village. There are several trails that pass Sam A Tsuen or Sam A Village (三椏村) where the teahouse is.

🛍 SHOPPING

LAI CHI WO
FARMERS MARKET
FOOD, ACCESSORIES

(荔枝窩農墟; www.facebook.com/HakkaHome LCW; ☉Sun & public holidays) Villagers in Lai Chi Wo make small batches of top-notch soya sauce, turmeric-laced sugar and scallion oil. You'll also find fresh rice and fruit, and popsicles with edible flowers. There's a farmers market on some Sundays, but you'll find at least a few of these items on sale in the village on most days.

🛏 SLEEPING

HOK TAU CAMPSITE
CAMPGROUND

(鶴藪營地; Hok Tau, Pat Sin Leng Country Park) **FREE** This campsite adjacent to the picturesque Hok Tau Reservoir (鶴藪水塘) is inside the 3100-hectare Pat Sin Range Country Park. It's also on Stages 9 and 10 of the Wilson Trail, which traverses the park.

Yuen Long

Yuen Long is an important transport hub and a gateway to the Mai Po Marshes and the nearby walled villages of Kat Hing Wai and Shui Tau Tsuen.

If you didn't manage to book a guided tour to Mai Po, Hong Kong Wetland Park is a more than worthy substitute: morning hours are the best time to go birdwatching. Watching the sunset in Pak Nai at the westernmost edge of Hong Kong is an unforgettable experience. A seafood dinner in Lau Fau Shan is the best way to end the day.

👁 SIGHTS

PING SHAN
HERITAGE TRAIL
HISTORIC BUILDING

See p158.

★ HONG KONG
WETLAND PARK
PARK

(香港濕地公園; ☎852 3152 2666; www.wetlandpark.gov.hk; Wetland Park Rd, Tin Shui Wai; adult/concession HK$30/15; ☉10am-5pm, closed Tue; ♿; ☐967, ☐705, 706) This 60-hectare ecological park is a window on the wetland ecosystems of the northwest New Territories. The natural trails, bird hides and viewing platforms make it a handy and excellent spot for birdwatching. The futuristic grass-covered headquarters houses interesting galleries (including one on tropical swamps), a film theatre, a cafe and a viewing gallery. If you have binoculars, bring them; otherwise be prepared to wait to use the fixed points in the viewing galleries and hides.

TANG CLAN
ANCESTRAL HALL
NOTABLE BUILDING

(鄧氏宗祠; Hang Tau Tsuen, Ping Shan; ☉9am-1pm & 2-5pm, closed Tue; Ⓜ Tin Shui Wai, exit E) **FREE** The sense of dignified grandiosity is unmistakable at Hong Kong's most magnificent ancestral hall (c 1273). The spaces and ornaments are larger than life, but keep to an understated palette. The basin feasts (parties where guests eat from basins piled with layers of food) thrown in the courtyards here by the Tangs are famous, as are the fashion shows by one of their best-known members – William Tang, a fashion designer who created uniforms for Dragon Air, the MTR and Hong Kong International Airport.

TANG CHING LOK
ANCESTRAL HALL
HISTORIC BUILDING

(清樂鄧公祠; Shui Mei; ☉9am-1pm & 2-5pm Wed, Sat & Sun; ☐64K) **FREE** A finely decorated 15th-century structure in the southwest corner of Shui Mei Village, Tang Ching Lok Ancestral Hall is a gathering point for descendants of the four oldest branches of the Tang family. Whenever a son is born, candles are lit and the child's name is officially entered into the lineage registry here. The central panel on the roof ridge shows the motif 'carp jumping over dragon's gate', which symbolises leaps in prestige and affluence following hard work.

PAK NAI
BEACH

(白泥; ☐minibus 33 from Ⓜ Tin Shui Wai) Literally 'white mud', Pak Nai is one of the best places to see the sunset in Hong Kong. This 6km stretch of coastline is dotted

> **WORTH A DETOUR**
>
> ## MAI PO NATURE RESERVE
>
> The 270-hectare **nature reserve** (米埔自然保護區; ☑852 2526 1011; www.wwf.org.hk; Mai Po, Sin Tin, Yuen Long; ⊙9am-5pm; ☐76K from Sheung Shui East Rail or Yuen Long West Rail stations) includes the Mai Po Visitor Centre at the northeastern end, where you must register; the Mai Po Education Centre to the south, with displays on the history and ecology of the wetland and Deep Bay; floating boardwalks and trails through the mangroves and mudflats; and a dozen hides. Disconcertingly, the cityscape of Shēnzhèn looms to the north.
>
> Access to Mai Po is restricted – it doesn't allow walk-ins. The best way to see it is by joining one of the several guided tours run by the World Wide Fund for Nature Hong Kong (WWF), which manages the reserve. You can book online (www.wwf.org. hk). Half-day English tours (HK$150) leave the visitor centre every Sunday at 2.30pm. Other tours include the Mangrove Broadwalk tour (adult/child HK$216/180) lasting four hours, the seasonal Night Safari, the Migration tour and Shrimp Harvesting. Note that the tours have different age requirements for child participants. The website has details.
>
> To visit the reserve unaccompanied, you'll need a permit issued by the Director of Agriculture, Fisheries and Conservation. Call 852 2708 8885 or email with a letter and supporting documents to mailbox@afcd.gov.hk to apply.
>
> Visitors are advised to wear comfortable walking shoes or boots but not bright clothing. It is best to visit at high tide (minimum 2m), when birds in their tens of thousands – mostly ducks, gulls, cormorants and kingfishers, but many rare species as well – flock to the area. The Hong Kong Observatory website (www.hko.gov.hk/tide/predtide.htm) and app have tidal information.
>
> Bus 76K, which runs between Yuen Long and the Fanling and Sheung Shui MTR East Rail stations, will drop you off at Mai Po Lo Wai, a village along the main road just east of the marsh. The car park is about a 20-minute walk from there. Red minibus 17 from San Fat St in Sheung Shui also goes to Mai Po Lo Wai. Alternatively, a taxi from Sheung Shui will cost HK$88.

with mangroves, fish ponds, farms, shacks and muddy beaches sprinkled with oyster shells. Sunset can be watched from most parts of Deep Bay Rd (it continues as Nim Wan Rd after Upper Pak Nai), the only road meandering along the coastline.

Green minibus 33 goes from Yuen Long via Lau Fau Shan. Check the website of Hong Kong Observatory (www.hko.gov.hk) for the sunset times.

🍴 EATING & DRINKING

HO TO TAI NOODLE SHOP — NOODLES $
(好到底麵家; ☑852 2476 2495; 67 Fau Tsoi St; wonton noodles HK$30; ⊙10am-8pm; 圓Tai Tong Rd) This 60-year-old Yuen Long institution is one of the world's cheapest Michelin restaurants. It is best known for the fresh Cantonese egg noodles and shrimp roe noodles that it churns out daily. Foodies from all corners come to slurp the delightful wonton noodles. An English menu is available from the cashier. The haunt is a three-minute walk south of Tai Tong Rd light-rail station.

DAI WING WAH — CANTONESE $
(大榮華酒樓; ☑852 2476 9888; 2nd fl, Koon Wong Mansion, 2-6 On Ning Rd; dishes HK$90-500, dim sum from HK$20; ⊙7am-11.30pm; 圓Tai Tong Rd) The brainchild of celebrated chef Leung Man-to, Dai Wing Wah is a traditional banquet-style restaurant specialising in walled-village dishes. Leung sources local ingredients from small farms and food producers whenever possible, and complements them with his innovations in cooking. Must-eats include lemon-steamed grey mullet, smoked oysters and steamed sponge cake with demarara sugar.

HANG HEUNG — BAKERY $
(恆香老餅家; ☑852 2476 3080; www. hangheung.com.hk; 66 Castle Peak Rd; ⊙9am-8pm; Ⓜ Yuen Long, exit B) Hong Kongers are familiar with the gold lettering on red

paper boxes that have been stained by lard from the warm and crumbly Chinese pastries inside. Often they're 'wife cakes' – flaky moons of sweetened wintermelon and white lotus seed paste. But they can also be date paste cakes or egg rolls. Of all of Hang Heung's branches, this old shop in red and gold is the best.

KAI KEE DESSERTS
DESSERTS $

(佳記甜品; ☑852 2479 4743; Shop 7, Chi Fu Centre, 7 Yau San St, Yuen Long; desserts HK$20-80; ☺12.30pm-2am) Yuen Long's long-standing dessert expert Kai Kee is famous for its grass jelly bowl – served as a mini mountain topped with mixed fruit and a drizzle of sago pearls. In summer you see families strolling here after dinner just for this. But Kai Kee offers well over a hundred other treats. From heirloom recipe almond soup to Thai-style sticky rice with mango, and everything in between, you'll find it here.

ACCRO COFFEE
CAFE

(☑852 9430 1433; Shop 8, Ground fl, Fook Cheong Bldg, 21-27 Ma Wang Rd, Yuen Long; ☺noon-midnight; Ⓜ Long Ping, exit B1) Excellent coffee – single-origin and blends – crafted by a world siphonist champion some ways removed from downtown Yuen Long. These are some of the best cuppas in the New Territories, so the cosy cafe gets crowded on weekends. If you're hungry, there's decent cheesecake and waffles with Earl Grey cream.

Tuen Mun

Industrial-residential Tuen Mun is not a particularly attractive part of Hong Kong, but several historic temples make it worth the trek. Foodwise, try the local speciality, roast goose, in the neighbourhood of Shem Tseng, or seafood along the coast.

◎ SIGHTS & EATING

TSING SHAN MONASTERY
BUDDHIST MONASTERY

(青山禪院; ☑852 2441 6666; www.tsingshan monastery.org.hk; Tsing Shan Monastery Path; ☺24hr; 🚌610, 615, 615P) Hong Kong's oldest temple sits at the foot of Castle Peak. It was founded as early as the 400s by Reverend Pui To (literally, 'travelling in a cup'), an Indian monk who crossed the seas in a wooden cup, although the complex you see today was rebuilt in the 20th century.

Check out shrines and temples for various deities and Bodhisattvas in the sprawling complex, including one to Pui To in a grotto. Some of these have slid into dilapidation; nonetheless, they're imbued with a spooky charm.

MIU FAT MONASTERY
BUDDHIST MONASTERY

(妙法寺; ☑852 2461 8567; 18 Castle Peak Rd; ☺9am-5pm; 🚃751) Miu Fat Monastery in Lam Tei, due north of Tuen Mun town centre, is one of Hong Kong's most eccentric Buddhist complexes, second to Sha Tin's 10,000 Buddhas Monastery. The main hall features, with true '70s flamboyance, not only dragons coiled over pillars, but huge stone elephants. Inside there's a golden likeness of Buddha and three larger statues of Lord Gautama. You can't miss the new extension, a 45m tower resembling a huge lotus blossom – it even glows at night.

This is an active monastery; you'll see brown-robed nuns in droves. To get here take light-rail line 751 from the Tuen Mun or Town Centre stops to Lam Tei station. The complex is on the opposite side of Castle Peak Rd; cross over the walkway and walk north 150m. Bus 63X, from the Mong Kok MTR station, also stops in front of the monastery.

SAM SHING HUI SEAFOOD MARKET
SEAFOOD $$

(三聖墟海鮮市場; Sam Shing St, Castle Peak Bay; meals HK$250-500; ☺10am-10pm; 🚐 minibus 140M from Tsing Yi) Along Castle Peak Beach, this busy working seafood market sits adjacent to rows of *dai pai dong* (food stalls), as well as fancier enclosed establishments, ready to cook up whatever you've picked. This is like Sai Kung seafood feasting, but with more locals than tourists and with no English spoken (but pointing and smiling should get you going – just be sure to ask for prices first).

Outlying Islands

Explore

Unless you plan on stargazing on Po Toi and Tung Lung Chau, all of Hong Kong's Outlying Islands can be visited on a day

WORTH A DETOUR

PO TOI

A solid favourite of weekend holidaymakers with their own seagoing transport, Po Toi is the largest of a group of five islands – one is little more than a huge rock. Hong Kong's territorial border lies just 2km to the south.

There's picturesque hiking on Po Toi, a small Tin Hau Temple across the bay from the pier and, on the southern coast, geological formations with monikers like Palm Cliff, Tortoise Rock and Monk Rock, a lighthouse, and mysterious 3000-year rock carvings of prehistoric totems on a cliff.

Po Toi is well known for the bamboo theatre that materialises on a cliff here during the Tin Hau Festival (23rd day of the third lunar month – April or May). The large ephemeral stage is built so it faces the gods in the Tin Hau Temple, as they are the main audience of the Cantonese opera performances. Below the cliff, dragon boats race and fishing junks decked out with flags dot the sea. The island gets quite crowded during this time and the wait for food at the restaurants is long, but the atmosphere is electrifying.

Ming Kee Seafood Restaurant (明記海鮮酒家; ☑852 2472 1408, 852 2849 7038; ⏲11am-11pm; 🚢Po Toi) is one of a handful of restaurants in the main village and is by far the most popular with day trippers; book ahead on weekends.

If you want to stargaze, the **Nam Kok Tsui Lighthouse** (南角咀燈塔; 🚢Po Toi) is the most ideal spot – a reasonable distance (1.5km) to hike from the pier with camping gear, and sunset views on the house. There's a flat area to the right of the path ascending to the (functioning) lighthouse where you can camp. Past the lighthouse, stairs lead to wind-whipped and wave-thrashed rocks called Nam Kok Tsui ('South Pointy Mouth'). You're officially at Hong Kong's southernmost tip.

---

trip, with the exception of Lantau. If you only have a day for Lantau, some options worth considering are: heading to Disneyland; taking the cable car to Po Lin Monastery, having lunch, followed by shopping in Tung Chung; beach- and village-hopping in Mui Wo; clam digging or kiteboarding on Shui Hau Beach; exploring the temples and stilt houses of Tai O Village supplemented by easy hiking. Or you can just devote an entire day to hiking sections of the spectacular Lantau Trail – rewarding enough on its own and more so if ending with a seafood dinner. Cheung Chau is much smaller than Lantau, but an equally memorable 14 hours can be spent grazing on fish balls and pastries near the pier, heading to Sai Wan to swim at secluded rock beaches, or strolling under fruit trees in the villages and along the cacti-fringed coast. If you stay the night, you could windsurf and indulge in a beach barbecue the next day. Seafood and hiking are de rigueur on Lamma Island, and there are several bays that make for pleasant swimming and kayaking. The island's unique bohemian vibe means you can spend a good half-day just hanging out in the villages, checking out the art scene and drinking with islanders.

The Best...

➡ **Sight** Po Lin Monastery & Big Buddha (p160)

➡ **Place to Eat** Lamma Rainbow (p181)

➡ **Activity** Lantau Peak (p183)

Top Tip

In autumn, the peak season for stargazing, the campsite on Tung Lung Chau can get crowded on weekends. You can go on a weekday. There are operators milling around Sai Wan Ho Pier. Just say you want to go to Tung Lung Chau and bargain. Remember to book them to take you back too if you're not returning on a regular weekend sailing.

Getting There & Away

➡ **Boat** Smaller 'fast ferries' cut travel time, but cost 50% to 100% more than large 'ordinary ferries'. Prices rise on holidays. Timetables displayed at piers and online.

Central (Pier 6)–Mui Wo (Lantau)

Adult ordinary/deluxe class/fast ferry HK$15.90/26.20/31.30; 50 to 55 minutes (large ferry); half hourly from 6.10am.

**Central (Pier 4)–Yung Shue Wan
(Lamma)** Adult HK$17.80; 30 minutes;
every half-hour to an hour from 6.30am.

Central (Pier 4)–Sok Kwu Wan (Lamma)
Adult HK$22; 40 minutes; every 1½
hours 7.20am to 11.30pm.

Central (Pier 5)–Cheung Chau
Adult ordinary/deluxe class/fast ferry
HK$13.60/21.30/26.80; 55 to 60 minutes
(large ferry); half hourly from 6.10am.

➡ **Kaito** Serve remote islands or
destinations, with less frequent services
than regular ferries and flexible schedules.
The Transport Department (www.td.gov.
hk) website has timetables.

Need to Know

➡ **Area Code** ☑852

➡ **Location** Lamma is the quickest escape
from downtown Hong Kong and only 3km
from Aberdeen; Lantau is the biggest and
most inhabited island and is where Hong
Kong International Airport is located.

Lamma

Lamma, Hong Kong's laid-back 'hippie island', is easily recognisable at a distance
by the three coal chimneys crowning its
hilly skyline. The chimneys stand out so
much because Lamma, home to 6000 or
so, is otherwise devoid of high-rise development. Here it's all about lush forests, hidden
beaches and chilled-out villages connected
by pedestrian paths. You won't see any cars
here, but be prepared for spotting the odd
snake.

There are two main settlements on the
island: Yung Shue Wan to the northwest
and Sok Kwu Wan on the east coast of the
island. Most visitors arrive in Yung Shue
Wan, a counterculture haven popular with
expats.

◉ SIGHTS

YUNG SHUE WAN VILLAGE

Map p180 (榕樹灣; ⊡Yung Shue Wan) Yung
Shue Wan (Banyan Tree Bay), with some
6000 inhabitants, may be close to the largest settlement on the island, but it remains
a small village with little more than a car-
free main street following the curve of the
bay. Despite encroaching development, the
village has somehow managed to retain
more than a whiff of rustic charm. The
main street is lined with cafes, bars, veggie
stalls and new-age shops, all popular with
locals and tourists alike.

TIN HAU TEMPLE TEMPLE

Map p180 (天后廟; Yung Shue Wan; ⊡Yung Shue
Wan) This temple has wooden plaques from
the Qing dynasty, which means it should be
over 100 years old. Its appearance, however,
originates from a 1960s reconstruction.
Note the lions guarding the entrance. They
look comical and slightly western. During the reconstruction, China was in the
throes of the Cultural Revolution with its
vow to destroy old customs. It was impossible to find a sculptor to create new lions,
and there being a dearth of such expertise
in Hong Kong, the task fell upon a Lamma
sculptor known for making western-style lions for customers in Southeast Asia. Unlike
Chinese felines who sit upright with their
backs to the temple, these ones lie horizon-
tally facing each other like the HSBC lions.

HUNG SHING YEH WAN BEACH

Map p180 (洪聖爺灣; ⊡Yung Shue Wan) A
25-minute walk southeast (1.7km) from the
Yung Shue Wan ferry pier, Hung Shing Yeh
beach is the most popular beach on Lamma.
Arrive early in the morning or on a weekday
and you'll probably find it deserted, though
you may find the view of the power station
across the bay takes some getting used to.
The beach is protected by a shark net and
has toilets, showers and changing rooms.

LAMMA ISLAND FAMILY TRAIL

From Yung Shue Wan, the most interesting way to see a good portion of the island is
to amble along the 4km-long Family Trail that runs between Yung Shue Wan and Sok
Kwu Wan, the island's second town (really little more than a strip of seafood restaurants). Those happy to be out in the hot sun should carry on to Tung O Wan, an idyllic
bay some 30 minutes or 2km further south, and perhaps return to Sok Kwu Wan via
Mo Tat Wan (total 5km).

Lamma

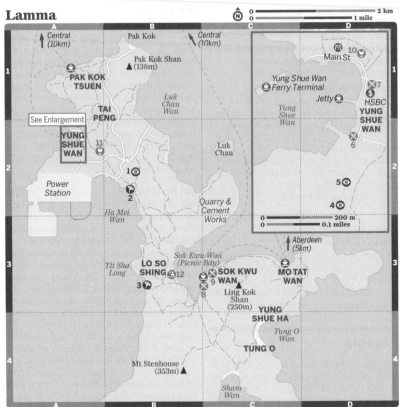

Lamma

◎ Sights
1 Herboland B2
2 Hung Shing Yeh Wan B2
3 Lo So Shing B3
4 Tin Hau Temple D2
5 Yung Shue Wan D2

✗ Eating
6 Bookworm Cafe D2
7 Candela D1
8 Lamma Rainbow C3
9 Wai Kee Seafood Restaurant C3

🍷 Drinking & Nightlife
10 Island Bar D1
11 Yardley Brothers Beer Shack A2

🏃 Sports & Activities
12 Sea Kayak Hong Kong B3

There are a few restaurants and drinks stands nearby, open in season.

HERBOLAND FARM

Map p180 (香草原; ☑852 9094 6206; off Hung Shing Yeh beach; ☺11am-5pm Sat & Sun; ⛴Yung Shue Wan) Nestled in the leafy fringes of Hung Shing Yeh beach is Herboland, the first organic herb farm in the territory. Stroll past fragrant bushes of rosemary and verbena, or choose from more than 40 types of herbal tea in the farm's blissful tea garden. Opening hours are irregular; check before you go.

✗ EATING

BOOKWORM CAFE CAFE $

Map p180 (南島書蟲; ☑852 2982 4838; 79 Main St, Yung Shue Wan; meals from HK$100; ☺9am-5pm Mon-Wed & Fri, 11am-8pm Sat & Sun; ✸🛜✐; ⛴Yung Shue Wan) 🌱 The granddaddy of

Hong Kong's healthy and eco-conscious dining scene, Bookworm Cafe lays claim to Lamma's widest range of vegetarian dishes. We like the book-lined walls, and the shepherdess pie which went well with the organic red wine. That said, the cafe could use more serving staff. Bookworm is also a secondhand bookshop.

⭐ **LAMMA RAINBOW** CHINESE, SEAFOOD $$
Map p180 (南丫天虹; ☑852 2982 8100; www.lammarainbow.com; Shops 1A-1B, Ground fl, 23-25 First St, Sok Kwu Wan; meals from HK$250; ⏱10am-10.30pm; ❖❖; ⛴Sok Kwu Wan) Gigantic Rainbow may boast 800 seats but you still need to book ahead for prime hours. Steamed grouper, lobster and abalone are the specialities at this waterfront restaurant, and they're excellent. Best to come with friends as portions are big. You have the option of being transported by its own ferries from Central pier 9 or Tsim Sha Tsui Public Pier; call or check the website for sailings.

WAI KEE SEAFOOD RESTAURANT SEAFOOD $$
Map p180 (威記海鮮酒家; ☑852 2982 8135; 3 & 4 First St, Sok Kwu Wan; ⏱10.30am-10pm) A small and popular seafood restaurant known for its pan-fried prawns with soy sauce and sautéed razor clams. The produce is fresh and prices are reasonable. Set meals for four or eight work out to about HK$200 per person but they're only good if you're not voracious and don't order beer (hard when deep-fried squid with salt and pepper is on the menu).

CANDELA TAPAS $$
Map p180 (☑852 6344 5288; 23 Main St, Yung Shue Wan; ⏱6pm-late; ☑) Chef Carlos' new restaurant offers affordable and delicious Spanish tapas. Residents and visitors have been flocking to Candela for the roasted pork, eggplant salad and *papas bravas* (fried potato cubes). Hours can vary; if you see staff working a paella in a large pan outside, you know it's open.

🍷 DRINKING & NIGHTLIFE

⭐**YARDLEY BROTHERS**
BEER SHACK CRAFT BEER
Map p180 (www.yardleybrothers.hk; 16B Tai Yuen Village, Yung Shue Wan; ⏱1-6pm Sat & Sun) These brewer brothers sell tasty craft beer on tap from a black booth on the way to the island's main beach. The refreshing Lamma Island IPA is perfect for a day by the water.

ISLAND BAR BAR
Map p180 (☑852 2982 1376; 6 Main St, Yung Shue Wan; ⏱3pm-late Mon-Fri, noon-late Sat & Sun; ⛴Yung Shue Wan) The closest bar to Yung Shue Wan's ferry pier, this institution is a favourite with older expats and hosts the best jam sessions (and quiz nights) on the island. Happy hour 5pm to 8pm.

🏃 SPORTS & ACTIVITIES

SEA KAYAK
HONG KONG KAYAKING
Map p180 (☑852 9313 9165; www.tours.seakayakhongkong.com; 54 Lo So Shing Village, Sok Kwu Wan) ✿ An environmentally conscious sea tour operator that offers kayaking tours of Hong Kong Global Geopark and the East Lamma Channel, among other places. There are trips and training courses every weekend. It's based in Lamma but goes everywhere. Make enquiries and book on the website; see coming expeditions on its Facebook page.

Lantau

The sheer size of Lantau, Hong Kong's largest island, makes for days of exploration. The north tip of the island, home to the airport, Disneyland and the high-rise Tung Chung residential and shopping complex, is highly developed. But much of the rest of Lantau is still entirely rural. Here you'll find traditional fishing villages, empty beaches and a mountainous interior criss-crossed with quad-burning hiking trails.

Most visitors come to Lantau to visit Mickey or see the justly famous 'Big Buddha' statue, but be sure you get beyond the north side for a taste of a laid-back island where cows graze in the middle of the road, school kids gather seaweed with their grandparents in the shallow bays, and the odd pangolin is said to still roam the forested hillsides.

The most inhabited town, Tung Chung, is on the northern coast, while Mui Wo, the second-largest settlement, is on the eastern coast. The airport, in Chek Lap Kok, is directly north of Tung Chung.

⊙ SIGHTS

PO LIN MONASTERY
& BIG BUDDHA   BUDDHIST MONASTERY
See p160.

★ TAI O   VILLAGE
Map p184 (🚌1 from Mui Wo, 11 from Tung Chung, 21 from Ngong Ping) On weekends, droves of visitors trek to the far-flung west coast of Lantau to see a fascinating way of life. Here in Tai O, historical home to the Tanka boat people, life is all about the sea. Houses are built on stilts above the ocean, sampans ply the dark-green waterways, and elderly residents still dry seafood on traditional straw mats and make the village's celebrated shrimp paste.

★ STILT HOUSES   HISTORIC BUILDING
Map p184 (棚屋; Kat Hing St, Tai O; 🚌1 from Mui Wo, 11 from Tung Chung, 21 from Ngong Ping) Tai O's remaining stilt houses stand over the waterway, scrunched up against each other for support. Some have ladders descending to boats, the vehicle of choice. These houses have a history of over two centuries. The earliest ones were made with pine bark, palm leaves and granite pillars quarried in Chek Lap Kok where the airport is. During typhoons, they had to be secured with rope or the rising water would wash them away. The ones in the '60s were sturdier and made with Borneo ironwood from retired fishing boats. Ironwood is a dense material that takes on a beautiful black sheen, as you can see, when exposed to water over long periods.

★ TAI O KWAN TAI TEMPLE   TAOIST TEMPLE
Map p184 (大澳關帝廟; Junction of Kat Hing St & Tai O Market St, Tai O; ⊗8am-6pm) Tai O's oldest temple, raised in the 15th century (Ming dynasty), is dedicated to Kwan Tai, a deified general known as the God of War. It was renovated in the Qing dynasty, with donations by court officials and Tai O merchants, whose names are etched on stone slabs inside the temple. Features introduced by the renovations include a copper bell and ornate roof decorations. The latter were made in Shiwan, a Chinese town synonymous with pottery. A red-faced Kwan Tai stands in the main hall. A symbol of valiance and loyalty, he is worshipped by fishers and farmers, as well as merchants, gangsters and the disciplinary forces.

★ SHUI HAU BEACH   BEACH
Map p184 (水口灣; 🚶) Lantau's largest stretch of mudflat, Shui Hau Beach, is lovely, with rippled black sand mirroring the sky and mangroves teeming with crustaceans and clams. At low tide, it attracts dozens of clam diggers. There's a store in the village where you can rent small rakes and leave your bags. The beach is down a path behind the store. The owners will cook your catch for you (for a fee). The store sells Hakka glutinous rice treats too.

HONG KONG
DISNEYLAND   AMUSEMENT PARK
Map p184 (香港迪士尼樂園; ☎852 183 0830; www.hongkongdisneyland.com; adult/child HK$619/458; ⊗10am-8pm Mon-Fri, to 9pm Sat & Sun; 🚶; 🅼 Disney Resort Station) Disneyland serves as a rite of passage for the flocks of Asian tourists who come daily to steal a glimpse of one of America's most famous cultural exports. It's divided into seven areas – Main Street USA, Tomorrowland, Fantasyland, Adventureland, Toy Story Land, Mystic Point and Grizzly Gulch – but it's still quite tiny compared to the US version, and most of the attractions are geared towards families with small children.

TRAPPIST
MONASTERY   MONASTERY
Map p184 (神樂院; ☎852 2987 6292; Tai Shui Hang; 🚤 kaito from Peng Chau, Discovery Bay) Northeast of Mui Wo and south of Discovery Bay is the Roman Catholic Lady of Joy Abbey, better known as the Trappist Monastery. The Trappists gained a reputation as one of the most austere religious communities in the Roman Catholic Church and the Lantau congregation was established at Peking in the 19th century. All of the monks here now are local Hong Kongers. The medieval-style stone chapel is a peaceful spot for quiet contemplation.

FAN LAU   AREA
Map p184 Only accessible on foot, Fan Lau (Divided Flow), a small peninsula on the southwestern tip of Lantau, has a couple of good beaches and the remains of Fan Lau Fort, built in 1729 to protect the channel between Lantau and the Pearl River estuary from pirates. It remained in operation until the end of the 19th century and was restored in 1985. The sea views from here are sterling.

WORTH A DETOUR

HAND-PAINTED POTTERY ON PENG CHAU

Chiu Kee Porcelain Studio (超記瓷器廠; Map p184; ☎852 9822 6506, 852 9193 8044; www.facebook.com/Winus-Lee-mini-ceramic-workshop-173182096098659; 7 Wing Hing St; ⏲noon-6pm), dating from the 1970s, is one of the precious few places around that still makes hand-painted pottery. You'll see the works of its founders, the late Mr Lam and his wife Mrs Lam, who now runs the shop. The tableware and crockery in traditional and contemporary styles make wonderful gifts and home accessories. Mrs Lam hosts two-hour ceramic painting workshops (HK$180 per person) at weekends. They're popular, so booking (by calling) is advised.

🍴 EATING & DRINKING

TAI O LOOKOUT   FUSION $$

Map p184 (☎852 2985 8383; www.taio heritagehotel.com; Tai O Heritage Hotel, Shek Tsai Po St, Tai O; sandwiches & mains HK$78-268; ⏲11am-9.30pm; ⛴1 from Mui Wo, 11 from Tung Chung, 21 from Ngong Ping) The rotating ceiling fans, wooden booths and tiled floor of this rooftop glasshouse restaurant ooze old-world charm, and no one would blame you if you came to just sip coffee and chill.

But the food – fried rice tossed with Tai O's famous shrimp paste, cheesecake with local mountain begonia – is well rated too.

HEMINGWAY'S   BAR

Map p184 (☎852 2987 8855; www.hemingways. hk; Shop G09, Discovery Bay Plaza, Discovery Bay; ⏲3pm-1am Mon-Fri, to 2am Sat & Sun; ⛴) Sleek and somewhat corporate-feeling, this Caribbean restaurant and bar is always packed with Disco Bay expats sipping rum cocktails and eating plates of plant-based meatball marinara and BBQ pulled jackfruit – the menu here is steadily transforming from vegetarian to vegan.

The umbrella-topped patio tables are a lovely place to watch the water.

CHINA BEACH CLUB   BAR

Map p184 (☎852 2983 8931; 18 Tung Wan Tau Rd, Silvermine Bay beach; ⏲noon-10pm Fri-Sun; ⛴Mui Wo) This cheerful restaurant has an airy rooftop and balcony overlooking Silvermine Bay beach for those who want to chill over their home-style Greek moussaka or just kick back with a cocktail or beer. The two-for-one cocktail 'hour' can go on well into the night.

🏃 SPORTS & ACTIVITIES

★LANTAU PEAK   HIKING

Map p184 (Fung Wong Shan) Known as Fung Wong Shan (Phoenix Mountain) in Cantonese, this 934m-high peak is the second-highest in Hong Kong after Tai Mo Shan (957m) in the New Territories. The view from the summit is absolutely stunning, and on a clear day it's possible to see Macau 65km to the west. Watching the sun rise from the peak is a popular choice among hardy hikers. Some choose to stay at the Ngong Ping SG Davis Hostel (p185) and leave around 4am for the two-hour summit push.

★SUNSET PEAK   HIKING

Map p184 (大東山; Tai Tung Shan) Hong Kong's third-highest peak (869m) is a good sweaty climb with lovely panoramic views of the surrounding mountains. Plan for three hours. The ambitious can combine it with Lantau Peak (this is popularly known as the 'two peak challenge'). Check out the creepy 'ghost houses' dotting the path to the peak – ruins of holiday huts built for holidaying missionaries in the 1930s.

LANTAU TRAIL   HIKING

Map p184 (鳳凰徑) The Lantau Trail is a 70km circular trail beginning and ending in Mui Wo. It's divided into 12 sections ranging from 2.5km to 10.5km, some of which can be done alone, others which must be hiked together. While a few sections are relatively flat, others are among the hillier (and most spectacular) hikes in Hong Kong.

FRIENDLY BICYCLE SHOP   CYCLING

Map p184 (老友記單車專門店; ☎852 2984 2278; 18A Mui Wo Ferry Pier Rd, Mui Wo; bike rental per hr HK$40; ⏲10am-6pm Wed-Fri, to 8pm

Lantau

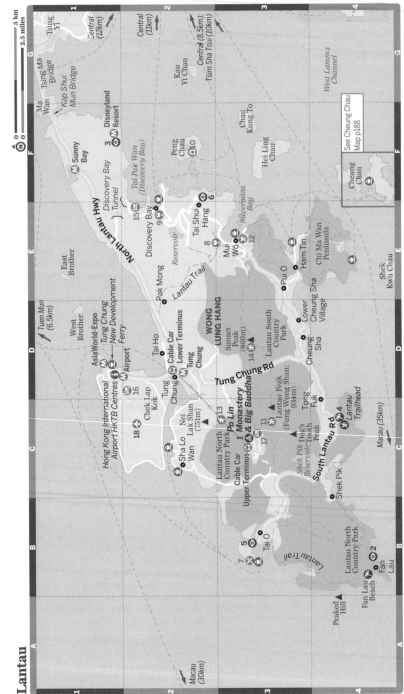

0 — 5 km
0 — 2.5 miles

Macau (30km)

Macau (35km)

Central (12km)
Central (11km)
Central (8.5km): Tsim Sha Tsui (10km)

West Lamma Channel

See Cheung Chau Map p188

Cheung Chau

Tsing Yi

Ma Wan
Tsing Ma Bridge
Kap Shui Mun Bridge

Tuen Mun (6.5km)

West Brother

East Brother

North Lantau Hwy

Sunny Bay

Disneyland Resort

Discovery Bay Tunnel

Discovery Bay

Kau Yi Chau

Chau Kung To

Hei Ling Chau

Tai Puk Wan (Discovery Bay)

Peng Chau

Tai Shui Hang

Silvermine Bay

Ham Tin

Chi Ma Wan Peninsula

Shek Kwu Chau

Pui O

Lower Cheung Sha

Cheung Sha Village

Lantau South Country Park

Sunset Peak (869m)

WONG LUNG HANG

Pak Mong

Reservoir

Lantau Trail

Mui Wo

AsiaWorld-Expo

Tung Chung New Development

Airport Ferry

Tai Ho

Cable Car Lower Terminus

Tung Chung

Tung Chung Rd

Nei Lak Shan (751m)

Po Lin Monastery & Big Buddha

Lantau Peak (Fung Wong Shan; 934m)

Tong Fuk

Lantau Trailhead

South Lantau Rd

Shek Pik Dog's Reservoir/Tooth Peak

Shek Pik

Lantau North Country Park

Cable Car Upper Terminus

Laintau North Country Park

Sha Lo Wan

Chek Lap Kok

Hong Kong International Airport HKTB Centres

Tai O

Lantau Trail

Lantau North Country Park

Fan Lau

Fan Lau Beach

Peaked Hill

Lantau

Sat & Sun) Rent bikes at this Mui Wo shop; it also does repairs. To get here, turn left out of the ferry pier and follow the sea road.

HONG KONG SHAOLIN
WUSHU CULTURE CENTRE   MARTIAL ARTS
Map p184 (香港少林武術文化中心; ☑852 2985 8898; www.shaolincc.org.hk; Shek Tsai Po St, Tai O; courses from HK$650) Located outside the centre of Tai O is this low-key martial-arts school and hostel. It's one of the few such schools in Hong Kong that runs intensive short courses for curious first-timers. Classes are offered on an irregular basis and special packages may be available sporadically, so check the website.

🛏 SLEEPING

NGONG PING SG DAVIS HOSTEL   HOSTEL $
Map p184 (昂坪戴維斯青年旅舍; ☑852 2985 5610; www.yha.org.hk; Ngong Ping; dm from HK$150, r from HK$380, tent HK$320; ☑2 from Mui Wo, or 21, 23 from Tung Chung) This hostel is near the Tian Tan Buddha statue and is an ideal place to stay if you want to watch the sunrise at Lantau Peak. The hostel is only open to HKYHA/HI cardholders or the guests of a cardholder.

From the Ngong Ping bus terminus, take the paved path to your left as you face the Tian Tan Buddha, pass the public toilets on your right and follow the signs.

★ AUBERGE   RESORT $$
Map p184 (香港愉景灣酒店; ☑852 2295 8288; www.aubergediscoverybay.com; 88 Siena Ave, Discovery Bay; r from HK$1400; ❄✳✿✉) A resort-type hotel with clean, spacious rooms, fabulous bathrooms and unobstructed views of the bay or the hills. Local couples and families like to come here for short getaways, lured by the relaxing vibe, the sumptuous breakfast, and the gym and spa. For children, there's a playroom and horse-drawn carriage rides. The hotel has a shuttle bus service to and from Sunny Bay and Disneyland.

ESPACE ELASTIQUE   B&B $$
Map p184 (歸田園居; ☑852 2985 7002; www. espaceelastique.com.hk; 57 Kat Hing St, Tai O; r Sun-Thu HK$700-1550, Fri & Sat HK$900-1850; ✿✉; ☑1 from Mui Wo, 11 from Tung Chung, 21 from Ngong Ping) This cosy four-room B&B is one of the best-kept gems on Lantau. All rooms are tastefully decorated; the 2nd-floor double room with a balcony overlooking the main Tai O waterway gets booked

WORTH A DETOUR

TUNG LUNG CHAU

The ninth largest of Hong Kong's 260 islands, craggy East Dragon Island lies to the east of Hong Kong Island and south of Kowloon. There are prehistoric **rock carvings** (🔊Tung Lung Chau) on the island's northern side; while **Tung Lung Fort** (東龍洲炮台; 🔊Tung Lung Chau) on the northeastern corner testifies to its military status in dynastic China. It is largely uninhabited and its most recent inhabitants, like the owners of **Holiday Store noodle shop** (假日士多; ☑852 2798 8877, 852 2560 9491; noodles HK$28; ⊘early-evening Sat, Sun & public holiday), moved here in the '60s and '70s and made a living growing vegetables and raising pigs. According to them, if it wasn't for the presence of paved roads and electricity, the island would look exactly as it did 40 years ago.

up quickly. The friendly owner Veronica provides multilingual travel advice, plus a hearty breakfast in the cafe. The jacuzzi on the rooftop is a delight. That said, it tends to favour customers who are staying at least three days to a week.

HONG KONG DISNEYLAND HOTEL   RESORT $$

Map p184 (☑852 3510 6000; www.hongkong-disneyland.com; Hong Kong Disneyland; r from HK$2500; ⊕❄@🛜🏊) Kids will be delighted with this palatial Disney resort, complete with a Mickey-shaped hedge maze, an enormous pool with a twisty water slide, and various kid-centric amenities: a reading hour headlined by Disney characters, a princess boutique and an indoor playroom. Adults should be happy as well with the relatively spacious, Victorian-themed rooms. See the website for the latest packages.

★TAI O HERITAGE HOTEL   BOUTIQUE HOTEL $$$

Map p184 (大澳文物酒店; www.taioheritagehotel.com; Shek Tsai Po St, Tai O; r HK$2000-2500; @🛜🏊; 🚌1 from Mui Wo, 11 from Tung Chung, 21 from Ngong Ping) Housed in a century-old former police station, this is Lantau's coolest hotel. All nine rooms are handsomely furnished in a contemporary style, offering top-of-the-line comfort. Our favourite is the inspector-office-turned–Sea Tiger room, the smallest digs (24 sq metres) but with picture windows ushering in the sea breeze.

Cheung Chau

This small, dumb-bell–shaped island is a popular getaway thanks to its beaches and its cute downtown, near the main pier, lined with snack shops and stores. Many of these operate out of village homes. Come here for an afternoon of temple and village touring, noshing on fish balls and exploring the rocky coastline. Or stay for a weekend at one of the many holiday rentals and treat yourself to a day of windsurfing lessons followed by an alfresco seafood dinner at a harbourside restaurant.

⊙ SIGHTS

★RECLINING ROCKS   NATURAL FEATURE

Map p188 (五行石; 🚶; 🚢Cheung Chau) In the southwestern corner of Cheung Chau are five giant eroded rocks on a cliff, like something from Chinese mythology. The largest of the scenic clusters seems to be perpetually teetering on the edge. Reclining Rocks are a 10-minute jaunt south from Cheung Po Tsai Cave, along the coastal Cheung Chau Family Trail. The cacti-framed scenery of Po Yue Wan (Stingray Bay) here is breathtaking. People come here to fish and just be by themselves.

PAK TAI TEMPLE   TAOIST TEMPLE

Map p188 (北帝廟; ☑852 2981 0663; ⊘7am-5pm; 🚢Cheung Chau) This colourfully restored temple from 1783 is the epicentre of the annual Cheung Chau Bun Festival, held in late April or early May. The most important and oldest temple on the island, it is dedicated to the Taoist deity Pak Tai, the 'Supreme Emperor of the Dark Heaven', military protector of the state, guardian of peace and order, and protector of fisherfolk.

CHEUNG CHAU MAIN STREET & VICINITY   VILLAGE

Map p188 (長州大街附近; 🚢Cheung Chau) The island's main settlement lies along the narrow strip of land connecting the headlands to the north and the south. The waterfront is a bustling place and the maze-like streets and alleyways are filled with old Chinese-style houses and tumbledown shops selling everything from plastic buckets to hell money and other combustible grave offerings. The streets close to the waterfront are pungent with the smell of incense and fish hung out to dry in the sun.

PAK TSO WAN
BEACH

Map p188 (白鰷灣, Italian Beach; 🚢Cheung Chau) If you are visiting the nearby cemetery, it's worth dropping down to Pak Tso Wan (known by local westerners as 'Italian Beach'), a sandy, isolated spot that is good for swimming and, according to Sai Wan locals, skinny-dipping.

TUNG WAN
BEACH

Map p188 (東灣; 🚢Cheung Chau) Tung Wan beach, east of the ferry pier, is not Cheung Chau's prettiest beach but it's the longest and most popular. The far southern end of Tung Wan is a great area for windsurfing. There are plenty of facilities here, as well as lifeguard stations overlooking the roped-off swimming area.

✖ EATING & DRINKING

⭐PIRATE BAY
FRENCH $

Map p188 (海盜灣; www.facebook.com/Pirate BayCheungChau; No 13-14, Tsan Tuen Rd; ⊙noon-7pm Thu-Sun; ✿🐾; 🚢Cheung Chau) Delicious crepes (the caramel is our favourite) by a French and Hong Konger couple, also hearty homemade chicken rillette, ratatouille and beef bourguignon. For the thirsty, there's French wine (fabulous with the cheese platter) and Asahi draught. There are off-the-menu goodies every week, like Moroccan vegan or chicken masala. It's the shop facing the sea with the pirate flag and wall art, and (likely) blasting '80s pop.

KAM WING TAI FISH BALL SHOP
CHINESE $

Map p188 (甘永泰魚蛋; ☑852 2981 3050; 106 San Hing St; balls HK$10-15; ⊙7am-5pm; 🚢Cheung Chau) The long line snaking along the alley should tell you something about this celebrated pit stop. Hakka-style snack balls of minced fish and meat are served piping hot. A stick of chewy assorted balls is highly recommended.

VALOR
CAFE

Map p188 (啡寮; ☑852 6699 5892; 4 Sun Hing St; ⊙10.30am-7pm; 🚢Cheung Chau) Valor offers great respite from Cheung Chau's crowded streets. The shop is tastefully understated with a display of ice-drip contraptions near the entrance. The well-made coffee is presented creatively. Ice-drip is served as is, in baby coconut shells, or turned into nitro-coffee. Fans of hot beverages can opt for the Yirgacheffe hand-drip or the salt-laced drinking chocolate.

CHEUNG CHAU BUN FESTIVAL

Taking place over four days in late April or early May, Cheung Chau's annual Bun Festival is one of Hong Kong's most engaging cultural experiences. Honouring the Taoist god Pak Tai, the festival involves days of parades, music and sweet buns galore. The main event is the scramble up the 'bun tower' – whoever grabs the top bun first wins.

Bun towers consist of bamboo scaffolding up to 20m high covered with sacred rolls. If you visit Cheung Chau a week or so before the festival, you'll see the towers being built in front of Pak Tai Temple.

At midnight on the designated day, hundreds of people clamber up the towers to snatch the buns for good luck. The higher the bun, the greater the luck, so everyone tries to reach the top. In 1978 a tower collapsed under the weight of the climbers, injuring two dozen people. The race didn't take place again for over two decades until it was revived – with strict safety controls – in 2005.

The third day of the festival features a procession of floats, stilt walkers and people dressed as characters from Chinese legends and opera. Most interesting are the colourfully dressed 'floating children' who are carried through the streets on long poles, cleverly wired to metal supports hidden under their clothing. The supports include footrests and a padded seat.

Offerings are made to the spirits of all the fish and livestock killed and consumed over the previous year. During the four-day festival, the whole island goes vegetarian.

Cheung Chau

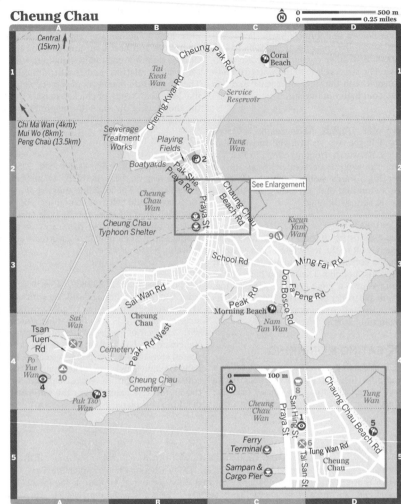

DAY TRIPS FROM HONG KONG OUTLYING ISLANDS

🏃 SPORTS & ACTIVITIES

A great way to see the harbour and soak up the fishing-village atmosphere is to charter a sampan for half an hour (expect to pay HK$80 to HK$150 depending on the day, the season and the demand). Most sampans congregate around the cargo pier in Cheung Chau Village, but virtually any small boat you see in the harbour can be hired as a water taxi. Just wave and two or three will come forward.

Be sure to agree on the fare first.

CHEUNG CHAU
WINDSURFING CENTRE   WINDSURFING

Map p188 (長洲滑浪風帆中心; ☎852 2981 8316; www.ccwindc.com.hk; Kwun Yam Wan beach, No 1 Hak Pai Rd; ⏰10am-7pm Thu-Tue; 🚢Cheung Chau) Windsurfing has always been a popular pastime on Cheung Chau, and Hong Kong's only Olympic gold medallist to date, Lee Lai-shan, who took the top prize in windsurfing at the 1996 Atlanta Olympics, grew up here. At the northern end of Kwun Yam Wan, Lee's uncle runs the Cheung Chau Windsurfing Centre, where you can try out the sport for yourself

Cheung Chau

(day-long beginner classes from HK$1800; sign up a week ahead).

🛏 SLEEPING

SAIYUEN   TENTED CAMP $$

Map p188 (西園; ☑852 2981 1010; www.saiyuen.com; DD CC Lot 12, Sai Wan; small tent HK$800-3300; ☻❄; ⛴Cheung Chau) The rolling gardens of this stunning 4.5-hectare country retreat have been converted into an adventure park (tickets 9am to 7.45pm) and glamping venue. Kids will love it here where fruit trees grow and goats roam free. You can choose to stay in teepees, safari tents, gers or 'stargazing' domes. All, with the exception of teepees, come with air-conditioners and shower cubicles. Overall, though, facilities are basic for 'glamping'. There's lots to do for the family, from ziplining to mud-baking chicken.

Shēnzhèn

Explore

The gleaming manifestation of China's economic miracle, Shēnzhèn (深圳) has risen from the marshy Pearl River Delta into one of the world's most mega megacities in less time than it took London's St Paul's Cathedral to be built. Millions of migrants have been drawn to its golden gates from the Chinese countryside since the 1980s; now, Shēnzhèn attracts high-flying tech graduates and global corporations.

But it's not all work, work, work. This free-spirited, forward-looking metropolis has thriving arts, nightlife and music scenes, multicultural dining and oodles of shopping. And when you step away from the skyscrapers and malls you'll discover fascinating 'urban villages', poor but vibrant migrant worker communities that were once clan villages before the city swallowed them up.

The Best...

➡ **Sight** OCT-LOFT (p190)
➡ **Place to Eat** Phoenix House (p194)
➡ **Place to Drink** Oil (p194)

Getting There & Away

Buses depart to Guǎngzhōu every 20 minutes from **Luóhú bus station** (罗湖汽车站; Luóhú Qìchēzhàn; Map p191; ☑0755 8232 1670; beneath Luóhú Commercial City). Fares cost ¥50 to ¥70 (two hours, 7am to 10pm). You can also reach other Guǎngdōng cities from here, including Dōngguǎn, Zhōngshān, Cháozhōu and Shàntóu.

For more buses to more distant destinations across China, head to Shēnzhèn's **Yínhú bus station** (Shangbubei Lu).

Dozens of high-speed trains per day shuttle between Shēnzhèn's Fútián and North stations, and Hong Kong West Kowloon rail terminus; you pass through mainland border and customs control before departure on both ends and don't have to get off the train when crossing the border. The first high-speed train to West Kowloon departs Shēnzhèn North at 6.44am, the last at 10.36pm. One-way 2nd-class tickets cost ¥75.

You can also catch the new high-speed line in the other direction to Guǎngzhōu South departing from Shēnzhèn North.

Shēnzhèn's metro also meets Hong Kong's Mass Transit Railway (MTR) at Luohu (Line 1) and Fútián Checkpoint (Line 4). Passengers have to disembark and cross border control on foot. You need a visa (p276) to visit mainland China.

Normal intercity services to Guǎngzhōu depart from Shēnzhèn train station (¥80, one hour, 20 minutes); Fútián train station (¥80, 50 minutes); and Shēnzhèn North station (¥75, 30 minutes).

Getting Around

Shēnzhèn has an excellent public transport network, with eight metro lines in operation at time of research and more in the works. Distance-based fares start from ¥2, with tokens purchased from bilingual machines (you'll need ¥1 coins or ¥5 notes).

One-day travel passes can be bought at metro-station service booths for ¥20, good for both metro and buses. Most bus trips in town cost around ¥1 to ¥2.

Flagfall for taxis is ¥12.50 (¥16 from 11pm to 6am), with a ¥4 fuel surcharge and ¥2.40 for every additional kilometre. For trips out of the city, you can usually negotiate a fee in advance.

Need to Know

➡ **Area Code** ☑0755

➡ **Population** 12.53 million

➡ **Tourist Office** (深圳旅遊咨詢中心; Shēnzhèn Tourist Consultation Centre; Map p191; ☑0755 8232 3045; ground fl, Shēnzhèn train station, east exit; ☺9am-6pm) Free and reasonably detailed maps available on request.

➡ **Currency** Shēnzhèn is part of mainland China, so its unit of currency is rénmínbì (RMB), also referred to as yuán (¥).

◉ SIGHTS

★OCT-LOFT   ARTS CENTRE

(华侨城创意文化园; Huáqiáochéng Chuàngyì Wénhuàyuán; www.octloft.cn; 2 Jinxiu Beilu, Nánshān District; 南山区锦绣北街2号; ☺10am-5.30pm; Ⓜ Line 1 to Qiaocheng East, exit A, Ⓜ Line 2 to Qiaocheng North, exit B) By far the best place for strolling or simply hanging out in the city is the breezy OCT-LOFT complex, a warren of repurposed communist-era factories criss-crossed by cobbled laneways. It's also a great place to browse a multitude of contemporary art spaces in between pit stops at the area's excellent cafes, design shops, music venues, bars, restaurants and Shēnzhèn's best bookstore (p195).

OCT-LOFT (OCT stands for Overseas Chinese Town) started out, appropriately for Shēnzhèn, as a TV manufacturing base before it was converted into a creative industries hub. Staying here is recommended, if you can snag a room at the hip Shēnzhèn Loft Youth Hostel (p196), formerly a factory workers' dormitory complex. Note that OCT-LOFT isn't actually served by OCT metro station.

★LIÁNHUĀ SHĀN PARK   PARK

(莲花山公园; Liánhuā Shān Gōngyuán; 6030 Hongli Lu, Fútián District; 福田区红荔路6030号; ☺6am-10.30pm; 🚻; Ⓜ Line 4 to Lianhua North, exit A2, Ⓜ Line 3, 4 to Children's Palace, exit F2) 𝐅𝐑𝐄𝐄 It's an easy half-hour amble up to the top of this tropical hill in the heart of Fútián District for Shēnzhèn's best skyline photographs. Appropriately, you'll be sharing the mind-blowing vistas with Deng Xiaoping (in statue form), whose economic reforms in the 1980s made this whole crazy mess of prosperity possible.

★SUNRISE ART CENTER   GALLERY

(太阳山艺术中心; Tàiyáng Shān Yìshù Zhōngxīn; ☑0755 2871 6049; www.sunrise-art.com.cn; 23 Laowei, Dàfēn Oil Painting Village, 大芬村老围23号; ¥20; ☺9.30am-6.30pm; Ⓜ Line 3 to Dafen, exit A1) Built from the vestiges of a century-old Hakka home, this idyllic courtyard gallery was created by Chen Qiuzhi, a contemporary ink artist from Ānhuī province. Several galleries display his work, and the wonderful cafe is just the spot to kick back with a tea or coffee after browsing the surrounding Dàfēn Oil Painting Village.

★DÀFĒN OIL PAINTING VILLAGE   ARTS CENTRE

(大芬村; Dàfēncūn; Dàfēn, Buji, Lónggǎng District; ☺9am-6pm; Ⓜ Line 3 to Dafen, exit A1) This folksy urban village of narrow lanes and alleys is a pleasure to visit in itself, but what makes Dàfēn simply unmissable are the hundreds of art studios and stores churning out reproduction oil paintings by hand, from Van Gogh's sunflowers (yours for less than ¥100) to enormous, gilt-framed scenes of mounted cavalry or galleons at sea rendered in lavish detail, costing upwards of ¥2000. Or why not go pop art with a Mona Lisa–meets-Minions mash-up?

All this has earned Dàfēn the nickname of 'the world's art factory', a reputation the authorities are now seeking to upgrade with the staging of international art festivals, improved road access and the con-

Shēnzhèn

Fán Lóu (500m);
Summer Tea House (750m)
Shēnzhèn ✈ (23km);
Shēnzhèn North 🚉 (23km);
Shēnzhèn ✈ (43km)

Dàfēn Oil Painting
Village (4km);
Guānlán
Print Village
(22km)

Litchi Park

Hongling Lu 红岭路

Bādèn Lu

Jiefang Lu 解放路

Shennan Donglu 深南路

● Laojie
🚇 2

Shennan Donglu 深南路

Muslim Hotel
Restaurant (800m);
Dàpéng Fortress (45km)

Shennan Donglu 深南路
深南路 ● Grand Theatre

Bus to Airport (750m);
Shēnzhèn Museum (5km);
Museum of Contemporary Art
& Planning Exhibition (5km);
Ping An Finance Center (5km);
Fútián 🚉 (5.5km);
Shékǒu Port (20km)

Jianshe Lu 建设路

● Guomao

Jiabin Lu

Youyi Lu

Renmin Nanlu 人民南路

Heping Lu

● Ludancun

Binhe Dadao

Renmin
South ●

Chunfeng Lu

Liánhuá Shān Park (6km); OCT-LOFT (11km);
Shēnzhèn Loft Youth Hostel (11km);
B10 Live House (11km);
OCT Art & Design Gallery (13km);
OCT Harbour (13km);
Splendid China (13km);
Window of the World (14km);
Design Society (24km)

Bao'an Nanlu

Bùjí River

Binhe Dadao

Shēnzhèn River

1 🏛

3 🛈
Shēnzhèn
Train Station

● Local
Bus Station

HONG KONG

Luóhú
● Bus Station

● Luohu

Shēnzhèn

struction of the new (and rather overblown) Dàfēn Art Museum. But for now, the place remains quirky and full of character.

For a wacky souvenir, you can even order a bespoke painting (you astride a unicorn, perhaps?) for a negotiable fee, and return to collect it a few days later. Dàfēn is also a good place to buy Chinese brushes and ink stones, which make excellent buys for the artistically inclined. To get to the village, exit the metro and take a left after Walmart.

★ **DESIGN SOCIETY**   GALLERY
(设计互联; Shèjì Hùlián; Sea World Culture & Arts Center; ☎0755 2667 1187; www.designsociety. cn; 1187 Wanghai Lu, Shékǒu; 蛇口望海路1187 号; ⊙10am-10pm; Ⓜ Line 2 to Sea World, exit A) **FREE** China's first dedicated museum of design, this architectural landmark opened on the Shékǒu shore in 2017 to considerable media fanfare. This was largely down to its inaugural exhibition, 'Values of Design', featuring 250 objects and curation from London's world-renowned V&A Museum, and set to run until August 2019. The fabulous building, designed by Japanese architect Fumihiko Maki, has plenty of room for humongous exhibitions, an excellent cafe (plus a small rooftop coffee kiosk with ocean views) and a dim sum restaurant.

ⓘ HUÁQIÁNG BĔI COMMERCIAL STREET

A sizeable chunk of Shēnzhèn's prosperity can be traced to this vast cottage industry of **tech** (华强北商业街; Huáqiángbĕi Shāngyèjiē; Huáqiáng Bĕilù; 华强北路; ⊙around 9am-7pm; Ⓜ Line 2, 7 to Huaqiangbei) that stretches across city blocks. Mall after mall selling every tiny electrical component imaginable has helped make Shēnzhèn the world's tech manufacturing hub. It's fascinating to browse around, and you'll also find stores selling all manner of cheap, 'made in Shēnzhèn' gadgets and gizmos.

A word of warning: avoid the temptation to buy Chinese Android smartphones. Government regulations restrict the installation of the Google suite of apps (including Play Store), effectively crippling them for non-Chinese users.

★ WINDOW OF THE WORLD
AMUSEMENT PARK

(世界之窗; Shìjiè Zhīchuāng; www.szwwco.com; 9037 Shennan Dadao; 深南大道9037号; adult/child ¥200/100; ⊙9am-10pm; 🖼; Ⓢ Line 1, 2 to Window of the World, exit H1) It's 'Around the World in 80 Minutes' (OK, more like half a day) at this endearingly kitsch theme park set in well-tended gardens. From the Houses of Parliament to the Pyramids, the world's great monuments are realised, tackily, in miniature. Some aren't so small – the Eiffel Tower clocks in at an impressive 108m, and Niagara Falls is quite the sight.

The Twin Towers still stand tall(ish) above micro Manhattan, floating in a boating lake overlooked by Mt Rushmore and Capitol Hill. There are a few child-friendly rides, too, including a miniature railway and grand canyon rapids. Tickets drop to ¥80 after 7.30pm.

DÀPÉNG FORTRESS
VILLAGE

(大鹏所城; Dàpéng Suǒchéng; Dàpéng Town, Lónggǎng District; 龙岗区大鹏市; adult ¥20, student & senior ¥10; ⊙10am-6pm; 🚌 E26 to Dàpéng bus station) This Ming dynasty-era walled town was erected 600 years ago to shore up the coastline against marauding Japanese pirates, and later became embroiled in the Opium Wars with the British in the 19th century. Old houses in narrow alleyways (some operating as restaurants and shops), fortress gates, temples, wells and other relics are the main attractions, many spruced up for visitors.

It's a bit of a mission to get here by public transport. From Fútián bus station, take bus E26 to Dàpéng bus station (60km, ¥10). Change to local bus B753 for the final 4km to the fortress (or take a taxi). The total journey time is around 2½ to three hours from Shēnzhèn. A taxi (one hour) should cost about ¥400 to ¥500 for the round-trip (negotiated in advance).

PING AN FINANCE CENTRE
NOTABLE BUILDING

(平安国际金融中心; Píng'ān Guójì Jīnróng Zhōngxīn; 5033 Yitian Lu, Fútián District; 益田路5033号; Ⓜ Line 1 to Shopping Park, exit D) The fourth-tallest building in the world when it topped out in 2015, the Ping An Finance Centre (599m) rises like a glass pencil above Shēnzhèn's ever-blooming Fútián District. The Free Sky Observation Deck offers suitably jaw-dropping views on a clear day.

It might be sobering to note that back in 1979, the city's tallest building was just five storeys. In 2017, Shēnzhèn built more skyscrapers than any other *country*.

OCT HARBOUR
WATERFRONT

(OCT Bay; 欢乐海岸; Huānlè Hǎi'àn; www.oct harbour.com; 2008 Binhai Dadao, Shahe Jiedao; 沙河街道滨海大道2008号; ⊙10am-10pm; 🖼; Ⓜ Line 9 to Shenzhen Bay Park, exit E) You could almost be in California at this palm-lined lifestyle complex set around artificial lakes and fountains, offering upscale dining, nightlife and shopping. There's plenty here for kids, from a huge Hello Kitty emporium to an IMAX cinema. Fireworks and lasers after nightfall add to the holiday atmosphere.

OCT ART & DESIGN GALLERY
GALLERY

(华美术馆; Huá Mĕishùguǎn; ☎0755 3399 3111; www.oct-and.com; 9009 Shennan Dadao; 深南大道9009号; adult/child ¥15/8; ⊙10am-5.30pm Tue-Sun; Ⓜ Line 1 to OCT, exit C) The interiors of this former warehouse are adorned with the works of Chinese and international graphic designers. Exhibits change frequently. It's a glass-encased steel structure with a hexagonal design motif, adjacent to the **Hé Xiāngníng Art Museum** (何凝美术馆; Héxiāngníng Mĕishúguǎn; ☎0755 2660 4540;

www.hxnart.com; 9013 Shennan Dadao; 深南大道9013; ⊙10am-5.30pm Tue-Sun) **FREE**.

MUSEUM OF CONTEMPORARY ART & PLANNING EXHIBITION
NOTABLE BUILDING

(MOCAPE; 当代艺术与城市规划展览馆; Dāngdài Yìshùyǔ Chéngshì Guīhuà Zhǎnlǎn Guǎn; 184 Fuzhong Lu, Fútián District; 福田区福中路184号; 10am-5pm Tue-Sun; Ⓜ Line 3, 4 to Children's Palace, exit A2) **FREE** One of those thrillingly space-age, 'only in China' architectural projects, this gargantuan exhibition space designed by Coop Himmelb(l)au anchors Shēnzhèn's Fútián Cultural District. Opened in 2016, the exterior is a vast curve of chrome planted among the city's high-rises, while the entrance hall is a soaring atrium with a cloud-like mirrored art installation (perfect to take selfies in). Gallery spaces within house temporary exhibitions with an emphasis on contemporary art and design.

SHĒNZHÈN MUSEUM
MUSEUM

(深圳博物馆新馆; Shēnzhèn Bówùguǎn Xīnguǎn; Ⓙ0755 8812 5800; www.shenzhenmuseum.com.cn; East Gate, Block A, Citizens' Centre, Fuzhong Sanlu, Fútián District; ⊙10am-6pm Tue-Sun; Ⓜ Line 4 to Shimin Zhongxin, exit B) **FREE** The hulking Shēnzhèn Museum provides a decent enough introduction to Shēnzhèn's brief but breakneck march into modernity, both before and after the implementation of Deng Xiaoping's policies of reform. Highlights include propaganda art popular in the 1940s and the colourful scale models in the folk-culture hall.

GUĀNLÁN PRINT VILLAGE
VILLAGE

(观澜版画村; Guānlán Bǎnhuà Cūn; http://en.guanlanprints.com; 169 Yuxin Rd, Lónghuá District; 龙华区裕新路169号; ⊙24hr) **FREE** Parts of this 300-year-old Hakka village have been preserved and repurposed into workshops and galleries showcasing print-making artists from China and overseas. Outside scheduled art events, it's a sleepy place to wander, with rows of quaint houses, tree-lined paths and lotus ponds, overlooked by a pair of five-storey *diāolóu* (watchtowers).

To get here, take Line 4 of the metro to Qinghu station, then change to bus M338 to the village. The journey from downtown Shēnzhèn takes about 1¾ hours. A taxi (45 minutes) costs about ¥100 each way.

SPLENDID CHINA
AMUSEMENT PARK

(锦绣中华; Jǐnxiù Zhōnghuá; Ⓙ0755 2660 0626; www.cn5000.com.cn; 9005 Shennan Dadao; 深南大道9005号; adult/child incl entry to China Folk Culture Village ¥200/100; ⊙10am-9pm; Ⓘ; Ⓜ Line 1 to OCT, exit D) Traverse the Middle Kingdom in miniature at this theme park featuring China's famous landmarks rendered on a Lilliputian scale. Included in the admission is **China Folk Culture Village** (中国民俗文化村; Zhōngguó Mínsú Wénhuà Cūn; www.cn5000.com.cn; 9003 Shennan Dadao; 深南大道9003号; adult/child incl entry to Splendid China ¥200/100; ⊙9am-10pm; Ⓜ Line 1 to OCT station, exit D), presenting faux minority villages complete with costumed dancing and cultural performances. A mini-monorail run by the Shēnzhèn Happy Line Tour Co links the parks together along with Window of the World and several hotels.

✗ EATING

★ FÁN LÓU
DIM SUM $

(繁楼; Ⓙ0755 8211 5186; 2nd fl, 2078 Baoan Nanlu; 宝安南路2078号2楼; dim sum ¥7-27; ⊙8am-10pm; Ⓜ Line 3, 9 to Hongling, exit C2) Excellent dim sum is served in square steamer baskets at this friendly and highly affordable restaurant. The tick-box picture menu is Chinese only; a simple payment key using Chinese characters denotes how much each dish costs. Note the mandatory ¥6 per person *zuò fèi* (sitting fee), which includes your choice of tea – *pǔ'ěr* (fermented tea from Yúnnán) is traditional.

★ HOI FAN
CANTONESE $

(开饭; Kāifàn; Ⓙ0755 8322 6165; Central Walk Shopping Mall, 3 Fuhua Yilu, Fútián District; 福田区福华一路3号怡景中心城; dishes from ¥30; ⊙11am-9.30pm; Ⓜ Line 1, 4 to Convention & Exhibition Center, exit B) Get an iced lemon coke with your 'kung-fu' crispy duck at this fun contemporary Canto chain, originally from Guǎngzhōu. The bilingual picture menu presents all manner of treats from roast-meat platters to Cantonese 'sweet and sour' fried eggs, steamed beef with preserved pickles and tender claypot chicken.

Find Hoi Fan on the northwest corner of Central Walk (on the outside concourse, not in the mall itself).

BOLLYWOOD CAFE
INDIAN $

Map p191 (宝莱坞印度餐厅; Bǎoláiwù Yìndù Cāntīng; Ⓙ0755 8222 0370; 3rd fl, 2055 Renmin Nanlu; 人民南路2055-3号; mains ¥45-68;

⊙10.30am-3.30pm & 5.30-11.30pm; Ⓜ Guomao) Here you'll find the best food from the Indian subcontinent in Shēnzhèn, if not all Guǎngdōng. Tandoor-baked breads and succulent meats are complemented by southern-style curries and dosa (savoury crêpes), and there's even a menu page given over to chaat, Mumbai's famous street snacks. A steady flow of Indian families and business-people attests to the authenticity.

To find Bollywood along the arcade of shopfronts, look for the yellow steps at street level. There's a second branch in Fútián District at 9 Zhenxing Lu.

MUSLIM HOTEL
RESTAURANT   CHINESE ISLAMIC $
(穆斯林宾馆大餐馆; Músīlín Bīnguǎn Dàcānguǎn; ☑0755 8225 9664; 2nd fl, Muslim Hotel, 2013 Wenjing Nanlu; 罗湖区文锦南路2013号; dishes ¥38-128; ⊙10am-11pm; Ⓜ Line 9 to Wenjin, exit D) Enjoy juicy roast mutton from the great plains of northern China at this halal restaurant run by the Hui (Chinese Muslims). The roast lamb legs, tender boiled ribs or dàpán jī ('big plate' stewed chicken) are best for groups, but solo diners can gorge on Lánzhōu noodle soup or bǎn miàn – chewy noodles stir-fried with tomatoes, peppers, carrots and mutton.

The restaurant is in a hotel done up like a mock mosque.

SUMMER TEA HOUSE   VEGETARIAN, DIM SUM $
(静颐茶馆; Jìngyí Cháguǎn; ☑0755 2557 4555; www.jingyi2000.com; 7th & 8th fl, Jìntáng Dàxià, 3038 Bao'an Nanlu; 综合大厦宝安南路3083号; dishes ¥50-80; ⊙10am-1am; ☑; Ⓜ Line 9 to Yuanling, exit C) An unexpected oasis of tranquillity in a dull office block, this wood-panelled teahouse has deep armchairs just begging for your bottom and a creative, all-veggie menu of mock-meat dishes. You could easily while away a couple of hours here sipping tea (¥6) and grazing on sweet dim sum snacks (¥45).

The iPad menu has photos and just enough English to get by.

★PHOENIX HOUSE   DIM SUM, CANTONESE $$
(凤凰楼; Fènghuánglóu; ☑0755 8207 6338, 0755 8207 6688; 4002 Huaqiang Beilu, East Wing, Pavilion Hotel; 华强北路4002号; lunch ¥60-100, dinner ¥100-350; ⊙8am-10pm; Ⓜ Line 3, 7 to Huaxin, exit C) One of the most popular Cantonese chains in town, so expect noisy waits for a table after 11.30am. Must-try dim sum here are the sweet durian puffs (榴莲酥; liúlián

sū) and chén cūn fěn (陈村粉), a speciality from the Guǎngdōng foodie heartland of Shùndé County, consisting of rice roll sheets steamed with pork and gravy.

MAGPIE   FUSION $$
(喜鹊派餐厅; Xǐquè Pài Cāntīng; ☑0755 8652 8782; 125, Block A5, OCT-LOFT; 华侨城东部工业区北区A5-125号; dishes ¥60-188; ⊙5pm-2am Tue-Sun, kitchen closes 10.30pm; Ⓜ Line 2 to Qiaocheng North, exit B) Dine on small-plate fusion fare at this hip and stylish restaurant in OCT-LOFT (p190). The Chinese chef owners draw inspiration from their Manchurian roots with ambitious creations such as horsemeat tartare with sweet-potato crisps, and venison Bolognese. There's definitely some molecular trickery at play, not least in the impressive cocktails.

Round off your dinner with a drink and a browse at Old Heaven Books in the same block.

🍷 DRINKING & NIGHTLIFE

You have to dig a little for great nightlife in Shēnzhèn, but when you do you're sure to strike gold. Boutique cocktail speakeasies are opening faster than you can muddle a mojito, and in Oil the city boasts one of the finest underground clubs in China. That's Shenzhen (www.thatsmags.com/shenzhen) is a handy source on what's hot and happening.

★OIL   CLUB
(油; Yóu; 11a Tairan Dasha, Tairan Balu; 车公庙泰然八路深然大厦11A号; around ¥80; ⊙10pm-late Fri & Sat; Ⓜ Line 9 to Xiasha, exit D) Quite possibly the best underground club in China, Oil is a compact, sweaty chapel to electronic beats, the darker and more esoteric the better. An adjoining cocktail bar (open nightly) provides the perfect prelude to Oil's weekend parties, which have been known to keep raging until 7am.

With a progressive music policy that invites cutting-edge underground DJs from around the world, Oil is an icon in the making, and the equal to anywhere in Běijīng or Shànghǎi – as long as it can stay open. Being on the side of an office complex that empties out after dark helps, but it does suffer the occasional police visit.

PEAT   COCKTAIL BAR
(2nd fl, Block A, Tairan Dasha, Tairan Shiyi Lu; 泰然十一路泰然大厦A座2楼; ⊙6.30pm-2am) Bartenders clamber up stepladders to ac-

COCO PARK BAR STREET

One of the liveliest concentrations of bars and clubs in Shēnzhèn can be found in Coco Park, an upscale shopping complex in high-rise Fútián District, which has its own, fairly commercial, bar street and plenty of restaurants.

cess their impressive cache of whiskies (some 500 to 600 bottles) in this smart bar sharing the same office-block location as nightclub Oil (though the vibe is completely different). Whisky-based cocktails (from ¥90) are the sort of smoky, booze-heavy drinks you twirl nonchalantly in your palm as you brood over life's great questions, cigar optional.

MIXY
COCKTAIL BAR

(☑0755 8670 1683; 3rd fl, West Market, 2 Xinglong Xijie; 兴隆西街2号西部市场3楼; ◷7.30pm-2am; Ⓜ Line 1 to OCT, exit B) A standout among Shēnzhèn's emerging boutique cocktail dens, Mixy reflects the personality of its eccentric owner Wu Xun, aka Planck, who rocks a pencil moustache and vintage Shànghǎi tailoring. Planck's outlandishly creative cocktails (around ¥100) are never less than accomplished, and the speakeasy vibe (Mixy is hidden above a wet market) adds to the fun.

BIONIC BREW
CRAFT BEER

(百优精酿啤酒; Bǎi Yōu Jīng Niàng Píjiǔ; ☑136 2466 8864; http://bionicbrew.com; Shop A1-1F02, 24 Shahe Jie Pedestrian St, Baishizhou, Nanshan District; 白石洲沙河街道商业步行街24栋A1-1F02铺; ◷6pm-1am, to 2am Fri & Sat; Ⓜ Line 1 to Baishizhou, exit A) Shēnzhèn's very own craft-beer brand, American-run Bionic Brew, pours four core beers as well as guest brews from elsewhere in China. But the best thing about this tiny, open-fronted bar is its thrillingly local setting, hemmed in by raucous *shāokǎo* (barbecue) joints in one of Shēnzhèn's few remaining 'urban villages'.

Cocktails are available too, including 'secret menu' concoctions like a whisky sour made with Bionic Brew's IPA. Whoops, not so secret anymore then. The taproom can be tricky to find – for detailed instructions check the website.

HEYTEA
TEAHOUSE

(喜茶; Xǐ Chá; ☑0755 8663 6383; www.heytea. com; B2 fl, Central Walk Mall, 3 Fuhua Yilu; 怡景中心城移一路3号; ◷10am-10.30pm; Ⓜ Line 1, 4 to Convention & Exhibition Center, exit B) You haven't been to Guǎngdōng unless you've tasted cheese tea. (This is not something LP ever expected to print!) There are umpteen branches of HEYTEA across Shēnzhèn, where folks queue up to sup big cups of milk tea topped with its trademark layer of cheesy foam (¥17), and take a selfie, of course. Say cheese!

☆ ENTERTAINMENT

For indie bands and underground DJs, Shēnzhèn is becoming a mandatory China tour stop after Běijīng and Shànghǎi. If you happen to be in town during May or October, cross your fingers that your visit coincides with the city's two excellent homegrown festivals, **OCT-LOFT Jazz Festival** (www.oct-loftjazz.com; OCT-LOFT; ◷Oct; Ⓢ Line 2 to Qiaocheng North, exit B, Ⓢ Line 1 to Qiaocheng East, exit A) and **Tomorrow Music Festival** (http://b10live.cn/tomorrowfestival; B10 Live House, OCT-LOFT; ◷May; Ⓢ Line 2 to Qiaocheng North, exit B).

★ B10 LIVE HOUSE
LIVE MUSIC

(B10现场; B10Xiànchǎng; ☑0755 8633 7602; www.b10live.cn; Xiangshan Dongjie; 香山东街华侨城创意文化园, OCT-LOFT; prices vary; Ⓜ Line 2 to Qiaocheng North, exit B) From hair metal to experimental jazz, all genres are equal at this warehouse live-music venue that welcomes eclectic performers from around the world. It's on the north side of Block B10 in the northern section of OCT-LOFT.

🛍 SHOPPING

★ OLD HEAVEN BOOKS
BOOKS

(旧天堂书店; Jiùtiāntáng Shūdiàn; ☑0755 8614 8090; oldheavenbooks@gmail.com; Shop 120, Bldg A5, OCT-Loft, Xiangshan Dongjie; 香山东街华侨城创意园北区A5栋120铺; ◷11am-10pm; Ⓜ Qiaochengdong, exit A) A delicious bookshop specialising in cultural and academic titles, Old Heaven also doubles as a vinyl-music store, cafe, live venue and community creative hub. It's a great place to plug in and catch up on that travel blog over a hazelnut latte. Performances take place here during the OCT-LOFT Jazz Festival.

Find it in the northern end of OCT-LOFT (p190), close to sister venue B10 Live House.

★HUÁQIÁNG
ELECTRONICS WORLD   ELECTRONICS

(华强电子世界(深圳二店); Huáqiáng Diànzǐ Shìjiè; 1007-1015 Huaqiang Beilu; 华强北路1007-1015号; ☺9.30am-6.30pm; 🚻; Ⓜ Line 7 to Huaqiangbei, exit D2) Miniscule spy cameras, jiving robots, e-skateboards, air-conditioned jackets (yep!) – for a sea of innovative, cut-price kidult toys, head to this multifloor electronics mall on Huáqiáng Běi Commercial St (p192). Haggling is the norm, with terrific bargains to be had.

Look for building 2 (二店) with its curved glass facade. Building 1 just sells electrical components (unless that's your thing).

🛏 SLEEPING

With multiple disparate downtowns, the conundrum in Shēnzhèn is choosing *where* to stay. High-rise Fútián District has the most luxury hotels, while scruffier Luōhú District is stuffed with budget and mid-range business hotels – the best orbit Lao Jie metro. Shékǒu, in the city's west, has decent midrange and upscale options, but is further from the sights. Consider anywhere in range of OCT-LOFT (p190), one of the most pleasant areas and very central.

★SHĒNZHÈN LOFT
YOUTH HOSTEL   HOSTEL $

(深圳侨城旅友国际青年旅舍;   Shēnzhèn Qiáochéng Lǚyǒu Guójì Qīngnián Lǚshè; ☑0755 8609 5773; 7 Xiangshan Dongjie, Nánshān District; 华侨城香山东街7号, OCT-LOFT; dm/d/f from ¥100/300/600; ⊜🌐@🛜; Ⓜ Line 1 to Qiaocheng East, exit A) Located in a tranquil part of OCT-LOFT, near the junction of Enping Jie and Xiangshan Dongjie, this immaculate YHA hostel has over 50 private rooms with showers and dormitory-type triples with shared bathrooms. The industrial building previously served as factory workers' lodgings. An adjoining cafe offers breakfast and drinks.

HYATT PLACE DONGMEN   HOTEL $$

Map p191 (东门凯悦嘉轩酒店; Dōngmén Kǎi Yuè Jiā Xuān Jiǔdiàn; ☑0755 6188 1234; https://shenzhen.place.hyatt.com; 3018 Jianshe Lu, Luōhú District; 罗湖区建设路3018号; d from ¥850; 🌐@🛜; Ⓜ Line 1, 3 to Laojie, exit D) Good deals can be had at this mid-sized hotel in the heart of Dōngmén's shopping and dining buzz. Rooms are spacious and contemporary, and all include breakfast. Many have sofa beds, effectively making them triples.

Macau

Macau Peninsula p199

Home to many of Macau's top historic attractions, including charming Portuguese colonial heritage and arts.

Taipa p210

Hiking, museums and a lovely traditional village that was once abuzz with fisherfolk and shipyards.

Coloane p214

Coastal village vibes, framed by temples, Portuguese restaurants, beaches and golf.

Cotai p218

Macau's answer to Las Vegas: come to gawp, dine and shop in architecturally unique megacasinos and entertainment complexes.

TOP SIGHT
RUINS OF THE CHURCH OF ST PAUL

The ruins of the Church of St Paul are Macau's most treasured icon. Once a Jesuit church in the early 17th century, all that remains now are the facade and the stairway. However, with the wonderful statues, portals and engravings that effectively make up a sermon in stone, the ruins are one of the greatest monuments to Christianity in Asia.

The church was designed by an Italian Jesuit and built in 1602 by Japanese Christian exiles and Chinese craftsmen. After the expulsion of the Jesuits, a military battalion was stationed here. In 1835 a fire erupted in the kitchen of the barracks, destroying everything, except what you see today.

The facade has five tiers. At the top is a dove, representing the Holy Spirit, surrounded by stone carvings of the sun, moon and stars. Beneath that is a statue of the infant Jesus accompanied by the implements of the Crucifixion. In the centre of the third tier stands the Virgin Mary being assumed bodily into heaven along with angels and two flowers: the peony, representing China, and the chrysanthemum, representing Japan. Just below the pediment, on the right side of the facade, is a dragon surmounted by the Holy Virgin. To the right of the Virgin is a carving of the tree of life and the apocalyptic woman (Mary) slaying a seven-headed hydra; the Japanese kanji next to her reads: 'The holy mother tramples the heads of the dragon'.

The facade is approached by six flights of 11 stairs each, with an attractive balustrade running up each side.

The small **Museum of Sacred Art & Crypt** (天主教藝術博物館和墓室, Museu de Arte Sacra e Cripta; Map p208; ⊙9am-6pm Wed-Mon, to 2pm Tue) FREE contains carved wooden statues, silver chalices and oil paintings, as well as the remains of Vietnamese and Japanese Christians martyred in the 17th century.

DON'T MISS

➜ Facade details
➜ The stairway
➜ Museum of Sacred Art
➜ Crypt & ossuary

PRACTICALITIES

➜ 大三巴牌坊, Ruinas de Igreja de São Paulo
➜ Map p208, D1
➜ Calçada de São Paulo
➜ admission free
➜ 🚌8A, 17, 26, disembark at Luís de Camões Garden

Macau Peninsula

Explore

While many visitors automatically equate Macau with gambling, the peninsula is far more about history than blackjack. This is the city's busy core, with dense working neighbourhoods, charming colonial buildings (and, yes, some casinos too – mostly the smaller, older ones). It's here that you'll come to see Macau's top historic attractions, vestiges of its past as a Portuguese colony such as the gaunt Ruins of the Church of St Paul, St Lazarus Church District and Guia Fortress and Chapel. It's also the heart of Macau's burgeoning arts scene, with a growing number of cool cafes and galleries to peruse, topped off by the Macau Museum of Art.

If you're coming from the Macau–Hong Kong Ferry Terminal, take bus 3 to Largo do Senado, Macau's main square, to begin your explorations. An hour or two before sundown, head to the southwestern corner of the peninsula. This is the old Portuguese quarter and it is breathtaking at sunset; if you prefer new architecture instead, go to the southeastern part of the peninsula for casinos (and award-winning dining) like Grand Lisboa.

The Best...

→ **Sight** Ruins of the Church of St Paul (p198)

→ **Place to Eat** Clube Militar de Macau (p206)

→ **Place to Drink** Macau Soul (p206)

Top Tip

You can download Macau EasyGo, a free app that allows you to check bus routes and stops, and track your bus – offline!

Getting There & Away

→ **Air** Macau International Airport (www.macau-airport.com) is only 20 minutes from the city centre, with frequent services to destinations including Bangkok, Chiang Mai, Kaohsiung, Kuala Lumpur, Manila, Osaka, Seoul, Singapore, Taipei, Tokyo, Moscow and Běijīng.

→ **Boat** Macau's main ferry terminal, Macau Maritime Ferry Terminal (p263), is in the outer harbour. Yuet Tung Shipping Co (p264) has ferries connecting Macau's Taipa Ferry Terminal (MOP$238, 1½ hours, seven times daily) with Shékǒu in Shēnzhèn and Shēnzhèn airport. TurboJet (p263) has the most sailings to Hong Kong and the trip takes one hour.

Need to Know

→ **Area Code** ☏853

→ **Location** Sixty kilometres southwest of Hong Kong.

→ **Currency** Macanese pataca (MOP$)/ Hong Kong dollar (HK$)

→ **Tourist Office** (旅遊局; Map p208; ☏853 8397 1120, tourism hotline 853 2833 3000; www.macautourism.gov.mo; Edificio Ritz, Largo do Senado; ◎9am-1pm & 2.30-5.35pm Mon-Fri)

→ **Casinos** Open 24 hours. You must be 21 or over to enter, and neatly dressed.

◉ SIGHTS

◉ Central Macau Peninsula

RUINS OF THE CHURCH OF ST PAUL   RUINS
See p198.

★**CHURCH OF ST JOSEPH**   CHURCH
Map p208 (聖若瑟聖堂, Capela do Seminario São José; Rua do Seminario; ◎10am-5pm; ☐9, 16, 18, 28B) St Joseph's, which falls outside the tourist circuit, is Macau's most beautiful model of tropicalised baroque architecture. Consecrated in 1758 as part of the Jesuit seminary, it features a scalloped canopy and a staircase leading to the courtyard from which you see the arresting white-and-yellow facade of the church and its dome. The latter is the oldest dome ever built in China. The interior with its three altars are lavishly ornamented with overlapping pilasters and attractive Solomonic 'spiral' columns.

★**MANDARIN'S HOUSE**   HISTORIC BUILDING
(鄭家大屋, Caso do Mandarim; ☏853 2896 8820; www.wh.mo/mandarinhouse; 10 Travessa de António da Silva; ◎10am-5.30pm Thu-Tue; ☐28B, 18) **FREE** Built around 1869, the Mandarin's

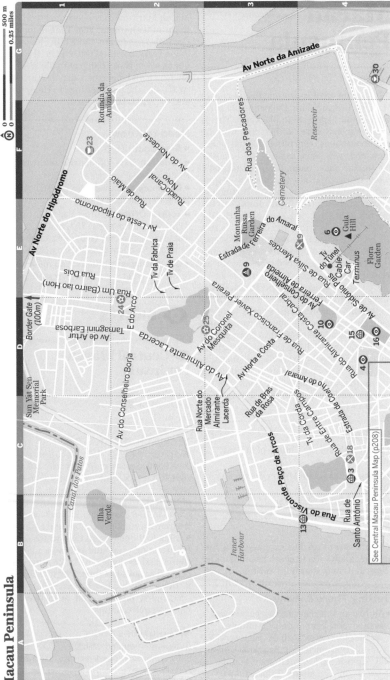

MACAU

Macau Peninsula

0.25 miles
500 m

Av Norte do Hipódromo

Av Norte da Amizade

Rotunda da Amizade

23

Av do Nordeste

Rua do Canal Novo

Rua de Maio

Av Leste do Hipódromo

Rua dos Pescadores

Reservoir

Cemetery

Tv de Praia

Tv da Fabrica

Rua Dois

Rua Um (Bairro Iao Hon)

E do Arco

24

Estrada de Ferreira do Amaral

Montanha Russa Garden

9

Guia Hill

6

30

Rua de Sidónio Pais

Tv do Túnel

Cable Car Terminus

Flora Garden

Border Gate (100m)

Av de Artur Tamagnini Barbosa

Av do Conselheiro Borja

Sun Yat Sen Memorial Park

Ilha Verde

Canal dos Patos

25

Av do Almirante Lacerda

Av do Coronel Mesquita

Ferreira de Almeida

Rua de Silva Mendes

Av de Sidónio Pais

Av do Conselheiro Costa Cabral

9

10

15

16

4

Rua de Francisco Xavier Pereira

Av Horta e Costa

Rua Norte do Mercado Almirante Lacerda

Rua de Bras da Rosa

Estrada de Coelho do Amaral

Tv da Cordas

Rua de Entre Campos

18

3

13

Rua do Visconde Paço de Arcos

Rua de Santo António

Inner Harbour

See Central Macau Peninsula Map (p208)

MACAU

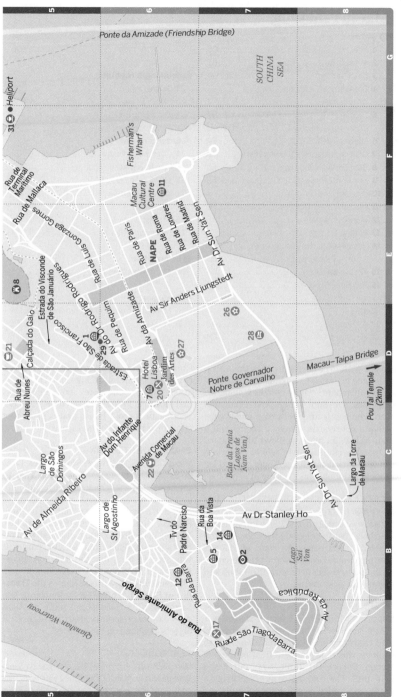

Ponte da Amizade (Friendship Bridge)

SOUTH CHINA SEA

31 Heliport

Rua de Terminal Marítimo

Rua de Mallaca

Rua de Luís Gonzaga Gomes

Fisherman's Wharf

Macau Cultural Centre

11

Rua de Paris

NAPE

Rua de Roma

Rua de Londres

Rua de Madrid

Av Dr Sun Yat Sen

Estrada do Visconde de São Januário

8

Calçada do Gaio

Estrada de São Francisco

Av Dr Rodrigo Rodrigues

Rua de Pequim

Av Sir Anders Ljungstedt

21

Rua de Abreu Nunes

1

29

Av da Amizade

Hotel Lisboa

Jardim das Artes

27

26

28

Macau–Taipa Bridge

7

20

Ponte Governador Nobre de Carvalho

Pou Tai Temple (2km)

Largo de São Domingos

Av do Infante Dom Henrique

Avenida Comercial de Macau

22

Baía da Praia (Lagos de Nam Van)

Av Dr Sun Yat Sen

Largo da Torre de Macau

Av de Almeida Ribeiro

Largo de St Agostinho

Tv do Padré Narciso

Rua da Boa Vista

Av Dr Stanley Ho

Lago Sai Van

Av da República

12

Rua da Barra

5

14

2

17

Rua de São Tiago da Barra

Qianshan Waterway

Macau Peninsula

House, with over 60 rooms, was the ancestral home of Zheng Guanying, an influential author-merchant whose readers included emperors, Dr Sun Yatsen and Chairman Mao. The compound features a moon gate, tranquil courtyards, exquisite rooms and a main hall with French windows, all arranged in that labyrinthine-style typical of certain Chinese period buildings. There are guided tours in Cantonese on weekend afternoons.

★ ST LAZARUS CHURCH DISTRICT   AREA
Map p208 (瘋堂斜巷, Calcada da Igreja de São Lázaro; www.cipa.org.mo; ⊡7, 8) A lovely neighbourhood with colonial-style houses and cobbled streets makes for some of Macau's best photo ops. Designers and other creative types like to gather here, setting up shop and organising artsy events.

★ SIR ROBERT HO TUNG LIBRARY   LIBRARY
Map p208 (何東圖書館; 3 Largo de St Agostinho; ⊙8am-8pm Tue-Sun, from 2pm Mon; ⊡9, 16, 18) This charming building, founded in the 19th century, was the country retreat of the late tycoon Robert Ho Tung, who purchased it in 1918. The colonial edifice, featuring a dome, an arcaded facade, Ionic columns and

Chinese-style gardens, was given a modern extension by architect Joy Choi Tin Tin in 2006. The new four-storey structure in glass and steel has Piranesi-inspired bridges connecting to the old house and a glass roof straddling the transitional space.

CHURCH OF ST DOMINIC   CHURCH
Map p208 (玫瑰堂, Igreja de São Domingos; Largo de São Domingos; ⊙10am-6pm; ⊡3, 6, 26A) In the heart of Macau's historic centre, this sunny yellow baroque church with a beautiful altar and a timber roof was founded by three Spanish Dominican priests from Acapulco, Mexico, in the 16th century, although the current structure dates from the 17th century. It was here, in 1822, that the first Portuguese newspaper was published on Chinese soil. The former bell tower now houses the **Treasure of Sacred Art** (聖物寶庫, Tresouro de Arte Sacra; Map p208; ⊙10am-6pm; FREE), an Aladdin's cave of ecclesiastical art and liturgical objects exhibited on three floors.

ALBERGUE SCM   GALLERY
Map p208 (婆仔屋文創空間, Albergue da Santa Casa da Misericórdia; ☏853 2852 2550; www.facebook.com/alberguescmmacau; 8 Calcada da Igreja

de São Lázaro; ☺noon-7pm Wed-Mon; ☐7, 8) **FREE** Once known as the Old Ladies' House, the poetic courtyard with two yellow colonial buildings was a shelter for Portuguese refugees from Shànghǎi in WWII and later a home for elderly women. It's now run by an art organisation, Albergue SCM, which mounts exhibitions in its gallery here and organises cultural events. On entry to the courtyard, you will be greeted by two magnificent camphor trees, possibly the most beautiful in Macau and older than the houses.

LOU KAU MANSION   HISTORIC BUILDING
Map p208 (盧家大屋, Casa de Lou Kau; ☑853 8399 6699; www.wh.mo/loukau; 7 Travessa da Sé; ☺10am-5.30pm Tue-Sun; ☐3, 4, 6A, 8A, 19, 33) **FREE** Built around 1889, this Cantonese-style mansion with southern European elements belonged to merchant Lou Wa Sio (aka Lou Kau), who also commissioned the **Lou Lim Ieoc Garden** (盧廉若公園, Jardim Lou Lim Ieoc; http://en.macaotourism.gov.mo; 10 Estrada de Adolfo de Loureiro; ☺6am-9pm; ☐2, 2A, 5, 9, 9A, 12, 16). Behind the grey facade, an intriguing maze of open and semi-enclosed spaces blurs the line between inside and outside. The flower-and-bird motif on the roof can also be found in the Mandarin's House and A-Ma Temple. Traditional craft workers often practise their art here during weekdays.

MONTE FORT   FORT
Map p208 (大炮台, Fortaleza do Monte; Praceta do Museu de Macau; ☺7am-7pm; ☐7, 8, disembark at Social Welfare Bureau) **FREE** Just east of the Ruins of the Church of St Paul (p198), from which it is separated by a pebbled path and picturesque foliage, Monte Fort was built by the Jesuits between 1617 and 1626 to defend the College of the Mother of God against pirates. It was later handed over to the colonial government. Barracks and storehouses were designed to allow the fort to survive a two-year siege, but the cannons were fired only once, during the aborted attempt by the Dutch to invade Macau in 1622.

LEAL SENADO   HISTORIC BUILDING
Map p208 (民政總署大樓; ☑853 2857 2233; 163 Avenida de Almeida Ribeiro; ☺9am-9pm Tue-Sun; ☐3, 6, 26A, 18A, 33, disembark at Almeida Ribeiro) Facing Largo do Senado is Macau's most important historical building, the 18th-century 'Loyal Senate', which houses the Instituto para os Assuntos Cívicos e Municipais (IACM; Civic and Municipal Affairs Bureau). It is so-named because the body sitting here

refused to recognise Spain's sovereignty during the 60 years that it occupied Portugal. In 1654, a dozen years after Portuguese sovereignty was re-established, King João IV ordered a heraldic inscription to be placed inside the entrance hall, which can still be seen today.

Inside the entrance hall is the **IACM Temporary Exhibition Gallery** (民政總署臨時展覽廳; Map p208; ☑853 2836 6866; www.icm. gov.mo/en/events; ☺9am-9pm Tue-Sun) **FREE**. On the 1st floor is the **Senate Library** (民政總署圖書館; Map p208; ☑853 2857 2233; ☺1-7pm Mon-Sat) **FREE**, which has a collection of some 18,500 books, and wonderful carved wooden furnishings and panelled walls.

TAP SEAC GALLERY   GALLERY
(塔石藝文舘, Galeria Tap Seac; ☑853 2836 6866; www.icm.gov.mo/ts; 95 Avenida Conselheiro Ferreira de Almeida; ☺10am-9pm; ☐7, 8) **FREE** One of a handful of 1920s houses surrounding **Tap Seac Square** (塔石廣場, Praca do Tap Seac), this one formerly belonging to an upper-class family has a European-style facade and Moorish arched doors. The gallery inside hosts excellent contemporary art exhibitions. The original patio in the middle of the house has been kept, which creates a light-filled, relaxing setting.

DOM PEDRO V THEATRE   HISTORIC BUILDING
Map p208 (崗頂劇院, Teatro Dom Pedro V; ☑853 2893 9646; www.wh.mo/theatre/en; Calçada do Teatro, Largo de St Agostinho; ☺10am-6pm Wed-Mon; ☐3, 4, 6A, 8A, 19) This sage green neoclassical theatre is one of the oldest western-style theatres in East Asia, and remains an important cultural venue today. It was built in 1860 by the local Portuguese in the style of European theatres at the time, but some features were added later, including the facade with white columns. Check out the corridor on the right of the main hall; it has beautiful windows in an art nouveau style, and a quaint staircase leading to the upper circle.

◉ Northern Macau Peninsula

★GUIA FORTRESS & CHAPEL   FORT, CHAPEL
(東望洋炮台及聖母雪地殿聖堂, Fortaleza da Guia e Capela de Guia; Flora Gardens; ☺fortress 9am-6pm, chapel 10am-5.30pm, lighthouse open only on special days; ☐2, 2A, 6A, 12, 17, 18, Flora

MACAU COFFEE CULTURE

Coffee culture is thriving on Macau Peninsula and there's no shortage of cafes serving strong espressos, single-origin brews and even the odd espresso martini. Some of our favourites:

Single Origin (單品; ☑853 6698 7475; 19 Rua de Abreu Nunes; coffee MOP$35; ⊙noon-8pm; 🖱; 🚌2, 4, 7, 7A, 8)

Cafe Philo (Map p208; www.facebook.com/pg/cafephilo; 17B Rua dos Artilheiros; ⊙12.30-7.30pm Tue-Sun; 🖱; 🚌7, 8, 18A, 19)

Terra Coffee House (Map p208; ☑853 2893 7943; 1 Largo de St Agostinho; ⊙10am-9.30pm Mon-Sat, noon-8pm Sun; 🖱; 🚌9, 16)

Terra Drip Bar (☑853 2847 3623; Block 4, 364 Rua 1 de Maio; ⊙noon-8pm Mon-Fri, from 10am Sat & Sun; 🖱; 🚌2A, 7, 18A)

Gardens stop) **FREE** As the highest point on the peninsula, Guia Fortress affords panoramic views of the city. At the top is the small but stunning Chapel of Our Lady of Guia, built in 1622 and retaining almost 100% of its original features, including frescoes with both Portuguese and Chinese details that are among Asia's most important. Next to the chapel stands the oldest modern lighthouse (c 1865) on the China coast – an attractive 15m-tall structure that is usually closed to the public.

The entrance to the fortress has an attractive display of old typhoon signals that were hoisted during storms – large, metallic physical symbols of the strong wind numbering system adopted by Macau (and Hong Kong). Inside the fortress is a new information gallery on the chapel and the complex. On the other side of the fortress is a tunnel showing old photos and replicas of how things used to look when it was an air-raid shelter.

You could walk to the fortress and chapel, but it's easier to take the Guia cable car that runs from the entrance of **Flora Gardens** (二龍喉公園, Jardim da Flora; Travessa do Túnel; cable car one-way/return MOP$2/3; ⊙garden 6am-8.30pm daily, cable car 8am-6pm Tue-Sun; ♿; 🚌2,17,18), Macau's largest public park.

AFA
GALLERY

(全藝社, Art for All Society; ☑853 2836 6064; www.afamacau.com; 1st fl, Art Garden, 265 Avenida Dr Rodrigo Rodrigues; ⊙10am-7pm Mon-Fri; 🚌8, 8A, 18A, 7) **FREE** Some of Macau's best contemporary art can be seen at this non-profit gallery, which has taken Macau's art worldwide and holds monthly solo exhibitions by the city's top artists. AFA is near the Mong Há Multi-Sport Pavilion. Disem-

bark from the bus at Rua da Barca or Rua de Francisco Xavier Pereira. Alternatively, it's a 20-minute walk from Largo do Senado.

CASA GARDEN
HISTORIC BUILDING

(東方基金會會址; 13 Praça de Luís de Camões; ⊙garden 9.30am-6pm daily, gallery open only during exhibitions 9.30am-6pm Mon-Fri; 🚌8A, 17, 26) **FREE** This beautiful colonial villa and park were built in 1770 as a merchant's residence. It later became the headquarters of the British East India Company when it was based in Macau in the early 19th century. The property has a small gallery that puts on excellent exhibitions with a cross-cultural (Portuguese and Macanese/Chinese) aspect. Visitors can wander the slightly forlorn-looking gardens.

KUN IAM TEMPLE
BUDDHIST TEMPLE

(觀音廟, Templo de Kun Iam; 2 Avenida do Coronel Mesquita; ⊙7am-5.30pm; 🚌1A, 10, 18A, stop Travessa de Venceslau de Morais) Macau's oldest temple was founded in the 13th century, but the present structures date to 1627. The roof ridges are ornately embellished with porcelain figurines and the halls are lavishly decorated, if a little weathered. Inside the main hall stands the likeness of Kun Iam, the Goddess of Mercy; to the left of the altar is a bearded arhat rumoured to represent Marco Polo. The first Sino-American treaty was signed at a round stone table in the temple's terraced gardens in 1844.

CEMETERY OF ST MICHAEL THE ARCHANGEL
CEMETERY

(西洋墳場, Cemitério de São Miguel Arcanjo; 2a Estrada do Cemitério; ⊙8am-6pm; 🚌7, 7A, 8) This cemetery, northeast of Monte Fort, contains tombs and sepulchres from the 19th and 20th centuries that are fine examples of baroque ecclesiastical art. Near the main entrance is the **Chapel of St Michael** (聖彌額爾小堂, Capela de São Miguel; ⊙10am-6pm), a doll-sized, mint-green church with a tiny choir loft and pretty porticoes. It was built in 1875.

PATANE LIBRARY   HISTORIC BUILDING

(沙梨頭圖書館; ☑853 2856 7576; www.library. gov.mo; 69-81 Rua da Ribeira do Patane; ⊙9.30am-8.30pm Tue-Sun, from 2pm Mon; ☐4,6,6A) A row of seven shophouses skirting the Inner Harbour has been renovated into an attractive public library. Built in the 1930s, the colourful two-storey structures have arcades harking to Southeast Asia and shuttered doors evoking Mediterranean countries. Old water pipes, door panels and railings belonging to previous tenants decorate the library's interior. If you go in the evening, you'll see elderly residents reading the newspaper and students with their school work.

⊙ Southern Macau Peninsula

⭐MACAU MUSEUM OF ART   MUSEUM

(澳門藝術博物館, Museu de Arte de Macau; ☑853 8791 9814; www.mam.gov.mo; Macau Cultural Centre, Avenida Xian Xing Hai; ⊙10am-6.30pm Tue-Sun; ☐1A, 8, 12, 23) FREE This excellent five-storey museum has well-curated displays of art created in Macau and China, including paintings by western artists such as George Chinnery, who lived in the enclave. Other highlights are ceramics and stoneware excavated in Macau, Ming and Qing dynasty calligraphy from Guǎngdōng, ceramic statues from Shíwān (Guǎngdōng) and seal carvings. The museum also features 19th-century western historical paintings from all over Asia, and contemporary Macanese art.

⭐CHAPEL OF OUR
LADY OF PENHA   HISTORIC BUILDING

(西望洋聖母堂, Capela de Nossa Senhora da Penha; Top of Penha Hill; ⊙9.30am-4pm; ☐3, 8, 9, 16) This graceful chapel atop Penha Hill was raised as a place of pilgrimage for Portuguese sailors in the 17th century, purportedly by survivors of a ship that had narrowly escaped capture by the Dutch. Most of what you see though came about in 1935. In the courtyard is a marble statue of Our Lady of Lourdes facing the sea; symmetri-cal staircases lead down to a grotto of the saint, complete with pews and altar. The grey chapel is visible across the lake.

AVENIDA DA REPÚBLICA   AREA

(民國大馬路; ☐6, 9, 16) Banyan-lined Avenida da República, along the northwest shore of Sai Van Lake, is Macau's oldest Portuguese quarter. There are several grand colonial villas not open to the public here. The former Bela Vista Hotel, one of the most-storied hotels in Asia, is now the **Residence of the Portuguese Consul-General** (葡國駐澳門領事官邸, Consulado-Geral de Portugal em Macau; Rua do Boa Vista). Nearby is the ornate Santa Sancha Palace, once the residence of Macau's Portuguese governors, and now used to accommodate dignitaries. Not too far away are beautiful, abandoned art deco–inspired buildings.

GALLERY OF MACAU'S
GAMING HISTORY   GALLERY

(澳門博彩業歷史資料館; Crystal Palace Casino, 3rd fl, Hotel Lisboa, 2-4 Avenida de Lisboa; ⊙9am-5.30pm; ☐3, 6, 26A) FREE Macau's gambling industry goes back to the 16th century, when labourers from China played a game called 'fan-tan' in makeshift stalls. While scholars have written about the subject, this is the first gallery devoted to it. The eye-opening exhibition walks you through Macau's gaming history via texts (Chinese only), fascinating old photos and vintage slot machines.

✗ EATING

⭐RIQUEXÓ CAFE   CAFETERIA $

(利多咖啡屋; ☑853 2856 5655; 69 Avenida Sidonio Pais; meals from MOP$60; ⊙noon 10pm) Modest Riquexó is *the* place for tasty, no-frills Macanese. Take your pick of the daily options, which may include *minchi,* a homey dish of minced meat sautéed with diced potatoes, and seasoned with soy and Worcester sauce. Then sit down in the cafe and look at the old photos of Macau on the white tiled walls as you wait for your order.

⭐HOU KONG CHI KEI   CANTONESE $

(濠江志記; ☑853 2895 3098; ground fl, Block 3, Lai Hou Gardens, Rua Coelho do Amaral; dishes MOP$48-228; ⊙6.30-10.30pm; ☐8A, 17, 26) Local families have been flocking to this unassuming restaurant for reasonably priced barbecued fish and pig-ear salad even before it received a Michelin mention. Now

---

LOCAL KNOWLEDGE

MACANESE CUISINE

A typical Macanese menu features an enticing stew of influences from Chinese, Asian and Portuguese cuisines, and the cooking of former Portuguese colonies in Africa, India and Latin America. Coconut, tamarind, chilli, jaggery (palm sugar) and shrimp paste can all feature. A famous Macanese speciality is *galinha à africana* (African chicken), made with coconut, garlic and chillies. Other popular dishes include *casquinha* (stuffed crab), *minchi* (minced pork or beef cooked with potatoes and onions) and *serradura* (a milk pudding).

---

reservation is a must on weekends. The fried taro fish balls and chunky oyster omelette are served piping hot and go swimmingly with Tsingtao beer.

★**CLUBE MILITAR DE MACAU** PORTUGUESE $$

Map p208 (陸軍俱樂部; ☑853 2871 4000; 975 Avenida da Praia Grande; meals MOP$200-500; ☻1.45-2.45pm & 7-10.30pm Mon-Fri, noon-2pm & 7-10.30pm Sat & Sun; ❈; ➡6, 28C) In a distinguished colonial building, with fans spinning lazily above, the Military Club takes you back in time to a quieter Macau. Simple and delicious Portuguese fare is complemented by reasonably priced wines and cheeses. The MOP$200 lunch buffet is great value, though à la carte offers more culinary refinement and a chance to taste the famous *leitão* (suckling pig). Reservations advised for dinner and weekends.

A LORCHA MACANESE, PORTUGUESE $$

(船屋葡國餐廳; ☑853 2831 3193; www.alorcha. com; 289 Rua do Almirante Sérgio; meals MOP$300-600; ☻12.30-2.30pm & 6.30-10.30pm Wed-Mon; ❈▦; ➡1, 5, 10) 'The Sailboat' is listed in every guidebook. One reason for its popularity is that it's within walking distance of the A-Ma Temple. If you go not expecting outstanding creativity, you'll enjoy its solid Portuguese and Macanese fare. Portions are generous.

★**EIGHT** CANTONESE $$$

Map p208 (8餐廳; ☑853 8803 7788; www. grandlisboahotel.com; 2nd fl, Grand Lisboa Hotel, Avenida de Lisboa; main dishes MOP$480-3000; ☻lunch 11.30am-2.30pm Mon-Sat, brunch 10am-3pm Sun, dinner 6.30-10.30pm daily; ℗❈☏; ➡3, 10, 28B) The Eight is a stellar three-Michelin star restaurant and model of Cantonese culinary refinement inside the Grand Lisboa. You can dine on a 'simple' meal of roast meat and Cantonese soup cooked to perfection, or splurge on marine delicacies such as abalone, to the accompaniment of water cascading down a wall and crystal-dripping chandeliers. Reservation a must.

TIM'S KITCHEN CHINESE $$$

(桃花源小廚; ☑853 8803 3682; www.hotel isboa.com; Shop F25, East Wing, Hotel Lisboa, 2-4 Avenida de Lisboa; meals MOP$500-13,800; ☻noon-2.30pm & 6.30-10.30pm; ➡3, 6, 26A) At Tim's, top ingredients are meticulously prepared using methods that highlight their original flavours, resulting in dishes that look simple but taste divine: a giant 'glass' prawn shares a plate with a sliver of Chinese ham; a crab claw lounges on a cushion of broth-soaked wintermelon. Seafood figures prominently on the menu, ranging from deep-fried scallops on mashed taro, to braised whole abalone.

🍷 DRINKING & NIGHTLIFE

★**MACAU SOUL** BAR

Map p208 (澳感廊; ☑853 2836 5182; www.macausoul.com; 31A Rua de São Paulo; ☻3-10pm Wed & Thu, to midnight Fri-Sun; ➡8A, 17, 26) An elegant haven in wood and stained glass, where twice a month a jazz band plays to a packed audience. On most nights, though, Thelonious Monk fills the air as customers chat with the owners and dither over their 400 Portuguese wines that include some rare varietals. Opening hours vary; phone ahead. Cash only.

★**BEER TEMPLE** PUB

Map p208 (☑853 2835 2803; www.facebook. com/beertemple.patiolazaro/; 4 Pátio São Lázaro; ☻noon-2am; ☏; ➡3, 4, 6A, 19) As the name suggests, the craft beer selection here is huge. If you can't decide, tell your staff your preference – fruit-forward, dry and bitter, or smelling like a pine forest, and they'll pick something out for you. Consume in the bar area with the high ceiling, loud music and shiny black surfaces.

CHE CHE CAFE
BAR

Map p208 (✆853 6288 0857; www.facebook. com/chechecafemacau; 70A Rua de Tomás Vieira; ⏰3pm-2am Mon-Sat; 🚌7, 8, 18A, 19) Owned by a member of post-rock band Why Oceans, Che Che is reassuringly dimly lit and laid-back. A faux-antique world map and a neon sign lamenting 'Love Will Tear Us Apart' jump out from dark walls. You may see culturally minded youth discussing film over a bottle of sake or pints of frothy beer.

MICO CAFE
BAR

Map p208 (78A Rua de Tomás Vieira; ⏰9pm-2am Wed-Mon; 🚌7, 8, 18A, 19) Macau's most elusive bar is not so due to its location – a few doors up from Che Che Cafe (p207), or that it's unknown, but because whether one gets in depends on the current mood of the owner Pedro. The quiet, half-lit space feels artsy and secretive. We think it's that, and the fine Portuguese wines, that make people keep trying to get in.

SKY 21 LOUNGE
LOUNGE

(✆853 2822 2122; www.sky21macau.com; 21st fl, AIA Tower, 215a-301 Avenida Comercial de Macau; ⏰6.30pm-2am Sun-Thu, to 3am Fri & Sat, happy hour 5-9pm; 🛜; 🚌18, 23, 32) A sleek lounge-bar with alfresco seating and rather costly drinks. There's beer pong from 10.30pm, and DJ action and/or live jazz on some days of the week, plus special parties on Saturdays. The highlight here is the killer views of the Macau skyline.

☆ ENTERTAINMENT

★ LIVE MUSIC ASSOCIATION
LIVE MUSIC

(LMA; 現場音樂協會; ✆853 2875 7511; www. facebook.com/lma.macau; 11th fl, Flat B, San Mei Industrial Bldg, 50 Avenida do Coronel Mesquita; 🚌7, 17, 18B) *The* go-to place for indie music in Macau, this excellent dive inside an industrial building hosts live acts from Macau and overseas. There are two or three bands a week, with past performers including Cold Cave, Buddhistson, Mio Myo and Pet Conspiracy. See its Facebook page for what's on.

Macau indie bands to watch out for include WhyOceans (www.whyoceans.com) and Turtle Giant (www.turtlegiant.com).

CINEMATHEQUE PASSION
CINEMA

Map p208 (戀愛電影館; ✆853 2852 2585; www. cinematheque-passion.mo; 11-13 Travessa da Paixão; tickets adult/student & senior MOP$60/30;

⏰ticket office 10am-11.30pm, archive 10am-8pm Tue-Sun; 🚌2, 3, 4, 6, 7) An attractive yellow house shelters Macau's art-house cinema and film archive. There are regular screenings of Macanese movies and films about the city. But even if you're not here for the flicks, it's worth going through the lobby to the back to see the garden and a view of the Ruins of the Church of St Paul. Most films come with English subtitles.

COMUNA DE PEDRA
DANCE

(石頭公社; ✆853 6628 0064; www.comuna depedra.blogspot.com; Iao Seng Industrial Bldg, Phase II, 9th fl, DB Rua Quatro do Bairro Iao Hon) This edgy but elusive contemporary-dance company has performed everywhere – in parks, on rooftops, in factories, and on stage in Macau and overseas. See its website for updates.

WYNN MACAU CASINO
CASINO

(永利娛樂場; ✆853 2888 9966; www.wynn macau.com; Wynn Macau, Rua Cidade de Sintra, Novos Aterros do Porto Exterior; ⏰24hr; 🚌8, 10A) Despite the outdoor Performance Lake, which gives a fountain show every 15 minutes to the tune of 'Money Makes the World Go Round' or Chinese tunes, the Wynn is one of Macau's more tranquil casino complexes. The gaming floors are relatively hushed, as is the small posh shopping area.

Less quiet is the Dragon of Fortune show in the Rotunda atrium, where every half an hour a golden animatronic dragon emerges from the floor breathing smoke. Other draws for the nongambler include a 24-carat gold tree that rises from the floor on the half hour, and an aquarium full of moon jellyfish.

GRAND LISBOA CASINO
CASINO

Map p208 (新葡京; ✆853 2838 2828; www. grandlisboa.com; Avenida de Lisboa; ⏰24hr; 🚌3, 10) A golden lotus-shaped tower, the delightfully tacky Grand Lisboa has become the landmark by which people navigate the peninsula's streets. Its four gaming floors are always jam-packed with serious gamblers. Less populated is the free daily 'Crazy Paris' cabaret dance show at the bar.

MGM GRAND MACAU
CASINO

(澳門美高梅; www.mgm.mo; Grande Praça, Avenida Dr Sun Yat Sen; ⏰24hr; 🚌3A, 8, 12) With softly lit casino floors and a bland upmarket shopping mall, you might think the MGM is less flashy than its brethren. But then you walk into the Grande Praça, a vast

Central Macau Peninsula

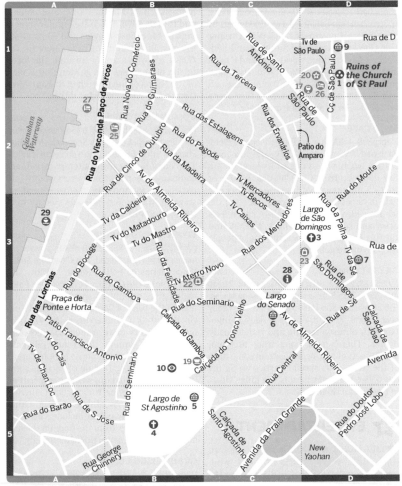

domed indoor plaza based on the streets of old Lisbon, centred on a ceiling-high tube-shaped aquarium of tropical fish.

🔒 SHOPPING

⭐ **LCM SHOP OF CANNED MACAU**   FOOD
Map p208 (澳門葡式辣魚店, LCM Loja das Conservas Macau; ☏853 6571 8214; www.facebook.com/lojadasconservasmacau; 9 Travessa do Aterro Novo; MOP$30-300; ⊙11am-9pm; ⛴4, 8A, 18A, 19) This shop carries dozens of canned seafood brands (representing hundreds of varieties) from Portugal, all labelled with

details on the history of the maker and the product. You'll find not only excellent sardine, tuna and mackerel, but also sea bream, *bacalhau* (salted cod), octopus and *sangacho de atum* (tuna blood). The last is good on a bed of greens with citrus dressing.

⭐ **PIN-TO LIVROS E MUSICA**   BOOKS
Map p208 (邊度有書有音樂; ☏853 2833 0909; www.facebook.com/pg/pintolivros; 47 Estrada de Coelho do Amaral; ⊙noon-9pm Tue-Sun; ⛴3, 6, 26A) One of Macau's best independent bookshops, Pin-to (which means 'where' in Cantonese) has a strong curation of titles in art

Central Macau Peninsula

and culture, including some in Portuguese and in English. The collections reflect the taste of owner Anson who can sometimes be seen reading by the staircase. You'll also find a dozen or so jazz and esoteric CDs, and two resident cats.

MERCEARIA PORTUGUESA   FOOD
Map p208 (☎853 2856 2708; www.mercearia portuguesa.com; 8 Calçada da Igreja de São Lázaro; ⊙1-9pm Mon-Fri, from noon Sat & Sun; ⌂7, 8) 'The Portuguese Corner', opened by a film director and actress, has a small but well-curated selection of provisions such as

tableware, soap and honey, wooden toys and jewellery from Portugal – all gorgeously packaged and reasonably priced.

VINTAGE MARKET
VINTAGE

Map p208 (古著市集; ☑853 6233 3900; www.facebook.com/vintagemarketmacau; 22A Rua da Sao Roque; ⊙3-9pm Mon-Fri, from 2pm Sat & Sun) Vintage overalls, biker jackets, twin sets and sheer dressing gowns – you'll find them here behind (very heavy) foldable yellow gates. The majority of the merchandise is from Australia, Thailand and North America, and it's supplemented by bold-looking handmade jewellery by local designers.

🛏 SLEEPING

Cheap guesthouses occupy central Macau, on and around Rua das Lorchas and Avenida de Almeida Ribeiro, with options aplenty on Rua da Felicidade (Street of Happiness), whose shuttered terraces were once Macau's main red-light district (scenes from *Indiana Jones and the Temple of Doom* were shot here). The high-end casino hotels generally occupy the southeast and the centre of town.

LOVE LANE SEVEN INN
INN $

Map p208 (戀愛七號旅館; ☑853 2836 6490; www.lovelane7.com; 7 Travessa da Paixão; d MOP$500-800; ❀❋☎; ☲8A, 17, 26) Occupying several floors behind a pink-and-green facade are seven rooms: a large one with two double beds; four standard rooms with private showers; and two small rooms with communal showers. Room 102 has stained-glass windows. Historical relics are dispersed throughout the building, including auspicious stone engravings.

OLD-SCHOOL MACAU

There's grace in the retro furniture and the casual way it's thrown together in this airy Cantonese teahouse (c 1963), **Lung Wah Tea House** (龍華茶樓; ☑853 2857 4456; 3 Rua Norte do Mercado Almirante-Lacerda; dim sum from MOP$14, tea MOP$10, staples MOP$48-110; ⊙7am-2pm; ❀; ☲23, 32). Take a booth by the windows overlooking the Red Market, where the teahouse buys its produce every day. There's no English menu; just point and take. Lung Wah also sells a fine array of Chinese teas.

★5FOOTWAY INN
INN $$

Map p208 (五步廊旅舍; ☑853 2892 3118; 8 Rua de Constantino Brito; d/tr incl breakfast from MOP$1400/2200; ❀❋☎; ☲1, 2, 5, 7, 10) This Singapore-owned accommodation converted from a love motel has 23 small clean rooms, vibrant paintings in communal areas and excellent English-speaking staff. Rates include a self-service breakfast. It's opposite the **Sofitel Macau at Ponte 16** (澳門十六浦索菲特大酒店; ☑853 8861 0016; www.sofitelmacau.com; Rua do Visconde Paço de Arcos), which means you can take its free shuttle buses to and from the ferry terminal. The rate for a double drops to MOP$500 on off-season weekdays.

★MANDARIN ORIENTAL
LUXURY HOTEL $$$

(文華東方酒店; ☑853 8805 8888; www.mandarinoriental.com/macau; Avenida Dr Sun Yat Sen; r/ste incl breakfast from MOP$3000/4800; ❀❋@☎❄) A great high-end option, the Mandarin has everything associated with the brand: elegance, superlative service, comfortable rooms and excellent facilities. Though relatively small, it's a refreshing contrast to the glitzier casino hotels.

Taipa

Explore

Taipa is a mere 6.3 sq km. This means that to an even greater extent than Macau Peninsula, everything is within walking distance; though you may prefer to supplement walking with bus or taxi rides. Roughly in the centre of Taipa is a roundabout called Rotunda do Estádio, named after a neighbouring sports stadium (*estádio*). To the south is Taipa Village (p211), only decades ago a fishing village with shipyards and duck farms before the sea was filled to make Cotai, home of the casinos. Taipa Village is the tourist epicentre with museums and sights to see, lanes to explore and lots to eat. To its immediate west is the Macau Jockey Club. To its north, past Avenida de Kwong Tung, is Pou Tai Temple and its two laudable vegetarian restaurants. You'll also find a few cafes, bars and places to eat on and around Avenida de Kwong Tung. The main hiking hills in Taipa are Big Taipa Hill on the eastern coast and Small Taipa Hill in the northwestern corner.

The Best...

➤ **Sight** Taipa Village (p211)

➤ **Place to Eat** Tapas de Portugal (p211)

➤ **Place to Drink** Goa Nights (p212)

Top Tip

Cycling is a good way to see Taipa Village when it's not too crowded. Yau Kei Store (p268), near Pak Tai Temple, has bikes for rent for MOP$10 to MOP$25 an hour. If you're bringing your own vehicle over, **Victo Cycle** (偉圖單車; ☑853 2883 0603; 205-241 Avenida de Kwong Tung, Taipa; ☺11am-8pm; ☐11, 16, 28A) has equipment and a repair service.

Getting There & Away

➤ **Bus** Between the peninsula and Taipa: 11, 22, 28A, 30, 33, AP1.

Need to Know

➤ **Area Code** ☑853

➤ **Location** Taipa is 2.5km from Macau Peninsula and 39.3km from Hong Kong.

 SIGHTS

★ TAIPA VILLAGE   VILLAGE

Map p212 (氹仔舊城區; ☐22, 26, 33) The historical part of Taipa is best preserved in this village in the south of the district. An intricate warren of alleys hold traditional Chinese shops and some excellent restaurants, while the broader main roads are punctuated by colonial villas, churches and temples. Rua do Cunha, the main pedestrian drag, is lined with vendors hawking free samples of Macanese almond cookies and beef jerky, and tiny cafes selling egg tarts and *serradura* pudding.

Avenida da Praia, a tree-lined esplanade with wrought-iron benches, is perfect for a leisurely stroll.

PAK TAI TEMPLE   TAOIST TEMPLE

Map p212 (北帝廟; Largo Camoes, Rua do Regedor, Taipa; ☺8.30am-5pm; ☐22, 26, 28A) Pak Tai Temple sits quietly in a breezy square framed by old banyan trees. It is dedicated to a martial deity, the Taoist God ('Tai') of the North ('Pak'), who allgedly defeated the Demon King terrorising the universe. A pair of Chinese lions guard the entrance to the temple. On the third day of the third lunar month each year, Cantonese opera performances take place here. Local residents come to chill in the square before the temple in late afternoon.

POU TAI TEMPLE   BUDDHIST TEMPLE

(菩提禪院, PouTaiUn; ☑85328811007; www.facebook.com/poutaimonastery; 5 Estrada Lou Lim Ieok; ☺9am-6pm; ☐21A, 22, 25, 25X, 26A, 28A) A picturesque monastery founded in the 19th century by Buddhist monks, Pou Tai is the most important Pure Land Buddhism or Amidism site in Macau. There's an enormous bronze statue of Lord Gautama in its main hall, and prayer pavilions and orchid greenhouses scattered around the complex. There are two vegetarian restaurants here in the main building.

TAIPA HOUSES-MUSEUM   MUSEUM

Map p212 (龍環葡韻住宅博物館, Casa Museum da Taipa; ☑853 2882 7103; Avenida da Praia, Carmo Zone; ☺10am-6.30pm Tue-Sun; ♿; ☐11, 15, 22, 28A, 30, 33, 34) **FREE** The pastel-coloured villas (c 1921) here were the summer residences of wealthy Macanese. House of the Regions of Portugal showcases Portuguese costumes; House of the Islands looks at the history of Taipa and Coloane, with displays on traditional industries, such as fishing and fireworks making; and Macanese House offers a snapshot of life in the early 20th century. There's a large and attractively landscaped lotus pond out front, with the towering casinos of Cotai in the distance, that art students like to sketch.

 EATING & DRINKING

★ TAPAS DE PORTUGAL   TAPAS $

Map p212 (葡慧園; ☑853 2857 6626; 9 Rua dos Clérigos; tapas from MOP$85; ☺noon-midnight; ☐22, 26) Tantalising Portuguese-style tapas are on offer at this cosy, warm-toned restaurant by the owner of Michelin-lauded **António** (安東尼奧; ☑853 2888 8668; www.antoniomacau.com; 7 Rua dos Clérigos; meals MOP$550-1200; ☺11.30am-4pm & 6pm-midnight; ❄). There are over 40 to choose from and savour with Portuguese wine. After your lamb tenderloin bruschetta, suckling-pig pie and scrambled eggs with asparagus and Iberico sausage on toast, you can order a main course of duck rice or the Macanese classic, African chicken.

Taipa

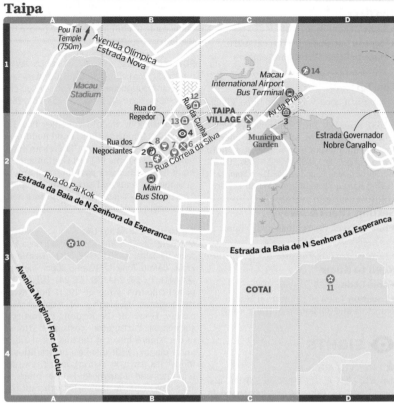

★BLISSFUL CARROT VEGETARIAN $
Map p212 (☑853 6298 8433; www.blissful
carrot.com; 79A Rua Direita Carlos Eugenio; rice
bowls from MOP$80; ☺10am-8pm Thu-Tue; ☑;
🚍11, 15, 22) 🍴 Fantastic takeaway shop and
online bakery for vegetarians. Our favourites are the plant-based rice bowls (nine versions!), almond milk and raw coconut pea-
nut butter cups. If you crave dairy, a grilled
cheese sandwich or quesadilla might do the
trick. It also sells organic wine and coffee.
Only biodegradable and sustainable packaging is used.

★SUM YUEN VEGETARIAN, CHINESE $$
(心橡素食; ☑853 2881 2698; www.facebook.
com/sumyuenmacau; 5 Estrada Lou Lim leok;
meals MOP$200-400; ☺10.30am-3pm & 5.30-
10.30pm; ❋☑🍴; 🚍21A, 22, 25, 25X, 26A, 28A)
You can pick from over 150 creative dishes
at this modern restaurant at Pou Tai Tem-
ple (p211). Avocado, yam and eggplant fig-

ure on the menu, in the form of sushi, tep-
panyaki or pudding, as do mushrooms and
bamboo piths as soup or stir-fry. The cook-
ing style is Chinese, with nods to Japan,
Europe and Southeast Asia.

You can have a feast here, and a healthy
one at that, especially if you come with
friends.

★GOA NIGHTS BAR
Map p212 (果阿之夜; ☑853 2856 7819; www.
goanights.com; 118 Rua Correria da Silva; ☺6pm-
1am Tue-Fri, noon-4pm & 6pm-1am Sat & Sun;
🚍22, 26) With lotus-shaped light stencils
on the walls, intimate Goa is a cocktail bar
that plays on the Portuguese-India theme.
The menu introduces nine aromatic con-
coctions that allude to Portuguese explor-
er Vasco da Gama through ingredients like
raw turmeric and chorizo fat. The most
unique, we felt, was the smooth, fruity and
spice-fragrant 'Lisbon'.

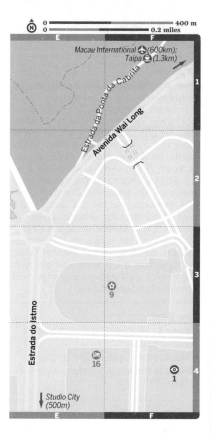

OLD TAIPA TAVERN PUB

Map p212 (好客鄉村餐廳, OTT; ☏853 2882 5221; 21 Rua dos Negociantes; ⊙2.30pm-2.30am Mon-Fri, from 1pm Sat & Sun; 🛜; 🚌22, 26, 28A) A location near the Pak Tai Temple (p211) makes laid-back OTT a sublime spot for a sundowner or two. You can enjoy the live sports broadcast over beer and pub grub, or take your drink to the temple courtyard and watch the comings and goings in the centre of Taipa Village.

BOOM GAY

(☏853 2882 1776; www.facebook.com/boom-barmacau; Nam Sun Garden Block 5, M Shop, Avenida de Kwong Tung; ⊙9pm-3am Mon-Sat; 🚌11, 16, 28A) Macau's only gay bar has pastel-coloured wall art and wire fences, bar-height tables for mingling and cosy corners for tête-à-têtes. There's live music most weekends and themed nights on other days, such as Techno Night and Red Night.

It also stages go-go dance shows and the occasional singing contest. If the door is closed, be sure to ring the bell.

🛍 SHOPPING

★O SANTOS LOJA PORTUGUESA FOOD & DRINKS

Map p212 (山度士葡國商店; ☏853 2857 6873; 2 Rua das Gaivotas; ⊙noon-9pm Wed-Mon; 🚌22, 26) Portuguese products in Macau are the rage these days, and this bright and welcoming store stocks wines, olive oil, sweets and canned seafood. Or if you're looking to bring home a couple of cockerel-themed cushions or a child-sized statue of the Virgin Mary, this is the place to go.

⭐ **CUNHA BAZAAR** GIFTS & SOUVENIRS

Map p212 (官也墟; www.cunhabazaar.com; 33-35 Rua do Cunha; ⓧ9.30am-10pm; 🚌22, 26, 33) This four-storey shop on the corner of Taipa Village's Rua do Cunha pedestrian street has the motherlode of made-in-Macau gifts, T-shirts, candies and more. You'll find traditional foods such as almond cookies and jerky on the ground floor, while the 1st floor is dedicated to goods bearing the image of Macau's own Soda Panda.

🏃 SPORTS & ACTIVITIES

BIG TAIPA TRAIL HIKING

Map p212 (大潭山步行徑, Trilho de Taipa Grande; 🚹; 🚌5, 21A, 50, 50X, N2) The well-paved 4000m Grand Taipa Trail, lying mostly within a country park on eastern Taipa Island, has broad slopes and steps rising to a peak of 160m – the highest point in Taipa from which you can see Cotai and Macau Peninsula. The route also takes you past exercise trails and a landscaped camellia garden.

The bus has a stop at the CEM Warehouse on Estrada Governador Nobre de Carvalho. Get off here and ascend the flight of steps that leads to the start of the trail.

🛏 SLEEPING

ALTIRA MACAU HOTEL $$

(新濠鋒酒店; 🕾853 2886 8866; www.altira macau.com; Avenida de Kwong Tung; r incl breakfast from MOP$1800; ◉☀@☎🏊) A rare luxury option in Taipa, Altira will suit those wanting to splurge outside the gaming hub of Cotai. It has a heated infinity pool, a spa, restaurants and a casino, discreetly tucked away. Rooms are top-notch with rather formal aesthetics. The waterfront rooms enjoy views of Macau Peninsula and the bridge – impressive at night when the lights come on.

Coloane

Explore

Most of Coloane's attractions lie along the southwestern and southeastern coasts. The former is where you'll find the popular Coloane Village with its palpable village vibe, temples and shipyards, and Portuguese restaurants operating from Chinese houses. Its southeast coast comprises Hac Sa Beach (p216) and country parks crisscrossed by hiking trails. Macau's two youth hostels are also here. A-Ma Cultural Village, with its Goddess of the Sea statue visible from kilometres away, occupies a hilltop in the centre of Coloane. Coloane's northeastern chunk, Ká Hó, is home to a large country park, an oil depot and industry. Along the coast here are a resort and golf club, and further up, a former leprosarium with a beautiful restored church.

The Best...

➡ **Sight** Ká Hó Church of Our Lady of Sorrows (p215)

➡ **Place to Eat** Espaco Lisboa (p217)

➡ **Place to Drink** Hon Kei Hand-Whipped Coffee (p217)

Top Tip

Cycling is how locals like to experience Coloane Village, especially the quiet temples and countryside at its southern end; bikes are available from **Dong Rong** (東榮單車行; Map p216; 🕾853 6687 3208; 2 Rua do Meio; bike rental per hour MOP$20; ⓧ11am-6pm) or **Island Bicycle** (路環小島單車; Map p216; 🕾853 6636 0060; www.facebook.com/islandbicycle coloane; 1 Rua Correia Lemo; per hr MOP$20-30; ⓧ10.30am-6.30pm Tue-Sun).

Getting There & Away

Getting to Coloane can be tricky. A public bus is your best bet.

➡ **Bus** Between the peninsula and Coloane via Taipa: 21A, 25, 26, 26A. There is a bus stop near the western end of Estrada de Cheoc Van in Coloane Village.

➡ **Taxi** Be aware that some taxis may refuse to take you to Coloane because they're not assured a return fare. And you may have difficulty finding one to pick you up here. Ask your hotel to book a taxi for you.

Need to Know

➜ **Area Code** 📞853

➜ **Location** Coloane is 5.6km from Macau Peninsula and 39.3km from Hong Kong.

 **SIGHTS**

COLOANE VILLAGE   VILLAGE

Map p216 (路環村) Coloane's 'urban centre' is an old fishing village on its southwestern coast. It is marked by Tam Kung Temple to the south and Lai Chi Vun Village (p218) to the north, with winding alleys, tiny squares, temples and modern villas in between. Coloane Village retains an idyllic air, especially in the late afternoon when the tour groups have left. Attractions here include delicious Portuguese and Macanese restaurants, the Chapel of St Francis Xavier and a couple of small but important temples.

★ KÁ HÓ CHURCH OF OUR LADY OF SORROWS   CHURCH

(九澳七苦聖母小堂, Missão de Nossa Senhora das Dores; Estrada de Nossa Senhora de Ká Hó, Nossa Senhora Village; 🚌15, 21A) Tent-like with a long, slanting roof, like hands in prayer, this church was raised in the Ká Hó leper colony in 1966. It was built for use by the female leprosy patients staying at the **leprosarium** (前九澳痲瘋病院; off Estrada de Nossa Senhora de Ká Hó, Nossa Senhora Village; 🚌15, 21A), along with their families and caretakers. Italian architect Oseo Acconci designed the simple and graceful structure. The sturdy wooden door has planks echoing the angularity of the roof and the bell tower. The bronze crucifix was by another Italian, sculptor Francisco Messima.

In the courtyard are statues of Our Lady and St Michael the Archangel, and a grotto of the Madonna.

The church is the newest addition to a village built for female leprosy patients that existed from the 1930s to the late 1990s. In 1963, a Salesian priest, originally from Sicily, came here, and improved conditions in the colony. The church and the restored colonial-style houses of the former leprosarium are reopening in phases.

Bus 15 from Hác Sá Beach goes to Ká Hó. Disembark at St Joseph School (九澳聖若瑟小學; Escola S Jose de Ká Hó) right at the exit of Ká Hó Village, a lacklustre cluster of houses next to a huge construction site. From the school, the walk here is 20 minutes. A cab ride from downtown Macau is about 20 minutes.

CHAPEL OF ST FRANCIS XAVIER   CHURCH

Map p216 (聖方濟各教堂, Capela de São Francisco Xavier; Rua do Caetano, Largo Eduardo Marques; ◐9.30am-5.30pm; 🚌15, 21A, 25, 26A) This chapel built in 1928 contains paintings of the infant Christ with a Chinese Madonna, a Korean missionary in period garments, and other reminders of Christianity and colonialism in Asia. It's a quirky place painted in yellow and embellished with red lanterns. In front of the chapel are a monument and fountain surrounded by four cannonballs that commemorate the successful, and final, routing of pirates in 1910.

A-MA CULTURAL VILLAGE   MEMORIAL

Map p216 (媽祖文化村, Aldeia Cultural de A-Má; 📞853 2836 6866; Estrada do Alto de Coloane; ◐temple 8am-7.30pm) Atop Alto de Coloane (170m), this 20m-high white jade statue of the goddess who gave Macau its name was erected in 1998. It's the best part of a touristy 'cultural village', which also features Tian Hou Temple. A free bus runs from the A-Ma ornamental entrance gate (媽祖文化村石牌坊) on Estrada de Seac

TAM KUNG FESTIVAL

Tam Kung Festival is huge in Coloane. The birthday of the Taoist sea deity falls on the eighth day of the fourth lunar month (May or June), with festivities lasting three to five days. Highlights include: a dazzling parade by residents dressed in traditional Chinese, Portuguese or fusion costumes; free Cantonese opera in a massive bamboo theatre that springs up by the harbour each year around this time; Portuguese folk dance and juggling; and lots of traditional food. The centre of festivities is **Tam Kung Temple** (譚公廟; Map p216; Avenida de Cinco de Outubro; ◐8.30am-5.30pm; 🚌15, 21A, 25, 26A). Inside the main altar is a long whale bone carved into a model of a dragon boat. To the left of the main altar is a path leading to the roof, which has views of the village and waterfront.

Coloane

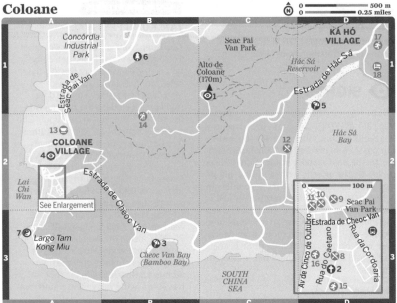

MACAU COLOANE

Coloane

Pai Van half-hourly from 8am to 6pm. You can also reach both by following the **Coloane Trail** (路環布行徑, Lùhuánbù Xíngjìng; Map p216) from **Seac Pai Van Park** (石排灣郊野公園; Map p216; Estrada de Seac Pai Van; ⊙8am-6pm; 📵21A, 26A, 50) FREE; it's a 90-minute walk.

Buses 21A, 25 and 50 go to Estrada de Seac Pai Van.

HÁC SÁ BEACH   BEACH

Map p216 (黑沙海灘; Estrada de Hác Sá; ⊙life-guard duty 10am-6pm Mon-Sat, from 9am Sun May-Oct; 📵21A, 25, 26A) Hác Sá (Black Sand) is Macau's most popular beach. The sand is indeed a blackish colour and makes the water look somewhat dirty, but it's natural. Lifeguards are on duty from May to October. The stalls just off the beach rent out parasols for MOP$60 a day, with a

MOP$100 deposit (but you'll need to bring your parasol back).

Map p216 (竹灣海灘; Estrada de Cheoc Van; ☺lifeguard duty 10am-6pm Mon-Sat, from 9am Sun, May-Oct; ◻21A, 25, 26A) About 1.5km down Estrada de Cheoc Van, which runs east and then southeast from Coloane Village, is the beach at Cheoc Van (Bamboo Bay). It's smaller but somewhat cleaner than Hác Sá beach. There are changing rooms and toilets and, in season, lifeguards on duty. There's also a large public outdoor pool.

✕ EATING & DRINKING

Map p216 (澳門安德魯餅店; ☏853 2888 2534; 1 Rua da Tassara; egg tarts MOP$9; ☺7am-10pm) Though the celebrated English baker Andrew Stow has passed away, his **cafe** (Map p216; ☏853 2888 2174; 9 Largo do Matadouro, Coloane; egg tarts MOP$9; ☺9am-6pm; ✷) and the original Lord Stow's Bakery here keep his memory alive by serving his renowned *pastéis de nata* (warm egg-custard tart with a flaky crust) and cheesecake (MOP$14) in different flavours, including black sesame and green tea.

Map p216 (雅憩花園餐廳; ☏853 2888 2086; 8 Rua do Caetano; mains MOP$80-250; ☺noon-1am; ◫; ◻21A, 25, 26A) Recommendable for the Chinese-Portuguese food, small-town atmosphere, views of the Chapel of St Francis Xavier, cheap prices and the owner – a guitar- and erhu-strumming ex-policeman named Feeling Wong.

Map p216 (法蘭度餐廳; ☏853 2888 2264; www.fernando-restaurant.com; 9 Estrada de Hác Sá; meals MOP$200-450; ☺noon-9.30pm; ◫; ◻21A, 25, 26A) Possibly Coloane's most famous restaurant, sprawling Fernando's contains two separate dining rooms and a large courtyard bar. Devoted customers and travellers pack the chequered tablecloth–covered tables to chow on plates of garlicky clams, golden roast suckling pig and piles of codfish rice. Expect lines during peak lunch and dinner times, especially on weekends. Cash only.

Map p216 (里斯本地帶; ☏853 2888 2226; 8 Rua das Gaivotas; meals MOP$250-800; ☺noon-3pm, 6.30-10pm, noon-10.30pm Sat & Sun, closed Wed; ◫; ◻21A, 25, 26A) 'Lisbon Space' is known for its classic Portuguese dishes, including several tasty versions of *açorda* – bread cooked to a paste with eggs, olive oil and parsley. Our favourite is the one with seafood that originated in the Alentejo region. But what makes this two-storey restaurant in Coloane Village unique is the combination of Portugal-inspired decor and a Chinese village house.

Map p216 (漢記手打咖啡; ☏853 2888 2310; S-26, Lai Chi Vun Village; coffee MOP$20; ☺8am-6pm Thu-Tue; ◫; ◻15, 26, 26A, 50) At this thriving cafe next to shipyards, instant coffee is hand-whipped with sugar to create a peanut-buttery texture. The owner Mr Leong was a shipyard worker who built this shanty with old wood after an arm injury left him unfit for his job. Besides coffee, patrons enjoy egg sandwiches and noodles with Spam at shared tables in the semi-open space.

The cafe is a 15-minute walk from Lord Stow's Bakery near the entrance to Coloane Village, past the Ponte Cais de Coloane pier and the shipyards of Lai Chi Vun Village. It's on the left side of the road.

🛏 SLEEPING

Map p216 (驚環海天度假酒店; ☏853 2887 1111; www.grandcoloane.com/en-us/; 1918 Estrada de Hác Sá; r off-season/peak season incl breakfast from MOP$700/900; ❄✷☎❔≋; ◻15, 21A) The former Westin Resort on Coloane's southeastern tip is now the Grand Coloane Resort. It has the same 1980s feel and is showing its age, but nonetheless provides a welcome getaway from downtown Macau. All 200 rooms are clean and spacious, with private terraces.

For the physically active, there's a gym, swimming pool, an **18-hole golf course** (澳門高爾夫球鄉村俱樂部; ☏853 2887 1188; www.macaugolfandcountryclub.com; weekday/weekend MOP$1980/3080; ☺6am-10pm; ◻15) and a playground with bouncy castle.

LOCAL KNOWLEDGE

COLOANE'S SHIPYARDS AND STILT HOUSES

Macau was a fishing village before gambling was legalised in the mid 19th century. Now the only vestiges of that idyllic past are found in Coloane. Along the coastline, on Rua dos Navegantes in Coloane's old fishing village, there are a few stilt houses and shipyards. These huts of colourful corrugated metal, extending like chunky chopsticks out into the harbour, were once landing spots for house boats. A couple have been turned into dried seafood shops, such as Loja de Peixe Tong Kei (棠記魚舖) at Largo do Cais, the square just off the charming old pier of Coloane. From the square, take the slope to the right of the Servicos de Alfangega building. After two minutes, you'll see the cavernous cadaver of a shipyard, also on stilts.

The Macau government bulldozed two shipyards in the 2010s then halted demolition due to a public outcry. There's been much talk of revitalising the shipyards into a museum, inns and boutiques, and everything in between. At the time of research, the site was awaiting heritage classification.

Cotai

Explore

Cotai rose out of the marshland that once divided Taipa and Coloane, with a name (from Co-loane and Tai-pa) to reflect this joining. Today, Cotai is Macau's answer to the Vegas Strip, an ever-growing collection of megacasinos and entertainment complexes drawing tens of millions of tourists every year. Even if you hate gambling, the casinos are marvels of giant-scale planning and detail – a faux Venice! A half-scale Eiffel Tower! Not to mention thrilling architecture – a beguiling art piece by Zaha Hadid!

The Best...

⇒ **Sight** MGM Cotai (p218)
⇒ **Place to Eat** Jade Dragon (p219)
⇒ **Place to Drink** Macallan Whisky Bar & Lounge (p219)

Top Tip

If you want to experience a bit of old Macau in Cotai, most casinos have food courts where you'll find a cluster of small eateries setting up shop. Many of these are old and reputable establishments that have been invited to open a branch in the casino. **Studio City's** (新濠影滙; ☑853 8865 8888; www.studiocity-macau.com; Estrada Flor de Lotus, Cotai; ⊙24hr; 🚻🚼; 🚌25, 26A) food court is actually designed to resemble a street in old Macau. All the famous pastry shops also have branches in casinos.

Getting There & Away

⇒ **Shuttle** Free shuttle buses run from the ferry terminals and the border gates to the casinos of Cotai; anyone can ride, not just hotel guests.

⇒ **Bus** Public bus 25 goes all the way from the peninsula's northern Border Gate, through Taipa and Cotai, all the way to Coloane; 26A covers a similar route.

⇒ **Taxi** There are plenty of taxi queues around the casinos in Cotai, but expect long lines and refusals to take you to far-flung locations (ie Coloane).

Need to Know

⇒ **Area Code** ☑853
⇒ **Location** Cotai is 3km from Macau Peninsula and 39.3km from Hong Kong.

◉ SIGHTS

MGM COTAI   CASINO
Map p212 (美獅美高梅; ☑853 8806 8888; www.mgm.mo/en/cotai; Avenida da Nave Desportiva; ⊙24hr) At the MGM Cotai's atrium, the walls are hung with LED screens showing razor-sharp images of landscapes from all over the world. These are interspersed with vertical gardens where purportedly 2000 plant species grow, including extinct 19th-century botanicals revived from seed banks. Topping it off is a glass canopy larger than a football field. It's quite an experience to traverse this space – lofty and futuristic, but with the grandeur and transience of an old train station.

EATING & DRINKING

GOLDEN PEACOCK
INDIAN **$$**

Map p212 (☑853 8118 9696; www.venetian macao.com; Shop 1037, Venetian Macao; mains MOP$98-316; ☺11am-3pm & 6-10.30pm; 🖋) Michelin-crowned Golden Peacock has a long and well-curated menu that covers all parts of India. Much thought is put into ingredient sourcing; spices and pickles are prepared in-house – and it shows. Dishes often surprise the palate in a pleasant way – the creamy Navratan korma or nine-gem curry stars French walnut oil, Himachal apple and Indian baby cucumber.

★JADE DRAGON
CANTONESE **$$$**

Map p212 (譽瓏軒; ☑853 8868 2822; Level 2, Shops at the Boulevard, City of Dreams; dim sum MOP$48-268, meals from MOP$800; ☺11am-3pm & 6-11pm) At Michelin-starred Jade Dragon, the genius of a Cantonese master is applied to top-notch ingredients and the results are mesmerising. We've all had barbecue pork and dumplings, but the real highlights here are its lychee-wood roasted Iberico pork or Kegani crabmeat pockets. The restaurant claims to consult experts on the health benefits of its creations (though we suspect the glistening barbecued goose was exempted).

★FOOK LAM MOON
CANTONESE **$$$**

Map p212 (福臨門; ☑853 8883 2221; www.fooklammoon-grp.com/en; 2nd fl, Galaxy Macau, Estrada da Baía de Nossa Senhora de Esperança; meals from MOP$800; ☺11am-3pm & 6-11pm; ☐25, 25X) This 1000-sq-metre branch of Hong Kong's revered Fook Lam Moon (aka 'tycoons' canteen'), lives up to its name in quality and price. This being a lavish casino restaurant, the menu favours marine delicacies such as dried abalone and sea cucumber, prepared with a perfection that has earned it a host of honours including Michelin stars.

★TASTING ROOM
FRENCH **$$$**

Map p212 (☑853 8868 6681; www.city-ofdreamsmacau.com; Level 3, Nüwa Hotel, City of Dreams, Estrada do Istmo; 7-course tasting menu MOP$1650; ☺noon-2.30pm & 6-10.30pm) Expat chef Fabrice Vulin gives his contemporary take on classical French cuisine at the elegant Tasting Room. Its affinity for unexpected texture and flavour combinations is evident: poached Gillardeau oysters lounge in a lettuce velouté with sea-water jelly; and, as a playful riff on the briny centrepiece, oyster leaves, a wild-growing plant that tastes surprisingly like oysters.

★MACALLAN WHISKY BAR & LOUNGE
BAR

Map p212 (☑853 8883 2221; www.galaxymacau.com; 2nd fl, Galaxy Macao, Estrada da Baía de Nossa Senhora de Esperança; ☺5pm-1am Mon-Thu, to 2am Fri & Sat; ☐25, 25X) Macau's best whisky bar is a traditional affair featuring oak panels, Jacobean rugs and a real fireplace. The 400-plus whisky labels include single malts from Ireland, France, Sweden and India, and a 1963 Glenmorangie. The 5pm to 8pm happy hour means you get your age in years discounted as a percentage from your drink (30 years old = 30% off, 100 years old = free).

ENTERTAINMENT

★HOUSE OF DANCING WATER
THEATRE

Map p212 (水舞間; ☑853 8868 6688; http://thehouseofdancingwater.com; City of Dreams, Estrada do Istmo; tickets MOP$580-1480; ☐50, 35) 'The House of Dancing Water', Macau's most expensively made show, is a breathtaking melange of stunts, acrobatics and theatre designed by Franco Dragone, the former director of Cirque du Soleil. The magic revolves around a cobalt pool the size of several Olympic-sized swimming pools. Over, around, into and under this pool a cast of 80, dressed in glorious costumes, perform hair-raising stunts.

CITY OF DREAMS
CASINO

Map p212 (新濠天地, COD; ☑853 8868 6688; www.cityofdreamsmacau.com; Estrada do Istmo; ☺24hr; 🛜🖶; ☐25, 26A) In addition to a sprawling gaming floor, this colossal hotel-casino-mall complex is home to four sleek hotels, several dozen restaurants (that include award-winning kitchens), kilometres of malls, and theatres large enough to host regional video game competitions. The 1600-sq-metre Kids' City is a sophisticated indoor climbing facility that evokes an enlarged futuristic Lego set.

VENETIAN
CASINO

Map p212 (澳門威尼斯人度假村酒店; ☑853 2882 8877; www.venetianmacao.com; Estrada da Baía de N Senhora da Esperança; ☺24hr; 🛜; ☐25, 26A) Said to be one of the 10 largest buildings in the world, the Venetian is 980,000 sq metres of what might be described as

BRIGHT LIGHTS, SIN CITY

Macau's gambling industry goes back to the 16th century when migrant labourers from China would gather to play a game called 'fan tan' in makeshift stalls on the streets and alleys near the harbour. But it wasn't until the 19th century when neighbour Hong Kong surpassed the port of Macau in importance that the government legalised gambling to boost revenue, and the city gained a reputation for being a gambling centre. In 2017, Macau's gaming revenue tripled that of Las Vegas. There are currently more than 40 casinos in Macau, with more in the pipeline. Macau Peninsula has most of the older, smaller casinos, while the Cotai area is home to the new breed of casino-hotel-shopping-entertainment behemoths.

Table games are the staple at casinos here – mostly baccarat, then roulette and a dice game called *dai sai* (big small). You'll hardly hear any whooping and clunking – slot machines make up only 5% of total casino winnings (versus Vegas' 60%). Drunks are also hard to come by, as Chinese players believe that booze dulls their skill. Over 80% of gamblers and 95% of high rollers come from mainland China. Note that smoking is now prohibited in all indoor areas in Macau, so its casinos are no longer the smoke-filled halls they once were.

For recreational players, the only thing to watch out for is harassment by tip hustlers – scam artists who hang around tables acting like your new best friend. They may steal your chips, nag you for a cut or try to take you to a casino that will tip them for bringing clients.

Casino Gothic architecture, packed to the gills with busloads of goggle-eyed tourists. Features include some 3000 hotel suites, a full-sized arena, an on-site medical and plastic surgery clinic and more than 46,000 sq metres of gaming floor.

GALAXY MACAU CASINO
Map p212 (澳門銀河綜合渡假城; ☑853 2888 0888; www.galaxymacau.com; Avenida Marginal Flor de Lotus; ⊙24hr; ☞🅟; 🚍25, 26A) Towering over Cotai like a sci-fi palace out of *Star Wars,* the ginormous gold-and-white Galaxy is one of the most extravagant megacasinos in the city (and that's saying something). It contains six hotels, more than 100 restaurants and kilometres of upmarket shopping, as well as a movie theatre and a jaw-dropping rooftop wave pool and lazy river (for hotel guests only).

🛏 SLEEPING

⭐**MGM COTAI** CASINO HOTEL **$$$**
Map p212 (美獅美高梅; ☑853 8806 8888; www. mgm.mo/en/cotai; Avenida da Nave Desportiva; r incl breakfast from MOP$4000; ☞✳🅐☞🆒) MGM Cotai has 1400 impeccable rooms, including duplex sky-lofts and private villas, all in a light and refreshing palette. There's also a gym with panoramic views, and a chic and soothing spa. But the star here is the four-storey atrium (p218) just past the reception lobby.

⭐**ST REGIS** CASINO HOTEL **$$$**
Map p212 (瑞吉金沙城中心酒店; ☑853 2882 8898; www.stregismacao.com; Estrada do Istmo; d incl breakfast from MOP$3000; ☞✳🅐☞) An excellent hotel belonging to Sands Macau, award-winning St Regis is all about meticulous, at-your-beck-and-call service and unobtrusive refinement. Many of the 400 well-appointed rooms have urban views as Sands is smack in the middle of Cotai. Check out its package deals that include cooking classes for the whole family and guided photo tours.

⭐**MORPHEUS** CASINO HOTEL **$$$**
Map p212 (摩珀斯酒店; ☑852 8868 8888; www. cityofdreamsmacau.com; City of Dreams, Estrada do Istmo; r incl breakfast from MOP$4000; ☞✳🅐☞🆒) Designed by the late Zaha Hadid, Morpheus, with 770 spacious rooms is the flagship luxury hotel of the City of Dreams (p219). The exoskeleton of the building has strong lines that are visible from the interior where generous stretches of white let them speak for themselves, like in a museum. It's definitely a hotel for design freaks.

Sleeping

Notorious for its boxy rooms, you won't get much bang for your buck in Hong Kong hotels. That said, service is usually very good and there's plenty of diversity, from dorm beds to chic apartments and palatial suites. Most hotels on Hong Kong Island are between Sheung Wan and Causeway Bay; in Kowloon, they fall around Nathan Rd, where you'll also find budget places.

Facilities

All rooms have air-conditioning, and all but the cheapest rooms have private bathrooms, in-room wi-fi and cable TV in English. Some hotels have computers for guests' use. All indoor areas of hostels and hotels are supposed to be nonsmoking. Pools are uncommon; even many high-end hotels only have indoor pools.

Guesthouses

Dominating the lower end of the accommodation market are guesthouses, usually a block of tiny rooms squeezed into a converted apartment. Often several guesthouses operate out of the same building. Some offer dormitory accommodation for those on tight budgets. Though rooms are small, all have air-con and most have TVs and free wi-fi. Depending on the season, try to negotiate a better deal, as a lot of places will be eager to fill empty rooms.

Hostels & Campsites

Gone are the days when Chungking Mansions (p229) was your only hope of a shoe-string bed in this pricey city. Hong Kong's hostel scene has come on in leaps and bounds in recent years, and there are now a couple of chains doing a roaring trade with grateful backpackers. Prices for a bed in a dormitory range from HK$180 to HK$350 a night, depending on the hostel.

The **Hong Kong Youth Hostels Association** (HKYHA; ☏852 2788 1638; www.yha.org.hk; annual membership HK$150) maintains seven hostels affiliated with Hostelling International (HI), which are popular with the Asian crowd. It also sells HKYHA and HI cards: you can't stay in one of these hostels unless you are a member. If you haven't applied for membership in your own country, visit the HKYHA office, sign up at check-in or come with somebody who's already a member, which will get you access. Be sure to take along a visa-sized photo and ID.

The Country & Marine Parks Authority (www.afcd.gov.hk) maintains 41 basic campsites in the New Territories and Outlying Islands.

Midrange Hotels

New places continue to emerge that are uniquely cool to look at and easy on the pocket, with rates hovering between HK$1000 and HK$2000 and dipping to budget range in the low season. Rooms at these places tend to be smallish and come with wi-fi connection, coffee-making facilities, limited cable TV, and room service.

Top-End Hotels

Hong Kong's luxury hotels are locked in an arms race for the dollars of affluent travellers. Their weapons are Michelin-starred restaurants, lavish spa complexes, smooth service and location, location, location. Prices for top-of-the-range hotels start from close to HK$3000 per room. A few of them offer comfort, amenities and service that compete with or surpass that of the world's finest five-star hotels.

Apartment Rentals

Recently there has been a rise in apartments catering to short-term travellers, both luxurious serviced apartments and homes-for-rent. Serviced apartments can sometimes cost no more than a standard hotel room, but come with room dividers, laundry, and kitchen facilities (good for families). For budget travellers, short-term room rentals can be half that of a budget hotel but still offer more privacy than a dorm bed. Renting a room in a home also offers opportunities for cultural exchange that can be lacking at hotels; many professional Hong Kongers speak English.

Airbnb (www.airbnb.com) is the main room/apartment rental provider; quality can vary drastically. There are a number of good serviced options around Sheung Wan, like the Putman (p225).

Where to Stay

Neighbourhood	For	Against
Central District (p224)	Close to the Star Ferry pier, famous skyscrapers and luxury malls; within walking distance of excellent bars and restaurants; good transport links.	Nearest eats, sleeps, bars and shops are pricey; office vibe; hectic and crowded.
The Peak & Northwest Hong Kong Island (p225)	Excellent nightlife and dining action; close to the Peak and the historic sites in Sheung Wan.	Sloping topography, hence more trips uphill and down; districts further west are quiet and away from the action.
Wan Chai & Northeast Hong Kong Island (p226)	Good for Hong Kong Park, Happy Valley Racecourse and shopping; abundant eating and drinking options; great transport links.	Wan Chai and Causeway Bay are traffic-choked and crowded; districts further east are a little worn and far away.
Aberdeen & South Hong Kong Island (p227)	Great for Aberdeen Typhoon Shelter, Stanley Market, Horizon Plaza, swimming and hiking around Repulse Bay and Shek O.	Not central, frequent traffic jams near Aberdeen Tunnel, limited sleeps, eats, bars and shops.
Kowloon (p228)	Convenient for many big museums and theatres, best views of the harbour; great for shopping, eating, even 'slumming'; cool mix of old and new, highbrow and low heel; great transport links.	Crowded and traffic-choked around Nathan Rd; some areas can be touristy and/or a little tacky.
New Territories (p161)	Fewer crowds, fresher air; handy for outdoor sports, nature tours, walled villages; prices generally lower.	Far from the action; fewer eats, sleeps, bars and shops; little to do at night.
Outlying Islands: Lamma, Lantau & Cheung Chau (p177)	Laid-back vibe, nice setting, good for seafood on Lamma, windsurfing on Cheung Chau, hiking the Lantau Trail and loads of beaches.	Longer time spent commuting; fewer eats, sleeps, bars and shops; activities dependent on weather.

SLEEPING

Lonely Planet's Top Choices

Peninsula Hong Kong (p230) World-class luxury and colonial elegance at the harbour end of Tsim Sha Tsui.

Tuve (p226) A tiny paradise for design fans in a pleasant neighbourhood full of restaurants.

Hotel Indigo (p226) Large, colourful rooms, attentive staff and a fabulous bar in a lively part of Wan Chai.

Mojo Nomad (p227) Flashy Aberdeen hostel with harbour views, organised activities and cool design.

Upper House (p227) A Zen-like atmosphere, yoga on the lawn and warm service overlooking the hills in Admiralty.

Jervois (p225) Elegant, spacious and bang in the middle of trendy Sheung Wan.

Best By Budget

$

Hop Inn on Carnavon (p228) Local art murals, sofas and a beer fridge sum up this Kowloon hostel.

Mojo Nomad (p227) Magnificent water views complemented by offbeat design.

Helena May (p224) Simple heritage rooms (some female-only) in a Central institution.

Mini Hotel Central (p224) Tiny rooms but plush lounge and hard-to-beat location.

$$

Tuve (p226) Sleek, industrial-chic rooms, an artsy reception area, and helpful staff in Tin Hau.

99 Bonham (p225) From the same local team as the Jervois; impeccable taste in a great location.

Hotel Jen (p225) The best deal on Hong Kong Island with a rooftop pool, in a pleasingly local area.

Little Tai Hang (p226) Charming hotel with Scandi-style furnishings in an equally charming neighbourhood.

$$$

Peninsula Hong Kong (p230) One of the most elegant and richly storied hotels in Asia.

Hotel Indigo (p226) Chinese-inspired design, state-of-the-art facilities and exceptional service.

Hotel Icon (p230) Affordable luxury with a rooftop pool.

Murray Hotel (p224) A pioneering luxury reinvention of a heritage building in Central.

Fleming (p227) An updated classic, with design flourishes that mimic Hong Kong's beloved retro ferries.

Best Design

Tuve (p226) It's all about design here, from the beds to the soft-drink bottles in the minifridge.

Madera Hong Kong (p229) Boldly coloured, whimsical decor reminiscent of the movie sets of Pedro Almodóvar.

Mira Moon (p227) Taking a famous Chinese legend to new and creative heights.

SLEEEP (p225) Hong Kong's first capsule hotel has won awards for its eco cred and gadgets.

NEED TO KNOW

Price Ranges

Nightly rates for a double room:

$ less than HK$900

$$ HK$900 to HK$1900

$$$ more than HK$1900

Monthly rates for a one-bedroom apartment:

$ less than HK$15,000

$$ HK$15,000 to HK$25,000

$$$ more than HK$25,000

High Season

When big trade fairs come to town, accommodation in Central, Wan Chai, Causeway Bay and Tsim Sha Tsui is very tight and prices rocket. Check exact dates at www.discoverhongkong.com.

➡ Trade-fair season and Labour Day holiday (January and March, and 1 May)

➡ Chinese New Year (late January or February)

➡ Ching Ming Festival (usually in April)

➡ National Day holiday (first 10 days of October)

Reservations

Booking a room is not essential outside peak periods. During quiet periods and the low season you can get big discounts. If you book direct, hotels will often throw in perks such as free breakfast.

Taxes

Most midrange and top-end hotels and a small number of budget places add 10% service.

SLEEPING

🛏 Central District

⭐ **MINI HOTEL CENTRAL**   BOUTIQUE HOTEL **$**

Map p302 (☑852 2103 0999; www.minihotel. hk/central; 38 Ice House St, Central; s/d from HK$400/460; @🅰) We've seen glasses of wine in ritzy Central more expensive than this budget hotel. Of course for this price there has to be a trade-off, and in Mini Hotel Central it's thin walls and 10-sq-metre rooms. Look beyond that, though, and it's an excellent deal: clean, stylish and modern, with glass-walled marbled bathrooms. Location could not be better.

The 'Mini' room category has no view; book a 'Smart' room if you want to see the sky. There's also a chic reception lounge to hang out in, filled with sumptuous mismatched furniture, a grand piano, beanbags and a dispensing machine selling the added extras (toothbrushes, shampoo, shower caps etc) that you'd get for free in pricier establishments.

⭐ **HELENA MAY**   HOTEL **$**

Map p298 (梅夫人婦女會主樓; ☑852 2522 6766; www.helenamay.com; 35 Garden Rd, Central; s/d HK$580/760, studios HK$850-980; 🚇23) If you like the peninsula's colonial setting but not its price tag, this grand dame could be your cup of tea. Founded in 1916 as a social club for single European women, it is now a private club for both sexes of all nationalities and a hotel with women-only rooms in the main building and popular en suite studios in an annex that allows men.

**BISHOP LEI
INTERNATIONAL HOUSE**   HOTEL **$**

Map p302 (宏基國際賓館; ☑852 2868 0828; www.bishopleihtl.com.hk; 4 Robinson Rd, Mid-Levels; s/d/ste from HK$540/580/760; @🖂; 🚇23, 40) This hotel uphill in residential Mid-Levels is one of the cheapest places to stay on Hong Kong Island with a pool (summer travellers, take note). Service is good, but the hotel is looking dated and standard rooms are small. It's a little out of the way, but only a five-minute walk from the top end of the Central–Mid-Levels Escalator.

LAN KWAI FONG HOTEL   BOUTIQUE HOTEL **$$**

Map p304 (蘭桂坊酒店; ☑852 3650 0000; www.lankwaifonghotel.com.hk; 3 Kau U Fong, Soho; r HK$2000-3000; 🅰; 🇲Sheung Wan, exit E2) The Chinese styling at this 162-room hotel, in staff uniforms and decor with a contemporary twist, adds a local touch that's hard to find in Hong Kong hotels. Service is top-notch and freebies include coffee and tea, wine (5pm to 8pm) and rooms with a smartphone for guest use. Best of all is the lovely open-air terrace/lounge hidden above the streets of Soho.

⭐ **POTTINGER**   BOUTIQUE HOTEL **$$$**

Map p302 (☑852 2308 3188; www.thepottinger. com; 74 Queen's Rd Central, enter from Stanley St, Central; r HK$2500-3000, ste from HK$5000; 🇲Central, exit D2) In the heart of Central, this unobtrusive boutique hotel has 68 airy, white-and-cream rooms with marble bathrooms and subtle Asian touches: carved wooden screens, calligraphy work, black-and-white photos of old Hong Kong. Free Fuji water is a nice touch. The Envoy, its excellent hotel bar, is a tribute to Sir Henry Pottinger, Hong Kong's first governor and the hotel's namesake.

MURRAY HOTEL   LUXURY HOTEL **$$$**

Map p298 (☑852 3141 8888; www.niccolohotels. com; 22 Cotton Tree Dr, Central; d from HK$3870; 🅰🖂; 🇲Central, exit J2) 🌿 The hottest new hotel opening in Hong Kong in 2018 was the Murray – a magnificent reinvention of a 1960s government office block beside Hong Kong Park. The building has distinctive deep-set angled windows that were a pioneering sustainability feature (designed to reduce solar heating) of the original architecture plans. Inside, the 336-room Niccolo hotel incorporates stone, glass, leather, wood and stainless steel into contemporary design.

There are also bars and restaurants at garden level and on the rooftop terrace, an indoor lap pool and a spa.

MANDARIN ORIENTAL   LUXURY HOTEL **$$$**

Map p298 (文華東方酒店; ☑852 2522 0111; www.mandarinoriental.com/hongkong; 5 Connaught Rd, Central; r HK$3250-7500, ste from HK$6000; @🅰🖂; 🇲Central, exit F) The venerable Mandarin has historically set the standard in Asia and its Hong Kong hotel is the original, maintaining a sense of gracious, old-world charm. The styling, service, food and atmosphere are stellar throughout and locals know it – the MO does 3000 food and drink covers a day and 70% is local business; afternoon tea is particularly popular.

🛏 The Peak & Northwest Hong Kong Island

SLEEEP
CAPSULE HOTEL $

Map p304 (☎852 9604 6049; www.sleeep.io; 242 Queen's Rd Central, Sheung Wan; capsule per hour/night from HK$79/399; 🖥; Ⓜ Sheung Wan, exit A2) 🏃 Frazzled city workers sometimes book into this award-winning futuristic hotel by the hour to recalibrate, and it's easy to see why: an aura of calm akin to a meditation studio surrounds SLEEEP – Hong Kong's first capsule hotel. There are only eight capsules, with shared shower facilities. The hotel is located on the steps between Queen's Rd Central and Gough St.

Each capsule comes with a large locker, ear plugs, and plenty of charging sockets. It's all very high tech, with movable magnetic light switches in the capsules, personalised electronic check-ins (you can choose your mattress and blanket thickness), and eco touches like hot water that captures residue from the air-con units. SLEEEP might not be the best option for longer stays, but it's a comfy, cheap sleep for short stopovers.

BUTTERFLY ON WATERFRONT
BOUTIQUE HOTEL $

Map p304 (☎852 3559 9988; www.butterflyhk. com; 94 Connaught Rd W, Sheung Wan; r from HK$650; 🖥; 🍴) Free smartphone, free on-the-go phone charger and wi-fi, free selfie stick, free portable fan – there's lots to like about this reasonably priced boutique hotel just off Dried Seafood St (aka Des Voeux Rd West and yes it does smell, unfortunately). Rooms are stylish enough and modern, and there's a 20% to 30% discount for booking more than one night, 30 days in advance.

★HOTEL JEN
HOTEL $$

(☎852 2974 1234; www.hoteljen.com/hong kong; 508 Queen's Rd W, Shek Tong Tsui; r from HK$900; 🖥; Ⓜ HKU, exit B2) Now part of the Shangri-La group, Hotel Jen feels more luxurious than its price tag suggests. The high-ceilinged, modern rooms are super-comfy with plump beds, and harbour views cost just a fraction more. In Hong Kong's stifling summers, the rooftop pool (with dreamy harbour views!) is a coveted amenity, and a rare one to find on Hong Kong Island at this price.

Hotel Jen's location is another perk; far enough away from Central to feel like a local neighbourhood, and walking distance to the increasingly hip communities of Kennedy Town and Sai Ying Pun, as well as the tram and HKU MTR station.

★99 BONHAM
BOUTIQUE HOTEL $$

Map p304 (☎852 3940 1111; www.99bonham. com; 99 Bonham Strand, Sheung Wan; r from HK$1500; 🖥; Ⓜ Sheung Wan, exit A2) This hotel has 84 unusually large rooms (for Hong Kong). They are stylishly minimalist, with luxury bathrooms and washed in a neutral palette. The hotel also has a small gym with free refreshments, free laundry on each floor, and a rooftop terrace with loungers and resplendent views. Extra-handy is the mobile phone with free data and local calls for use during your stay.

JERVOIS
BOUTIQUE HOTEL $$

Map p304 (☎852 3994 9000; www.thejervois. com; 89 Jervois St, Sheung Wan; 1-bed ste HK$1900-3900, 2-bed ste HK$3650-6100; 🖥; Ⓜ Sheung Wan, exit A2) If you can bag a room at the lower end of the price range (book direct, online), the elegant Jervois is an excellent deal. Its 49 one- and two-bed suites are each configured with a lounge area partitioned from the bedroom, a kitchenette and huge windows allowing abundant natural light. One-bed suites are around 65 sq m; two-bed suites are double that.

All rooms come with a smartphone for guest use, and luxurious grey-and-white marble bathrooms. There's also a laundry room (though the two-bed pads have their own), and a petite roof terrace with peeking harbour views. Rates are discounted in low season.

PUTMAN
APARTMENT $$$

Map p304 (☎852 2233 2233; www.theputman. com; 202-206 Queen's Rd Central, Sheung Wan; r HK$1300-3700, ste from HK$2550; 🖥; Ⓜ Sheung Wan, exit A or E) Behind the art deco–inspired glass facade, this designer outfit has three cool-toned standard rooms and 25 one-bedroom suites. You get space (the apartments are 120 sq metres and the rooms are 30 to 40 sq metres) and impeccable taste here. Each one-bed flat occupies an entire storey, with floor-to-ceiling windows, eco toiletries and designer kitchens big enough to accommodate dining tables.

🛏 Wan Chai & Northeast Hong Kong Island

YESINN
HOSTEL **$**

Map p310 (☑852 2213 4567; www.yesinn.com; 2nd fl, Nan Yip Bldg, 472 Hennessy Rd, Causeway Bay; dm HK$100-300, r HK$500-800; @🛜; Ⓜ Causeway Bay, exit B) This funky, sociable hostel attracts backpackers from all over the world to its brightly painted female and mixed dorms with curtained-off bunks and lockers, as well as private rooms in another building across the street. The petite reception area is made up for by the excellent roof deck, the site of monthly, hostel-sponsored barbecues.

The hostel entrance is at the side of the building on the corner. The neon, shopping and late-night eats of Causeway Bay are a two-minute hop away. YesInn has sister hostels in Fortress Hill and Kowloon.

CHECK INN
HOSTEL **$**

Map p308 (卓軒旅舍; ☑852 2955 0175; Room A, 3rd fl, Kwong Wah Mansion, 269-273 Hennessy Rd, Wan Chai; dm/r from HK$160/650; @🛜; Ⓜ Wan Chai, exit A2) Clean, spacious and brightly lit dorms are furnished with huge bunk beds and lockers at this well-located Wan Chai hostel. The reception and hang-out area (2nd floor) has sofas, free coffee and iMacs facing a wall of windows. Friendly staff host the occasional activity for guests, such as hiking up Victoria Peak.

★ HOTEL INDIGO
DESIGN HOTEL **$$**

Map p308 (☑852 3926 3888; www.ihg.com; 246 Queen's Rd E, Wan Chai; r from HK$1600; @🛜⬚; Ⓜ Wan Chai, exit A3) With an enticing location on hip Queen's Rd East, and colourful, tech-forward rooms that are exceedingly spacious for the price, Indigo is an excellent mid- to upper-range proposition. A petite pool and quiet bar high up on the rooftop seal the deal.

★ TUVE
BOUTIQUE HOTEL **$$**

Map p310 (☑852 3995 8800; www.tuve.hk; 16 Tsing Fung St, Tin Hau; r from HK$1200; 🛜; Ⓜ Tin Hau, exit A1) From the dungeon-like entrance to the brass-and-concrete slab of a front desk, everything here spells design. Industrial glam continues in the rooms where concrete walls are accented with gold, and grey marble plays off against wood tones and wired glass, all grounded by immaculate white linen.

Curiously, Tuve's design was inspired by a series of art panoramas of Sweden's Lake Tuve taken by photographer Kim Høltermand. Even the drinks in the minibar were hand-picked by its owner, a product designer, for their compliance with overall aesthetics. Design fanatics will have a field day, but if your lodging tastes tend towards the traditional, Tuve might not be for you.

★ HOTEL VIC ON THE HARBOUR
HOTEL **$$**

(☑852 3896 9888; www.hotelvic.com; 1 North Point Estate Lane, North Point; r HK$1500-2500; @🛜⬚; Ⓜ North Point, exit A1) New in 2018, this polished waterfront behemoth claims that all 671 rooms have a harbour view (the 'deluxe harbour-front' category offers the best-value eye candy). Tasteful and contemporary, all rooms have capsule coffee machine, wi-fi smartphone and free minibar. A neat rooftop pool has an infinity-style harbour backdrop, while the gym (also with fab views) has virtual-reality exercise machines.

Built on a wedge of reclaimed harbour in up-and-coming North Point, the hotel offers regular shuttle buses to other parts of the city, even though the MTR is only a few minutes away.

★ LITTLE TAI HANG
HOTEL **$$**

Map p310 (☑852 3899 8888; www.littletaihang.com; 98 Tung Lo Wan Rd, Tai Hang, Tin Hau; r from HK$1250; @🛜; Ⓜ Tin Hau, exit B) The hip and characterful Tai Hang hood now has a worthy hotel in Little Tai Hang: 91 charmingly turned out guestrooms with Scandi furnishings and lovely linen. The pick of the rooms are the Corner Studios (above 8th floor) boasting enormous sunken Japanese bath-tub overlooking Victoria Park and the harbour.

METROPARK HOTEL
HOTEL **$$**

Map p310 (維景酒店; ☑852 2600 1000; www.metroparkhotelcausewaybay.com; 148 Tung Lo Wan Rd, Causeway Bay; r from HK$1100; @🛜⬚; Ⓜ Tin Hau, exit B) This tower hotel overlooking Victoria Park makes the most of its easterly aspect, with more than half of its 250 or so rooms boasting sweeping city-harbour views. Decor does feel dated throughout, but the rooftop pool, with sunloungers and gorgeous vistas, makes up for it. Another big plus is the location, skirting the hip, locally flavoured Tai Hang neighbourhood.

MIRA MOON
BOUTIQUE HOTEL $$

Map p308 (問月酒店; ☑852 2643 8888; www.miramoonhotel.com; 388 Jaffe Rd, Wan Chai; r HK$1500-3000; @🛜; MWan Chai, exit A1) Decor at this 91-room boutique hotel riffs on the Chinese fairy tale of the Moon Goddess and the Jade Rabbit – stylised rabbit wall art, oversized lanterns, graphic peony floor mosaics. Free-standing bath-tubs in the 'Half Moon' and 'Full Moon' rooms are to die for, while the more budget-friendly 'New Moon' category is shower-only. Service is warm and accommodating.

All rooms come with portable wi-fi hot-spot device and iPad room controller. Amenities include a 24-hour gym, a Spanish-Chinese fusion tapas restaurant and petite Champagne bar by reception.

OZO WESLEY
BUSINESS HOTEL $$

Map p306 (遨舍衛蘭軒酒店; ☑852 2292 3000; www.ozohotels.com; 22 Hennessy Rd, Wan Chai; r from HK$900; @🛜; MAdmiralty, exit F) The 250 small but well-appointed rooms at this midrange business hotel between Admiralty and Wan Chai are great value for the quality and location, and so tend to book out early. A good breakfast is served; there's a gym but no pool.

PARK LANE HONG KONG
HOTEL $$

Map p310 (柏寧酒店; ☑852 2293 8888; www.parklane.com.hk; 310 Gloucester Rd, Causeway Bay; r from HK$1600; @🛜; MCauseway Bay, exit E) Sandwiched between Victoria Park and the commercial buzz of Causeway Bay, the 832-room Park Lane is a fine choice for those who want to be both in and out of the action. All but three of the floors had been refurbished at time of research, with guest rooms looking spiffy. Skye Bar (p117) on the 27th floor is fabulous.

The hotel also runs daily free yoga classes on the rooftop 'Sky Garden', and there's a good gym. For harbour views, request a 'Premium Deluxe' room.

★UPPER HOUSE
BOUTIQUE HOTEL $$$

Map p306 (☑852 2918 1838; www.upperhouse.com; 88 Queensway, Pacific Pl, Admiralty; r/ste from HK$4500/12,000; @🛜; MAdmiralty, exit F) For ultraluxe living in designer style, there is no finer Hong Kong hotel – provided you're willing to forgo a pool. Piggybacking on to the top floors of the JW Marriott (hence the 'Upper'), even the smallest rooms, the Studio 70s, are twice as large as other top-end digs and have walk-in closet, complimentary minibar and deep-soaking tub with a view.

★FLEMING
BOUTIQUE HOTEL $$$

Map p308 (☑852 3607 2288; www.thefleming.com; 41 Fleming Rd, Wan Chai; r from HK$1900; @🛜; MWan Chai, exit A) An updated classic, this Wan Chai boutique hotel evokes the golden age of travel, with 66 clubby rooms bedecked in colonial whites, bottle greens, hardwoods and brass fixtures. Said to be inspired by Hong Kong's cross-harbour ferry, it's more like staying on the royal yacht *Britannia* (before she sailed out of Hong Kong Harbour for the final time in 1997).

The smallest rooms are a poky 21 sq metres but all come with bespoke bathroom amenities, feather-soft beds and delightful design details such as the 'do not disturb' dials mimicking an old ship's telegraph. A handsome Mediterranean restaurant, Osteria Marzia, is the setting for breakfast. The Fleming sits in the corner between Fleming and Jaffe Rds.

🛏 Aberdeen & South Hong Kong Island

★MOJO NOMAD
HOSTEL $

Map p312 (☑852 3728 1000; www.mojonomad.com; 100 Shek Pai Wan Rd, Aberdeen; d HK$200-260, f from HK$1700; ⌗@🛜; 🚌31, 42, 48, 71, 72) One of Hong Kong's best budget options, Mojo Nomad has 196 beds and 64 rooms spread over 20 floors a street shy of Aberdeen Typhoon Shelter and its moored boats. The divine view is displayed to full effect by wall-to-wall windows in the harbour-facing rooms (which includes all family rooms). Units overlooking a hillside cemetery are HK$20 to HK$40 cheaper. Dormitory beds drop to HK$150 to HK$180 in the off season.

Triple rooms come with a bunk bed and a single. Dormitories consist of four bunk beds each, two private bathrooms, numbered lockers and reading lights. There's a laundry, a kitchen, and a communal area with a TV room, computers, work space and a booth for private calls. Activities, like movie nights and tours, are organised daily by the friendly staff.

★T HOTEL
HOTEL $$

(T酒店; ☑852 3717 7388; www.thotel.edu.hk; VTC Pokfulam Complex, 145 Pok Fu Lam Rd, Pok Fu

Lam; r/ste from HK$1040/2760; ☻❄@☎; ☐7, 91 from Central, 973 from Tsim Sha Tsui) Ah, we almost don't want to tell you about this gem! The 30-room T in the serene neighbourhood of Pok Fu Lam is entirely run by students of the hospitality training institute. The young trainees are attentive, cheerful and eager to hone their skills. Rooms, all on the 6th floor, are sparkling and spacious, with ocean or mountain views.

The suites are larger than many serviced apartments, and come with guest toilets and a kitchenette. The two restaurants, run by the culinary school in the complex, provide good-value Chinese and international meals. The hotel also has a sky lounge, again with gorgeous views, and a spa. From University metro station, it's a 10-minute taxi ride here.

OVOLO SOUTHSIDE
BOUTIQUE HOTEL $$

Map p312 (Ovolo 南區; ☏852 2165 1000; www. ovolohotels.com; 64 Wong Chuk Hang Rd, Wong Chuk Hang; r HK$700-$1800; ☐73, 973, 42, 171, 99, Ⓜ Wong Chuk Hang, exit A2) Converted from a warehouse, Ovolo Southside complements its original setting with chic industry-inspired decor. Views of the hills from the upper floors, mostly attentive service, happy-hour perks at the rooftop bar, and a free minibar more than make up for small rooms and bathrooms.

🛏 Kowloon

★HOP INN ON CARNARVON
HOSTEL $

Map p316 (☏852 2881 7331; www.hopinn.hk; 9th fl, James S Lee Mansion, 33-35 Carnarvon Rd, Tsim Sha Tsui; dm HK$180-280, s HK$460-580, d HK$620-650; @☎; Ⓜ Tsim Sha Tsui, exit A2) A sofa-strewn lounge, adjoining roof terrace (and obligatory cheap beer fridge) make this laid-back hostel a great place to wind down after a day pounding the mean streets of Kowloon. Polished concrete floors lead to neatly swept singles, doubles, triples and four- to eight-person dorms, several with murals by local artists.

★URBAN PACK
HOSTEL $

Map p314 (休閒小窩; ☏852 2732 2271; www. urban-pack.com; Unit 1410, 14th fl, Haiphong Mansion, 99-101 Nathan Rd, Tsim Sha Tsui; dm HK$200-500, r from HK$500; ☎; Ⓜ Tsim Sha Tsui, exit A1) A laid-back, sociable hostel with a great location between Kowloon Park and Harbour City, Urban Pack is run by two friendly Canadian-Chinese, Albert and Jensen. Compact dorms with privacy blinds, doubles and twin bunk rooms occupy various units of a commercial building, with separate areas for hanging out. A tour program includes bar crawls and Happy Valley races.

★YESINN @YMT
HOSTEL $

Map p318 (1B Wing Sing Ln, Yau Ma Tei; dm/d from HK$170/600; @☎; Ⓜ Yau Ma Tei, exit C) Boasting an enviable location in the neon-clad heart of Yau Ma Tei, YesInn is a great base from which to soak up those local Hong Kong vibes. Pick from petite four-/eight-person dorms or rather nice doubles (some of the twins are bunks); a sociable kitchen has the obligatory beer fridge. Just a shame staff can be frosty.

INNSIGHT
GUESTHOUSE $

Map p314 (悠悠客舍; ☏852 2369 1151; www. innsight.hk; 3rd fl, 9 Lock Rd, Tsim Sha Tsui; s/d from HK$480/600; @☎; Ⓜ Tsim Sha Tsui, exit H) The best feature of this welcoming, no-frills guesthouse is the fabulous location within strolling distance of the Star Ferry. A homely check-in area leads to simple singles and doubles – nothing fancy but you get towels, air-con, a TV and that all-important window.

YHA MEI HO HOUSE YOUTH HOSTEL
HOSTEL $

(美荷樓青年旅舍; ☏852 3728 3500; www. meihohouse.hk; Block 41, Shek Kip Mei Estate, 70 Berwick St, Sham Shui Po; dm HK$400-549, r from HK$900; @☎; ☐A21, Ⓜ Sham Shui Po, exit D2) Converted from public housing units in a hilly corner of Kowloon, this heritage youth hostel has everything you need: a laundry, on-site convenience store, immaculate rooms and dorm-style lodgings, lockers with inbuilt chargers and an excellent bar-restaurant, House 41. It even has a museum (p142). The price is high for a hostel, however.

★OTTO HOTEL
HOTEL $$

Map p314 (☏852 3551 6888; http://theotto.hk; 8 Cameron Rd, Tsim Sha Tsui; d/tw from HKD$1100; ☎; Ⓜ Tsim Sha Tsui, exit B2) A good balance of price and quality, Otto has 56 immaculate, well-soundproofed rooms and a fantastic location in the heart of TST just seconds from the MTR. Smallish rooms are cleverly designed so even the cheapest category has space for two, including walk-in rain showers and a writing desk. 'Premium Queen' rooms have views overlooking Kowloon Mosque & Islamic Centre (p139).

Off-season discounts nudge Otto into the budget category.

★**SALISBURY YMCA**   HOTEL $$

Map p314 (香港基督教青年會; ☎852 2268 7888; www.ymcahk.org.hk/thesalisbury; 41 Salisbury Rd, Tsim Sha Tsui; s/d/ste from HK$1250/1450/2450; @ ⚛ ✉; Ⓜ East Tsim Sha Tsui, exit L6) If you can manage to book a room at this fabulously located YMCA hotel, you'll be rewarded with professional service and excellent exercise facilities. The 372 rooms and suites are comfortable but basic, so keep your eyes on the harbour: that view would cost you five times as much at the Peninsula next door.

★**ATTITUDE ON GRANVILLE**   BOUTIQUE HOTEL $$

Map p316 (☎852 2105 3888; www.attitudegranville.com; 20 Granville Rd, Tsim Sha Tsui; ⚛r from HK$1350; @ ⚛; Ⓜ Tsim Sha Tsui, exit B1) 'Boutique hostel' or 'student chic' seem like appropriate labels for this wacky hotel rocking a nostalgic HK aesthetic mashed up with pop art, murals and, er, stuffed sheep. Eighty-one guestrooms start at a compact 15 sq metres for the 'Urban Double' – go larger and you'll get a desk (raised on breeze blocks!) and hand-painted graphic art on the walls.

Across the street is sister venue Soravit on Granville, with an entirely different Southeast Asian design scheme. Go figure.

MADERA HONG KONG   DESIGN HOTEL $$

Map p318 (木的地酒店; ☎852 2121 9888; www.hotelmadera.com.hk; 1-9 Cheong Lok St, Yau Ma Tei; r from HK$1100, ste HK$2500; @ ⚛; Ⓜ Jordan, exit B1) A walk-through museum exhibit of old-time Hong Kong greets arrivals at this playful hotel close to Temple Street Night Market (p135) and Jordan MTR station. Lower-category rooms are more than adequate, but splurge and you get a handsome suite decked out in warm wood tones (*madera* means 'wood' in Spanish), and fine city views.

CHUNGKING MANSIONS

Say 'budget accommodation' and 'Hong Kong' in one breath and everyone thinks of Chungking Mansions. Built in 1961, CKM is a labyrinth of homes, guesthouses, Indian restaurants, souvenir stalls and foreign-exchange shops spread over five 17-storey blocks in the heart of Tsim Sha Tsui. According to anthropologist Gordon Mathews, it has a resident population of about 4000 and an estimated 10,000 daily visitors. More than 120 different nationalities – predominantly South Asian and African – pass through its doors in a single year.

Though standards vary significantly, most of the guesthouses at CKM are clean and quite comfortable. It's worth bearing in mind, however, that rooms are usually the size of cupboards and you have to shower right next to the toilet. The rooms typically come with air-con and TV and, sometimes, a window. Virtually all have wi-fi and some even offer daily housekeeping and luxuries like toothbrushes!

Bargaining for a bed or room is always possible, though you won't get very far in high season. You can often negotiate a cheaper price if you stay more than, say, a week, but never try that on the first night – stay one night and find out how you like it before handing over more rent. Once you pay, there are usually no refunds.

Though there are dozens of ever-changing hostels in Chungking Mansions, some reliable ones include **Dragon Inn** (龍滙賓館; Map p314; ☎852 9304 7843; www.dragoninn.info; Flat B5, 3rd fl, B Block; s HK$180-400, d HK$360-680, tr/q HK$480/520; ⚛; Ⓜ Tsim Sha Tsui, exit D1), **Holiday Guesthouse** (Map p314; ☎852 2316 7152, 852 9121 8072; fax 2316 7181; Flat E1, 6th fl, E Block; s HK$250-600, d HK$350-700; ⚛; Ⓜ Tsim Sha Tsui, exit D1) and **Canada Hostel** (Park Inn, Icon Inn; Map p314; ☎852 2368 1689; Flat A1, 15th fl, A Block; s/d from HK$180/200; @ ⚛; Ⓜ Tsim Sha Tsui, exit D1), the latter in fact being a cluster of nine different guesthouses, so that you never quite know what you've actually booked. But that's half the fun...right?

SLEEPING KOWLOON

Make sure you catch at least one sunset on the rooftop of Horizonte Lounge (p150), the hotel's tiny 29th-floor bar.

MIRA
DESIGN HOTEL **$$**

Map p314 (☏852 2368 1111; www.themira hotel.com; 118-130 Nathan Rd, Tsim Sha Tsui; r/ste from HK$1700/2800; @🛜🛝; MTsim Sha Tsui, exit B1) Right in the heart of Tsim Sha Tsui, Mira impresses with colour-themed rooms, designer fixtures and a darkened entrance so cool you wouldn't be surprised to see a bouncer. The in-room gadgets aren't too shabby either: wi-fi hot spot, iPod dock, smart TV etc. Service can be inconsistent, though staff are generally helpful.

★PENINSULA HONG KONG
HOTEL **$$$**

Map p314 (香港半島酒店; ☏852 2920 2888; www.peninsula.com; Salisbury Rd, Tsim Sha Tsui; r/ste from HK$4000/6000; @🛜🛝; MTsim Sha Tsui, exit E) Lording it over the southern tip of Kowloon, the throne-like Peninsula (c 1928) is one of the world's great hotels. It was once called 'the finest hotel east of Suez', and your dilemma will be how to get here: landing on the rooftop helipad or arriving in one of the hotel's 16-strong fleet of Rolls Royce Phantoms.

Another dilemma is choosing which of the 300 classic, European-style rooms is for you; staying in the 20-storey annex offers spectacular harbour views, but the original building has glorious heritage interiors. Taking afternoon tea here is a wonderful experience – dress neatly and be prepared to queue for a table.

★HOTEL ICON
HOTEL **$$$**

Map p316 (唯港薈; ☏852 3400 1000; www.hotel-icon.com; 17 Science Museum Rd, Tsim Sha Tsui; r/ste from HK$2100/4000; @🛜🛝; MEast Tsim Sha Tsui, exit P1) Return guests heap praise on this high-spec hotel with its luxurious rooms, complimentary mini-bar, sweeping harbour views and rooftop pool; it's the worst-kept hospitality secret in Hong Kong. Associated with a hospitality training school, it represents good value for the quality, plus you're never more than a metre or so from a keen-to-please staff member.

EATON
HOTEL **$$$**

Map p318 (香港逸東酒店; ☏852 2782 1818; www.hongkong.eatonhotels.com; 380 Nathan Rd, Yau Ma Tei; r HK$2350-3200, ste from HK$3250; @🛜🛝; MJordan, exit B1) Leave the bedlam of Nathan Rd behind as you enter the Eaton's designer surrounds, all earthy woods and mismatched furnishings.The 'Executive Room' category has king beds facing a curvaceous crescent of windows overlooking Kowloon. Enclosed by a peristyle (colonnaded porch), the spa-like rooftop pool has major wow factor.

Dining is a strength of the Eaton; a basement food court, sharing the lobby's funky design aesthetic, has everything from nostalgic HK snacks to Japanese rice bowls to a tiny craft-beer bar. Yat Tung Heen in the lower basement serves Michelin-lauded lunchtime dim sum.

INTERCONTINENTAL HONG KONG
HOTEL **$$$**

Map p316 (香港洲際酒店; ☏852 2721 1211; www.intercontinental.com; 18 Salisbury Rd, Tsim Sha Tsui; r/ste from HK$3000/4000; @🛜🛝; MTsim Sha Tsui, exit F) The InterContinental might look like an '80s office block, but so what when you have the finest waterfront spot in the territory? Impeccable service ensures that the business VIPs and rock stars keep coming back, while colonial nods include a pair of metallic-blue Rolls Royce phantoms, door staff liveried in white and incessant brass polishing.

In-room check-in, butler service and sunken bath-tubs come as standard, but not all rooms have harbour views. If you have the wallet for it, InterCon has five fabulous eateries with multiple Michelin stars between them. The lobby lounge bar (p147) has the best views in Hong Kong.

KERRY HOTEL
LUXURY HOTEL **$$$**

(香港嘉里酒店; ☏852 2252 5888; www.shangri-la.com/hongkong/kerry; 38 Hung Luen Rd, Hung Hom; r from HK$2300; 🛜🛝) A curvaceous resort-style hotel commanding a generous wedge of Hung Hom harbourfront, the Kerry is somewhat out on a limb, though that means it has ample space for gardens, alfresco dining venues, a lagoon-like infinity pool, and harbour views from two-thirds of the 546 guestrooms. Rooms are also echo-big and luxurious, the smallest clocking in at 42 sq metres.

The Red Sugar rooftop bar is a stellar perch for sundowner cocktails. Usefully, Kerry is right beside the Hung Hom Ferry Pier connecting with Central, Wan Chai and North Point.

Understand Hong Kong

Hong Kong Today

Just a decade ago, most Hong Kong residents would say the return to Chinese rule did not bring many changes, but since then, rising tensions with Běijīng have begun to dominate Hong Kong politics and public sentiment, putting the 'One Country, Two Systems' experiment in question. A city that was known for its political antipathy during the 150 years of British rule has become highly politicised.

Best on Film

Infernal Affairs (2002) The crime thriller that inspired Scorsese's *The Departed*.

Night and Fog (2010) Auteur Ann Hui's darkly realistic drama on domestic violence and the lives of migrant women.

The Grandmaster (2013) Wong Kar-wai's stylish martial-arts drama about the life of Wing Chun grandmaster Ip Man.

Chungking Express (1994) Cult classic following the love lives of two Hong Kong policemen.

Trivisia (2016) Engaging and reflective action crime thriller produced by Johnnie To and Yau Nai-hoi.

Best in Print

City at the End of Time: Poems by Leung Ping-kwan (ed Esther Cheung; 2012) Leung Ping-kwan, aka Yesi was Hong Kong's unofficial poet laureate.

The Hungry Ghosts (Anne Berry; 2009) Restless spirits haunt this excellent tale.

The Piano Teacher (Janice YK Lee; 2009) Easy read following midcentury Hong Kong society lovers.

Hong Kong Shop Cats (Marcel Heijnen; 2016) Book of photojournalism cataloging the city's furry friends.

Hong Kong: A Cultural History (Michael Ingham; 2007) The definitive title in this category.

The State of Play

Hong Kong has witnessed much political strife since the turn of the decade. Critics of the government have focused on a long list of increasingly intractable issues, from slow democratic reform and the perceived collusion between the government and big businesses, to stifling property prices and the perceived drain on public resources by mainland migrants.

Since the Běijīng-stamped appointment of Carrie Lam to Hong Kong's top post in 2017, there has been little change and a sense of political foreboding lingers in the air. The combination of divisive party politics and the lack of a democratic mandate has caused many to condemn the government as weak, and hopelessly so when faced with vested interests as strong as the largest developers.

Basic Economics

In 2018 Hong Kong was named the least affordable housing market in the world for the eighth consecutive year, showing just how depressingly expensive it has become to live in the city. The property market is flush with cash from mainland speculators and Hong Kong has more billionaires than most countries, but many more struggle to meet basic levels of subsistence; some live in spaces no bigger than 10 sq metres. Despite reasonable economic growth in the past few years, Hong Kong's economy has become increasingly reliant on the financial sector and the spending power of mainland tourists.

In Běijīng's Shadow

Once savvy and confident, many Hong Kongers are worried about what they see as the government's attempt at homogenisation. From his seat in Běijīng, President Xi Jinping has stepped up interventions in Hong Kong affairs. What is most feared is a premature erosion of the autonomy negotiated for the Special Administrative Region (SAR). The opening in 2018 of the new Kowloon West cross-border rail terminus, partially governed by mainland laws despite being well inside Hong Kong turf, has only served to heighten these concerns of encroachment.

The seemingly headlong rush for the Chinese tourist dollar, with the attendant proliferation of luxury stores and galleries, has bred discontent among critics. Resulting rent hikes across the board are fuelling inflation and forcing traditional shops out of business.

Cultural differences between Hong Kongers and mainland migrants, and the influx of tariff-dodging parallel traders to border towns are other sources of conflict. Interestingly, one saving grace is that China may not be quite as enthralled with Hong Kong as it once was, because the SAR's importance to the Chinese economy is waning. At the time of the 1997 handover, Hong Kong accounted for almost 20% of China's GDP; today it is less than 3%.

Yet despite the general mood of anxiety, all is not doom and gloom. If anything, these challenges are strengthening the identity of Hong Kong's local community and bringing into greater focus the core values it holds dear (namely, the rule of law and civil liberties).

Rebellion & Rebound

In September 2014, protesters – many of them students – took to the streets to speak out against planned reforms to the local electoral system which they claimed would limit the potential for universal suffrage. The protests grew into a thousands-strong pro-democracy campaign known variously as Occupy Central and the Umbrella Movement. The protests lasted for three months and since then, several student leaders have launched a new political party.

Yet local defiance may have begun to waver. The annual 1 July protest march, organised by the Civil Human Rights Front every year since the handover in 1997, hit a three-year low on the 21st anniversary of Hong Kong's return to China in 2018. Local activists are worried that apathy is beginning to set in. New chief executive Carrie Lam has made it clear that she feels the best way to preserve Hong Kong's distinct systems is to succumb to the city's 'one country' future.

On the flip side, part of the city's growing assertion of its identity is an increasing drive to preserve its heritage. Many Hong Kongers bristle at any perceived threat to the use of Cantonese or traditional Chinese characters, or to the wellbeing of country parks and old neighbourhoods. Collectives have flowered to document the social history of storied neighbourhoods caught in the tide of urban redevelopment. The perennial tussle for space has also seen the growth of alternative cultural venues and farms. As always, Hong Kong is demonstrating its extraordinary ability to rebound, adapt and excel.

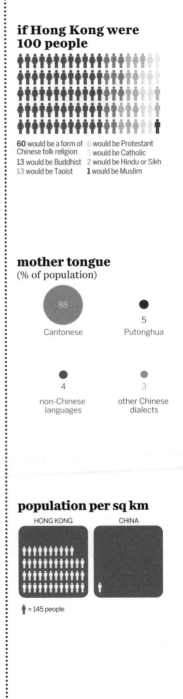

if Hong Kong were 100 people

60 would be a form of Chinese folk religion
13 would be Buddhist
13 would be Taoist
6 would be Protestant
5 would be Catholic
2 would be Hindu or Sikh
1 would be Muslim

mother tongue
(% of population)

88 Cantonese

5 Putonghua

4 non-Chinese languages

3 other Chinese dialects

population per sq km

HONG KONG   CHINA

≈ 145 people

History

The name Hong Kong came from the Cantonese *heung gawng* (fragrant harbour), which was inspired by the sandalwood piled at what is now Aberdeen. In the long scale of history, Hong Kong as we know it today has existed for a mere blink of an eye. But there was a lot going on in the region before that morning in 1841 when British marines clambered ashore and planted the Union flag on the western part of Hong Kong Island.

Early Inhabitants

Hong Kong has supported human life since at least the Middle Neolithic Period (c 4000–2500 BC). Artefacts uncovered at almost 100 archaeological sites in the territory suggest that the inhabitants of these settlements shared similar cultural characteristics to the people who lived in the Pearl River delta. The remnants of Bronze Age habitations (c 1500–220 BC) unearthed on Lamma and Lantau Islands, among other places – as well as the eight extant geometric rock carvings along Hong Kong's coastline – also indicate that these early peoples practised some form of folk religion involving animal worship.

Archaeologists say Hong Kong's Stone Age inhabitants enjoyed a relatively nutritious diet of iron-rich vegetables, small mammals, shellfish and fish harvested far offshore. Early Chinese historical records call the diverse maritime peoples along China's southeastern coasts the 'Hundred Yue' tribes, which potentially included some of Hong Kong's prehistoric inhabitants.

The Five Great Clans

Hong Kong's mighty 'Five Clans' – Han Chinese, whose descendants hold political and economic clout to this day – began settling the area around the 11th century. The first and most powerful of the arrivals was the Tang, who initially settled around Yuen Long (the walled village of Kat Hing Wai is part of this cluster).

The Tang clan was followed by the Hau and the Pang, who spread around present-day Sheung Shui and Fanling. These three clans were followed by the Liu in the 14th century and the Man a century later.

The Cantonese-speaking newcomers called themselves *bun day* (Punti), meaning 'indigenous' or 'local' – something they clearly were not. They looked down on the original inhabitants, the Tanka, many

TIMELINE	4000–1500 BC	214 BC	AD 1000–1400
	Small groups of Neolithic hunter-gatherers and fisherfolk settle in coastal areas; a handful of tools, pottery and other artefacts are the only remnants left by these nomads.	Chinese emperor Qin Shi Huang conquers present-day Guǎngxī, Guǎngdōng and Fújiàn after a long period of war. Hong Kong comes under greater cultural influence from the north.	Hong Kong's Five Clans – Tang, Hau, Pang, Liu and Man – settle in what is now the New Territories and build walled villages in the fertile plains and valleys.

of whom had been shunted off the land and had moved onto the sea to live on boats.

An Imperial Outpost

Clinging to the southern edge of the Chinese province of Canton (now Guǎngdōng), the peninsula and islands that became the territory of Hong Kong counted only as a remote pocket in a neglected corner of the Chinese empire.

The Punti flourished until the struggle that saw the moribund Ming dynasty (1368–1644) overthrown. The victorious Qing (1644–1911), angered by the resistance put up by southerners loyal to the old order, enforced evacuation inland of all the inhabitants of China's southeastern coastal area, including Hong Kong, in the 1660s.

More than four generations passed before the population was able to recover to its mid-17th-century level, boosted in part by the influx of the Hakka (Cantonese for 'Guest People'), who moved here in the 18th century and up to the mid-19th century. A few vestiges of their language, songs, folklore and cooking survive, most visibly in the wide-brimmed, black-fringed bamboo hats sported by Hakka women in the New Territories.

Arrival of the Outer Barbarians

For centuries the Pearl River estuary had been an important trading artery centred on the port of Canton (now Guǎngzhōu). Some of the first foreign traders (or 'outer barbarians') were Arab traders who entered – and sacked – the settlement as early as the 8th century AD. Similarly, the Ming emperors regarded their subjects to the south as an utterly uncivilised bunch. It was therefore fitting that the Cantonese should trade with the 'outer barbarians'.

Regular trade between China and Europe began in 1557 when Portuguese navigators set up a base in Macau, 65km west of Hong Kong. Dutch traders came in the wake of the Portuguese, followed by the French. British ships appeared as early as 1683 from the East India Company concessions along the coast of India, and by 1711 the company had established offices and warehouses in Guǎngzhōu to trade for tea, silk and porcelain.

The First Opium War & British Hong Kong

China did not reciprocate Europe's voracious demand for its products, for the most part shunning foreign-manufactured goods. The foreigners' ensuing trade deficit was soon reversed, however, after the British discovered a commodity that the Chinese did want: opium.

The discovery of coins and pottery from the Eastern Han dynasty (AD 25–220) on Lantau and at several important digs, including a tomb at Lei Cheng Uk in central Kowloon, attests to the growing Han influence in Hong Kong at the start of the first millennium.

In 1276 the boy emperor Duan Zong and his younger brother, Bing, were forced to flee to Hong Kong as the Mongols swept aside the remaining army of the Song dynasty. After Mongol ships defeated the tattered remnants of the imperial fleet on Pearl River, the dynasty was definitively ended.

1557	1644	1683	1757
Portuguese navigators set up a base in Macau, and are followed by Dutch and then French traders. Regular trade begins between China and Europe.	The Ming dynasty (1368–1644) is overthrown by the Qing dynasty, which reigns until 1911.	British East India Company ships begin to arrive, and by 1711 the company has established offices and warehouses in Guǎngzhōu, to trade for tea, silk and porcelain.	An imperial edict restricts European trade to the cohong (local merchants guild) in Guǎngzhōu; growing discontent with the trading system sets the stage for the First Opium War.

The British, with a virtually inexhaustible supply of the drug from the poppy fields of India, developed the trade aggressively. Consequently, opium addiction spread out of control in China, and the country's silver reserves (used to pay for opium) became perilously drained.

In late 1838 Emperor Dao Guang (r 1820–50) appointed Lin Zexu, governor of Húnán and Húběi and a Mandarin of great integrity, to stamp out the opium trade. His rather successful campaign would ultimately lead to the First Opium War (or First Anglo-Chinese War) of 1839–42.

In January 1841 a naval landing party hoisted the British flag at Possession Point (now Possession St) on Hong Kong Island. Subsequently, the Treaty of Nanking abolished the monopoly system of trade, opened five 'treaty ports' to British residents and foreign trade, exempted British nationals from all Chinese laws and ceded the strategically useful island of Hong Kong to the British 'in perpetuity'.

Hong Kong, with its deep, well-sheltered harbour, formally became a British possession on 26 June 1843, and its first governor, Sir Henry Pottinger, took charge. A primitive, chaotic and lawless settlement soon sprang up.

Growing Pains

What would later be called the Second Opium War (or Second Anglo-Chinese War) broke out in October 1856. The victorious British forced the Chinese to sign the Convention of Peking in 1860, which ceded Kowloon Peninsula and Stonecutters Island to Britain. Britain was now in complete control of Victoria Harbour and its approaches.

As the Qing dynasty slid into major chaos towards the end of the 19th century, the British government petitioned China to extend the colony into the New Territories. The June 1898 Convention of Peking handed Britain a larger-than-expected slice of territory that included 235 islands and ran north to the Shumchun (Shēnzhèn) River, increasing the colony's size by 90%.

Alarmed by the spread of addiction and the silver draining from the country to pay for opium, the Qing emperor issued an edict in 1799 banning the trade of opium in China. The ban had little effect and the lucrative trade continued.

Build-Up to WWII

While Hong Kong's major trading houses, including Jardine Matheson and Swire, prospered from their trade with China, the colony hardly thrived in its first few decades. Fever, bubonic plague and typhoons threatened life and property, and at first the colony attracted a fair number of criminals and vice merchants.

1773	1799	1841	1842
Opium smuggling to China skyrockets after the British East India Company monopolises production and export of Indian opium.	China's silver reserves, used to pay for opium, drain rapidly as opium addiction sweeps through China. The Qing emperor issues an edict banning opium trade in the country.	During the First Opium War against China, British marines plant the Union flag on the western part of Hong Kong Island, claiming the land for the British Crown.	China cedes Hong Kong Island to Britain.

Gradually Hong Kong began to shape itself into a more substantial community. Nonetheless, from the late 19th century right up to WWII, Hong Kong lived in the shadow of the treaty port of Shànghǎi, which had become Asia's premier trade and financial centre – not to mention its style capital.

The colony's population continued to grow thanks to the waves of immigrants fleeing the Chinese Revolution of 1911, which ousted the decaying Qing dynasty and ushered in several decades of strife, rampaging warlords and famine. The Japanese invasion of China in 1937 sparked another major exodus to Hong Kong's shores.

Hong Kong's status as a British colony would offer the refugees only a temporary haven. The day after Japan attacked the US naval base at Pearl Harbor on 7 December 1941, its military machine swept down from Guǎngzhōu and into Hong Kong.

Conditions under Japanese rule were harsh, with indiscriminate killings of mostly Chinese civilians; western civilians were incarcerated at Stanley Prison on Hong Kong Island. Many Hong Kong Chinese fled to Macau, administered by neutral Portugal.

'Albert is so amused at my having got the island of Hong Kong', wrote Queen Victoria to King Leopold of Belgium in 1841. At the time, Hong Kong was little more than a backwater of about 20 villages and hamlets.

HISTORY BUILD-UP TO WWII

THE TRIADS

Hong Kong's Triads, which continue to run the territory's drug, prostitution, people-smuggling, gambling and loan-sharking rackets, weren't always the gangster operations they are today.

They were founded as secret and patriotic societies that opposed the corrupt and brutal Qing (Manchu) dynasty and aided the revolution that eventually toppled it in 1911. The fact that these organisations had adopted Kwan Tai (or Kwan Yu), the god of war and upholder of righteousness, integrity and loyalty, as their patron, lent them further respectability. The Triads descended into crime and vice during the Chinese Civil War (1945–49), and came in droves to Hong Kong after the communists came to power in 1949. Today they are the Chinese equivalent of the Mafia.

The communists smashed the Triad-controlled drug racket in Shànghǎi after the 1949 revolution. Having long memories and fearing a repeat could occur with the looming 1997 handover, many Hong Kong–based hoods moved their operations to ethnic-Chinese communities in countries such as Thailand, the Philippines, Australia, Canada and the US. Since 1997, however, many Triads have moved back into Hong Kong and have even expanded their operations onto the mainland.

The definitive work on the Triads is *Triad Societies in Hong Kong* by WP Morgan (1960), a former sub-inspector with the Royal Hong Kong Police.

1860	1894	1895	1898
China loses the Second Opium War against Britain and under the Convention of Peking cedes Kowloon Peninsula and Stonecutters Island to Britain.	Bubonic plague breaks out in Hong Kong, killing 2500 of mainly local Chinese; trade suffers badly.	Future Chinese national hero Sun Yatsen plots an insurrection in southern China from his base in Hong Kong; it fails and the British ban Sun from the territory.	China hands the New Territories to Britain on a 99-year lease, which begins on 1 July 1898 and ends at midnight on 30 June 1997.

The Road to Boomtown

After Japan's withdrawal from Hong Kong, and subsequent surrender in August 1945, the colony looked set to resume its hibernation. But events both at home and on the mainland forced the colony in a new direction.

The Chinese Civil War (1945–49) and the subsequent communist takeover of China caused a huge number of refugees – both rich and poor – to flee to Hong Kong. The refugees brought along capital and cheap labour, which would prove vital to Hong Kong's economic take-off. On a paltry, war-torn foundation, local and foreign businesses built a huge manufacturing (notably textiles and garments) and financial services centre that transformed Hong Kong into one of the world's great economic miracles.

Hong Kong's stability received a hard battering at the height of the Cultural Revolution in 1967, as local pro-communist groups instigated a series of anticolonial demonstrations, strikes and riots. The violence soon mushroomed into bombings and arson attacks, and the colony's economy was paralysed for months. The riot came to an end in December 1967, when Chinese Premier Zhou Enlai ordered the pro-communist groups to stop.

A Society in Transition

After the 1967 crisis the colonial government initiated a series of reforms to alleviate social discontent and to foster a sense of belonging to Hong Kong. In the next decade the government introduced more labour laws, and invested heavily in public housing, medical services, education and recreational activities for youth.

In the early years of British Hong Kong, opium dens, gambling clubs and brothels proliferated; just a year after the Britain took possession, an estimated 450 sex workers worked out of 24 brothels, including a fair number of foreign prostitutes clustered in Lyndhurst Tce, which today is home to a hip bar scene.

Although Hong Kong's stock market collapsed in 1973, its economy resumed its upward trend later in the decade. The 'Open Door' policy of Deng Xiaoping, who took control of China in the confusion after Mao Zedong's death in 1976, revived Hong Kong's role as the gateway to the mainland and it boomed. By the end of the 1980s, Hong Kong was one of the richest places in Asia, second only to Japan in terms of GDP per capita.

The 1997 Question

Few people gave much thought to Hong Kong's future until 1979, when the governor of Hong Kong, Murray MacLehose, raised the issue with Deng Xiaoping on his first official visit to Běijīng. Britain was legally bound to hand back only the New Territories – not Hong Kong Island and Kowloon, which had been ceded to it forever. However, the fact that

1911	1937	1941	1962
The colony's population expands as large groups of immigrants flee the Chinese Revolution on the mainland.	Pouncing on a country weakened by a bloody civil war, Japan invades China; as many as 750,000 mainlanders seek shelter in Hong Kong over the next three years.	British forces surrender to Japanese forces on Christmas Day; the population in Hong Kong is more than halved during almost four years of Japanese occupation.	The great famine caused by the Great Leap Forward in China drives 70,000 people to flee into Hong Kong in less than three months.

nearly half of Hong Kong's population lived in the New Territories by that time made it an untenable division.

It was Deng Xiaoping who decided that the time was ripe to recover Hong Kong, forcing the British to the negotiating table. The views of Hong Kong people were not sought. The inevitable conclusion laid to rest the political jitters and commercial concerns that in 1983 had seen the Hong Kong dollar collapse and subsequently be pegged to the US dollar.

Despite soothing words from the Chinese, British and Hong Kong governments, over the next 13 years the population of Hong Kong was to suffer considerable anxiety over the possible political and economic consequences of the handover due in 1997.

One Country, Two Systems

Under the December 1984 Sino-British Joint Declaration on the Question of Hong Kong of December 1984, Hong Kong would be reborn as a Special Administrative Region (SAR) of China. This meant its capitalist system would be permitted to continue, while across the border China's version of socialism would continue. The Chinese catchphrase for this was 'One Country, Two Systems'.

The Basic Law for Hong Kong, the future SAR's constitution, preserved Hong Kong's English common-law judicial system and guaranteed the right of property and ownership, as well as other key civil liberties. The SAR would enjoy a high degree of autonomy with the exception of foreign affairs and matters of defence.

Despite these assurances, many families and individuals had little faith in a future Hong Kong under Chinese rule, and a so-called brain drain ensued when tens of thousands left the colony for the US, Canada, Australia and New Zealand towards the end of the 1980s.

Tiān'ānmén & Its Aftermath

The concern of many Hong Kong people over their future turned to out-and-out fear on 4 June 1989, when the Chinese army killed pro-democracy demonstrators in Běijīng's Tiān'ānmén Square.

Tiān'ānmén was a watershed for Hong Kong. Sino-British relations deteriorated, the stock market fell 22% in one day and a great deal of capital left the territory for destinations overseas.

The Hong Kong government sought to rebuild confidence by announcing plans for a new airport and shipping port in what was the world's most expensive (HK$160 billion or US$20.6 billion) infrastructure project of the day.

In the early 1970s, the construction of the first three 'New Towns' (Sha Tin, Tsuen Wan and Tuen Mun) commenced, marking the start of a massive and unprecedented public-housing program that would, and still does, house millions of Hong Kong people.

Following the Tiān'ānmén Square protests of 1989, an underground smuggling operation, code-named Yellow Bird, was set up in Hong Kong to spirit many activists to safety overseas. Meanwhile Hong Kong–based Chinese officials who had criticised the killings were either removed from their posts or sought asylum in the West.

1967	1971	1976	1982
Riots and bombings by pro-communist groups rock Hong Kong; armed Chinese militia cross the border, killing five policemen and penetrating 3km into the New Territories before pulling back.	A former child actor called Bruce Lee lands his first adult leading role in the kung fu film *The Big Boss;* it becomes a smash around the world.	Deng Xiaoping takes control of China after Mao Zedong's death, and revives Hong Kong's role as the gateway to the mainland.	British PM Margaret Thatcher visits Běijīng to begin talks on Hong Kong's future. Two years of closed-door wrangling between the Chinese and British ensues.

The Tiān'ānmén protests had strengthened the resolve of those people who either could not or would not leave, giving rise to the territory's first official political parties. In a bid to restore credibility, the government introduced a Bill of Rights in 1990 and the following year gave Hong Kong citizens the right to choose 18 of the 60 members of the Legislative Council (LegCo), which until then had essentially been a rubber-stamp body chosen by the government and special-interest groups.

To this day, Hong Kong is the only place in China where the crackdown on the Tiān'ānmén pro-democracy uprising of 4 June 1989 can be openly commemorated.

Democracy & the Last Governor

One of the first parties to emerge was the United Democrats of Hong Kong, led by outspoken democrats Martin Lee and Szeto Wah. The pair, initially courted by China for their anticolonial positions and appointed to the committee that drafted the Basic Law, subsequently infuriated Běijīng by publicly burning copies of the proto-constitution in protest over Tiān'ānmén. China denounced them as subversives.

Chris Patten, Hong Kong's 28th – and last – British governor, arrived in 1992, pledging that democracy reforms would be sped up. China reacted by levelling verbal attacks at Patten and threatening the post-1997 careers of any pro-democracy politicians or officials. When these tactics failed, China targeted Hong Kong's economy. Talks on certain business contracts and infrastructure projects straddling 1997 suddenly came to a halt, including the new airport program.

Sensing that it had alienated even its supporters in Hong Kong, China backed down and in 1994 gave its blessing to the new airport at Chek Lap Kok. It remained hostile to direct elections, however, and vowed to disband the democratically elected legislature after 1997. It eventually did what it promised by installing an interim rubber-stamp body which would serve until June 1998.

As for the executive branch of power, China organised an 'election' in December 1996 to select Hong Kong's first postcolonial leader. But Tung Chee Hwa (1937–), the Shànghǎi-born shipping magnate hand-picked to be the SAR's first chief executive, won approval by retaining Patten's right-hand woman, Anson Chan, as his chief secretary and Donald Tsang as financial secretary. In a media briefing given to reporters when he accepted the post, Tung ushered the curtain call to a century and a half of British rule and summed up Chinese feelings about the upcoming handover with the words: 'Now we are finally masters of our own house'.

In the wake of the Tiān'ānmén Square protests, local Hong Kong people with money and skills made a mad dash to emigrate to any country that would take them. During the worst period more than 1000 people were leaving each week, especially for Canada and Australia.

1984	1989	1990	1991
Hong Kong's future is sealed in the Sino-British Joint Declaration on the Question of Hong Kong; the city's capitalist system will continue after 1997.	More than a million Hong Kong people march in support of the pro-democracy movement in Běijīng; the Chinese army kills protesting students in and around Tiān'ānmén Square.	The government introduces a Bill of Rights and in 1991 gives Hong Kong citizens the right to choose 18 of the 60 members of the Legislative Council (LegCo).	In a forward step for the LGBTQ+ community, the Crimes (Amendment) Ordinance removes criminal penalties for homosexual acts between consenting adults over 18.

CHINA'S HONG KONG INVASION PLAN

The peaceful agreement that eventually settled the status of Hong Kong was by no means a foregone conclusion in the decades leading up to it. The key negotiators have since revealed just how touchy China felt about Hong Kong and how close it came to retaking the territory by force.

Margaret Thatcher, the British prime minister who negotiated the deal, purportedly said later that Deng Xiaoping, then China's leader, told her during 1982 talks that he 'could walk in and take the whole lot this afternoon'. She replied that China would lose everything if it did.

More than three decades later, Lu Ping, the top Chinese negotiator, confirmed that this was no bluff on Deng's part. Deng feared that announcing the date for the 1997 handover would provoke serious unrest in Hong Kong, and China would be compelled to invade as a result.

According to Lu, China had also been hours away from invading during 1967, at the height of the chaotic Cultural Revolution, when a radical faction of the People's Liberation Army (PLA) was poised to invade the British colony during pro-communist riots. The invasion was called off only by a late-night order from Premier Zhou Enlai to the local army commander, Huang Yongsheng, a radical Maoist who had been itching to invade.

On the night of 30 June 1997, the handover celebrations held in the purpose-built extension of the Hong Kong Convention & Exhibition Centre in Wan Chai were watched by millions of people around the world. Chris Patten shed a tear while Chinese President Jiang Zemin beamed and Prince Charles was outwardly stoic.

Post-1997: Hong Kong Under Tung

Almost as soon as the euphoria of the 1997 handover faded, things started going badly in Hong Kong. The financial crisis that had rocked other parts of Asia began to be felt in Hong Kong at the end of 1997. A strain of deadly avian flu saw the city slaughter more than one million chickens.

In the first few years after the handover, the mainland government largely chose to tread lightly in Hong Kong, honouring the spirit of the handover agreement to a great extent. Tung Chee Hwa's first term is remembered as much for his confusing housing policy, which many blamed for a sustained fall in property prices, as for such vacuous infrastructure proposals as a Chinese medicine port. Despite his poor standing in the polls, Tung was returned for a second five-year term in March 2002.

1997	2003	2008	2009
The rain falls, outgoing governor Chris Patten cries and Hong Kong returns to Chinese sovereignty; avian flu breaks out, leaving six dead. Tung Chee Hwa becomes Hong Kong's first chief executive.	Severe acute respiratory syndrome (SARS) shuts down Hong Kong for weeks. The Closer Economic Partnership Agreement with the mainland provides favourable business opportunities.	Lung King Heen becomes the first Chinese restaurant in the world to receive three Michelin stars, heralding a new era for gourmet Cantonese cuisine.	Hong Kong's population exceeds seven million and the unemployment rate grows to almost 5% in the face of the world's worst economic crisis since the Great Depression.

Today's Triads still recite an oath of allegiance to the Ming, but their loyalty these days is to the dollar rather than the vanquished Son of Heaven.

Controversy continued to dog his time in office, however, most notably in March 2003, when the government's failure to contain the severe acute respiratory syndrome (SARS) epidemic at an early stage provoked a torrent of blame. The outbreak killed 299 people, infected 1755 and all but closed Hong Kong down for weeks.

In July 2003 the government caused further controversy when it tried to turn Article 23 of the Basic Law into legislation; the National Security Bill raised fears that Hong Kong's press freedom and civil liberties would be undermined. In the face of massive public protests – of 500,000 people or more – the government shelved the bill indefinitely, but the incident changed Běijīng's stance on Hong Kong.

The Clamour for Democracy

In March 2005 Tung announced his resignation as chief executive. His replacement was the bow-tie-wearing chief secretary Sir Donald Tsang, who had continuously served as Hong Kong's financial secretary from before the handover up to 2001, when he became the city's number-two public official.

Compared to Tung, Tsang was a welcome replacement for both the Běijīng powerbrokers and the Hong Kong public. In 2007 Tsang was easily re-elected with Běijīng's blessing. However, he soon suffered an erosion of public confidence when he was seen to renege on a series of promises, including delaying a highly anticipated consultation on reforming the electoral process for the chief executive and legislature to make the 2012 polls more democratic.

A measure of just how successful the handover had generally been came in a 2007 BBC interview with Margaret Thatcher. Marking the 10th anniversary of the handover of Hong Kong from Britain to China, Thatcher, to her own surprise, deemed China's overall performance a success.

The clamour for democracy reached a crescendo in 2010 as two landmark political events took place in successive months. In May five pro-democracy lawmakers were re-elected to LegCo after they collectively resigned four months earlier in the hope that the resulting by-elections would serve as a de facto referendum on universal suffrage. The pro-Běijīng parties boycotted the contests, however, and the quintet's campaign came unstuck, even though they could claim to have been returned to the chamber by a respectable vote.

The pro-democracy parties had in fact been divided over the political strategy behind the forced by-elections, and the long-running differences among the key players imploded the following month when the biggest of them all, the Democratic Party, sided with the government in a new political reform package that would see LegCo earn a slightly increased percentage of popularly elected seats at the expense of delayed universal suffrage for the entire legislature and for the election of Hong Kong's chief executive.

2010	2011	2012	2014
LegCo approves HK$66.9 billion for the Hong Kong portion of the Guǎngzhōu–Hong Kong high-speed rail link, following 25 hours of heated debate.	A minimum wage of HK$28 per hour takes effect, and inflation hits a 16-year high.	Property surveyor Leung Chun-ying begins a five-year term as the fourth Hong Kong Special Administrative Regions (SAR) chief executive a in a scandal-plagued election.	Tens of thousands of pro-democracy protesters take to the streets in the Umbrella Movement, a three-month-long civil disobedience campaign against reforms limiting universal suffrage.

The calls for democracy have continued since, most notably around the election – by a 1200-member body of predominantly pro-Běijīng notables – of the SAR's fourth chief executive in March 2012. Leung Chunying, a stalwart in Hong Kong politics with impeccably close links to Běijīng, defeated the long-time hopeful and former civil-service chief Henry Tang.

In June 2014 an unofficial referendum on making the election of the city's chief executive more democratic garnered votes from more than 787,000 Hong Kong residents – the equivalent of more than 22% of the city's 3.5 million registered voters. Following this, on 1 July 2014, thousands of people turned out for a pro-democracy protest march on the anniversary of the handover. The protest organisers claimed 510,000 attendees, though the police put the figure at 98,600. Discontent continued to bubble beneath the surface and in September 2014 it erupted into a larger pro-democracy campaign that became known as the Umbrella Movement.

A Changed City?

Apart from ever more glitzy skyscrapers, visitors returning to Hong Kong since July 1997 would see and feel little material difference walking around the city. Perhaps the most striking thing they might notice is the influx of a new breed of visitor: mainland Chinese, who in the past two decades have grown to make up nearly 70% of the territory's visitor numbers.

In many ways Hong Kong has benefited from closer ties with the mainland. The growth in Hong Kong's tourism would have been impossible without the influx of mainland tourists, and the Closer Economic Partnership Agreement signed with the mainland government in 2003 provided favourable business opportunities to Hong Kong's investors and industries.

While closer ties with the mainland have often been met with uneasy feelings, might history one day identify an equal and opposite reaction going on? Hong Kong's dazzling success and core values arguably exert 'soft' power that influences thinking on the mainland. It might be hard to measure, but in the enclave that sheltered and inspired the fathers of powerful mainland movements (Sun Yatsen and Zhou Enlai), it should not be dismissed.

Hong Kong is the only place under Chinese rule that still mourns those killed in 1989 at Běijīng's Tiān'ānmén Square. Every year on 4 June, tens of thousands of people gather at Victoria Park to attend a candlelight vigil held in commemoration of those who lost their lives – though they come under increasing pressure not to do so.

HISTORY **A CHANGED CITY?**

2015	2016	2018	2018
Five booksellers connected with books banned on the mainland go missing; one resurfaces in Hong Kong asking police to end the investigation into his missing-person case.	At Lunar New Year, a government crackdown on unlicensed hawkers turns violent as riot police clash with protesters in Mong Kok.	In July 2018 there was a landmark ruling by Hong Kong's Court of Final Appeal, stating that the same-sex partner of a British expat should be granted a spousal visa.	Fourteen years after it was decommissioned, the Central Police Station (1841) and magistracy reopens as a major heritage and arts complex called Tai Kwun, transforming Soho.

Arts

Hong Kong's arts scene grows more vibrant by the day and its fine-art market is now considered one of the best in the world. There are musical ensembles of all persuasions, an assortment of theatre groups, Chinese and modern-dance troupes, and numerous art organisations. The West Kowloon Cultural District is one of Asia's most ambitious cultural projects. Government funds allow organisers to bring in top international performers, and the number of international arts festivals hosted here seems to grow each year.

Visual Arts

Top Museums for Hong Kong Art

Hong Kong Museum of Art (Tsim Sha Tsui)

JC Contemporary, Tai Kwun (Soho)

Hong Kong Arts Centre (Wan Chai)

Asia Society Hong Kong (Admiralty)

Hong Kong is one of the three most important art-auction centres in the world, along with New York and London. Theoretically, it can only get stronger, given that China has already surpassed the US as the world's largest market for art and antiques. Despite some industry concern about the ability of the Chinese market to promote stable, long-term growth, Hong Kong will continue to ride the bull wave nimbly – and with gusto – for as long as the overheated market keeps its lid on. Art Basel, the world's premier art fair, launched a Hong Kong edition in 2013; Hong Kong Art Walk is an annual event that runs alongside it, involving dozens of galleries in town – both now fall under the umbrella of what has been designated Hong Kong Arts Month. There's also the Affordable Art Fair, so that mere mortals can get in on the act without having to drop megabucks.

Contemporary Hong Kong art tends not to bother too much with grandiose narratives about nationhood and religion, preferring to take an introverted view of the world and expressing visions of Chinese-ness and increasingly Hong Kong–ness outside of the national frame. There are hundreds of small commercial galleries in Hong Kong, particularly in Central, many of them selling very serious works of art.

The opening of the M+, tentatively slated for late 2019 though it has been dogged by delays, will definitely be a highlight of Hong Kong's cultural arena. The M+ is a museum for 20th- and 21st-century visual culture, and is part of the West Kowloon Cultural District (WKCD), the city's most ambitious arts development project to date.

The best sources for information on Hong Kong and Asian art are *Asian Art News* (www.asianartnews.com), the free monthly *Art Map* (www.artmap.com.hk; Chinese only), the Asia Art Archive (www.aaa.org.hk) and the Hong Kong International Association of Art Critics (www.aicahk.org).

Roots

In general, Chinese painters of the past were interested in traditional forms and painting processes – not necessarily composition and colour. Brush strokes and the utensils used to produce them are of vital importance and interest. In traditional Chinese art, change for the sake of change was never the philosophy or the trend; Chinese artists would compare their work with that of the master and judge it accordingly.

The influential Lingnan School of Painting, founded by the water-colourist Chao Shao-an (1905–98) in the 1930s and relocated to Hong Kong in 1948, attempted to move away from this tradition. It combined traditional Chinese, Japanese and western artistic methods to produce a rather decorative style, and dominated the small-art market in Hong Kong for the next two decades.

The most distinct group of painters and sculptors to appear in Hong Kong were the proponents of the New Ink Painting movement who came to prominence in the late 1960s. Most had strong links to China or its cultural heritage. The movement aimed at reconciling Chinese and western ideas by steering traditional Chinese ink painting towards abstract expressionism. Lui Shou-kwan (1919–75), who arrived in Hong Kong in 1948, was the earliest and the best known of the New Ink Painting artists. Lui worked for the Yau Ma Tei ferry as a pier inspector and taught in his spare time. Speaking no English, his only experience of the west was through pictures and books borrowed from the British Council library. Many of the artists who became associated with the movement were his students.

The only major artist to break free of the dominant style of the era was Luis Chan (1905–95). Born in Panama, Chan came to Hong Kong at the age of five, where he learnt to paint from art magazines and a correspondence course. Stylistically, Chan was a loner with no apparent allegiance to any painting tradition. He was also a genius who, particularly in his post-1960s works, transformed Hong Kong into a fantastical realm of dreams and hallucinations. His 1976 painting *Ping Chau* is a bizarre interpretation of the somnolent outlying island that is at once puzzling and endearing.

Avant-Garde

The 1980s and '90s saw the coming of age of artists born after WWII, many of whom had received their training abroad. Less burdened by the need to reconcile east and west, they devoted their efforts to defining avant-garde art, often through western mediums. They were also politically engaged. Wong Yan-kwai (1955–), a painter educated in France, was arguably the most influential artist of that period and is still one of the most accomplished today. His powerful paintings in vibrant colours are free of any social or historical context. Wong's mural graces Club 71 in Central.

London-trained Antonio Mak (1951–94) is Hong Kong's most famous contemporary sculptor and is known for his figurative pieces in cast bronze. He focused on the human figure as well as on animals important in Chinese legend and mythology (eg horses and tigers), and was greatly influenced by Rodin.

ART SPACES & GALLERIES

Nonprofit exhibition spaces in Hong Kong include Para Site in North Point, one of Asia's most active independent nonprofit art groups; Fotanian Open Studios (www.fotanstudios.org), with its annual opening day of artists' lofts in vacated factory buildings set against the rolling hills of Fo Tan; the nine-storey Jockey Club Creative Arts Centre (JCCAC; www.jccac.org.hk), which was converted from an industrial building and houses artists' studios; and Cattle Depot Artist Village, a one-time slaughterhouse that is home to a colony of local artists. The best time to visit the Fotanian Open Studios and the JCCAC is during their open studios (see their websites for the dates).

Admission is free to almost all commercial galleries in Hong Kong.

Salisbury Gardens, leading to the entrance of the Hong Kong Museum of Art in Tsim Sha Tsui, is lined with modern sculptures by contemporary Hong Kong sculptors. Dotted among the greenery of Kowloon Park is Sculpture Walk, with 30 marble, bronze and other weather-resistant works by both local and overseas artists, including a bronze by Mak called *Torso* and one by Britain's Sir Eduardo Paolozzi (1924–2005) called *Concept of Newton*.

Only a handful of King of Kowloon's works are left on Hong Kong's streets and there was public outcry in 2017 when one of them was painted over in a playground closed for renovations. See the concrete pillar that bears his imperial treatise at the Star Ferry pier in Tsim Sha Tsui.

Contemporary

Compared to their predecessors, Hong Kong's young artists – those born in the '70s and '80s – take a more internalised view of the world. They are overwhelmingly unfussed with orthodox Chinese culture and older generations' attempts to amalgamate east and west. Instead, they're often looking for – or perhaps, trying to retrieve – something that is uniquely Hong Kong. Nonetheless, their works show eloquence in a host of mediums, from Wilson Shieh's cheeky urban paintings using Chinese *gōngbǐ* (fine-brush) techniques to Jaffa Lam's sculpture installations.

Chow Chun-fai's background across a wide spectrum of media has seen him work between different art forms, such as photographs from classical paintings, or paintings from films. Adrian Wong's playful works involve his family connections to prominent names in the local entertainment industry, and indigenous superstitions. Kacey Wong's exciting installations can usually move about and invariably involve some kind of Hong Kong theme or common household treasure recast in a jovial light. His *Sleepwalker* (2011) contraption imbues the bunk bed – an indispensable fixture in Hong Kong's tight living spaces – with life and speaks to a mass aspiration, or doomed desperation, for a more humane habitat.

Photography

Hong Kong is endowed with internationally competitive photographers, and some of their works can be seen in the Hong Kong Heritage Museum, Blindspot Gallery and during the excellent biennial Hong Kong International Photo Festival.

Working in black and white, documentary photographer Yau Leung captured some of the most stunning and iconic images of 1960s Hong Kong, while art photographer So Hing-keung focuses on the shadows, figurative and literal, of the city in creations known for their psychological depth. Hong Kong–born, London-based visual artist Kurt Tong explores his multilayered identity, family heritage and memories through thoughtful documentary photography. *In Case it Rains in Heaven* (2010), his best-known project, is presented like a high-end shopping catalogue of stylised portraits of paper-made objects burnt as offerings for the deceased. The combustible items honoured by Tong run the gamut of modern human desires in Chinese societies.

Street Art & Other Arts

Street graffiti was almost nonexistent or largely unrecognised in Hong Kong until the passing in 2007 of the self-proclaimed 'King of Kowloon' (aka Tsang Tsou-choi), who for decades had smothered the city with his trademark rambling, childlike calligraphy that cursed the Queen of England for 'usurping' his rightful land. His irrepressible daily reveries and inimitable visual style eventually inspired many artists and designers, and won him exhibitions both at home and abroad.

Street art has noticeably grown in Hong Kong since, perhaps with the King's benediction. This trend in part stems from a new-found confidence among a younger generation of artists to express their dis-

Mural by Alex Croft on Graham St, Soho

satisfaction with the social problems of the day using means that are more open and combative. The website Hong Kong Street Art (http://hkstreetart.com) shows where you can see samples of the genre.

HKWalls (http://hkwalls.org) is an annual street-art festival held around March that showcases the works of local and international artists on the streets of Hong Kong. Unlike much of the graffiti you see in town, the organisers of HKWalls actually seek approval from businesses to use their walls before covering them with art. Events were held in Wong Chuk Hang and Soho in 2017 and 2018.

After the April 2011 arrest in mainland China of the prominent artist and activist Ai Weiwei, a number of artists in Hong Kong came forth with a dose of creative surprise to raise public awareness of his case and to rally for his release. Most memorably, Ai-inspired graffiti stencils appeared on pavements, overpasses and walls for five nights straight around the city, thanks to a lone operator known only as 'Tangerine'.

Contemporary ceramics is another field in which Hong Kong artists enjoy an edge beyond the city's borders. Fiona Wong, one of the city's best-known ceramic artists, makes life-sized sculptural works of clothing, shoes and other familiar items. A couple of small studios to look out for are Pottery Workshop Gallery in Central and Chiu Kee Porcelain Studio on Peng Chau Island.

Hollywood Rd in Central is a hot spot for street art. Start at the intersection with Graham St and work your way west, finishing around Tai Ping Shan St, and you'll pass an ever-changing open-air gallery. Or even an artist in the process of creating a new piece.

Music

Hong Kongers may not be quick to get up and jive when music is played, but they certainly enjoy music – in their homes, the air-conditioned comfort of a concert hall or a casual bar or karaoke lounge. Thanks to the city's mixed heritage, you'll find a decent range of music, from eastern to western, and classical to contemporary.

Western Classical

Western classical music is very popular in Hong Kong. The territory boasts the Hong Kong Philharmonic Orchestra, the Hong Kong Sinfonietta and the City Chamber Orchestra of Hong Kong. Opportunities to see big-name soloists and major orchestras abound throughout the year, especially during the Hong Kong Arts Festival. The Hong Kong International Piano Competition, with its star-studded jury, is held every three years in October/November. The Hong Kong Academy for Performing Arts (www.hkapa.edu) has free concerts almost daily.

Jazz

The best times to experience world-class jazz in the city are during the Hong Kong International Jazz Festival and the Hong Kong Arts Festival. Hong Kong also has a small but zealous circle of local musicians, including guitarist Eugene Pao, the first local jazz artist to sign with an international label, and pianist Ted Lo, who has played with Astrud Gilberto and Herbie Hancock.

Traditional Chinese

You won't hear much traditional Chinese music on the streets of Hong Kong, except perhaps the sound of the doleful *di-daa,* a clarinet-like instrument played in funeral processions; the hollow-sounding *gu* (drums) and crashing *luo* (gongs) and *bat* (cymbals) at lion dances; the *erhu,* a two-stringed fiddle favoured by beggars for its plaintive sound; or strains of Cantonese opera wafting from the radio of a minibus driver. You can sample this kind of music, albeit in a form adapted to a symphony-orchestra model, at concerts given by the Hong Kong Chinese Orchestra (www.hkco.org). For more authentic fare, catch a Chinese opera or check out the Temple Street Night Market, where street performers deliver operatic excerpts.

Canto-Pop

Hong Kong's home-grown popular-music scene is dominated by 'Canto-pop' – compositions that often blend western rock, pop and R & B with Chinese melodies and lyrics. Rarely radical, the songs invariably deal with such teenage concerns as unrequited love and loneliness; to many they sound like the American pop songs of the 1950s. The music is slick and eminently singable – thus the explosion of karaoke bars throughout the territory. Attending a Canto-pop concert is to see the city at its sweetest and most over the top, with screaming, silly dancing, day-glo wigs and enough floral tributes to set up a flower market.

Canto-pop scaled new heights from the mid-1980s to mid-1990s and turned singers such as Anita Mui, Leslie Cheung, Alan Tam, Priscilla Chan and Danny Chan into household names in Hong Kong and among Chinese communities around the world. The peak of this Canto-pop golden age came with the advent of the so-called Four Kings: thespian/singer Andy Lau, Mr Nice Guy Jacky Cheung, dancer-turned-crooner Aaron Kwok and teen heart-throb Leon Lai.

It never quite reached that altitude again. Subsequent arrivals such as Běijīng waif Faye Wong, Sammi Cheung, Kelly Chen and proto-hunk Nicholas Tse took their turns on the throne for a time. But today most stars are a packaged phenomenon. Singers from the mainland and Taiwan – singer-songwriter Jay Chou is one example – are competing with local stars and gaining new fans here, and the strongest influences on local music are now coming from Japan and Korea. There are also acts making their marks from the edge of the mainstream, such as Ellen

Antonio Mak's work employs much visual 'punning'. In his *Bible from Happy Valley* (1992), a racehorse is portrayed with a winglike book made of lead across its back. The word 'book' in Cantonese has the same sound as 'to lose (at gambling)'.

The Leisure and Cultural Services Department (www.lcsd.gov.hk) regularly stages free arts and entertainment shows at its venues throughout the territory.

Lo and Eman Lam, two 'urban folk' singer-songwriters, and My Little Airport, a dapper act whose irreverent multilingual lyrics are often speckled with cute Chinglish.

Theatre

Much, though not all, theatre in Hong Kong is western in form, if not content. Traditional Chinese theatre can still be experienced, but western theatre has been very influential. Most productions are staged in Cantonese, and a large number are new plays by Hong Kong writers. The fully professional Hong Kong Repertory Theatre (www.hkrep. com) and Chung Ying Theatre Company (www.chungying.com) put on Cantonese productions, very often with English titles. Theatre du Pif (www.thtdupif.com), formed by a professional Scottish-Chinese couple, puts on innovative works incorporating text, movement and visuals, in English and/or Cantonese. Hong Kong Players (www.hongkongplayers. com), consisting of expatriate amateurs, mounts classical and modern productions in English, while Zuni Icosahedron (www.zuni.org.hk) creates conceptual multimedia works known for their experimental format.

Among the more popular venues are the Fringe Club theatres in Central. The Hong Kong Cultural Centre, Hong Kong Academy for the Performing Arts, Hong Kong City Hall and the Hong Kong Arts Centre all host foreign productions, ranging from large-scale western musicals to minimalist Japanese theatre.

Chinese Opera

Chinese opera *(hei kuk)*, one of the three oldest dramatic art forms in the world, is a colourful, cacophonous spectacle featuring music, singing, martial arts, acrobatics and acting. Admittedly, it can take some getting used to. Female characters, whether played by men or women, sing in falsetto. The instrumental accompaniment often takes the form of drumming, gonging and other unmelodious punctuation. And the whole affair can last four to six hours. But the costumes are splendid and the plots are adapted from legends and historical tales with universal themes. If you happen to attend a performance by a leading Cantonese opera troupe such as Chor Fung Ming, you'll experience some of the best moments of Chinese opera.

Cantonese opera *(yuet-kek)* is a regional variety of Chinese opera that flourished in Hong Kong, particularly in the 1950s when opera virtuosi fleeing China composed and performed a spate of original works in the territory. But eventually the limelight shifted to the sleek, leather-clad kid on the block – cinema – and things have been going downhill for Cantonese opera ever since. It is still very popular with retirees, but younger fans are few and far between.

A shortage of performance venues has been a problem in the past, but theatre options are improving. Sunbeam Theatre in North Point and the restored Yau Ma Tei Theatre in Kowloon both promote Chinese opera, but more recently the Ko Shan Theatre in Hung Hom, Kowloon, has become a champion of local opera culture. Its new wing, opened in 2014, includes a 600-seater auditorium and busy weekly performances, and it's also home to a new Cantonese Opera Education & Information Centre, with a small exhibition, videos and costumes.

The best way to experience Cantonese opera is by attending a 'performance for the gods' *(sun kung hei)* in a temporary theatre. During major Chinese festivals, such as the Lunar New Year, Mid-Autumn Festival and Tin Hau Festival, rural communities invite troupes to perform. The performances usually take place on a makeshift stage

Liu Yichang (1918–2018), Hong Kong's most respected senior writer, was the author of the stream-of-consciousness novella *Tête-bêche* which inspired Wong Kar-wai's *In the Mood for Love*.

set up in a temple or a bamboo shed, and it is a jovial, laid-back event for the whole family that lasts several days. For a more formal experience, try the Hong Kong Arts Festival. At other times, you might stumble upon a performance at the Temple Street Night Market nearby. You can also check out the enlightening Cantonese-opera display at the Hong Kong Heritage Museum.

Other varieties of Chinese opera being performed in Hong Kong by local and/or visiting troupes include Peking opera, a highly refined form that uses almost no scenery but different kinds of traditional props; and Kun opera, the oldest form and one designated a Masterpiece of the Oral and Intangible Heritage of Humanity by Unesco.

A Xiqu Centre, a top-notch venue for the performance, production, education and research of Chinese traditional theatre, was due to open in the West Kowloon Cultural District at the time of press.

Renditions journal (www.cuhk.edu. hk/rct/ renditions/ index.html) has excellent info on Chinese literature published in English. Hong Kong University Press (www.hku-press.org) also publishes works by local Chinese writers.

Literature

Hong Kong has long suffered from the misconception that it does not have a literature of its own, but, in fact, the city has seen a thriving microclimate in the vast landscape of Chinese literature, where the same sun shining on other parts of China has spawned distinct smells, textures and voices.

From the 1920s to the 1940s, Hong Kong was a haven for Chinese writers on the run. These émigrés continued their writing here, their influence lasting until the 1970s when the first generation of writers born and/or raised locally came into their own. The relative creative freedom offered by the city has spawned works in a variety of genres and subjects, from prose poems to experimental novels, from swordplay romance to life as a make-up artist for the dead.

Hong Kong Collage: Contemporary Stories and Writing (ed Martha PY Cheung; 1998) is an important collection of fiction and essays by 15 local writers. *To Pierce the Material Screen: an Anthology of Twentieth Century Hong Kong Literature* (ed Eva Hung; 2008) is a two-volume anthology featuring established figures, younger names and emerging voices, and spans 75 years. In *From the Bluest Part of the Harbour: Poems from Hong Kong* (ed Andrew Parkin; 1996), 12 poets reveal the emotions of Hong Kong people in the run-up to 1997 (when Hong Kong returned to Chinese sovereignty). For critical articles on Hong Kong literature, check out the special Hong Kong issue (winter 2008) of the *Journal of Modern Literature in Chinese* (Lingnan University of Hong Kong).

The major literary festival in the city is the Hong Kong Literary Festival. *Cha* (www.asiancha.com), Hong Kong's home-grown literary journal, features poetry, prose and photography about Asia.

Cinema

Once known as the 'Hollywood of the Far East', Hong Kong was for decades the third-largest motion-picture industry in the world (after Mumbai and Hollywood) and the second-largest exporter. Now it produces a few dozen films each year, down from well over 200 in the early 1990s. Yet Hong Kong film continues to play an important role on the world cinema stage as it searches for a new identity in the greater China market.

Martial Arts

Hong Kong cinema became known to the west when a former child actor appeared as a sinewy hero in a kung fu film. But before Bruce Lee (1940–73) unleashed his high-pitched war cry in *The Big Boss* (1971), the kung fu genre was alive and kicking. The *Wong Fei-hung* series, featuring the adventures of a folk hero, has been named by the *Guinness Book of Records* as the longest-running cinema serial dedicated to one man, with roughly a hundred episodes made from 1949 to 1970 alone. The works of the signature directors of the period – Chang Cheh, whose macho aesthetics seduced Quentin Tarantino, and King Hu, who favoured a more refined style of combat – continue to influence films today.

The 1970s saw the start of another trend spearheaded by actor-director-screenwriter Michael Hui, who produced comedies satirising the realities and dreams of Hong Kong people. *Games Gamblers Play* (1974) was the highest grossing film of its time, even surpassing the movies of Bruce Lee.

Jackie Chan & Jet Li

The decade after Bruce Lee's death saw the leap to stardom of two martial artists: Jackie Chan and Jet Li. Chan's blend of slapstick and action, as seen in *Snake in the Eagle's Shadow* (1978), a collaboration with action choreographer Yuen Wo-ping (who choreographed the action on *Crouching Tiger, Hidden Dragon* and *The Matrix*), became an instant hit. He later added stunts to the formula, resulting in the hits *Police Story* and the *Rush Hour* series. Li garnered international acclaim when he teamed up with director Tsui Hark in *Once Upon a Time in China* (1991). Despite his reputation for tampering with a print just hours before its premiere, Tsui introduced sophisticated visuals and rhythmic editing into the martial-arts genre, most notably in Hong Kong's first special-effects extravaganza, *Zu: Warriors from the Magic Mountain* (1983). As a producer, he helped to create John Woo's gangster classic *A Better Tomorrow* (1986).

Contemporary Martial-Arts Films

Fast-forward to the 21st century, when a Bruce Lee craze briefly returned on the 35th anniversary of his death with the release of *Ip Man* (2008), a fawning semispeculative biopic of Lee's mentor. A sequel, *Ip Man 2* (2011), was more chop socky and less solemn, though the nationalist-hero treatment still applied, with a Sinophobic British pugilist in postwar Hong Kong replacing Japanese soldiers as the enemy. Also cashing in on Lee's revived legend is *Bruce Lee, My Brother* (2010), a coming-of-age comedy based on a published recollection of childhood memories that the master's siblings shared of their famous brother.

Once Upon a Time in China (1991) is the first of Tsui Hark's five-part epic that follows folk hero Wong Fei-hung (Jet Li) as he battles government officials, gangsters and foreign entrepreneurs to protect his martial-arts school in 19th-century China.

Similarly nostalgic is *Gallants* (2010), a retro comedy in which various kung fu stars of yesteryear pay a feisty homage to an old genre. The low-budget film won Best Picture at the 2011 Hong Kong Film Awards. *Ashes of Time Redux* (2008) is a shorter cut of Wong Kar-wai's haunting 'non-action action movie' of the same name from 1994.

New Wave

Tsui Hark belonged to the New Wave, a group of film-makers of the late 1970s and '80s who grew up in Hong Kong, and were trained at film schools overseas as well as in local TV. Their works had a more contemporary sensibility, unlike those of their émigré predecessors, and were more artistically adventurous.

Ann Hui, Asia's top female director, is a New Waver who has won awards both locally and overseas. *Song of the Exile* (1990), a tale about the marriage between a Japanese woman and a Chinese man just after the Sino-Japanese War, won Best Film at both the Asian Pacific Film Festival and the Rimini Film Festival in Italy.

International Acclaim

The 1990s saw Hong Kong gaining unprecedented respect on the global film-festival circuit. Besides Ann Hui, Wong Kar-wai received Best Director at the Cannes Film Festival for *Happy Together* in 1997. Auteur of the cult favourite *Chungking Express* (1994), Wong is famous almost as much for his elliptical mood pieces as for his disregard of shooting deadlines. In the same year, Fruit Chan bagged the Special Jury Prize at the Locarno International Film Festival with *Made in Hong Kong,* an edgy number shot on film stock Chan had scraped together while working on other projects.

Tough Times & New Direction

Due to changes in the market, in the 1990s the Hong Kong film industry sank into a gloom from which it has not recovered. The return to China also presented problems related to censorship and self-censorship. But there have been sunny patches too. *Infernal Affairs* (2002), directed by Andrew Lau and Alan Mak, made such an impact on its release that it was heralded as a box-office miracle, though it suffered some loss in translation in Martin Scorsese's remake, *The Departed. Election* (2005) and *Election 2* (2006), by master of Hong Kong noir Johnnie To, also enjoyed immense critical and box-office success.

The Warlords (2007), directed by Peter Chan, is a period war film about sworn brothers forced to betray one another by the realities of war – showing it's possible to please both Hong Kong and mainland audiences.

Echoes of the Rainbow (2010), a rather maudlin tale about the battling spirit of Hong Kong people in the turbulent 1960s, won a Crystal Bear at the Berlin Film Festival. Meanwhile, veteran thespian Deanie Ip won the Best Actress award at the Venice Film Festival for her role as a traditional housemaid in Ann Hui's *A Simple Life* (2011), an elegant drama about ageing and loneliness.

The past decade has also seen a string of big-budget Hong Kong–China collaborations, most notably the *Ip Man* series and *Bodyguards and Assassins* (2009), a story of anti-Qing intrigue set in 1905 Hong Kong. The trend of growing cooperation with the wealthy – and lucrative – Chinese market looks set to take hold as local film-makers seek new ways to finance their celluloid (or digital) fantasies.

That said, despite budgetary constraints, new directors' local films, like Wong Ka-yan (2015), Weeds on Fire (2016) and Trivisa (2016), managed to garner critical acclaim, signalling a brighter future for Hong Kong cinema. The low-budget directorial debut by Wong Chun, *Mad World* (2016), followed a man whose mental illness is exacerbated

HONG KONG IN FILM

Hong Kong has been the setting of many western-made films, including *Love is a Many-Splendored Thing* (1955), starring William Holden, and Jennifer Jones as his Eurasian doctor paramour, with great shots on and from Victoria Peak; *The World of Suzie Wong* (1960), with Holden again, and Nancy Kwan as the pouting bar girl from Wan Chai; and *The Man with the Golden Gun* (1974), with Roger Moore as James Bond, filmed partly in a Tsim Sha Tsui topless bar.

More recently, in *The Dark Knight* (2008), Christian Bale's Batman performed one of his trademark escapes from Two International Finance Centre (although a planned scene in which the superhero would drop from a plane into the harbour was axed after the film's producers found the water quality could pose a potential health danger). The Hong Kong skyline made a perfect backdrop for streetscape scenes from the future in *Ghost in the Shell* (2017); and Lara Croft's adventures in *Tomb Raider* (2018) take off in Aberdeen's harbour.

by Hong Kong's cramped living conditions. It won a slew of awards, including international acclaim at the Toronto International Film Festival, and was put up for Oscar consideration.

In 2016 Financial Secretary John Tsang also announced that an extra HK$20 million would be injected into the Film Development Fund to subsidise distribution and promotion of locally made Cantonese films.

Ten Years (2015), a dystopian indie film offering a vision of Hong Kong in 10 years' time with freedoms diminishing as the mainland authorities exert increasing influence, was voted Best Film at the Hong Kong Film Awards. As the film is banned on the mainland, it is believed that the triumph was due less to the film's artistic merit than to it being a statement that Hong Kong cinema will not bow to fear.

Film Festivals & Awards

The Hong Kong International Film Festival (www.hkiff.org.hk), now in its third decade, is the best in Asia and boasts a laudable if precarious balance of art-house choices and titles offering red-carpet opportunities. The Hong Kong Film Awards is also among the most respected in this part of the world. The Hong Kong Film Archive is a treasure trove of Hong Kong films and resources on them.

Architecture

Welcome to the most dazzling skyline in the world. We defy you not to be awed as you stand for the first time at the harbour's edge in Tsim Sha Tsui and see Hong Kong Island's majestic panorama of skyscrapers march up those steep, jungle-clad hills. This spectacle arises from the rapidity of construction in Hong Kong, where buildings are knocked down and replaced with taller, shinier versions almost while your back is turned. The scarcity of land, the strains of a growing population and the rapacity of developers – as well as the opportunism of the common speculator – drive this relentless cycle of destruction and construction.

Heritage Preservation

The government's lack of interest in preserving architecturally important buildings went almost entirely unregretted by most through the 20th century. The destruction of the iconic Star Ferry Terminal in Central marked a surprising reversal in public apathy. Heartfelt protests greeted the wrecking balls in late 2006, but to no avail.

However, in the wake of the protests, the government announced that the Streamline Moderne–style Wan Chai Market would be partially preserved (though a luxury apartment tower has risen over it).

Meanwhile the nearby Pawn, a flashy drinking hole converted from four old tenements and a century-old pawn shop, is a running sore with heritage activists who argue that the Urban Renewal Authority has short-changed the public by refusing to list the building's rooftop terrace as an unrestricted public space. Similarly, the former Marine Police Headquarters in Tsim Sha Tsui, now yet another hotel-cum-shopping centre, has disappointed many after the original landscape was razed.

Now attention has turned to the Central Market, a modernist style icon whose reinvigoration has been on the table for so long it's become a source of escalating public indignation. After delays of nearly 12 years, work on the site finally started in mid-2017. The Urban Renewal Authority has been tasked with redeveloping the site for affordable culture and retail, with a completion date of 2021/22 – locals are waiting with bated breath to find out what that realistically means.

There have been some bright spots, however, most notably when the government stopped the demolition of the magnificent King Yin Lei (1937), a private, Chinese Renaissance–style mansion on Stubbs Rd near Happy Valley. Even more significantly, the government launched in 2008 a scheme for the 'revitalisation' of historic monuments, which allows NGOs to pitch for the use of these buildings. The program has seen the restoration of the Old Tai O Police Station and the distinctive pre-WWII shophouse Lui Seng Chun.

PMQ in Sheung Wan, the Blue House cluster in Wan Chai and, most recently, Tai Kwun, the former Central Police Station complex, are three examples of visionary community-minded revitalisation projects that received major funding and are proving hugely successful. Then there's the Murray – a reimagining of 1960s government offices on Cotton Tree

---

Precolonial Buildings

....

Tsui Sing Lau Pagoda (Yuen Long)

....

Tang Ancestral Hall (Yuen Long)

....

Yu Kiu Ancestral Hall (Yuen Long)

....

Sam Tung Uk Museum (Tsuen Wan)

Drive as a luxury hotel, which opened to much fanfare in 2018 and has been hailed as an example of best practice in enhancing heritage buildings for the 21st century.

Despite these positive examples of heritage preservation, the reality remains that the imperatives of the property market, in the name of urban redevelopment, continue to dictate the city's future and its connection with the past. The deep, protracted uncertainty over the fate of the West Wing of the former Government Secretariat in Central – a fine model of understated elegance and a vital place of contact between the former colonial administration and the people – shows that no building in Hong Kong, no matter how valued its architectural and historical heritage, is truly safe from the bulldozers.

Traditional Chinese Architecture

About the only examples of 19th-century Chinese architecture left in urban Hong Kong are the popular Tin Hau temples, including those at Tin Hau near Causeway Bay, Aberdeen, Stanley and Yau Ma Tei. Museums in Chai Wan and Tsuen Wan have preserved a few 18th-century Hakka village structures. More substantial physical reminders of the past lie in the New Territories and the Outlying Islands, where walled villages, fortresses and even a 15th-century pagoda can still be seen.

When East-Met-West Architecture

Largely the preserve of the wealthy and the religious, fusion architecture has appeared in Hong Kong since the 1920s.

The abandoned Shek Lo Mansion in Fanling (1925) resembles a Kāipíng *diāolóu* (a fortified tower that blends Chinese and western architectural elements) across the border in Guăngdōng. The Anglican St Mary's Church is a somewhat-comical orientalist exercise from 1937 while a Tao Fung Shan Christian centre features Buddhist-inspired buildings designed by a Dane.

Tai Hang's Lin Fa Kung is a small Kwun Yam temple with a unique octagonal design and side entrances reminiscent of a medieval Catholic chapel.

Revitalised Heritage

Tai Kwun (Soho)
....
PMQ
(Sheung Wan)
....
Blue Mansion
(Wan Chai)
....
Lui Seng Chun
(Sham Shui Po)
....
Béthanie
(Pok Fu Lam)
....
Explosives Magazine
(Admiralty)
....
Mei Ho House Youth Hostel
(Sham Shui Po)

DISTINCTIVELY URBAN VISTAS

For thrill-seekers, a seemingly ordinary tram ride across the northern shore of Hong Kong Island often feels more like an impossible hurtle through an endless canyon of high-rises. Indeed, similar psycho-geography can be experienced in much of urban Hong Kong. While the bulk of the buildings here may be uninspired office and apartment blocks sprouting cheek by jowl throughout the territory, there are perverse spectacles to be found as various forms of the built environment routinely challenge conventional notions of scale and proportion to achieve their purpose.

A classic example is the tumbledown Oceanic Mansion (1010–30 King's Rd), a forbidding cliff of pulverised dwellings that soars above a tight, sloping bend in the shadows of a country park in Quarry Bay. Near the western end of the tramline in Kennedy Town, Hill Rd Flyover is a towering urban racetrack that lures traffic from the rarefied heights of Pok Fu Lam to the siren call of Central, *Blade Runner*–like; underneath it there's a miniscule urban public space with benches harbouring weary retirees.

The same sense of space or freedom can rarely be manufactured by the many luxury real-estate projects you will see in Hong Kong, however, even if they've been romantically given names such as Sorrento, Leguna Verde or Cullinan. Tiny living spaces remain the norm in this city. Those interested in the future of the city's urban landscape can visit the City Gallery.

Lippo Centre (p104), Admiralty

Colonial Architecture

Most of the colonial architecture left in the city is on Hong Kong Island, especially in Central, such as the Old Supreme Court Building (1912) and Government House, residence of all British governors from 1855 to 1997. In Sheung Wan there is Western Market (1906), and in the Mid-Levels the Edwardian-style Old Pathological Institute, now the Hong Kong Museum of Medical Sciences (1905). The Old Stanley Police Station (1859) and nearby Murray House (1848) are important colonial structures on the southern part of Hong Kong Island.

The interesting Hong Kong Antiquities & Monuments Office, located in a British schoolhouse that dates from 1902, has information and exhibits on current preservation efforts.

Modernism

Bank of China Tower and Old Bank of China Building (Central)

Lippo Centre (Admiralty)

International Finance Centre (Central)

HSBC Building (Central)

Hong Kong International Airport (Lantau)

Contemporary Architecture

Hong Kong's verticality was born out of necessity – the scarcity of land and the sloping terrain have always put property at a premium in this densely populated place. Some buildings, such as Central Plaza and International Commercial Centre, have seized height at all costs; a privileged few, such as the Hong Kong Convention & Exhibition Centre and the windowless Hong Kong Cultural Centre, have pulled off audacious moves to go horizontal. Internationally celebrated modern architecture in the city includes the HSBC Building in Central and the Hong Kong International Airport in Chep Lap Kok (opened in 1998) – both by English architect Norman Foster, in Late-Modern high-tech style – as well as IM Pei's soaring symphony of triangular geometry that is the Bank of China Tower.

Hong Kong Architecture 1945–2015: From Colonial to Global (2016), by Charlie Xue Qiuli, charts the city's reinvention as a vertical modern metropolis.

Religion & Belief

Hong Kong is arguably the only city in China where religious freedom is both provided for by the law and respected in practice. Almost everyone here is brought up on certain spiritual beliefs, even though these may not always add up to the profession of a religion. And most of the time, they don't – Hong Kongers are not a particularly religious bunch.

Early Influences

The city's early inhabitants were fishers and farmers who worshipped a mixed bag of deities – some folk, some Taoist, notably the Kitchen God, the Earth God, and the Goddess of the Sea (Tin Hau). Many sought divine protection by symbolically offering their children to deities for adoption. All villages have ancestral shrines. Traditional practices are alive in Hong Kong today, often colourfully intertwined with those of imported religions including Buddhism and Christianity.

Confucianism

For 2000 years the teachings of Confucius (551–479 BC) and the subsequent school of thought called Confucianism informed the familial system and all human relationships in imperial China. Yet in the revolutionary fervour of the 20th century, the philosophy that was the bedrock of Chinese civilisation was blamed for a host of evils from feudal oppression and misogyny to all-round backwardness.

Family Ethos

Traditionally, Confucian doctrines helped Chinese rulers to maintain domestic order. Emperors led by a 'mandate of heaven'; government positions were filled by top-scoring candidates on exams in the Confucian classics. For historical reasons, Confucianism in this institutionalised form never existed in Hong Kong. Yet Confucian values are at the core of familial and social relationships in the former British colony. Two pillars of Confucian thought are respect for knowledge and filial piety. Hong Kong parents attach huge importance to academic performance; youngsters are trained to work hard as well as to treat parents and teachers with courtesy. Many adults live with their folks (though this is related to the city's exorbitant rent); almost everyone is expected to provide for their parents, though whether they do or not is another matter.

Buddhism

Buddhism is Hong Kong's dominant religion. It was first introduced here in about the 5th century, when the monk Pui To set up a hermitage in the western New Territories. The area, a stop on the ancient route linking Persia, Arabia and India to Guǎngzhōu, is regarded as the birthplace of Buddhism in the territory.

Although a tiny fraction of the population is purely and devoutly Buddhist, about a million practise some form of the religion, and use

Some 80% of funeral rites in Hong Kong are presided over by Taoist priests. These are noisy affairs with cymbals and *suona* (a Chinese reed instrument). Some have elaborate rituals featuring props from coins to flaming swords that are meant to ensure the soul lets go of its worldly relationships.

A small Parsee community migrated to Hong Kong from Mumbai in the early colonial period. Despite their small number, the Parsees' influence has been great. At one time, three of the 13 board members of the Hong Kong & Shanghai Banking Corporation (HSBC) were Parsee. It was also a Parsee who founded the Star Ferry.

its funeral and exorcism rites. Generally speaking, the ritual of taking refuge in the Three Jewels (Buddha, Darma, Sangha) is regarded as the Buddhist initiation rite. Some followers abstain from meat on certain days of the month, others for longer periods. Very few are strict vegetarians.

Buddhist organisations here do not play an active political role, unlike some of their counterparts in Southeast Asia. They focus instead on providing palliative care and spiritual services. Every year on Remembrance Day (11 November), they hold a ceremony for the souls of the victims of the two World Wars and the Japanese invasion. Buddhist funerals are dignified affairs that can be quite elaborate, with some ceremonies lasting 49 days – the time it purportedly takes an average soul to find the conditions for its rebirth. Prayers are chanted every seven days to help the soul find rebirth in a higher realm ('happy human' versus 'cockroach', for instance). On the seventh day, souls are believed to revisit their homes. Everyone in the family stays in their room to avoid crossing paths with the loved one.

Taoism

Taoism is an indigenous Chinese religion more than 2000 years old. Though never declared a national faith, its presence is ubiquitous in most aspects of Chinese life. Unlike evangelical religions stressing crusading and personal conversion, Taoism simply offers its services, whether it's treatment for illness or protection from evil spirits, to everyone within its locale.

The Hong Kong horse-racing season, and all construction and filming projects, are preceded by Taoist rituals to appease the nature deities and ensure good feng shui. Necromancy, which strives for harmony between humanity and nature, is a practise influenced by Taoism.

During the first two weeks of the Lunar New Year, millions of all creeds and faiths pay their respects at Taoist temples. Taoist priests preside over the majority of funeral rites in Hong Kong. There are about 150 Taoist temples in Hong Kong and another one to two hundred that worship a combination of Taoist and folk deities.

There are about 300,000 Muslims of various nationalities in Hong Kong. The city's earliest Muslims were seamen who settled in the area around Lower Lascar Row (Cat St) in Central; the word Lascar means 'Indian sailor'. You can tour the beautiful mint-green Jamia Mosque in the Mid-Levels to learn more.

Christianity

Hong Kong's Christian community has more than 800,000 followers, with Protestants outnumbering Roman Catholics and having more young believers. About a third of the Catholics are Filipina domestic helpers. Most churches offer services in Cantonese and English, and some also in Tagalog.

Christianity has been in Hong Kong since the mid-19th century. In the early days, the Hong Kong Catholic Church provided support to the missionaries travelling to and from China, and served the Catholics in the British Army as well as Portuguese merchants and their families from Macau. In the ensuing decades, both Catholics and Protestants began working for the local community, founding schools, hospitals and welfare organsations. These services were, as they are now, open to followers and nonfollowers alike.

Survival Guide

Transport

GETTING THERE & AWAY

Hong Kong

Most international travellers arrive and depart via Hong Kong International Airport. Travellers to and from mainland China can use ferry, road or rail links to Guǎngdōng and points beyond. Hong Kong is also accessible from Macau via ferry or helicopter.

More than 100 airlines operate between Hong Kong International Airport and some 190 destinations around the world. Flights include from New York (16 hours), Los Angeles (14 hours), Sydney (9½ hours), London (13 hours) and Běijīng (3½ hours).

There are regular buses connecting Hong Kong with major destinations in neighbouring Guǎngdōng province. Regular trains run to Guǎngzhōu (two hours), Běijīng (24 hours) and Shànghǎi (19 hours). Visas (p276) are required to cross the border to the mainland.

Frequent scheduled ferries link the China Ferry Terminal in Kowloon and/or the Hong Kong–Macau Ferry Terminal on Hong Kong Island with a string of towns and cities on the Pearl River Delta, including Macau. Trips to Macau on the high-speed ferries take one hour.

High-speed trains began operation from Kowloon West Railway Station to Shēnzhèn and Guǎngzhōu in September 2018.

Flights, cars and tours can be booked online at lonely planet.com.

Hong Kong International Airport

Designed by British architect Sir Norman Foster, the **Hong Kong International Airport** (HKG; Map p184; ☑852 2181 8888; www.hkairport. com) is on Chek Lap Kok, a largely reclaimed area off Lantau's northern coast. Highways, bridges (including the 2.2km-long Tsing Ma Bridge, one of the world's longest suspension bridges) and a fast train link the airport with Kowloon and Hong Kong Island.

The two terminals have a wide range of shops, restaurants, cafes, ATMs and money changers including:

China Travel Service (CTS; 中國旅行社; Zhōngguó Lǚxíngshè; ☑customer service 852 2998 7888, tour hotline 852 2998 7333; www.ctshk. com) Has a counter at Arrivals Hall A in Terminal 1 and can organise China visas (normally takes two to five working days).

Hong Kong Hotels Association (香港酒店業協會; HKHA; Map p184;☑852 2769 8822, 852 2383 8380; www.hkha. org; Hong Kong International Airport; ⊙7am-midnight) Counters are located inside the Buffer Halls. HKHA deals with midrange and top-end hotels only and does not handle hostels, guesthouses or other budget accommodation.

There are flights between Hong Kong and around 50 cities in mainland China, including Běijīng, Chéngdū, Kūnmíng and Shànghǎi. One-way fares are a bit more than half the return price. Hong Kong is the hub city for Cathay Pacific (www.cathay pacific.com), a five-star airline. Other carriers include the following:

Air China (www.airchina.hk) The national carrier, based in Běijīng.

Cathay Dragon (www.cathay pacific.com) Owned by Cathay Pacific, Cathay Dragon was previously known as 'Dragonair'; its flight schedules have been amalgamated into the main website. It specialises in regional flights to mainland China.

Hong Kong Airlines (www. hongkongairlines.com) Cheaper airline covering nearly 40 destinations in Asia Pacific and North America.

AIRPORT EXPRESS
The **Airport Express line** (☑852 2881 8888; www.mtr. com.hk; 1-way Central/Kowloon/ Tsing Yi HK$110/100/65; ⊙every 10 min, 5.50am-1.15am) is the fastest (and most expensive, other than a taxi) way to get to and from the airport.

The trains have plug sockets and free wi-fi.

Departures From 5.54am to 12.48am heading to Central, calling at Tsing Yi island and then Kowloon en route to the city; the full trip takes 24 minutes. Tickets are available from vending machines at the airport and train stations.

Fares There is a marginal saving if you book a return rather than single; one-way is also HK$5 cheaper if you use an Octopus card. Return fares for Central/Kowloon/Tsing Yi, valid for a month, cost HK$205/185/120. Children three to 11 years pay half-price. An Airport Express Travel Pass allows three days of mostly unlimited travel on the MTR and Light Rail and one-way/return trips on the Airport Express (HK$250/350).

Shuttle buses Airport Express also operates shuttle buses on Hong Kong Island (H1 to H4) and in Kowloon (K1 to K5), with free transfers for passengers between Central and Kowloon stations and major hotels. The buses run every 15 to 20 minutes between 6.12am and 11.12pm. Schedules and routes are available at www.mtr.com.hk/en/customer/services/complom_free_bus.html.

AsiaWorld-Expo The Airport Express is the same train that deposits visitors at the AsiaWorld-Expo venue; a two-minute journey in the opposite direction to the city centre.

BUS
There are good bus links to/from the airport. These buses have plenty of room for luggage, and announcements are usually made in English, Cantonese and Mandarin notifying passengers of hotels at each stop. For more details on the routes, check the Transport section at www.hkairport.com.

Departures Buses run every 10 to 30 minutes from about 6am to around midnight. Airport buses use the designation 'A' ahead of their route number. There are also quite a few night buses (designated 'N').

Fares Major hotel and guesthouse areas on Hong Kong Island are served by the A11 (HK$40) and A12 (HK$45) buses; the A21 (HK$33) covers similar areas in Kowloon. Bus drivers in Hong Kong do not give change, but it is available at the ground transportation centre at the airport, as are Octopus cards. Normal returns are double the one-way fare. Unless otherwise stated, children aged between three and 11 years and seniors over 65 pay half-fare.

Tickets Buy your ticket at the booth near the airport bus stand.

Mainland China
BUS
The Hong Kong–Zhūhǎi–Macau Bridge opened in 2018. From the Hong Kong port area, a 24-hour licensed shuttle-bus service operates daily to both Macau

and Zhūhǎi, with departures every five to 15 minutes. A one-way daytime trip costs HK$65 and HK$70 at night. Bus services A11, A21, A22, A29, A31, A33X, A35, A36 and A41 have been extended from the airport to reach the port area and shuttle pick-up.

CTS Express Coach (Map p298; ☑852 2365 0118; http://ctsbus.hkcts.com) Buses to mainland China.

Eternal East Cross Border Coach (Map p314; ☑852 3760 0888, 852 3412 6677; www.eebus.com; 13th fl, Kai Seng Commercial Centre, 4-6 Hankow Rd, Tsim Sha Tsui; ☺7am-8pm) Mainland destinations from Hong Kong include Shēnzhèn, Guǎngzhōu and other Guǎngdōng cities.

FERRIES
Regular scheduled ferries link the China Ferry Terminal in Kowloon and/or the Hong Kong–Macau Ferry Terminal in Sheung Wan on Hong Kong Island with a string of towns and cities on the Pearl River Delta – but not central Guǎngzhōu or Shēnzhèn.

Mainland destinations from Hong Kong include the following:

Shékǒu One hour

Shùndé Two hours

Zhōngshān 1½ hours

Zhūhǎi 70 minutes

SkyPier is a fast ferry service that links Hong Kong airport with nine Pearl River Delta

---

CLIMATE CHANGE & TRAVEL
Every form of transport that relies on carbon-based fuel generates CO_2, the main cause of human-induced climate change. Modern travel is dependent on aeroplanes, which might use less fuel per kilometre per person than most cars but travel much greater distances. The altitude at which aircraft emit gases (including CO_2) and particles also contributes to their climate change impact. Many websites offer 'carbon calculators' that allow people to estimate the carbon emissions generated by their journey and, for those who wish to do so, to offset the impact of the greenhouse gases emitted with contributions to portfolios of climate-friendly initiatives throughout the world. Lonely Planet offsets the carbon footprint of all staff and author travel.

ports including Shēnzhèn, Guǎngzhōu and Macau. The service enables travellers to board ferries directly without clearing Hong Kong customs and immigration. Book a ticket prior to boarding from the ticketing counter located at Transfer Area E2 at least 60 minutes before ferry departure time. For more information, see the 'Mainland Connections' tab under Transport on the airport website (www.hongkong airport.com).

TRAIN

The Kowloon West high-speed rail terminus opened in September 2018. Costing HK$9 billion, the terminus comprises joint immigration and customs for travel to mainland China and is partly governed by mainland laws. Built to hook up to mainland China's high-speed rail infrastructure, it has roughly halved the time it takes to reach Guǎngzhōu, to 48 minutes, and makes Shēnzhèn accessible in just 14 minutes. You can also catch direct high-speed trains from here to Běijīng (nine hours) and Shànghǎi (seven hours). Tickets can be booked on the MTR website (www.high speed.mtr.com.hk).

Nonbullet intercity trains to Guǎngzhōu and the rest of Guǎngdōng province and further afield leave from Hung Hom station.

Intercity train tickets can be purchased at the Intercity Through Train Customer Service Centre in Hung Hom Station, and ticket offices at Mong Kok East, Kowloon Tong and Shatin MTR stations, plus the Tourist Services counter at Admiralty MTR station. Sales open 30 days in advance for the Guǎngzhōu line and 60 days in advance for Běijīng and Shànghǎi.

Běijīng & Shànghǎi
➡ High-speed trains to Běijīng West railway station (2nd class/1st class/business HK$1223/1958/3826) depart at 8.05am, arriving at 5.01pm the same day.

➡ High-speed trains to Shànghǎi Hóngqiáo railway station (2nd class/1st class/business HK$1144/1869/3563) depart at 11.10am, arriving at 7.27pm the same day.

➡ MTR intercity trains run between Hung Hom and both Shànghǎi and Běijīng, departing on alternative days.

Guǎngzhōu
➡ Dozens of the new high-speed trains per day leave from West Kowloon rail terminus for Guǎngzhōu South station; you pass through mainland border and customs control before departure.

➡ One-way 2nd-class tickets cost HK$244.

➡ Slower MTR intercity trains leave Hung Hom station for Guǎngzhōu East train station; the trip takes approximately two hours.

➡ One-way tickets cost HK$210/105 for adult/child aged five to nine.

Shēnzhèn
➡ Dozens of the new high-speed trains per day leave from West Kowloon rail terminus calling at Shēnzhèn's Fútián and North stations; you pass through mainland border and customs control before departure.

➡ The first high-speed train to Shēnzhèn departs West Kowloon at 7am, the last at 10.50pm.

➡ One-way 2nd-class tickets cost HK$85.

➡ There are also two foot-border crossings for Shēnzhèn, at Lo Wu and Lok Ma Chau, both of which have their own station on the MTR East Rail line, 200m from the mainland border.

➡ The MTR's Tourist Cross-Boundary Travel Pass (1/2 consecutive days HK$100/140) allows unlimited travel on the MTR and two single journeys to/from Lo Wu or Lok Ma Chau stations.

➡ The first MTR train to Lo Wu/Lok Ma Chau leaves Hung Hom station at 5.30am/5.35am, the last at 11.07pm/9.35pm, and the trip takes about 45/49 minutes.

LEFT LUGGAGE

MTR train and ferry Left-baggage services are in major stations, including Hung Hom station, Kowloon station and Hong Kong station; the West Tower of Shun Tak Centre in Sheung Wan, from where the Macau ferry departs; and the China ferry terminal in Tsim Sha Tsui. Some services charge per locker (HK$20 to HK$30 per hour, depending on size) but others can be per item (HK$69 per item for 24 hours at Hong Kong Station, for example).

Airport The Hong Kong International Airport provides a **left baggage service** (Map p184; ☑852 2261 0110; www.hongkongairport.com/eng/passenger/arrival/t1/baggage/left-baggage.html; Level 3, Terminal 2, Hong Kong International Airport; per hour/day HK$12/140; ⊗5.30am-1.30am).

Accommodation Most hotels, guesthouses and hostels have left-luggage rooms and will store your bags after checkout if you have a late flight. Some will also store luggage for longer periods, but may charge.

➡ The border crossing at Lo Wu opens at 6.30am and closes at midnight. The crossing at Lok Ma Chau is open around the clock.

➡ Lo Wu is the main checkpoint for foot passengers and tourists. Queues can be bad at both checkpoints during peak times.

Macau

Most travellers arrive in Macau by ferry from Hong Kong. If you are coming from mainland China, you can take the ferry or a bus from Guǎngdōng, or fly from select cities in mainland China.

Macau International Airport is connected to a number of destinations in Asia. If you are coming from outside Asia and destined for Macau, your best option is to fly to Hong Kong International Airport and take a ferry to Macau without going through Hong Kong customs.

Bus

Macau is an easy gateway by land into mainland China. Simply take bus 3A, 27, AP1 to the **Border Gate** (關閘; Portas do Cerco; ☉6am-1am) and walk across. A second – and much less busy crossing – is the **Cotai Frontier Post** (路氹邊檢大樓; ☉24 hrs) on the causeway linking Taipa and Coloane, which allows visitors to cross the Lotus Flower Bridge by shuttle bus (MOP$5) to Héngqín in Zhūhǎi. Buses 15 (6am or 6.45am to 7pm or 8pm, every 30 or 35 minutes, from MOP$2.80) and 50 (MOP$2.80–MOP$10) will drop you off at the crossing.

If you want to travel further afield in China, buses run by **Kee Kwan Motor Road Co** (歧關車路有限公司; ☎853 2888 1228; ☉9am-9.30pm) leave the bus station at the Border Gate. Buses for different locations in Guǎngzhōu (about MOP$90, 3½ hours) depart every 15 minutes or so, and for Zhōngshān (MOP$33, one hour) every

20 minutes. There are buses to Guǎngzhōu (MOP$175, four hours) from Macau International Airport.

In 2018 the long-anticipated Hong Kong–Zhūhǎi–Macau Bridge opened to traffic, reducing transit times and costs for getting around the Pearl River Delta. A 24-hour licensed shuttle-bus service (HK$65, every five to 15 minutes) operates daily to Hong Kong port, where you can pick up local buses to the airport and city.

Ferry

Ferry and catamaran tickets can be booked in advance at the ferry terminals, through travel agencies or online. You can also buy tickets on the spot, though advance booking is recommended if you travel on weekends or public holidays, as tickets are often in high demand. There is a standby queue at the pier for passengers wanting to travel before their ticketed sailing. You need to arrive at the pier at least 15 minutes before departure, but you should allow 30 minutes because of occasional long queues at immigration.

You are limited to 10kg of carry-on luggage in economy class, but oversized or overweight bags can be checked in.

TO/FROM HONG KONG

The vast majority of travellers make their way from Hong Kong to Macau by ferry. The journey takes just an hour and there are frequent departures throughout the day, with reduced service between midnight and 7am.

Most ferries depart from the Hong Kong–Macau Ferry Terminal on Hong Kong Island or the China Ferry Terminal in Kowloon, and arrive at the **Macau Maritime Ferry Terminal** (澳門外港客運碼頭, Terminal Marítimo de Passageiros do Porto Exterior) in the outer harbour or the Taipa Ferry Terminal.

TurboJet (噴射飛航; ☑Hong Kong enquiry 852 2859 3333, Macau 853 2855 5025, toll-free mainland China & Taiwan 00800 3628 3628; www. turbojet.com.hk; Macau Ferry Terminal; economy/superclass Mon-Fri MOP$153/315, Sat & Sun MOP$166/337, night crossing MOP$189/358) has regular departures from the Hong Kong–Macau Ferry Terminal (every 15 minutes) and the China Ferry Terminal (every 30 minutes to 1½ hours) to Macau from 7am to midnight, and less frequent service after midnight. Fares for economy/ superclass are HK$171/346; it costs about 10% more on weekends and 20% more for the night service (12.30am to 6am).

CotaiJet (金光飛航; ☑853 2885 0595; www. cotaiwaterjet.com/index.html; Taipa Ferry Terminal, Estrada de Pac On, Taipa; weekdays to Hong Kong regular/1st class MOP$160/282, weekend MOP$175/299, evenings MOP$200/327; ☑26, N2, 36) has high-speed catamarans connecting the Hong Kong–Macau Ferry Terminal and the **Taipa Ferry Terminal** (氹仔客運碼頭, Terminal Marítimo de Passageiros da Taipa; Estrada de Pac On, Taipa; ☑26, N2, 36) every 15 minutes between 7am and midnight. Fares for Cotai class/Cotai 1st are HK$171/293; it costs about 10% more on weekends and 20% more for night service after 6pm. Free shuttles at the ferry terminal in Taipa will take you to destinations along the Cotai Strip.

TO/FROM MAINLAND CHINA

TurboJet has 11 departures from the Macau Maritime Ferry Terminal daily to the port of Shékǒu (economy/ super class MOP$257/412, 60 minutes) in Shēnzhèn. Eleven ferries return from Shékǒu between 8am and 6.45pm. TurboJet also has four departures to Shēnzhèn airport (MOP$252/437, one hour) from 10.30am to

6pm, and two departures to Nánshā in Guǎngzhōu (MOP$185/288, one hour) at 11.45am and 3.50pm.

Yuet Tung Shipping Co (粵通船務有限公司; Map p208; ☑853 2833 1067, 853 2885 0272; www.ytmacau. com; Point 11A Inner Harbour, Inner Harbour Ferry Terminal) has ferries connecting Macau (Taipa Ferry Terminal) with Shékǒu (MOP$238, 1½ hours, six daily), departing between 8.30am and 8:30pm.

GETTING AROUND

Hong Kong

Bicycle

Cycling in urbanised Kowloon or Hong Kong Island would be suicide, but in the quiet areas of the islands (including southern Hong Kong Island) and the New Territories, a bike can be a lovely way to get around. It's more recreational than a form of transport, though – the hilly terrain will slow you down (unless you're mountain biking). Be advised that shops and kiosks renting out bicycles tend to run out early on weekends if the weather is good.

Boat

Despite Hong Kong's comprehensive road and rail public-transport system, the territory still relies very much on ferries to get across the harbour and to reach the Outlying Islands. The cross-harbour Star Ferry services are faster and cheaper than buses and the MTR. They're also great fun and afford stunning views. While Lantau can be reached by MTR and bus, for the other Outlying Islands ferries remain the only game in town. Ferries to Kowloon and the Outlying Islands depart from Central Piers 1 to 7.

STAR FERRY

➜ There are two **Star Ferry** (天星小輪; Map p298; ☑852 2367 7065; www.starferry. com.hk; Pier 7, Central; adult HK$2.20-3.70, child HK$1.50-2.20; ☺every 6-12min, 6.30am-11.30pm; ⓜHong Kong, exit A2) routes, but by far the most popular is the one running between Central (Pier 7) and Tsim Sha Tsui. The other links Wan Chai with Tsim Sha Tsui.

➜ There are two ticket types: upper deck (slightly more expensive) and lower deck. Fares are nominally higher on weekends and public holidays.

➜ Buy a ticket at one of the payment kiosks or use an Octopus card (most convenient).

OUTLYING ISLANDS FERRIES

➜ Regular ferry services link the main Outlying Islands to Hong Kong.

➜ Fares are reasonable, nominally higher on weekends and public holidays, and the ferries are comfortable and usually air-conditioned.

➜ The boats have toilets, and some have a basic bar that serves snacks and cold drinks.

➜ The ferries can get very crowded on Saturday afternoon and all day Sunday, especially in the warmer months.

FERRY SERVICES

Ferries to the Outlying Islands depart from the Central Piers. The nearest MTR station is Hong Kong; follow the elevated walkway east out of the IFC Mall (MTR exit A1 or A2) and then due north to reach the piers (follow signs for the Star Ferry). Tickets can be bought on the day from kiosks at the entrance to each pier.

Cheung Chau Ferries run every half-hour from Pier 5. One-way fares start from HK$13.60; tickets for the fast ferry cost about 50% more.

Discovery Bay Ferries depart from Pier 3 every half-hour around the clock (less frequent after midnight). One-way fares start from HK$46; the trip takes 25 minutes. On Saturdays and Sundays, four ferries a day go from here to Disneyland Resort.

Lamma Ferries depart from Pier 4 to Lamma Island's main town of Yung Shue Wan every half-hour to an hour until around 11.30pm. Some departures head to the smaller town of Sok Kwu Wan. One-way fares start from HK$17.80.

Lantau and Peng Chau Ferries depart from Pier 6, heading to the Lantau village of Mui Wo (every 20 to 50 minutes) or the nearby small island of Peng Chau (every 30 to 40 minutes). One-way fares for either destination start at HK$15.90.

Bus

Hong Kong's extensive bus system will take you just about anywhere in the territory, but it's not always easy to follow. Since Kowloon and the northern side of Hong Kong Island are so well served by the MTR, most visitors use the buses primarily to explore the southern side of Hong Kong Island, the New Territories and Lantau Island.

Departures Most buses run from 5.30am or 6am until midnight or 12.30am. There are a small number of night buses that run from 12.45am to 5am or later, designated with the letter 'N'.

Fares Bus fares cost HK$4 to HK$46, depending on the destination. Fares for night buses cost from HK$7 to HK$32. You will need exact change or an Octopus card.

Bus stations On Hong Kong Island the most important bus stations are the terminus in Central underneath Exchange Sq and the one on Queensway at Admiralty. From these sta-

NEED TO KNOW

Top Tips

→ Use the tram or walk if your destination is one MTR station away.

→ Download the app for the MTR system before you leave home.

→ If short of time, combine the MTR with taxis for destinations that are some walking distance from the MTR station.

→ Carry the business card from your hotel with its name in Chinese characters so you can show your taxi driver; many do not speak English.

When to Travel

→ Avoid rush hours (7.30am to 9.30am and 5pm to 7pm), when the MTR's interchange stations (Central, Admiralty, Tsim Sha Tsui and Kowloon Tong) are jam-packed.

→ Vehicular traffic on major roads and the cross-harbour tunnels can also be painfully slow during peak hours.

Travel at Night

Hong Kong's night buses, running every half-hour or so, cover most of the city. Their numbers are prefixed with the letter 'N'. But while they're comfortable and safe, sometimes it's worth taking a taxi as they are inexpensive and get you to bed more quickly.

How to Hail a Taxi

→ Look for a stationary or approaching cab with a lit 'For Hire' sign.

→ When the car is approaching, stand in a prominent place on the side of the road and stick out your arm. Drivers should pull over when they see you.

→ Taxis do not stop if there are double yellow lines on the side of the road, or at bus stops.

Etiquette

→ Have your ticket or Octopus card ready before you go through the barrier in the MTR station. Or feel the impatience at your back if you slow down the human traffic by three seconds.

→ Stand on the right side of the escalator or risk being asked to move aside by commuters in a hurry – plenty in Hong Kong.

→ Drinking and eating on MTR, trams and buses is not allowed.

→ Let passengers disembark first before entering the MTR carriage. The train won't leave the station until all doors are properly closed.

→ Priority seats are clearly marked on buses and the MTR.

→ Hong Kongers are not very good at giving up their seats to pregnant women and the elderly.

---

tions you can catch buses to Aberdeen, Repulse Bay, Stanley and other destinations on the southern side of Hong Kong Island. In Kowloon the Star Ferry bus terminal has buses heading up Nathan Rd and to the Hung Hom train station.

Route information Figuring out which bus you want can be difficult. Citybus (www.nwstbus.com.hk) and New World First

Bus, owned by the same company, plus Kowloon Motor Bus (www.kmb.hk) provide user-friendly route searches on their websites. KMB also has a route app for smartphones.

Lantau Most parts of Lantau Island are served by New Lantao Bus (www.newlantaobus.com). Major bus stations are located in Mui Wo ferry terminal and Tung Chung MTR station.

Car & Motorcycle

Hong Kong's maze of one-way streets and dizzying expressways isn't for the faint-hearted. Traffic is heavy and finding a parking space is difficult and very expensive. If you are determined to see Hong Kong under your own steam, do yourself a favour and rent a car with a driver.

Road rules Vehicles drive on the left-hand side of the road

HAILING A CROSS-HARBOUR TAXI

Hailing a cross-harbour taxi can be a frustrating task. There are three main ways to snag one:

➜ Look for a taxi with its lights on, but its 'Out of Service' sign up. This generally means the taxi is looking for a cross-harbour fare.

➜ Find a (rare) cross-harbour taxi stand.

➜ Hail a cab with a sort of 'walk like an Egyptian' gesture, snaking your arm as if in imitation of a wave. Taxis potentially interested in cross-harbour fares will stop to negotiate.

in Hong Kong, as in the UK, Australia and Macau, but *not* in mainland China. Seatbelts must be worn by the driver and all passengers, in both the front and back seats. Police are strict and give out traffic tickets at the drop of a hat.

Driving licence Hong Kong allows most foreigners over the age of 18 to drive for up to 12 months with a valid licence from home. It's still a good idea to carry an International Driving Permit (IDP) as well. Car-rental firms accept IDPs or driving licences from your home country. Drivers must usually be at least 25 years of age.

Minibus

Minibuses are vans with no more than 19 seats. They come in two varieties: red and green.

Green minibuses (HK$4 to HK$24) Cream-coloured with a green roof or stripe; they make designated stops and operate fixed fares, much like regular buses. You must put the exact fare in the cash box when you get in or you can use your Octopus card. Two useful routes are the 6 (HK$6.60) from Hankow Rd in Tsim Sha Tsui to Tsim Sha Tsui East and Hung Hom station in Kowloon, and the 1 (HK$10.20) to Victoria Peak from next to Hong Kong station. There's a good directory of routes, costs and frequencies at www.16seats.net.

Red minibuses Cream-coloured with a red roof or stripe, they pick up and discharge passengers wherever they are hailed or asked to stop along fixed routes. Information such as the destination and price are only displayed in Chinese.

MTR

The Mass Transit Railway is the name for Hong Kong's rail system comprising underground, overland and Light Rail (slower tram-style) services. Universally known as the 'MTR', it is clean, fast and safe, and transports around four million people daily.

It costs only slightly more than bus travel (fares HK$4 to HK$25), and is the quickest way to get to most destinations in Hong Kong. Routes, timetables and fares can be found at www.mtr.com.hk.

TRAINS

There are around 90 stations on nine underground and overland lines, and a Light Rail network that covers the northwest New Territories. Smoking, eating and drinking are not permitted in MTR stations or on the trains, and violators are subject to a fine of HK$5000.

Departures Trains run every two to 14 minutes from around 6am to sometime between midnight and 1am.

Exits MTR exit signs use an alphanumerical system and there can be as many as a dozen to choose from. There are easy-to-

navigate maps of the local area in each ticket hall; use them to decipher which exit will serve you best.

Fares Tickets are extremely cheap compared with those in many other world cities: between HK$5 and HK$30, though fares to stations bordering mainland China (Lo Wu and Lok Ma Chau) cost up to HK$53.50. Children aged between three and 11 years and seniors over 65 pay half-fare. Ticket machines accept notes and coins and dispense change.

Tickets Once you've passed through the turnstile to begin a journey you have 90 minutes to complete it before the ticket becomes invalid. If you have underpaid (by mistake or otherwise), you can make up the difference at an MTR service counter next to the turnstiles.

Peak hours If possible, it's best to avoid the rush hours: 7.30am to 9.30am and 5pm to 7pm weekdays.

LIGHT RAIL LINES

The MTR's Light Rail system is rather like a modern, air-conditioned version of the trams in Hong Kong, but it's much faster. It runs in the northwest New Territories.

Departures Operates from about 5.30am to between 12.15am and 1am. Trams run every four to 12 minutes, depending on the line and time of day.

Fares HK$5.50 to HK$7.50, depending on the number of zones (from one to five) travelled; children and seniors over 65 pay from HK$2.50 to HK$4.

Tickets You can buy single-journey tickets from vending machines on the platforms, valid for 120 minutes. There are no gates or turnstiles and customers are trusted to validate their ticket or Octopus card when they board and exit – make sure you tap on the right processor (entry or exit) because you could get charged twice if you tap on 'entry' at the end of your journey.

TICKETS & PASSES
Octopus card (www.octopus cards.com) A rechargeable smartcard valid on the MTR and most forms of public transport. The card costs HK$150 (HK$70 for children and seniors), which includes a HK$50 refundable deposit (minus a HK$9 handling fee if returned within 90 days) and HK$100 worth of travel. Octopus fares are about 5% cheaper than ordinary fares on the MTR. You can buy one and recharge at any MTR station; the minimum rechargeable amount is HK$50. Exact change is required to travel on buses and trams so Octopus is the most convenient way to pay.

Airport Express Travel Pass (one way/return HK$250/350) As well as travel to/from the airport, it allows three consecutive days of mostly unlimited travel on the MTR, Light Rail and MTR Bus.

MTR Tourist Day Pass (adult/child three to 11 years

HK$65/30) Valid on the MTR for 24 hours after the first use.

Taxi
Hong Kong taxis are a bargain compared with those in other world-class cities. With more than 18,000 cruising the streets of the territory, they're easy to flag down, except during rush hour, when it rains or during the driver shift-change period (around 4pm daily). Taxi drivers in Hong Kong always use their meter.

Taxis are colour-coded:

Red with silver roofs Urban taxis – those in Kowloon and on Hong Kong Island. Can go anywhere except Lantau.

Green with white tops New Territories taxis.

Blue Lantau taxis.

You need to take a red taxi in the New Territories if your destination is in Hong Kong, Kowloon or the city centres of the new towns in New Territories.

Availability When a taxi is available, there should be a red 'For Hire' sign illuminated on the meter that's visible through the windscreen. At night the 'Taxi' sign on the roof will be lit up as well. Taxis will not stop at bus stops or in restricted zones where a yellow line is painted next to the kerb.

Extra fees There is a luggage fee of HK$6 per bag, but (depending on the size) not all drivers insist on this payment. Wheelchairs are free. There are no extra late-night charges and no extra passenger charges.

Passengers must pay the toll if a taxi goes through the many Hong Kong harbour or mountain tunnels or uses the Lantau Link to Tung Chung or the airport. Though the Cross-Harbour Tunnel costs only HK$10, you'll have to pay HK$20 if, say, you take a Hong Kong taxi from Hong Kong Island to Kowloon. If you manage to find a Kowloon taxi returning 'home', you'll pay only HK$10. (It works the other way round as well, of course.) Taxi bookings made by phone cost HK$5 extra.

Language Some taxi drivers speak English well; others don't know a word of English. It's never a bad idea to have your destination written down in Chinese. Some hotels provide cards to give to taxi drivers with the hotel name (and often some popular tourist destinations) written in Chinese.

Lost property If you leave something behind in a taxi, call the Road Co-op Lost & Found hotline (852 2385 8288); most drivers turn in lost property.

Paying Try to carry smaller bills and coins; most drivers are hesitant to make change for HK$500.

Seatbelts The law requires that everyone in a vehicle wears a seatbelt. Both driver and passenger(s) will be fined if stopped by the police and not wearing a seatbelt.

Tipping You can tip up to 10%, but most Hong Kong people just leave the little brown coins and a dollar or two.

TAXI FARES

TYPE OF TAXI	FIRST 2KM (HK$)	EVERY ADDITIONAL 200M & MINUTE OF WAITING
Urban taxi (red)	24	HK$1.70 (HK$1.20 if fare exceeds HK$83.50)
New Territories taxi (green)	20.50	HK$1.50 (HK$1.20 if fare exceeds HK$65.50)
Lantau taxi (blue)	19	HK$1.50 (HK$1.50 if fare exceeds HK$154)

Tram

Hong Kong's venerable old trams are tall, narrow double-deckers. They are slow, but they're cheap and a great way to explore the city above ground level. Try to get a seat at the front window on the upper deck for a first-class view while rattling through the crowded streets.

➡ The flat fare is HK$2.60 for adults, HK$1.30 for kids. Drop your coins (exact change only) into the box beside the driver, or use the Octopus touch pad.

➡ Use the turnstiles at the back of the trams to get on; pay at the front when you disembark.

➡ The route is very simple, moving along one set of tracks that runs along the northern coast of Hong Kong Island (with a couple of minor offshoots), from Kennedy Town in the west to Shau Kei Wan in the east.

➡ Hong Kong Tramways also offers an hour-long **Tram-Oramic Tour** (☑852 2548 7102; www.hktramways.com; adult/child HK95/65), which lets you experience the city on an open-top, 1920s-style tram with an audio guide.

PEAK TRAM

The **Peak Tram** (Map p298; ☑852 2522 0922; www.thepeak. com.hk; Lower Terminus, 33 Garden Rd, Central; 1-way/ return adult HK$37/52, child 3-11yr & seniors over 65yr HK$14/23; ◷7am-midnight; Ⓜ Central, exit J2) is not really a tram but a cable-hauled funicular railway that has been scaling the 396m ascent to the highest point on Hong Kong Island since 1888. It is

thus the oldest form of public transport in the territory. It's such a steep ride that the floor is angled to help standing passengers stay upright.

➡ Avoid going on Sunday and public holidays when there are usually long queues. Octopus cards can be used.

➡ Bus 15C (HK$4.20, every 15 to 20 minutes) takes passengers between the bus terminus near the Star Ferry pier and the lower tram terminus at Garden Rd.

Macau

Bicycle

Bikes can be **rented** (友記 士多; Map p212; ☑853 2882 7975; 11 Rua dos Negociantes; MOP$10-25; ◷11am-8pm; ☐11, 15, 22, 28A) in Taipa Village for around MOP$20 per hour. You are not allowed to cross the Macau–Taipa bridges on a bicycle.

Public Transport

Public buses and minibuses run by **TCM** (www.tcm.com. mo) and **Transmac** (☑853 2827 1122; www.transmac. com.mo) operate from 6am until shortly after midnight. All routes charge a standardised fare (MOP$6) which is dropped into a box upon entry (exact change only), or you can pay with a Macau Pass that allows you to enjoy a discount of MOP$3 or MOP$4 per trip. The Macau Pass can be purchased from various supermarkets and convenience stores. The card costs MOP$130 at first purchase, which includes a refundable deposit of

MOP$30. A minimum of MOP$50 is required to add money to the card each time. Expect buses to be very crowded.

The *Macau Tourist Map* has a full list of bus-company routes and it's worth picking one up from one of the Macau Government Tourist Office (MGTO) outlets. You can also check the routes on the TCM website. The two most useful buses on the peninsula are buses 3 and 3A, which run between the Maritime Ferry Terminal and the city centre, near the post office. Both continue up to the border crossing with the mainland, as does bus 3X, which can be boarded along Avenida Almeida Ribeiro. Bus 12 runs from the ferry terminal, past the Lisboa Hotel and then up to Lou Lim Ieoc Garden and Kun Iam Temple. The best services to Taipa and Coloane are buses 21A, 25 and 26A. Buses to the airport are AP1, 26, MT1 and MT4.

Taxi

Taxi is a convenient and inexpensive option in Macau. The flag-fall charge is MOP$19 for the first 1.6km, and MOP$2 for every 240m thereafter. A MOP$5 surcharge applies to taxi trips boarded at Macau International Airport, Taipa Ferry Terminal, the University of Macau and journeys from Macau Peninsula to Coloane.

For a taxi, call either ☑853 8500 0000 or ☑853 2828 3283, or have your hotel call a taxi for you. You can also try using the Macau Taxi Fare app. There's no Uber in Macau.

Directory A–Z

Accessible Travel

People with mobility issues face substantial obstacles in Hong Kong, particularly on Hong Kong Island, because of its extremely hilly topography, pedestrian overpasses and crowded – often obstructed – streets. Those with hearing or visual impairments will find several aids to help them, including Braille panels in lift lobbies and audio units at traffic signals.

Online Resources

Lonely Planet Download Lonely Planet's free Accessible Travel guides from http://lptravel.to/AccessibleTravel.

Transport Department (www.td.gov.hk) Guides to public transportation, parking and pedestrian crossings for people with disabilities in Hong Kong.

Access Guide (www.accessguide.hk) A useful guide to accessibility of sights, hotels, transport, shopping and dining

venues, run by the Hong Kong Society for Rehabilitation.

Mobility Issues

Ladder streets (streets so steep that they consist of steps instead of pavements) are particularly common in Central and Sheung Wan on Hong Kong Island, heading south away from the harbourfront.

Hong Kong's minibuses are not suitable for wheelchair users; about 70% of Hong Kong's full-size bus

---

PRACTICALITIES

Media

There are several English-language newspapers and radio stations in Hong Kong.

South China Morning Post (www.scmp.com) The city's biggest daily broadsheet toes the government line, has an excellent website and is a good source of both current affairs and lifestyle news, particularly new restaurant reviews.

China Daily (www.chinadaily.com.cn) The Běijīng mouthpiece prints an English-language edition and covers news from across Asia.

Time Out Hong Kong (www.timeout.com/hong-kong) The international what's-on guide has a dedicated Hong Kong edition with its finger on the pulse of local life, especially events, eating and drinking.

Smoking

Banned in all public indoor spaces and some outdoor areas, but the law isn't always strictly enforced in some bars and restaurants.

Weights & Measures

Although the international metric system is in official use in Hong Kong, traditional Chinese weights and measures are still common. At local markets, meat, fish and produce are sold by the *léung,* equivalent to 37.8g, and the *gàn* (catty), which is equivalent to about 600g. There are 16 *léung* to the *gàn.* Gold and silver are sold by the *tael,* which is exactly the same as a *léung.*

services are. Wheelchairs can negotiate the lower decks of most ferries. Taxis are easy to flag down, but note that most are not large enough to accommodate wheelchairs.

Discount Cards

Many of Hong Kong's attractions are free, but look out for combination tickets that save pennies on big-ticket sights like the Peak's Sky Terrace 428, Madame Tussauds and Disneyland. Good pass deals exist for tourists using the MTR to travel widely.

Hostel Card

There are several Hostelling International (HI) hostels in Hong Kong but to stay at one you need to be a member. The annual membership card costs HK$150 and can be bought at any affiliated hostel at the time of check-in, if you don't already have one.

Seniors Card

Those aged 65 and above can travel on most forms of transport for HK$2 per trip (more than a 50% discount on MTR, for example). The Elder Octopus card can be obtained from any MTR Customer Centre, which automatically applies the discount when valid.

Student, Youth & Teacher Cards

Hong Kong Student Travel, based at **Sincerity Travel** (學聯旅遊; Map p314; ☑852 2730 2800; www.hkst.com. hk; Room 833-8343, Star House, Salisbury Rd, Tsim Sha Tsui; ⊘9.30am-6pm Mon-Sat; 🚢Star Ferry), can instantly issue you any of the following cards for HK$100. Make sure you bring your student ID or other credentials along with you.

International Student Identity Card (ISIC) Provides discounts on some forms of transport and admission to some sights.

International Youth Travel Card (IYTC) Gives similar discounts to the ISIC card for anyone aged 12 to 30 but not a student.

International Teacher Identity Card (ITIC) Holders may enjoy discounts at certain bookshops.

Hong Kong Museums Pass

Most of Hong Kong's museums are free to enter so the value of this pass is questionable. It does, however, get you free entry to special exhibitions. The annual pass costs HK$50 for individuals and HK$100 for families up to four. Apply online or at a participating museum, including the Hong Kong Space Museum and Hong Kong Science Museum.

Electricity

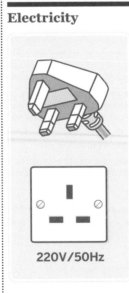

220V/50Hz

Embassies & Consulates

About 120 countries have representative offices in Hong Kong. Most are based on Hong Kong Island, in or around Central, and open in the mornings and afternoons Monday to Friday.

Australian Consulate (Map p308; ☑852 2827 8881; http:// hongkong.china.embassy. gov.au; 23rd fl, Harbour Centre, 25 Harbour Rd, Wan Chai; ⊘9am-5pm Mon-Fri; Ⓜ Wan Chai, exit C)

Canadian Consulate (Map p298; ☑852 3719 4700; 5th fl, Tower 3, Exchange Sq, 8 Connaught Pl, Central; Ⓜ Central, exit A)

Dutch Consulate (Map p308; ☑852 2599 9200; www. netherlandsandyou.nl; Suite 3001, 30th fl, Central Plaza, 18 Harbour Rd, Wan Chai; ⊘9am-noon & 2-4.30pm Mon-Fri)

French Consulate (Map p306; ☑852 3196 6100; www.consul france-hongkong.org; 26th fl, Tower II, Admiralty Centre, 18 Harcourt Rd, Admiralty; ⊘8.30am-12.30pm Mon-Fri; Ⓜ Admiralty, exit C2)

German Consulate (Map p306; ☑852 2105 8788; www. hongkong.diplo.de; 21st fl, United Centre, 95 Queensway, Admiralty; ⊘8.30-11.30am Mon-Fri; Ⓜ Admiralty, exit C2)

Indian Consulate (Map p306; ☑852 3970 9900; www.cgihk. gov.in; Unit A, 16th fl, United Centre, 95 Queensway, Admiralty; ⊘9am-5.30pm Mon-Fri; Ⓜ Admiralty, exit C1)

Irish Consulate (Map p302; ☑852 2535 0700; www.dfa. ie/irish-consulate/hong-kong; 20th fl, 33 Des Voeux Rd Central, Central; ⊘10am-noon & 2.30-4.30pm Mon-Fri; Ⓜ Central, exit C)

Japanese Consulate (Map p298; ☎852 2522 1184; www. hk.emb-japan.go.jp; 46-47th fl, 1 Exchange Sq, 8 Connaught Pl, Central; ⊗9.15am-noon & 1.30-4.45pm Mon-Fri; ⓂCentral, exit D1)

Kazakhstani Consulate (Map p304; ☎general enquiries 852 2548 3841, visa application 852 2548 3773; www.mfa.gov.kz/en/hongkong; Unit 2503-2504, 25th fl, Cosco Tower, 183 Queen's Rd Central, Sheung Wan; ⊗9.30am-12.30pm & 3-5pm Mon, Tue, Thu & Fri; ⓂSheung Wan, exit E1)

Laotian Consulate (Map p304; ☎852 2544 1186; 14th fl, Arion Commercial Centre, 2-12 Queen's Rd West, Sheung Wan; ⊗9am-noon & 1.30-5pm; 🚌5)

Nepalese Consulate (Map p316; ☎852 2369 7813; 715 China Aerospace Tower, Concordia Plaza, 1 Science Museum Rd, Tsim Sha Tsui; ⓂHung Hom, exit D1)

New Zealand Consulate (Map p308; ☎852 2525 5044; www. eit.ac.nz; Room 6501, 65th fl, Central Plaza, 18 Harbour Rd, Wan Chai; ⊗8.30am-1pm & 2-5pm Mon-Fri; ⓂWan Chai, exit C)

UK Consulate (Map p306; ☎852 2901 3000; www.gov. uk/government/world/hong-kong; 1 Supreme Court Rd, Admiralty; ⊗8.30am-5.15pm Mon-Fri; ⓂAdmiralty, exit F)

US Consulate (Map p298; ☎852 2523 9011; https://hk.usconsulate.gov; 26 Garden Rd, Central; ⊗8.30am-noon & 1.30-4pm Mon-Fri; ⓂCentral, exit J2)

Emergency & Useful Numbers

To make a phone call to Hong Kong, dial your international access code, Hong Kong's country code, then the eight-digit number.

Hong Kong country code	☎852
International access code	☎001
Local directory enquiries	☎1081
Reverse-charge/collect calls	☎10010
Police emergency	☎999
Police	☎852 2527 7177
Antiscam public helpline	☎18222
Weather/tropical cyclone warning enquiries	☎187 8200

Health

The occasional avian- or swine-flu outbreak notwithstanding, health conditions in the region are good. Travellers have a low risk of contracting infectious diseases compared with much of Asia. The health system is generally excellent. The mosquitoes that carry dengue fever are present in Hong Kong, so it's worth taking antimosquito measures (and to prevent bites in general; especially in summer). If your health insurance doesn't cover you for medical expenses abroad, consider supplemental insurance.

Insurance

Visitors without a Hong Kong identity card can use public hospitals by paying private market rates, which are multiple times the normal rate. Check the Hospital Authority website (www.ha.org.hk) for exact fees. However, if you have the appropriate supporting documents, many private health insurances reimburse these fees.

A health-insurance plan with international coverage may allow you to receive inpatient medical and certain surgical treatments in Hong Kong, but do check with your insurer about coverage of outpatient services, ie services that do not require overnight stay in hospital.

Recommended Vaccinations

There are no required vaccinations for entry into Hong Kong, unless you will be travelling to the mainland or elsewhere in the region.

Environmental Hazards

Mosquitoes These are prevalent in Hong Kong. You should always use insect repellent during warm and hot weather, and if you're bitten and have a bad reaction, consider using antihistamines.

Centipedes Lamma is home to large red centipedes, which have a poisonous bite that causes swelling and discomfort in most cases, but can be more dangerous (and supposedly in very rare cases deadly) for young children.

Wild boars & dogs Wild boars and aggressive dogs are a minor hazard in some of the more remote parts of the New Territories. Wild boars are shy and retiring most of the time, but are dangerous when they feel threatened, so give them a wide berth and avoid disturbing thick areas of undergrowth.

Snakes There are many snakes in Hong Kong, and some are deadly, but you are unlikely to encounter any. Still, always take care when bushwalking, particularly on Lamma and Lantau islands. Go straight to a public hospital if bitten; private doctors do not stock antivenene.

Tap Water

Hong Kong tap water conforms to World Health Organization standards and is considered safe to drink, though many locals prefer bottled for reasons of flavour and prestige.

Medical Services

The standard of medical care in Hong Kong is generally excellent but expensive. Always take out travel insurance before you travel. Health care is divided into public and private, and there is no interaction between the two.

CLINICS

There are many English-speaking general practitioners, specialists and dentists in Hong Kong, who can be found through your consulate, a private hospital or the *Yellow Pages* (www.yp.com.hk). If money is tight, take yourself to the nearest public-hospital emergency room and be prepared to wait. The general enquiry number for hospitals is ☑852 2300 6555, or visit www.ha.org.hk.

HOSPITALS & EMERGENCY ROOMS

In the case of an emergency, all ambulances (☑999) will take you to a government-run public hospital where, as a visitor, you will be required to pay a hefty fee for using emergency services. Treatment is guaranteed in any case; people who cannot pay immediately will be billed later. While the emergency care is excellent, you may wish to transfer to a private hospital once you are stable.

Hong Kong Island

Queen Mary Hospital (瑪麗醫院; ☑852 2255 3838; www3.ha.org.hk/qmh; 102 Pok Fu Lam Rd, Pok Fu Lam; ☑30X, 40M, 90B, 91, minibus 8, 10) Public, with a 24-hour accident and emergency service.

Ruttonjee Hospital (律敦治醫院; Map p308; ☑852 2291 2000; www.ha.org.hk; 266 Queen's Rd E, Wan Chai; ⓂWan Chai, exit A3) Public.

Kowloon

Hong Kong Baptist Hospital (香港浸信會醫院; ☑852 2339 8888; 222 Waterloo Rd, Kowloon Tong) Private.

Princess Margaret Hospital (瑪嘉烈醫院; ☑852 2990 1111; www.ha.org.hk; 2-10 Princess Margaret Hospital Rd, Lai Chi Kok) Public, with a 24-hour accident and emergency service.

Queen Elizabeth Hospital (伊利沙伯醫院; Map p318; ☑852 2958 8888; 30 Gascoigne Rd, Yau Ma Tei; ☑112, ⓂJordan, exit C1) Public.

New Territories

Prince of Wales Hospital (威爾斯親王醫院; Map p166; ☑852 2632 2211; 30-32 Ngan Shing St, Sha Tin) Public.

PHARMACIES

➡ Pharmacies are abundant; they bear a red-and-white cross outside and there should be a registered pharmacist available inside.

➡ Many medications can be bought over the counter without a prescription, but always check it is a known brand and that the expiry date is valid.

➡ Sanitary pads, tampons and condoms are widely available in pharmacies, especially Watson's and Mannings, and large supermarkets. Birth-control pills are available over the counter in pharmacies.

Internet Access

Free wi-fi is available in virtually all hotels, at the airport, in MTR stations, on some buses and in various public areas including shopping malls, key cultural and recreational centres, and almost all urban cafes and bars.

In short, Hong Kong is well hooked up.

Wi-fi hot spots There are more than 15,000 public hot spots in Hong Kong. They will pop up as 'CSL' or 'Wi.Fi.HK' on your device; you can search where the latter hot spots are by downloading the Wi.Fi.HK mobile app.

Portable wi-fi devices Some hotels now offer portable wi-fi devices as a free add-on for guests, or have them available to hire for a nominal fee.

Computer access If you don't have a smartphone, tablet or laptop, desktop computers are available for guests at some hotels and in some public locations such as Hong Kong's Central Library.

Legal Matters

➡ Carry your passport all the time. As a visitor, you are required to show your identification if the police request it.

➡ *All* forms of narcotics are illegal in Hong Kong. Whether it's heroin, opium, ice, ecstasy or marijuana, the law makes no distinction. If police or customs officials find dope or even smoking equipment in your possession, you can expect to be arrested immediately.

➡ If you run into legal trouble, contact the **Legal Aid Department** (☑24hr hotline 852 2537 7677; www.lad.gov.hk), which provides residents and visitors with representation, subject to a means and merits test.

LGBTQ+ Travellers

Hong Kong has a small but growing LGBTQ+ scene and the annual Pride Parade in November now attracts rainbow flag-wavers by the thousands. That said, Hong Kong Chinese society remains fairly conservative, and it can still be risky for gays and lesbians to come out to family members or their employers. It is not common to see LGBTQ+ couples making displays of affection in public.

In 1991 the Crimes (Amendment) Ordinance removed criminal penalties for homosexual acts between consenting adults over the age of 18. Since then LGBTQ+ groups have been lobbying for legislation to address the issue of discrimination on the grounds of sexual orientation, but the government has been criticised for failing to recognise and embrace the community.

In July 2018 there was a landmark ruling by Hong Kong's Court of Final Appeal, stating that the same-sex partner of a British expat should be granted a spousal visa – a move that has given the local LGBTQ+ community hope that change (and, importantly, greater equality) is on the horizon.

Pink Alliance (https://pink alliance.hk) For information about LGBTQ+ culture and events in Hong Kong.

Dim Sum Magazine (http://dimsum-hk.com) Hong Kong's first free gay lifestyle magazine covers local lifestyle, news and entertainment.

Money

ATMs

➡ Most ATMs are linked up to international money systems such as Cirrus, Maestro, Plus and Visa Electron.

➡ Withdrawal fees will typically be between HK$20 and HK$50 per transaction, and the local ATM provider may levy an extra surcharge.

➡ American Express (Amex) cardholders can withdraw cash from AEON ATMs in Hong Kong if you have signed up to Amex Express Cash service before arrival.

Changing Money

The local currency is the Hong Kong dollar (HK$). Hong Kong has no currency controls; locals and foreigners can bring, send in or take out as much money as they like. No foreign-currency black market exists in Hong Kong; if anyone on the street does approach you to change money, assume it's a scam.

Money changers Licensed money changers, such as Chequepoint, abound in touristed areas such as Tsim Sha Tsui and Central. While they are convenient (usually open on Sundays, holidays and late into the evenings) and take no commission per se, the less-than-attractive exchange rates offered are equivalent to a 5% commission. These rates are clearly posted, though if you're changing several hundred US dollars or more you might be able to bargain for a better rate. Before the actual exchange is made, the money changer is required by law to give you a form to sign that clearly shows the amount due to you, the exchange rate and any service charges. Try to avoid the exchange counters at the airport or in hotels, which offer some of the worst rates in Hong Kong.

Credit Cards

➡ Credit (and debit) cards are widely used in midrange to upmarket shops, restaurants and bars, and it is safe to pay with them.

➡ The most widely accepted cards are Visa, MasterCard,

Amex, Diners Club and JCB – pretty much in that order. It may be an idea to carry two, just in case.

➡ Note that transactions using an international credit or debit card will incur a handling fee from your home bank.

Opening Hours

Some shops and restaurants are closed on the first and second days of the Lunar New Year, some for a longer period of time. The following list summarises standard opening hours.

Banks 9am to 4.30pm or 5.30pm Monday to Friday, 9am to 12.30pm Saturday

Museums 10am to between 5pm and 9pm; many close on Mondays as well as sometimes Sundays

Offices 9am to 5.30pm or 6pm Monday to Friday (lunch hour 1pm to 2pm)

Restaurants 11am to 3pm and 6pm to 11pm

Shops Usually 10am to 8pm

Post

Hong Kong Post (www. hongkongpost.com) is generally excellent; local letter delivery takes one to two working days and there is Saturday delivery. The staff at most post offices speak English. Mailboxes on the streets are green and clearly marked in English.

Receiving Mail

If you need anything sent to you while travelling in Hong Kong, address it c/o Poste Restante, GPO Hong Kong, and it will go to the GPO on Hong Kong Island. Pick it up at counter No 29 from 7am to 8pm Monday to Saturday and 8am to 7pm on Sunday. If you want your letters to go to Kowloon, have them addressed as follows: c/o Poste Restante, Tsim Sha Tsui Post Office, 10 Middle Rd, Tsim Sha Tsui, Kowloon. Overseas mail is normally held for two months and local mail for two weeks.

Sending Mail

On Hong Kong Island, the **General Post Office** (中央郵政局; Map p298; 2 Connaught Pl, Central; ⊙8am-6pm Mon-Sat, noon-5pm Sun; Ⓜ Hong Kong, exit A1, A2) is just east of the Hong Kong MTR station. In Kowloon, the **Tsim Sha Tsui Post Office** (尖沙咀郵政局; Map p314; Ground & 1st fl, Hermes House, 10 Middle Rd, Tsim Sha Tsui; ⊙9am-6pm Mon-Sat; Ⓜ East Tsim Sha Tsui, exit L1) is just east of the southern end of Nathan Rd. Post-office branches elsewhere keep shorter hours and usually don't open on Sunday.

Allow nine to 14 working days for delivery of letters, postcards and packages to Australia, seven to 16 for the USA, and around 10 days for Europe, by airmail.

Courier Services

Many MTR stations have DHL outlets, including the **MTR Central branch** (Map p298; ☑852 2877 2848; www. dhl.com.hk/en.html; Ⓜ Central, exit H, F; ⊙9am-7.30pm Mon-Fri, to 4pm Sat) and the **MTR Admiralty branch** (Map p308; ☑852 2400 3388; www. dhl.com.hk; Shop G2, Great Eagle Centre, 23 Harbour Rd, Wan Chai; ⊙24hr Sun-Fri; Ⓜ Wan Chai, exit C).

Postal Rates

Local letter mail is HK$2 for up to 30g; local packages are HK$5.20 up to 100g.

Airmail letters weighing up to 30g cost about HK$5 to Europe and HK$7.60 to North America. Packages weighing up to 50g cost HK$13.50 to Europe and North America, plus up to HK$2 for every 10g

over. Rates to Australia are broadly similar, and it's a little cheaper to send letters or packages to the rest of Asia.

Speedpost

The fastest way to send letters and small parcels is via Hong Kong Post's Speedpost (www.hongkongpost.com/ speedpost), which covers 210 destinations worldwide. The fee and delivery timeframes vary massively depending on the destination; every post office has a schedule of fees and a timetable. Fees include registered delivery.

Public Holidays

Western and Chinese culture combine to create an interesting mix – and number – of public holidays in Hong Kong. Determining the exact date of some of them is tricky, as there are traditionally two calendars in use: the Gregorian solar (or western) calendar and the Chinese lunar calendar.

New Year's Day 1 January

Chinese New Year 25 January 2020, 12 February 2021

Ching Ming 4 April 2020, 5 April 2021

Easter 10–13 April 2020, 2–5 April 2021

Labour Day 1 May

Buddha's Birthday 30 April 2020, 19 May 2021

Dragon Boat (Tuen Ng) Festival 7 June 2019, 25 June 2020, 14 June 2021

Hong Kong SAR Establishment Day 1 July

Mid-Autumn Festival 13 September 2019, 2 October 2020, 22 September 2021

China National Day 1 October

Chung Yeung 7 October 2019, 26 October 2020, 14 October 2021

Christmas Day 25 December

Boxing Day 26 December

Telephone

As in the rest of the world, public telephones are increasingly rare. More and more hotels are including free mobile handsets with 4G data and free local calls as part of the room deal.

International Direct Dial (IDD) service If the phone you're using has registered for the IDD 0060 service (or if you have the IDD Global Calling Card), dial ☑0060 first, then ☑852, and then the number; rates will be cheaper at any time.

Rates All local calls in Hong Kong are free. However, hotels charge from HK$3 to HK$5 for local calls from your room landline.

Mobile Phones

Any GSM-compatible phone can be used here. If you have an unlocked handset, buying a local SIM card with 4G mobile data and free local calls is convenient and easy.

The Hong Kong Tourist Board sells a prepaid Tourist SIM, which includes 4G mobile data, unlimited CSL wi-fi hot-spot usage and unlimited calls. A five-day pass costs HK$88 and includes 1.5GB of data; the eight-day pass is HK$118 for 5GB. It can be purchased at the HKTB counters in the airport arrivals hall or at 7-Elevens and dozens of other retailers in the city. Other SIM-card options are available at CSL stores and 7-Elevens.

Coverage Mobile phones work everywhere, including in the harbour tunnels and on the MTR.

Handsets There are **CSL** (Map p298; Ground fl, 113 Des Voeux Rd, Central; ⊙10am-8pm Mon-Sat, 10.30am-7pm Sun; Ⓜ Hong Kong Station, exit A1, A2) stores all over the city that sell cheap handsets and mobile accessories, should you need to replace your phone while in Hong Kong.

Rates Local calls cost between 6¢ and 12¢ a minute (calls to the mainland are about HK$1.50–HK$3 per minute with IDD 0060 – significantly more without it).

Phonecards

Buy an International Direct Dial (IDD) Global Calling Card for cheaper rates on global calls; they are available at CSL and 7-Eleven stores.

Time

➡ Hong Kong Time is eight hours ahead of London (GMT); 13 hours ahead of New York (EST); the same time as Singapore, Manila and Perth; and two hours behind Sydney (AEST).

➡ Hong Kong does not have daylight-saving time.

Toilets

➡ Hong Kong has a vast number of free western-style public toilets, including decent facilities in Central, all MTR stations, markets and parks.

➡ Equip yourself with tissues, as toilet paper isn't always available.

➡ Many public toilets have wheelchair access, and baby-changing shelves in both men's and women's rooms.

➡ Hong Kong's Toilet Rush mobile app will show you where the nearest public toilets are to your location.

Tourist Information

Hong Kong Tourism Board (www.discoverhong kong.com) visitor centres

have helpful and welcoming staff, and reams of information – most of it free. There are two branches in town, as well as visitor centres in the airport.

Hong Kong International Airport (Map p184; Chek Lap Kok; ⏰7am-11pm) In Halls A and B on the arrivals level in Terminal 1, and the E2 transfer area.

The Peak (港島旅客諮詢及服務中心; www.discoverhong kong.com; Peak Piazza, The Peak; ⏰11am-8pm) In a vintage tram, between the Peak Tower and the Peak Galleria.

Kowloon (香港旅遊發展局; Map p314; Star Ferry Concourse, Tsim Sha Tsui; ⏰8am-8pm; 🚢Star Ferry) Right by the ferry terminal.

Lo Wu (羅湖旅客諮詢及服務中心; Map p191; 2nd fl, Arrival Hall, Lo Wu Terminal Bldg, New Territories; ⏰8am-6pm) At this border crossing to Shēnzhèn, mainland China.

Visas

Hong Kong

Visas are not required for Brits (up to 180 days); or Australians, Canadians, EU citizens, Israelis, Japanese, New Zealanders and US citizens (up to 90 days).

Citizens of British Dependent Territories and British Overseas citizens can stay for up to 90 days without a visa. Holders of some African (including South African), South American and Middle Eastern passports can visit for up to 30 days without a visa.

Anyone requiring a visa or wishing to stay longer than the visa-free period must apply before travelling to Hong Kong. See www.fmprc.gov.cn for your nearest Chinese consulate or embassy where the application must be made.

You must apply for a visa extension in person at the **Hong Kong Immigration Department** (Map p308; ☑852 2824 6111; www.immd.gov.hk; 2nd fl, Immigration Tower, 7 Gloucester Rd, Wan Chai; ⏰8.45am-4.30pm Mon-Fri, 9-11.30am Sat; Ⓜ Wan Chai, exit C) within seven days of visa expiry; they are granted the same day.

If you plan to visit mainland China, you must have a visa.

You can check all visa requirements at www.immd.gov.hk/eng/services/visas/visit-transit/visit-visa-entry-permit.html.

Macau

UK travellers can enter Macau with just their passports for six months. Most other travellers can do the same between 30 and 90 days, including citizens of Australia, Canada, EU, New Zealand, South Africa, UK and the US. Travellers who do require visas can get them, valid for 30 days, on arrival in Macau. They cost MOP$100/50/200 per adult/child under 12 years/family. You can apply for a visa extension from the Taipa branch of the **Immigration Department Office Building** (出入境事務廳; Serviço de Migração; ☑853 2872 5488; Immigration Department Office Bldg, Travessa Um do Cais de Pac On; ⏰9am-5pm Mon-Fri).

Nationals of Australia, Canada, the EU, UK, New Zealand and most other countries (but not US citizens) can purchase their China visas at Zhūhǎi on the border, but it will ultimately save you time if you get one in advance as lines can be long. These are available in Macau or Hong Kong from **China Travel Service** (CTS; 中国旅行社; Zhōngguó Lǚxíngshè; ☑853 2870 0888; www.cts.com.mo; Nam Kwong Bldg, 207 Avenida do Dr Rodrigo Rodrigues, Macau; ⏰9am-6pm), usually in one day.

Mainland China

Everyone except Hong Kong Chinese residents must have a visa to enter mainland China. Visas can be arranged by **China Travel Service** (CTS; 中國旅行社; Zhōngguó Lǔxíngshè; ☎customer service 852 2998 7888, tour hotline 852 2998 7333; www.ctshk. com), the mainland-affiliated agency; a good many hostels and guesthouses; and most Hong Kong travel agents.

At the time of writing, holders of Canadian, Australian, New Zealand, US and most EU passports can get a single visa on the spot for around HK$150 at the Lo Wu border crossing, the last stop on the MTR's East Rail. This visa is for a maximum stay of five days within the confines of the Shēnzhèn Special Economic Zone (SEZ). However, the rules about who can get what change frequently, the queues for these visas can be interminable, and there have been reports of tourists being rejected on shaky grounds (such as certain passport stamps).

Taking that into consideration, it is highly recommended that you shell out the extra money and get a proper China visa before setting off, even if you're headed just for Shēnzhèn. If you have at least a week to arrange your visa yourself, you can go to the **China Visa Application Service Centre** (Map p308; ☎852 2992 1999; www.visaforchina. org; 20th fl, Capital Centre, 151 Gloucester Rd, Wan Chai; ⊗9am-5pm Mon-Fri; Ⓜ Wan Chai, exit A3). For further details see www.fmprc.gov.cn.

Language

Cantonese is the most popular Chinese dialect in Hong Kong and the surrounding area. Cantonese speakers can read Chinese characters, but will pronounce many characters differently from a Mandarin speaker.

Several systems of Romanisation for Cantonese script exist, and no single one has emerged as an official standard. In this chapter we use Lonely Planet's pronunciation guide designed for maximum accuracy with minimum complexity.

Pronunciation

Vowels

a	as the 'u' in 'but'
ai	as in 'aisle' (short sound)
au	as the 'ou' in 'out'
ay	as in 'pay'
eu	as the 'er' in 'fern'
eui	as in French *feuille* (eu with i)
ew	as in 'blew' (short and pronounced with tightened lips)
i	as the 'ee' in 'deep'
iu	as the 'yu' in 'yuletide'
o	as in 'go'
oy	as in 'boy'
u	as in 'put'
ui	as in French *oui*

Consonants

In Cantonese, the ng sound can appear at the start of a word. Practise by saying 'sing along' slowly and then do away with the 'si'.

WANT MORE?

For in-depth language information and handy phrases, check out Lonely Planet's *China phrasebook*. You'll find it at **shop. lonelyplanet.com**, or you can buy Lonely Planet's iPhone phrasebooks at the Apple App Store.

Note that words ending with the consonant sounds p, t, and k must be clipped in Cantonese. You can hear this in English as well – say 'pit' and 'tip' and listen to how much shorter the 'p' sound is in 'tip'.

Many Cantonese speakers, particularly young people, replace an 'n' sound with an 'l' if a word begins with it – náy (you), is often heard as láy. Where relevant, this change is reflected in our pronunciation guides.

Tones

Cantonese is a language with a large number of words with the same pronunciation but a different meaning, eg gwàt (dig up) and gwàt (bones). What distinguishes these homophones is their 'tonal' quality – the raising and the lowering of pitch on certain syllables. Tones in Cantonese fall on vowels (a, e, i, o, u) and on the consonant n.

To give you a taste of how these tones work, we've included them in our red pronunciation guides in this chapter – they show six tones, divided into high and low pitch groups. High-pitch tones involve tightening the vocal muscles to get a higher note, whereas low-pitch tones are made by relaxing the vocal chords to get a lower note. The tones are indicated with the following accent marks:

à	high
á	high rising
a	level
à̱	low falling
á̱	low rising
a̱	low

Basics

Hello.	哈佬 。	hàa·ló
Goodbye.	再見 。	joy·gin
How are you?	你幾好啊嗎 ？	láy gáy hó à maa
Fine.	幾好 。	gáy hó

Excuse me. (to get attention)	對唔住 。	deui·ǹg·jew
Excuse me. (to get past)	唔該借借 。	ǹg·gòy je·je
Sorry.	對唔住 。	deui·ǹg·jew
Yes.	係 。	hai
No.	不係 。	ǹg·hai
Please...	唔該...	ǹg·gòy...
Thank you.	多謝 。	dàw·je
You're welcome.	唔駛客氣 。	ǹg·sái haak·hay

What's your name?
你叫乜嘢名 ? — láy giu màt·yé méng aa

My name is...
我叫... — ngáw giu...

Do you speak English?
你識唔識講
英文啊 ? — láy sìk·ǹg·sìk gáwng
yìng·mán aa

I don't understand.
我唔明 。 — ngáw ǹg mìng

Accommodation

campsite	營地	yìng·day
guesthouse	賓館	bàn·gún
hostel	招待所	jiù·doy·sáw
hotel	酒店	jáu·dim

Do you have a... room?	有冇...房 ?	yáu·mó... fáwng
single	單人	dàan·yàn
double	雙人	sèung·yàn

How much is it per...?	一...幾多錢 ?	yàt...gáy·dàw chín
night	晚	máan
person	個人	gaw yàn

air-con	空調	hùng·tiù
bathroom	沖涼房	chùng·lèung·fáwng
bed	床	chàwng
cot	BB床	bi·bì chàwng
window	窗	chèung

Directions

Where's...?
...喺邊度? — ...hái bìn·do

What's the address?
地址係 ? — day·jí hai

KEY PATTERNS

To get by in Cantonese, mix and match these simple patterns with words of your choice:

When's (the next tour)?
(下個旅遊團
係)幾時 ? — (haa·gaw léui·yàu·tèwn hai) gáy·sì

Where's (the station)?
(車站)喺邊度 ? — (chè·jaam) hái·bìn·do

Where can I (buy a padlock)?
邊度可以
(買倒鎖) ? — bìn·do háw·yí (máai dó sáw)

Do you have (a map)?
有冇 (地圖) ? — yáu·mó (day·tò)

I need (a mechanic).
我要 (個整車
師傅) 。 — ngáw yiu (gaw jíng·chè sì·fú)

I'd like (a taxi).
我想 (坐的士) 。 — ngáw séung (cháw dìk·sí)

Can I (get a stand-by ticket)?
可唔可以 (買
張後補飛)呀 ? — háw·ǹg·háw·yí (máai jèung hau·bó fày) aa

Could you please (write it down)?
唔該你 (寫落嚟)? — ǹg·gòy láy (sé lawk lài)

Do I need (to book)?
駛唔駛 (定飛
先)呀 ? — sái·ǹg·sái (deng·fày sìn) aa

I have (a reservation).
我 (預定)咗 。 — ngáw (yew·deng) jáw

behind	後面	hau·min
left	左邊	jáw·bìn
near...	...附近	...fu·gan
next to...	...旁邊	...pàwng·bìn
on the corner	十字路口	sap·ji·lo·háu
opposite	對面	deui·min
right	右邊	yau·bìn
straight ahead	前面	chìn·min
traffic lights	紅綠燈	hùng·luk·dàng

Eating & Drinking

What would you recommend?
有乜嘢好介紹 ? — yáu màt·yé hó gaai·siu

What's in that dish?
呢道菜有啲乜嘢 ? — lày do choy yáu dì màt·yé

That was delicious.
真好味 。 — jàn hó·may

Cheers!
乾杯 ! — gàwn·bui

I'd like the bill, please.
唔該我要埋單 。 — ǹg·gòy ngáw yiu màai·dàan

I'd like to book a table for...	我想訂張檯，…嘅。	ngáw séung deng jèung tóy ...ge
(eight) o'clock	（八）點鐘	(bàat) dím·jùng
(two) people	（兩）位	(léung) wái

I don't eat...	我唔吃…	ngáw ǹg sìk...
fish	魚	yéw
nuts	果仁	gwáw·yàn
poultry	雞鴨鵝	gài ngaap ngàw
red meat	牛羊肉	ngàu yèung yuk

Key Words

appetisers	涼盤	lèung·pún
baby food	嬰兒食品	yìng·yi sìk·bán
bar	酒吧	jáu·bàa
bottle	樽	jèun
bowl	碗	wún
breakfast	早餐	jó·chàan
cafe	咖啡屋	gaa·fè·ngùk
children's menu	個小童菜單	gaw síu·tung choy·dàan
(too) cold	（太）凍	(taai) dung
dinner	晚飯	máan·fàan
food	食物	sìk·mat
fork	叉	chàa
glass	杯	bui
halal	清真	chìng·jàn
high chair	高凳	gò·dang
hot (warm)	熱	yit
knife	刀	dò
kosher	猶太	yàu·tàai
local specialities	地方小食	day·fàwng siú·sìk
lunch	午餐	ńg·chàan
market	街市	gàai·sí
main courses	主菜	jéw·choy
menu (in English)	（英文）菜單	(yìng·màn) choy·dàan
plate	碟	díp
restaurant	酒樓	jáu·làu
(too) spicy	（太）辣	(taai) laat
spoon	羹	gàng
supermarket	超市	chiù·sí
vegetarian food	齋食品	jàai sìk·bán

Meat & Fish

beef	牛肉	ngàu·yuk
chicken	雞肉	gài·yuk
duck	鴨	ngaap
fish	魚	yéw
lamb	羊肉	yèung·yuk
pork	豬肉	jèw·yuk
seafood	海鮮	hóy·sìn

Fruit & Vegetables

apple	蘋果	pìng·gwáw
banana	香蕉	hèung·jiù
cabbage	白菜	baak·choy
carrot	紅蘿蔔	hùng·làw·baak
celery	芹菜	kàn·choy
cucumber	青瓜	chèng·gwàa
fruit	水果	séui·gwáw
grapes	葡提子	pò·tài·jí
green beans	扁荳	bín·dau
lemon	檸檬	ling·mùng
lettuce	生菜	sàang·choy
mushroom	蘑菇	màw·gù
onion(s)	洋蔥	yèung·chùng
orange	橙	cháang
peach	桃	tó
pear	梨	láy
pineapple	菠蘿	bàw·làw
plum	梅	muì
potato	薯仔	sèw·jái
spinach	菠菜	bàw·choy
tomato	番茄	fàan·ké
vegetable	蔬菜	sàw·choy

Other

bread	麵包	mìn·bàau
egg	蛋	dáan
herbs/spices	香料	hèung·liú
pepper	胡椒粉	wù·jiù·fán
rice	白飯	baak·faan
salt	鹽	yìm
soy sauce	豉油	sì·yàu
sugar	砂糖	sàa·tàwng
vegetable oil	菜油	choy·yàu
vinegar	醋	cho

SIGNS

入口	**Entrance**
出口	**Exit**
廁所	**Toilets**
男	**Men**
女	**Women**

Drinks

beer	啤酒	bè·jáu
coffee	咖啡	gaa·fè
juice	果汁	gwáw·jàp
milk	牛奶	ngàu·láai
mineral water	礦泉水	kawng·chèwn·séui
red wine	紅葡萄酒	hùng·pò·tò·jáu
tea	茶	chàa
white wine	白葡萄酒	baak·pò·tò·jáu

Emergencies

Help!	救命！	gau·meng
Go away!	走開！	jáu·hòy
I'm lost.	我蕩失路 。	ngáw dawng·sàk·lo
I'm sick.	我病咗 。	ngáw beng·jáw

Call a doctor!
快啲叫醫生！ faai·dì giu yì·sàng

Call the police!
快啲叫警察！ faai·dì giu gíng·chaat

Where are the toilets?
廁所喺邊度？ chi·sáw hái bìn·do

I'm allergic to...
我對…過敏 。 ngáw deui ... gaw·mán

Shopping & Services

I'd like to buy...
我想買… ngáw séung máai ...

I'm just looking.
睇下 。 tái haa

Can I look at it?
我可唔可以睇下？ ngáw háw·ǹg·háw·yí tái haa

How much is it?
幾多錢？ gáy·dàw chín

That's too expensive.
太貴啦 。 taai gwai laa

Can you lower the price?
可唔可以平啲呀？ háw·ǹg·háw·yí pèng dì aa

There's a mistake in the bill.
帳單錯咗 。 jeung·dàan chaw jáw

QUESTION WORDS

How?	點樣？	dím·yéung
What?	乜嘢？	màt·yé
When?	幾時？	gáy·sì
Where?	邊度？	bìn·do
Who?	邊個？	bìnz·gaw
Why?	點解？	dím·gáai

ATM	自動提款機	ji·dung tài·fún·gày
credit card	信用卡	seun·yung·kàat
internet cafe	網吧	máwng·bàa
post office	郵局	yàu·gúk
tourist office	旅行社	léui·hàng·sé

Time & Dates

What time is it?	而家幾點鐘？	yì·gàa gáy·dím·jùng
It's (10) o'clock.	（十）點鐘 。	(sap)·dím·jùng
Half past (10).	（十）點半 。	(sap)·dím bun

morning	朝早	jiù·jó
afternoon	下晝	haa·jau
evening	夜晚	ye·máan
yesterday	寢日	kàm·yat
today	今日	gàm·yat
tomorrow	听日	tìng·yat

Monday	星期一	sìng·kày·yàt
Tuesday	星期二	sìng·kày·yi
Wednesday	星期三	sìng·kày·sàam
Thursday	星期四	sìng·kày·say
Friday	星期五	sìng·kày·ńg
Saturday	星期六	sìng·kày·luk
Sunday	星期日	sìng·kày·yat

January	一月	yàt·yewt
February	二月	yi·yewt
March	三月	sàam·yewt
April	四月	say·yewt
May	五月	ńg·yewt
June	六月	luk·yewt
July	七月	chàt·yewt
August	八月	baat·yewt
September	九月	gáu·yewt
October	十月	sap·yewt
November	十一月	sap·yàt·yewt
December	十二月	sap·yi·yewt

Transport

Public Transport

boat	船	sèwn
bus	巴士	bàa·sí
plane	飛機	fày·gày

NUMBERS

1	一	yàt
2	二	yi
3	三	sàam
4	四	say
5	五	ńg
6	六	luk
7	七	chàt
8	八	baat
9	九	gáu
10	十	sap
20	二十	yi·sap
30	三十	sàam·sap
40	四十	say·sap
50	五十	ńg·sap
60	六十	luk·sap
70	七十	chàt·sap
80	八十	baat·sap
90	九十	gáu·sap
100	一百	yàt·baak
1000	一千	yàt·chìn

taxi	的士	dìk·sí
train	火車	fáw·chè
tram	電車	dìn·chè

When's the... (bus)?	... (巴士) 幾點開？	... (bàa·sí) gáy dím hòy
first	頭班	tàu·bàan
last	尾班	máy·bàan
next	下一班	haa·yàt·bàan

A ... ticket to (Panyu).	一張去 (番禺)嘅 ...飛 。	yàt jèung heui (pùn·yèw) ge ... fày
1st-class	頭等	tàu·dáng
2nd-class	二等	yi·dáng
one-way	單程	dàan·chìng
return	雙程	sèung·chìng

What time does it leave?
幾點鐘出發？ — gáy·dím jùng chèut·faa

Does it stop at...?
會唔會喺 ...停呀？ — wuí·ǹg·wuí hái ...tìng aa

What time does it get to...?
幾點鐘到... ？ — gáy·dím jùng do...

What's the next stop?
下個站 叫乜名？ — haa·gaw jaam giu màt méng

I'd like to get off at...
我要喺... 落車 。 — ngáw yiu hái... lawk·chè

Please tell me when we get to...
到...嘅時候， 唔該叫聲我 。 — do...ge si·hau ǹg·gòy giu sèng ngáw

Please stop here.
唔該落車 。 — ǹg·gòy lawk·chè

aisle	路邊	lo·bìn
cancelled	取消	chéui·siù
delayed	押後	ngaat·hau
platform	月台	yéwt·tòy
ticket window	售票處	sau·piu·chew
timetable	時間表	si·gaan·biú
train station	火車站	fó·chè·jaam
window	窗口	chèung·háu

Driving & Cycling

I'd like to hire a...	我想租 架...	ngáw séung jò gaa...
4WD	4WD	fàw·wiù·jàai·fù
bicycle	單車	dàan·chè
car	車	chè
motorcycle	電單車	dìn·dàan·chè

baby seat	BB座	bi·bì jaw
diesel	柴油	chàai·yàu
helmet	頭盔	tàu·kwài
mechanic	修車師傅	sàu·chè sì·fú
petrol	汽油	hay·yàu
service station	加油站	gàa·yàu·jaam

Is this the road to...?
呢條路係唔係去 ...㗎？ — lày tiu lo hai·ǹg·hai heui ...gaa

Can I park here?
呢度泊唔泊得 車㗎？ — làu·do paak·ǹg·paak·dàk chè gaa

How long can I park here?
我喺呢度可以 停幾耐？ — ngáw hái làu·do háw·yí tìng gáy·loy

Where's the bicycle parking lot?
喺邊度停單車？ — háy·bìn·do tìng dàan·chè

The car/motorbike has broken down at ...
架車/電單車 係...壞咗 。 — gaa chè/dìn·dàan·chè hái...waai jáw

I have a flat tyre.
我爆咗肽 。 — ngáw baau·jáw tàai

I've run out of petrol.
我冇晒油 。 — ngáw mó saai yáu

I'd like my bicycle repaired.
我想修呢架車 。 — ngáw séung sàu làu gaa chè

GLOSSARY

arhat – Buddhist disciple freed from the cycle of birth and death

bodhisattva – Buddhist striving towards enlightenment

cha chaan tang – local tea cafe serving western-style beverages and snacks and/or Chinese dishes

cheongsam – a fashionable, tight-fitting Chinese dress with a slit up the side (*qípáo* in Mandarin)

dai pai dong – open-air eating stall, especially popular at night, but fast disappearing in Hong Kong

dim sum – literally 'touch the heart'; a Cantonese meal of various tidbits eaten as breakfast, brunch or lunch and offered from wheeled steam carts in restaurants; see also yum cha

dragon boat – long, narrow skiff in the shape of a dragon, used in races during the Dragon Boat Festival

feng shui – Mandarin spelling for the Cantonese *fung sui* meaning 'wind water'; the Chinese art of geomancy that manipulates or judges the environment to produce good fortune

Hakka – a Chinese ethnic group who speak a different Chinese language than the Cantonese; some Hakka people still lead traditional lives as farmers in the New Territories

hell money – fake-currency money burned as an offering to the spirits of the departed

HKTB – Hong Kong Tourism Board

junk – originally Chinese fishing boats or war vessels with square sails; diesel-powered, wooden pleasure yachts, which can be seen on Victoria Harbour

kaido – small- to medium-sized ferry that makes short runs on the open sea, usually used for nonscheduled services between small islands and fishing villages; sometimes spelled kaito

kung fu – the basis of many Asian martial arts

mah-jong – popular Chinese game played among four persons using tiles engraved with Chinese characters

MTR – Mass Transit Railway

nullah – uniquely Hong Kong word referring to a gutter or drain and occasionally used in place names

Punti – the first Cantonese-speaking settlers in Hong Kong

sampan – motorised launch that can only accommodate a few people and is too small to go on the open sea; mainly used for interharbour transport

SAR – Special Administrative Region of China; both Hong Kong and Macau are now SARs

SARS – Severe Acute Respiratory Syndrome

si yau sai chaan – 'soy sauce western'; a cuisine that emerged in the 1950s featuring western dishes of various origins prepared in a Chinese style

tai tai – any married woman but especially the leisured wife of a businessman

taichi – slow-motion shadow-boxing and form of exercise; also spelt tai chi or t'ai chi

Tanka – Chinese ethnic group that traditionally lives on boats

Triad – Chinese secret society originally founded as patriotic associations to protect Chinese culture from the influence of usurping Manchus, but today Hong Kong's equivalent of the Mafia

wan – bay

wet market – an outdoor market selling fruit, vegetables, fish and meat

yum cha – literally 'drink tea'; common Cantonese term for dim sum

MENU DECODER

Fish & Shellfish

baau·yew	鮑魚	abalone
daai·haa	大蝦	prawn
haa	蝦	shrimp
ho	蠔	oyster
lung haa	龍蝦	rock lobster
yau·yew	魷魚	squid
yew	魚	fish
yew chi	魚翅	shark's fin
yew daan	魚蛋	fish balls, usually made from pike

Meat & Poultry

gai	雞	chicken
jew sau	豬手	pork knuckle
jew·yuk	豬肉	pork
ngaap	鴨	duck
ngau yuk	牛肉	beef
ngaw	鵝	goose
paai guat	排骨	pork spareribs
yew jew	乳豬	suckling pig

Pastries

bo lo baau	菠蘿包	pineapple bun
gai mei baau	雞尾包	cocktail bun

Rice & Noodle Dishes

baak·faan	白飯	steamed white rice
chaau·faan	炒飯	fried rice
chaau·min	炒麵	fried noodles
faan	飯	rice
fan·si	粉絲	cellophane noodles or bean threads
haw·fan	河粉	wide, white, flat rice noodles that are usually pan-fried
juk	粥	congee
min	麵	noodles
sin·haa haa wan·tan	鮮蝦餛飩	wontons made with prawns
wan·tan min	餛飩麵	wonton noodle soup

Sauces

gaai laat	芥辣	hot mustard
ho yau	蠔油	oyster sauce
laat jiu jeung	辣椒醬	chilli sauce
si yau	豉油	soy sauce

Soups

aai yuk suk mai gang	蟹肉粟米羹	crab and sweet corn soup
baak·choy tawng	白菜湯	Chinese cabbage soup
daan faa·tawng	蛋花湯	'egg flower' (or drop) soup; light stock into which a raw egg is dropped
dung·gwaa tawng	冬瓜湯	winter-melon soup
wan·tan tawng	餛飩湯	wonton soup
yew·chi tawng	魚翅湯	shark's-fin soup
yin waw gang	燕窩羹	bird's-nest soup

Vegetarian Dishes

chun gewn	春卷	vegetarian spring rolls
gai lo may	雞滷味	mock chicken, barbecued pork or roast duck
gam gu sun jim	金菇筍尖	braised bamboo shoots and black mushrooms
law hon jaai	羅漢齋	braised mixed vegetables
law hon jaai yi min	羅漢齋伊麵	fried noodles with braised vegetables

Under Fish & Shellfish:

yau·jaa·gwai	油炸鬼	'devils' tails'; dough rolled and fried in hot oil

Cantonese Dishes

haak cheuk haa	白灼蝦	poached prawns served with dipping sauces
chaa siu	叉燒	roast pork
ching chaau gaai laan	清炒芥蘭	stir-fried Chinese broccoli
ching jing yew	清蒸魚	whole steamed fish served with spring onions, ginger and soy sauce
geung chung chaau haai	薑蔥炒蟹	sautéed crab with ginger and spring onions
haai yuk paa dau miu	蟹肉扒豆苗	sautéed pea shoots with crab meat
ho yau choi sam	蠔油菜心	*choisum* with oyster sauce
ho yau ngau yuk	蠔油牛肉	deep-fried spare ribs served with coarse salt and pepper
jaa ji gai	炸子雞	crispy-skin chicken
jiu yim yau·yew	椒鹽魷魚	squid, dry-fried with salt and pepper
mui choi kau yuk	霉菜扣肉	twice-cooked pork with pickled cabbage
sai laan faa daai ji	西蘭花帶子	stir-fried broccoli with scallops
siu ngaap	燒鴨	roast duck
siu yew gaap	燒乳鴿	roast pigeon
siu yew jew	燒乳豬	roast suckling pig
yìm guk gai	鹽焗雞	salt-baked chicken, Hakka-style

Dim Sum

chaa siu baau	叉燒包	steamed barbecued-pork buns
cheung fan	腸粉	steamed rice-flour rolls with shrimp, beef or pork
ching chaau si choi	清炒時菜	fried green vegetable of the day
chiu jau fan gwaw	潮州粉果	steamed dumpling with pork, peanuts and coriander
chun gewn	春卷	fried spring rolls
fan gwaw	粉果	steamed dumplings with shrimp and bamboo shoots
fu pay gewn	腐皮卷	crispy tofu rolls
fung jaau	鳳爪	fried chicken feet
haa gaau	蝦餃	steamed shrimp dumplings
law mai gai	糯米雞	sticky rice wrapped in a lotus leaf
paai gwat	排骨	small braised spare ribs with black beans
saan juk ngau yuk	山竹牛肉	steamed minced-beef balls
siu maai	燒賣	steamed pork and shrimp dumplings

Chiu Chow Dishes

bing faa gwun yin	冰花官燕	cold, sweet bird's-nest soup served as a dessert
chiu·jau lo Oseui ngaw	潮州滷水鵝	Chiu Chow braised goose
chiu·jau yew tong	潮州魚湯	aromatic fish soup
chiu·jau yi min	潮州伊麵	pan-fried egg noodles served with chives
dung jing haai	凍蒸蟹	cold steamed crab
jin ho beng	煎蠔餅	oyster omelette
sek lau gai	石榴雞	steamed egg-white pouches filled with minced chicken
tim·sewn Ohung·siu haa/ haai kau	甜酸紅燒蝦 蟹球	prawn or crab balls with sweet, sticky dipping sauce

Northern Dishes

bak·ging tin ngaap	北京填鴨	Peking duck
chong baau yeung yuk	蔥爆羊肉	sliced lamb with onions served on sizzling platter
gaau·ji	餃子	dumplings
gon chaau	乾炒牛肉絲	dried shredded beef
ngau yuk si		with chilli sauce
haau yeung·yuk	烤羊肉	roast lamb
sewn laat tong	酸辣湯	hot-and-sour soup with shredded pork (and sometimes congealed pig's blood)

Shanghainese Dishes

baat bo faan	八寶飯	steamed or pan-fried glutinous rice with 'eight treasures', eaten as a dessert
chong yau beng	蔥油餅	pan-fried spring onion cakes
chung·ji wong yew	松子黃魚	sweet-and-sour yellow croaker with pine nuts
daai jaap haai	大閘蟹	hairy crab (an autumn and winter dish)
fu gwai gai/ hat yi gai	富貴雞/ 乞丐雞	'beggar's chicken'; partially deboned chicken stuffed with pork, Chinese pickled cabbage, onions, mushrooms,ginger and other seasonings, wrapped in lotus leaves, sealed in wet clay or pastry and baked for several hours in hot ash

gon jin say gwai dau	乾煎四季豆	pan-fried spicy string beans
hung·siu si·ji·tau	紅燒獅子頭	Braised 'lion's head meatballs' – over-sized pork meatballs
jeui gai	醉雞	drunken chicken
lung jeng haa jan	龍井蝦仁	shrimps with 'dragon-well' tea leaves
seung·hoi cho chaau	上海粗炒	fried Shànghǎi-style (thick) noodles with pork and cabbage
siu lung baau	小籠包	steamed minced-pork dumplings

Sichuan Dishes

ching jiu ngau yok si	青椒牛肉絲	sautéed shredded beef and green pepper
daam daam min	擔擔麵	noodles in savoury sauce
gong baau gai ding	宮爆雞丁	sautéed diced chicken and peanuts in sweet chilli sauce
jeung chaa haau ngaap	樟茶烤鴨	duck smoked in camphor wood
maa ngai seung sew	螞蟻上樹	'ants climbing trees'; cellophane noodles braised with seasoned minced pork
maa paw dau fu	麻婆豆腐	stewed tofu with minced pork and chilli
say·chewn ming haa	四川明蝦	Sichuan chilli prawns
wui gwaw yuk	回鍋肉	slices of braised pork with chillies
yew heung ke ji	魚香茄子	sautéed eggplant in a savoury, spicy sauce

Behind the Scenes

SEND US YOUR FEEDBACK

We love to hear from travellers – your comments keep us on our toes and help make our books better. Our well-travelled team reads every word on what you loved or loathed about this book. Although we cannot reply individually to your submissions, we always guarantee that your feedback goes straight to the appropriate authors, in time for the next edition. Each person who sends us information is thanked in the next edition – the most useful submissions are rewarded with a selection of digital PDF chapters.

Visit **lonelyplanet.com/contact** to submit your updates and suggestions or to ask for help. Our award-winning website also features inspirational travel stories, news and discussions.

Note: We may edit, reproduce and incorporate your comments in Lonely Planet products such as guidebooks, websites and digital products, so let us know if you don't want your comments reproduced or your name acknowledged. For a copy of our privacy policy visit lonelyplanet.com/privacy.

OUR READERS

Many thanks to the travellers who used the last edition and wrote to us with helpful hints, useful advice and interesting anecdotes:

Alice Weissmann, Bill Clifford, Jim Revell, Maximus Sandler, Michelle Bedolla, Nick Patton, Nora Yong, Parag Mody, Seymour White

WRITER THANKS

Lorna Parkes

As always, huge thanks to the family that kept things together while I disappeared into the sub-tropics to do this update, especially my husband Rob, who never baulks when I tell him how long my research trips are going to be. Thanks also to the enthusiastic Hong Kongers I met during my trip, who were full of recommendations and tips over dim sum and jazz. Last but not least, thanks to Austin and Lily for waiting patiently for my return home.

Piera Chen

Massive thanks to Yvonne Ieong, Cora Si, Anson Ng and Francisco Chan of Macau for always being generous and helpful. Thanks also to Eric, Jackal and Gabriel for wonderful company and good food. Gratitude goes to Alvin Tse, Linda To and Sophia Wong of Hong Kong for much-needed support. And finally a big thank you to my husband, Kontau, and my daughter, Clio, for their love and patience.

Thomas O'Malley

Thanks to the late Sir Matthew Nathan for giving his name to the road I walked up and down a gazillion times. Thanks to Megatron, the Happy Valley nag who galloped home at 66/10 and paid for my dinner. Thanks to the incorruptible Megan Eaves, editor extraordinaire. Thanks also to Jennie, Chris, Cindy, Megatron (oops, done him already). Also, to my co-writers, Lorna and Piera and, finally, to my lovely Ophelia (not a horse).

ACKNOWLEDGEMENTS

Cover photograph: Temple in Tai Po, New Territories, Danita Delimont Stock/AWL ©

THIS BOOK

This 18th edition of Lonely Planet's *Hong Kong* guidebook was researched and written by Lorna Parkes, Piera Chen and Thomas O'Malley. The previous two editions were written by Piera Chen and Emily Matchar. This guidebook was produced by the following:

Destination Editor
Megan Eaves
Senior Product Editor
Kate Chapman
Regional Senior Cartographer Julie Sheridan
Product Editor Amanda Williamson
Book Designer Wibowo Rusli
Assisting Editors Carly Hall, Trent Holden, Kate Kiely, Kellie Langdon, Kate Mathews, Anne Mulvaney, Charlotte Orr, Monique Perrin
Assisting Cartographers Katerina Pavkova, Anthony Phelan
Cover Researcher Wibowo Rusli
Thanks to Gwen Cotter, Min Dai, James Hardy, Andi Jones, Wayne Murphy

BEHIND THE SCENES

See also separate subindexes for:

✗ EATING P292

🍷 DRINKING & NIGHTLIFE P294

☆ ENTERTAINMENT P295

🔒 SHOPPING P295

Index

✗ EATING

Hong Kong Maps

Sights

- Beach
- Bird Sanctuary
- Buddhist
- Castle/Palace
- Christian
- Confucian
- Hindu
- Islamic
- Jain
- Jewish
- Monument
- Museum/Gallery/Historic Building
- Ruin
- Shinto
- Sikh
- Taoist
- Winery/Vineyard
- Zoo/Wildlife Sanctuary
- Other Sight

Activities, Courses & Tours

- Bodysurfing
- Diving
- Canoeing/Kayaking
- Course/Tour
- Sento Hot Baths/Onsen
- Skiing
- Snorkelling
- Surfing
- Swimming/Pool
- Walking
- Windsurfing
- Other Activity

Sleeping

- Sleeping
- Camping

Eating

- Eating

Drinking & Nightlife

- Drinking & Nightlife
- Cafe

Entertainment

- Entertainment

Shopping

- Shopping

Information

- Bank
- Embassy/Consulate
- Hospital/Medical
- Internet
- Police
- Post Office
- Telephone
- Toilet
- Tourist Information
- Other Information

Geographic

- Beach
- Gate
- Hut/Shelter
- Lighthouse
- Lookout
- Mountain/Volcano
- Oasis
- Park
- Pass
- Picnic Area
- Waterfall

Population

- Capital (National)
- Capital (State/Province)
- City/Large Town
- Town/Village

Transport

- Airport
- Border crossing
- Bus
- Cable car/Funicular
- Cycling
- Ferry
- Metro/MTR/MRT station
- Monorail
- Parking
- Petrol station
- Skytrain/Subway station
- Taxi
- Train station/Railway
- Tram
- Underground station
- Other Transport

Note: Not all symbols displayed above appear on the maps in this book

Routes

- Tollway
- Freeway
- Primary
- Secondary
- Tertiary
- Lane
- Unsealed road
- Road under construction
- Plaza/Mall
- Steps
- Tunnel
- Pedestrian overpass
- Walking Tour
- Walking Tour detour
- Path/Walking Trail

Boundaries

- International
- State/Province
- Disputed
- Regional/Suburb
- Marine Park
- Cliff
- Wall

Hydrography

- River, Creek
- Intermittent River
- Canal
- Water
- Dry/Salt/Intermittent Lake
- Reef

Areas

- Airport/Runway
- Beach/Desert
- Cemetery (Christian)
- Cemetery (Other)
- Glacier
- Mudflat
- Park/Forest
- Sight (Building)
- Sportsground
- Swamp/Mangrove

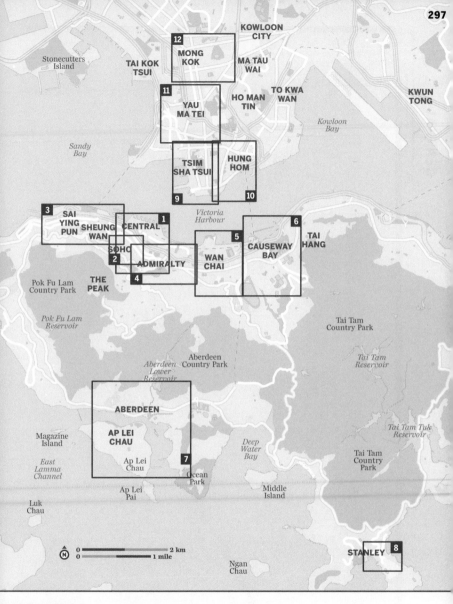

MAP INDEX

CENTRAL

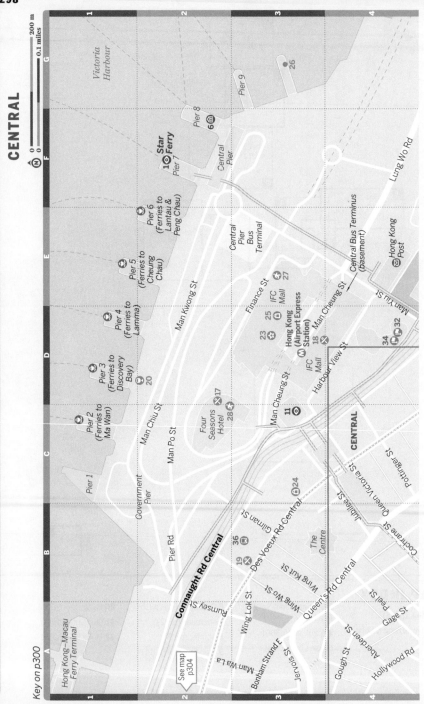

Key on p300

See map p304

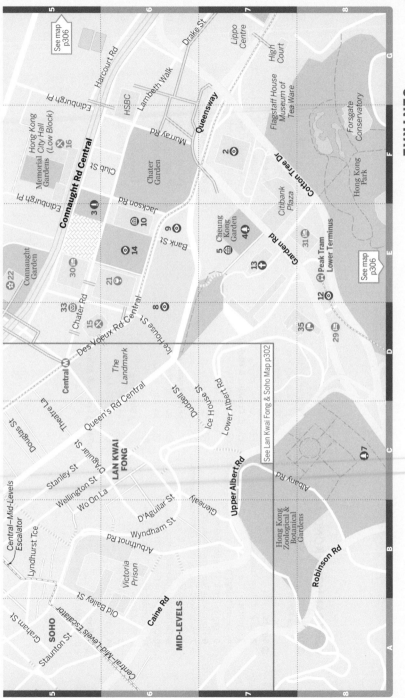

CENTRAL

See map p306

Drake St

Lippo Centre

High Court

Harcourt Rd

Edinburgh Pl

HSBC

Lambeth Walk

Queensway

Flagstaff House Museum of Tea Ware

Forsgate Conservatory

Hong Kong City Hall (Low Block) ✕ 16

Murray Rd

Memorial Gardens

Connaught Rd Central

Club St

Chater Garden

2 ◉

Cotton Tree Dr

Hong Kong Park

Edinburgh Pl

Jackson Rd

3 🍴

Citibank Plaza

Connaught Garden

30 🛍

14 ◉

9 ◉

Bank St

5 Cheung Kong Garden 🏛

4 ◉

Garden Rd

31 🛍

Peak Tram Lower Terminus

22 ✪

10 🏛

21 🍴

13 ✚

12 ◉

See map p306

33 🛍

15 ✕

8 ◉

Chater Rd

Ice House St

Des Voeux Rd Central

35 🛍

29 🛍

Central Ⓜ

The Landmark

Queen's Rd Central

Duddell St

Ice House St

Lower Albert Rd

See Lan Kwai Fong & Soho Map p302

Theatre La

Douglas St

Stanley St

D'Aguilar St

LAN KWAI FONG

Upper Albert Rd

Albany Rd

Central–Mid-Levels Escalator

Lyndhurst Tce

Wellington St

Wo On La

D'Aguilar St

Glenealy

Wyndham St

Arbuthnot Rd

Hong Kong Zoological & Botanical Gardens

7 ◉

Graham St

SOHO

Staunton St

Central–Mid-Levels Escalator

Old Bailey St

Victoria Prison

Caine Rd

MID-LEVELS

Robinson Rd

LAN KWAI FONG & SOHO *Map on p302*

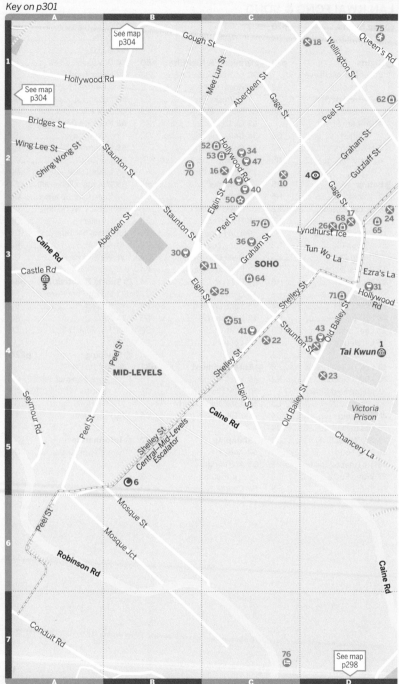

Key on p301

LAN KWAI FONG & SOHO

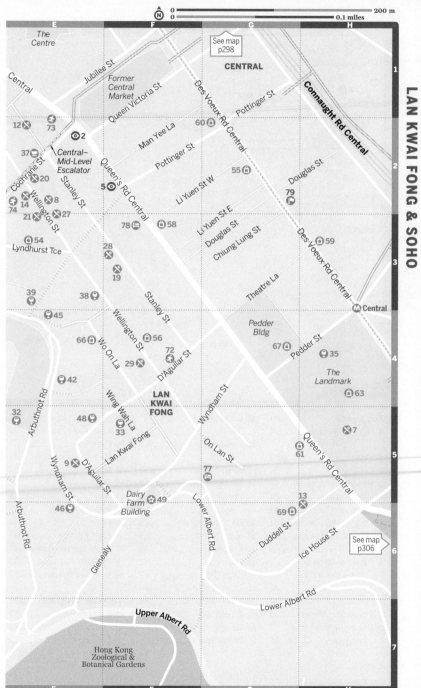

SHEUNG WAN & SAI YING PUN

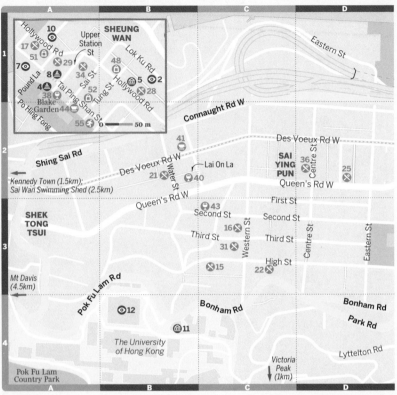

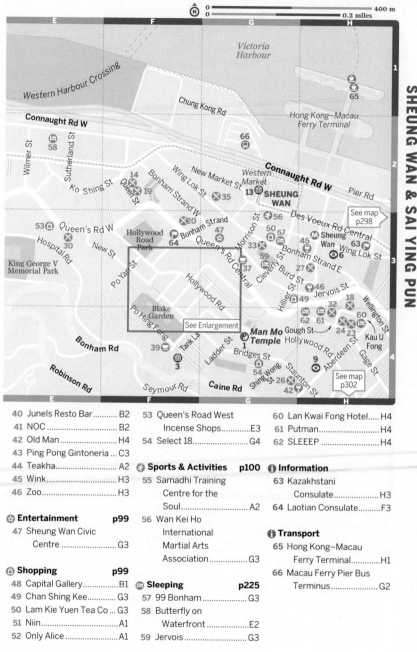

0   400 m
0   0.2 miles

Victoria Harbour

Western Harbour Crossing

Chung Kong Rd

Connaught Rd W

Hong Kong–Macau Ferry Terminal

Wilmer St
Sutherland St
Ko Shing St
Queen St

Bonham Strand W
Wing Lok St
New Market St
Western Market

Connaught Rd W

Pier Rd

SHEUNG WAN

See map p298

Des Voeux Rd Central

Queen's Rd W
Hospital Rd
New St

Hollywood Road Park

Bonham Strand
Queen's Rd Central

Morrison St

Bonham Strand E
Sheung Wan
Wing Lok St

King George V Memorial Park

Po Yan St

Hollywood Rd

Cleverly St
Burd St

Hillier St
Jervois St

Wellington St

Po Hing Fong

Blake Garden

See Enlargement

Man Mo Temple

Gough St
Hollywood Rd

Kau U Fong

Gage St

Bonham Rd

Tank La
Ladder St

Bridges St

Aberdeen St

See map p302

Robinson Rd

Seymour Rd
Caine Rd
Shing Wong St
Staunton St

---

40 Junels Resto Bar........... B2
41 NOC B2
42 Old Man H4
43 Ping Pong Gintoneria ... C3
44 Teakha........................... A2
45 Wink............................... H3
46 Zoo................................. H3

🎭 Entertainment   p99
47 Sheung Wan Civic
   Centre G3

🛍 Shopping   p99
48 Capital Gallery.............. B1
49 Chan Shing Kee............. G3
50 Lam Kie Yuen Tea Co ... G3
51 Niin................................ A1
52 Only Alice A1

53 Queen's Road West
   Incense Shops............. E3
54 Select 18....................... G4

⚽ Sports & Activities   p100
55 Samadhi Training
   Centre for the
   Soul............................. A2
56 Wan Kei Ho
   International
   Martial Arts
   Association G3

🛏 Sleeping   p225
57 99 Bonham.................... G3
58 Butterfly on
   Waterfront E2
59 Jervois G3

60 Lan Kwai Fong Hotel..... H4
61 Putman.......................... H4
62 SLEEEP H4

ℹ Information
63 Kazakhstani
   Consulate.................... H3
64 Laotian Consulate.......... F3

ℹ Transport
65 Hong Kong–Macau
   Ferry Terminal............. H1
66 Macau Ferry Pier Bus
   Terminus..................... G2

ADMIRALTY

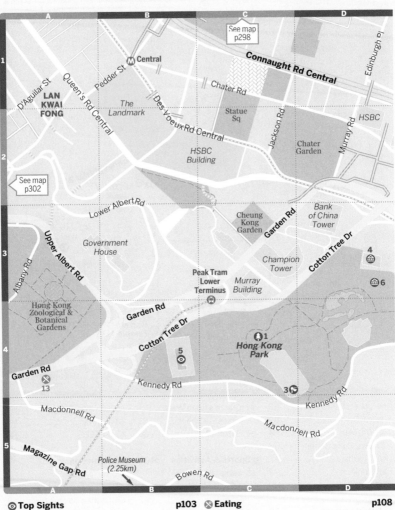

See map p298
See map p302

Police Museum (2.25km)

◎ Top Sights	p103
1 Hong Kong Park	C4

◎ Sights	p104
2 Asia Society Hong Kong Centre	F5
3 Edward Youde Aviary	C4
4 Flagstaff House Museum of Tea Ware	D3
5 Hong Kong Visual Arts Centre	B4
6 KS Lo Gallery	D3
7 Lippo Centre	E3
8 Tamar Park	F1

⊗ Eating	p108
AMMO	(see 2)
Great Food Hall	(see 18)
9 Honbo	H4
10 La Creperie	H4
11 Le Petit Saigon	G4
Lock Cha Tea Shop	(see 6)
12 Pici	G4
13 Pure Veggie House	A4
San Xi Lou	(see 13)

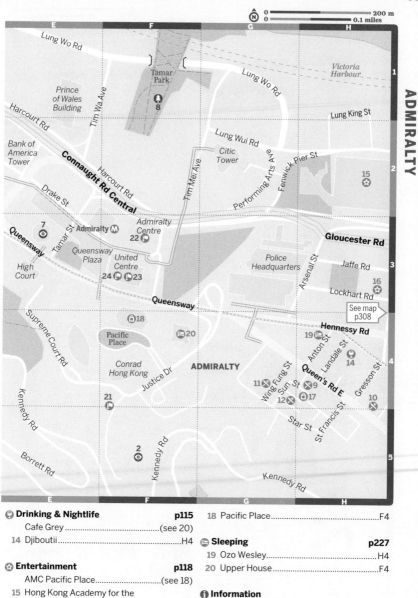

WAN CHAI

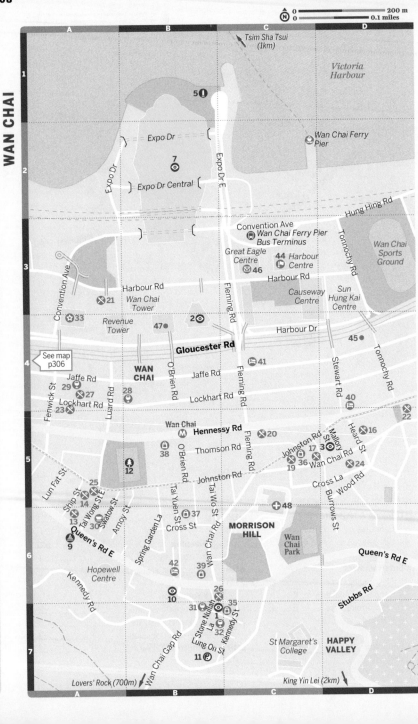

200 m
0.1 miles

Tsim Sha Tsui
(1km)

Victoria
Harbour

5

Wan Chai Ferry
Pier

Expo Dr

Expo Dr Central

7

Expo Dr E

Hung Hing Rd

Convention Ave
Wan Chai Ferry Pier
Bus Terminus

Great Eagle
Centre
46

44 Harbour
Centre

Tonnochy Rd

Wan Chai
Sports
Ground

Convention Ave

Harbour Rd

21

Wan Chai
Tower

Harbour Rd

Causeway
Centre

Sun
Hung Kai
Centre

33

Revenue
Tower

47

2

Flemin g Rd

Harbour Dr

45

Gloucester Rd

WAN
CHAI

O'Brien Rd

Jaffe Rd

41

Jaffe Rd

29
27

Luard Rd

28

Lockhart Rd

Fleming Rd

Stewart Rd

Tonnochy Rd

40

Fenwick St

Lockhart Rd

23

Wan Chai
M

Hennessy Rd

20

Johnston Rd

22

Heard St

16

Mallory St

3

38

O'Brien Rd

Thomson Rd

Fleming Rd

17

19
36

Wan Chai Rd

24

Cross La

Wood Rd

Burrows St

12

Johnston Rd

25

Lun Fat St

Ship St

14

Tai Wong St E

Swatow St

Amoy St

Tai Yuen St

Tai Wo St

Spring Garden La

Cross St

37

48

MORRISON
HILL

Wan Chai
Park

Queen's Rd E

13
30

Queen's Rd E

9

Stubbs Rd

Hopewell
Centre

Kennedy Rd

42

39

Wan Chai Rd

10

26

HAPPY
VALLEY

31

Stone Nullah La

1

35

Kennedy St

32

Lung On St

St Margaret's
College

11

Lovers' Rock (700m)

Wan Chai Gap Rd

King Yin Lei (2km)

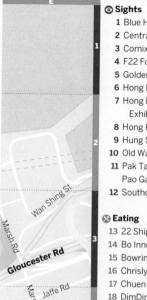

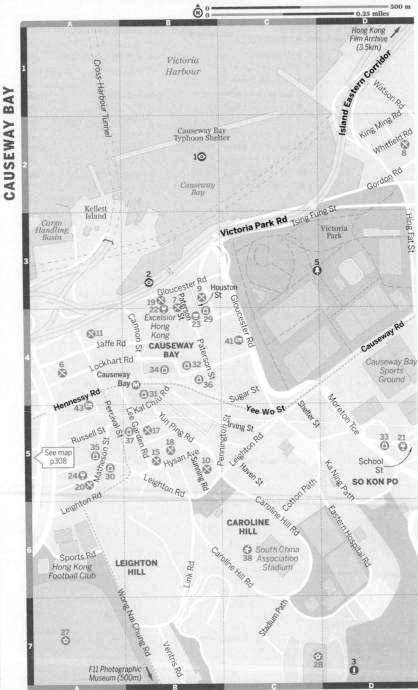

N

0 ____ 500 m
0 ____ 0.25 miles

Hong Kong Film Archive (3.5km)

Victoria Harbour

Cross-Harbour Tunnel

Causeway Bay Typhoon Shelter

1

Island Eastern Corridor

Watson Rd

King Ming Rd

Whitfield Rd

8

Gordon Rd

Causeway Bay

Kellett Island

Cargo Handling Basin

Victoria Park Rd

Tsing Fung St

Victoria Park

5

Hing Fat St

2

Gloucester Rd

Houston St

9

19
7
22
23
Paterson St
29

Excelsior Hong Kong

Cannon St

CAUSEWAY BAY

Jaffe Rd

11

41

Gloucester Rd

Causeway Rd

6

Lockhart Rd

Causeway Bay M

34

32

36

Paterson St

Causeway Bay Sports Ground

Hennessy Rd

43

31

Lee Kai Chiu Rd

Sugar St

Yee Wo St

Shelter St

Moreton Tce

Russell St

Percival St

37

17

Yun Ping Rd

Irving St

Leighton Rd

Ka Ning Path

33
21

School St

SO KON PO

35

15

18

Hysan Ave

Sunning Rd

10

Pennington St

Haven St

24
20
30
Matheson St

Leighton Rd

Leighton Rd

Cotton Path

Caroline Hill Rd

Eastern Hospital Rd

Sports Rd

Hong Kong Football Club

LEIGHTON HILL

Link Rd

Caroline Hill Rd

CAROLINE HILL

South China Association Stadium
38

Wong Nai Chung Rd

27

Ventris Rd

Stadium Path

28

3

F11 Photographic Museum (500m)

ABERDEEN

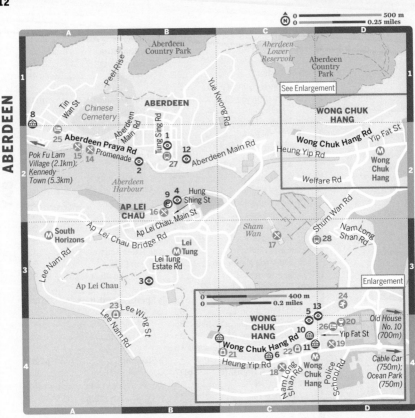

STANLEY

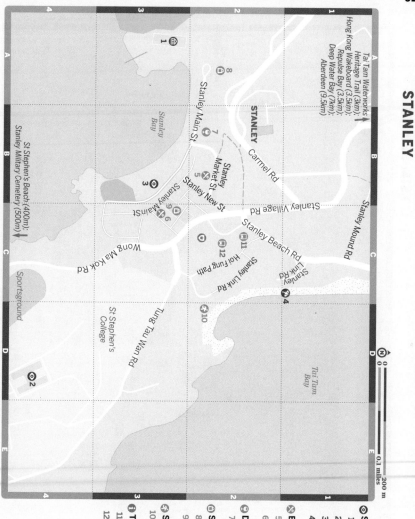

Tai Tam Waterworks
Heritage Trail (3km);
Hong Kong Wakeboard
Repulse Bay (3.5km);
Deep Water Bay (7km);
Aberdeen (9.5km)

STANLEY

Stanley
Bay

Stanley Main St

Stanley
Market St

Stanley New St

Carmel Rd

Stanley Village Rd

Stanley Mound Rd

Stanley Beach Rd

St Stephen's Beach (400m);
Stanley Military Cemetery (500m)

Sportsground

Wong Ma Kok Rd

Hoi Fung Path

Stanley Link Rd

Stanley Link Rd

Tung Tau Wan Rd

St Stephen's
College

Tai Tam
Bay

0   200 m
0   0.1 miles

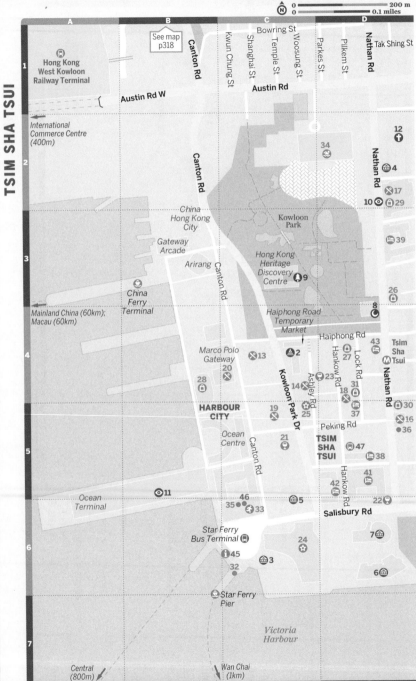

TSIM SHA TSUI

See map p318

0 — 200 m
0 — 0.1 miles

Hong Kong West Kowloon Railway Terminal

Canton Rd

Austin Rd W

Bowring St

Kwun Chung St
Shanghai St
Temple St
Woosung St
Parkes St
Pilkem St
Nathan Rd
Tak Shing St

Austin Rd

International Commerce Centre (400m)

34

12

Nathan Rd

4

17

10 29

China Hong Kong City

Kowloon Park

39

Gateway Arcade

Canton Rd

Arirang

Hong Kong Heritage Discovery Centre

9

China Ferry Terminal

Mainland China (60km); Macau (60km)

26

Haiphong Road Temporary Market

8

Haiphong Rd

Tsim Sha Tsui

Marco Polo Gateway

13

2

27

43

Hankow Rd
Lock Rd
Nathan Rd

Ashley Rd

23

28

20

Kowloon Park Dr

14

18

31

37

HARBOUR CITY

19

25

30

Ocean Centre

21

Peking Rd

16

36

TSIM SHA TSUI

47

38

Canton Rd

41

42

Hankow Rd

22

Ocean Terminal

11

35 46
33

5

Salisbury Rd

7

Star Ferry Bus Terminal

45

24

3

32

6

Star Ferry Pier

Victoria Harbour

Central (800m)

Wan Chai (1km)

TSIM SHA TSUI

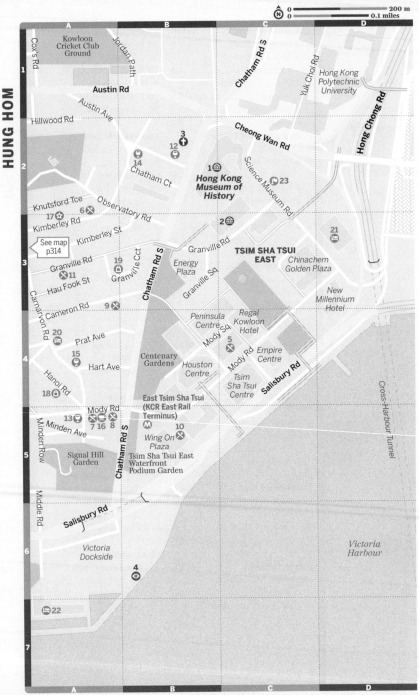

HUNG HOM

See map
p314

HUNG HOM

YAU MA TEI

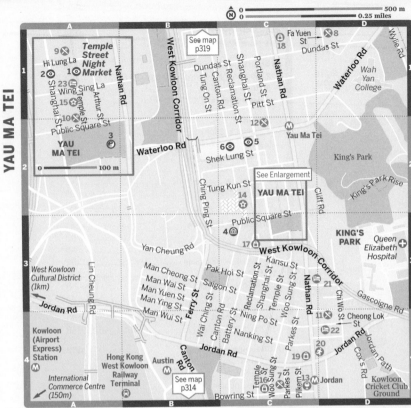

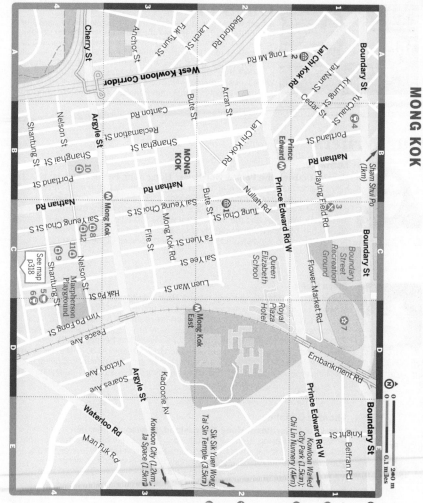

Our Story

A beat-up old car, a few dollars in the pocket and a sense of adventure. In 1972 that's all Tony and Maureen Wheeler needed for the trip of a lifetime – across Europe and Asia overland to Australia. It took several months, and at the end – broke but inspired – they sat at their kitchen table writing and stapling together their first travel guide, *Across Asia on the Cheap*. Within a week they'd sold 1500 copies. Lonely Planet was born.

Today, Lonely Planet has offices in Franklin, London, Melbourne, Oakland, Dublin, Beijing and Delhi, with more than 600 staff and writers. We share Tony's belief that 'a great guidebook should do three things: inform, educate and amuse'.

Our Writers

Lorna Parkes

Central District, the Peak & Northwest Hong Kong Island Londoner by birth, Melburnian by palate and former Lonely Planet staffer in both cities, Lorna has contributed to numerous Lonely Planet books and magazines. She's discovered she writes best on planes, and is most content when researching food and booze. Wineries and the tropics (not at the same time!) are her go-to happy places, but Yorkshire will always be special to her. Follow her @Lorna_Explorer.

Lorna also wrote the Plan Your Trip, Understand Hong Kong and Survival Guide chapters.

Piera Chen

Aberdeen & South Hong Kong Island, New Territories, Outlying Islands, Macau Piera is a travel writer who divides her time among Hong Kong (hometown), Taiwan and Vancouver when not on the road. She has authored over a dozen travel guides and contributed to as many travel-related titles. Piera has a BA in literature from Pomona College. Her early life was peppered with trips to Taiwan and China to visit relatives, and then to Southeast Asia, where her father was working. But it was during her first trip to Europe that dawn broke. She remembers being fresh off a flight in Rome, looking around and thinking, 'I want to be doing this everyday.' And she has.

Thomas O'Malley

Wan Chai & Northeast Hong Kong Island, Kowloon, Shēnzhèn A British writer based in Běijīng, Tom is a world-leading connoisseur of cheap eats, dive bars, dark alleyways and hangovers. He has contributed travel stories to everywhere from the BBC to *Playboy*, and reviews hotels for the *Telegraph*. Under another guise, he is a comedy scriptwriter. Follow him by walking behind at a distance.

Published by Lonely Planet Publications Pty Ltd
ABN 36 005 607 983
18th edition – Jun 2019
ISBN 978 1 78657 808 2
© Lonely Planet 2019   Photographs © as indicated 2019
10 9 8 7 6 5 4 3 2 1
Printed in Singapore